CORE CSS

CASCADING STYLE SHEETS

2ND EDITION

D0731321

PRENTICE HALL PTR
CORE SERIES

Core MySQL, Atkinson

Core PHP Programming, 3/e, Atkinson

Core Python Programming, Chun

Core Jini, 2/e, * Edwards

Core Java 2, Vol I–Fundamentals, * Horstmann/Cornell

Core Java 2, Vol II–Advanced Features, * Horstmann/Cornell

Core JSP, Hougland & Tavistock

Core Perl, Lerner

Core CSS, 2/e, Schengili-Roberts

Core C++: A Software Engineering Approach, Shtern

Core Java Web Server, Taylor & Kimmet

Core JFC, 2/e, Topley

Core Swing: Advanced Programming, Topley

Core Web3D, Walsh & Bourges-Sévenier

*Sun Microsystems Press titles

CORE CSS

CASCADING STYLE SHEETS

2ND EDITION

KEITH SCHENGILI-ROBERTS

Prentice Hall PTR
Upper Saddle River, NJ 07458
www.phptr.com

Library of Congress Cataloging-in-Publication Data

A catalog record for this book can be obtained from the Library of Congress

Editorial/production supervision: *Nicholas Radhuber*
Cover design director: *Jerry Votta*
Cover design: *Nina Scuderi*
Manufacturing manager: *Alexis Heydt-Long*
Acquisitions editor: *Gregory Doench*
Editorial assistant: *Brandt Kenna*
Marketing manager: *Curt Johnson*

© 2004 by Pearson Education, Inc.
Publishing as Prentice Hall Professional Technical Reference
One Lake Street
Upper Saddle River, New Jersey 07458

Prentice Hall books are widely used by corporations and government agencies for training, marketing, and resale.

The publisher offers excellent discounts on this book when ordered in quantity for bulk purchases or special sales. For more information, please contact:
U.S. Corporate and Government Sales
1-800-382-3419
corpsales@pearsontechgroup.com

For sales outside the U.S., please contact:
International Sales
1-317-581-3793
international@pearsontechgroup.com

Product and company names mentioned herein are the trademarks or registered trademarks of their respective owners.

All rights reserved. No part of this book may be
reproduced, in any form or by any means,
without permission in writing from the publisher.

Printed in the United States of America
First printing.

ISBN 0-13-009278-9

Pearson Education LTD.
Pearson Education Australia PTY, Limited
Pearson Education Singapore, Pte. Ltd.
Pearson Education North Asia Ltd.
Pearson Education Canada, Ltd.
Pearson Educación de Mexico, S.A. de C.V.
Pearson Education—Japan

This book is dedicated to my youngest daughter,
Annie Evelyn Roberts.

It's her turn.   ;-)

Contents

ACKNOWLEDGMENTS   XXIX

PREFACE   XXXI

    Who You Are   xxxii

    How This Book Is Organized   xxxiii

    Conventions Used in This Book   xxxv

    Further Information   xxxv

    Additional Material   xxxvi

    Feedback   xxxvii

CHAPTER 1
THE BIRTH OF CSS   2

    1.1   The World Wide Web Consortium Introduces Cascading Style Sheets   5

    1.2   XHTML, CSS2 and CSS3   7

    1.3   Re-emergence of the Browser Wars?   10

CHAPTER 2
(X)HTML AND ITS RELATIONSHIP TO CSS   14

2.1   Adding Cascading Style Sheets to Web Pages   17

2.2   The <style> Element   18

      <style> and CSS3   20

2.3   The <span> and <div> Elements   21

2.4   The <link> Element   24

CHAPTER 3
BROWSER ADOPTION OF CSS   28

3.1   Internet Explorer 3.x   30

3.2   Internet Explorer 4.x   31

3.3   Internet Explorer 4.5 (Macintosh) and 5.x (Windows and Macintosh)   32

3.4   Internet Explorer 5.5   34

3.5   Internet Explorer 6.0   35

3.6   Opera 3.5   37

3.7   Opera 4.x – 6.x   38

3.8   Netscape Navigator 4.x   39

3.9   Mozilla and Netscape Navigator 6.x and 7.x   40

3.10   Other Browsers   47

      Popular Linux Browsers   47

      Emacspeak   48

      Amaya   48

      Hardware Browsers   50

CHAPTER 4
IMPLEMENTATION OF BASIC CSS CONCEPTS   52

4.1   Grouping   53

      Browser Compatibility   55

4.2   Inheritance   56

      Browser Compatibility   57

4.3 class and id as Selectors   58

    Browser Compatibility   61

4.4 Contextual Selectors   62

    Browser Compatibility   65

4.5 Comments   66

    Browser Compatibility   67

4.6 CSS2 Selectors   67

    Universal Selector   68

    Child Selectors   68

    Adjacent Sibling Selectors   70

    Attribute Selectors   71

4.7 CSS3 Selectors   76

    Additional Attribute Selectors   76

    Structural Pseudo-Classes   77

    Various Non-Structural Pseudo-Class Selectors   79

CHAPTER 5
THE CASCADE   82

5.1 Cascading Order   83

    Browser Compatibility   86

5.2 !important   88

    Browser Compatibility   89

5.3 Cascade-Order Sources   90

CHAPTER 6
CSS UNITS   94

6.1 Length Units   95

    Browser Compatibility   99

6.2 Percentage Units   101

    Browser Compatibility   103

6.3 URLs   103

    Browser Compatibility   105

6.4   Strings   106

    Browser Compatibility   107

6.5   Time Units   108

    Browser Compatibility   108

6.6   Angle Units   108

    Browser Compatibility   110

6.7   Frequency Units   110

    Browser Compatibility   111

CHAPTER 7
PSEUDO-CLASSES AND PSEUDO-ELEMENTS   112

7.1   anchor Pseudo-Element   114

    Browser Compatibility   115

7.2   first-line Pseudo-Element   117

    Browser Compatibility   118

7.3   first-letter Pseudo-Element   119

    Browser Compatibility   121

7.4   lang Pseudo-Class   122

    Browser Compatibility   122

7.5   left, right and first Pseudo-Classes   123

7.6   focus and hover Pseudo-Classes   123

    Browser Compatibility   125

7.7   first-child Pseudo-Class   125

    Browser Compatibility   127

7.8   Pseudo-Elements in Selectors and Combining Multiple Pseudo-Elements   128

CHAPTER 8
MEDIA TYPES AND MEDIA QUERIES   130

8.1   Browser Compatibility   134

8.2   Media Queries   135

8.3   width and height Media Queries   136

8.4   device-width and device-height Media Queries   136

8.5   device-aspect-ratio Media Query   137

8.6   color Media Query   137

8.7   color-index Media Query   138

8.8   monochrome Media Query   138

8.9   resolution Media Query   139

8.10   scan Media Query   139

8.11   grid Media Query   140

CHAPTER 9
FONT PROPERTIES   142

9.1   font-family Property   144

      Browser Compatibility   150

9.2   font-size Property   150

      Browser Compatibility   157

9.3   font-style Property   158

      Browser Compatibility   159

9.4   font-variant Property   160

      Browser Compatibility   161

9.5   font-weight Property   162

      Browser Compatibility   167

9.6   font Property   167

      Browser Compatibility   170

9.7   font-stretch Property   170

      Browser Compatibility   172

9.8   font-size-adjust Property   173

      Browser Compatibility   175

9.9   The @font-face Pseudo-Element   175

      Browser Compatibility   181

9.10   CSS3 Font Decoration Properties   182

      font-effect Property   182

      font-smooth Property   183

font-emphasize-style Property   184

font-emphasize-position Property   184

font-emphasize Property   185

CHAPTER 10
TEXT PROPERTIES   186

10.1   letter-spacing Property   187

       Browser Compatibility   189

10.2   word-spacing Property   190

       Browser Compatibility   192

10.3   line-height Property   193

       Browser Compatibility   195

10.4   vertical-align Property   196

       Browser Compatibility   198

10.5   text-align Property   198

       Browser Compatibility   200

10.6   text-decoration Property   201

       Browser Compatibility   203

10.7   text-indent Property   204

       Browser Compatibility   206

10.8   text-transform Property   207

       Browser Compatibility   208

10.9   text-shadow Property   209

       Browser Compatibility   211

10.10   glyph-orientation-horizontal and glyph-orientation-vertical Properties   211

10.11   text-script Property   214

10.12   min-font-size and max-font-size Properties   215

10.13   text-justify-trim Property   216

10.14   line-break Property   216

10.15   word-break-cjk Property   216

10.16   word-break-inside Property   217

10.17   word-break Property   217

10.18   wrap-option Property   218

10.19   linefeed-treatment Property   219

10.20   white-space-treatment Property   219

10.21   all-space-treatment Property   220

10.22   white-space Property   220

10.23   text-overflow-mode Property   222

10.24   text-overflow-ellipsis Property   222

10.25   text-overflow Property   223

10.26   kerning-mode Property   223

10.27   kerning-pair-threshold Property   224

10.28   punctuation-trim Property   224

10.29   text-line-through Set of Properties   225

text-line-through-color Property   225

text-line-through-mode Property   226

text-line-through-style Property   226

text-line-through Property   226

10.30   text-overline Set of Properties   228

text-overline-color Property   229

text-overline-mode Property   229

text-overline-style Property   229

text-overline Property   230

10.31   text-underline Set of Properties   232

text-underline-color Property   232

text-underline-mode Property   232

text-underline-style Property   233

text-underline-position Property   233

text-underline Property   234

10.32   text-blink Property   236

CHAPTER 11
TEXT PROPERTY EXTENSIONS   238

11.1   Internet Explorer Text-Formatting CSS Extensions   239

11.2   layout-flow Property   239

11.3   writing-mode Property   244

    CSS3 and writing-mode   246

11.4   layout-grid Sub-Family of Properties   247

    layout-grid-mode Property   248

    layout-grid-type Property   248

    layout-grid-line and layout-grid-char Properties   250

    layout-grid Property   255

11.5   text-autospace Property   258

    CSS3 and text-autospace   261

11.6   text-justify Property   261

    CSS3 and text-justify   263

11.7   text-kashida-space Property   264

    CSS3 and text-kashida-position   266

11.8   text-underline-position Property   266

    CSS3 and text-underline-position   267

11.9   word-break Property   268

    CSS3 and word-break   270

11.10   text-align-last Property   271

    Browser Compatibility   272

    CSS3 and text-align-last   273

CHAPTER 12
BOX PROPERTIES   274

12.1   border-"style" Properties   276

12.2   border-style Property   277

    Browser Compatibility   279

12.3   border-color Property   280

    Browser Compatibility   282

12.4   border-width Property   283

        Browser Compatibility   286

12.5   border-bottom Property   286

        Browser Compatibility   288

12.6   border-left Property   289

        Browser Compatibility   291

12.7   border-right Property   292

        Browser Compatibility   293

12.8   border-top Property   294

        Browser Compatibility   296

12.9   border-bottom-width Property   297

        Browser Compatibility   298

12.10   border-left-width Property   299

        Browser Compatibility   301

12.11   border-right-width Property   302

        Browser Compatibility   303

12.12   border-top-width Property   304

        Browser Compatibility   306

12.13   border Property   307

        Browser Compatibility   309

12.14   border-radius Set of Properties   310

12.15   border-image Set of Properties   312

12.16   border-fit Set of Properties   314

12.17   border-image-transform Set of Properties   317

12.18   border-break Property   319

12.19   box-shadow Property   319

12.20   clear Property   321

        CSS3 and clear   323

        Browser Compatibility   323

12.21   clear-after Property   324

12.22   float Property   325

        CSS3 and float   330

Browser Compatibility   331

12.23   float-displace Property   331

12.24   indent-edge-reset Property   332

12.25   height Property   332

CSS3 and height   334

Browser Compatibility   334

12.26   width Property   335

CSS3 and width   336

Browser Compatibility   336

12.27   padding-bottom Property   337

Browser Compatibility   339

12.28   padding-left Property   339

Browser Compatibility   341

12.29   padding-right Property   341

Browser Compatibility   343

12.30   padding-top Property   343

Browser Compatibility   345

12.31   padding Property   345

Browser Compatibility   348

12.32   margin-bottom Property   349

Browser Compatibility   351

12.33   margin-left Property   352

Browser Compatibility   353

12.34   margin-right Property   354

Browser Compatibility   356

12.35   margin-top Property   357

Browser Compatibility   359

12.36   margin Property   360

Browser Compatibility   362

12.37   min-width, max-width, min-height and max-height Properties   362

12.38   fit and fit-position Properties   363

12.39   marquee Properties   365

CHAPTER 13

COLOR   368

13.1   color Property   370

    Browser Compatibility   374

13.2   Gamma Correction under CSS3   375

13.3   opacity Property   376

13.4   rendering-intent Property   377

13.5   color-profile Property   378

13.6   @color-profile   379

13.7   XII Color Keywords   379

CHAPTER 14

BACKGROUND PROPERTIES   386

14.1   background-color Property   387

    Browser Compatibility   389

14.2   background-image Property   391

    Browser Compatibility   393

14.3   background-repeat Property   394

    Browser Compatibility   396

14.4   background-attachment Property   397

    Browser Compatibility   400

14.5   background-position Property   401

    Browser Compatibility   406

14.6   background Property   407

    Browser Compatibility   409

14.7   background-position-x and background-position-y Properties   410

14.8   CSS3 Properties   415

14.9   background-clip Property   415

14.10   background-origin   416

14.11   background-size   418

14.12   background-quantity   419

14.13   background-spacing   420

CHAPTER 15
CLASSIFICATION PROPERTIES AND GENERATED/AUTOMATIC CONTENT   422

15.1   white-space Property   423

    Browser Compatibility   425

15.2   list-style-type Property   426

    Browser Compatibility   434

15.3   list-style-image Property   435

    Browser Compatibility   436

15.4   list-style-position Property   437

    Browser Compatibility   439

15.5   list-style Property   440

    Browser Compatibility   442

15.6   The content Property plus the before and after Pseudo-Elements   443

    Browser Compatibility   446

15.7   quotes Property   446

    Browser Compatibility   449

15.8   counter-increment and counter-reset Properties   449

    Browser Compatibility   451

15.9   marker-offset Property   452

    Browser Compatibility   453

CHAPTER 16
VISUAL FORMATTING AND DETAILED VISUAL FORMATTING   456

16.1   display Property   457

    Browser Compatibility   464

16.2   Positioning Properties: position, top, left, right and bottom   465

    Browser Compatibility   471

16.3   z-index Property   473

    Browser Compatibility   475

16.4   direction and unicode-bidi Properties   476

Browser Compatibility   478

16.5   min-width, max-width, min-height and max-height Properties   479

Browser Compatibility   482

CHAPTER 17
VISUAL EFFECTS   486

17.1   overflow Property   487

Browser Compatibility   489

17.2   overflow-x and overflow-y Properties   490

17.3   clip Property   492

Browser Compatibility   494

17.4   visibility Property   495

Browser Compatibility   500

17.5   zoom Property   500

17.6   ime-mode Property   503

CHAPTER 18
PAGED MEDIA   506

18.1   size Property   507

Browser Compatibility   509

18.2   marks Property   510

Browser Compatibility   511

18.3   Page-Break Properties   512

Browser Compatibility   514

18.4   page Property   515

Browser Compatibility   516

18.5   windows and orphans Properties   517

Browser Compatibility   519

CHAPTER 19
TABLES   520

19.1   caption-side Property   521

Browser Compatibility   523

19.2   table-layout Property   524

Browser Compatibility   526

19.3   border-collapse, border-spacing and empty-cells   527

border-collapse Property   527

border-spacing Property   531

empty-cells Property   533

19.4   speak-header Property   536

Browser Compatibility   536

19.5   Table-like Layout Using CSS   537

Two-Column Layout   537

Three-Column Layout   540

CHAPTER 20
USER INTERFACE   542

20.1   cursor Property   544

Browser Compatibility   548

cursor and CSS3   549

20.2   outline Sub-Family of Properties   549

20.3   outline-width Property   550

Browser Compatibility   552

20.4   outline-style Property   553

Browser Compatibility   554

20.5   outline-color Property   554

Browser Compatibility   555

20.6   outline Property   556

Browser Compatibility   556

20.7   accelerator Property   557

Browser Compatibility   559

20.8   CSS3 Properties   559

20.9   resizer Property   559

20.10   key-equivalent Property   560

20.11   tab-index Property   561

20.12   user-input Property   562

20.13   user-modify Property   562

20.14   user-select Property   563

20.15   user-focus, user-focus-key and user-focus-pointer Properties   564

20.16   toggle-group and group-reset Properties   564

20.17   Mozilla User-Interface-Related Extensions   565

20.18   CSS3 Additions to Existing User-Interface Properties   567

CHAPTER 21
AURAL CASCADING STYLE SHEETS   568

21.1   speak Property   570

21.2   volume Property   571

21.3   Pause Sub-Set of Properties   573

21.4   Cue Sub-Set of Properties   576

21.5   play-during Property   577

21.6   azimuth Property   579

21.7   elevation Property   582

21.8   speech-rate Property   584

21.9   voice-family Property   586

21.10   pitch Property   587

21.11   pitch-range Property   589

21.12   stress Property   590

21.13   richness Property   591

21.14   Speech Sub-Group of Properties   592

CHAPTER 22
RUBY   596

22.1   What Is Ruby?   597

22.2   The <ruby> Tag Set   598

22.3   ruby-align Property   602

        Browser Compatibility   605

22.4   ruby-overhang Property   605

Browser Compatibility   607

22.5   ruby-position Property   608

Browser Compatibility   610

CHAPTER 23
MULTI-COLUMN LAYOUT   612

23.1   Introduction   613

23.2   column-count Property   616

23.3   column-width Property   616

23.4   column-gap Property   617

23.5   column-width-policy Property   617

23.6   column-space-distribution Property   618

23.7   Column Rule Properties   620

column-rule-color Property   620

column-rule-style Property   621

column-rule-width Property   621

column-rule Property   622

23.8   column-span Property   622

CHAPTER 24
SCROLLBARS   624

24.1   The Parts of a Scrollbar   625

24.2   Scrollbar Properties   626

24.3   Browser Compatibility   634

CHAPTER 25
FILTERS AND TRANSITIONS   636

25.1   Visual Filters in Internet Explorer   637

25.2   Static Filters   638

AlphaFilter Filter   639

Blur and MotionBlur Filters   641

DropShadow and Shadow Filters   645

Emboss and Engrave Filters   649

Wave filter   651

BasicImage Filter   653

Glow Filter   656

Chroma Filter   658

Light Filter   660

Compositor Filter   663

ICMFilter Filter   665

MaskFilter Filter   667

Matrix Filter   669

25.3   Transition Filter Overview   672

Blinds and Barn Transition Filters   674

Checkerboard and Fade Transition Filters   676

GradientWipe, RadialWipe and Strips Transition Filters   678

RandomBars and RandomDissolve Transition Filters   681

Iris and Spiral Transition Filters   683

Stretch and Slide Transition Filters   685

Inset Transition Filter   687

Pixelate Transition Filter   688

Wheel Transition Filter   689

Zigzag Transition Filter   690

APPENDIX A
CSS1 AND CSS2 COMPATIBILITY CHARTS   692

APPENDIX B
ALPHABETICAL LISTING OF CSS PROPERTIES AND VALUES   706

accelerator   707

azimuth   708

background   709

background-attachment   710

background-color   710

background-image   711

background-position   711

background-position-x   712

background-position-y   712

background-repeat   713

border   713

border-bottom   714

border-bottom-color   715

border-bottom-style   715

border-bottom-width   716

border-collapse   716

border-color   717

border-left   718

border-left-color   718

border-left-style   719

border-left-width   719

border-right   720

border-right-color   721

border-right-style   721

border-right-width   722

border-spacing   722

border-style   723

border-top   724

border-top-color   724

border-top-style   725

border-top-width   726

border-width   726

bottom   727

caption-side   727

clear   728

clip   728

color   729

content   729

counter-increment   730

counter-reset   731

cue   732

cue-after   733

cue-before   733

cursor   734

direction   734

display   735

elevation   736

empty-cells   737

float   737

font   738

font-family   739

font-size   740

font-size-adjust   740

font-stretch   741

font-style   741

font-variant   742

font-weight   742

height   743

layout-flow   743

layout-grid   744

layout-grid-char   745

layout-grid-line   745

layout-grid-mode   746

layout-grid-type   746

left   747

letter-spacing   747

line-break   748

line-height   748

list-style   749

list-style-image   750

list-style-position   750

list-style-type   751

margin   751

margin-bottom   752

margin-left   752

margin-right   753

margin-top   753

marker-offset   754

marks   755

max-height   755

max-width   756

min-height   757

min-width   757

orphans   758

outline   758

outline-color   759

outline-style   760

outline-width   760

overflow   761

padding   762

padding-bottom   762

padding-left   763

padding-right   763

padding-top   764

page   764

page-break-after   765

page-break-before   766

page-break-inside   767

pause   768

pause-after   768

pause-before   769

pitch   769

pitch-range   770

play-during   770

position   771

quotes   772

richness   773

right   774

ruby-align   774

ruby-overhang   775

ruby-position   776

scrollbar-3dlight-color   776

scrollbar-arrow-color   776

scrollbar-base-color   777

scrollbar-darkshadow-color   777

scrollbar-face-color   778

scrollbar-highlight-color   778

scrollbar-shadow-color   778

scrollbar-track-color   779

size   779

speak   780

speak-header   780

speak-numeral   781

speak-punctuation   782

speech-rate   782

stress   783

table-layout   784

text-align   784

text-align-last   785

text-autospace   785

text-decoration   786

text-indent   787

text-justify   787

text-kashida-space   788

text-overflow   789

text-shadow   789

text-transform   790

text-underline-position   790

top   791

unicode-bidi   791

vertical-align   792

visibility   793

voice-family   793

volume   794

white-space   795

widows   795

width   796

word-break   797

word-spacing   797

writing-mode   798

z-index   798

APPENDIX C
CSS3 MOBILE PROFILE   800

Mobile Properties   801

Mobile At-rules   807

Mobile Selectors   807

INDEX   809

Acknowledgments

There are always people helping out behind the scenes to make any book possible. For this project, I had to sequester myself for days at a time in order to write code, test it, check the specification to see how it ought to have worked, re-write the code, and then check it against other platforms and browsers. A lot of people aided me in my work, and this is the space in which I'd like to take the time to thank them in print.

First of all, I'd like to thank my wife Erika and daughters Vanessa and Annie for allowing me to take the time to write this book. Thanks also to my technical editors Amy Ball and Bill Wood IV for the great editing job, and to Dave Truman for taking my text and creating a printable book out of the results. For those few screenshots and diagrams that no browser is currently capable of handling, I'd like to thank graphics wizards Andy Yadegar and Ali Dib for whipping them up for me. Many of the pictures of ancient Roman Coins scattered throughout the illustrations in this book were kindly provided by Robert Kokotailo of the Calgary Coin Gallery.

Thanks also to Linux-wizard Peter Liska who helped set up versions of Linux on a couple of test systems in order for me to check CSS compatibility under this operating system. Last but not least, thanks to Prentice Hall editors Brandt Kenna, Eileen Clark and especially Greg Doench for their patience as this book developed over the course of more than a year's worth of writing.

Preface

Welcome to the second edition of *Core CSS*. When the initial edition came out in 2000, while CSS had been around for a few years, it was largely underutilized on the Web. And there was a good reason for this: browser support for CSS properties was, to put it kindly, "spotty." In the past few years things have changed substantially: the Mozilla project pushed for a standards-compliant rendering engine — including CSS — that has since been incorporated into the most recent versions of Netscape Navigator; and Internet Explorer 5.0 and later 6.0 made real advances in supporting CSS properties. As older, non-CSS-compliant browsers fade into the background, Web design has advanced accordingly and is beginning to take full advantage of the formatting possibilities that CSS opens up for both eye-popping and better functioning Web sites.

While the browser manufacturers have been playing "catch-up" and have largely (with some notable exceptions) instituted the CSS1 and CSS2 standards devised by the World Wide Web Consortium (W3C), the W3C has not stood still. While still in draft status, the various modules that will one day comprise the CSS3 specification are well on the way towards providing a comprehensive set of tools for Web authors seeking to format just about anything and everything you can think of that has to do with a Web page. While none of these CSS3 modules have been finalized — and things may still change substantially — many of the new directions that are being charted by the W3C in this area are covered in this book as a "heads up" as to what future Web developers can come to expect.

One of the original reasons behind the creation of CSS was to prevent competing browsers developers from the runaway development of new HTML tags that only worked in their particular browser. This has seemingly not stopped the temptation by browser manufacturers to continue to "push the envelope," and in particular, recent versions of Microsoft's Internet Explorer have included a number of browser-specific CSS properties. These are covered in the various sections of the book, both out of a sense of completeness as well as wanting to provide readers who may be working in a "closed-shop" environment (i.e., where they know that their clients are all using this browser) with information they can genuinely use. As a member of the W3C, Microsoft is also helping to chart the progress of the future CSS development, and many as yet browser-specific CSS properties may not be so in the future.

When I am asked why I write computer books, I usually respond that I write books I wished already existed that I could use daily in my work. A number of books have appeared since the first edition of *Core CSS* came out, but none of them have been as comprehensive — especially when it came to covering CSS2 or Internet Explorer properties — as I would have liked. The majority of the code in the first book has been completely re-written for this edition, and dozens more examples better show what particular CSS properties can do and how they work — or do not work — in modern browsers.

Who You Are

You are a Web author who is looking to expand the capabilities of your Web pages. You know that CSS opens the doors to a wide range of possibilities, but want to learn more about how to make the most of it. Or perhaps you know that CSS will solve some of your most pernicious Web formatting problems, but shy away from using it because you have heard that it can produce varying results when viewed under different browsers or under different operating systems. Maybe you are looking for a single source that tells you what you need to know about a property at a glance, instead of having to traverse a dozen Web sites to get the same information. If you fit any of these circumstances, then this book is for you.

This book takes a practical, pragmatic look at the current state of affairs regarding CSS and guides the reader through how CSS works. This book provides the information Web authors need in order to understand not only how CSS should work, but also how it actually works in current major browsers. It does not confine itself only to one operating system, but takes a look at how CSS works under browsers working under multiple operating systems. With this knowledge, Web authors will know which CSS properties are "safe" for use, and which to avoid.

More than that though, this book also provides information as to the future of CSS with an in-depth look at what will likely prove to be the foundation of the future CSS3 specification.

You do not have to be an expert at understanding how Web pages work, but the book does assume you have a basic understanding of both HTML and the Web. The book assumes no prior knowledge of CSS. It will not only serve those Web authors who are just starting out using CSS, but also act as a handy reference for those occasions when you need to look up how a particular CSS property works.

How This Book Is Organized

The first edition of this book separated CSS1 and CSS2 properties. Now that much of CSS2 has been adopted within the major browsers, it no longer made sense to keep things separate. This has been extended further to include draft CSS3 properties into the (sometimes rough) families of properties to which they belong. While these properties are not currently in use — and some of them may not end up looking the same as they do in this book when they are finally released — they are important as an indicator of the way CSS development is progressing, so that forward-looking Web authors can get a heads up. The CSS3 properties outlined here are my "best guesses" based on my own Web-authoring experience. In some cases there are wholly separate chapters devoted to Internet Explorer-only CSS properties, but many of them fall into already-defined families of properties and are included in those chapters. In addition to all of the chapters in this book are some appendices designed to provide the Web author with quick reference material to have on hand when writing CSS code.

Chapter 1 ("The Birth of CSS") explores how CSS in its current form came to be. The following two chapters (Chapter 2, "(X)HTML and Its Relationship to CSS" and Chapter 3, "Browser Adoption of CSS") provide information on how CSS can be accessed within Web page code, and how the major browser manufacturers have increasingly adopted CSS within their browsers. Chapter 4 ("Implementation of Basic CSS Concepts") looks at how some of the basic concepts behind CSS — such as inheritance, grouping CSS code and cascading rules — are implemented in the major browsers. Chapters 5 and 6 ("The Cascade" and "CSS Units," respectively) extend this concept further by looking at how the "C" of "CSS" works, and explains the many different fundamental units of measure that can be used in conjunction with certain CSS properties. Chapter 7 ("Pseudo-Classes and Pseudo-Elements") looks at how these CSS elements which allow for special or conditional types of formatting can be utilized. Chapter 8 ("Media Types and Media Queries") introduces the concept of media types and examines how Web pages can be modified so that they can be displayed through such things as print or "talking browsers."

Chapters 9 and 10 ("Font Properties" and "Text Properties") begin the "meat and potatoes" part of the book for most readers, looking in detail at the properties used daily by an increasing number of Web authors. Chapter 11 ("Text Property Extensions") is the first chapter devoted wholly to Internet Explorer-specific properties, most of which are aimed at formatting Web pages for an international audience. Chapter 12 ("Box Properties") brings us back to the "meat and potatoes" area of CSS formatting, explaining in detail the box set CSS properties, which can determine how a wide variety of Web elements such as headers, images and paragraphs can be enhanced. The topic of Chapter 13 ("Color") used to be part of the background family of properties, but the draft CSS3 module has charted a new course for using color on the Web, all of which is looked at in this section. Background properties — including a number of draft CSS innovations in this area — are covered in Chapter 14 ("Background Properties").

Chapter 15 ("Classification Properties and Generated/Automatic Content") is the start of what for many readers will be the more esoteric uses to which CSS can be put to, and yet represents much of where the real rendering power behind CSS lies. This chapter looks at how its functions enable Web authors to control and enhance content that is automatically generated by the browser, including such things as the numbering and display of lists. Chapter 16 ("Visual Formatting and Detailed Visual Formatting") represents the core of what is popularly known as the "CSS positioning" properties. Chapter 17 ("Visual Effects") looks primarily at properties designed to produce stunning effects using dynamic code. Chapter 18 ("Paged Media") explores those properties related to crafting Web pages so that they can be printed (rather than displayed on a screen) in the precise way that a Web author desires. Chapter 19 ("Tables") looks at the somewhat rag-tag collection of table-related formatting properties, but then rounds off the chapter by looking at ways of creating table-like formatting structures using only CSS. In addition to covering what is already possible to do with user-interface properties in Chapter 20 ("User Interface") — such as providing greater control over the display of such things as cursors and the outlines that surround buttons or text fields in forms that denote a "focus" for user input — it also includes an extensive preview as to how you can affect the functionality of Web pages when now-draft CSS3 properties become available. Mastering the properties covered in these sections guarantees that you will be at the forefront of CSS-based Web design.

Chapter 21 ("Aural Cascading Style Sheets") begins a section of the book covering either under-implemented CSS properties or those specific to working with a particular browser. This chapter explores a relatively new class of properties designed to enable the Web author to determine how a Web page could be spoken aloud by a browser with speech capabilities — sadly, this is poorly implemented in the major browsers. Chapter 22 ("Ruby") looks at the properties used in formatting a particular type of Chinese text layout; these properties are specific to Internet Explorer but are now being actively considered by the W3C for inclusion in the future CSS3 specification. Columnar layout properties, based in part on some old browser-specific HTML tags in Netscape Navigator, are explored in Chapter 23 ("Multi-Column Layout"). Chapter 24 ("Scrollbars") briefly looks at some properties designed to change the appearance of scrollbars specific to recent versions of Internet Explorer. The final chapter (Chapter 25 "Filters and Transitions") is a sizable one devoted to Internet Explorer's CSS-based way of adding some interesting and often dynamic visual effects.

Appendix A is a CSS compatibility chart, looking at all of the "Safe," "Unsafe" and "Partial"-ly implemented CSS1 and CSS2 properties for various versions of the browsers Web authors are likely to run into. Appendix B provides an alphabetical listing of all CSS1, CSS2 and Internet Explorer CSS properties (minus the admittedly oddball filter and transition properties) as a quick reference. Appendix C looks at the CSS3 Mobile Profile and contains properties that are expected to be implemented in scaled-down browsers intended for use while "on the go."

Conventions Used in This Book

`Courier` font is used to indicate HTML code, both in the listings and in the shorter code extracts that you'll find included in the text. The same font is also used to indicate HTML tags and CSS property names (such as `background-color`). In a few cases, we show a code extract and then explain how to modify it to change its behavior. In this case, the code that is added or modified is shown in **`bold courier font`**.

Icons are used to call out material that is of significance and to which the reader should be alerted:

Core Tip

Tip: *This is particularly useful information that will save the reader time, highlight a valuable programming tip, or offer specific advice on increasing productivity.*

Further Information

CSS is an ever-evolving subject. At the time of writing, the CSS3 specification was still very much in draft status, and I was writing against an ever-moving target. The definitive place to find information about CSS is the extensive material devoted to the official specifications that can be found at the World Wide Web Consortium's Web site, which can be found at:

`http://www.w3.org/Style/CSS`

It is also a good idea for any Web master to keep abreast of the latest developments in browser technology. The two acknowledged major players in the industry (for both Mac and PC) are Microsoft and Netscape. You can find out more about the latest developments and releases of Microsoft's Internet Explorer at:

`http://www.microsoft.com/windows/ie`

Similarly, you can find out more about Netscape Navigator by going to Netscape's home page at:

```
http://home.netscape.com
```

Mozilla is an offshoot project of Netscape Corporation that was charged with the mission of producing a browser incorporating open standards such as CSS. The latest version of their browser understands CSS1 fully, as well as much of CSS2. Keeping tabs on this browser is important as it has laid the groundwork upon which subsequent versions of Netscape Navigator (so far, versions 6.x and 7.x) have been based. More information about the Mozilla browser can be found at:

```
http://www.mozilla.org
```

Microsoft and Netscape are not the only two browsers out there. While keeping several versions of their browsers on your system is handy for testing purposes, you should also think about adding other browsers to you Webmaster's "toolbox" when checking whether your CSS code functions the way you intend it to. Foremost of these "other" browsers is Opera, which has repeatedly led the way in adopting the latest developments from the CSS specifications. You can find out more information about Opera from the Opera Software Web site at:

```
http://www.opera.com
```

If you are using Linux as an operating system, you have two main choices when it comes to Web browsers: either the Linux version of Netscape Navigator/Mozilla, or Konqueror, which is included as part of the KDE desktop environment. This browser correctly renders most of CSS1 and much of CSS2. More information about this browser — which is unavailable under MS-Windows, can be found at:

```
http://www.konqueror.org
```

Additional Material

A Web site has been created containing all of the example code from this book. If you are looking to grab a working code example or to find out the latest browser compatibility information, please visit the following site:

```
http://www.corecss.com
```

Feedback

No computer book is perfect and this book is unlikely to be an exception to that rule. Even though this book has been subject to a long period of revision and technical review, there are bound to be errors and other places where improvements could be made. If you find an error or if there is something that you think might make the book more useful, please send an e-mail to the author at the following e-mail address:

```
author@corecss.com
```

THE BIRTH OF CSS

Topics in This Chapter

- The Birth of the Web and HTML
- The World Wide Web Consortium Introduces Cascading Style Sheets
- XHTML, CSS2 and CSS3
- Re-emergence of the Browser Wars?

Chapter 1

The World Wide Web began in 1991 as the result of a project by computer engineer Tim Berners-Lee at the European Centre for Nuclear Research (CERN) in Geneva, Switzerland. His goal was to get different computers to communicate with each other and display information across the Internet. Berners-Lee's work soon blossomed into the Web we know today.

The Web was founded on two major protocols: the Hypertext Transport Protocol ("HTTP"), which transfers Web page information across the Internet, and the Hypertext Markup Language (better known as "HTML"), which formats the way in which a page is displayed within a Web browser. In the days of the original HTML 1.0 specification, things were pretty simple, as there were only a few HTML tags, designed primarily to handle such things as modest text formatting, hypertext links and the inclusion of images within a Web page.

The Web quickly grew in popularity, especially with the release of the Mosaic browser from the National Center for Supercomputing Applications in 1993, the first relatively easy-to-use browser for the popular Microsoft Windows and Macintosh operating systems. The initial version of Netscape Navigator, one of the first major commercial browsers, followed soon after, in 1994.

Arguably the first shot of what would become to be known as the "browser wars" was fired by Netscape when they sought to make their Web browser stand out from the crowd by creating new HTML tags for Webmasters — tags whose effects could *only* be viewed within Netscape's browser. Many of these new tags provided desirable options for Webmasters, giving them the ability to add such things as tables, frames and enhanced text formatting. This strategy not only lured Webmasters to create pages using these new tags, but also drew in viewers who realized they were "missing out" on things if they didn't have the Netscape browser. This strategy was one of the things that helped Netscape to quickly grab a majority of the Web-browser market. This strategy worked well for Netscape — while it may seem hard to believe now, back in the mid-1990s there were several dozen commercial Web browsers vying for market share, the majority of which have long since fallen by the wayside. (In fact, the author worked on one of these, the now largely forgotten "Cyberjack," produced by Delrina — best known at the time for its "WinFax" fax software — released in 1995.) One of Netscape's main competitors at the time was Spyglass, which had a license to sell a commercial version of the Mosaic browser. It was at this time that Microsoft's Bill Gates realized the impact the Web was going to make on the future of computing and communications, and so Microsoft decided to get into the browser market by purchasing the rights to Spyglass's browser code. The initial version of Microsoft's Internet Explorer came shortly thereafter.

Microsoft soon began to incorporate new HTML tags into their browser, in an attempt to get Webmasters to preferentially use their code and viewers to use Internet Explorer in order to see these new features in action. Thanks to the many features that these new tags brought to Web design, and the fact that Microsoft offered their browser for free, Internet Explorer soon took off in popularity.

Thus the "browser wars" began in earnest as Netscape and Microsoft competed for "mind share" by creating new HTML tags in an attempt to sway Webmasters to incorporate them into their Web pages.

Unfortunately for the Web community, this conflict means that Internet Explorer and Netscape Navigator don't agree about a lot of things. Both companies have introduced all sorts of HTML enhancements and technologies, some of which have been wildly successful (such as Netscape's HTML table standard or Internet Explorer's `<font>` tag) and some of which have failed to gain wide acceptance (such as Netscape's abortive layers standard or Internet Explorer's Active Channels feature). Even when the two companies incorporate the same technology within their browsers, there are often incompatibilities between the implementation of the technology (a point with which any JavaScript developer will readily agree).

These days, Webmasters still have to jump through hoops in order to make Web pages function and display properly in the two major browsers. Some Webmasters simply decide to craft their Web pages to look best in one browser, to the detriment of those using a different browser. A few Webmasters go so far as to write code that will detect the type of browser being used, and then deliver a Web page optimized for that browser. While in some ways this might be seen as an ideal circumstance, few Webmasters have the time or resources to do this properly. The majority simply design their Web sites to work optimally within the two major browsers, but this restricts the Web author to code Web pages that often cater to the "lowest common denominator" in Web design and functionality.

Many of the non-standard HTML tags introduced in both Netscape Navigator and Internet Explorer make it hard or impossible for people using command-line browsers (such as Lynx) or people with disabilities (such as blind users who use browsers that read content aloud) to "view" a Web site.

As a result of these issues, most professional Webmasters test their Web pages against different versions of each of the major browsers and several of the less popular browsers in order to examine their Web pages for general compatibility.

Clearly, something had to be done before HTML became too awkward and unwieldy for use. This is where the World Wide Web Consortium enters the picture.

1.1 The World Wide Web Consortium Introduces Cascading Style Sheets

Tim Berners-Lee created the Web at CERN, and the initial standards for HTML 1.0 and HTML 2.0 were governed by them. But CERN's main focus is particle physics research, not the Web, and so in 1994 CERN abdicated its role as the standards-setting body for HTML. It passed the torch to a newly created body called the World Wide Web Consortium, better known simply as "W3C." The W3C has convinced major software companies, including Netscape Communications, Microsoft, IBM, Novell, Sun Microsystems and many more, to become members of this standards body. This arrangement provides the software firms with lines of communication to other member firms and to a body recognized as authoritative in the devising and setting of a workable standard for HTML.

The W3C is designed to be a neutral meeting ground, where competing companies can come together to contribute to and comply with future Web standards. The W3C recognized the need to bring some stability to HTML, as the multiple tags introduced during the "browser wars" threatened to introduce widespread incompatibilities into working HTML. The W3C tried to consolidate existing HTML standards, first with the official HTML 3.2 specification, later with the HTML 4.0, and most recently the XHTML 1.0 specification and the XHTML 1.1 recommendation. These specifications adopted many of the HTML tags made popular in both Internet Explorer and Netscape Navigator, even though these tags often failed to conform to one of HTML's main guiding principles: that markup should reflect the structure of a document rather than its physical layout.

HTML was originally designed with the intention of displaying the logical structure of a document, as opposed to dealing with the finer issues of formatting text and image layout. This was done because there are many different varieties of computers out there, and they could not be expected to display content in exactly the same way. By defining logical constants as the basis for Web documents, it was left up to the Web browser programmer to create software that could adequately represent these structures in a way that would look best under a particular computer or a specific operating system. In this way, HTML was designed to be as widely compatible with as many computer platforms as possible.

But much of the drive by the browser manufacturers to provide Webmasters with proprietary tags was spurred by Webmasters' demand for better control over the layout of elements on a Web page, similar to what already exists in desktop publishing programs. Over time, however, these extra tags have increased the overall complexity of Web pages, in addition to producing many Web sites along the way that could not be viewed properly when viewed under the "wrong" browser. The HTML 4.0 specification in particular tried to consolidate the existing state of HTML at that point in time, but it was felt that action had to be taken in order to curb the development of further HTML tags by the browser manufacturers.

Thus the idea of Cascading Style Sheets (CSS) was born.

CSS is an effort by the W3C to minimize the need for the introduction of new *physical* formatting tags (such as the font or table tags) by browser manufacturers — chiefly Microsoft and Netscape — by making such tags unnecessary. CSS is a compromise, providing the page layout features that Webmasters want by adding CSS formatting elements to existing HTML tags.

CSS retains much of the logical structure of a Web page while delivering many of the page layout features in a way that is easy to understand and powerful in the effects it produces. Under currently implemented CSS, it is possible to do the following on a Web page:

- specify the exact point size of text
- add indentations to text
- set margins within a Web page
- add new formatting elements to a Web page, such as borders around text
- use such measurement units as inches and centimeters to set precise sizes for text or images displayed on a Web page
- create a distinctive style for individual Web pages or sets of Web pages
- change the fundamental way a tag is supposed to be displayed onscreen
- precisely lay out text, images and other objects using absolute screen references
- set precisely where a background image is displayed, and whether it should be repeated across or down a Web page
- alter the spacing between letters, between words or lines of text, and much more

CSS's long list of features provides many of the page layout and typographical functions Webmasters have been looking for, although it still provides less layout or typographic control than desktop publishing programs. CSS is really a mechanism for modifying how content is displayed on a Web page, and is not designed as a comprehensive layout tool. Despite this, CSS provides Webmasters much finer control over where and how things appear on a Web page than can be achieved using regular HTML.

1.2   XHTML, CSS2 and CSS3

HTML development has not stood still in the meantime. The XHTML 1.0 standard, released in January 2000, succeeded the HTML 4.01 specification. The "X" in "XHTML" points to another Web coding standard called "XML," short for "eXtended Markup Language." XML is a way to embody and describe data elements, and is used in the construction of many Web-based databases. The new XHTML 1.0 specification (and the XHTML 1.1 recommendation, which is likely to become a formal specification soon) is a way of taking the descriptive data features of XML and combining them with the ease with which that data can be displayed using HTML. So the XHTML 1.0 specification merges aspects of XML into HTML — in fact XHTML is HTML redefined using XML expressions.

The XHTML 1.0 specification also requires Web authors to write their code to a more conforming style — in other words, no more "sloppy" coding — in order for an XHTML-compliant browser to understand it. Some of the new rules imposed by the XHTML include:

- certain XHTML elements must always appear on a page (such as `<!doctype>`, `<html>`, `<title>` and `<body>`)
- tags and attributes must be in lowercase
- all XHTML elements must be "closed" (i.e., there must always be a closing tag, even if a tag is "stand-alone")
- any attribute values must be in quotes.

This is not a book on XHTML, so no lengthy explanation of these points will be offered here, but it is worth pointing out that all of the code examples in this book have been rewritten in order to conform with the XHTML specification where possible.

Development on the CSS specification continues, and so in order to further enhance and extend the capabilities of Web browsers without the need for new HTML tags, the W3C first introduced CSS2 in 1998. CSS2 was not designed to succeed the CSS1 specification, but rather to extend it with new functionality, and to better define many of the existing properties covered in the previous CSS1 specification. Among other things, CSS2 includes support for the following:

- definitions that support new media display types, such as print

- "aural" style sheets
- special features designed to better support Web pages across different languages
- much more precise control over font selection, including better font-matching mechanisms, "creating" fonts and support for downloadable fonts
- properties that will make table displays more versatile
- an extended box family of properties
- greater ability to control the visibility of content, including controlling overflowing content and clipping sections of it from display
- the ability to set minimum and maximum widths and heights for on-screen elements
- automated functions that help generate content for such things as counters and automatic numbering
- greater control over user-interface elements, such as the display of cursors
- the ability for Web authors to specify exactly where elements should be positioned onscreen.

Probably the single most innovative concept introduced in the CSS2 specification is the introduction of aural style sheets — in other words, information that tells the Web browser how a page should *sound* when read. Aural style sheet information embedded in the code on a Web page is designed to tell a browser how the text on a Web page should be interpreted and read by speaking devices. In large part, aural design is there to aid the visually impaired, but it has other, far-reaching uses; it will likely be important when you can tap into the Web while on the go. Aural style sheets foreshadow the day when a computer reads Web pages aloud while you are driving in your car or in situations where your hands are otherwise occupied.

While a Web page may look great on your computer monitor, it doesn't always look so marvelous when the same Web page is printed. The introduction of the "paged media" concept in CSS2 tries to overcome aspects of the Web that do not lend themselves well to other media types, such as printed text. The paged media components of CSS2 allow Web authors to determine where such things as page breaks should occur when a page is printed, and where they want to set divisions both on the Web (on-screen) and off (printed). This also means that you can set such things as headers and footers to the printed page, whether a page should be displayed in landscape or portrait style, even where such things as crop marks should be displayed. CSS2 extends this control even further, to the extent that you can now distinguish between left- and right-facing pages, setting different margin values for each side. In addition to making Web pages more "print friendly," these new properties enable Web authors to better render Web pages for other specific media devices, including Braille readers, WebTV devices, small handheld computers and more.

Font characteristics are also expanded in CSS2. Using CSS1, you can set the size, type and color of a font. CSS2 allows Web authors to specify more precisely the type of font to be displayed, by providing information a browser can use in order to find a closer match to the fonts present on the user's system. CSS2 goes further still by providing browsers with downloadable font types if a font specified on a Web page does not exist on a user's computer, so Web authors can specify the exact font to be displayed. This new mechanism also supports Unicode, making it much easier for Web authors to add characters from non-European languages.

These and other such CSS2 features will provide Web authors with many wonderful new ways to shape and craft their Web pages. At the time of this writing, however, none of these features can be found in the popular Web browsers. It may take a while before CSS2 catches on in a big way, since many of these changes rely on the browser manufacturers to add significant new features to their products. In short, CSS2 provides Web authors with many new and useful tools, but as the "big two" browsers have yet to implement this specification fully, we still have to wait a while before we can use all of its properties.

An update to CSS2, called CSS2.1, was released in August 2002. It does not introduce anything really new, and is really more of an errata list of minor errors and things that were missed in writing up the original CSS2 specification. Still, it helps firm up the CSS2 specification as a whole prior to moving on to CSS3.

While browser manufacturers continue to play "catch-up" with implementing the properties comprising the CSS2 specification, the W3C continued work on a subsequent CSS3 specification. They took a new, modularized approach towards making the new specification, wanting to get updates and changes to CSS faster than simply issuing a single, "monolithic" specification after months or years of development. This way, the W3C can more easily keep in step with the browser manufacturers' demands for the addition of new CSS features, allowing for a more flexible road map for driving the development of CSS as a whole.

The various modules introduced under the umbrella of CSS3 development include further refinements and enhancements to existing CSS properties as well as those in completely new areas. These enhancements and additions include such things as:

- more versatile selectors, allowing you to set conditional settings for formatting purposes (i.e., such as being able to apply a formatting style only to the first paragraph after a header, for example)
- greater control over color, including such things as gamma correction
- ruby layout properties, used primarily for adding commentary text in languages like Japanese
- the ability to add and format columnar displays
- user-interface properties allowing for greater control over such things as selectable form elements
- selected CSS properties aimed at mobile communication devices

- descriptions of how Scalable Vector Graphics (SVG) should be displayed
- additional styles for formatting lists in other languages
- numerous other enhancements that provide greater control over such things as the placing of background images, font and text display, line formatting properties, refinements to cascading rules and much more.

This book looks at the latest developments in the CSS3 specification (except SVG, a topic too large to conveniently cover here), with several new chapters devoted to the wholly new sets of properties (such as ruby and columns) and enhancements added to chapters covering existing CSS1 and CSS2 properties.

Core Tip

For the very latest information on new W3C developments with CSS, see the "CSS: Under Construction" page at:
`http://www.w3c.org/Style/CSS/current-work`.

The W3C is not the final word in CSS development. Ultimately it is the browser manufacturers that have to implement the latest CSS recommendations and final specifications. And there is evidence that some browser manufacturers are not willing to wait for the W3C before implementing features they deem necessary now.

1.3   Re-emergence of the Browser Wars?

One can justifiably ask about the relevancy of a "browser war" now that the major battles seem to have been handily won by Internet Explorer, which currently commands somewhere in the region of 90% of all browsers used. For many Web authors, it's no longer a matter of ensuring a Web site is compatible with all of the major browsers, but instead making sure that it is workable when used by the most recent versions of Internet Explorer. Knowing how to tailor pages to work best with this browser is knowledge most Web authors want to know.

Despite Internet Explorer's preponderance on the browser scene, it would be foolish to dismiss the existence of other browsers out there. In fact, it may be fair to say that the browser wars have simply entered a new phase, and CSS has become one of the battlegrounds as browser manufacturers add their own extensions to it. On the good side, it seems as though browser manufacturers have been converted to the potential of implementing as many of the officially sanctioned CSS properties as possible in order to win mind share amongst Web authors.

Starting with Internet Explorer 4.0 Microsoft has been adding their own extensions to CSS. Some of these CSS properties have later become recommendations under developing CSS specifications — such as Ruby — while others are wholly new properties that as yet have no parallel under the official W3C specifications, like the scrollbar formatting properties and transition filters. In all, over 40 cumulative CSS properties have been added to various versions of Internet Explorer, and these are all covered in detail in this book.

While the user base for such browsers as Netscape Navigator has been greatly diminished since the start of the browser wars, it is far from dead. In fact, with the deep pockets of AOL behind it as well as the collected efforts of the open source development community behind the Mozilla browser (whose code base has been going into versions of Netscape Navigator since version 6.0) it certainly should not be written off. It is interesting to note that Mozilla/Netscape have been adding their own CSS extensions within the releases of these twinned browsers — in fact a staggering 160+ CSS extensions have been added to various versions of these browsers. But for the most part these extensions are anticipations of developments of the CSS specification by the W3C, and they are also "unofficial" extensions, none of them officially documented (the extensions to Internet Explorer are well covered by Microsoft for aspiring developers). These extensions are not included in this book due to their ever-changing nature, and because for the most part they parallel developments in upcoming CSS specifications.

While its command of the browser market is relatively small, Opera is another browser that should not be ignored. While it has long been at the forefront of CSS compatibility, it has also introduced its own small subset of CSS extensions — so far, three in total (again, they are covered in this book). Though Opera has a small user base when compared to Internet Explorer, the company that produces it has been aggressively pushing it for use in forthcoming portable hardware browsers, and it is also available under a wide variety of operating systems.

Though versions of Internet Explorer are available for various releases of Microsoft Windows as well as the Macintosh OS, there is no version of it available for the increasingly popular Linux operating system — nor is there likely to be in the foreseeable future. There are a number of different browsers available for this operating system, including Opera and Netscape Navigator, as well as Linux-only browsers such as Galleon, Emacspeak and Konqueror. Many of these browsers have good-to-excellent support for CSS, though thankfully none of them seem to have added their own CSS extensions. Taken together, they may represent a small portion of the browsers used to visit your Web site, but they too are worth noting, if only for the ways they implement CSS — sometimes, like Emacspeak, they are well in advance of other leading browsers.

It is probably too early to say whether or not the browser wars are over, since it seems likely that they are entering a new phase — one in which the operating system or hardware platform is likely to prove as important for Web authors to consider as browser-specific extensions belonging to any one browser. No matter how you look at it, CSS compatibility has become a real factor in garnering mind share amongst the user base and with Web authors. Greater adoption of CSS properties within the major browsers means that today's Webmasters can no longer afford to overlook using CSS as an integral part of their Web site designs.

One thing is clear: CSS is here to stay. The more you know about how to use it effectively, the more professional you and your Web site designs will be.

(X)HTML AND ITS RELATIONSHIP TO CSS

Topics in This Chapter

- Ways CSS Can Be Incorporated into HTML Code
- The `style` Element
- The `span` Element
- The `div` Element
- The `link` Element
- The `style` Attribute
- The `class` Attribute
- The `id` Attribute

Chapter 2

CSS does not replace HTML code (or XHTML code for that matter) on a Web page; instead, it is added to existing HTML elements, augmenting them. You do not have to change the way you write HTML code for your Web pages, as CSS can simply sit on top of your existing code. In fact, once you get used to using CSS, you may find yourself using fewer HTML elements in favor of CSS. For example, the `font` element is superceded by various CSS properties (such as `font-size`, `font-family`, `font-weight`, `line-height`, etc.) that give you far greater control over how text is displayed onscreen. And once you understand the basics of CSS, you'll find it easy to understand and to use.

CSS works by adding CSS properties to a specific HTML element, which tell the browser how the element should be modified in its display. A typical CSS statement (or "rule") consists of two parts:

- the element to be changed, known as the "selector"
- a statement that describes how the "selector" should be displayed, known as the "declaration"

Listing 2.1 is a simple example of some HTML code that includes a few simple CSS rules. The effects of this code can be seen in Figure 2–1.

Listing 2.1	*Simple CSS Example*

```
<html>
<head>
<title>Simple CSS Example</title>
<style>
p {color: lime}
em {color: red}
body {font-size: xx-large}
</style>
</head>
<body>
This text on this page is displayed using a double-extra-large
font size.
<p>
This text is displayed at the same size, but is lime green.
</p>
<p>
This text is the same as the previous paragraph, <em>but this
emphasized text is in red</em>.
</p>
</body>
</html>
```

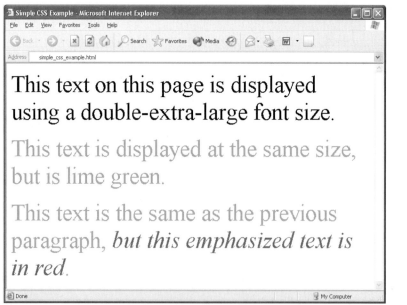

Figure 2–1   Web page displaying the effects of some simple CSS code.

There are three separate sets of CSS modifications being made to the HTML elements that appear in the previous code example. In the first example, set between the `style` element in the header of the Web page, the first selector is the paragraph element (`<p>`, but without the usual brackets; for an explanation of why this is so please read on) and the declaration assigns a lime color value to it ("`color: lime`"). The second selector is the emphasis element, which is set to the color red ("`color: red`"). The third CSS example is set to the `body` element, which is the selector, modifying it with the declaration "`font-size: xx-large`". This applies the effect of a double-extra large font (the equivalent of `<font size="7">`) to all of the text appearing on the Web page. As you can see from Figure 2–1, the more specific emphasis element turns the text it encloses to red — it does not stay green as does the rest of the text in that paragraph. This is an example of the cascading effect (the "C" in "CSS") which says that more specific references override more general ones. (This is explored in depth in Chapter 5, "The Cascade").

This is a relatively simple example of what can be done with a few CSS elements, but the combined effects of some well-chosen CSS code can easily make your Web pages stand out from the crowd.

2.1　Adding Cascading Style Sheets to Web Pages

There are several ways in which CSS information can be specified within a Web page. In this section, we look at the HTML elements and attributes that enable Web authors to add CSS code to their Web pages.

The different ways in which CSS information can be added to a Web page are as follows:

- It can be embedded within the header of a Web page
- It can be embedded within the body of a Web page (usually in certain sections or individual elements)
- It can be specified within a separate Web page

Each of these will be explored in this section.

There are four HTML elements and three HTML attributes that can be used to add CSS to a Web page. The HTML elements are `<style>`, `<span>`, `<div>` and `<link>`. The HTML attributes are `style`, `class` and `id`. The three elements are most commonly used to modify a section of a Web page or a particular set of HTML elements. The attributes, which can be added to almost every existing HTML element, are designed to modify the display of the particular HTML element with which it is associated.

As noted previously, there is a special formatting style used to signify the CSS modifications to be associated with a particular HTML element. The specified element (the selector) is not surrounded by the usual angle brackets, but is instead left "naked" at the beginning of a line. The declaration is contained within "curly" brackets ("{" and "}"), and a simple space separates the selector and the declaration.

Core Tip

Many beginners to CSS often make the simple mistake of adding angle brackets to the selector, or using the wrong style of bracket type in the declaration. Browsers are finicky when it comes to CSS rules, and it is important to get this right.

2.2   The <style> Element

As we saw in the initial CSS example, it is possible to add CSS code within the header of a Web page. This is done by using the <style> element, which is used to set CSS properties to a Web element that is applied to the whole of a Web document.

The <style> element is always contained within the header of a Web page, and unless overridden elsewhere in the Web page, its effects are applied globally to the selected HTML elements contained within it.

The <style> element has several attributes: accesskey, dir, disabled, lang, language, media, tabindex, title, and type, all of which are optional — and frankly, only a few of which are used routinely in practice. It is important to know the values of the attributes in those cases where it may be useful, however.

The accesskey attribute enables Web authors to assign a keyboard key to the <style> element. This keyboard "shortcut" enables the user to hit ALT plus the designated key which then selects the element.

The dir attribute is a standard HTML attribute that sets the text direction, and can take the values ltr and rtl (for "left-to-right" and "right-to-left," respectively). This does not necessarily switch the direction for displayed text, but instead is there to tell the browser which way it is meant to be read.

The disabled attribute — which is an unofficial attribute for <style> and is only supported within Internet Explorer version 4.0 and higher — indicates that the particular CSS function should not be "enabled" (in other words, that its effects should not be displayed). This is for use in circumstances where you may wish to disable the CSS formatting display in a particular place on the Web page. If you use this particular attribute, the content associated with the selected element is still displayed, but is not formatted in the CSS style indicated.

`lang` is another standard HTML attribute, and is used to set the language code (i.e., "english" or "french"). Internet Explorer 4.0 and up add an additional `language` attribute, which associates the element with a scripting language (like JavaScript or VBScript).

The `media` attribute is used to specify the type of medium for which the CSS formatting is to be used. There are nine distinct values: `all`, `aural`, `braille`, `handheld`, `print`, `projection`, `screen`, `tv` and `tty`, each reflecting the different types of media the Web page can be "viewed" in. The default value is `screen` (i.e., a computer screen). If a device exists to translate the Web page into a different medium (such as a digital video projector for the `projection` value, or a Palm device for the `handheld` value), the device will use the CSS elements associated with the particular style used for it. Actual support for most of these attributes has always been spotty, and on the whole you are probably better off trying to tailor your code for specific devices if you expect heavy use in these other media displays. (Also, as we will see, there are a number of media types called by the `@media` "at-rule" which accomplishes much the same thing, and is much more flexible. This is covered in detail in Chapter 8, "Media Types and Media Queries.")

`tabindex` is another accessibility attribute (like `accesskey`), and in this case it sets the tab order for the element. This relates to the order in which selectable elements on a page can be accessed when you hit the tab key repeatedly. Normally, when you do this, elements are selected in order from the top of the page to the bottom. But when you set an integer value to `tabindex`, you can interrupt this flow and make the element it is associated with either a priority tab-able item or not.

The `type` attribute simply specifies the MIME type contained by the `<style>` element. There are two possible values for this at the moment: "text/css", which applies to CSS, and "text/javascript", which applies to JavaScript code. For the most part, the `text/css` value is simply assumed, and the two major browsers do not have any problems interpreting CSS code when this value is not present. This attribute is widely recognized in all major browsers.

There used to be a common recommendation to surround the `style` element with comment elements (i.e., "`<!--`" and "`-->`") in case older browsers which do not recognize the element display the content contained within them. This concern is pretty much a thing of the past these days, and if you are truly concerned about your CSS code being displayed in an older browser, it's old enough so that you wouldn't seriously be coding CSS for it anyway.

\<style\> and CSS3

The CSS3 specification has introduced some interesting variations for the \<style\> element. These variations greatly extend the uses to which this element can be used for adding CSS code to a page. When adopted by browser manufacturers, they will enable Web authors to add code directly to the style attribute that otherwise would have had to have been added to the header of a Web page — greatly increasing coding flexibility. Say, for example, you are working with a standard template file for a Web site that contains the HTML header, and you either don't have ready access to changing it, or don't want to add code to the header of a page when you only intend to implement a single formatting instance limited to a single page. This would be a situation where the CSS3 extensions to the \<style\> element would help you out of a potential jam.

The first variant allows Web authors to add pseudo-elements to a particular Web element. Curly braces are wrapped around the "standard" CSS properties for a given element, and then the pseudo-element code is added, and the CSS properties associated with the pseudo-element are similarly wrapped in curly braces. The following code snippet makes this clear:

```
<p style="{background-color: black; color: white} ::first-letter
{color: red}">Some sample text</p>
```

(Note that in CSS3 double colons are recommended over single colons for pseudo-elements, hence "::first-letter" instead of ":first-letter"). Pseudo-elements are covered in detail in Chapter 7, "Pseudo-Elements, Pseudo-Classes and Selectors."

The second variation allows you to set the display properties on a link — something that hitherto would have had to have been set either in the header of a page or in an external style sheet. Like the first variant, the CSS properties are wrapped in curly braces, as the following line of code shows:

```
Visit <a href="http://www.captmondo.com" style={color: navy}
:link {background: aqua}
:visited {background: red}
:hover {background: yellow}
:active {background: green}">captmondo.com</a>.
```

The third variation allows you to reference an external style sheet directly within an element. Again, this allows you to easily supercede any CSS code that may already be contained in the document, providing the flexibility of creating style sheets on an element-by-element basis if need be. The following line of code shows how this could be done:

```
<span style="@import url(funky.css)">Funky-looking text</span> set
against decidedly un-funky text.
```

2.3   The <span> and <div> Elements

Other HTML elements can be used to apply CSS to a specific section of a Web page, enabling the Web author to set special CSS characteristics for that section, visually differentiating it from the rest of the Web page. This can be accomplished by using the <span> and <div> elements.

The <span> element is designed to temporarily override any existing CSS information that may have already been specified, and is meant to be used as an inline element. The <div> element works in the same manner, but is supposed to be applied to block-level elements.

Inline elements refer to those common formatting HTML elements that are usually contained within a line of text, such as <b> or <i>. These elements do not necessarily begin or end a separate line onscreen. Elements such as <h1> or <p> do, and they are known as block elements. <span> and <div> work in the same way, but are simply meant to be applied to different types or groups of HTML elements. As you will see later in the book, some CSS elements can only be used with either inline or block-level HTML elements.

The <span> and <div> elements both have only one required attribute: style. The style attribute sets the CSS element to be displayed directly within the element itself (instead of from the header, from within the <style> elements). You'd use style primarily in circumstances where you want to set CSS values to a particular element on a Web page. When you are not setting CSS to a specific element in this way, you can "call" specific CSS values using the id and class attributes.

Using style, you can directly set the CSS rule to apply to a specific HTML element (or with the aid of the <span> and <div> elements, to a group of such elements contained within them). Its structure has already been explained, but you will note one important addition in the sample code provided for the <div> element: how to add more than one CSS attribute to an HTML element. This can be accomplished by adding a semicolon (";") between two or more CSS statements, forming a compound CSS rule that is associated with the specific HTML element.

The other two attributes you are most likely to use are id and class. Using these two attributes you can identify which CSS rules that have previously been set by the <style> element in the header of a Web page should be used to format a given HTML element. The id attribute is meant to be used when you want to add CSS formatting to a single element, and class should be used when you want to apply the same type of CSS formatting to multiple elements. For an example of these attributes at work, take a look at the code depicted in Listing 2.2 (whose results are shown in Figure 2–2).

Listing 2.2	*id and class Example*

```
<html>
<head>
<title>id and class Example</title>
</head>
<style>
#blue {color: #0000ff}
.red {color: #ff0000}
body {font-size: 30px}
</style>
<body>
<h1 id="blue">A Big Blue Header</h1>
<p>
Some regular text. <span class="red">Some red text.</span>
</p>
<p>
<div class="red">A block of red text.</div>
</p>
<h2 class="red">A Red Sub-Header</h2>
So have you noticed by now that class="red" has been applied to
multiple elements, and id="blue" only to one?
</body>
</html>
```

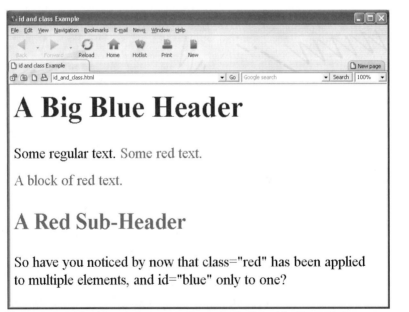

Figure 2–2   The id and class example code displayed in Opera 6.0.

As you can see from the code used in Listing 2.2, the `id="blue"` statement (`id` can be applied to almost any HTML element) has been added to the `<h1>` element, producing a blue header. The `class="red"` statement has been added to a number of elements, including `<div>`, `<span>` and `<h2>` elements. Note also that you specify a CSS rule to be called by an `id` attribute by placing a "#" in front of it, and that you place a period (".") immediately prior to a CSS rule that is to be called by the `class` attribute.

You can make `id` and `class` statements more specific by adding specific Web elements at the beginning of the rule. For example, if you substituted ".red" with "div.red", only the `<div>` elements that called the red `class` would be colored red — any other elements, even if they called the red `class`, would *not* be colored red.

It is worth noting that if you make a mistake and use `id` for formatting multiple instances of Web page elements, most browsers won't give you any problems. So you may well wonder what the functional difference between `id` and `class` is at this point. Since the `id` attribute is supposed to be used only once, it is given greater "weight" when it comes to cascading, and when used it will override an element using the more general `class` attribute.

Unlike many other HTML attributes, values assigned to `id` and `class` are case sensitive. So if you specified a `.red` and a `.Red` class, the browser will read them as separate classes. Further, any value assigned to `id` should be unique, so using a `#blue` and a `#BLUE` id on the same page is invalid, and is likely to cause problems.

The `<span>` and `<div>` elements share all of the same attributes (minus a few, primarily browser-specific variants belonging to `<div>`). In practice you'll probably rarely need to use any of them other than the default `style` attribute, but they are worth knowing for those circumstances where they can be useful.

The `dir` attribute is a standard HTML attribute that sets the text direction, and can take the values `ltr` and `rtl` (for "left-to-right" and "right-to-left," respectively). This does not necessarily switch the direction for displayed text, but instead is there to tell the browser which way it is meant to be read.

`lang` is another standard HTML attribute, and is used to set the language code (i.e., "english" or "french").

Finally, `title` sets the text display for the tooltip. The tooltip is the text that is displayed whenever your mouse passes over a particular element onscreen.

The code examples for both `<span>` and `<div>` also serve to introduce the meaning behind the "Cascading" part of the term "Cascading Style-Sheets." Quite simply, more specific CSS rules tend to override global ones. The designers of CSS realized that there would be situations in which a Web author would want to do just that. When this situation occurs, the browser "cascades" from the more general to the more specific rule. This cascading order is defined by the following rules:

Situation: A browser is presented with a number of CSS statements, some of which conflict with each other.

1. If a statement is applied to a "parent" HTML element (such as
    `<body>`) and elements that are its "children" do *not* have explicit CSS
    statements of their own, the CSS statement that applies to the parent
    rules.
2. The CSS statements are then sorted by explicit weight, and any
    marked `!important` (covered in Chapter 5, "The Cascade") take pre-
    cedence over the others.
3. Any style sheet information that may be imported through the `<link>`
    element will be overruled by any CSS statements contained within the
    Web page.
4. More specific CSS statements overrule more general ones.
5. If two or more CSS statements appear that have the same weight, the
    one specified last wins. This concept is explored in more depth in
    Chapter 5, "The Cascade."

2.4   The \<link\> Element

There is a third way CSS information can be added to a Web page: by specifying CSS
elements in a completely different Web page, which are then linked to the original
page. By specifying the display and layout attributes in a separate Web page, you can
customize the style for a set of Web pages that use ordinary HTML code. This is
potentially most appealing for Web authors who manage large Web sites, since all
you have to do is make changes to a single page which are then reflected globally
throughout your Web site.

To use the `<link>` element, you must first create a simple text file that contains
nothing but CSS formatting information in much the same format as used by the
`<style>` element, as you can see from the code displayed in Listing 2.3 and Listing
2.4 (each representing separate pages named `formatting.css`).

Listing 2.3	*formatting.css #1*

```
<!-- formatting.css #1 -->
body {font-size: x-large}
b {font-size: xx-large; color: red}
i {font-size: large; color: blue}
p {color: gray}
h1 {color: white; background: black}
```

Listing 2.4 *formatting.css #2*

```
<!-- formatting.css #2 -->
body {font-size: x-large; margin: 1in}
b {color: green; background: yellow}
i {color: black}
p {background: gray; color: white}
h1 {border-color: red}
```

Then, you "link" to one of these pages containing pure CSS code from a Web page using the <link> element in the header of that Web page. The code displayed in Listing 2.5 contains a <link> element that references the CSS code page, called for-matting.css.

Listing 2.5 *link Element Example Page*

```
<html>
<head>
<title>link Element Example</title>
<link rel="stylesheet" href="formatting.css" type="text/css">
</head>
<body>
<h1>Link Example</h1>
<p>
This Web page will appear very different depending on the content
of the <b>formatting.css</b> page that it is linked to. This
demonstrates the power behind the use of the <i>LINK</i> tag to
easily make global changes to a number of different Web pages at
once.
</body>
</html>
```

When you use one or the other of the two CSS code pages (Listings 2.3 and 2.4) as the master formatting.css page, you will see how they affect the formatting of elements on the Web page. Figure 2–3 and Figure 2–4 show how each of these two CSS code files are interpreted by the browser.

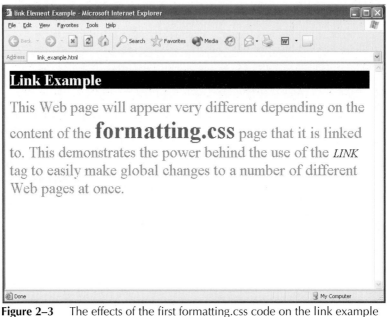

Figure 2–3   The effects of the first formatting.css code on the link example Web page.

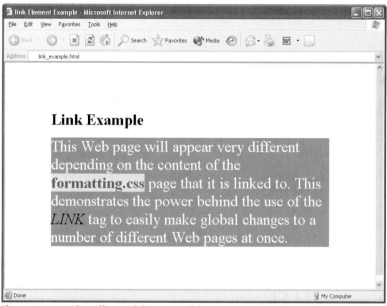

Figure 2–4   The effects of the second formatting.css code on the same link example Web page.

Core Tip

Looking for some "ready-made" CSS code template pages to link to? Try the World Wide Web Consortium's set of such pages, which you can try out and download from their Core Styles page at:
`http://www.w3.org/StyleSheets/Core/.`

This is a mere taste of what can be done using CSS within Web pages. The examples shown here have employed only a small sub-set of the CSS elements available, but nevertheless demonstrate the power behind CSS.

BROWSER ADOPTION OF CSS

Topics in This Chapter

- Internet Explorer 3.x
- Internet Explorer 4.x
- Internet Explorer 4.5 (Macintosh) and 5.x (Windows and Macintosh)
- Internet Explorer 5.5
- Internet Explorer 6.0
- Opera 3.5
- Opera 4.x – 6.x
- Netscape Navigator 4.x
- Mozilla and Netscape Navigator 6.x and Netscape 7.x
- Other Browsers

Chapter 3

While both Netscape and Microsoft have agreed to implement CSS in their respective browsers, it took them both several versions before either of them got it right.

Despite the fact that recent versions of many of the most popular browsers have greatly increased their support for CSS, this support is not still 100%. Even this improved support is a relatively recent development, and Web authors need to know which CSS properties are safe, unsafe or may behave quirkily under certain circumstances in particular browsers. This means that Web authors who want to use CSS still need to know which CSS elements they can and can't use, as well as the significant differences in the ways adopted CSS elements behave in the major browsers. Much of the information contained in this book deals with the ways CSS is currently implemented in the two major browsers, looking at the way particular CSS elements work.

The piecemeal way in which Netscape Navigator and Internet Explorer have adopted CSS elements arguably held CSS back from wider adoption within the Web authoring community. In the "bad old days" (which, in terms of CSS, means the days prior to the release of Internet Explorer 5.5 and Netscape Navigator 6.0) there were many cases where CSS elements supported in Internet Explorer were not supported in Netscape Navigator, vice versa, or were simply not supported in either. Sometimes only certain values of a CSS element were supported, or they only worked when associated with certain HTML tags. There were even cases where a CSS element had been adopted for use within a beta (or "preview") version of a browser and then later dropped in the next beta release — presumably an oversight, but not exactly something to inspire confidence in CSS for a Web author. One other lesson that has been learned the hard way by many Web authors is the fact that the "same" browser may produce different results for a given Web page when used under different operating systems. From a browser developer's perspective this is only natural — given that the code base for a browser is unlikely to be exactly the same across different platforms, you can always expect slightly different results. But in some cases these differences were not so slight, amounting to serious CSS implementation bugs in a given browser. Today, though, the situation is much improved, but for Web authors who like to be thorough and ensure that their Web pages are viewable to all, it is worth knowing which browser-specific pitfalls to avoid.

In general, if a certain feature is already supported within one browser, you can most likely use a CSS element to set it, too. For example, the `text-decoration` element has a value called `blink` that flashes the text on and off repeatedly. It is supported within Netscape Navigator — where you could use the `<blink>` tag to do much the same sort of thing — but up until recently not in Internet Explorer, which never supported the `<blink>` tag. On the other hand, there is a feature seen only in Internet Explorer called "watermarking" that allows the Web author to create a background image that remains fixed upon the page even when a user scrolls up or down. There is a CSS value ("`background-attachment: fixed`") that does the same thing. Not surprisingly, this CSS element is supported within Internet Explorer, but again, up until recently, not within Netscape Navigator. This sort of thing makes for a good rough guide to the type of behavior you can expect from the various browsers.

The widespread adoption of CSS within the most recent popular browsers can be seen as a real success for the W3C, and ultimately for Web authors who now have a fairly reliable new set of powerful formatting tools to use on their Web pages. Now that pretty much all of the CSS1 and much of the CSS2 specification have been adopted within the two major browsers, the use of CSS code on Web pages has exploded. Yet any good Web author will still want to know the details of what CSS properties work — and which don't — in specific browsers.

An understanding of the strengths and weaknesses of a given browser will help you to choose which CSS elements will be most effective in your Web pages.

3.1   Internet Explorer 3.x

Internet Explorer 3.x was the first major browser to implement CSS, although only in a rudimentary fashion. It did not implement many CSS properties, and those that were implemented were rarely implemented fully. Very few people use Internet Explorer 3.x today, so it is probably not worthwhile to try and design pages that would look good in it. This is just as well, since designing Web pages that use the few CSS properties implemented in Internet Explorer 3.x is pretty much an exercise in frustration, anyway. In short, don't plan on designing a CSS-oriented Web site that has to be "safe" for whatever Internet Explorer 3.x users are still out there.

For this reason, in the summary listing of "safe" and "unsafe" elements provided at the end of this book, Internet Explorer 3.x is not included, as it would render too many CSS elements as "unsafe."

3.2 Internet Explorer 4.x

Microsoft greatly extended CSS compatibility within the initial 4.x version of Internet Explorer. This version of Internet Explorer was the first to show that a major browser vendor was serious about implementing CSS.

This version of Internet Explorer was not without its drawbacks, however. While it supported much of the `background`, `border`, `font`, `margin`, `list` and `padding` CSS element families at least partially, it could not support a number of other elements, such as `display` or `clear`/`float` in the Macintosh version at all. There were also some minor variances worth noting in the ways the browser implemented the same CSS elements across different operating systems. Problems implementing the `text-align` property have been noted, as have more general problems when implementing some basic CSS functions, such as containment, inheritance and dealing with certain length units.

This version of Internet Explorer has subsequently been superceded by versions 5.x and 6.x, and the vast majority of Internet Explorer users now use one of these later releases. However, it is worthwhile keeping its limitations in mind for those few users who may still be using it.

Microsoft's tendency to start adding their own browser-specific CSS properties began with this release of Internet Explorer. The `filter` property was added to this version, enabling Web authors to add a number of transitioning effects (see Chapter 25, "Filters and Transitions"). Compared to later versions of the browser, this was a relatively minor addition, but arguably started a trend towards adding fresh browser-specific properties in future versions of Internet Explorer.

Another interesting development with this version of the browser was that it implemented — at least partially — some positioning properties (like `top`, `left` and `vertical-align`) which were being considered at the time for inclusion for the CSS2 specification, which was in a draft status at the time. Microsoft was truly looking forward with this development, though it would take version 5.5 before CSS2 properties were substantially supported.

3.3   Internet Explorer 4.5 (Macintosh) and 5.x (Windows and Macintosh)

Released back in March 1999, Internet Explorer 5.x was the first version of a *major browser* that implemented significant CSS properties. But "first" was not "perfect." Prior to its release, many people had hoped that this version would fully support CSS1, but, unhappily, it did not.

Prior to the release of Internet Explorer 5.x for Windows, Microsoft had made major improvements with the release of the Macintosh 4.5 release of Internet Explorer (IE), adding full or improved support for several CSS elements that were previously unsupported or only partially supported. The work on this browser pointed the way in which CSS support was going. Upon this framework lay the basis of much of the work that was subsequently done to the Windows version of Internet Explorer 5.0. For the most part, Internet Explorer 5.0 handled CSS1 code well. It is worth noting, however, that the Macintosh 4.5 version was actually better in a few cases, such as its more comprehensive handling of the border and background family of elements. In addition to this, it was better when it came to handling the `display` and `float` properties (when used on text elements), though significantly, whereas the Windows versions of Internet Explorer 4.0 fully implemented the `!important` property, Macintosh IE 4.5 did not, so there were important differences between these browsers.

Presumably the improvements that went into Internet Explorer 4.5 for the Macintosh was carried over into the general code base for Internet Explorer 5.0. The 5.0 version of the browser included greater support for such things as the white-space, word-wrap, border-collapse, table-layout and more. Significantly, it also began to support the majority of positioning properties, and a number of internationalization properties. It is notable though that these versions of Internet Explorer (including the Macintosh version 5.0 which came along a little bit later) were relatively weak when it came to supporting the float properties, especially where more complex layouts were attempted.

The Macintosh version of Internet Explorer 5.1 included a feature that would later appear in version 6 of the browser for Windows: the DTD-switch. When the `!doctype` element is used, it tells the browser to follow whatever DTD is specified. This switch enables the Web author to set a page to either strict or standard conformance for the (X)HTML and CSS code contained in a given Web page. So if the `!doctype` is set to a strict rather than a transitional setting, non-compliant code is not rendered properly, if at all. In the case of Internet Explorer, this means that many of their own CSS extensions — such as the scrollbar extensions — are not rendered if the page is set to strict. In order to keep the code examples in this book simple and easy-to-render in any compliant browser, no explicit `!doctype` settings are specified.

It was also this release of Internet Explorer where Microsoft started to add a considerable number of new browser-specific CSS extended properties, and they are:

- `accelerator`
- `ime-mode`
- `layout-flow`
- `layout-grid`
- `layout-grid-char`
- `layout-grid-line`
- `layout-grid-mode`
- `layout-grid-type`
- `line-break`
- `overflow-x`
- `overflow-y`
- `ruby-align`
- `ruby-overhang`
- `ruby-position`
- `text-autospace`
- `text-justify`
- `word-break`

All of these extended CSS properties are covered in various sections throughout the book.

At the time of writing, version 5.1 is the latest version of Internet Explorer available for Macintosh users running OS9, and a version 5.2 is available for those Macintosh users running OS X.

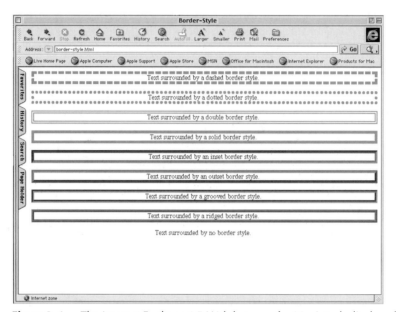

Figure 3–1   The Internet Explorer 4.5 Web browser for Macintosh displayed.

3.4   Internet Explorer 5.5

Internet Explorer 5.5 was released in July 2000, well over a year after the previous 5.0 release. This version constituted a major improvement in complying with both CSS1 and CSS2 properties, managing to fill in major "gaps" in its support for properties hitherto unsupported in the previous version of the browser. This version saw improved support in many areas, including such things as support for the `:first-letter` and `:first-line` pseudo-properties.

One oddity about this browser is that it has incorporated a lot of "bozo code" which ensures in many cases that improperly coded CSS properties are accepted as valid. For example, it accepts improperly formatted CSS code such as hexadecimal color values that don't begin with a hash symbol ("#"), invalid id and class names, and it automatically assumes values to be pixel values if not otherwise specified (so for example, `font-size: 20` would be rendered as `font-size: 20px`). While this might seem like a good thing, the sloppy Web author who doesn't check their invalid code in other browsers may never notice the problem the code will cause in browsers that expect properly formatted CSS.

Additionally, the following browser-specific properties were added to Internet Explorer 5.5:

- `background-position-x`
- `background-position-y`
- `layout-flow`
- `scrollbar-3dlight-color`
- `scrollbar-arrow-color`
- `scrollbar-base-color`
- `scrollbar-darkshadow-color`
- `scrollbar-face-color`
- `scrollbar-highlight-color`
- `scrollbar-shadow-color`
- `text-autospace`
- `text-justify`
- `text-kashida-space`
- `text-underline-position`
- `word-wrap`
- `writing-mode`
- `zoom`

3.5   Internet Explorer 6.0

In terms of CSS, Internet Explorer 6.0 only included a limited number of improvements over the previous 5.5 version for Windows. With only some minor exceptions, all of the CSS1 properties are supported, and there is much improved — though not full — CSS2 compliance. On the CSS1 front, these improvements now include support for the `min-height` and `word-spacing` properties, as well as the `pre` value for the `white-space` property. The Windows version of this browser also carries over the DTD-switch first implemented in the Macintosh version of Internet Explorer 5.5 (see that section for more detail on this). When the `!doctype` element is set to a strict value, it is important to note that the width and height properties will conform to the way they are intended to work as per the CSS1 specification

The following browser-specific properties were added to Internet Explorer 6.0:

- `min-height`
- `text-overflow`

Core Tip

If you have ever looked at the Help > About Internet Explorer page, you'll have noticed that it doesn't just say "Version 5.5" or "Version 6.0," but something like "Version 5.50.4308.2900" or "Version 6.00.2600.0000." This is because there are often a number of different builds of a given browser for particular circumstances, such as preview releases, different builds tailored for various versions of Windows, etc. For a definitive list of all of Windows versions of Internet Explorer, see "How to Determine Which Version of Internet Explorer Is Installed" at: http://support.microsoft.com/default.aspx?scid=kb;EN-US;q164539

Figure 3–2   Microsoft's Internet Explorer 6.0 browser displayed.

3.6   Opera 3.5

Though not considered a "major" browser by many — its overall share of the browser market is small compared to Internet Explorer or Netscape Navigator — Opera deserves mention because of its extensive support for CSS. The first major release of Opera in terms of CSS support was version 3.5, which was released in November 1998. The makers of Opera have always prided themselves in terms of adopting the latest CSS specifications from the World Wide Web Consortium and for the longest time CSS support in Opera was far and away better than in any other browser. Opera 3.5 implemented more CSS properties than did the subsequent releases of Netscape Navigator and Internet Explorer. There were only a handful of CSS1 properties it did not fully support, and there were few cases where it didn't at least partially support some CSS property. If you were interested in seriously playing around with CSS code back in 1999, this version of Opera became your "reference" browser for how things *ought* to have worked. While you are unlikely to run across this release of Opera "in the wild" these days, it represents an important landmark in terms of the adoption of CSS within browsers, and provided a powerful boost to Web authors pushing for standards compliance in more popular browsers.

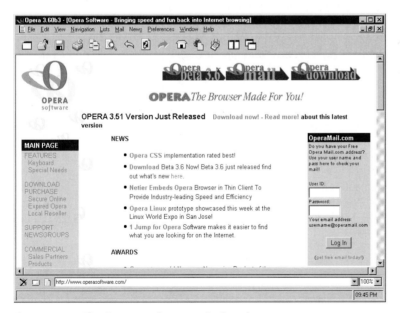

Figure 3–3   The Opera 3.5 browser displayed.

3.7   Opera 4.x – 6.x

Subsequent releases of Opera have built upon its solid reputation for supporting the latest CSS code. Opera 4.0 came out in June 2000, and was the first browser to begin seriously implementing CSS2 properties. This included support for such things as the CSS2 table-related properties, dimension properties (i.e., `width`, `min-height`, etc.) and provided better support for absolute positioning than did Internet Explorer 4's relatively tentative support in this area. This version of Opera also included a single browser-specific CSS extension, called `replace`, which is designed primarily to render images in XML documents.

Beginning with Opera 5.0, the browser became freely available, though in what's called an "ad-ware" format, where banner ads appeared within the browser itself. To get rid of the ads, you had to buy the browser, though it is worth noting that the ad-based and ad-less versions of the browser do not affect the way CSS code is rendered. This version of the browser had few substantial improvements for its CSS support, but in part that is because its support is quite good already. This version of the browser does have some problems when it comes to displaying absolute positioning code, and its handling of extremely large and small font sizes is odd — resembling that displayed by Internet Explorer.

Opera 6.0 came out in November 2001, with full support for CSS1, and increasingly better support for CSS2 properties. This version of the browser has limited support for such things as `:hover` psuedo-class and the `@page` at-rule, `overflow` and still has some problems with absolute positioning. It does have the best support yet available for handling the `@media` at-rule of all contemporary browsers. This version of the browser also includes two additional browser-specific CSS extensions: `set-link-source` and `use-link-source`, both primarily for use in setting destination URLs in XML documents. All of these properties are covered in various sections in the book.

If you are planning to use CSS code extensively in your Web pages, it is a good idea to keep a "reference" copy of the latest version of the Opera browser. You can see how your CSS code should work, and then compare that to what you see in Internet Explorer and Netscape Navigator. Opera also boasts wide support across many different platforms, including BeOS, Linux, Solaris, Macintosh, OS/2, Symbian OS, QNX as well as Windows.

Core Tip

If you are looking for the latest information about CSS support in the Opera browser, go to `http://www.opera.com/docs/specs/#css`.

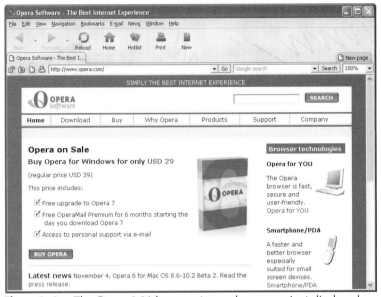

Figure 3–4   The Opera 6.01 browser (non-ad-ware version) displayed.

3.8   Netscape Navigator 4.x

Netscape Navigator 4.x was the least capable of the major browsers when it came to rendering CSS properties. CSS was first implemented in the 4.0 version of the browser, but there has been little to no improvement in the later 4.5, 4.6 and final 4.79 versions that have appeared subsequently. It was weak in its support of some background, border and font families of elements, in several cases not supporting them at all.

The CSS implementation of Netscape Navigator is at least consistent between the different operating systems — if your CSS code works in the Windows version of Netscape Navigator, you can be sure that it also works in the Macintosh and Linux versions of the browser.

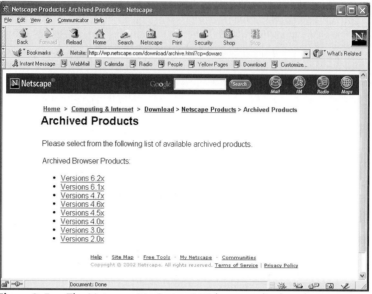

Figure 3–5   The Netscape Navigator 4.79 browser displayed.

Core Tip

Earlier versions of Netscape Navigator can be downloaded from the "Archived Products" section of the Netscape Web site at:

`http://wp.netscape.com/download/archive.html.`

3.9   Mozilla and Netscape Navigator 6.x and 7.x

Mozilla is the open-source offshoot of Netscape. Back in February 1998, Netscape Corporation decided to freely release the source code for their browser, with the idea of opening up development efforts. One of the reasons behind the "open source" software movement is that it is a way for the contributions of many hundreds or thousands of outside programmers to help add features, find and fix bugs, and in general make the program more robust and flexible. In return, the program — including its source code — is available to all. This is the same line of thinking that led to the development of the Linux operating system. Like Internet Explorer, Mozilla is freely available for anyone to download, but unlike Internet Explorer, programmers can take the source code to Mozilla and adapt it to their own needs — with the proviso that any code changes/improvements be shared.

Jumping ahead one version number from version 4.x (there was never a 5.x release of Netscape Navigator) Netscape Corporation incorporated Mozilla's browser engine code (called "Gecko") into version 6.0 of their browser. This immediately put Netscape back in the running when it came to CSS compliance, especially when compared to the haphazard implementation of CSS in Netscape Navigator 4.x.

In June 2002, Mozilla 1.0 was released, containing arguably the best CSS implementation of all current browsers. This is significant since Netscape Corporation is expected to use Mozilla 1.0 as the basis for the release of *its* next browser (likely to be named 6.5, or perhaps 7.0 if they decide to play a game of "versioning leap-frog" with Microsoft). There are also hints that the next version of Netscape Navigator will also become the core of the AOL browser, so this is yet another reason to get seriously interested in this browser if you aren't already (it is likely that by the time this book goes to press that these issues will have been resolved).

With only a few exceptions, Mozilla 1.0 supports all CSS1 and most CSS2 properties. Netscape 6.x, which was released prior to the 1.0 version of Mozilla, is not as fully CSS compliant, and its differences are noted in this book. In particular, Mozilla's handling of floats is hard to beat, as a lot of effort went into ensuring that the Gecko rendering engine got this right. What CSS-related bugs that do exist in Mozilla are well known, so it is likely only a matter of time before the browser can claim full CSS compliance.

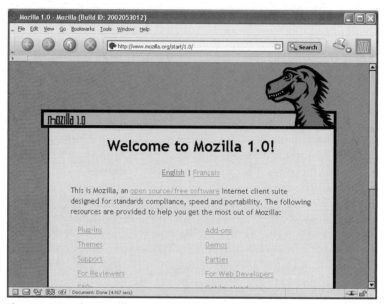

Figure 3–6   The Mozilla 1.0 browser displayed.

With the advent of the Mozilla browser came a long series of CSS extensions. What makes these different from those introduced in Internet Explorer is that none of these extensions are "official" — they are present in the browser but there is absolutely nothing in the way of documentation about them from Netscape. What's more, there's no guarantee that any of them will work, as some of them appear to be present solely as "placeholders," providing the programmers with a way of testing out future implementations of properties contained in draft versions of the CSS specification, or just a simple way of accessing features within the browser. All of the Mozilla CSS extensions are preceded by the prefix "-moz," and in many cases they are tacked onto some names for CSS3 properties currently in development. The following is a list of these Mozilla CSS extensions:

Table 3.1   *Mozilla CSS Extensions*

`-moz-Dialog`	`-moz-DialogText`
`-moz-Field`	`-moz-FieldText`
`-moz-address`	`-moz-all`
`-moz-anonymous-block`	`-moz-anonymous-positioned-block`
`-moz-any-link`	`-moz-appearance`

Table 3.1   *Mozilla CSS Extensions (continued)*

-moz-arabic-indic	-moz-bengali
-moz-bg-inset	-moz-bg-outset
-moz-binding	-moz-border-bottom-colors
-moz-border-colors	-moz-border-diagonal
-moz-border-left-colors	-moz-border-radius
-moz-border-radius-bottomleft	-moz-border-radius-bottomright
-moz-border-radius-topleft	-moz-border-radius-topright
-moz-border-right-colors	-moz-border-top-colors
-moz-bound-element	-moz-box
-moz-box-align	-moz-box-direction
-moz-box-flex	-moz-box-flex-group
-moz-box-ordinal-group	-moz-box-orient
-moz-box-pack	-moz-box-sizing
-moz-bulletinboard	-moz-buttonlabel
-moz-center	-moz-checkbox
-moz-cjk-earthly-branch	-moz-cjk-heavenly-stem
-moz-deck	-moz-deck-hidden
-moz-devanagari	-moz-dialog
-moz-dialogtext	-moz-display
-moz-display-comboboxcontrol-frame	-moz-dll
-moz-dragtargetzone	-moz-drop-marker
-moz-dropdown-btn-out	-moz-dropdown-btn-pressed
-moz-dropdown-list	-moz-dummy-option
-moz-editor-invert-value	-moz-field
-moz-fieldtext	-moz-file
-moz-first-line-fixup	-moz-fixed
-moz-float-edge	-moz-focus-inner

Table 3.1   *Mozilla CSS Extensions (continued)*

`-moz-focus-outer`	`-moz-grid`
`-moz-grid-group`	`-moz-grid-line`
`-moz-groupbox`	`-moz-gujarati`
`-moz-gurmukhi`	`-moz-hangul`
`-moz-hangul-consonant`	`-moz-icon`
`-moz-image-region`	`-moz-initial`
`-moz-inline-box`	`-moz-inline-grid`
`-moz-inline-stack`	`-moz-internal-item-list`
`-moz-japanese-formal`	`-moz-japanese-informal`
`-moz-kannada`	`-moz-key-equivalent`
`-moz-khmer`	`-moz-lao`
`-moz-left`	`-moz-line-frame`
`-moz-list-bullet`	`-moz-mac-accentdarkestshadow`
`-moz-mac-accentdarkshadow`	`-moz-mac-accentface`
`-moz-mac-accentlightesthighlight`	`-moz-mac-accentlightshadow`
`-moz-mac-accentregularhighlight`	`-moz-mac-accentregularshadow`
`-moz-mac-focusring`	`-moz-mac-menuselect`
`-moz-mac-menushadow`	`-moz-mac-menutextselect`
`-moz-malayalam`	`-moz-math-font-size`
`-moz-math-font-style`	`-moz-math-font-style-anonymous`
`-moz-math-font-style-stretchy`	`-moz-math-inline`
`-moz-math-symbol`	`-moz-math-table`
`-moz-math-text`	`-moz-message-or-folder`
`-moz-myanmar`	`-moz-native`
`-moz-opacity`	`-moz-option-selected`
`-moz-oriya`	`-moz-outline`
`-moz-outline-color`	`-moz-outline-radius-bottomleft`

Table 3.1 *Mozilla CSS Extensions (continued)*	
`-moz-outline-radius-bottomright`	`-moz-outline-radius-topleft`
`-moz-outline-radius-topright`	`-moz-outline-style`
`-moz-outline-width`	`-moz-outliner`
`-moz-outliner-`	`-moz-outliner-cell`
`-moz-outliner-cell-image`	`-moz-outliner-cell-text`
`-moz-outliner-column`	`-moz-outliner-image`
`-moz-outliner-indentation`	`-moz-outliner-line`
`-moz-outliner-row`	`-moz-outliner-separator`
`-moz-outliner-twisty`	`-moz-outliner-xxxx`
`-moz-outlinerrow`	`-moz-page`
`-moz-page-sequence`	`-moz-persian`
`-moz-popup`	`-moz-pre-wrap`
`-moz-radio`	`-moz-resizer`
`-moz-right`	`-moz-scrollbars-horizontal`
`-moz-scrollbars-none`	`-moz-scrollbars-vertical`
`-moz-select-scrolled-content`	`-moz-show-background`
`-moz-simp-chinese-formal`	`-moz-simp-chinese-informal`
`-moz-singleline-textcontrol-frame`	`-moz-smiley`
`-moz-stack`	`-moz-tamil`
`-moz-telugu`	`-moz-thai`
`-moz-trad-chinese-formal`	`-moz-trad-chinese-informal`
`-moz-urdu`	`-moz-url`
`-moz-use-text-color`	`-moz-user-focus`
`-moz-user-input`	`-moz-user-modify`
`-moz-user-select`	`-moz-window-icon`

As there is no formal documentation for these properties, the function of many of these properties is wholly conjectural. Where there are obvious links to CSS3 properties, they are explored within the book, as they provide something of a "heads up" as to what's coming in terms of some interesting CSS3 properties. One final note about these properties: they tend to "come and go" depending on different browser versions and there is no guarantee they will work, or even display anything at all — sometimes a placeholder is just that.

As the very latest major browser revision covered in this book, expect Mozilla (and Netscape 7.x) to lead the way in terms of support for CSS.

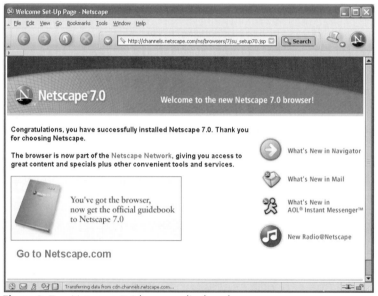

Figure 3–7   Netscape 7.0 browser displayed.

3.10 Other Browsers

Despite the overwhelming prominence of Internet Explorer, and to a lesser extent Netscape Navigator, Mozilla and Opera, there are many other browsers out there.

Popular Linux Browsers

If you are a user of the Linux operating system, Internet Explorer is simply not an option, as Microsoft has not released a version of their browser for this operating system (nor are they likely to in the foreseeable future). Versions of Netscape and/or Mozilla are often distributed with various versions of the most popular "flavors" of Linux, such as Red Hat, Debian, Mandrake and SuSE. Other than some minor differences in the way that such things as buttons and other user interface elements (like radio buttons and checkboxes) appear, there are few functional differences between the way CSS has been implemented in the Windows and Linux versions of Netscape/Mozilla.

Linux is also host to other Web browsers of note. One of these is Galeon (`http://galeon.sourceforge.net/`), which is designed to work with the GNOME desktop. It is based upon Gecko, the name for the Mozilla rendering engine. In short, if it works in Mozilla, in works in Galeon.

Konqueror (`http://www.konqueror.org/`) is another Linux browser worth noting. Konqueror comes as part of the KDE desktop environment and it uses its own rendering engine. The most recent version of the browser supports the majority of CSS1 and CSS2 properties. In addition to extensive support for CSS it also supports ECMAscript 262 support (read: JavaScript), is HTML 4.0 compliant and provides full support for bidirectional text such as Arabic and Hebrew. Konqueror is included in the "Browser Compatibility" listings for CSS properties throughout the book.

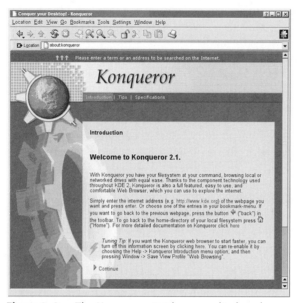

Figure 3–8   The Konqueror 2.1 browser displayed.

Emacspeak

The only browser currently capable of playing back Aural Cascading Style Sheet (ACCS) code is Emacspeak (`http://www.cs.cornell.edu/Info/People/raman/emacspeak/`), which is available only under the Linux operating system. Billing itself as "the complete audio desktop," when used with either a hardware- or software-based speech synthesizer and is set to voice lock mode, Emacspeak supports many ACCS properties. A freely available software speech synthesizer, IBM's Via-Voice Text-to-Speech (TTS) is often used with this browser to produce spoken Web pages. While it is not as popular as the other Linux browsers, if you are interested in checking out ACCS code, it is currently the only option available.

Amaya

Amaya (`http://www.w3.org/Amaya/`) is the open-source browser developed by the W3C itself in order to test out the latest developments in the standards and protocols they have helped develop. In fact Amaya is a combination browser and editor, so Web authors can use its WYSIWYG ("What You See Is What You Get") interface in order to play around with XHTML and CSS.

It is not what you might call a thing of beauty — in fact it is far and away one of the worst-looking modern browsers you are likely to run across. Despite the fact that it is created by the W3C, its implementation of CSS for the most part is little better than the 4.x versions of either Netscape Navigator or Internet Explorer — in other words, pretty flaky. While an over-generalization, it supports many (though not all) CSS1 properties, and is weak when it comes to CSS2 properties. Being open source, not only is it free, but it is also available for a number of operating systems, including Windows 95-XP, various flavors of Linux and Solaris.

Core Tip

For a list of the CSS properties supported by the latest version of Amaya, go to: `http://www.w3.org/Amaya/User/CSSStatus.html.`

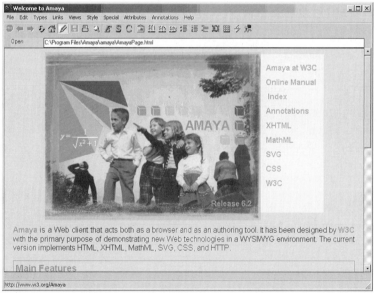

Figure 3–9   The Amaya 6.2 browser displayed.

Hardware Browsers

With the introduction of the CSS Mobile specification (see Appendix C, "CSS3 Mobile Profile"), you can expect more and more hardware-based Web browsers that are capable of displaying this subset of CSS. For example, in the near future you can expect cell phones that are XHTML and CSS Mobile compliant. As an example of this, in Japan Mitsubishi Electric recently launched cell phones and an embedded hardware browser which can accept XHTML Basic 1 and CSS Mobile compliant code. You can expect this trend to continue in the future.

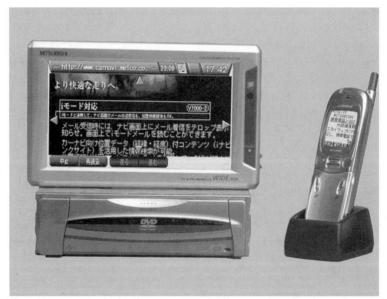

Figure 3–10   Mitsubishi Electric's CSS Mobile compliant hardware browser and cell phone.

IMPLEMENTATION OF BASIC CSS CONCEPTS

Topics in This Chapter

- Containment in HTML
- Grouping
- Inheritance
- `class` as Selector
- `id` as Selector
- Contextual Selectors
- Comments
- CSS2 Selectors
- CSS3 Selectors

Chapter 4

This chapter will explain how some of the more basic concepts behind CSS are implemented. In order for browsers to understand and implement CSS formatting, they must be aware of the ways in which CSS properties can be combined within the XHTML elements contained on a Web page. Recognition of these basic CSS concepts within Web browsers is crucial to the implementation of CSS within a browser. Thankfully, all of these features are at least partially implemented in the major browsers, going back even to their earliest vaguely CSS-compatible versions.

4.1   Grouping

Grouping is a basic CSS concept designed to make things simpler for Web authors by allowing them to combine several CSS rules in a single statement. This can be very handy, and can considerably shorten the length of your CSS code as you customize exactly how you want different HTML tags to appear on a Web page. Grouping allows you to add the same basic formatting rules to common groups of formatting elements, such as headers or paragraphs.

Quite often, Web authors may only want to add a single CSS rule to a given HTML tag, as in the following code snippet:

```
<style>
h1 {font-family: helvetica}
</style>
```

But what if you wanted to format all of your major headers using the Helvetica font? You could write it all out, assigning the CSS rule to each and every header you intend to use on the Web page, or you could simply use the CSS grouping concept to add the same formatting to all of those headers, as shown in the following code snippet:

```
<style>
h1, h2, h3 {font-family: helvetica}
</style>
```

This code ensures that the Helvetica font will be used for all of the `<h1>`, `<h2>` and `<h3>` headers on the Web page.

The grouping concept also means that you can add several CSS properties to a single HTML tag, customizing it so that it is displayed exactly the way you want. For example, the following CSS code example adds several CSS declarations to a single HTML tag:

```
<p style="font-size: 12pt; font-family: courier;
font-variant: normal; color: navy">
This paragraph is displayed using a number of CSS
declarations that have been grouped together.
</p>
```

Grouping allows your code to be more compact, while at the same time making it easier to read (and understand). It also arguably encourages better layout for CSS properties, as it is a natural thing to want to format similar elements (such as headers) using common formatting elements, such as the font they should all display. By grouping CSS properties in this manner, you can easily set a genuine "style sheet" for a page or set of pages that is short, concise and fosters good (rather than wild) layout. Figure 4–1 shows the effects of the CSS code examples from this section — notice how the grouping of the Helvetica font applied to the header code presents an orderly progression of headers that share the same look.

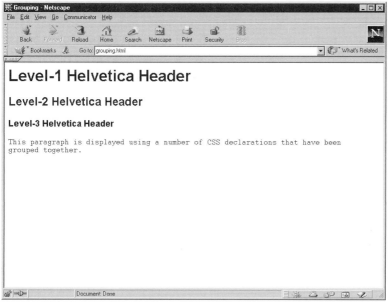

Figure 4–1   A Web page displaying grouped properties as seen in
Netscape Navigator 4.79.

Browser Compatibility

Grouping is fully supported in all but Internet Explorer 3.0, which was the very first
browser to implement rudimentary CSS concepts. Grouping is such a fundamental
concept in CSS that it was rapidly adopted within all subsequent browsers. It is considered safe for general use.

- Internet Explorer 3.0: Unsafe.
- Internet Explorer 4.0: Safe.
- Internet Explorer 4.0 – 4.5 (Mac): Safe.
- Internet Explorer 5.0: Safe.
- Internet Explorer 5.1 – 5.2 (Mac): Safe.
- Internet Explorer 5.5: Safe.
- Internet Explorer 6.0: Safe.
- Netscape Navigator 4.0 – 4.79: Safe.
- Netscape Navigator 4.0 (Mac & UNIX): Safe.
- Netscape Navigator 6.0: Safe.
- Netscape Navigator 7.0: Safe.
- Mozilla 1.0: Safe.
- Opera 3.6 – 4.0: Safe.

- Opera 5.0 – 6.0: Safe.
- Konqueror: Safe.

The only thing of note is that with Internet Explorer 3.0 single CSS values are permitted but not when grouped together, hence its Unsafe rating.

4.2 Inheritance

One of the chief concepts behind CSS is that CSS properties should be able to take on, or "inherit," the display properties of dominant HTML tags. For example, if you set specific properties for the `<body>` tag, all of the HTML elements that fall under this tag (which includes all displayable Web elements) should take on these same display properties. In other words, the "child" elements (tags such as `<p>`, `<i>`, `<b>`, etc.) should take on the display properties set by the "parent" (in this case, `<body>`). In effect, all of the child elements will take on the display properties set to the parent; further changes made to any child element are additive. This can be seen in Figure 4–2, which is derived largely from the code from Listing 4.1.

Listing 4.1	*Sample Code Showing Inheritance*

```
<head>
<title>Inheritance</title>
</head>
<style>
p.large-italic-blue {font-size: 24pt; font-style: italic; color:
blue}
</style>
<body>
<p class="large-italic-blue">
The text in this paragraph should appear in an italic blue-colored
24 point font. The only exception to this is <b>this bold
section</b>. Note how the bold section (the "child") still retains
the formatting belonging to the rest of the paragraph (the
"parent").
</p>
</body>
</html>
```

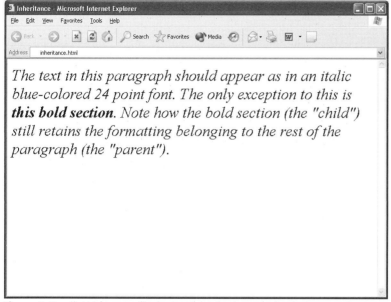

Figure 4–2   A Web page displaying inherited properties in Internet Explorer 6.0.

As you can see from Figure 4–2, all of the text in the paragraph is set to large, blue italic text. The section that appears in bold (which is a "child" element to the paragraph it is contained within) retains all of these formatting elements, and adds its own.

The concept of inheritance is extended in the CSS2 specification, where the explicit `inherit` property is added to the majority of CSS properties, in order for child elements to be able to take on any parent value that may already be present on a Web page. It is simply a way of ensuring that the same elements on a Web page are displayed the same way.

Browser Compatibility

Inheritance is another fundamental CSS concept, and is implemented in all but Internet Explorer 3.0 and 4.0 (Macintosh version only — the Windows version is fine). It is considered safe for general use.

- Internet Explorer 3.0: Unsafe.
- Internet Explorer 4.0: Safe.
- Internet Explorer 4.0 – 4.5 (Mac): Partial.
- Internet Explorer 5.0: Safe.
- Internet Explorer 5.1 – 5.2 (Mac): Safe.

- Internet Explorer 5.5: Safe.
- Internet Explorer 6.0: Safe.
- Netscape Navigator 4.0 – 4.79: Safe.
- Netscape Navigator 4.0 (Mac & UNIX): Safe.
- Netscape Navigator 6.0: Safe.
- Netscape Navigator 7.0: Safe.
- Mozilla 1.0: Safe.
- Opera 3.6 – 4.0: Safe.
- Opera 5.0 – 6.0: Safe.
- Konqueror: Safe.

The only thing of note is that the 4.x versions of Internet Explorer for the Macintosh experience problems with inheritance under some extreme circumstances.

4.3   class and id as Selectors

In preparation for the full implementation of CSS, the forward-looking HTML 4.0 specification (released in December 1997) added two new attributes: `class` and `id`. These new attributes can be applied universally to almost any Web element meant to be displayed within the body of a Web page. This makes sense, since CSS is designed to alter the display of visible elements on a Web page, and by definition that means that Web elements are displayed within the body of a Web page, and not, say, in the header of a Web page.

The idea behind `class` and `id` is that they identify the HTML tags with which they are associated as "targets" for CSS declarations that have previously been defined within the header of a Web page. `class` and `id` differ in that class is intended for general formatting across many elements on a Web page, whereas `id` is meant for specific formatting to a single instance — it is particularly useful when programming dynamic elements via JavaScript, for example, when you want to only affect a single element.

CSS attributes to be associated with either `class` or `id` are initially set within the header of a Web page. CSS rules for both `class` and `id` are defined within a pair of `<style>` tags contained within the header, much like any other CSS rules that may be set there. What makes `class` and `id` stand out is their specificity, as any CSS rule that uses these elements will overrule any other CSS properties that may already be associated with a given HTML tag.

Individual selectors are given "names" that are later called upon by a `class` attribute associated with that tag, separated by a period in the header of the Web page, as seen in the following CSS rule:

```
<style>
h1.red {color: red}
</style>
```

In this case the name "red" has been associated with the <h1> tag. An <h1> tag can call upon this CSS rule by using `class` and the name associated with this rule in the body of the Web page, as can be seen in the following line of code:

```
<h1 class ="red">A Big, Red Header</h1>
```

In this case, the CSS declaration `{color: red}` will be applied to this header. If `class ="red"` was not used in the previous example, the header would be displayed using the browser's default values for displaying a top-level header. This gives you an idea of the flexibility that `class` can provide; it enables Web authors to call upon a CSS rule anywhere within a Web page without having to explicitly set a CSS rule for each and every HTML tag to be modified.

In fact, if you just want to assign `class` as a property that can be applied to any type of Web element, you can do so by eliminating a reference to a specific Web element. So for example, if you wanted to have a general class for making things red, you could use the following code in the header of a Web page:

```
<style>
.red {color: red}
</style>
```

Note the "." that precedes the class name — it must be there for it to be applicable to all Web elements on a page. To use this code you just have to call the "red" class within any element (paragraphs, headers, tables, etc) you want to make red.

When using `id`, a CSS rule is preceded by a hash symbol ("#") and then the "name," as can be seen in the following line of code:

```
#green {color: #33ff33; font-weight: bold}
```

Just as with `class`, individual HTML tags call upon these names (and their corresponding rules) by adding the `id` attribute to the tag and then specifying the name in quotes, as can be seen in this line of code:

```
<h1 id="green">a light green, bold header</h1>
```

Whereas `class` can be used with multiple elements on a Web page, `id` is meant for use with only a single element. Listing 4.2 demonstrates how you can use multiple `id` and `class` attributes in a Web page.

Listing 4.2	*Sample Code Depicting class and id as Selectors*

```
<html>
<head>
<title>class and id as Selectors</title>
<style>
.green {color: green}
#green {color: #33ff33; font-weight: bold}
body {font-size: xx-large}
</style>
</head>
<body>
<div>A normal line of text.</div>
<div class="green">A Dark Green Header</div>
<div id="green">A Light Green, Bold Header</div>
<div class="GREEN">Another Dark Green Header</div>
</body>
</html>
```

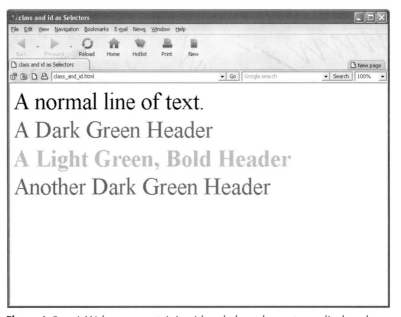

Figure 4–3   A Web page containing id and class elements, as displayed within Opera 6.0.

As you can see, even though the name "GREEN" is applied in two different instances, the browser is able to make the distinction between which set of CSS rules should be applied to each header, based on whether it is called by `id` or `class`. You can also see from this example that the names used do not have to be case-sensitive — both "GREEN" and "green" are equally effective as names.

Both `class` and `id` are powerful tools for the Web author, as they are endlessly versatile. It is possible to use either of them in an externally referenced style sheet where you can set all possible combinations of the elements you might want to display on a page. Instead of having to explicitly write out the CSS code for it, create a `class` and `id` in a style sheet, and then reference them as needed with a given Web page. In this way many Web authors create a single, separately referenced style sheet that collects together extensive formatting solutions. Throughout this book you will find many examples of relatively simple classes of CSS code used within the code examples.

Browser Compatibility

In terms of browser compatibility, both `id` and `class` should be considered safe to use. In fact, the "Partial" ratings given to earlier versions of Internet Explorer result from the fact that they didn't meet the requirements of the official CSS specification exactly, and these are in situations that are either unlikely to appear or otherwise do not interfere with these properties' functions.

- Internet Explorer 3.0: Unsafe.
- Internet Explorer 4.0: Partial.
- Internet Explorer 4.0 – 4.5 (Mac): Partial.
- Internet Explorer 5.0: Partial.
- Internet Explorer 5.1 – 5.2 (Mac):
- Internet Explorer 5.5: Safe.
- Internet Explorer 6.0: Safe.
- Netscape Navigator 4.0 – 4.79: Partial.
- Netscape Navigator 4.0 (Mac & UNIX): Partial.
- Netscape Navigator 6.0: Safe.
- Netscape Navigator 7.0: Safe.
- Mozilla 1.0: Safe.
- Opera 3.6 – 4.0: Safe.
- Opera 5.0 – 6.0: Safe.
- Konqueror: Safe.

Internet Explorer 4.0 on up are given a Partial rating because they accept digits as part of the name of a selector; this is against specification, though it does not otherwise affect functionality.

Netscape Navigator 4.x rates a Partial because it does not properly recognize the hash symbol ("#") after a specified associated HTML element, (e.g., `P#FRED {COLOR:`

RED;}), as it should according to the official specification. Subsequent versions of this browser (along with Mozilla 1.0) fix this.

`class` and `id` as selectors have been properly implemented since version 3.6 of Opera.

Konqueror also fully and properly implements `class` and `id` as selectors.

4.4 Contextual Selectors

Another basic CSS concept is that Web browsers should be able to selectively apply CSS formatting rules based upon the context in which a particular CSS property appears on a Web page. We have already seen an example of this in the previous section, as the browsers are able to distinguish which CSS rule should be applied to an `id` or `class` property when the name "green" was used.

In a more general sense, contextual selectors are meant to be applied in certain situations or when combinations of HTML tags appear on a Web page.

For example, say you have a couple of nested, unordered lists on a Web page, and you want them to be displayed differently when they appear, for emphasis. You could set things so that those list elements that appear in the "main" list appear larger and in a different color than those that appear in the sub-list, as can be seen in Listing 4.3.

Listing 4.3	*Simple Example Code Using Contextual Selectors*

```
<html>
<head>
<title>Contextual Selectors #1</title>
<style>
ul li {font-size: x-large; color: black;}
ul ul li {font-size: large; color: gray;}
</style>
</head>
<body>
<ul>
<li>An extra-large list item in a black font.
    <ul>
    <li>A large sub-list in a gray font
    <li>Another large sub-list item in a gray font
    </ul>
<li>Another extra-large list item in a black font
</ul>
</body>
</html>
```

You can see the results in Figure 4–4, which applies this code to a Web page that contains a set of nested, unordered lists.

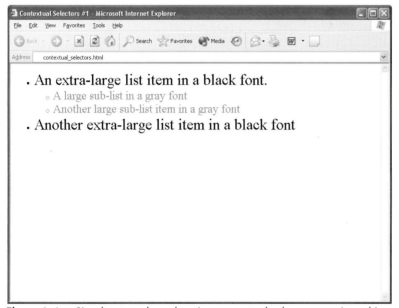

Figure 4–4   Simple example code using contextual selectors, as viewed in Internet Explorer 6.0.

This basic CSS concept can be applied to many other useful situations. For example, you can set nested, ordered lists to display different numeral types using the `list-item` CSS property, so that the "outer" list elements are preceded by decimals and the nested list is preceded by roman numerals. It can also be handy in situations where you want to distinguish between elements that would ordinarily be rendered in the same way. For example, say you set all of your `<i>` and `<em>` tags to the color value "green". But if you have both tags in a single sentence, then you will lose any distinction between the two elements. The contextual selector rule means that you can apply a special CSS rule that allows you to set a different set of display properties whenever these two tags appear together. Listing 4.4 (and Figure 4–5) display both of these examples at work:

| Listing 4.4 | *Contextual Selectors #2* |

```
<html>
<head>
<title>Contextual Selectors #2</title>
<style>
ol {list-style: decimal}
ol ol {list-style: lower-roman}
i {color: green}
em {color: green}
i em {color: lime}
body {font-size: large}
</style>
</head>
<body>
<ol>
<li>This list item should be preceded by a decimal number
<li>As should this one
    <ol>
    <li>This nested sub-list is preceded by a roman numeral
    <li>As is this one
    </ol>
<li>Back to decimal numbers as we return to the "outside" list.
</ol>
The words in this sentence that <i>are italicized</i> should be in
green.
<p>
The words in this sentence that <em>are emphasized</em> should
also be in green.
<p>
<i>This sentence is all in italics, and the <em>emphasized
words</em> should appear differently.</i>
</body>
</html>
```

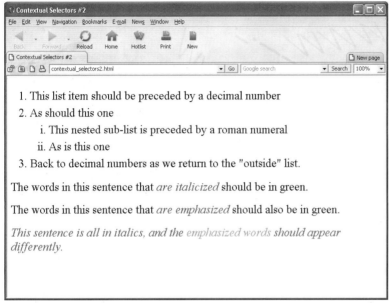

Figure 4–5 A nested, unordered list displaying the effects of contextual selectors, as viewed from within Opera 6.0.

Note how the special contextual CSS rule applies a different color value when the <i> and <em> tags are both being applied within the same sentence, overriding the value when both appear singly.

Browser Compatibility

This property is completely safe to use, and has been implemented in the earliest CSS-compatible browsers.

- Internet Explorer 3.0: Safe.
- Internet Explorer 4.0: Safe.
- Internet Explorer 4.0 – 4.5 (Mac): Safe.
- Internet Explorer 5.0: Safe
- Internet Explorer 5.1 – 5.2 (Mac): Safe.
- Internet Explorer 5.5: Safe.
- Internet Explorer 6.0: Safe.
- Netscape Navigator 4.0 – 4.79: Safe.
- Netscape Navigator 4.0 (Mac & UNIX): Safe.
- Netscape Navigator 6.0: Safe.
- Netscape Navigator 7.0: Safe.

- Mozilla 1.0: Safe.
- Opera 3.6 – 4.0: Safe
- Opera 5.0 – 6.0: Safe.
- Konqueror: Safe.

4.5   Comments

Experienced Web authors are aware of how handy comments can be to Web code. When writing a Web page at the code-level, comments can be used to explain why certain actions or formatting decisions are made, or to mark distinct sections in code. For the same reasons, it is handy to be able to add comments to CSS code, so that you (or someone else) have an idea of what is going on in your code, and why.

In XHTML, comments are added to Web pages by using "`<!--`" at the beginning of the comment and "`-->`" at the end of the comment, as in the following code snippet:

```
<!-- This HTML comment will not be displayed -->
```

CSS comments follow a different model, based upon the commenting style used in the C programming language. The beginning of a CSS comment begins with a "`/*`" and ends with the opposite, "`*/`". Here's how this can be applied:

```
/* This CSS comment will not be displayed */
```

You have to be careful to be sure that when you add CSS comments, they are contained *within* CSS code statements, otherwise they may be displayed within the Web page. For example, you can insert a CSS comment within the boundaries of the `<style>` tag in the header of a Web page, as in the following code snippet:

```
<style>
h1 {font-size: x-large; color: black; background: gray}
/* sets the formatting for the top-level headers */
</style>
```

If you are adding a comment to inline CSS code, make sure that it appears within the boundaries of the HTML tag, as in this code snippet:

```
<h1 style="font-size: large; color: #333333; background: yellow; /*
regular top-level header formatting style has been over-ruled in
this case */">another, smaller header</h1>
```

Still, Web authors have to be careful to get the order of the comments right ("/*" followed by "*/"), and to make sure that the comments fall within the CSS code and not outside of it.

Browser Compatibility

Comments are fully supported in the latest versions of Internet Explorer and Netscape Navigator. Since it is arguably a relatively easy thing for the browser manufacturers to implement (for after all, no actual change in the display of an element is required), the ability to add comments is found in virtually all CSS-compliant browsers. This property is safe to use, and is only unsupported in the earliest CSS-compliant browsers (Internet Explorer 3.0). Still Web authors have to be careful to get the order of the comments right ("/*" followed by "*/"), and to make sure that the comments fall within their CSS code and not outside of it; otherwise it will most likely be displayed.

- Internet Explorer 3.0: Unsafe.
- Internet Explorer 4.0: Safe.
- Internet Explorer 4.0 – 4.5 (Mac): Safe.
- Internet Explorer 5.0: Safe
- Internet Explorer 5.1 – 5.2 (Mac): Safe.
- Internet Explorer 5.5: Safe.
- Internet Explorer 6.0: Safe.
- Netscape Navigator 4.0 – 4.79: Safe.
- Netscape Navigator 4.0 (Mac & UNIX): Safe.
- Netscape Navigator 6.0: Safe.
- Netscape Navigator 7.0: Safe.
- Mozilla 1.0: Safe.
- Opera 3.6 – 4.0: Safe.
- Opera 5.0 – 6.0: Safe.
- Konqueror: Safe.

4.6   CSS2 Selectors

The CSS2 specification came with a number of new selectors. These selectors allow Web authors much greater flexibility over how to associate CSS properties to Web elements. Only those wholly new selector types and those relevant to standard HTML are covered in this chapter.

Universal Selector

The universal selector is specified with the standard Windows/UNIX "wildcard" character, which is an asterisk ("*"). It allows the Web author to select all cases of a certain selector in a Web document. When an "*" is added in front of a given selector, it formats all of the instances for that selector (without the "*") throughout the document, so that *[lang="en"] is equivalent to [LANG="EN"] wherever it appears in a Web page.

Browser Compatibility

A lot of the early browsers did not have the universal selector. It has been implemented in almost all recent browsers,

- Internet Explorer 3.0: Unsafe.
- Internet Explorer 4.0: Unsafe.
- Internet Explorer 4.0 – 4.5 (Mac): Unsafe.
- Internet Explorer 5.0: Safe.
- Internet Explorer 5.1 – 5.2 (Mac): Safe.
- Internet Explorer 5.5: Safe
- Internet Explorer 6.0: Safe.
- Netscape Navigator 4.0 – 4.79: Unsafe.
- Netscape Navigator 4.0 (Mac & UNIX): Unsafe.
- Netscape Navigator 6.0: Safe.
- Netscape Navigator 7.0: Safe.
- Mozilla 1.0: Safe.
- Opera 3.6: Unsafe
- Opera 4.0 – 6.0: Safe
- Konqueror: Safe

Internet Explorer started implementing the universal selector beginning with version 5.0.

Netscape Navigator started implementing this selector beginning with version 6.0. Ditto Mozilla by version 1.0.

Opera was the first past the gate with implementing this selector, and was compatible beginning with version 4.0.

Konqueror also implements the universal selector.

Child Selectors

A child selector is applied whenever an element is considered to be the "child" of some "parent" element. It uses a "less than" symbol (">") between at least two Web elements.

List elements can be considered the "children" of the "parent" ordered or unordered list tags. In a similar way, all displayed content on a Web page can be considered to be the child of the body tag. The child selector enables the Web author to specify that when a given child element appears after a certain parent element, it should be formatted in a way described. The following code sample provides two examples of this:

```
ol > li {font-size: 12pt}
ul > li {font-size: 10pt}
```

In this case, all of the list items that are displayed in an ordered list will be rendered in a 12-point font, and those in an unordered list will be rendered in a 10-point font.

Browser Compatibility

A lot of the early browsers did not have child selectors. They have been implemented in almost all recent browsers,

- Internet Explorer 3.0: Unsafe.
- Internet Explorer 4.0: Unsafe.
- Internet Explorer 4.0 – 4.5 (Mac): Unsafe.
- Internet Explorer 5.0: Unsafe.
- Internet Explorer 5.1 – 5.2 (Mac): Safe.
- Internet Explorer 5.5: Unsafe.
- Internet Explorer 6.0: Unsafe.
- Netscape Navigator 4.0 – 4.79: Unsafe.
- Netscape Navigator 4.0 (Mac & UNIX): Unsafe.
- Netscape Navigator 6.0: Safe.
- Netscape Navigator 7.0: Safe.
- Mozilla 1.0: Safe.
- Opera 3.6 – 4.0: Unsafe
- Opera 5.0 – 6.0: Safe
- Konqueror: Safe

As of the time of writing, Windows versions of Internet Explorer still do not implement child selectors. Macintosh versions of Internet Explorer starting with 5.1 do implement them.

Netscape Navigator started implementing these selectors beginning with version 6.0. Ditto Mozilla by version 1.0.

Opera started implementing child selectors beginning with version 5.0.

Konqueror implements child selectors.

Adjacent Sibling Selectors

Adjacent sibling selectors allow Web authors to decide how one Web element should appear if it appears immediately after another specified element that shares the same parent. In such a case, you could define how different header tags should interact with each other (because their immediate parent is the body tag), but not, say, a header and a cell in a table, which fall under different parent elements (the header to the body tag; the cell to the table tag). Adjacent sibling selectors use the plus symbol "+" between two or more elements, and specify that if a certain condition occurs between these two elements, formatting should occur according to the rule stated by the selector. In the following case, whenever a second-level header immediately follows a top-level header, the second-level header will be indented by 1 inch:

```
h1 + h2 {text-indent: 1in}
```

If there are any second-level headers on the Web page that do not appear immediately after a top-level header, they will not be indented.

Browser Compatibility

A lot of the early browsers did not have adjacent sibling selectors. They have been implemented in almost all recent browsers,

- Internet Explorer 3.0: Unsafe.
- Internet Explorer 4.0: Unsafe.
- Internet Explorer 4.0 – 4.5 (Mac): Unsafe.
- Internet Explorer 5.0: Unsafe.
- Internet Explorer 5.1 – 5.2 (Mac): Safe.
- Internet Explorer 5.5: Unsafe.
- Internet Explorer 6.0: Unsafe.
- Netscape Navigator 4.0 – 4.79: Unsafe.
- Netscape Navigator 4.0 (Mac & UNIX): Unsafe.
- Netscape Navigator 6.0: Safe.
- Netscape Navigator 7.0: Safe.
- Mozilla 1.0: Safe.
- Opera 3.6 – 4.0: Unsafe.
- Opera 5.0 – 6.0: Safe
- Konqueror: Safe

Windows versions of Internet Explorer still do not implement adjacent selectors. However, Macintosh versions of Internet Explorer beginning with 5.1 do.

Netscape Navigator started implementing these selectors beginning with version 6.0. Ditto Mozilla by version 1.0.

Opera started implementing adjacent selectors beginning with version 5.0.

Konqueror implements adjacent selectors.

Essentially, the rule here is that if a browser understands child selectors, it also understands adjacent selectors.

Attribute Selectors

The set of attribute selectors greatly extends the functionality of the `class` and `id` attributes. This class of selectors allows the Web author to format Web objects that utilize attributes on a conditional basis — so you can select a particular combination of elements to be formatted when it appears within a Web page.

The CSS2 specification added four of these attribute selectors. In each case, an attribute value is enclosed within square brackets, and is then followed by further CSS code which does the actual formatting. Here are quick descriptions for their use and purpose:

- `element[attribute]` — Matches the name of the attribute contained within square brackets.
- `element[attribute="value"]` — A match is made when the attribute equals the value of "value."
- `element[attribute~="value"]` — A match is made when the attribute roughly matches the value of "value," in cases where the text "value" may be part of a larger word.
- `element[attribute|="value"]` — A match is made whenever the attribute matches the first few letters of a value whose first few letters match the text "value."

The initial example is pretty simple: wherever you have a particular type of attribute appear against a specific element, the browser formats it accordingly. For example, take a look at the following code snippet:

```
<style>
h2[class] {color: red}
</style>
```

In this case, any `<h2>` header in the page that uses `class` — whatever its value — will be colored red. So a header like `<h2 class="header">This header is in red</h2>` matches the criteria, whereas `<h2 id="header">This header is not</h2>` does not, because it uses the `id` attribute instead. You can see how this can be a powerful tool, allowing you to rapidly add some further modifying CSS code to further format existing CSS code on your Web page — in this case, any `<h2>` header that uses the `class` attribute.

Things get more interesting when you come to the second example, which is where you can start adding further conditional statements to the selector, allowing you to be more selective over what gets formatted. Consider the following code snippet:

```
<style>
h2[class="header"] {color: red}
</style>
```

In this case, only `<h2>` headers containing a class attribute set to the value "header" would be formatted red. If there is an `<h2>` header on the page with a class value set to anything else, it won't be considered a match, and therefore won't be turned to red. You can even use a "null" value with this particular arrangement, which can be quite useful in some circumstances. Let's say you have a dynamically generated Web page, and occasionally you get elements that are automatically generated but are empty, such as a "Next" link at the end of a slide-show Web presentation, for example. So what you could do is insert the following code in the header of your Web page:

```
<style>
a[href=""] {visibility: hidden}
</style>
```

In this case, whenever you get an anchor tag that doesn't contain any content — in other words, when it doesn't actually link to anything — this particular attribute selector will render it invisible.

The third type of attribute selector allows you to choose a particular value within an attribute whenever there is more than one value present. This is available because there are certain times when you may in fact wish to call upon more than one type of `class` or `id` attribute formatting within a page. You can in fact, have a single Web element on a page formatted by more than one class attribute for example, with each value separated by a comma. The "~=" in the third type of attribute selector tells the browser to select against a particular value whenever it appears, whether it be the first, second, or third (or more) value that appears within the value for a given attribute. Listing 4.5 should help make this concept clear:

Listing 4.5	*Attribute Selector Example #1*

```
<html>
<head>
<title>Attribute Selector Example #1</title>
<style>
body {font-size: 45px}
p.goldilocks {font-weight: bold}
p[class~="gold"] {color: gold}
</style>
</head>
<body>
<p>The story of Goldilocks and the Three Bears</p>
<p class="goldilocks">Once there was a little girl whose name was
Goldilocks.</p>
<p class="goldilocks gold">She ran into some trouble with a trio
of bears.</p>
</body>
</html>
```

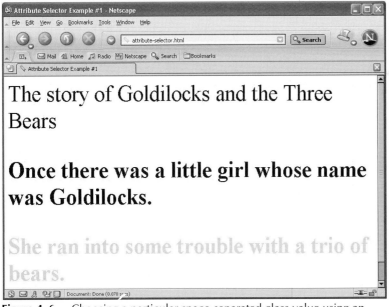

Figure 4–6   Choosing a particular space-separated class value using an attribute selector, as seen in Netscape 7.0.

As you can see in Figure 4–6, what happens is that the first paragraph is formatted normally, the second is rendered in bold, and the third paragraph is displayed in bold and in a gold color, the gold formatting coming from the `p[class~="gold"] {color: gold}` matching the `"gold"` value in `<p class="goldilocks gold">`.

The fourth type of attribute selector is for use when you are trying to match a particular type of hyphen-separated (instead of space-separated) values contained within an attribute. It uses "`|=`" and what it tells the browser is to look and match against a given value only when it first appears in a given sequence of hyphen-separated values contained within an attribute. Again, a look at some actual code, as seen in Listing 4.6, may help make things more clear:

Listing 4.6	*Attribute Selector Example #2*

```
<html>
<head>
<title>Attribute Selector Example #2</title>
<style>
body {font-size: 50px}
p[class|="hum"] {color: white; background-color: red}
</style>
</head>
<body>
<p class="hum-bug">hum-bug</p>
<p class="bug-hum">bug-hum</p>
<p class="hum-bug-hum">hum-bug-hum</p>
<p class="bug-hum-bug">bug-hum-bug</p>
</body>
</html>
```

As you can see in Figure 4–7, in this case we have a Web page where we have the attribute selector looking for matches to `p[class|="hum"]`, which uses `{color: white; background-color: red}` to turn the text white against a red background. In the paragraphs contained within the body of the page, only two paragraphs meet this condition: those beginning with `<p class="hum-bug">` and `<p class="hum-bug-hum">`, because the value "`hum`" appears at the beginning of the sequence of hyphen-separated values. The other two paragraphs are not matched against since "`hum`" does not appear at the beginning of the hyphenated sequence of values.

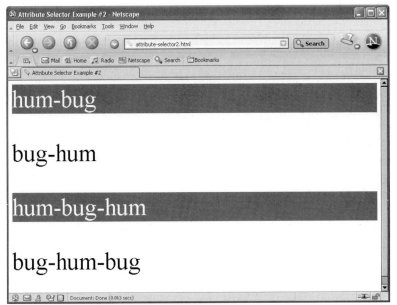

Figure 4–7   Choosing a particular hyphenated class value using an attribute selector, as seen in Netscape 7.0.

Browser Compatibility

Because these selectors are a CSS2 feature, a lot of the early browsers are automatically ruled out.

- Internet Explorer 3.0: Unsafe.
- Internet Explorer 4.0: Unsafe.
- Internet Explorer 4.0 – 4.5 (Mac): Unsafe.
- Internet Explorer 5.0: Unsafe.
- Internet Explorer 5.1 – 5.2 (Mac): Unsafe.
- Internet Explorer 5.5: Unsafe.
- Internet Explorer 6.0: Unsafe.
- Netscape Navigator 4.0 – 4.79: Unsafe.
- Netscape Navigator 4.0 (Mac & UNIX): Unsafe.
- Netscape Navigator 6.0: Safe.
- Netscape Navigator 7.0: Safe.
- Mozilla 1.0: Safe.
- Opera 3.6 – 4.0: Unsafe.
- Opera 5.0 – 6.0: Safe
- Konqueror: Safe

No versions of Internet Explorer support attribute selectors.

Netscape Navigator started implementing attribute selectors beginning with version 6.0. Ditto Mozilla by version 1.0.

Opera started implementing adjacent selectors beginning with version 5.0.

Konqueror implements attribute selectors.

4.7   CSS3 Selectors

The proposed CSS3 module that deals with selectors further extended the types of selectors available to Web authors. There are three main types of new selectors that came with the CSS3 specification:

- Additional attribute selectors
- Structural pseudo-classes
- Various non-structural pseudo-class selectors

All of these are looked at in turn in this section.

Additional Attribute Selectors

Three new attribute selectors have been added under the CSS3 specification. They are:

- element `[attribute^="value"]` — where an element whose "attribute" value begins exactly with the string "value"
- element `[attribute$="value"]` — where an element whose "attribute" value ends exactly with the string "value"
- element `[attribute*="value"]` — where an element whose "attribute" value contains the substring "value"

This is a modest extension to the existing attribute selectors introduced under the CSS2 specification, providing still greater control over how selectors can be activated when the browser matches them against certain strings of text

The "`[^=]`" selector is useful in those cases where you want to exactly match the attributes to a given string. For example, the following code snippet is designed to work only with a `div` element that uses only the string "`prev`"; "previous" and "previously" would not match.

```
div[rel^="prev"]
```

The "`$=`" selector is for when you want to match up an element that exactly equals the end of a string value contained within the quotes. So, for example, the following code snippet would only work with a `div` element that ends with "ing"; "missing" and "hitting" would be a match, whereas "inglenook" wouldn't.

```
div[rel$="ing"]
```

The "`*=`" selector works by looking for any match to the string contained within quotes. This is a much broader selector than the other two introduced under CSS3 — it is essentially a refined universal selector. As with the previous code sample, the following code sample also looks for the string "ing", but it would match "missing", "hitting" as well as "inglenook", "singer" or "bingo".

```
div[rel*="ing"]
```

Structural Pseudo-Classes

Despite the many different types of selectors that already exist, there are still situations that they do not cover. For example, selecting against information based within the document structure that cannot easily be represented through a combination of current selectors. That is where the new CSS3 structural pseudo-classes come in. What they do is allow the Web author to do such things as apply different formatting to successive paragraphs or other elements on a Web page, the first child element (whatever it may be) that follows under a parent element, and so forth.

The following are the structural pseudo-class types introduced under CSS3:

- `:root` — an element that is root of the document
- `:nth-child(n)` — an element which is the n-th child of its parent
- `:nth-last-child(n)` — an element which is the n-th child of its parent, counting from the last one
- `:nth-of-type(n)` — an element which is the n-th sibling of its type
- `:nth-last-of-type(n)` — an element which is the n-th sibling of its type, counting from the last one
- `:last-child` — an element which is the last child of its parent
- `:first-of-type` — an element which is the first sibling of its type
- `:last-of-type` — an element which is the last sibling of its type
- `:only-child` — an element which is the only child of its parent
- `:only-of-type` — an element which is the only sibling of its type
- `:empty` — an element that has no children (including text nodes)

The `:root` pseudo-class selector applies formatting only to the root of a document. For a Web page, this is always the `<html>` element. This selector comes into play primarily when used with XML documents, as it can set the specific formatting applicable to different sub-types of XML documents (of which XHTML is one).

The `:nth-child(n)` pseudo-class selector can be used to set different formatting to elements in sequence. It addition to a numeric value (which sets the repeat pattern) it can also take the named values `odd` and `even`. In the following code snippet, you can see how it can be used to set different formatting values to `odd` and `even` rows to successive table row elements:

```
tr:nth-child(odd)
tr:nth-child(even)
```

The next code snippet does exactly the same thing as the previous example, except that it uses numeric values instead; "`(2n+1)`" is the equivalent of "`(odd)`" and "`(2n)`" is the equivalent of "`(even)`".

```
tr:nth-child(2n+1)
tr:nth-child(2n)
```

The `:nth-last-child(n)` pseudo-class selector works in a similar fashion to `:nth-child(n)` except that it counts from the last child element or elements of a parent. For example, the following code snippet selects the final row of a table:

```
tr:nth-last-child(-n+1)
```

The `:nth-of-type(n)` pseudo-class selector works by working with sibling elements and applies formatting based on either a numeric value or by using odd and even values. The following code snippet alternates the position of floated tables:

```
table:nth-of-type(2n+1) {float: right}
table:nth-of-type(2n) {float: left}
```

The `:nth-last-of-type(n)` pseudo-class selector looks for the n-th sibling of its type. This allows you to do some interesting things, such as selecting to format the first and last elements on a Web page. The following example shows how you could use this to select the first and last paragraphs on a page:

```
body > p:nth-of-type(n+2):nth-last-of-type(n+2)
```

If you just want to select the very last child element, you can use the `:last-child` pseudo-class selector. So if you wanted to selectively format the final row of a table, you could use the following code:

```
table > tr:last-child
```

There are twin `first-of-type` and `last-of-type` pseudo-property selectors, useful for selecting the first and last child elements in relation to a given parent. For example, the following code snippet selects the very first and very last table data elements in a table.

```
tr > td:first-of-type
tr > td:last-of-type
```

There are two "only" types of pseudo-property selectors: `:only-child` and `:only-of-type`. The first represents an element that has no siblings, the second represents an element with no siblings that have the same element name. The first is equivalent to `:first-child:last-child` and the second to `:first-of-type:last-of-type`, although both "only" pseudo-property selectors are both lower in specificity (and hence, lower in the cascading order).

The final pseudo-property selector is `:empty`, which represents an element that does not have any children.

Various Non-Structural Pseudo-Class Selectors

In addition to the new structural pseudo-classes there are also a number of new non-structural pseudo-class selectors that are applicable to specific elements.

Here is a list of the non-structural pseudo-classes added under the CSS3 specification:

- `:target` — refers to the target of the referring URL
- `:enabled` and `:disabled` — a user interface element which is either enabled or disabled
- `:checked` and `:indeterminate` — a user interface element which is checked or in an indeterminate state
- `:contains("string")` — an element containing the substring "string" in its textual contents
- `::selection` — the portion of an element currently selected or highlighted by the user
- `:not(this)` — an element that does not match simple selector "this"
- `E ~ F` — element F when preceded by element E

The `:target` psuedo-class selector is for use in conjunction with URL values that point to a specific named anchor (i.e., a name element) using a hash ("#") symbol. So you can use the following code to format the target of this type of URL in the color blue:

```
*:target {color: navy}
```

The `:enabled` and `:disabled` psuedo-class selectors are to be used in conjunction with user interface elements (such as a checkbox or radio button) to set how enabled or disabled elements should be formatted. The `:checked` and `:indeterminate` psuedo-class selectors are also to be used with user interface elements. The `:checked` psuedo-class selector is activated whenever a user interface element (again, such as a checkbox or radio button) is selected by the user. The `:indeterminate` psuedo-class is for formatting user interface elements that are in a state that is neither selected nor unselected (an example of this would be a group of radio buttons that has no pre-selected default choice).

The :contains("string") is a pseudo-class selector that looks for a match to the string value contained within quotes and formats it accordingly. So, for example, the following code snippet looks for the word "ambidextrous" in a paragraph, and if it finds a match, formats that paragraph (along with all other paragraphs that may contain that word).

```
p:contains("ambidextrous") {color: aqua}
```

The ::selection pseudo-class selector formats any element that is selected or highlighted by the user. So for example, the following code sets a white background to whatever text is contained within a given paragraph:

```
p::selection {background-color: white}
```

An interesting new pseudo-class is :not(this), which is also called the negation pseudo-class. It allows you to select the opposite or negative state of an element. For example, the following code snippet would selectively format input elements that were not disabled.

```
input:not([disabled])
```

The final new pseudo-class selector added to the CSS3 specification is an indirect adjacent combinator, which uses the tilde ("~") character to separate two selectors. Both selectors must appear in a Web document and the first must precede the other — although not necessarily one immediately after the other — for it to work. For example, the following code snippet selects for any code element that follows at some point after a level-1 header.

```
h1 ~ code
```

THE CASCADE

Topics in This Chapter

- Cascading Order
- The `!important` Property
- Cascade-Order Sources

Chapter 5

One of the key design features behind CSS is that it is possible to specify more than one style sheet at a time within a document. This is called "cascading." This chapter takes a look at the rules governing how cascading works, and how you can increase the "weight" of a CSS statement by using the `!important` property.

5.1   Cascading Order

Cascading order is one of the fundamental features of the CSS specification. It determines how much "weight" is to be applied to a given CSS rule, based on the situation in which it appears. In essence, more specific CSS statements overrule more general ones, and if two or more CSS statements with the same weight appear in a Web page, it is the last one that is applied. This is an over-simplification, but can be a useful way to remember how things are supposed to work.

Here are the actual cascading rules, presented in more detail:

*   If a statement is applied to a "parent" XHTML tag (such as `<body>`) and tags that are its "children" (like `<p>`, or `<div>`, or anything that appears within the body of a Web page) as long as they do not conflict with more specific elements on the Web page, the CSS formatting is "inherited" by the child elements. So if the body of a Web page is set

to black, all of the elements contained on the Web page will also appear in black.

- The CSS statements are then sorted by explicit weight, and any marked `!important` (covered in the next section) take precedence over the others.
- Any style sheet information that may be imported through the `<link>` tag will be overruled by any CSS statements contained within the Web page.
- More specific CSS statements overrule more general ones. So if the body of a Web page is set to black, a paragraph set to white will override the more general statement set to the page.
- If two or more CSS statements appear that have the same weight, the one specified last wins. So if you have a rule that colors all paragraphs white contained in the header of a page, a CSS rule contained within the page itself that sets a specific paragraph to yellow would win out over the more general rule.

The code in Listing 5.1 shows a number of conflicting cascading effects, whose effects can be seen in Figure 5–1.

Notice how the initial color value set to the `<li>` tag is olive, but this is overruled by the following statement, which says that any `<li>` tag associated with an ordered list (`<ol>`) should be displayed in navy. This specific CSS statement overrules the previous, more general one. Similarly, the next statement associates the color yellow whenever an `<li>` tag is contained within an unordered listing (`<ul>`). You can go to another level of specificity when you reference a CSS statement using either a `class` or `id` statement in the code; in each of the two cases presented in this Web page, these values carry more weight than the default value specified. The two CSS statements are a case where there are two identical CSS statements with the same weight. In this case, the latter of the two ("`color: silver`") is what will be applied by the browser.

The final example is somewhat tricky, and its background needs to be explained. First, there are two imported style sheets referenced by this Web page via two separate `<link>` elements: `one.css` and `two.css`. `one.css` contains the following code:

```
.decoration {text-decoration: underline}
```

The separate `two.css` page contains this code:

```
.decoration {text-decoration: overline}
```

Despite these CSS rules, as you can see on the final page the affected text is in fact struck-through! This is because of the `.decoration {text-decoration: line-through}` contained within the header of the page itself — it is more specific, and thereby wins out over the previous CSS rules. If the more specific rule within the page was not there, `two.css` would win out over `one.css` since it came after it, and is therefore the more specific rule.

Listing 5.1   *Cascading Order*

```
<html>
<head>
<title>Cascading Order</title>
<link rel="stylesheet" type="text/css" href="one.css">
<link rel="stylesheet" type="text/css" href="two.css">
<style>
li {color: olive}
ol li {color: navy}
ul li {color: yellow}
li.lime {color: lime}
ol li#maroon {color: maroon}
.order {color: blue}
.order {color: silver}
.decoration {text-decoration: line-through}

body {font-size: 25px; font-color: black}
</style>
</head>
<body>

<ol>
<li>This first-level list item should be navy
<li>Ditto with this line; neither should be olive
<ul>
<li>This unordered sub-list item should be yellow
<li class="lime">This one ought to be lime colored
</ul>
<li id="maroon">This should be maroon
<li>This list-item should default to navy.
</ol>

<p class="order">
This paragraph should be rendered in a silver color, taking on the
second value defined for the class
"<code>order</code>".
</p>
```

Listing 5.1 *Cascading Order (continued)*

```
<p class="decoration">
This text should be struck-through and not appear with an overline
or underline, as the overline code and underline codes which
appear in the two linked style sheets should be overridden by the
code contained in this page.
</p>

</body>
</html>
```

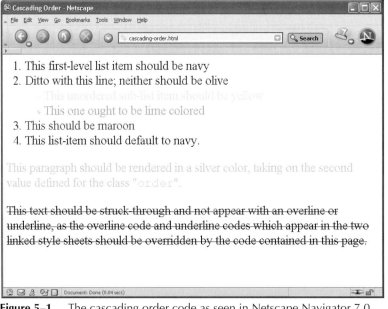

Figure 5–1   The cascading order code as seen in Netscape Navigator 7.0.

Browser Compatibility

- Internet Explorer 3.0: Unsafe
- Internet Explorer 4.0: Unsafe
- Internet Explorer 4.0 – 4.5 (Mac): Unsafe
- Internet Explorer 5.0: Partial
- Internet Explorer 5.5: Safe

- Internet Explorer 6.0: Safe

- Netscape Navigator 4.0 – 4.79: Partial

- Netscape Navigator 4.0 (Mac & UNIX): Partial

- Netscape Navigator 6.0: Safe

- Netscape Navigator 7.0: Safe

- Mozilla 1.0: Safe

- Opera 3.6 – 4.0: Safe.

- Opera 5.0 – 6.0: Safe

- Konqueror: Safe

The code example from Listing 5.1 will put any browser to the test when it comes to cascading rules. Opera 3.6 was the first browser to get everything completely right.

Internet Explorer versions 3.x and 4.x fail the test code — for these early versions of this browser one should be careful about not getting too complicated when it comes to laying out cascading order of items on a page. Internet Explorer 5.0 did much better when it came to interpreting cascading order, but it stumbles over one instance in the test code from Listing 5.1, misapplying the rules to the final line of text, displaying the text both as crossed out — which it should be — and with an overline. What happens is that it is applying the rule from `two.css` when it should be completely overridden by the more specific `class="decoration"` rule contained within the Web page. It should be noted that this is the only place where Internet Explorer 5.0 has problems, and it is easy enough to remedy as long as you can keep track of any CSS code being applied through external style sheets. Beginning with version 5.5 of Internet Explorer the people at Microsoft got this right, along with all subsequent versions of this browser.

Netscape Navigator 4.x handles this code very poorly. If you look at the test code from Listing 5.1, the text contained in the ordered lists is in black, the numbers in navy, and the second unordered bullets are lime colored; only the final two paragraphs are rendered correctly. In short, it knows how to deal with conflicts between local and imported style sheets, but fails when it comes to resolving conflicting internal rules. It is rated as Partial, although its behavior verges into Unsafe territory. If you are planning on writing CSS code for an audience that uses at least in part this version of the browser, ensure your code has as few CSS conflicts as possible. Otherwise, if you run into troubles, it may be difficult to predict exactly which CSS elements will be overridden. By the advent of Netscape Navigator 6.0, these problems had been fixed.

5.2   !important

The !important property enables Web authors to increase the "weight" applied to a certain rule, ensuring that it overrules any other CSS properties that might otherwise be specified. The !important property is useful in situations where you want to ensure that a certain formatting style is always applied to a document.

Listing 5.2   *!important*

```
<html>
<head>
<title>!important</title>
<style>
p {color: blue !important}
p {color: red}
p.fuchsia {color: fuchsia}
body {font-size: 34px; font-weight: bold}
</style>
</head>
<body>
<p>
This line of text should be in blue.
</p>

<p style="color: red">
This line of text should also be in blue, even though it is set to
red.
</p>

<p class="fuchsia">
This line of text should also be in blue, even though it is set to
fuchsia.
</p>

<p style="color: red !important">
This text should be in red, as it is set to !important. This
specific setting overrides the global !important reference for
this page, following proper cascading rules.
</p>

</body>
</html>
```

In the code sample included with the definition of this term, the initial paragraph tag is set to the color blue, and !important is attached to it. Two further paragraph tags are set to different colors, but the end result, as shown in Figure 5–2, is that the initial blue value applied to the first paragraph overrules all of the other values that have been set.

In the normal order of things, the initial value given to the paragraph tag would be overruled by those values that follow it. In this case the !important property is given the most "weight" by the browser, and consequently forces all of the text in the other paragraphs of the Web page to appear blue.

The !important property is best used in situations where you want to ensure that a particular CSS rule is applied to a page, perhaps when you are unsure of all of the properties being imported through linked CSS style sheets, or if you wish to override CSS code that you know appears later in the Web page.

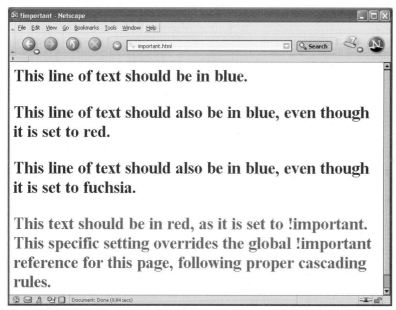

Figure 5–2   !important in action, as seen in Netscape Navigator 7.0.

Browser Compatibility

- Internet Explorer 3.0: Unsafe
- Internet Explorer 4.0: Safe
- Internet Explorer 4.0 – 4.5 (Mac): Safe
- Internet Explorer 5.0: Safe

- Internet Explorer 5.5: Safe
- Internet Explorer 6.0: Safe
- Netscape Navigator 4.0 – 4.79: Unsafe
- Netscape Navigator 4.0 (Mac & UNIX): Unsafe
- Netscape Navigator 6.0: Safe
- Mozilla 1.0: Safe
- Opera 3.6 – 4.0: Safe.
- Opera 5.0 – 6.0: Safe
- Konqueror: Safe

Support for this property used to be pretty spotty, although it is now fully supported in the most recent browsers. Internet Explorer beginning with version 4.0, Opera from version 3.6 and Netscape Navigator 6.0 on up deal with this property properly.

The browser of possible concern for Web authors in this case is Netscape Navigator 4.x, which did not support this property at all. While its numbers of users are dwindling, at the time of writing it still has a substantial enough user base that Web authors should use this property judiciously in their Web code.

5.3   Cascade-Order Sources

There are three different sources from which style sheets can originate: from the Web author, those (if any) created by the user viewing your Web page, and from the default settings used by the browser for rendering style sheets. It is important to know that these are also given specific "weights" in the cascading order, since under the right circumstances, a Web author's style sheet code can be overridden by these other settings.

Most browsers enable individual users to set their own viewing preferences when viewing Web pages. A fairly typical change that is often made is to make default text on a page larger than normal, making it more readable for those whose vision may be weak. Other quick changes that some browsers allow include letting the user set preferences for colors displayed on a Web page, or for specific fonts, links styles or even tables. While these are only the most typical changes, knowledgeable users can in fact set up separate style sheets that detail their display preferences for how Web pages should appear within browsers that allow this feature. This means that users can style Web pages using the full gamut of formatting possibilities available to CSS. Figure 5–3 shows how these settings can be explicitly set in several recent Web browsers.

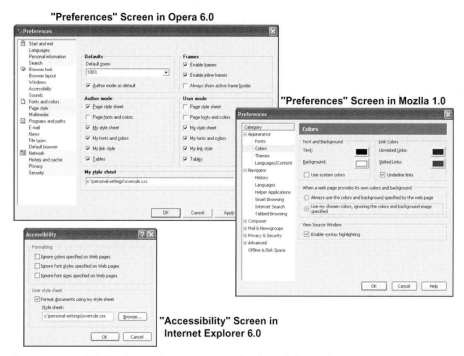

Figure 5–3   CSS display preference screens for three different browsers.

In terms of cascading order, it is important to remember that a user's preferences for displaying Web pages can — although not always — overrule whatever CSS settings you may have embedded in your pages. There's no way to detect whether a user's own style sheet is being used, and there's little a Web author can do about it, as this cascading rule gives the user ultimate control over how things appear on screen (which is arguably the way things ought to be).

Browsers have their own ways of interpreting CSS properties, and in fact incorporate their own "default style sheets" that tell the browser how to display regular HTML code. So, for example, such a style sheet might tell a browser that text surrounded by the `<strong>` tag should be rendered in a bold font, and that text surrounded by `<a>` tags should be displayed as a link. Any CSS properties you (or a user) may impose will automatically overrule the default settings, and this is necessary, since otherwise no CSS formatting would be possible.

The official cascading order for all of these different style sheet origins runs as follows (from most important to least important):

- User important style sheets
- Web Author important style sheets

- Web Author normal style sheets
- User normal style sheets
- The browser's default style sheet (also known as the "User Agent" style sheet)

As you can see, by default any `!important` settings a user may have set will always overrule any settings you have embedded into your Web pages — even the ones you consider `!important`. By the same token, any CSS code you implement will override a user's specific settings if they have not been explicitly set to `!important`.

CSS UNITS

Topics in This Chapter

- Length Units
- Percentage Units
- Color Formats
- URLs
- Strings
- Time Units
- Angle Units
- Frequency Units

Chapter 6

One of the most appealing things about CSS to many Webmasters is that it provides much finer control over setting the size, width and color of HTML elements on a Web page. CSS also has its own unique ways of handling URLs and strings of text, and since the advent of properties controlling the "layout" of sound in CSS2 (covered in detail in Chapter 21, "Aural Cascading Style Sheets"). CSS also provides control over timing, angles and frequencies. All of these units of measure and other ways of specifying unique properties are covered in this chapter.

6.1   Length Units

One of the chief benefits of CSS to Webmasters is the fact that you can finally tune borders, font sizes and margins using exact units of length. There are eight standard units of measure available, ranging from simple, common units of length to typographic measurement units, all of which can be used with CSS properties: inches, millimeters, centimeters, picas, points, pixels, m-lengths and x-heights. All of these units of measure can be specified by using a two-letter short form:

- inches = in
- millimeters = mm
- centimeters = cm
- pica = pc

- point = pt
- pixels = px
- m-length = em, and
- x-height = ex.

Units of measure are not case-sensitive; you could use either "CM" or "cm" to set a measure for a given CSS rule when using centimeters.

Inches are a standard measure of length in the imperial system of measurement, and most people should be familiar with it. There are 25.4 millimeters to an inch. Millimeters and centimeters are standard units of length under the metric system. There are 10 millimeters to the centimeter, and there are 2.54 centimeters to the inch.

Picas and points are standard typographical units of measure. There are 72 points to the inch, 12 points to 1 pica, and 6 picas equal 1 inch. In Web browsers, the typical default value for text display is 12 points for variable-width fonts (such as Times Roman), and 10 points for fixed-width fonts (such as Courier).

m-length and x-height refer to the length and height of the letters "m" and "x," respectively, in a given font. In a fixed-width font such as Courier, the "m" and "x" lengths should be the same.

Pixels are a standard unit of measure for gauging height and width on computer screens. Depending on the type of computer monitor being used and the resolution being displayed, a typical pixel measures between 0.25 and 0.35 millimeters.

These units of measure can be divided into three types: absolute, relative and device-dependent. Inches, millimeters, centimeters, points and picas are all absolute measures. In theory, you should be able to take a ruler to your computer screen and verify that 1 inch on screen corresponds to a standard inch in length.

m-length and x-height are relative units of measure that depend on the font currently being used. Since these lengths are font dependent, the m-length and x-height of a given 10-point font will necessarily be smaller than that of a 16-point font.

Pixels are a device-dependent unit of measure, as different monitors set to different screen resolutions can yield very different absolute resolutions. Since the results will always be consistent between monitors, however, it is considered safe to use pixels, although there may be differences in terms of the absolute scale of the item being displayed.

Listing 6.1 uses all of the standard units of length in a single Web page, the values of each designed to produce a left margin setting the equivalent of 1 inch.

Listing 6.1   *Length Units*

```
<html>
<head>
<title>Length Units</title>
<style>
.no_left_margin {margin-left: 0}
.inch {margin-left: 1in}
.mm {margin-left: 25.4mm}
.cm {margin-left: 2.54cm}
.pica {margin-left: 6pc}
.point {margin-left: 72pt}
.ex {margin-left: 12ex}
.em {margin-left: 6em}
.pixel {margin-left: 96px}

body {font-family: "Courier New", Courier, monospace}
</style>
</head>

<body>
<p class="no_left_margin">
This paragraph has no left margin. All of the other paragraphs
that follow have margins that should be set the equivalent of one
inch.
</p>
<p class="inch">
This paragraph has a left margin set to 1 inch.
</p>
<p class="mm">
This paragraph has a left margin set to 25.4 millimeters.
</p>
<p class="cm">
This paragraph has a left margin set to 2.54 millimeters.
</p>
<p class="pica">
This paragraph has a left margin set to 6 picas.
</p>
<p class="point">
This paragraph has a left margin set to 72 points.
</p>
<p class="ex">
This paragraph has a left margin set to 12 ex.
</p>
```

Listing 6.1	*Length Units (continued)*

```
<p class="em">
This paragraph has a left margin set to 6 em. The major browsers
calculate 1 ex = 1/2 em, which
is not technically correct, but at least it is consistent. ;-)
</p>
<p class="pixel">
This paragraph has a left margin set to 96 pixels (which is
equivalent to 1 inch on the monitor
displaying this code).
</p>

</body>
</html>
```

Figure 6–1 shows how the code example is displayed in Internet Explorer 6.0.

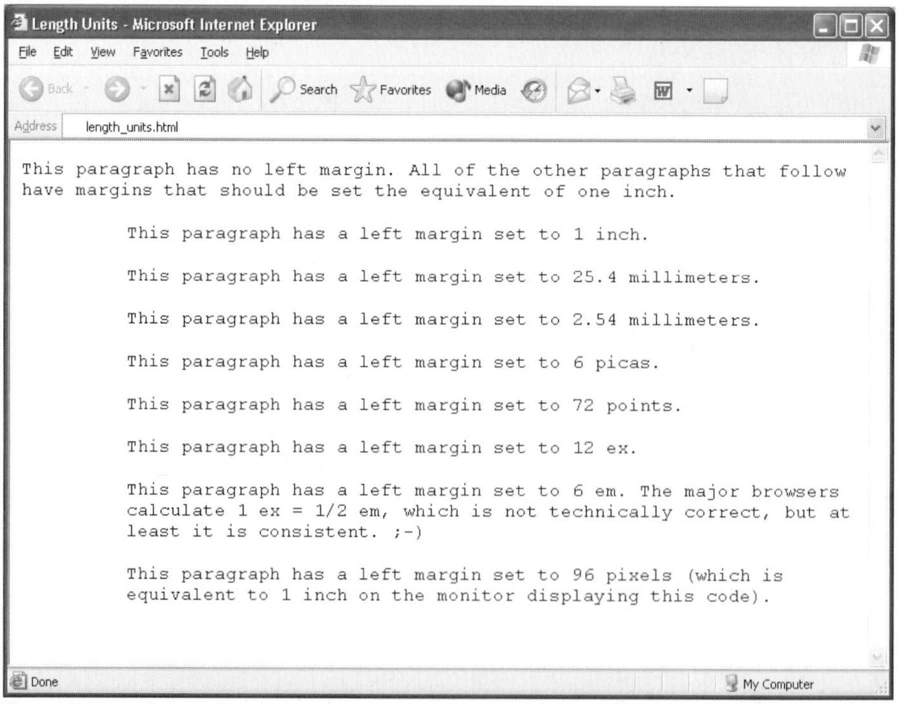

Figure 6–1   Various units of measure set to an equivalent indent value of 1 inch from the left margin, as seen in Internet Explorer 6.0.

Browser Compatibility

In general, this property has been well supported in the major browsers, save for some problems dealing with x-height and m-length measures. In practice, however, there is little call for using m-length or x-height when a more convenient measure can be used instead, so it is recommended that em and ex measures be avoided when possible for general browser compatibility, especially when trying to set sizes of non-text objects.

- Internet Explorer 3.0: Partial.
- Internet Explorer 4.0: Partial.
- Internet Explorer 4.0 – 4.5 (Mac): Partial.
- Internet Explorer 5.0: Partial.
- Internet Explorer 5.5: Safe.
- Internet Explorer 6.0: Safe.
- Netscape Navigator 4.0 – 4.79: Partial.
- Netscape Navigator 4.0 (Mac & UNIX): Partial.
- Netscape Navigator 6.0: Partial.
- Netscape Navigator 7.0: Partial.
- Mozilla 1.0: Partial.
- Opera 3.6 – 4.0: Partial.
- Opera 5.0 – 6.0: Safe.
- Konqueror: Safe.

In versions of Internet Explorer up to version 5.0, and Netscape Navigator up to version 4.x, m-length and x-height units were not rendered properly. This was because the browsers calculated 1 ex as equivalent to 1/2 em, which is not always technically correct. This behavior was consistent between the two major browsers, so at least they displayed things the same, even if technically speaking it was not quite correct, which is why they are given a "Partial" rating. Microsoft got around to correcting this in Internet Explorer 5.5 and up, as it renders m-length and x-height lengths consistently, as can be seen in Figure 6–1.

Netscape Navigator 6.x and 7.x render m-lengths correctly, but still have problems with x-height measures. They are rated as "Partial" to note the variance in the way that recent Netscape browsers handle this. Recent Netscape browsers derive the em behavior directly from how the operating system determines relative font size settings, which differs from the way Internet Explorer determines the value for a given em value. This behavior appears to be consistent among the different operating systems Netscape operates under. You can see how Netscape Navigator 7.0 renders the same test code in Figure 6–2, rendering the line set using ex slightly behind all of the other lines on the page.

The early versions of Opera (3.6 and 4.0) had the same problems with m-length and x-height units as did the early versions of Internet Explorer. These were fixed by version 5.0.

Konqueror supports length units properly.

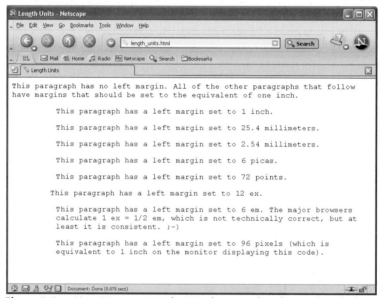

Figure 6–2   How Netscape 7.0 for Windows renders the same code from Listing 6.1; the line set using ex measure is interpreted differently.

Core Tip

It should be noted that when units of length are specified, there should be no space between the number and the unit of measure. In other words, when specifying an inch, write it as "1in", not "1 in". Internet Explorer is forgiving of this sort of thing, but all other browsers stick strictly to the specification and will not accept the measurement value used when there's a space between the number and the unit of measure.

6.2   Percentage Units

In addition to using units of measure in your CSS code, you can also use percentage units to set the width and height of various elements displayed on screen. The behavior is really no different than when using percentage values in standard HTML code, such as using `<table  width="50%">` in order to set table to half the width of the browser window. Similarly, percentage values in CSS are always relative to another value, typically the height or width of the browser window. Percentages are always specified using a numeral followed by a percentage sign, in exactly the same way as with a standard HTML tag.

Listing 6.2	*Percentages*

```
<html>
<head>
<title>Percentages</title>
<style>
p.margin-left {margin-left: 25%}
p.margin-right {margin-right: 25%}
p.halfway-left {margin-left: 50%}
p.halfway-right {margin-right: 50%}

body {font-size: x-large; font-weight: bold}
</style>
</head>
<body>

<p class="margin-left">
This text is indented 25% of the browser window to the
<em>left</em>. Here's some extra text to make this more
apparent.
</p>

<p class="margin-right">
This text is indented 25% of the browser window to the
<em>right</em>. Here's some extra text to make this more
apparent.
</p>

<p class="halfway-left">
This text is indented to half of the browser window, and is
indented 50% from the <em>left</em> of the browser window.
</p>
```

| Listing 6.2 | *Percentages (continued)* |

```
<p class="halfway-right">
This text is indented to half of the browser window, and is
indented 50% from the <em>right</em> of the browser window.
</p>

</body>
</html>
```

One of the advantages of using percentage values in CSS is that they give you greater flexibility than can be achieved using standard HTML code, and should give you consistent displays across different computer monitor resolutions. Figure 6–3 displays the example code from Listing 6.2, and shows how you can easily set the left and right margins for text (or other elements) on a Web page.

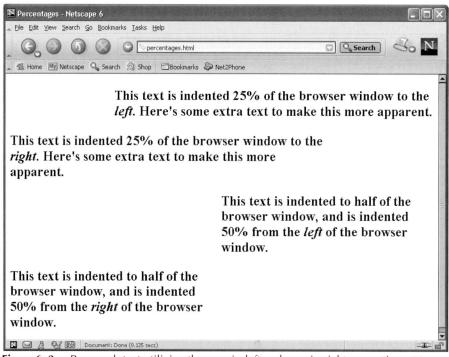

Figure 6–3   Paragraph text utilizing the margin-left and margin-right properties set to 25% and 50% values, respectively, as depicted in Netscape Navigator 6.2.

Browser Compatibility

Percentage values are fully supported by all browsers that support CSS. This is one of those rare CSS properties that has always been completely safe to use.

- Internet Explorer 3.0: Safe.
- Internet Explorer 4.0: Safe.
- Internet Explorer 4.0 – 4.5 (Mac): Safe.
- Internet Explorer 5.0: Safe.
- Internet Explorer 5.5: Safe.
- Internet Explorer 6.0: Safe.
- Netscape Navigator 4.0 – 4.79: Safe.
- Netscape Navigator 4.0 (Mac & UNIX): Safe.
- Netscape Navigator 6.0: Safe.
- Netscape Navigator 7.0: Safe.
- Mozilla 1.0: Safe.
- Opera 3.6 – 4.0: Safe
- Opera 5.0 – 6.0: Safe.
- Konqueror: Safe.

6.3   URLs

It is possible to add URL references within some CSS code, allowing Webmasters to add such things as backgrounds to Web pages, tables and other displayable elements, or links to external CSS formatting pages.

Specifying URLs in CSS is slightly different than specifying URLs in HTML (as opposed to XHTML, in which the CSS version is supposed to be used instead of the deprecated HTML code). In HTML, you would reference a background image using a standard URL format, as in the following line of code:

```
<body background="http://www.frantics.net/images/background.jpg">
```

To specify this same URL in CSS code, you place the actual URL in round brackets, preceded by "URL" to denote it as such, as in the following example CSS code:

```
<body style="background:
url(http://www.frantics.net/images/background.jpg)>
```

Figure 6–4 shows how the Listing 6.3 example code works. Note how the additional margin settings added to the CSS code tile the background image within certain boundaries — something that cannot be accomplished using regular HTML.

| Listing 6.3 | *URLs* |

```
<html>
<head>
<title>URLs</title>
<style>
body {background:
url(http://www.frantics.net/images/background.jpg); margin-right:
100px; margin-left: 100px}
p {color: white; font-size: x-large}
</style>
</head>
<body>
<p>
This Web page uses a background image imported from an outside
source, and has margins set to 100 pixels on both sides so that the
text does not stray over the "sides" set by the background image.
</p>
<p>
The twin sides of the coin depicted on either side of this page is
from a single silver coin of the ancient Roman Emperor Antonius
Pius, who reigned from 138 until 161AD.
</p>
</body>
</html>
```

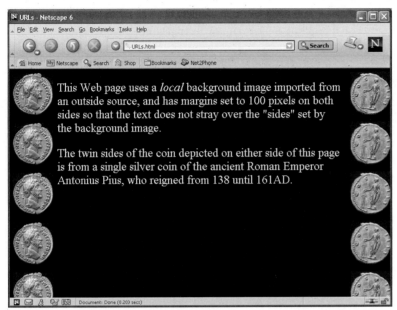

Figure 6–4   Netscape Navigator 6.2 displaying the sample code that sets a background image using CSS code.

Browser Compatibility

This is another rare case of a completely safe CSS property to use, since all browsers that have claimed to support CSS in some way support this particular property.

- Internet Explorer 3.0: Safe.
- Internet Explorer 4.0: Safe.
- Internet Explorer 4.0 – 4.5 (Mac): Safe.
- Internet Explorer 5.0: Safe.
- Internet Explorer 5.5: Safe.
- Internet Explorer 6.0: Safe.
- Netscape Navigator 4.0 – 4.79: Safe.
- Netscape Navigator 4.0 (Mac & UNIX): Safe.
- Netscape Navigator 6.0: Safe.
- Netscape Navigator 7.0: Safe.
- Mozilla 1.0: Safe.
- Opera 3.6 – 4.0: Safe
- Opera 5.0 – 6.0: Safe.
- Konqueror: Safe.

6.4   Strings

"String" is a programming term that relates to displaying or manipulating functions based on text. The string equivalent of the hexadecimal color value `#FF0000` is "red", and both are equally understood by browsers when used in either XHTML objects or as values within a given CSS property.

Normally, quote marks are not used when specifying text values in CSS. The sole exception to this rule is when you need to set a specific font value. The `font-family` property allows Web authors to select a particular font on a user's system by placing it within quotes, for example:

```
font-family: "Arial Black", Arial, sans-serif
```

In this case, the "Arial Black" will only make a match with a font of exactly the same name on the user's system — it will not match similar font names, such as "Arial Narrow" or "Arial Rounded MT Bold." Additionally, in this case it is important to use quotes because of the space contained within the name of this font, as "Arial Black" and Arial Black (without quotes) are not equivalent; in the latter case, the browser will first search for a font called Arial, then for one called Black. Of course, whenever you do use such a specific font setting, it is in your interest to use a setting that is commonly found on most computing systems. You are relatively safe with a setting like "`Times Roman`", as opposed to a less-common font such as "`Poor Richard`", "`Matisse ITC`" or "`Franklin Gothic Demi`".

In CSS, strings of text — like those used when generating automatic content — can be contained within sets of single or double quotes. So, for example, the following code snippet contains two valid strings:

```
"The quick brown fox jumped over the lazy dog."
'The quick brown fox jumped over the lazy dog.'
```

If you needed to have the quote symbols displayed along with the text, use the backslash character, which works as an escape character for the quote. The next code snippet contains code that would display the word "fox" with quotes.

```
span:after {content: "The quick young \"fox\" jumped over the lazy
dog." }
strong:after {content: 'The quick young \'fox\' jumped over the
lazy dog.' }
```

If you needed to include a displayed line break within some CSS code, you can either use an escape character immediately before an actual line break, or use the "carriage-return" escape character "`\A`" to do the same thing. The following code snippet features two equivalent lines of code, and would display a line break after the word "fox":

```
span:after {content: "The quick young fox \
jumped over the lazy dog." }
span:after {content: 'The quick young fox \A jumped over the lazy
dog.' }
```

For more information on the `content` property, see Chapter 15, "Classification Properties and Generated/Automatic Content."

Browser Compatibility

All browsers understand specific font family references within quotes. However, the way strings of text are utilized in automatically generated content is a relatively recent introduction, and its adoption has been relatively slow in the major browsers, and hence the specific properties that deal with strings (such as the `content` property, described in detail in Chapter 15) are far from robust in their operation.

- Internet Explorer 3.0: Unsafe.
- Internet Explorer 4.0: Unsafe.
- Internet Explorer 4.0 – 4.5 (Mac): Unsafe.
- Internet Explorer 5.0: Unsafe.
- Internet Explorer 5.5: Unsafe.
- Internet Explorer 6.0: Unsafe.
- Netscape Navigator 4.0 – 4.79: Unsafe.
- Netscape Navigator 4.0 (Mac & UNIX): Unsafe.
- Netscape Navigator 6.0: Partial.
- Netscape Navigator 7.0: Partial.
- Mozilla 1.0: Unsafe.
- Opera 3.6: Unsafe
- Opera 4.0-6.0: Partial.
- Konqueror: Unsafe.

Internet Explorer does not as yet support strings.

From version 6.x on up, when the `content` property was first supported, Netscape also supported quotes within quotes for generated text, but like Opera, it does not display line breaks properly. For this reason, it is also rated as Partial.

Opera led the way by supporting strings and quotes within quoted text in version 4.0 of its browser, as it was the first to support generated text via CSS. However, its implementation is not perfect, as it does not display a line break when one should appear, so it is rated as Partial.

Strings are not yet supported within Konqueror.

6.5   Time Units

Some Aural Cascading Style Sheet (ACSS) properties allow the Web author to set the time duration for a sound. There are two available time units: ms (milliseconds) and s (seconds). To use them, all you have to do is put an integer number in front of them within a valid property. The following code snippet shows how this could work:

```
<body style="speak:normal">
Some spoken text.
<p style="pause-before:50ms">A slight pause.</p>
<p style="pause-before:2s">A longer pause.</p>
</body>
```

Negative time unit values are not allowed.

For more information on ACSS, see Chapter 21, "Aural Cascading Styles Sheets."

Browser Compatibility

At the time of writing, none of the major browsers have implemented any of the ACCS properties, hence none of them support any CSS-based time units.

- Internet Explorer 3.0: Unsafe.
- Internet Explorer 4.0: Unsafe.
- Internet Explorer 4.0 – 4.5 (Mac): Unsafe.
- Internet Explorer 5.0: Unsafe.
- Internet Explorer 5.5: Unsafe.
- Internet Explorer 6.0: Unsafe.
- Netscape Navigator 4.0 – 4.79: Unsafe.
- Netscape Navigator 4.0 (Mac & UNIX): Unsafe.
- Netscape Navigator 6.0: Unsafe.
- Netscape Navigator 7.0: Unsafe.
- Mozilla 1.0: Unsafe.
- Opera 3.6 – 4.0: Unsafe.
- Opera 5.0 – 6.0: Unsafe.
- Konqueror: Unsafe.

6.6   Angle Units

There are a few Aural Cascading Style Sheet (ACSS) properties that enable the user to set exactly where a sound should be placed within a stereo sound field. These properties can take angle values to help you place where the sound should "appear". In addition, one of the proposed new ways of setting colors in CSS3 would also use angle units (for more information on this, look up the color property in Chapter 13, "Color").

Three types of angle units are available: deg (degrees), grad (grads) and rad (radians). All of the values can take negative values, although positives are assumed by default if not explicitly set using a "-" symbol. Of these three types of angle values, people are most familiar with degrees values, which range from 0 – 360. The following code snippet shows a couple of lines of ACSS code that use a degree setting to place a couple of speaking voices:

```
<p style="azimuth:90deg">Hamlet: How does the Queen?<p>
<p style="azimuth:270deg">King: She sounds to see them bleed.</p>
```

In this case, the voice of Hamlet would appear to the right ("90deg"), and that of the King to the left (270deg).

Figure 6–5 shows the placement of positive and negative degree values around a circle.

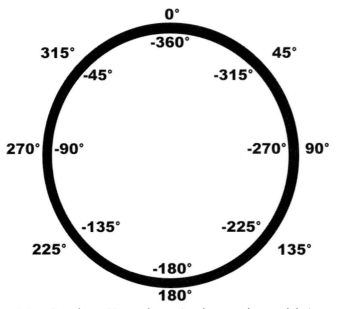

Figure 6–5   Sample positive and negative degree values and their placement around a circle.

Less well known are the radian and grad values. Here's how they work: there are 360 degrees in a circle, which is equal to 2π radians. There are 57.29577951 degrees in each radian, and each degree is equal to 0.01745329252 radians. A value of 90 degrees is equivalent to 1.57079633 radians, and 270 degrees to 4.71238898 radians (expressed to 8 decimal places — whenever you are dealing with π you are dealing with infinitely-repeating irrational numbers). The grad is a metric unit of circumference, used primarily in Europe. For the 360 degrees of a circle you get 400 grads, dividing the circle into four equal quarters. Each of these quarters equals 100 grads, so 90 degrees equals 100 grads, and 270 degrees equals 300 grads.

Browser Compatibility

At the time of writing, none of the major browsers have implemented any of the ACCS properties, or the new ways of setting color values using angle units in CSS3, so correspondingly they don't support any CSS-based angle units.

- Internet Explorer 3.0: Unsafe.
- Internet Explorer 4.0: Unsafe.
- Internet Explorer 4.0 – 4.5 (Mac): Unsafe.
- Internet Explorer 5.0: Unsafe.
- Internet Explorer 5.5: Unsafe.
- Internet Explorer 6.0: Unsafe.
- Netscape Navigator 4.0 – 4.79: Unsafe.
- Netscape Navigator 4.0 (Mac & UNIX): Unsafe.
- Netscape Navigator 6.0: Unsafe.
- Netscape Navigator 7.0: Unsafe.
- Mozilla 1.0: Unsafe.
- Opera 3.6 – 4.0: Unsafe.
- Opera 5.0 – 6.0: Unsafe.
- Konqueror: Unsafe.

6.7   Frequency Units

With the advent of the Aural Cascading Style Sheets (ACCS) specification came the introduction of units of value for sound frequencies. There are two such units of frequency that can be specified in selected ACSS properties: Hz (Hertz) and kHz (kilohertz). For the most part, when specifying frequency values, use Hz for relatively low sounds (like a human voice) and kHz for higher sounds (like high-pitched tones). These values cannot be expressed in negative values and this is obvious when you think about it — if a 0 value is silence, what could be less than that? Also, it is worth noting that these values are not case sensitive — hz, khz, HZ, KHz are all equivalent

The following code snippet shows how the Hertz frequency unit might be put to use:

```
<p style="voice-family:male; pitch:170hz">
Hamlet: What hour now?
</p>
<p style="voice-family:male; pitch:120hz">
Horatio: I think it lacks of twelve.
</p>
```

In this case, Hamlet's voice is deliberately pitched higher than Horatio's, helping the listener to distinguish between the two speakers.

Browser Compatibility

At the time of writing, none of the major browsers have implemented any of the ACCS properties, so correspondingly they don't support any CSS-based frequency units, which are the only properties which are applicable.

- Internet Explorer 3.0: Unsafe.
- Internet Explorer 4.0: Unsafe.
- Internet Explorer 4.0 – 4.5 (Mac): Unsafe.
- Internet Explorer 5.0: Unsafe.
- Internet Explorer 5.5: Unsafe.
- Internet Explorer 6.0: Unsafe.
- Netscape Navigator 4.0 – 4.79: Unsafe.
- Netscape Navigator 4.0 (Mac & UNIX): Unsafe.
- Netscape Navigator 6.0: Unsafe.
- Netscape Navigator 7.0: Unsafe.
- Mozilla 1.0: Unsafe.
- Opera 3.6 – 4.0: Unsafe
- Opera 5.0 – 6.0: Unsafe.
- Konqueror: Unsafe.

PSEUDO-CLASSES AND PSEUDO-ELEMENTS

Topics in This Chapter

- `anchor` Pseudo-Element
- `first-line` Pseudo-Class
- `first-letter` Pseudo-Class
- `lang` Pseudo-Class
- `left`, `right` and `first` Pseudo-Classes
- `focus` and `hover` Pseudo-Classes
- `first-child` Pseudo-Class
- Pseudo-Elements in Selectors and Combining Multiple Pseudo-Elements

Chapter 7

It is common for Web browsers to display a link differently based upon whether or not it has already been visited by the user, and to acknowledge that the user is clicking on it. Web authors have had the ability to set the colors of links on their Web pages for some time now using HTML, but CSS gives Web authors a new way to do things, providing the flexibility to change more than the color of the links. The pseudo-classes `anchor`, `first-line` and `first-letter` deal with these situations.

There are a number of common typographical layout techniques (such as drop-cap letters, or special text formatting applied to the first line or letter of text in a paragraph) that, while commonplace in print media, are not easy to reproduce using standard HTML. These do not conform to the idea of typical structural elements contained in a Web page, but are better thought of as pure typographical layout formatting features. CSS enables the Web author to accomplish this using the pseudo-elements `first-line` and `first-letter`.

This chapter looks at the all of these pseudo-classes and pseudo-elements, showing how they can be used.

(Note: The `before` and `after` pseudo-elements are examined in detail in conjunction with the `content` property in Chapter 15, "Classification Properties and Generated/Automatic Content").

7.1   anchor Pseudo-Element

The anchor pseudo-element controls how links are handled on a Web page. Many browsers display a link differently depending on whether or not it has already been visited, or is actively being clicked on by the user. The anchor pseudo-element is actually a set of sub-properties that give the Web author full control over how links appear on a Web page.

The anchor pseudo-element is comprised of the following sub-properties: a:link, a:active and a:visited. a:link defines how an unclicked and unvisited link (in other words, a link "at rest") should appear on a Web page. The a:active property defines how a link should appear when it is clicked or otherwise selected by the user. The a:visited property determines what the link should look like after it has been visited. These CSS pseudo-properties are designed to work in exactly the same way as the anchor attributes you can add to the <body> tag using HTML, as the following line of code shows:

```
<body link="fuchsia" vlink="black" alink="olive">
```

In this case, the HTML attribute <link> is equivalent to the CSS a:link, <vlink> is equivalent to a:visited and <alink> is equivalent to a:active. Figure 7–1 displays CSS code that is equivalent to this HTML code — in this code, the "resting" link is displayed in fuchsia, active links in olive and visited links in black.

Listing 7.1	*Links Example Code*

```
<html>
<head>
<title>anchor Property</title>
<style>
a:link {color: fuchsia}
a:active {color: olive}
a:visited {color: black}
#redlink {color: #ff0000; font-size: x-large}

body {font-size: 25px; font-family : Arial, Helvetica, sans-serif;
font-weight: bold}
</style>
</head>
<body>
```

Listing 7.1	*Links Example Code (continued)*

```
None of the links on this page should be a <a
href="link1.html">navy color</a> as they are over-ridden by the
subsequent anchor values. Before they are clicked they should
appear as a <a href="link2.html">fuschia color</a>, an <a
href="link3.html">olive color</a> when clicked and <a
href="link4.html">black</a> once it has been visited.
<p>
The link in this line should appear <a href="link4.html"
id="redlink">red and larger</a> than the rest of the text, and
should not change when it is clicked, or after it has been visited.
</p>
</body>
</html>
```

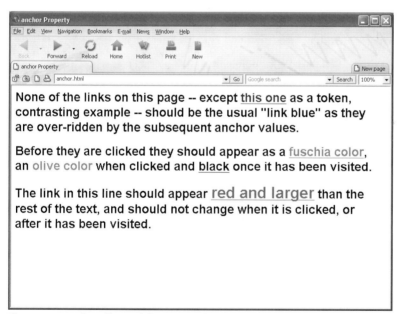

Figure 7–1   The effects of the CSS anchor pseudo-properties displayed in Opera 6.0.

Browser Compatibility

Despite the fact that this group of pseudo-elements is not rendered correctly in the earliest browsers, you are relatively safe using them in Web pages. The best tactic to take is to not make the color scheme you choose for your links critical to navigating the Web page. In other words, don't use a background color normally associated with a link value, such as blue or red.

- Internet Explorer 3.0: Unsafe.

- Internet Explorer 4.0: Safe.

- Internet Explorer 4.0 – 4.5 (Mac): Safe.

- Internet Explorer 5.0: Safe.

- Internet Explorer 5.1 – 5.2 (Mac): Safe.

- Internet Explorer 5.5: Safe.

- Internet Explorer 6.0: Safe.

- Netscape Navigator 4.0 – 4.79: Partial

- Netscape Navigator 4.0 (Mac & UNIX): Partial

- Netscape Navigator 6.0: Partial

- Netscape Navigator 7.0: Partial

- Mozilla 1.0: Partial.

- Opera 3.6 – 6.0: Safe.

- Konqueror: Safe.

Internet Explorer 3.0 doesn't know what to make of the test code in Listing 7.1, rendering all of the links the same. Microsoft got things right by version 4.0, however.

Netscape Navigator 4.x had some trouble with the test code seen in Listing 7.1 — it handles the `a:link` and `a:visited` links properly, but does not color the `a:active` link the proper value, and is in fact treated as if the settings applied to `a:link`. There's another problem in Netscape Navigator 4.x that occurs with these pseudo-elements when it comes to dealing with cascading rules. If, for example, you added a `{color: navy}` to the top of the header of the page in Listing 7.1, you might expect that all the tags on the Web page would appear in a navy color, but due to cascading rules, all of the subsequent color values assigned to the regular, active and visited links should overrule this setting. In Netscape Navigator 4.x, this does not happen, and all of the links would be rendered in a navy color. It does, however properly interpret the link with the specific anchor value "redlink", which renders the link in red (using the hexadecimal value "`#ff0000`") and in a larger font size than the rest of the text, obeying the cascading rules. Netscape got it largely right with the release of Netscape Navigator 6.0 — all of the example links in Listing 7.1 work properly save for the last one where the link referenced via an `id` value is not rendered properly — but in all other respects things work as intended.

Opera has fully implemented the anchor pseudo-element since version 3.6.

7.2   first-line Pseudo-Element

`first-line` is a pseudo-element meant to reproduce the type of text sometimes seen in the first lines of newspapers and magazines, setting it apart from the rest of the text in a paragraph. It changes the way the first line of text in a paragraph is displayed. Using the `first-line` pseudo-element, you can change the color, background, spacing or other ways in which the first line of text in a paragraph is displayed.

Listing 7.2 shows how this can be used in practice. The results can be seen in Figure 7–2.

Listing 7.2	*first-line*

```
<html>
<head>
<title>first-line Pseudo-Element</title>
<style>
div:first-line {font-variant: small-caps; color: navy; background:
yellow}
body {font-size: 25px; font-family : Verdana, Geneva, Arial,
Helvetica, sans-serif}
</style>
</head>
<body>
<div>
The first line, and only the first line of this paragraph, should
be displayed in a navy color, be in small caps and have a yellow
background. All of the subsequent lines of this paragraph should
appear in the default text color, which is black. Here is some
extra text in order to make the effect clear.
</div>
<p>
The first paragraph is displayed within a <code>div</code> block
instead of the usual paragraph. If the <code>first-line</code>
pseudo-element was set to <code>p</code> instead, the first line
of each paragraph would be similarly displayed.
</p>
<p>
So, be careful when using this pseudo-element.
</p>
</body>
</html>
```

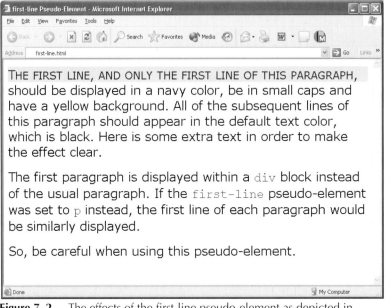

Figure 7–2   The effects of the first-line pseudo-element as depicted in Internet Explorer 6.0.

Notice that only the first *line* of text in a paragraph is altered in its display, as opposed to the first *sentence* of the initial paragraph. Note also how the size of the line of text determines how much text will be rendered in the first-line format; the first line of text that appears in the small table has a shorter first line, and subsequently fewer words are formatted under the first-line properties specified.

The first-line pseudo-element is designed to handle only certain types of additional CSS formatting properties: the various font color and background properties, plus the word-spacing, letter-spacing, text-decoration, text-transform, line-height and clear CSS properties.

Browser Compatibility

As with many other pseudo-elements, full compatibility within the major browsers has only been a relatively recent thing.

- Internet Explorer 3.0: Unsafe
- Internet Explorer 4.0: Unsafe
- Internet Explorer 4.0 – 4.5 (Mac): Unsafe
- Internet Explorer 5.0: Unsafe
- Internet Explorer 5.1 – 5.2 (Mac): Safe

- Internet Explorer 5.5: Safe
- Internet Explorer 6.0: Safe
- Netscape Navigator 4.0 – 4.79: Unsafe
- Netscape Navigator 4.0 (Mac & UNIX): Unsafe
- Netscape Navigator 6.0: Safe
- Netscape Navigator 7.0: Safe
- Mozilla 1.0: Safe
- Opera 3.6 – 6.0: Safe
- Konqueror: Safe

Internet Explorer started implementing this pseudo-element correctly only with version 5.5 of its browser. Previous versions simply ignored the pseudo-element when it appeared.

Netscape Navigator only started to recognize `first-line` in version 6.0 of its browser. Previous versions ignored it when it was present.

Not surprisingly, Opera got it right first, and since version 3.6 of its browser it has successfully supported this pseudo-element.

Konqueror properly supports this pseudo-element.

7.3   first-letter Pseudo-Element

`first-letter` is another pseudo-element, designed specifically to give either a "drop-cap" or "initial-cap" appearance to the first letter than appears in a paragraph, an effect often seen in print publications like newspapers and magazines.

This particular pseudo-element takes a bit of planning in order to get the effect to look just right. Listing 7.3 demonstrates how a proper drop-cap effect can be accomplished using the `first-letter` pseudo-element.

Listing 7.3	*first-letter*

```
<html>
<head>
<title>First-Letter</title>
<style>
p {font-size: 25px; line-height: 25pt}
p:first-letter {font-size: 50px; float: left; color: navy;
font-weight: bold}
</style>
</head>
```

Listing 7.3	*first-letter (continued)*

```
<body>
<p>
The first letter in this sentence will be 50 pixels in size, navy
in color, bold and float to the left of the text -- set to half its
size -- that follows it. Some extra text is needed to properly show
off the box-like properties of the pseudo-element style specified,
so that the final line of text flows underneath the first letter.
</p>
<p>
"Look at that!" he said, pointing to the fact that the quotation
mark and the capital "L" in "Look"
were both rendered in the first-letter pseudo-element style
specified. This is working exactly the way it is designed to do, as
it is supposed to be associated with the first letter.
</p>
</body>
</html>
```

Figure 7–3 shows how this code is displayed in the Internet Explorer 6.0.

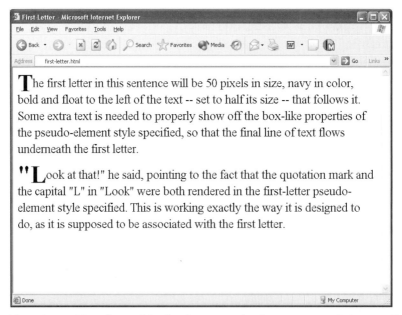

Figure 7–3   The effects of the first-letter pseudo-element as seen in Internet Explorer 6.0.

Note how the first letter in each of the paragraphs displayed takes on the values assigned to the `first-letter` pseudo-element: the letter should be 50 pixels in size, navy in color, bold and float to the left of the text that follows it. Note the line of code that precedes the `first-letter` pseudo-element sets the text and the line-height that follows the first letter to 25 pixels in height. This is done so that the text aligns properly with the top of the first letter; otherwise the following text would float slightly above the first letter.

The second line of text shows another intended effect of the `first-letter` pseudo-element: any quotation mark that precedes the first-letter takes on the same properties as the first letter itself. This is desirable, as paragraphs often begin with quotation marks. Note that this is not designed to work with other symbols, such as a round bracket (i.e., a parenthesis) or mathematical symbols.

In order to create an initial cap instead of a drop cap in the code example shown earlier, all you would have to do would be to remove the `float: left;` rule from the code to produce the desired effect.

Many of the same formatting restrictions that apply to `first-line` apply to the `first-letter` pseudo-element: it can take the various font color and background properties, plus the `word-spacing`, `letter-spacing`, `text-decoration`, `text-transform`, `line-height` and `clear` CSS properties.

Browser Compatibility

With this pseudo-element, the basic rule of thumb is if `first-line` works, then so will `first-letter`.

- Internet Explorer 3.0: Unsafe
- Internet Explorer 4.0: Unsafe
- Internet Explorer 4.0 – 4.5 (Mac): Unsafe
- Internet Explorer 5.0: Unsafe
- Internet Explorer 5.1 – 5.2 (Mac): Safe.
- Internet Explorer 5.5: Unsafe
- Internet Explorer 6.0: Unsafe
- Netscape Navigator 4.0 – 4.79: Unsafe
- Netscape Navigator 4.0 (Mac & UNIX): Unsafe
- Netscape Navigator 6.0: Safe
- Netscape Navigator 7.0: Safe
- Mozilla 1.0: Safe
- Opera 3.6 – 6.0: Safe
- Konqueror: Safe

Internet Explorer started implementing the `first-letter` pseudo-element correctly only with version 5.5 of its browser. Previous versions simply ignored the pseudo-element when it appeared.

Netscape Navigator only started to recognize `first-letter` in version 6.0 of its browser. Previous versions ignored it when it was present.

Opera got things right first with version 3.6 of its browser.

7.4   lang Pseudo-Class

The `lang` pseudo-class sets the language associated with a particular Web element. A good example of where this can be put to use is in setting the type of quote marks that should appear in pages, such as those typified by Listing 7.2. While in English you can expect double- and single-quote characters, other languages have different ways of displaying quoted text. For example, the following code could be used to dynamically set the type of quote that should appear given the language of the text.

```
<style>
q:lang(en) {quotes: '"' '"'}
q:lang(FR) {quotes: '«' '»'}
q:lang(DE) {quotes: '»' '«'}
</style>
```

This pseudo-class is roughly the CSS equivalent of the HTML `lang` attribute common to all HTML 4.0 tags. The `lang` pseudo-class is more flexible however, allowing a page or even a particular element to be differently formatted depending on the language being used, something not available to the `lang` HTML attribute.

Browser Compatibility

Unfortunately, this pseudo-class is not supported within any major browser.

- Internet Explorer 3.0: Unsafe
- Internet Explorer 4.0: Unsafe
- Internet Explorer 4.0 – 4.5 (Mac): Unsafe
- Internet Explorer 5.0: Unsafe
- Internet Explorer 5.5: Unsafe
- Internet Explorer 6.0: Unsafe
- Netscape Navigator 4.0 – 4.79: Unsafe
- Netscape Navigator 4.0 (Mac & UNIX): Unsafe
- Netscape Navigator 6.0: Unsafe
- Netscape Navigator 7.0: Unsafe
- Mozilla 1.0: Unsafe
- Opera 3.6 – 6.0: Unsafe
- Konqueror: Unsafe

7.5   left, right and first Pseudo-Classes

The left, right and first pseudo-classes are all used with the @page media type. They are used to stipulate specific styles for the left, right and initial page of a Web document that is formatted for print. The following code snippet shows them all in use:

```
<style>
@page :first {margin-left: 1.5in;
margin-right: 1.5in;}
@page :left {margin-left: 1.5in;
margin-right: 1in;}
@page :right {margin-left: 1in;
margin-right: 1.5in;}
</style>
```

In this case, the margin formats are set for how the initial page should be printed, and then all subsequent left-hand and right-hand pages.

For more information on using these pseudo-classes, see Chapter 18, "Paged Media."

7.6   focus and hover Pseudo-Classes

The focus and hover pseudo-classes are meant to convey information to the user whenever a cursor passes over a selected Web element, and are always associated with the anchor tag ("<a>"). With the focus pseudo-class, the cursor will change to indicate that the Web element it is associated with has "focus" (meaning that it is available to take user input in some form). The hover pseudo-class indicates to the user that the element the cursor has passed over can be "activated" in some way. These new pseudo-classes are closely associated with the link, visited and active pseudo-elements introduced under CSS1. Listing 7.4 shows how this might be put to use within the header of a given Web page; the effects are seen in Figure 7–4.

Listing 7.4	*focus and hover Pseudo-Class Example Code*

```
<html>
<head>
<title>:hover and :focus Example</title>
```

Listing 7.4	*focus and hover Pseudo-Class Example Code (continued)*

```
<style>
a:link {color: red} /* Unvisited links */
a:visited {color: blue} /* Visited links */
a:active {color: lime} /* Active links */
a:hover {color: yellow} /* User Hover over link turns it yellow */
a:focus {color: green} /* User focus on a link turns it green */

body {font-family: Arial, Helvetica, sans-serif; font-size: 40px;
font-weight: bold}
</style>
</head>

<body>
<a href="link1.html">Here's a link</a>.
<a href="link2.html">Here's another link</a>.
<a href="link3.html">And another link</a>.
</body>
</html>
```

Here's a link. **Here's another link. And another link.**

**a:hover {color: yellow}
activated by cursor**

Here's a link. Here's another link. **And another link.**

**a:focus {color: green}
activated by keyboard
tabbing**

Figure 7–4   a:hover activated by a cursor hovering over it, and a:focus taking effect when it is tabbed to via the keyboard.

Due to cascading rules, :hover must be used after :link and/or :visited in order to work.

Browser Compatibility

- Internet Explorer 3.0: Unsafe.
- Internet Explorer 4.0: Safe.
- Internet Explorer 4.0 – 4.5 (Mac): Safe.
- Internet Explorer 5.0: Safe.
- Internet Explorer 5.1 – 5.2 (Mac): Safe.
- Internet Explorer 5.5: Safe.
- Internet Explorer 6.0: Safe.
- Netscape Navigator 4.0 – 4.79: Unsafe.
- Netscape Navigator 4.0 (Mac & UNIX): Unsafe.
- Netscape Navigator 6.0: Safe.
- Netscape Navigator 7.0: Safe.
- Mozilla 1.0: Safe.
- Opera 3.6 – 4.0: Unsafe.
- Opera 5.0 – 6.0: Safe.
- Konqueror: Safe.

These pseudo-classes are relatively well supported in Internet Explorer, with both `:hover` and `:focus` equally well supported beginning with version 4.0.

Support for both of these pseudo-classes is a relatively recent thing for Netscape users, beginning with Netscape Navigator 6.0.

Opera, which usually has a good history for supporting such pseudo-classes, did not support this one in the early releases of this browser. By version 5.0 they had gotten things right.

There is full support for this pseudo-class in Konqueror.

7.7　first-child Pseudo-Class

The `first-child` pseudo-class is an innovation introduced under the CSS2 specification. It is designed to format an object only when it matches the first selected element to appear after another. So if you have a `div` element as the "parent" and several successive `p` "child" elements contained within it, this pseudo-class allows you to format only the first paragraph, while leaving subsequent paragraphs alone. Listing 7.5 shows how this can be put to use.

Listing 7.5	*first-child Pseudo-Class Example*

```
<html>
<head>
<title>first-child Example</title>
<style>
div > p:first-child {color: navy; font-family: Arial, Helvetica,
sans-serif}
body {font-size: 30px;}
</style>
</head>
<body>
<div>
<p>
First sample sentence. It is the first child to follow a
<code>div</code> element, and so it is formatted according to the
<code>first-rule</code> rule.
</p>
</div>
<div>
<h2>Note:</h2>
<p>
Second sample sentence. The <code>first-child</code> pseudo-class
doesn't apply in this case.
</p>
</div>
<p>
Third sample sentence. The <code>first-child</code> pseudo-class
doesn't apply in this case either.
</p>
</body>
</html>
```

The results of the code from Listing 7.5 can be seen in Figure 7–5. Only the initial paragraph on the page meets the conditional statement contained in the header, as it is the first paragraph to follow a `div` element ("`div > p:first-child`"). Neither of the two subsequent paragraphs meet this condition, and so the formatting is not applied.

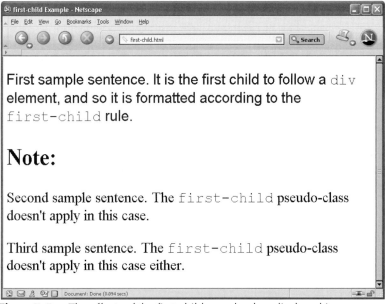

Figure 7–5   The effects of the first-child pseudo-class displayed in
Netscape Navigator 7.0.

Browser Compatibility

The `first-child` pseudo-class was introduced under CSS2, which automatically
means that older browsers simply won't recognize it.

- Internet Explorer 3.0: Unsafe.
- Internet Explorer 4.0: Unsafe.
- Internet Explorer 4.0 – 4.5 (Mac): Unsafe.
- Internet Explorer 5.1 – 5.2: Safe.
- Internet Explorer 5.0: Unsafe.
- Internet Explorer 5.5: Unsafe.
- Internet Explorer 6.0: Unsafe.
- Netscape Navigator 4.0 – 4.79: Unsafe.
- Netscape Navigator 4.0 (Mac & UNIX): Unsafe.
- Netscape Navigator 6.0: Safe.
- Netscape Navigator 7.0: Safe.
- Mozilla 1.0: Safe.
- Opera 3.6 – 4.0: Unsafe.
- Opera 5.0 – 6.0: Unsafe.
- Konqueror: Unsafe.

Internet Explorer does not yet implement this property.

Support for this pseudo-class is limited even in more recent versions of the major browsers — only Netscape Navigator 6.0 (and Mozilla 1.0) on up can correctly format elements that use this pseudo-class.

No other browser interprets the test code from Listing 7.5 correctly, ignoring the conditional statement completely.

7.8 Pseudo-Elements in Selectors and Combining Multiple Pseudo-Elements

By looking at the previous code examples covered in this chapter, you may have wondered how you can combine pseudo-selectors with other CSS properties, or how to differentiate between combinations of pseudo-elements. Pseudo-elements can be combined with classes in selectors so that they can be specifically selected. Pseudo-elements can also be tacked onto a selector. Listing 7.6, which is an adaptation of what was seen earlier in the `first-line` section, shows both pseudo-elements combined with classes at work.

Listing 7.6 *Pseudo-Elements in Selectors*

```
<html>
<head>
<title>pseudo-elements in selectors</title>
</head>
<style>
p.initial:first-line {font-variant: small-caps; color:
navy; font-size: 20pt;}
body p:first-letter {color: blue; font-size: 30pt;}
body {font-size: 20pt;}
</style>
<body>
<p class="initial">
The first line, and only the first line of this paragraph, should
be displayed in a navy color and in small caps, and because the
<code>initial</code> class is selected for this paragraph, the
first letter of the first line will appear as a large, blue
letter. All of the subsequent lines of this paragraph should
appear in the default text color, which is black.
</p>
```

Listing 7.6	*Pseudo-Elements in Selectors (continued)*

```
Here is some more text. The <code>first-line</code> and
<code>first-letter</code> pseudo-element values do not apply to
this sentence because it is outside of previous closed paragraph.
<p>
This is a new paragraph, but because the <code>initial</code>
class is not selected, only the <code>first-letter</code> value
will be displayed.
</p>
</body>
</html>
```

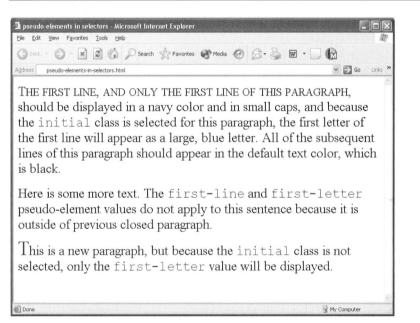

Figure 7–6 Mixing pseudo-elements and selectors, as seen in Internet Explorer 6.0.

You can see the results of Listing 7.6 in Figure 7–6. Note how the first paragraph combines the display values set by first-line and first-letter, but that the third paragraph only shows the effects of first-letter. That is because the effects of the first-line pseudo-element are set using the class p.initial, which is selected for in the first paragraph by using the code <p class="initial">. The first-letter pseudo-element has been tacked onto the body selector, which applies the value of a large blue letter to the first letter that appears in a paragraph. Note how the second paragraph, which is not contained within a paragraph tag, does not take on either of these values (nor is it supposed to, since it lies outside of the end-paragraph tag).

MEDIA TYPES AND MEDIA QUERIES

Topics in This Chapter

- Media Types: `all` – `tv`
- Browser Compatibility
- Media Queries
- `width` and `height` Media Queries
- `viewport-aspect-ratio` Media Query
- `color`, `color-index` and `monochrome` Media Queries
- `resolution` Media Query
- `scan` Media Query
- `grid` Media Query

Chapter 8

Media types introduce the concept that devices other than standard computer screens may be expected, now or in the future, to display Web content. Under the CSS2 specification, there are ten CSS2 media types: `all`, `aural`, `braille`, `embossed`, `handheld`, `print`, `projection`, `screen`, `tty` and `tv`. Each has particular characteristics, and is designed to provide Web authors with the option of specifying how a Web page should appear on very different display devices.

These properties are to be used with the "at-rule" `@media`, which is always specified in the header of a Web document. It selects the type of display device upon which a page can be displayed. Each of these different media types is defined in terms of media groupings. A continuous medium means that the medium is not broken up into discrete chunks, like the pages of a book; a paged medium, on the other hand, is. A visual medium is one that relies upon the viewer to see the page displayed, whereas an aural medium is one that speaks the page aloud, and a tactile medium means the Web page is intended to be felt (usually through a "display" mechanism that can be read by the visually impaired). A medium that relies upon grids can handle character grids, whereas a bitmap medium represents all displays (text and images) as bitmaps. Some media are interactive, which enable the user to work with and affect the flow of information, while others are static, meaning that the flow of information is fixed. In some cases, media types are capable of handling seemingly contradictory media groups, but this is wholly dependent on the type of media groups that may be used with a specific type of display device.

The `all` media type is generally suitable for all display devices. The `aural` media type is intended for use with "talking browsers" (a computer equipped with a speech synthesizer, for example), and is associated with the `continuous`, `aural`, and interactive/static media groups. With the `braille` media type, Web content is intended for use on a Braille tactile interactive feedback device. It is associated with the `continuous`, `tactile`, `grid` and interactive/static media groups. `embossed` is similar to `braille`, except the Web content is to be printed in Braille instead of being read through an interactive, mechanical Braille "display" device, and so it is associated with the `paged` media group instead of `continuous`. The `handheld` media group is designed for people who use Palm PCs and similar PDA (personal data assistant) devices, which typically have relatively small screens — often with monochrome displays — and are likely limited in the bandwidth available to them. Its associated media groups include `continuous/paged`, `visual`, `grid/bitmap` and interactive/static.

The `print` media group is designed to print Web content, or to be viewed on screen in a print-preview form. Its associated media groups are `paged`, `visual`, `grid/bitmap` and `static`. `projection` is a media group designed for projecting Web content on a remote screen, either directly or from printed transparencies. It is associated with the `paged`, `visual`, `bitmap` and `static` media groups. The `screen` media type is designed for standard color computer displays, and is associated with the `continuous`, `visual`, `grid` and interactive/static media groups. The `tty` media type is meant for displaying Web pages on such devices as teletype displays or terminals that use a fixed-pitch character grid. It is associated with the `continuous`, `visual`, `grid` and interactive/static media groups.

Finally, there is the `tv` media type, which allows for Web content to be displayed on a television screen, which implies relatively low screen resolution (compared to a computer screen), color display, sound and limited scrolling capabilities. It is associated with the `continuous/paged`, `visual/aural`, `bitmap` and interactive/static media groups.

Table 8.1 provides a simple breakdown of all of the media groups to which the various media types belong.

Table 8.1 *Media Types and Their Associated Media Groups*

Media Types   *Media Groups*

	CONTINUOUS	PAGED	VISUAL	AURAL	TACTILE	GRID	BITMAP	INTERACTIVE	STATIC
AURAL	X			X				X	X
BRAILLE	X				X	X		X	X
EMBOSSED		X			X	X		X	X
HANDHELD	X	X	X			X	X	X	X
PRINT		X	X				X		X
PROJECTION		X	X				X		X
SCREEN	X		X				X	X	X
TTY	X		X			X		X	X
TV	X	X	X	X			X	X	X

These media types enable Web authors to specify how things should "appear" when seen through various display devices. As a result, they are always set to apply globally to the Web document as a whole, as there is no point in trying to only specify how particular Web elements should appear. Listing 8.1 provides an example of how these media type values can be used.

Listing 8.1 *Media Types Example*

```
<html>
<head>
<title>Media Types Example</title>
<style>
@media screen {body {font-size: medium}}
@media print {body {font-size: small}}
@media handheld {body {font-size: x-small}}
@media tv {body {font-size: large}}
</style>
</head>
```

Listing 8.1	*Media Types Example (continued)*

```
<body>
The quick brown fox jumped over the lazy dogs.
</body>
</html>
```

As you can see from Listing 8.1, the size of the displayed font will change depending on the device being used to view the Web page. It is set to `medium` for a computer screen, `small` for print (to minimize the number of pages to be printed), `x-small` for handheld devices (to cram more text onto the screen), and `large` for a TV screen, which is likely to be viewed from a distance.

8.1   Browser Compatibility

Only the more recent browsers support the `@media` rule and will format a Web page according to its associated media type.

- Internet Explorer 3.0: Unsafe.
- Internet Explorer 4.0: Unsafe.
- Internet Explorer 4.0 – 4.5 (Mac): Unsafe.
- Internet Explorer 5.0: Unsafe.
- Internet Explorer 5.1 – 5.2 (Mac): Safe.
- Internet Explorer 5.5: Safe.
- Internet Explorer 6.0: Safe.
- Netscape Navigator 4.0 – 4.79: Unsafe.
- Netscape Navigator 4.0 (Mac & UNIX): Unsafe.
- Netscape Navigator 6.0: Safe.
- Netscape Navigator 7.0: Safe.
- Mozilla 1.0: Safe.
- Opera 3.6 – 4.0: Unsafe
- Opera 5.0 – 6.0: Safe.
- Konqueror: Safe.

Internet Explorer began to implement the `@media` rule and its associated media types beginning with version 5.1 for the Macintosh, and version 5.5 for Windows.

The `@media` rule began to be supported in Netscape Navigator 6.0 and Mozilla 1.0.

Opera began supporting the `@media` rule beginning with version 5.0.

For a long time, support for media types was lacking in Konqueror, but support has been added to the latest builds of this browser/desktop environment.

8.2   Media Queries

The latest draft CSS3 ushers in the idea of "media queries," which extends the idea of media types (such as "tv" and "print") so that the display properties of a Web page can be more precisely customized for these devices by the Web author. The idea is to better tailor the display of Web pages without having to change anything in terms of content. It also allows room for expansion to media types other than those already mapped out under the CSS2 specification.

Since this has not been finalized, what follows should be considered a "heads up" of what we may soon expect from browsers of the future — there is no guarantee that this is exactly how they will be implemented.

Media queries are expressions that are either true or false; either they are correctly laid out and match an existing setting, or they are rejected by the browser and not used.

Media "query" may not in fact be the best name for this function, as it does not actively seek out a setting and then programmatically return a result that can then be further manipulated. Instead, they are passive settings contained within the header of a Web page or embedded in a separate style sheet. But they will change the display of content given the right values for a given media query. In practice, it is a way of cascading display parameters — if a match is found, it is used, otherwise the next available setting is used instead. If no match is found, a default setting is used. Think of media queries as being akin to a font property with various specific and generic font types listed and you'll get the idea.

Media queries can either be written in HTML, using the link element, or written in CSS, using the @media rule. When taking the HTML path, you use the media attribute to set the media query, which is then linked to an external page containing specific information on formatting for a given display device. When setting things using @media, you name the media types in sequential order, and then link to the defining external formatting style sheet. Both types can also use operational expressions such as "only", "and" and "not".

Whether written in HTML or CSS, the rule format is the same:

```
media query + media type(s) + media feature + URL
```

Listing 8.2 shows two equivalent media queries, the first written using HTML, the second using CSS.

Listing 8.2	*Equivalent Media Queries Expressed as HTML and CSS*

```
<link rel="stylesheet" media="tv and (color), projection"
href="http://www.corecss.com/dummyexample/" />

@media tv and (color), projection {@import
url(http://www.corecss.com/dummyexample)}
```

8.3   width and height Media Queries

The `width` and `height` media features describe the horizontal and vertical measures for the display a page can be formatted against. They take standard length units, and can be applied to the `visual` and `tactile` media types. They can also accept `min-` and `max-` prefixes. These properties are designed to specify the viewport of a device (a browser window, for example).

The following code snippet sets the width range for a screen device:

```
@media screen and (min-width: 600px) and (max-width: 800px)
{@import url(http://www.corecss.com/dummyexample/)}
```

Note that the `height` property of the rendering display surface for continuous media is the height of the viewport (the browser window), whereas for static media, like `print`, it would be the height of the page. The following code snippet provides an example of this:

```
@media print and (min-height: 8.5in) and (max-height: 11in)
{@import url(http://www.corecss.com/dummyexample/)}
```

8.4   device-width and device-height Media Queries

`device-width` and `device-height` describe the horizontal and vertical measure, respectively, for an output device. They can be applied to the `visual` and `tactile` media types, take standard length units and the `min-` and `max-` prefixes can be used with them. They differ from the `width` and `height` properties in that they correspond to the dimensions of a particular display, rather than the viewport. The difference is akin to that of the size of a browser window versus the size of the full display containing the browser.

The following example sets the media query for devices with a `device-width` value of 800 pixels, and a `device-height` of 600 pixels:

```
<link rel="stylesheet" media="screen and (device-width: 800px) and
(device-height: 600px)" href="http://www.corecss.com/dummyexample/"
/>
```

8.5   device-aspect-ratio Media Query

The `device-aspect-ratio` property applies only to bitmap media types, and takes two numerical values separated by a "/" that describe the aspect ratio of the display. It can also accept the `min-` and `max-` prefixes.

While not limited to television or projection displays, most aspect ratios you will run across reference these technologies — you do not typically see print sizes referenced by their aspect ratio, for example. Standard television displays use a 4:3 aspect ratio (which is relatively square), and widescreen HDTV uses a 16:9 aspect ratio (which is significantly wider than it is tall). This way of determining the relative screen size of a device is a convenient shortcut for a wide range of devices; for example, while NTSC and PAL (the broadcast standards for North America and Europe, respectively) television screens have different equivalent pixel values, they share the same 4:3 aspect ratio.

The following code snippet shows a media query configured for a wide-screen display:

```
@media screen and (device-aspect-ratio: 16/9) {@import
url(http://www.corecss.com/dummyexample/)}
```

To determine the aspect ratio for a device, simply find the ratio of horizontal pixels versus the number of horizontal pixels.

8.6   color Media Query

The `color` property can be used against all visual media types. It is used to describe the number of bits used by the target display in order to depict individual color values. It can accept the `min-` and `max-` prefixes.

Monochrome monitors have a color value of `0`, so by default color has a minimum value of 1. 4-bit color display can display 16 colors, 8-bit systems can display 256 colors and 24-bit displays are capable of displaying over 16 million colors. If a minimum value of 2 is specified, it formats the page to be displayed for systems that are capable of 2-bit color, which would include 4-bit on up to 24-bit and beyond.

The following code example shows a color media query set to a minimum of 2-bit color display:

```
<link rel="stylesheet" media="all and (min-color: 2)"
href="http://www.corecss.com/dummyexample/" />
```

8.7   color-index Media Query

Like the `color` property, `color-index` applies to all visual media types, and it can also take the `min-` and `max-` prefixes. This media feature describes the number of color entries in the lookup table of the target device — in other words, the total number of colors a device can simultaneously display. The ranges you will typically run across are 16 colors, 256 colors, 65,536 colors and 16,777,215 colors, corresponding to 4-bit, 8-bit, 16-bit and 24-bit color depths, respectively.

The following code snippet shows a `color-index` media query set to a minimum of 65,536 colors:

```
@media screen and (min-color-index: 65,536) {@import
url(http://www.corecss.com/dummyexample/)}
```

This particular media query is good for discriminating the color depth of a given device, which is handy if, for example, a page relies upon displaying such things as high-resolution graphics correctly with minimal distortion of color values.

8.8   monochrome Media Query

The `monochrome` media feature describes the number of bits per pixel in a monochrome frame buffer. It works the same way as the `color` property — it can be applied to all visual media, and can accept the `min-` and `max-` prefixes — although due to its nature, monochrome displays tend not to use too many bits to describe the monochrome "depth."

A value of 1 will describe a basic "black and white" display, and higher values describe most grayscale devices (for example, a non-color Palm V has a palette of 16 shades of gray, while earlier models used a whopping 4 shades of gray). A value of 0 specifies that the display is not monochrome (and is therefore a color display).

The following example code could be used to display different formatting information based on whether the target device is capable of displaying only color or in monochrome:

```
<link rel="stylesheet" media="print and (min-monochrome: 0)"
href="http://www.corecss.com/dummyexample/color/" />
```

In this case this media query is specifically looking for color printers, and the style sheet it links to would format the page for them.

8.9   resolution Media Query

The `resolution` media feature is applicable to bitmap media types and can accept the min- and max- prefixes.

This media feature is used to describe the density of the pixels used for displaying content. Many computer printers, for example, have print resolutions between 300 – 1200 dots per inch (dpi), whereas a typical monitor displays its content at a considerably lower 72 dpi.

The following code snippet provides formatting information from printers capable of at least a 600-dpi resolution (typical of most modern laser printers):

```
@media print and (min-resolution: 600dpi)
{http://www.corecss.com/dummyexample/color/}
```

8.10 scan Media Query

The `scan` media feature can be only be used to describe the scanning process used by `tv` media type devices. It cannot take min- or max- prefixes, and must take one of two values: `progressive` or `interlace`. The `progressive` value will match most current television screens and older computer monitors, which use consecutive sets of scan lines that progressively fill the screen. The `interlace` value is a process used on most high-resolution television sets and most current computer monitors, which use a single set of scan lines to fill the screen. For most Web authors, the functional difference between the two is that progressive displays tend to be relatively low resolution and appear "fuzzy," whereas interlaced displays tend to render sharper, crisper images.

The following media query example would specify where the browser could go to find formatting information for a TV display that uses progressive scanning:

```
<link rel="stylesheet" media="tv and (scan: progressive)"
href="http://www.corecss.com/dummyexample/" />
```

8.11 grid Media Query

The `grid` media feature has a simple purpose: it queries whether or not the display device is grid- or bitmap-based. It applies to all media types and does not accept `min-` or `max-` prefixes. This property seeks out grid-based displays, such as a tty terminal, or a phone display using only a single fixed font. A value of `1` is a positive match. A value of `0` matches any non-grid type of display.

The "`em`" unit of measurement takes on special significance with grid-based displays, since a value of 1 em is commonly understood to be the width of one grid cell horizontally and the height of one grid cell vertically, so it makes for an ideal unit of measure for use with this media query. The following code snippet shows it put to use with the `grid` media query:

```
@media handheld and (grid: 0) and (min-width: 35em) {
http://www.corecss.com/dummyexample/color/   }
```

FONT PROPERTIES

Topics in This Chapter

- `font-family`
- `font-size`
- `font-style`
- `font-variant`
- `font-weight`
- `font`
- `font-stretch`
- `font-size-adjust`
- `@font-face`
- CSS3 Font Decoration Properties

Chapter 9

Web authors have always wanted to have greater control over the formatting of font properties on Web pages. Netscape tried to oblige the Web authoring community by introducing the `<font>` tag in Netscape Navigator 1.0, which allowed authors to change the size of the displayed text by using the `size` attribute. Microsoft added two new attributes, `color` and `face`, with the release of Internet Explorer 1.0, the first of which was adopted within Netscape Navigator 2.0 and the second in version 3.0. Despite these efforts by Netscape and Microsoft to improve the `<font>` tag, Web authors will find far greater flexibility with the CSS `font` family of properties.

It is worth pointing out that the `<font>` tag (and the related `<basefont>` tag) are "deprecated" (in other words, "not recommended for use") within the HTML 4.0 specification. This is the W3C's way of trying to drive Web authors to use CSS properties described here to achieve the same effects. While it is retained within the current HTML 4.0 specification and support for the `<font>` tag is not likely to be dropped any time soon within the two major browsers, it is still valuable to learn how the CSS font family of properties should be used.

Under CSS1, the font family consists of a number of properties designed to specify and alter the way fonts are displayed on screen. While they have many capabilities, it is still possible in many instances for the CSS1 properties to "fall through the cracks," with the intended font display coming out incorrectly.

To prevent this, CSS2 goes further, filling in the "gap" by adding properties that can describe exactly the type of font to be displayed, improve font matching, and enable fonts to be "created" by providing a means for the browser to download the appropriate font from an online source.

To this extensive family of properties, CSS2 adds `font-stretch` and `font-size-adjust` as well as an additional "@rule" for specifying the name of a font descriptor, called `@font-face`. The CSS3 font module adds another four: `font-effect`, `font-emphasize-position`, `font-emphasize-style` and `font-smooth`. Taken together, these new elements round out the family of font properties under CSS2 and what's currently proposed under CSS3.

9.1   font-family Property

`font-family` determines how a font should be displayed. Instead of naming a specific font, as the `<font>` tag does, the `font-family` CSS property instead sets the display characteristics of that font.

It can take any of the following values: `cursive`, `fantasy`, `monospace`, `sans-serif` and `serif`. One of the drawbacks of the `<font>` tag is that you had to specify a particular font name (such as "`Arial`", "`Times Roman`" or "`Courier`") in order to try and get it to appear on screen. The `font-family` CSS property tries to get around this by specifying the type or "family" of font to be displayed. Given a particular value, the browser does its best to come up with a match, so if you specify `monospace` you may get a Courier font to appear on screen, whereas if you specify `serif`, you may get a Times Roman font instead. This CSS property is still dependent on the user's computer to come up with a matching font family, but the font family categories encompass a broad spectrum of fonts that could only be accomplished with a `<font>` tag containing multiple values attached to the `face` attribute.

In other words, you could choose to include the following HTML code in order to get a serif font displayed on a user's screen:

```
<font face="Garamond, AGaramond, Times, Times Roman, CG Times, Home,
Goudy"><b>This sentence is displayed in a serif font</b></font>
```

Or you could use the following, more concise CSS code instead:

```
<b style="font-family: serif">This sentence is displayed in a serif
font</b>
```

Listing 9.1 shows the five different values that can be applied to `font-family`. The results are displayed in Figure 9–1.

Listing 9.1 *font-family Code Example*

```html
<html>
<head>
<title>font-family Example</title>
<style>
body {font-size: 30px}
</style>
</head>
<body>
<p>
<strong style="font-family: cursive">This sentence is displayed
using a cursive font.</strong>
</p>
<p>
<strong style="font-family: fantasy">This sentence is displayed
using a fantasy font.</strong>
<p>
</p>
<strong style="font-family: monospace">This sentence is displayed
using a monospace font.</strong>
</p>
<p>
<strong style="font-family: sans-serif">This sentence is displayed
using a sans-serif font.</strong>
</p>
<p>
<strong style="font-family: serif">This sentence is displayed
using a serif font.</strong>
</p>
</body>
</html>
```

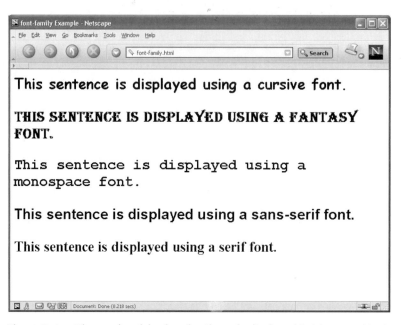

Figure 9–1 The results of the font-family code displayed in Netscape Navigator 7.0.

The illustration shows how the browser tries to interpret and then apply the correct font family based on what it can find on the user's system. The initial line of code specifies that a cursive font (that is, one that looks like handwriting) should be displayed in the browser. This doesn't happen because the browser is unable to find a close match, although it does its best and displays a font that certainly looks different from the default browser font. The browser is able to find `font-family` matches for the rest of the code, and displays the text accordingly. There is an inherent trade-off when you use the `font-family` CSS property in this manner: what you lose in specificity you gain in terms of the greater likelihood of getting a font match and brevity of code.

There is one thing that ought to be noted whenever you are using such brief values for `font-family`: different browsers may end up displaying different fonts, although they will be from the same family of fonts. So if a system has a number of fantasy-style fonts on it, different browsers may pick a different "default" fantasy font to use. A good example of this can be seen in Figure 9–2, in which the code in Listing 9.1 (depicted in Netscape Navigator 7.0 in Figure 9–1) displays different results in Internet Explorer 6.0 and Opera 6.0.

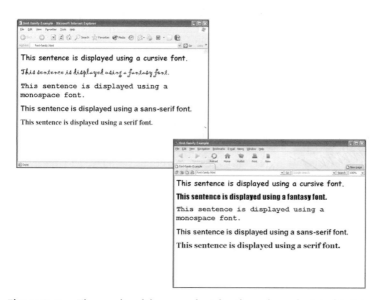

Figure 9–2   The results of the same font-family code as depicted in Internet Explorer 6.0 and Opera 6.0.

While the code in Listing 9.1 is a fairly simple way of specifying font appearance on a Web page, `font-family` is robust, and can also take more specific font name information in a manner similar to the `<font>` tag. For example, you might want to make sure that, of all of the serif fonts available, a Times font (such as Times New Roman) takes precedence. This is done by specifying the name of the specific font you want in single quotes, backed up by a more general font name, followed by a `font-family` value that the font belongs to. The following code snippet shows what that code would look like in the case of trying to specify the Times New Roman font:

```
<h1 style="font-family: 'Times New Roman', Times, serif">Serif
font</h1>
```

The browser interprets the code by moving from the specific font name, if it can't find a match, to the family to which the font belongs, and then to the generic font family type if no match has been found. To see this in action, compare the following code and illustration to the first one:

Listing 9.2 *font-family Code Example Displaying Basic Family Types*

```html
<html>
<head>
<title>font-family Example 2</title>
<style>
body {font-size: 30px}
</style>
</head>
<body>
<p>
<b style="font-family: 'Freestyle Script', cursive">This sentence
is displayed using a cursive font.</b>
</p>
<p>
<b style="font-family: 'Dauphin', Dauphin, fantasy">This sentence
is displayed using a fantasy font.</b>
</p>
<p>
<b style="font-family: 'Courier', Courier, monospace">This
sentence is displayed using a monospace font.</b>
</p>
<p>
<b style="font-family: 'Verdana', Verdana, sans-serif">This
sentence is displayed using a sans-serif font.</b>
</p>
<p>
<b style="font-family: 'Garamond', Garamond, serif">This sentence
is displayed using a serif font.</b>
</p>
</body>
</html>
```

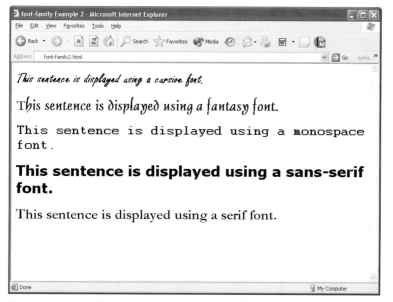

Figure 9–3   Results of the more specific font-family code displayed in Internet Explorer 6.0.

Note that although the same font families are being used, the more specific references select a different type of font within a font family. Keep in mind that whatever font you choose must find a match on the user's system in order to work. There are only a few fonts that work well among PC, Macintosh and UNIX systems. You could use the following code snippet to be certain of displaying a sans-serif font on a user's system:

```
body {Arial, Verdana, Geneva, Helvetica, sans-serif}
```

If you wanted to display a serif font instead, this code snippet should do the trick:

```
body {Times New Roman, Times, Georgia, serif}
```

And if you wanted to set a monospaced font, you can expect good results from the following:

```
body {Courier New, Courier, monospace}
```

Note that there are no comparable "safe" settings for the cursive or fantasy font families.

Browser Compatibility

Given that the `<font>` element has been in use within the major browsers for a long time, and it therefore wasn't much of stretch to adopt the same characteristics to the `font-family` property, this element is safe to use in all but the earliest, vaguely CSS-compatible browsers.

- Internet Explorer 3.0: Unsafe.
- Internet Explorer 4.0: Safe.
- Internet Explorer 4.0 – 4.5 (Mac): Safe.
- Internet Explorer 5.0: Safe.
- Internet Explorer 5.1 – 5.2 (Mac): Safe.
- Internet Explorer 5.5: Safe.
- Internet Explorer 6.0: Safe.
- Netscape Navigator 4.0 – 4.79: Safe.
- Netscape Navigator 4.0 (Mac & UNIX): Safe.
- Netscape Navigator 6.0: Safe.
- Netscape Navigator 7.0: Safe.
- Mozilla 1.0: Safe.
- Opera 3.6 – 4.0: Safe.
- Opera 5.0 – 6.0: Safe.
- Konqueror: Safe.

While not adopted within Internet Explorer 3.0, `font-family` was adopted fully in subsequent editions.

Netscape Navigator has supported `font-family` since version 4.x.

Similarly, Opera has long supported this property, as does Konqueror.

9.2   font-size Property

The `font-size` property is used to set the size of the text to be displayed. It can do this in any one of three ways: by specifying the size relative to the default browser font, relative to the last specified font size, or with a precise size value.

In many ways, the `font-size` CSS property is like the `<font>` tag when its `size` attribute is used, but again the CSS property provides greater flexibility than the HTML tag.

The `font-size` property provides seven specific name values for setting the size of the font displayed. Ranging from smallest to largest, they are: `xx-small`, `x-small`, `small`, `medium`, `large`, `x-large` and `xx-large`. They are equivalent to the `<font>` tag using the attributes ranging from `size="1"` to `size="7"`. Listing 9.3 (whose results can be seen in Figure 9–4) shows how the text is displayed using all of `font-size`'s values.

| Listing 9.3 | *font-size Code Example* |

```
<html>
<head>
<title>font-size Example</title>
</head>
<body>
<p>
<b style="font-size: xx-small">This sentence is set to
<code>xx-small</code>.</b>
</p>
<p>
<b style="font-size: x-small">This sentence is set to
<code>x-small</code>.</b>
</p>
<p>
<b style="font-size: small">This sentence is set to
<code>small</code>.</b>
</p>
<p>
<b style="font-size: medium">This sentence is set to
<code>medium</code>.</b>
</p>
<p>
<b style="font-size: large">This sentence is set to
<code>large</code>.</b>
</p>
<p>
<b style="font-size: x-large">This sentence is set to
<code>x-large</code>.</b>
</p>
<p>
<b style="font-size: xx-large">This sentence is set to
<code>xx-large</code>.</b>
</p>
</p>
</body>
</html>
```

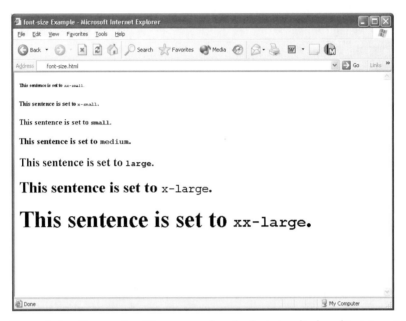

Figure 9–4   The results of the name values for font-size displayed in Internet Explorer 6.0.

It is also possible to set the font displayed to a value that is one size larger or smaller than the base font size value being used. This is analogous to the way you can set the HTML tag `<basefont>` to a particular value, and then set the font size relative to that value (by using `<font size="+1">` or `<font size="-1">`). This can be done in CSS by using the values `larger` and `smaller`.

In the following code example, the `font-size` for the `<body>` tag has been set to the name value `x-large`. The last two paragraphs of bolded text are set to one size larger and one size smaller than the default value.

Listing 9.4	*Relative font-size Values*

```
<html>
<head>
<title>font-size Example #2</title>
<style>
b {font-family: monospace}
body {font-size: x-large}
</style>
</head>
```

Listing 9.4	*Relative font-size Values (continued)*

```
<body>
<p>
<b>this sentence is displayed using a large monospaced font, which
is set as the base font value.</b>
</p>
<p>
<b style="font-size: larger">this sentence is set to one size
larger than the base value.</b>
</p>
<p>
<b style="font-size: smaller">this sentence is set to one size
smaller than the base value.</b>
</p>
</body>
</html>
```

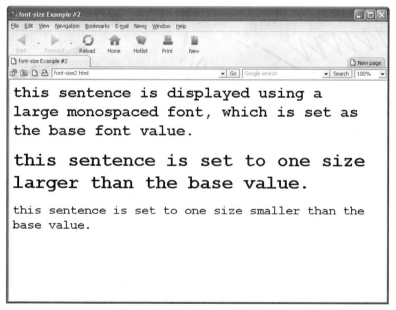

Figure 9–5   font-size displaying the effects of the larger and smaller settings, as seen in Opera 6.0.

Keep in mind when using the `larger` and `smaller` values that they are relative to the base font size that has been set; they are not relative to each other. If that were the case, the `smaller` value seen in Figure 9–5 would be the same size as the first line, which is set to the default value of x-large. Instead, it is one size smaller than extra large, equivalent to a value of large.

The most powerful feature of the font-size property is that you can specify a particular size (or more properly, height) of a font using a standard unit of measure. For example, you can set a font to be a quarter-inch height, or a centimeter, set a specific point value for the font, a pixel value or more (for more information on units of length, see Chapter 6, "CSS Units"). The code example Listing 9.5 (whose results can be seen in Figure 9–6) shows how this can be accomplished.

Listing 9.5	*font-size Set to Specific Units of Length*

```
<html>
<head>
<title>font-size Example #3</title>
</head>
<body>
<h1 style="font-size: 0.25in">Header text set to 0.25 inches in
height</h1>
<h1 style="font-size: 1cm">Header text set to 1 centimeter in
height</h1>
<h1 style="font-size: 10pt">Header text set to 10 points in
height</h1>
<h1 style="font-size: 25px">Header text set to 25 pixels in
height</h1>
<h1 style="font-size: xx-large">For comparison, this header is set
to xx-large</h1>
</p>
</body>
</html>
```

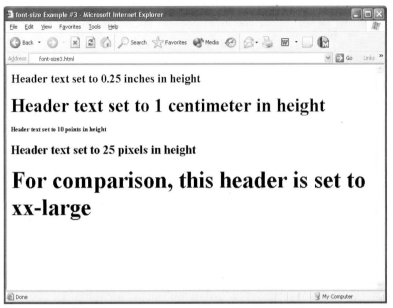

Figure 9–6 Specific measurement unit sizes for font-size displayed.

font-size can also take a percentage value. The percentage value that is specified is relative to the size of the base font. The code seen in Listing 9.6 shows how percentage values work with font-size. As you can see in Figure 9–7, the 100% value corresponds exactly to the default font size. 200% displays the font at twice the default size, and 50% reduces the displayed font to half the size of the default font size.

Listing 9.6 *font-size Set to a Percentage Value*

```
<html>
<head>
<title>font-size Example #4</title>
<style>
body {font-size: 16pt}
</style>
</head>
<body>
Here is some body text displayed set to 16pt
<p style="font-size: 100%">
This line of text is set to font-size: 100%, so it should be the
<em>same size</em> as the default font size depicted in the
previous line (i.e. 16pt).
```

Listing 9.6 *font-size Set to a Percentage Value (continued)*

```
</p>
<p style="font-size: 200%">
This line of text is set to font-size: 200%, so it should be
<em>twice</em> the size
of the default font size (i.e. 32pt).
</p>
<p style="font-size: 50%">
This line of text is set to font-size: 50%, so it should be
<em>half</em> the size of the default font size (i.e. 8pt).
</p>
</body>
</html>
```

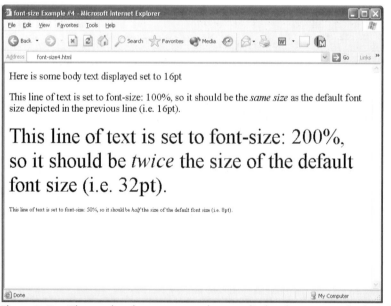

Figure 9–7   The results of percentage values applied to font-size as displayed in
Internet Explorer 6.0.

Core Tip

Be careful whenever you are writing code containing measurement units, as Netscape Navigator is finicky when it comes to reading them. Make sure there is no space between the numerical value and the measurement value ("1in") or Netscape will not recognize it as a legitimate value and will ignore it. Internet Explorer is much more forgiving, and will display a value correctly if there is a space between the number and measurement unit ("1 in"), which is, for most people, a more natural way of writing the figure.

Browser Compatibility

One of the main problems with this property is that two of the major browsers — Internet Explorer and Netscape Navigator — differ in how they interpret the standard name values for `font-size` values. Otherwise, support for this property is very good.

- Internet Explorer 3.0: Safe.
- Internet Explorer 4.0: Safe.
- Internet Explorer 4.0 – 4.5 (Mac): Safe.
- Internet Explorer 5.0: Safe.
- Internet Explorer 5.1 – 5.2 (Mac): Safe.
- Internet Explorer 5.5: Safe.
- Internet Explorer 6.0: Safe.
- Netscape Navigator 4.0 – 4.79: Safe.
- Netscape Navigator 4.0 (Mac & UNIX): Safe.
- Netscape Navigator 6.0: Safe.
- Netscape Navigator 7.0: Safe.
- Mozilla 1.0: Safe.
- Opera 3.6 – 4.0: Safe.
- Opera 5.0 – 6.0: Safe.
- Konqueror: Safe.

Internet Explorer has implemented this property since their earliest CSS-compatible version of their browser.

Netscape Navigator also fully implements this property, and has done so since version 4.x.

Opera and Konqueror also fully implement this property.

As a final word on browser compatibility: be careful when using the name values (i.e., `x-small`, `medium`, `xx-large`, etc) as they are interpreted differently by the various browsers. The Netscape Navigator browsers are consistently one size smaller than their equivalent setting in Internet Explorer, so a `large` setting in Internet Explorer is equivalent to a `medium` setting in Netscape Navigator. Opera and Konqueror both follow Internet Explorer's lead in this area. For consistency, you might want to avoid using the name values for `font-size`, and instead use specific length values that do not vary as much between browsers and platforms, such as specifying a point (`pt`) or pixel (`px`) height.

9.3   font-style Property

The `font-style` property exists primarily as a way of telling a font to display itself in an italic setting. It takes one of three possible values: `italic`, `normal` and `oblique`. `normal` tells the browser to use the default (i.e., non-italic) setting for a font. `italic` and `oblique` are equivalent, and should display a font in its italic (or "oblique") setting. So why are there two settings that achieve the same thing? There is no standard way of indicating a "slanted" font, which is usually used for emphasis. In addition to being called italic and oblique, other names for this style of font include "incline", "cursive", "kursiv" and "slanted". The definition adopted by the W3C adopts `italic` as the cursive companion font to the "regular" form of a given font, while `oblique` is considered the slanted, angled form the regular font — in other words, script versus slanted. This distinguishes between slightly slanted normal faces which might otherwise be labeled oblique, and Greek language fonts which might improperly be called italic, but in the vast majority of instances you are likely to run across they are equivalent. You can see this in Figure 9–8, which displays the default Times font as italic when set to the `italic` and `oblique` values seen in Listing 9.7.

Listing 9.7   *font-style*

```
<html>
<head>
<title>font-style Example</title>
</head>
<body>
<h1 style="font-style: normal">A normal header</h1>
<h1 style="font-style: italic">An italicized header</h1>
<h1 style="font-style: oblique">An oblique header (which should
appear the same as the italicized header above)</h1>
</body>
</html>
```

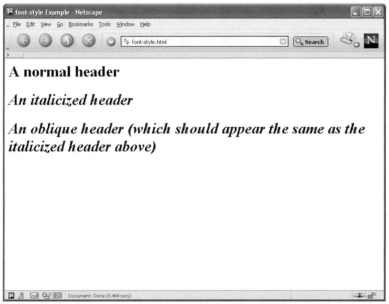

Figure 9–8   The results of the name values for font-size displayed in Netscape Navigator 7.0.

In terms of functionality, font-style essentially replaces the italics (<i>) and emphasis (<em>) HTML elements in usage, whose functions it emulates. However, the tag form is much easier to remember and to write than its CSS equivalent — and for the moment, the tag is also better supported within the major browsers.

Browser Compatibility

The font-style property has been widely emulated since the advent of CSS, and the Partial ratings seen here represent the brief lack of support for the oblique value.

- Internet Explorer 3.0: Partial.
- Internet Explorer 4.0: Safe.
- Internet Explorer 4.0 – 4.5 (Mac): Safe.
- Internet Explorer 5.0: Safe.
- Internet Explorer 5.1 – 5.2 (Mac): Safe.
- Internet Explorer 5.5: Safe.
- Internet Explorer 6.0: Safe.
- Netscape Navigator 4.0 – 4.79: Partial.
- Netscape Navigator 4.0 (Mac & UNIX): Partial.
- Netscape Navigator 6.0: Safe.

- Netscape Navigator 7.0: Safe.
- Mozilla 1.0: Safe.
- Opera 3.6 – 4.0: Safe.
- Opera 5.0 – 6.0: Safe.
- Konqueror: Safe.

Internet Explorer has supported this property fully since version 4.0. The Partial rating given to version 3.0 is for its lack of support for the `oblique` value.

Similarly, Netscape Navigator 4.x gets a Partial rating for not supporting the `oblique` value. This was fixed with the advent of Netscape Navigator 6.0 (and Mozilla 1.0).

Opera was the first to get things right, implementing `font-style` fully since version 3.6.

Konqueror supports this property fully.

9.4   font-variant Property

The rather obscurely named `font-variant` essentially tells the browser whether or not a given font should be displayed using small capital letters (better known as "small caps").

There are only two values for `font-variant`: `normal` (the default value) and `small-caps`. Listing 9.8 shows the effects of both values displayed within Netscape Navigator 7.0 (seen in Figure 9–9), as well as the difference between small-caps and regular text.

Listing 9.8   *font-variant Example Code*

```
<html>
<head>
<title>font-variant Example</title>
<style>
body {font-size: 60px}
</style>
</head>
<body>
<div style="font-variant: normal">Text Using the normal Setting
for <code>font-variant</code></div>
```

| Listing 9.8 | *font-variant Example Code (continued)* |

```
<p>
<div style="font-variant: small-caps">Text Using Small-Caps
Setting for <code>font-variant</code></div>
</p>
<body>
</html>
```

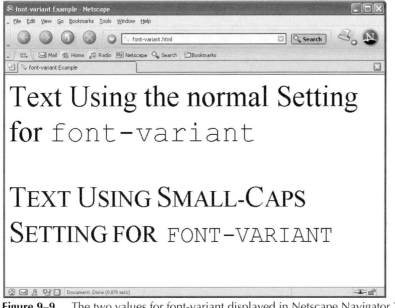

Figure 9–9 The two values for font-variant displayed in Netscape Navigator 7.0.

Browser Compatibility

- Internet Explorer 3.0: Unsafe.
- Internet Explorer 4.0: Safe.
- Internet Explorer 4.0 – 4.5 (Mac): Safe.
- Internet Explorer 5.0: Safe.
- Internet Explorer 5.1 – 5.2 (Mac): Safe.
- Internet Explorer 5.5: Safe.
- Internet Explorer 6.0: Safe.
- Netscape Navigator 4.0 – 4.79: Unsafe.
- Netscape Navigator 4.0 (Mac & UNIX): Unsafe.
- Netscape Navigator 6.0: Safe.

- Netscape Navigator 7.0: Safe.

- Mozilla 1.0: Safe.

- Opera 3.6 – 4.0: Safe.

- Opera 5.0 – 6.0: Safe.

- Konqueror: Safe.

In the early versions (5.0 and before) of Internet Explorer, *all* the text — not just the initial capital letters of each word — set to `font-style:` `small-caps` is displayed in all caps. This is not exactly according to specifications, although it is good enough to qualify as conforming to the specification. This "problem" was fixed in subsequent versions of Internet Explorer.

This property has only been supported in Netscape Navigator since version 6.0 (and Mozilla 1.0).

Opera has always displayed `font-style:` `small-caps` more in the spirit of the specification, using true small caps. It has adopted this property fully since version 3.6.

Konqueror has always adopted this property.

9.5   font-weight Property

The `font-weight` property is used to set the "thickness" of a given font. Think of it as the "bold" counterpart to `font-style`, with more options.

There are three ways you can set `font-weight`: as an absolute value ranging from 100 to 900, as a relative measure to the default value and as an absolute name value.

The first way introduces a new concept to Web authors, that of absolute numerical values for the weight of a font. In typographical terms, the values roughly correspond to the following series of values, from smallest to heaviest: Book, Medium, Bold, Heavy, Black and Extra Black. You may have noticed that this series is not composed of nine different values, and this has been taken into account in the official CSS specification. Wherever "holes" appear in font weight, the browser is supposed to fill them in by representing the missing values as either the next available value up or down. According to the specification, the value 400 corresponds to the normal, default weight — roughly equivalent to "medium" in typographic terminology — and 700 to the Bold weight. The major browsers render these two values correctly, but there is no smooth progression from the least to heaviest weight. This effect can be seen in Figure 9–10, which uses the test code seen in Listing 9.9.

Listing 9.9	*font-weight Example Code Using Numeric Values*

```
<html>
<head>
<title>font-weight Example</title>
</head>
<body>
<p style="font-weight: 100">Line of text to font-weight: 100.</p>
<p style="font-weight: 200">Line of text to font-weight: 200.</p>
<p style="font-weight: 300">Line of text to font-weight: 300.</p>
<p style="font-weight: 400">Line of text to font-weight: 400.</p>
<p style="font-weight: 500">Line of text to font-weight: 500.</p>
<p style="font-weight: 600">Line of text to font-weight: 600.</p>
<p style="font-weight: 700">Line of text to font-weight: 700.</p>
<p style="font-weight: 800">Line of text to font-weight: 800.</p>
<p style="font-weight: 900">Line of text to font-weight: 900.</p>
<p>For comparison, this line of text is set to the default font
weight value.</p>
<p><strong>For comparison, this line of text is set to the default
bold font value.</strong></p>
<body>
</html>
```

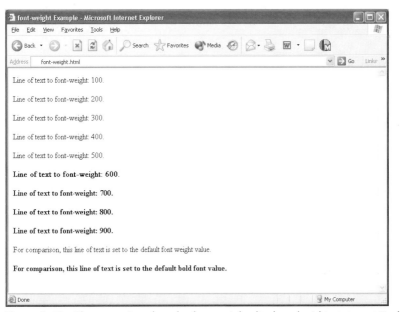

Figure 9–10   The numeric values for font-weight displayed within Internet Explorer 6.0.

As you can see, there are basically only three different font weights supported — at least as seen within Internet Explorer; Netscape Navigator only supports regular and bold — and there is no smooth progression of font weight to be seen. This arrangement does not vary much among the most commonly-used Web fonts. Typically, if there is any difference with a given font, it is because there is one *less* font state available to display, which is usually the 600 value, equivalent to an "expanded, bold" setting. It should be noted that despite being unable to display a smooth progression of font values, all of the major browsers are considered in compliance of the CSS specification if it is at least attempted — and in their defense, quite often the fonts themselves don't support much in the way of differentiated values.

font-weight also has two relative name values, bolder and lighter, which work in the same way as the larger and smaller relative name values associated with font-size. bolder is supposed to make the selected text heavier than the default, and lighter is supposed to make the selected text less heavy than the default. You can see how this works in the code of Listing 9.10, as displayed in Internet Explorer in Figure 9–11.

Listing 9.10	*Media Types Example*

```
<html>
<head>
<title>font-weight Example 2</title>
<style>
body {font-weight: 600; font-size: 45px}
</style>
</head>
<body>
<p>This text should be rendered in a bold font.</p>
<p style="font-weight: bolder">This text should be bolder than the
previous line of text.</p>
<p style="font-weight: lighter">This text should be lighter than
the first line of text.</p>
</body>
</html>
```

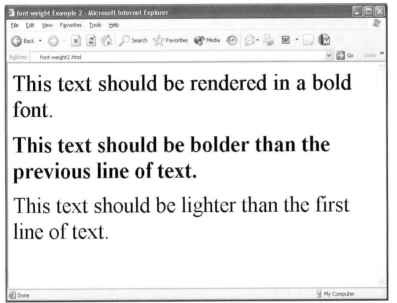

Figure 9–11 The bolder and lighter values for font-weight displayed in Internet Explorer.

Keep in mind when using the `bolder` and `lighter` values that they are relative to the base font weight that has been set; they are not relative to each other. If that were the case, the smaller value seen in Figure 9–11 would be the same weight as the first line, which is set to the "default" value of `600`, which produces a bold font. What actually happens is that the browser takes the default value, and for the `bolder` value adds `100`, and subtracts `100` when `lighter` is used, so in this case the `bolder` setting is equivalent to `700`, and the `lighter` to `500`. Since this is how the browser tackles the bolder and lighter settings, and knowing that there is not always a smooth progression between numeric font weights, you may not always get a bolder or lighter font displayed — you may get a numerically heavier or lighter font, but there may not be a visible difference.

Finally, `font-weight` also supports the two absolute name values `normal` and `bold`. These two values do pretty much what you would expect: they turn bolding "on" or "off" for selected text. Listing 9.11 shows these two values in action; the results are seen in Figure 9–12.

Listing 9.11 *font-weight Using the normal and bold Values*

```
<html>
<head>
<title>font-weight Example 3</title>
<style>
body {font-weight: 700; font-size: 40px}
</style>
</head>
<body>
<p>This text is rendered in a default bold face.</p>
<p style="font-weight: normal">This text is rendered using
<code>font-weight: normal</code>, and it "turns off" the default
bold value.</p>
<p style="font-weight: bold">This text is rendered using
<code>font-weight: bold</code>, and should match the first
line.</p>
</body>
</html>
```

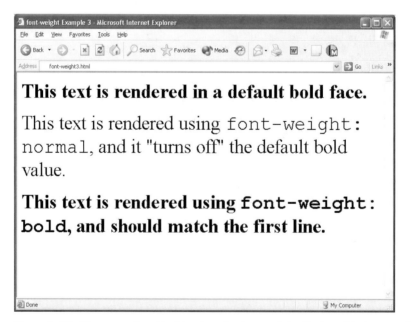

Figure 9–12 The normal and bold values for font-weight displayed in Internet Explorer 6.0.

Figure 9–12 shows off the effects of the `normal` and `bold` settings: `normal` turns off what would otherwise be bolded text, and `bold` turns it back on. Notice that the `bold` setting does not make the bolded text any bolder than it would otherwise be.

Browser Compatibility

The `font-weight` property has received widespread support since the advent of CSS in the major browsers.

- Internet Explorer 3.0: Unsafe.
- Internet Explorer 4.0: Safe.
- Internet Explorer 4.0 – 4.5 (Mac): Safe.
- Internet Explorer 5.0: Safe.
- Internet Explorer 5.1 – 5.2 (Mac): Safe.
- Internet Explorer 5.5: Safe.
- Internet Explorer 6.0: Safe.
- Netscape Navigator 4.0 – 4.79: Safe.
- Netscape Navigator 4.0 (Mac & UNIX): Safe.
- Netscape Navigator 6.0: Safe.
- Netscape Navigator 7.0: Safe.
- Mozilla 1.0: Safe.
- Opera 3.6 – 4.0: Safe.
- Opera 5.0 – 6.0: Safe.
- Konqueror: Safe.

Internet Explorer has supported this property fully since version 4.0.

Netscape Navigator has also supported `font-weight` fully since version 4.x, although it should be noted that the numerical `font-weight` values may not display exactly the same results as you would get in Internet Explorer — depending on the font, the expanded bold value (equivalent to `600`) may not appear as expanded. This is within the boundaries of CSS compliance, and so is given a Safe rating, but Web authors should be aware of this difference.

Opera has implemented `font-weight` fully since version 3.6.

Konqueror supports this property fully.

9.6   font Property

This is a "shortcut" property that allows the Web author to quickly set fonts in the manner possible under the `font-family`, `font-size`, `font-style`, `font-variant` and `font-weight` CSS properties. Interestingly enough, it also allows you to set line-height as well. Also, note by their absence the inability to add values belonging to the font-stretch and font-size-adjust properties introduced under CSS2 — this is deliberate, as the designers of CSS wanted the font property to be backwards compatible.

For the most part, though, you can do anything with the font value that you can do with any of the other font family properties. If you are planning on using a number of font family properties in your code, you may find this simple but versatile CSS property useful to make all the font settings you want.

The code in Listing 9.12 and its subsequent illustration in Figure 9–14 show how you can "compress" your font CSS code into a single, concise statement.

Listing 9.12   *font Example*

```
<html>
<head>
<title>font Example</title>
</head>
<body>
<div style="font-weight: bold; font-size: 36pt; line-height: 45pt;
font-family: sans-serif">This sentence combines a number of
separate font family css values.</div>
<p>
<div style="font: bold 36pt/45pt sans-serif">The font in this
sentence should look the same as that in the previous
sentence.</div>
</p>
</body>
</html>
```

The one new thing in this code is the "36pt/45pt" value, in which the first value corresponds to font-size: 36pt, and the second value to line-height: 45pt — this is how line height can be set using the font property.

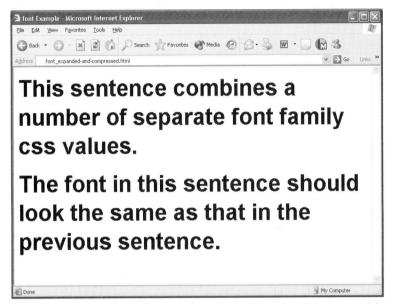

Figure 9–13 Equivalent output produced by expanded and compressed font values.

An additional problem when using the `font` property is browsers are sensitive to the ordering of the modifiers. If, instead of using `<div style="font: bold 36pt/45pt sans-serif">` you used `<div style="font: 36pt/45pt bold sans-serif">`, you would get very different results depending on the browser being used. Internet Explorer renders that code in a 40-point font that is neither bold nor sans-serif, while Netscape Navigator only renders the text in bold. The property order for laying out font values is `font-style`, `font-variant`, `font-weight`, `font-size`, `line-height` and `font-family`. You can omit certain properties in this sequence, but the list of values used should follow this order.

Beginning with the CSS2 specification, the `font` property could also be set to a number of additional values designed to give you control over the system fonts used on such things as buttons, icons, status-bars and more. The system font values for the `font` property are `caption`, `icon`, `menu`, `message-box`, `small-caption` and `status-bar`. The `caption` value is for use with such things as buttons and drop-down menus. The `icon` value is for labeling icons, `menu` is for menu lists, `message-box` changes the font displayed in dialog boxes. The `small-caption` value changes the font used for labeling small controls, and `status-bar` controls the font displayed in window status bars. The following code snippet shows how you could set the font characteristics for the buttons on a page:

```
caption {font: bold italic 20pt serif}
```

Browser Compatibility

As a shortcut property, support for the `font` property is necessarily only as good as the sum of its many sub-properties.

- Internet Explorer 3.0: Unsafe.
- Internet Explorer 4.0: Safe.
- Internet Explorer 4.0 – 4.5 (Mac): Safe.
- Internet Explorer 5.0: Safe.
- Internet Explorer 5.1 – 5.2 (Mac): Safe.
- Internet Explorer 5.5: Safe.
- Internet Explorer 6.0: Safe.
- Netscape Navigator 4.0 – 4.79: Unsafe.
- Netscape Navigator 4.0 (Mac & UNIX): Unsafe.
- Netscape Navigator 6.0: Safe.
- Netscape Navigator 7.0: Safe.
- Mozilla 1.0: Safe.
- Opera 3.6 – 4.0: Safe.
- Opera 5.0 – 6.0: Safe.
- Konqueror: Safe.

Internet Explorer has supported the `font` property fully since version 4.0 (although the system fonts, introduced under CSS2, were supported from version 5.0 onwards).

Netscape Navigator 4.x did not implement the `font-variant` property, and also had problems with `font-style`, so these values only are Unsafe. They were fully supported with the advent of Netscape Navigator 6.0 (and Mozilla 1.0). The CSS2 system fonts are supported beginning with Netscape Navigator 6.0.

Opera has implemented `font` property since version 3.6. More recent versions of the browser also implement the CSS2 system font extensions.

Konqueror supports this property fully.

9.7 font-stretch Property

The `font-stretch` property is designed to provide a normal, condensed or expanded font face. This property differs from the CSS1 property `font-weight`; `font-weight` deals with the "boldness" assigned to a font, while `font-stretch` is capable of actually changing the relative width of the individual characters that comprise the displayed font.

font-stretch does exactly what it says: it either compresses or stretches the appearance of a displayed font. font-stretch comes with nine different named values. Ranging from most condensed to most expanded, these values are ultra-condensed, extra-condensed, condensed, semi-condensed, normal, semi-expanded, expanded, extra-expanded and ultra-expanded. The universally applicable CSS2 value inherit, which takes the parent value set for font-stretch, is also available.

Listing 9.13, whose results are mocked-up in Figure 9–14, shows how you can use these values and the effects they have on the displayed font: As you can see in this case, the wider value is equal to the semi-expanded value, and the narrower value is equal to the semi-condensed value. That is because these values are relative to whatever font-stretch value has been set. In this case, as no font-stretch value has been set, they are set to the default, which is normal, so wider is one size larger, and narrower is one size smaller.

Listing 9.13	*font-stretch Example*

```
<html>
<head>
<title>font-stretch Example</title>
</head>
<body>
<h3 style="font-stretch: ultra-condensed">An Ultra-Condensed
Header</h3>
<h3 style="font-stretch: extra-condensed">An Extra-Condensed
Header</h3>
<h3 style="font-stretch: condensed">A Condensed Header
</h3>
<h3 style="font-stretch: semi-condensed">A Semi-Condensed
Header</h3>
<h3 style="font-stretch: narrower">A Narrower Header</h3>
<h3 style="font-stretch: normal">A Normal Header</h3>
<h3 style="font-stretch: wider">A Wider Header</h3>
<h3 style="font-stretch: semi-expanded">A Semi-Expanded
Header</h3>
<h3 style="font-stretch: expanded">An Expanded Header</h3>
<h3 style="font-stretch: extra-expanded">An Extra-Expanded
Header</h3>
<h3 style="font-stretch: ultra-expanded">An Ultra-Expanded
Header</h3>
</body>
</html>
```

An Ultra-Condensed Header

An Extra-Condensed Header

A Condensed Header

A Semi-Condensed Header

A Narrow Header

A Normal Header

A Wider Header

A Semi-Expanded Header

An Expanded Header

An Extra-Expanded Header

An Ultra-Expanded Header

Figure 9–14   The intended effects — sometimes subtle — of the various font-stretch values illustrated.

Browser Compatibility

- Internet Explorer 3.0: Unsafe.
- Internet Explorer 4.0: Unsafe.
- Internet Explorer 4.0 – 4.5 (Mac): Unsafe.
- Internet Explorer 5.0: Unsafe.
- Internet Explorer 5.1 – 5.2 (Mac): Unsafe.
- Internet Explorer 5.5: Unsafe.
- Internet Explorer 6.0: Unsafe.
- Netscape Navigator 4.0 – 4.79: Unsafe.
- Netscape Navigator 4.0 (Mac & UNIX): Unsafe.
- Netscape Navigator 6.0: Unsafe.
- Netscape Navigator 7.0: Unsafe.
- Mozilla 1.0: Unsafe.
- Opera 3.6 – 4.0: Unsafe.
- Opera 5.0 – 6.0: Unsafe.
- Konqueror: Unsafe.

None of the major browsers as yet supports this CSS2 property.

9.8   font-size-adjust Property

The `font-size-adjust` property gives Web authors control over the legibility of the font displayed. It effectively extends the functionality of the `font-size` property by addressing an inherent problem with specifying font sizes: not all font sizes are equal. A courier font set to 12 points does not take up the same space on screen as 12-point Times Roman, 12-point Helvetica or just about any other font. You can see this illustrated in Figure 9–15, which uses a number of different fonts all set to the same point size.

Shelly Volante 12 Point

The quick brown fox jumped over the lazy dog.

Verdana 12 Point

The quick brown fox jumped over the lazy dog.

Garamond 12 Point

The quick brown fox jumped over the lazy dog.

Arial 12 Point

The quick brown fox jumped over the lazy dog.

Comic Sans MS 12 Point

The quick brown fox jumped over the lazy dog.

Century Gothic 12 Point

The quick brown fox jumped over the lazy dog.

Figure 9–15   Different fonts set to the same point size (12 points).

This is primarily due to the different aspect values of various fonts, which is the value of the size of the font divided by its x-height. While fonts of the same point size may have a different display size, fonts of the same aspect value appear to have the same size. `font-size-adjust` enables Web authors to set the aspect value for the fonts on a Web page, so that they all appear with the same legibility, as Figure 9–16 depicts.

Shelly Volante

The quick brown fox jumped over the lazy dog.

Verdana

The quick brown fox jumped over the lazy dog.

Garamond

The quick brown fox jumped over the lazy dog.

Arial

The quick brown fox jumped over the lazy dog.

Comic Sans MS

The quick brown fox jumped over the lazy dog.

Century Gothic

The quick brown fox jumped over the lazy dog.

Figure 9–16   The same fonts with similar legibility values mocked-up.

`font-size-adjust` takes one of three values: a numerical value, which is equivalent to the aspect value, plus the named values `none`, which does not preserve the aspect value between fonts, and `inherit`, which takes on whatever parent value exists for `font-size-adjust`.

The general rule is, the larger the aspect value, the more legible the font will appear. `font-size-adjust` uses the following formula to calculate the aspect value:

```
y(a/a') = c
```

where:

y = the "font size" of first font chosen

a = the aspect value of the target font

a' = the aspect value of the *available* font

c = the proper "font size" to apply to the available font

In the event that a font match can't be made, the `font-size-adjust` property takes the next available font, and applies the aspect value of the chosen font to the font that is available. This ensures that the font that is displayed is as legible as the one the Web author had originally intended to appear.

The following code snippet provides an idea as to how this property could be used:

```
<h1 style="font-size: 12pt; font-family: courier; font-size-adjust:
1.5;">Font-Size-Adjusted Header</h1>
```

In this case, the chosen font family is Courier. If this is not available on the user's system, then the closest available font is chosen, and then the formula from the `font-size-adjust` property is applied to the value "1.5", and the resulting font is set to that value.

Browser Compatibility

- Internet Explorer 3.0: Unsafe.
- Internet Explorer 4.0: Unsafe.
- Internet Explorer 4.0 – 4.5 (Mac): Unsafe.
- Internet Explorer 5.0: Unsafe.
- Internet Explorer 5.1 – 5.2 (Mac): Unsafe.
- Internet Explorer 5.5: Unsafe.
- Internet Explorer 6.0: Unsafe.
- Netscape Navigator 4.0 – 4.79: Unsafe.
- Netscape Navigator 4.0 (Mac & UNIX): Unsafe.
- Netscape Navigator 6.0: Unsafe.
- Netscape Navigator 7.0: Unsafe.
- Mozilla 1.0: Unsafe.
- Opera 3.6 – 4.0: Unsafe.
- Opera 5.0 – 6.0: Unsafe.
- Konqueror: Unsafe.

None of the major browsers as yet support the `font-size-adjust` property.

9.9   The @font-face Pseudo-Element

The new `@font-face` pseudo-element provides the mechanism by which Web authors can specify fonts that can be downloaded by the user and then displayed directly within the Web page. It can take a number of values, many of them derived from the many CSS2 font specific properties, and it works in exactly the same way.

The following is a sample Web page that will attempt to download the font "`mildly-funky`" and then display that font when requested in a Web page:

Listing 9.14	*@font-face Code Example*

```
<html>
<head>
<title>@font-face example</title>
<style>
@font-face {font-family: "mildly-funky"; src:url("http://
www.funky-fonts-are-us.com/newfonts/mild-funky"); font-style:
normal, italic;}
body {font-family: "mildly-funky", normal}
h1 {font-family: "mildly-funky", italic}
</style>
</head>
<body>
<h1>This heading uses an Italic Mildly Funky Downloaded
Font</h1>
The text in the remaining body of the Web page uses the
same font as in the header, but uses the normal (i.e.,
unitalicized) version of it.
</body>
</html>
```

In this case, the `@font-face` pseudo-element looks up a reference for the "Mildly-Funky" font on the fictitious Web site "`http://www.FunkyFontsAreUs.com`" in the "`/newfonts/mild-funky`" directory. Subsequently, style sheet information is provided that tells the browser to use that font for both the body of the document and any top-level headers, rendering the first in a normal, non-italic way, and the latter in an italic version of the "Mildly-Funky" font. As you can see from this example, the `@font-face` pseudo-element relies upon other values to help "shape" the font that gets used on screen. It can use any of the following CSS2 properties as values, all of which work in exactly the same way as their property equivalents: `font-family`, `font-style`, `font-variant`, `font-stretch`, `font-size`, `font-weight`. As these are already covered in other parts of this book, there is no need to repeat the same information here.

The `@font-face` pseudo-element also uses a number of new values: `unicode-range`, `units-per-em`, `src`, `panose-1`, `stemv`, `stemh`, `slope`, `cap-height`, `x-height`, `ascent`, `descent`, `widths`, `bbox`, `definition-src`, `baseline`, `centerline`, `topline` and `mathline`. These need some additional explanation.

The `unicode-range` value is an optional value used by Web authors who want to make sure that a font being downloaded is capable of displaying certain characters. There are many fonts that can only provide a specific number of characters corresponding to a certain range within the Unicode font specification. `unicode-range` takes a hexadecimal number (which can include wildcard characters) that refers to a specific Unicode character range. Table 9.1 displays the languages and their ranges via a hexadecimal matrix for the full Unicode specification.

Table 9.1 *The Hexadecimal Range for the Unicode Specification and the Languages Covered*

	0	1	2	3	4	5	6	7	8	9	A	B	C	D	E	F
0				Basic Latin									Latin 1 Supplement			
1			Latin Extended-A								Latin Extended-B					
2		Latin Extended-B				IPA Extensions							Spacing Modifiers			
3			Combining Diacritics					Greek								
4						Cyrillic										
5	???	???	???		Armenian						Hebrew					
6						Arabic										
7		(Syriac)			???	Phoenician		(Thaana)			???	???	???	???		
8	Avestan			Aramaic		???	???	Tifinagh			Samaritan ?		???	???		
9		Devanagari							Bengali							
0A		Gurmukhi							Gujarati							
0B		Oriya							Tamil							
0C		Telugu							Kannada							
0D		Malayalam							Sinhala							
0E		Thai							Lao							
0F					(Tibetan with Extensions under Ballot)											
10		(Myanmar)							Georgian							
11						Hangul Jamo										
12						Ethiopic										
13		Ethiopic					Eth.Ext.			Cherokee						
14-15				Unified Canadian Aboriginal Syllabics												
16	Unified Canadian Aboriginal Syllabics						Ogham			Runic						
17	Tagalog		Hanunóo		Buhid		Tagbanwa			(Khmer)						

Table 9.1 *The Hexadecimal Range for the Unicode Specification and the Languages Covered (continued)*

18	(Mongolian)						Cham		
19	New Tai Lü		???	Dehong Dai		Pahawh Hmong?			
1A	Lanna Tai		???	Viêt Thái			???	???	
1B	Buginese	Javanese?		Meitei/Manipuri			Lisu?		
1C	(Batak)	Kirat/Limbu		Siddham			???	???	
1D	Róng/Lepcha		Kayah Li ?	Phags-pa ?			???	???	
1E	Latin Extended Additional								
1F	Greek Extended								
20	General Punctuation			Subs/Supers		Currency	Diac. Symbs.		
21	Letterlike Symbols		Number Forms		Arrows				
22	Mathematical Symbols								
23	Miscellaneous Technical								
24	Control Pictures	OCR		Enclosed Alphanumerics					
25	Box Drawing			Blocks	Geometric Shapes				
26	Miscellaneous Symbols								
27	Dingbats					???	???	???	
28	Braille Patterns								
29	Glagolitic		???	???	Old Hungarian	???	???	???	???	???
2A	(Ethiopic Extended)		???	???	Ol Cemet'	Sorang Sng.		???	???
2B	Newari ?		???	???	Varang Kshiti		???	???	???	???
2C-2D	???				???				
2E	???				(CJK Radicals)				
2F	(Kangxi Radicals)						???	(IDC)	
30	CJK Syms. & Punct.	Hiragana			Katakana				
31	Bopomofo	Hangul Compatibility Jamo		M	Ext.Bo p.	???	???	???	???
32	Enclosed CJK Letters & Months								
33	CJK Compatibility								

Table 9.1 *The Hexadecimal Range for the Unicode Specification and the Languages Covered (continued)*

34-4C	CJK Ideographic Extension A								
4D	CJK Ideographic Extension A				???	???	???	???	
4E-9F	CJK Unified Ideographs								
A0-A3	(Yi)								
A4	(Yi)		(Yi Radicals)		???	???	???	???	
A5-AB	???		???						
AC-D6	Hangul Syllables								
D7	Hangul Syllables			???	???	???	???	???	
D8-DF	High-half Zone of UTF-16								
E0-F8	Private Use Area								
F9-FA	CJK Compatibility Ideographs								
FB	Alphabetic Pres. Forms	Arabic Presentation Forms A							
FC-FD	Arabic Presentation Forms A								
FE	???	???	Half	CJKcomp	Small	Arabic Presentation Forms B			
FF	Halfwidth & Fullwidth Forms								Sp.

Key:

??? — Unassigned space

Name ? — Tentatively reserved for given language set

(Name) — Incompletely defined language set

So if you wanted to make sure that the font you are downloading has all of the characters in the standard Latin-1 font (used by most Western languages), you would write the following code:

```
unicode-range: U+00??
```

This covers the Unicode range of `0000` to `00FF`, which contains all the characters in the Latin-1 font. If the selected downloadable font does not cover this Unicode range of characters, it will not be downloaded or displayed. If you wanted to make sure your font included all fractional characters, you would specify "`U+215?`" and if you wanted to ensure that your font covered all Tibetan characters, you would specify "`U+0F??`". Not all sections in the Unicode specification have been confirmed or allotted, and these spaces either contain question marks or are blank. For a complete listing of all of the names and ranges for existing Unicode characters, visit `http://www.unicode.org/roadmaps/`, from which the information in Table 9–1 is largely derived.

The `units-per-em` value takes an integer that sets the width of the letter "m" (a standard square measure used for defining font character size) for the font being downloaded. Common values for this are 250 under the Intellifont standard, 1000 for Type 1, and 2048 for TrueType, OpenType and TrueType GX.

`src` takes a URL value and determines the source from which the font file should be downloaded. An example of how this can be used can be seen in the code sample provided earlier.

`panose-1` is used to match the downloadable font to a standard TrueType font classification. It takes a 10-digit value that categorizes the key display features of the Latin typeface (used by most Western languages).

`stemv` and `stemh` take a numeric value and set the vertical and horizontal stem width (meaning the width for the "stroke" that makes up a character) for the downloaded font. If these are used, the `units-per-em` value must be as well. The slope value also takes an integer value, and it sets the vertical stroke angle for the font being downloaded.

`cap-height` takes an integer value and is used to set the height for a font's uppercase characters. `x-height` works in the same way, but is used to set the height of the lowercase characters instead. If these are used, the `units-per-em` value must be as well.

`ascent` and `descent` set the maximum unaccented height and depth, respectively, for a font. Essentially, they set the height for the highest displayed part of a font (such as the top of a "T" or "I") and the depth of the lowest displayed part of a font (such as the lowest part of the letters "g" or "j"), in their unaccented forms. Characters that are accented in some way (such as "Ñ" or "Ç") are excluded from this measure. If these values are used, the units-per-em value must be as well.

When a font has to be synthesized, the `widths`, `bbox` and `definition-src` values come into play. These descriptors are intended to help provide a description for the font to be synthesized. `widths` sets the value for the width of individual characters (also known as "glyphs"), and it takes a Unicode range followed by a numeric value that sets the width for each glyph represented in the Unicode range. In the following code snippet, `widths` is used to set the widths of all Latin-1 fonts to a value of `1500`.

```
widths: U+00?? 1500
```

The `bbox` value sets the maximum bounding box (in other words, the maximum size of the "box" in which all glyphs for a font appear). It takes four numeric values, which set the dimensions for the lower-left x, lower-left y, upper-right x, and upper-right y for the bounding box for the font.

The `definition-src` value works in the same way as `src`, and points to a specific font resource.

Finally, there are four descriptors that define the alignment values for the font. They are `baseline`, `centerline`, `topline` and `mathline`. `baseline`, `centerline` and `topline` set the lower-baseline, central baseline and top-baseline values for the font. `mathline` sets the mathematical baseline for the font. All of these values take a numeric value, and, if specified, all of the descriptors must be used in conjunction with the `definition-src` value.

Browser Compatibility

*   Internet Explorer 3.0: Unsafe.
*   Internet Explorer 4.0: Unsafe.
*   Internet Explorer 4.0 – 4.5 (Mac): Unsafe.
*   Internet Explorer 5.0: Unsafe.
*   Internet Explorer 5.1 – 5.2 (Mac): Unsafe.
*   Internet Explorer 5.5: Unsafe.
*   Internet Explorer 6.0: Unsafe.
*   Netscape Navigator 4.0 – 4.79: Unsafe.
*   Netscape Navigator 4.0 (Mac & UNIX): Unsafe.
*   Netscape Navigator 6.0: Unsafe.
*   Netscape Navigator 7.0: Unsafe.
*   Mozilla 1.0: Unsafe.
*   Opera 3.6 – 4.0: Unsafe.
*   Opera 5.0 – 6.0: Unsafe.
*   Konqueror: Unsafe.

None of the major browsers support the `@font-face` at-rule.

9.10 CSS3 Font Decoration Properties

The font-decoration properties — font-effect, font-smooth, font-emphasize-style, font-emphasize-position and font-emphasize — are wholly new properties currently proposed under the CSS3 font module. Several of them are designed primarily for use with East Asian typography and work in much the same way as the text decoration properties. As CSS3 is still a work-in-progress at the time of writing, none of the following properties are set in stone, or supported in any of the major browsers, but this section provides an overview of what to expect in the future.

It should be noted that these properties are *not* designed to be contained within the shortcut font property, and in fact the font decoration properties contain a new shortcut property called font-emphasize that handles the values for two other font decoration properties: font-emphasize-style and font-emphasize-position.

font-effect Property

This property is used to add special effects — such as having the text appear to be "punched in," "raised" or appear as an outline — to the selected font.

This property can take one of four values: none, engrave, emboss or outline. The none value is the default, applying no special effect to the chosen font. The engrave value makes the text appear as though it is embedded, or punched into the Web page. Conversely, the emboss value makes the text appear as though it is raised above the Web page's surface. The outline value only displays the outside edge of the selected font — it is as though the font has been hollowed out. Figure 9–17 shows the intended display effects of these values, set against a gray background to make the emboss and engrave effects more noticeable.

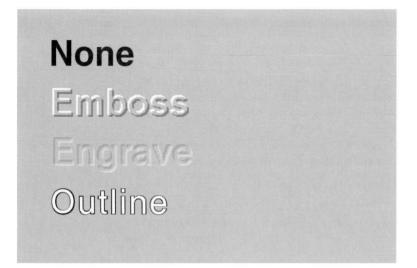

Figure 9–17   The intended effects of the font-effect property's four values.

font-smooth Property

Anti-aliasing is a measure used to make a font appear either jagged or smooth. Small fonts don't always scale well, so a font that looks perfectly fine at a relatively small 8 or 10 points in size may look downright ugly and jagged when expanded to 30 points or more. The `font-smooth` property provides direct control over the anti-aliasing value attached to the targeted font.

This property takes one of four values: `auto`, `never`, `always` and a length measurement value. The `auto` value is the default. The `never` value tells the browser not to apply any anti-aliasing to the target font — if you deliberately want a jagged look, you would use this value. The `always` value conversely tells the browser to add anti-aliasing to a font of any size. Conceivably, this could be a problem when something like a monospaced font is rendered in a very small size, as the anti-aliasing might make it less readable. The length unit value is applied to a font if it is greater than the amount of font smoothing value that is already in place against a given font.

Keep in mind that not all displays are capable of displaying anti-aliased fonts. Many portable computing devices and things like large LED billboards may be incapable of depicting the shaded gray or color values necessary for anti-aliasing a displayed font.

font-emphasize-style Property

The `font-emphasize-style` property is designed to add emphasis marks that are specific to East Asian fonts. In the same way that a Latin-based font might use the strong or emphasis elements to emphasize text, so the `font-emphasize-style` property allows you to do the same with East Asian characters.

It takes one of four values: `none`, `accent`, `dot` and `circle`. The `none` value — which adds no emphasis symbol — is the default. The `accent` value adds a slanted, apostrophe-like character to the text, the `dot` value adds a filled-in disc symbol, and the `circle` value adds a hollowed-out version of `dot`. You can see examples of these values against Japanese and Chinese characters in Figure 9–18.

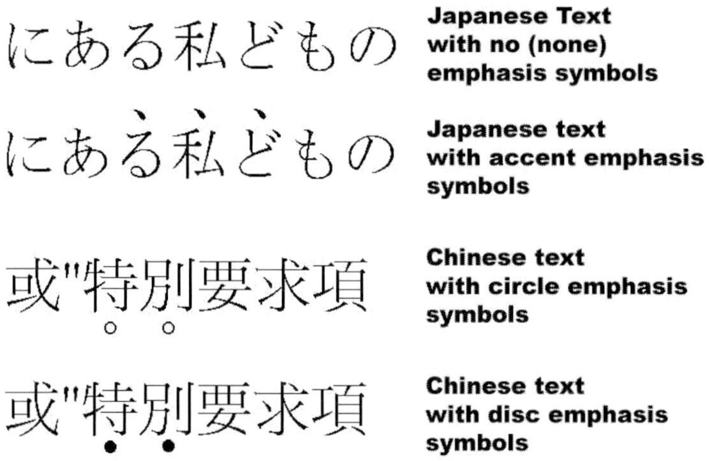

にある私どもの   Japanese Text
with no (none)
emphasis symbols

にある私どもの   Japanese text
with accent emphasis
symbols

或"特別要求項   Chinese text
with circle emphasis
symbols

或"特別要求項   Chinese text
with disc emphasis
symbols

Figure 9–18   The various accent values for font-emphasize-style mocked-up against Japanese and Chinese text.

It should be noted that this property can affect the line height of a row of characters, spacing out the entire row the accented characters appear within.

font-emphasize-position Property

Different Asian character sets require that accent symbols be placed either to one side or the top or bottom of a given character. The `font-emphasize-position` property lets the Web author set where any accent characters should appear.

The `font-emphasize-position` property has two values: `before` and `after`. Given that Asian text can be displayed either horizontally or vertically, these values should be thought of in terms of a given row or column of characters. In a vertical arrangement `before` places the accent character to the right (remember that Asian text reads right-to-left), and `after` to the left. In a horizontal arrangement, `before` means above the text, and `after` places the accent character below the text.

The before value is the preferred position for Japanese and Traditional Chinese text, while the after value is for use with Simplified Chinese text. You can see how these two values might be applied to such text in Figure 9–18 (the example used for `font-emphasize-style`): the second Japanese row of characters has an accent above (or `before`), characters, and the Chinese rows of characters have accents set below (or `after`).

font-emphasize Property

The `font-emphasize` position property is a shortcut property, allowing you to set the values for `font-emphasize-style` and `font-emphasize-position` at one time. It takes all of the values belonging to these other two properties `none`, `accent`, `dot`, `circle`, `before` and `after` in combination.

Using this property, the following code snippet should produce the results seen in second line of Japanese text in Figure 9–18.

```
<div style="font-family: "MS Mincho"; font-size: 16pt">
&#12395;&#12354;<span style="font-emphasize: accent
before">&#12427;&#31169;&#12393;</span>&#12418;&#12398;
</div>
```

TEXT PROPERTIES

Topics in This Chapter

- Letter and Word Spacing, Line Height, Alignment, Indent
- Text Case and Shadow
- Multi-Lingual Sizing, Flow, Justification
- White Space and Embedded Spacing
- Text Overflow and Text Kerning
- `punctuation-trim`
- text-line-through Properties
- text-overline Properties
- text-underline Properties
- `text-blink`

Chapter 10

The family of text properties enables Web authors to change the manner in which text is displayed on-screen. They differ from the font family of properties in that the text family is designed to accomplish a number of typographical display options, irrespective of the font being used. Using the text family of properties, you can alter the spacing between lines, words or individual letters in your text, change the alignment of your text and much more. CSS3 looks as if it will greatly expand the capabilities of this set of properties, providing finer control over a number of text formatting features and extending support for formatting non-Western language text.

The initial part of this chapter looks at all of the properties first initiated in the CSS1 and CSS2 specifications and how they have been implemented in the major browsers. The second part of the chapter (beginning with `glyph-orientation-vertical` and `glyph-orientation-horizontal`) looks at all of the new CSS3 properties that have been proposed. The next chapter ("Text Property Extensions") looks at existing Internet Explorer-only properties relating to text formatting, many of which could be adopted within the CSS3 text module.

10.1 letter-spacing Property

The `letter-spacing` property does just that: it adds spacing between individual letters on a Web page. It can take one of two possible values: the default keyword value `normal`, or a specific measurement value. When used effectively, the `letter-spacing` property enables the Web author to help spread out what text they have across the Web page. This technique is common in page layout programs to better space words across a single line of text, usually to fully justify it (i.e., to have even left and right margins). This technique may not fully translate to the Web, since it is exceedingly difficult to know where a specific word will appear on-screen, making it hard to fully justify the line of text in this manner. The `letter-spacing` property can be used effectively for eye-catching displays, however.

The `letter-spacing` property can take any unit of measure that has been allotted to CSS (see the CSS Units chapter for more detailed information on which units of measure can be used).

The best use for the `letter-spacing` property is for emphasis. It is great for making your headers stand out, or for emphasizing particular words or phrases in your text. It is tricky to use `letter-spacing` for its intended typographical purpose of fully justifying text across a line, and that use is not recommended (`text-align` is better suited for this purpose).

Listing 10.1 shows some good — and not-so-good — examples of the `letter-spacing` property in action.

Listing 10.1	*letter-spacing Example Code*

```
<html>
<head>
<title>letter-spacing Example</title>
</head>
<body style="font-size: large">
<h1 align="center" style="letter-spacing: 0.5cm">This Header
Stands Out</h1>
<h2 align="center" style="letter-spacing: 0.3cm">On the Web,
Letter Spacing is Best Used for Emphasis</h2>
<p>
Again, within a line of regular text, the letter-spacing property
is best used for <em style="letter-spacing: 0.2cm">emphasis</em>,
as it really stands out from the rest of the text being displayed.
<p>
In typographical circles, letter spacing is most often used
<b style="letter-spacing: 0.1cm; font-weight: normal;">to help a
line</b> of text to be fully justified across the width of the
page. However, <b style=" letter-spacing: 0.1cm; font-weight:
normal;">on the Web it</b> is hard to know exactly where a line of
text will be placed on the page.
<p>
Try not to go <em style="letter-spacing: 0.5in">overboard</em>
when using this property (even emphasis can go too far)!
</body>
</html>
```

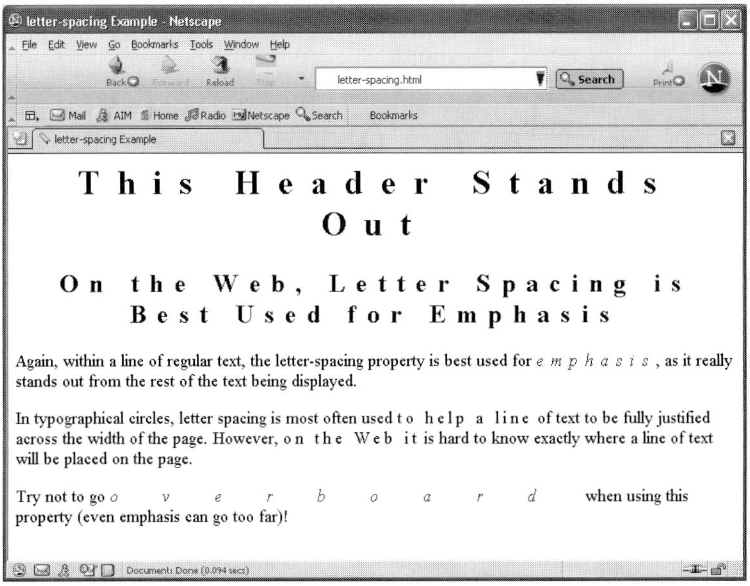

Figure 10–1 The use and abuses of the letter-spacing property, as seen in Netscape Navigator 7.0.

Figure 10–1 gives you a good idea as to how the `letter-spacing` property should and should not be used. When used in moderation, the `letter-spacing` property helps to emphasize headers or words in a line of text. It does not hold up well when trying to justify a line of text (as it is impossible to know the exact width of the browser window your viewers will be using), or when you use an extreme value to space out the individual letters. Use this property sparingly.

When using the `letter-spacing` property in a paragraph, a good compromise would be to use it in conjunction with tags (such as `<em>`, `<b>` or `<i>`) that will still convey the emphasis you want to get across to the reader.

Browser Compatibility

This property has been widely adopted, although in Netscape Navigator this has only been the case since version 6.0.

- Internet Explorer 3.0: Unsafe
- Internet Explorer 4.0: Safe
- Internet Explorer 4.0 – 4.5 (Mac): Safe
- Internet Explorer 5.0: Safe
- Internet Explorer 5.1 – 5.2 (Mac): Safe.

- Internet Explorer 5.5: Safe
- Internet Explorer 6.0: Safe
- Netscape Navigator 4.0 – 4.79: Unsafe.
- Netscape Navigator 4.0 (Mac & UNIX): Unsafe.
- Netscape Navigator 6.0: Safe.
- Netscape Navigator 7.0: Safe.
- Mozilla 1.0: Safe.
- Opera 3.6 – 4.0: Safe.
- Opera 5.0 – 6.0: Safe.
- Konqueror: Safe.

The `letter-spacing` property has been implemented successfully in Internet Explorer since version 4.0.

The 4.0 version of Netscape Navigator did not implement this property — any `letter-spacing` value is ignored. This property was supported fully beginning with version 6.0 (and in Mozilla 1.0).

Opera was an early adopter of the `letter-spacing` property, and has been fully implemented since version 3.6 of that browser.

Konqueror fully implements this property.

10.2 word-spacing Property

What the `letter-spacing` property does for letters, the `word-spacing` property does for words. Again, it was designed primarily for typographical reasons, typically to fully justify text across a line, but as we have already seen in the example for the `letter-spacing` property, this use is not recommended for the Web. Instead, the `word-spacing` property is best used for emphasis. The `word-spacing` property was not supported in either of the two major browsers until relatively recently.

The `word-spacing` property can take any unit of measure that has been allotted to CSS (see the CSS Units chapter for more detailed information on what unit of measure can be used).

Again, like the `letter-spacing` property, the best use for the `word-spacing` property is for emphasis. It is great for making your headers stand out, or for emphasizing particular words or phrases in your text. It is tricky to use `word-spacing` for its intended typographical purpose of fully justifying text across a line, so that particular use is not recommended.

The following code example and accompanying illustration displays `word-spacing` put to effective and not-so-effective uses:

Listing 10.2	*word-spacing Example Code*

```html
<html>
<head>
<title>word-spacing Example</title>
</head>
<body style="font-size: large">
<h1 align="center" style="word-spacing: 2cm">This Header Stands
Out</h1>
<h2 align="center" style="word-spacing: 2cm">On the Web, word
spacing is best used for emphasis</h2> While word-spacing can be
applied to non-block elements, it is most-effective when applied
to a paragraph or to a phrase in a line of text,
<i style="word-spacing: 2cm">like this one</i>.
<p>
For word-spacing to be effective, it must be applied to more than
a single word, such as the word at the end of this
<b style="word-spacing: 2cm;">sentence</b>. Word-spacing will not
work, as you might expect, on individual words -- you need at least
<b style="word-spacing: 2cm;">two words</b> to see the effect
displayed.
</p>
<p style="word-spacing: 3in">Try not to go overboard when using
this property (even emphasis can go too far)!
</p>
</body>
</html>
```

Using code similar to that used in the `letter-spacing` section, Figure 10–2 shows how `word-spacing` should and should not be used. Again, it is best used for emphasis. Notice that you have to have at least two words for the effects of `word-spacing` to be seen — it will not work on a single word in isolation. It does not hold up well when trying to justify a line of text, since it is impossible to know the exact width of the browser window your viewers will be using. Again, if your aim is at justifying the text, `text-align` is more appropriate for the job. When it is set to an extreme value, as can be seen in the final paragraph displayed in Figure 10–2, it can make the resulting text hard to read.

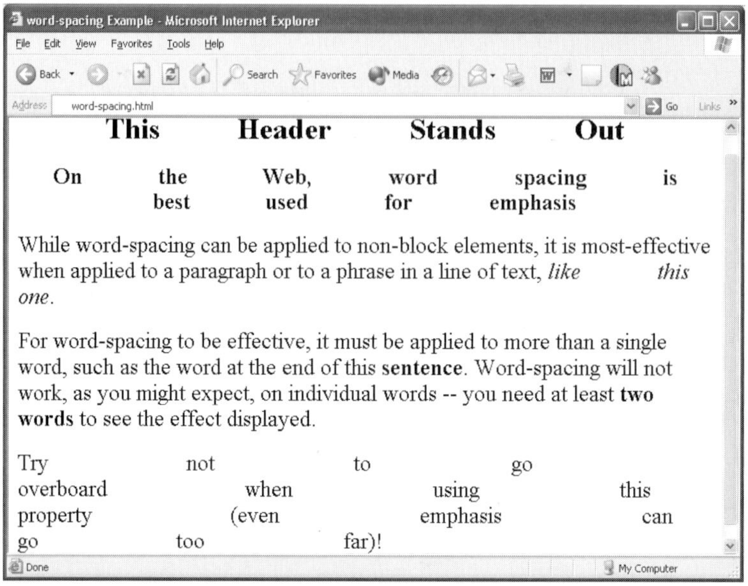

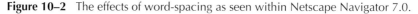

Figure 10–2   The effects of word-spacing as seen within Netscape Navigator 7.0.

Browser Compatibility

This property is now well supported, although only in the most recent versions of the two major browsers.

- Internet Explorer 3.0: Unsafe
- Internet Explorer 4.0: Unsafe
- Internet Explorer 4.0 – 4.5 (Mac): Safe
- Internet Explorer 5.0: Unsafe
- Internet Explorer 5.1 – 5.2 (Mac): Safe.
- Internet Explorer 5.5: Unsafe
- Internet Explorer 6.0: Safe
- Netscape Navigator 4.0 – 4.79: Unsafe.
- Netscape Navigator 4.0 (Mac & UNIX): Unsafe.
- Netscape Navigator 6.0: Safe.
- Netscape Navigator 7.0: Safe.
- Mozilla 1.0: Safe.
- Opera 3.6 – 4.0: Partial.
- Opera 5.0 – 6.0: Safe.
- Konqueror: Safe.

The `word-spacing` property has only been supported in Windows versions of Internet Explorer since version 6.0, although it has been implemented fully in Macintosh versions of this browser since version 4.0.

Netscape Navigator did not implement this property until version 6.0 (and in Mozilla 1.0).

Early versions of Opera get a Partial rating because, while they did begin implementing this property with version 3.6, behavior was buggy. In version 3.6 – 4.0 of Opera, when `word-spacing` is applied to inline elements, the paragraph it is contained within may end up being "shifted" to the left-hand side of page, with the text that has been set to `word-spacing` shifted over to the right (which is what happens with the example code). This problem does not occur with block-level elements. By version 5.0, this problem was fixed.

Konqueror fully implements this property.

10.3 line-height Property

The `line-height` property is designed to allow a Web author to set the distance between lines of text on a Web page. Using this property, you can space out the text that appears on your Web page, creating effects like "double spacing." It can take one of three sets of values: the default `normal` value (equivalent to "single spacing"), a specific height value using a measurement value, or a percentage value relative to the font's height. The `line-height` property can take any unit of measurement that has been allotted to CSS (see the CSS Units chapter for more detailed information on which units of measure can be used).

It is best to use the `line-height` property in conjunction with the `font-size` property. That way, you can simply set the exact size for the font of the text to be displayed, and precisely control the amount of vertical line spacing for that text. For example, if you want a "double-spacing" effect, you set a value for `font-size`, and then simply double that value for `line-height` to get the intended effect. You can see code for that effect in Listing 10.3, whose results are displayed in Figure 10–3.

Listing 10.3   *line-height Example Code*

```
<html>
<head>
<title>line-height Example</title>
</head>
<body style="font-size: 20pt">
```

Listing 10.3 *line-height Example Code (continued)*

```
<p>
These lines of text do not use the <code>line-height</code>
property, so you are seeing the normal, default value for
line-height used by this browser for this font size.
</p>
<p style="line-height: 33pt">
If you want your Web page to appear as if it is "double-spaced"
on-screen you can use the line-height attribute to set the
separation value between the lines of text. You can set this value
more precisely if you have also set a specific font-size
beforehand. That way, you simply double its value with line-height
to get the intended effect.
</p>
<p style="line-height: 10pt">
Be careful about using <code>line-height</code> values smaller
than that used for <code>font-size</code>, as you can get lines of
text that run into each other, potentially making them unreadable.
</p>
</body>
</html>
```

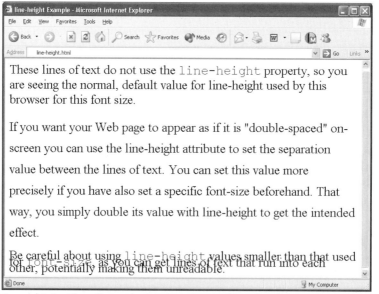

Figure 10–3   The effects of using font-size and line-height in conjunction with each other on a Web page as seen in Internet Explorer 6.0.

You can also use a percentage value for line-height, which is relative to the height of the existing font size, so if you set line-height to a value of 200%, for example, it will always display the text on the Web page as double-spaced.

The font property also allows you to set font-size and line-height directly. For example, the following two code snippets are equivalent:

```
<body style="font-size: 14pt; line-height: 16pt">
```

```
<body style="font: 14pt/16pt">
```

For more information on the font property, see Chapter 9, "Font Properties."

Browser Compatibility

The line-height property has long been implemented by the major browsers and is considered safe to use.

- Internet Explorer 3.0: Partial.
- Internet Explorer 4.0: Safe.
- Internet Explorer 4.0 – 4.5 (Mac): Safe.
- Internet Explorer 5.0: Safe.
- Internet Explorer 5.1 – 5.2 (Mac): Safe.
- Internet Explorer 5.5: Safe.
- Internet Explorer 6.0: Safe.
- Netscape Navigator 4.0 – 4.79: Safe.
- Netscape Navigator 4.0 (Mac & UNIX): Safe.
- Netscape Navigator 6.0: Safe.
- Netscape Navigator 7.0: Safe.
- Mozilla 1.0: Safe.
- Opera 3.6 – 4.0: Safe.
- Opera 5.0 – 6.0: Safe.
- Konqueror: Safe.

The line-height property has been implemented fully since version 4.0 of Internet Explorer. Version 3.0 gets a Partial rating, as it implements specific values for line-height but not percentage values.

Netscape Navigator has implemented this property fully since version 4.0.

Opera has implemented line-height since version 3.6.

Konqueror fully implements this property.

10.4 vertical-align Property

The `vertical-align` property is designed to let a Web author align the placement of text on a Web page with respect the vertical placement of another element on the Web page — most typically an image. It belongs to the text family of CSS properties and its numerous values equate to various positioning values normally associated with text.

The `vertical-align` property can take any one of eight different values: `baseline`, `middle`, `sub`, `super`, `text-top`, `text-bottom`, `bottom` and `top`. In addition, it can also take on a percentage value that is set relative to the `line-height` property above the baseline by whatever percentage value is specified.

`baseline` aligns the baseline of the element to that of the parent element, while `middle` aligns the text to the middle of the associated element. `sub` and `super` are the equivalent of subscript and superscript. `text-top` aligns the top of the element to the top of the parent, and `text-bottom` does the same thing, but to the bottom of the parent element instead. `bottom` and `top` are two additional values designed to be used in relation to the existing line of text or object on which the element is situated, so that `top` aligns the element to the tallest element on that line of text, and `bottom` does the same for the lowest element. The important thing to remember with these values is that they are relative to the *entire* vertical height of the line. Even if a given line of text does not include any descenders — letters which have a "tail," like "g," "y" or "q" — the `text-bottom` value acts as if such a tail exists, placing its text lower than that of the `baseline` value. This effect is better demonstrated than explained — you can see the effects of all of the values for `vertical-align` in Figure 10–4, which uses the example code in Listing 10.4.

Listing 10.4 *vertical-align Example Code*

```
<html>
<head>
<title>vertical-align Example</title>
<style>
body {font-size: 33px; font-weight: bold}
span {font-size: 15px}
</style>
</head>
<body>
Some regular text <span style="vertical-align:
super">superscript-aligned text</span><br />
Some regular text <span style="vertical-align:
sub">subscript-aligned text</span><br />
```

Listing 10.4	*vertical-align Example Code (continued)*

```
Some regular text <span style="vertical-align:
text-top">text-top-aligned text</span><br />
Some regular text <span style="vertical-align:
text-bottom">text-bottom-aligned text</span><br />
<span style="vertical-align: baseline">baseline-aligned
text</span> And some text that follows it for comparison.<br />
<span style="vertical-align: bottom">bottom-aligned text</span>
And some text that follows it for comparison.<br />
<span style="vertical-align: middle">middle-aligned text</span>
And some text that follows it for comparison.<br />
<span style="vertical-align: top">top-aligned text</span> And some
text that follows it for comparison.<br />
<span style="vertical-align: 65%">65%-aligned text</span> And some
text that follows it for comparison.<br />
</body>
</html>
```

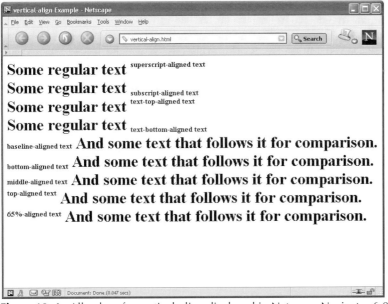

Figure 10–4   All values for vertical-align displayed in Netscape Navigator 6.0.

Browser Compatibility

The `vertical-align` property has a problematic history of implementation in the major browsers; only recently have they gotten things "right."

- Internet Explorer 3.0: Partial.
- Internet Explorer 4.0: Partial.
- Internet Explorer 4.0 – 4.5 (Mac): Partial.
- Internet Explorer 5.0: Safe.
- Internet Explorer 5.1 – 5.2 (Mac): Safe.
- Internet Explorer 5.5: Safe.
- Internet Explorer 6.0: Safe.
- Netscape Navigator 4.0 – 4.79: Safe.
- Netscape Navigator 4.0 (Mac & UNIX): Safe.
- Netscape Navigator 6.0: Safe.
- Netscape Navigator 7.0: Safe.
- Mozilla 1.0: Safe.
- Opera 3.6 – 4.0: Partial.
- Opera 5.0 – 6.0: Safe.
- Konqueror: Safe.

The 3.0 and 4.0 Windows versions of Internet Explorer really only got the `sub` and `super` values for `vertical-align` right — all other values were problematic. Support for all values was much better with the release of version 5.0, although it should be noted that the Macintosh 4.x version of the browser does not interpret the percentage value for `vertical-align` properly, shifting the parent text well down on the page. By Windows version 6.0, they seem to have gotten things right.

With Netscape Navigator 4.x, the values for `vertical-align` were only applied when they were used in conjunction with an image used as the parent, hence the Partial rating. By version 6.0 (and Mozilla 1.0) they had gotten it right.

Opera 3.6 and 4.0 had real problems implementing this property: `middle` didn't work properly when used with images, and percentage values produced odd results. These glitches had been sorted out by version 5.0.

Konqueror fully implements this property.

10.5 text-align Property

The `text-align` property is very handy for quickly aligning text on a Web page. It can take one of five values: `left`, `right`, `center`, `justify` and `inherit`. It is designed to be applied to block-level elements, such as headers or paragraphs, rather than inline formatting elements (such as <b> or <i>, for example).

For the most part, the values for text-align are self-explanatory. The inherit value takes on whatever parent value may hold for text-alignment. For those unfamiliar with the term, justification refers to how text is displayed between the margins. Full justification (which is what the justify value sets) means the browser will space the text contained within the paragraph fully across the two margins. In Figure 10–5 you'll notice how the unjustified sentence that follows the justified example is "ragged" — the words at the end of the right-margin are not flush against it.

The code seen in Listing 10.5 and Figure 10–5 shows how the text-align property can be used to format block-level elements (in this case, paragraphs) within a browser.

Listing 10.5	*text-align Example Code*

```
<html>
<head>
<title>text-align Example</title>
<style>
body {font-size: 16pt; font-family: sans-serif}
</style>
</head>
<body>
<p style="text-align: center">
Centered text.
</p>
<p style="text-align: left">
Left-aligned text.
</p>
<p style="text-align: right">
Right-aligned text.
</p>
<p style="text-align: justify">
This line contains justified text. Since the only way to properly
see this effect is to have enough text to cover at least a couple
of lines, this is more wordy than the other examples.
</p>
<p>
This paragraph is not justified. Notice that the text at the right
margin of this paragraph is "ragged" as compared to the previous
paragraph, meaning that the words do not fill in all of the space
between the left and right margins of the browser window.</p>
</body>
</html>
```

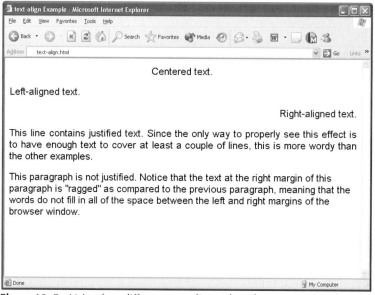

Figure 10–5   Using four different text-align values for paragraphs of text in Internet Explorer 6.0.

Browser Compatibility

The text-align property has long been implemented by the major browsers and is considered safe to use.

- Internet Explorer 3.0: Partial.
- Internet Explorer 4.0: Safe.
- Internet Explorer 4.0 – 4.5 (Mac): Partial.
- Internet Explorer 5.0: Safe.
- Internet Explorer 5.1 – 5.2 (Mac): Safe.
- Internet Explorer 5.5: Safe.
- Internet Explorer 6.0: Safe.
- Netscape Navigator 4.0 – 4.79: Safe.
- Netscape Navigator 4.0 (Mac & UNIX): Safe.
- Netscape Navigator 6.0: Safe.
- Netscape Navigator 7.0: Safe.
- Mozilla 1.0: Safe.
- Opera 3.6 – 4.0: Safe.
- Opera 5.0 – 6.0: Safe.
- Konqueror: Safe.

The `text-align` property has been implemented fully since version 4.0 of Internet Explorer. Version 3.0 gets a Partial rating, as it did not implement the `justify` value. Versions 4.0 – 4.5 for the Macintosh receive a Partial rating for the same reason. Version 5.x (both Windows and Macintosh) was the first to implement all values properly.

Netscape Navigator has implemented this property fully since version 4.0. It is worth pointing out that Netscape Navigator 4.x supported `text-align` beyond the intents of specification by applying the alignment values to non-block elements, such as tables. This use for `text-align` is not recommended, as it may lead to some unexpected results, and in any event this behavior was fixed by version 6.0 (ditto Mozilla 1.0).

Opera has implemented `text-align` properly since version 3.6.

Konqueror fully implements this property.

10.6 text-decoration Property

The `text-decoration` property enables Web authors to set "decorative" properties to their text displays. This does not mean, as you might first think, that you can add such things as curlicues or baroque fluting to the individual letters in your text. Instead, `text-decoration` is designed to let you add underlines, overlines or strikethroughs to your text, or even make your text blink on and off.

The `text-decoration` property can take any one of five keyword values: `blink`, `line-through`, `overline`, `underline` and `none`. The `blink` value is analogous to setting text within the `<blink>` tag, first instituted in the original version of Netscape Navigator. This tag is considered "infamous" by many, as there is no control over the rate of blinking, and over time it is guaranteed to annoy the user reading the page. Unfortunately, the `text-decoration` property offers no extra control over the rate or duration of blinking. The `line-through` value behaves in the same way as the little-used `<s>` tag, which puts a line through the text. Struck-through text is universally recognized to indicate that edits to the text have been made. The `overline` value adds a line above the text being displayed, and has no HTML tag equivalent. The `underline` value works in the same way as the little-used `<u>` tag, placing a line underneath the text. Caution should be used when using this value, as some users may mistake it for a hyperlink, which is also typically underlined. The `none` value, which is the default, can also be put to good use. It can remove the underline normally associated with hyperlinks, so that if you have a need for such a thing, it can easily be accomplished using this value. All of these values are used in Listing 10.6, and the results can be seen in Figure 10–6.

Listing 10.6	*text-decoration Example Code*

```
<html>
<head>
<title>text-decoration Example</title>
<style>
body {font-size: 28px; font-family: sans-serif}
</style>
</head>
<body>
<h1 style="text-decoration: overline">Header with an Overline</h1>
<h1 style="text-decoration: underline">Header with an
Underline</h1>
<strong style="text-decoration: line-through; color: red">I
decided to cut this sentence out. The intention is to let you know
that this sentence has been removed, but you can still see it so
that you can view my edits.</strong>
<p>
<em style="text-decoration: blink">This text blinks. Annoying,
isn't it?</em>
</p>
<p>
<a href="no-link.html">This link has an underline</a>. <a
href="no-link.html" style="text-decoration: none">This link is not
underlined</a>.
</p>
</body>
</html>
```

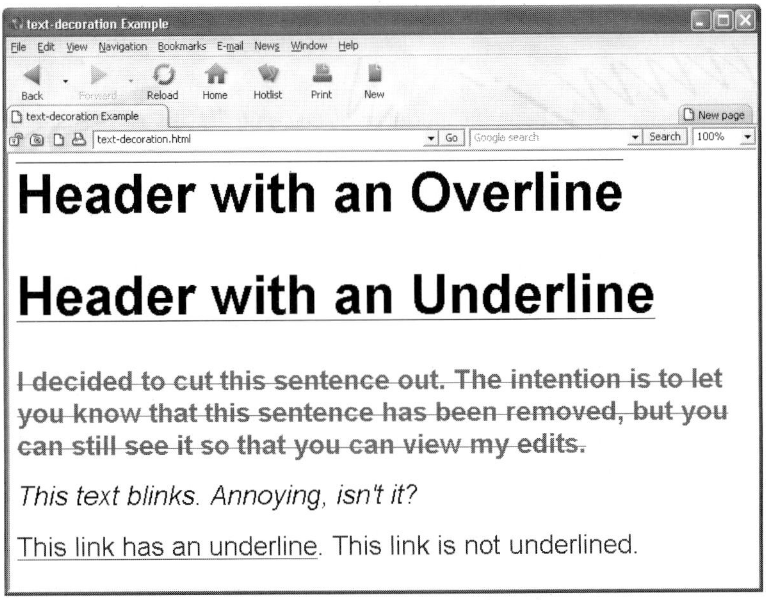

Figure 10–6   The values for text-decoration displayed in Opera 6.0.

Browser Compatibility

The text-decoration property has long been implemented within the major browsers, with the sole exception of the blink value. In an odd bureaucratic quirk, the CSS2 specification states that a browser does not have to implement this value in order to be considered "compliant." However, if only for the sake of clarity, those browsers that do not support this value are rated as "Partial" in the following listing.

- Internet Explorer 3.0: Partial.
- Internet Explorer 4.0: Partial.
- Internet Explorer 4.0 – 4.5 (Mac): Partial.
- Internet Explorer 5.0: Partial.
- Internet Explorer 5.1 – 5.2 (Mac): Partial.
- Internet Explorer 5.5: Partial.
- Internet Explorer 6.0: Partial.
- Netscape Navigator 4.0 – 4.79: Partial.
- Netscape Navigator 4.0 (Mac & UNIX): Partial.
- Netscape Navigator 6.0: Safe.
- Netscape Navigator 7.0: Safe.
- Mozilla 1.0: Safe.
- Opera 3.6 – 4.0: Safe.

- Opera 5.0 – 6.0: Safe.
- Konqueror: Partial.

All but the `blink` value for `text-decoration` have been fully implemented in Internet Explorer since version 3.0. It should be noted that Internet Explorer 5.5 introduced a new property for dealing with "underlines" as applied to non-Western text: `text-underline-position`. For more information on this Internet Explorer-only property, see Chapter 11, "Text Property Extensions."

Netscape Navigator 4.x implemented all of the values for this property save for the `overline` value. This had been fixed by version 6.0 (and Mozilla 1.0).

Opera has implemented the `text-decoration` property — including the `blink` value — since version 3.6.

Konqueror implements this property save for the `blink` value.

10.7 text-indent Property

The `text-indent` property is used for indenting text from the left margin. It differs in function from the various margin properties in that it only indents the first line of text from the left margin. It can either take a specific measurement value or a percentage value that corresponds to the width of the browser window.

The `text-indent` property can take any unit of measure that has been allotted to CSS (see the CSS Units chapter for more detailed information on which units of measure can be used). It can also take a percentage value, which is relative to the width of the browser window.

The `text-indent` property is meant for use with block-level elements, so it is not meant to be used for such things as tables or inline elements (such as an emphasized word within a line of text). The sample code in Listing 10.7, whose results are displayed in Figure 10–7, provides an idea as to how `text-indent` can be used:

Listing 10.7 *text-indent Example Code*

```
<html>
<head>
<title>text-indent Example</title>
<style>
body {font-size: 26px; font-family: sans-serif}
.indent {text-indent: 2in}
</style>
</head>
```

Listing 10.7 *text-indent Example Code (continued)*

```
<body>
<h1 class="indent">This header is indented by 2 inches.</h1>
<div class="indent">So is this text.</div>
<p style="text-indent: 50%">The first line of text in this
paragraph is indented by 50% of the browser window's width.
</p>
<p>
Some text. <span class="indent">Note how this line of text is
<em>not</em> indented</span>, as <code>text-indent</code> does not
apply to inline elements that are not at the beginning of a line.
</p>
<p style="text-indent: -1in">This first words in this text do not
appear onscreen, as <code>text-indent</code> is set to a value of
-1 inch.
</p>
</body>
</html>
```

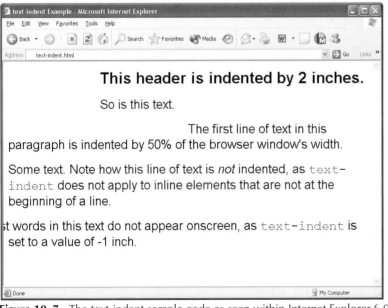

Figure 10–7   The text-indent sample code as seen within Internet Explorer 6.0.

Browser Compatibility

The `text-indent` property has long been implemented by the major browsers, although it should be noted that you can get some odd behavior when this property is applied to things like tables and inline elements, with which it was not designed for use.

- Internet Explorer 3.0: Safe.

- Internet Explorer 4.0: Safe.

- Internet Explorer 4.0 – 4.5 (Mac): Safe.

- Internet Explorer 5.0: Safe.

- Internet Explorer 5.1 – 5.2 (Mac): Safe.

- Internet Explorer 5.5: Safe.

- Internet Explorer 6.0: Safe.

- Netscape Navigator 4.0 – 4.79: Safe.

- Netscape Navigator 4.0 (Mac & UNIX): Safe.

- Netscape Navigator 6.0: Safe.

- Netscape Navigator 7.0: Safe.

- Mozilla 1.0: Safe.

- Opera 3.6 – 4.0: Safe.

- Opera 5.0 – 6.0: Safe.

- Konqueror: Safe.

Internet Explorer has implemented `text-indent` since version 3.0.

Netscape Navigator has implemented this property fully since version 4.0. That isn't the full story, however. If `text-indent` is applied to a table in this version of the browser, it ends up indenting the table, rather than the table's contents (which is more in line with the default behavior for this property when applied to a table). In addition, in this version of Netscape Navigator you will get an effect when the property is applied inline — which strictly speaking, according to the specification, shouldn't be allowed. In relation to the example code from Listing 10.7, you get a 2-inch gap between the text in the fourth paragraph of Listing 10.7, where none should appear. This glitch was ironed out by version 6.0 (ditto Mozilla 1.0).

Opera has implemented `text-indent` since version 3.6.

Konqueror fully implements this property.

10.8 text-transform Property

The text-transform property is another of those CSS properties whose name doesn't adequately describe its function. Many new users might be forgiven for thinking that perhaps it does something to change or otherwise "transform" the text on the page to something else altogether. While the term is correct in typographical terms, for the layperson, all it really does is control the case (as in "upper-" or "lower-" case) of the words it encloses.

text-transform has four different values: capitalize, lowercase, uppercase and none. Each of these values is fairly self-explanatory; they affect the text they enclose in the ways they describe, although it should be said that capitalize in this case means "initial capitals." You can find all four values for text-transform used in Listing 10.8, whose results can be seen in Figure 10–8.

Listing 10.8	*text-transform Example Code*

```
<html>
<head>
<title>text-transform Example</title>
</head>
<body>
<h1 style="text-transform: capitalize">Header in initial caps</h1>
<h2 style="text-transform: lowercase">HEADER ALL IN LOWERCASE
LETTERS</h2>
<h3 style="text-transform: uppercase">header all in uppercase
letters</h3>
<h4 style="text-transform: none">Nothing special happens with this
header</h4>
</body>
</html>
```

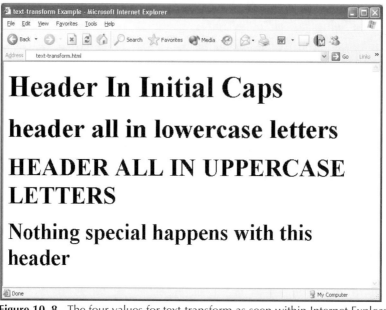

Figure 10–8 The four values for text-transform as seen within Internet Explorer 6.0.

Note in particular how the browser takes the second and third headers and reverses the case in which they were written.

Browser Compatibility

The text-transform property is considered safe for use, as it has been implemented since the advent of the earliest CSS-compatible browsers.

- Internet Explorer 3.0: Unsafe.
- Internet Explorer 4.0: Safe.
- Internet Explorer 4.0 – 4.5 (Mac): Safe.
- Internet Explorer 5.0: Safe.
- Internet Explorer 5.1 – 5.2 (Mac): Safe.
- Internet Explorer 5.5: Safe.
- Internet Explorer 6.0: Safe.
- Netscape Navigator 4.0 – 4.79: Safe.
- Netscape Navigator 4.0 (Mac & UNIX): Safe.
- Netscape Navigator 6.0: Safe.
- Netscape Navigator 7.0: Safe.
- Mozilla 1.0: Safe.
- Opera 3.6 – 4.0: Safe.

- Opera 5.0 – 6.0: Safe.

- Konqueror: Safe.

The `text-transform` property has been implemented fully since version 4.0 of Internet Explorer.

Netscape Navigator has implemented this property fully since version 4.0.

Opera has implemented `text-transform` since version 3.6.

Konqueror fully implements this property.

10.9 text-shadow Property

The `text-shadow` property does exactly what it describes — it adds a background shadow to the selected text. This shadow can appear behind and to the left or right of the text, or even in front of the text. Since it is a "shadow," the shadow never actually overlays the text itself, although the shadow may overlay itself, depending on how sharp or how blurry you make the ends of the shadow. According to the CSS specification, the shadow does not extend the box of its Web element, and it can therefore overlay any text that may lie immediately adjacent to the affected text.

There are several different combinations of values that can be set for `text-shadow`. There are two different space-separated values that set how much the shadow is offset from the text. The first number sets the horizontal length of the shadow from the text, and the second number does the same for the vertical length. By default, the first numeric value sets the shadow to the right of the text, and the second numeric value sets the shadow below the text. `text-shadow` can accept negative values for these as well, so it is possible to set the shadow to the left and above the text by using negative values. `text-shadow` can take a third numeric length value, which sets the amount of "blur" at the boundaries of the shadow. How this should work is not explicitly stated in the CSS2 specification, so results may vary from browser to browser if and when this property is implemented.

The shadow can also take a specific color value, which can either be set as a standard color name or a numerical color value. If no color value is set, the shadow takes on the default value set by the `color` property — and if that isn't explicitly set, it is whatever color value is associated with the text (the default is therefore black). You can also set more than one shadow to a given selection of text.

Listing 10.9 displays several different values for the `text-shadow` property. You can see how this code ought to be displayed in Figure 10–9.

Listing 10.9   *text-shadow Example*

```
<html>
<head>
<title>text-shadow Example</title>
</head>
<body>
<div align="center">
<h1 style="text-shadow: 5px 5px">Drop Shadow</h1>
<p>
<h1 style="text-shadow: -5px -5px red">Drop Shadow</h1>
</p>
<p>
<h1 style="text-shadow: -5px 5px 5px silver">Drop Shadow</h1>
</p>
<p>
<h1 style="text-shadow: gray 10px 10px, lime -5px 5px">Drop
Shadow</h1>
</p>
</div>
</body>
</html>
```

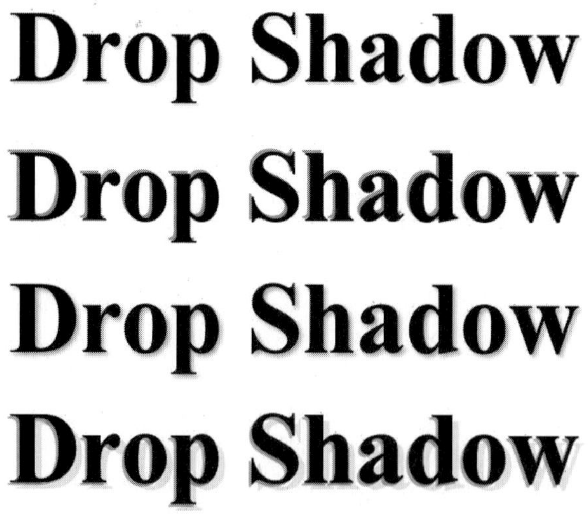

Drop Shadow

Drop Shadow

Drop Shadow

Drop Shadow

Figure 10–9   A mock-up of how the example code for text-shadow ought to be displayed within a compliant browser.

Note how in the final example two separate shadow values are set: one which is gray and offset 10 pixels down and right, the second set to lime and offset from the text by 5 pixels to the left (the effect of the "-5" value) and down.

Browser Compatibility

Unfortunately, no browser has implemented this CSS2 property as yet.

- Internet Explorer 3.0: Unsafe.
- Internet Explorer 4.0: Unsafe.
- Internet Explorer 4.0 – 4.5 (Mac): Unsafe.
- Internet Explorer 5.0: Unsafe.
- Internet Explorer 5.1 – 5.2 (Mac): Unsafe.
- Internet Explorer 5.5: Partial. Unsafe.
- Internet Explorer 6.0: Partial. Unsafe.
- Netscape Navigator 4.0 – 4.79: Unsafe.
- Netscape Navigator 4.0 (Mac & UNIX): Unsafe.
- Netscape Navigator 6.0: Unsafe.
- Netscape Navigator 7.0: Unsafe.
- Mozilla 1.0: Unsafe.
- Opera 3.6 – 4.0: Unsafe
- Opera 5.0 – 6.0: Unsafe.
- Konqueror: Unsafe.

10.10 glyph-orientation-horizontal and glyph-orientation-vertical Properties

The `glyph-orientation-horizontal` and `glyph-orientation-vertical` properties proposed under CSS3 are designed to solve a common problem when formatting mixed Western and non-Western scripts together, because the orientation of one is usually "wrong" in relation to the other. If, for example, Japanese text is arranged in vertical columns, any English words that appear are usually rotated 90 degrees, which is the default way of displaying Western-language text in this format. These two properties are intended to allow you to set the rotation value for a particular type of script, correcting this type of problem.

Both `glyph-orientation-horizontal` and `glyph-orientation-vertical` take the same values: `auto` (the default) or an angle of rotation value. The four standard rotation values are `0deg`, `90deg`, `180deg` and `270deg`, and these are the values any conforming browser must support. The `auto` value is equal to the `0deg` value, which sets the glyph or character to its default rotation position inline to the text. The corresponding degree values rotate the character or glyph in respect to this initial state. It is important to realize that `0deg` does not necessarily mean "up" — for example, English text in a vertical column with Japanese text is normally placed on its "side," which would seem to correspond to a value of `90deg`, but because it is the default, is in fact equal to `0deg`.

The functional difference between the two values is that you would use `glyph-orientation-horizontal` to rotate glyphs that are laid out horizontally (i.e. mainly English with mixed Japanese characters) or `glyph-orientation-vertical` for rotating characters that are laid out vertically (i.e., main Japanese text mixed with English words).

Listing 10.10 shows how this could be put to use for the `glyph-orientation-vertical` property, which gets the basic idea across for the two properties. In this first case no rotation is applied to the English words, whereas in the second case `glyph-orientation-vertical` is set to a value of `270deg`, rotating the English letters so that they are oriented properly.

Listing 10.10	*glyph-orientation-vertical Example Code*

```
<html>
<head>
<title>glyph-orientation-vertical Example</title>
</head>
<style>
span.chinese {font-family: ËÎÎå,MingLiU; font-weight: bold;
font-size: 40pt}
span.english {font-family: arial; font-weight: bold; font-size:
40pt}
span.english-oriented {font-family: arial; font-weight: bold;
font-size: 40pt; glyph-orientation-vertical: 270deg}
</style>
<body>

<div style="layout-flow: horizontal">
<span class="chinese">
&#27489;&#36814;&#28459;&#28216;</span>
<span class="english">PanelX &#150;</span>
<span class="chinese">
&#24179;&#38754;&#39023;&#31034;&#23631;&#26989;&#30028;&#30340;
</span>
<span class="english">Portal </span>
<span class="chinese">&#21450;</span>
<span class="english">Exchange</span>
</div>
```

Listing 10.10	*glyph-orientation-vertical Example Code (continued)*

```
<div style="layout-flow: vertical-ideographic">
<span class="chinese">
&#27489;&#36814;&#28459;&#28216;</span>
<span class="english-oriented">PanelX &#150;</span>
<span class="chinese">
&#24179;&#38754;&#39023;&#31034;&#23631;&#26989;&#30028;&#30340;<
/span>
<span class="english-oriented">Portal </span>
<span class="chinese">&#21450;</span>
<span class="english-oriented">Exchange</span>
</div>

</body>
</html>
```

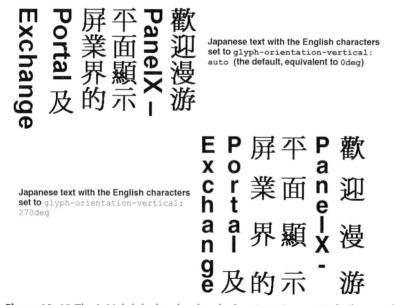

Figure 10–10 The initial default value for glyph-orientation-vertical when applied to English text, and when set to 270deg.

10.11 text-script Property

The `text-script` property is to non-Western text what `word-spacing` is for Western-language text. Many Asian and Middle-Eastern styles of writing have their own ways of properly justifying text across a line. This may seem like a simple process, but compressing or stretching a line of characters so that they are justified across a full line (or column, for vertical text) can be a tricky thing when you consider that cursive scripts like Arabic join their individual "letters" together, or that some South-East Asian scripts, like Thai or Lao, do not leave spaces between words.

The `text-script` property has seven proposed values: `auto` (the default), `inter-word`, `inter-ideograph`, `inter-cluster`, `kashida`, `newspaper` and `distribute`. When the `auto` value is used, it is up to the browser to do what it thinks is best, which is essentially a trade-off between performance and the quality of the presentation. The `inter-word` value simply spreads the text evenly across the line by increasing the space between words. In a similar manner, the `inter-ideograph` value adds sufficient spacing between each individual Chinese, Japanese or Korean character. So if you used `inter-ideograph` on a line of mixed Chinese and English text, for example, you'd get even spacing between each Chinese character but no extra spacing between the individual letters making up the English words. The `inter-cluster` value works the same way as `inter-ideograph`, but is intended for use with South-East Asian scripts, like Khmer, Lao, Myanmar and Thai. Similarly, the `kashida` value works the same way as `inter-ideograph`, but is intended for Arabic text. The `newspaper` value is comprised of a sophisticated mix of the `inter-word` and `inter-letter` spacing. This value tells the browser to first try to compress letter spacing to ensure that words fit on a line, and if that doesn't work, expand the spaces between the words, and then increase the spacing in the letters between the words, if necessary. This is relatively processor-intensive, and when implemented should be used sparingly. This value would be most effective when arranging text in relatively narrow columns — much like what you see in most newspapers. The `distribute` value works in much the same way as `newspaper`, but it does not discriminate between letter and word spacing. If you used this value on a combination of Chinese and English text, you could expect to see even spacing between all characters, both Chinese and English. In addition to these values, there are also the ubiquitous `initial` and `inherit` values, the former likely to become common to all CSS3 properties (possibly *all* CSS properties) and the second and the latter common to the vast majority of CSS properties since the CSS2 specification. The `initial` value takes on whatever the default value for a property is, which in this case is `auto`, and the `inherit` value takes on whatever parent value may already be set for this property.

Most of the effects — and values — of this property are mimicked by the Internet Explorer-specific property `text-justify`. For more information on this property, as well as a working code sample whose effects are displayed, see `text-justify` in Chapter 11, "Text Property Extensions."

10.12 min-font-size and max-font-size Properties

You might think that the new CSS3 properties called `min-font-size` and `max-font-size` would be used for setting the minimum and maximum font size that could be used globally on a page — perhaps in cases where you have a dynamic value assigned to stretching or squeezing font sizes. Instead, `min-font-size` and `max-font-size` are designed to be used in a very specific case; they are only for use in conjunction with the `text-align-last` property when it is set to `size`.

`text-align-last: size` tells the browser to stretch or squeeze the content on the final line of text in a paragraph (or some other block element) so that it fits across the line. This includes changing the font size of the text in order to make that content fit. So `min-font-size` and `max-font-size` are used to set the upper and lower constraints. Both `min-font-size` and `max-font-size` can take one of four values: a specific numeric font-size value, `auto` (the default), `initial` and `inherit`. `initial` and `inherit` are values common to all CSS3 text properties — `initial` is used to explicitly set a property to its normal default value, and `inherit` takes on whatever parent value may already been set for the property. The `auto` value means there is no default limit to the minimum or maximum size for the font. You can expect to use the numeric font size value the most with these properties, as they give you direct control over how much a font in the final line of text in a block element can be re-sized. The following code snippet provides an idea as to how you can expect to use these properties:

```
<style>
text-align-last: size
min-font-size: 10pt
max-font-size: 30pt
</style>
```

For more information on the `text-align-last` property, see Chapter 11, "Text Property Extensions."

10.13 text-justify-trim Property

This CSS3 text property is designed primarily for use with Asian character sets to help set the type of justification to be used. Specifically, it compresses things at the font level, so that any spaces that occur around a given character are reduced — all without actually affecting the character itself.

The `text-justify-trim` property has five values: `none`, `punctuation`, and `punctuation-and-kana`, as well as `initial` and `inherit`. The `none` value ensures that no font space between characters and punctuation is removed. The `punctuation` value (which is the default) allows the browser to remove any extra space from punctuation characters. The `punctuation-and-kana` value allows for full font-space compression between punctuation characters and regular characters. The `initial` value is a way to specifically set a property to its default value (useful on those occasions when you may not know what that is offhand) and the `inherit` value forces the browser to take on whatever parent value may exist for the property.

It should be noted that this value should not be used if `text-script` is set to `inter-word` because these two properties would conflict with each other.

10.14 line-break Property

The `line-break` property is a CSS3 property designed to be applied primarily to Chinese, Japanese and Korean (CJK) character sets. This property sets the type of line-breaking rule to be applied to text. It has four values: `normal` and `strict`, plus the usual `initial` and `inherit` values. The `normal` value (which is the default) sets the normal line-breaking mode for CJK characters, which is typically between any small katakana or hiragana characters that may appear on a line. When the `strict` value is used, these same small katakana or hiragana characters are not used to start a line of text. The `initial` value sets the property to its default value, and the `inherit` value tells the browser to take whatever parent value may be available for the property.

10.15 word-break-cjk Property

The `word-break-cjk` property is designed to give the Web author control over how line breaks should occur within words in Chinese, Japanese or Korean text (the "CJK" of `word-break-cjk`") when mixed with text from another language.

There are five values for this property: `normal`, `break-all`, and `keep-all`, as well as the ubiquitous `initial` and `inherit`. The `normal` value is the default, which allows line-breaking behavior within characters. The `break-all` value works the same way as `normal`, but is intended for Asian characters, and yet is designed to allow any non-Asian characters to break as they normally might. The `keep-all` value is designed not to allow word breaks for Chinese, Japanese or Korean characters, although it works the same way as `normal` for any non-Asian language. The `initial` value can be used to force the property to its default value, and the `inherit` value tells the property to take on whatever parent value may be available.

This property works in exactly the same way as the `word-break` property specific to Internet Explorer. For more information on this property (including a practical example), see the section devoted to this property in Chapter 11, "Text Property Extensions."

The values for both `word-break-cjk` and `word-break-inside` are combined within the shortcut value `word-break`.

10.16 word-break-inside Property

The `word-break-inside` property is part of the same small family of properties as `word-break-cjk`, and it also deals with where line breaks should occur in text.

The `word-break-inside` property has four values: `normal` and `hyphenate`, as well as the usual `initial` and `inherit`. The `normal` value is the default and tells the browser that any given word should stay on a single line. This value can be overridden if the `word-break-cjk` value is set to `break-all`, or if the `wrap-option` property (see below) is set to `emergency`. The `hyphenate` value tells the browser that it is okay to break a given word at an appropriate point within the word (such as between syllables, a hyphenation technique typical of Western languages). The `initial` value is CSS3's way of allowing you to explicitly set the default value for a given property when you don't know what it is, and the `inherit` value takes on any parent value that may have been set.

The values for both `word-break-inside` and `word-break-cjk` are combined within the shortcut value `word-break`.

10.17 word-break Property

The `word-break` property is a shortcut property for setting the values for both the `word-break-inside` and `word-break-cjk` properties. It should be noted that there are currently two versions of this property: one with this same name that is Internet

Explorer-specific and is functionally equivalent to `word-break-cjk`; and the proposed CSS3 version, which goes further and incorporates the values for `word-break-inside` as well.

The `word-break` property's values are `normal`, `break-all`, `keep-all` and `hyphenate`, as well as the usual `initial` and `inherit`. Its default value is `normal`, which is similarly the same default value for `word-break-inside` and `word-break-cjk`.

Since Microsoft creates Internet Explorer and is an active member of the World Wide Web Consortium (and therefore had a hand in the creation of the CSS3 text module), you can probably expect that future editions of Internet Explorer will match the functionality of the CSS3 version of the `word-break` property.

10.18 wrap-option Property

The `wrap-option` property is designed to provide direct control over how text should or should not wrap when it reaches the end of the line of the block it is contained within. This may seem rather odd at first, since you could argue that the same sort of thing could be accomplished using the `<br>` tag to arbitrarily truncate a line of text, but the `wrap-option` property tells the browser to be on the lookout for an imbedded linefeed character — specifically, the `U+000A` character block, which is typically used by text-editing programs to denote a line break. How the browser is to deal with the text that comes before and after this character depends on the value used.

The `wrap-option` property has six values: `wrap`, `hard-wrap`, `soft-wrap` and `emergency`, as well as the usual `initial` and `inherit` values. `wrap`, which is the default value, tells the browser to wrap the text in the target block at the best available opportunity to do so, using whatever settings for `line-break` and `word-break` may be present. As well, this value is to give priority in making a line break whenever an embedded linefeed character is encountered within the text. `hard-wrap` instead tells the browser to only wrap text when it encounters an embedded linefeed character. The `soft-wrap` value is similar to `wrap`, save for the fact that no line-breaking algorithm is invoked, so that it is entirely up to the browser to determine where to best break the line. The oddly named `emergency` value also works similarly to `wrap`, except that it is intended to break very long words that may appear within a line when ordinarily they would be constrained by the `line-break` or `word-break` properties — it essentially prevents a long word from awkwardly "protruding" from the end of a block of text. The `initial` value is a way of setting a property explicitly to its default value. The `inherit` value simply tells the property to take on whatever parent value may already be present.

10.19 linefeed-treatment Property

Like the `wrap-option` property (as well its fellow white-space sub-family of properties), the `linefeed-treatment` property is designed to work with embedded linefeed characters. In this case, when a `U+000A` character block is encountered, this property determines how to interpret this character as a linefeed.

This property has nine values, `auto`, `ignore`, `preserve`, `treat-as-space`, `treat-as-zero`, `width-space`, and `ignore-if-after-linefeed`, as well as the `initial` and `inherit` values. The `auto` value is the default, and tells the browser that it should treat linefeed characters as either a space character, a space character with zero width, or no character at all (the choice is to be made by the browser). The `ignore` value does just that — any linefeed characters are treated as if they weren't there. The `preserve` value says that linefeed characters indicate a boundary to the current text and sets a visual linefeed. The `treat-as-space` transforms any linefeed characters into a space character, nullifying their effect. The `treat-as-zero-width-space` is more specific, telling the browser that it should treat linefeeds like a space character with no width. The `ignore-after-linefeed` is there for cases where they may be multiple sequential linefeed characters — only one linefeed is accepted. The `initial` value is a way to explicitly set a property to its default value. Finally, the `inherit` value takes on whatever parent value may pre-exist for this property.

10.20 white-space-treatment Property

The `white-space-treatment` property falls into the same sub-family as `wrap-option`, `linefeed-treatment`, `all-space-treatment` and `white-space`, each dealing with embedded space- or line-formatting characters. The `white-space-treatment` property works with embedded space characters (`U+0020`) along with any other white-space characters, with the exception of linefeeds.

It has seven values, `ignore`, `preserve`, `ignore-if-before-linefeed`, `ignore-if-after-linefeed`, and `ignore-if-surrounding-linefeed`, plus `initial` and `inherit`. The `ignore` value transforms white-space characters into no character at all. The `preserve` value retains the effects of the white spaces, extending the spaces between words or characters. The `ignore-if-before-linefeed` discards any spacing characters appearing immediately before a linefeed character, and the `ignore-if-after-linefeed` character does the same for any white spaces that appear after a linefeed. The `ignore-if-surrounding-linefeed` value is the default value, eliminating any spacing characters appearing either immediately before or after a linefeed character. The `initial` value is equal to the default value for the property, and `inherit` takes on whatever parent value that may be available for this property.

10.21 all-space-treatment Property

The `all-space-treatment` property also belongs to the sub-family of properties dealing with embedded spacing and linefeed characters.

The property has four values: `preserve` and `collapse`, as well as the ubiquitous `initial` and `inherit` values common to all CSS3 properties. The `preserve` value retains the intended effect of all spacing characters, such as linefeeds and spaces — even the tab character (U+0009), which sets an equivalent to 8 spaces of width. The `collapse` value does just the opposite, rendering all embedded linefeeds, tabs, spaces and so on as a single space. The `initial` value allows a Web author to explicitly set a property to its default. The `inherit` value takes on whatever parent value may be present.

10.22 white-space Property

The `white-space` property is a shortcut property at the head of the sub-family of properties controlling embedded white-space characters. As a shortcut property, it is a bit of an oddball, as its values actually set a bunch of relational values for its sub-properties; in effect, you get several values set at once. This makes sense, since some of the effects of specific values for some of the properties in this sub-family could easily conflict with each other — that is, trying to retain all spacing characters using `all-space-treatment: preserve` while `white-space-treatment: ignore` is set will make for a very confused browser.

It takes seven properties: `normal`, `pre`, `nowrap`, `pre-wrap`, and `pre-lines`, as well as `initial` and `inherit`. The following table shows the meaning of each value, corresponding to the equivalent set of values for its sub-properties.

Table 10.1 *Relationship of Values for the white-space Property*

white-space	wrap-option	linefeed-treatment	white-space-treatment	all-space-treatment
normal	wrap	auto	ignore-if-surrounding-linefeed	collapse
pre	hard-wrap	preserve	preserve	preserve
nowrap	hard-wrap	auto	ignore-if-surrounding-linefeed	collapse
pre-wrap	wrap	preserve	preserve	preserve
pre-lines	wrap	preserve	ignore-if-surrounding-linefeed	collapse

With the `normal` value, spacing characters are collapsed and linefeeds are treated as if they are spaces. The `pre` value works very much like the `<pre>` tag: linefeeds and spaces are preserved. `nowrap` essentially ignores any linefeed characters or extra white spaces, and any lengthy words may overflow the "box" they are contained within. `pre-wrap` works the same way as the `pre` value, but it preserves the effects of any linefeed characters it encounters. `pre-lines` is similar to `pre-wrap`, except that it ignores any additional characters that may surround any linefeed characters, and collapses any other white space characters. The `normal` value is the default value, which is also the value `initial` takes. `inherit` takes on whatever parent value may already exist for this property.

The following code snippet shows how this property could be put to use, treating text in paragraphs that contain embedded spacing and linefeed characters equivalent to the way the `<pre>` tag works:

```
<style>
p white-space: pre
</style>
```

This code snippet differs from how the `<pre>` tag would itself work in that it is only applied to embedded characters — any paragraph that does not contain these characters will be displayed normally.

10.23 text-overflow-mode Property

The `text-overflow-mode` property is part of a small sub-family of properties (which also includes `text-overflow-ellipsis` and `text-overflow`) that control what happens when text overflows its boundary at the end of a line, and the `overflow` property prevents the text from simply flowing to a new line. This property allows you to present "hint" characters, like an ellipsis ("..."), suggesting to the viewer that more text is to follow.

The `text-overflow-mode` property has five properties: `clip`, `ellipsis`, and `ellipsis-word`, as well as `initial` and `inherit`. The `clip` value simply snips off the end of the text without leaving any "hint" characters behind. When `ellipsis` is used, an ellipsis is inserted at the *end of the line* where the text overflow occurs. The `ellipsis-word` value works the same way, but instead of inserting an ellipsis at the end of the line, it replaces the final word that would have overflowed the line — so instead of the ellipsis appearing right up against the boundary of the containing box, it simply replaces what would have been the word prior to the normal ellipsis appearing. The symbol used to indicate the "hint" (which need not be an ellipsis) is controlled by the `text-overflow-ellipsis` property. The `initial` value is equivalent to the default value, which in this case is `clip`, and the `inherit` value takes on any parent value that may be present.

10.24 text-overflow-ellipsis Property

The `text-overflow-ellipsis` property controls the type of "hint" character that is displayed when text overflows its line and its behavior is constrained by the `overflow` property from simply flowing to the next line. This property is designed to work in conjunction with `text-overflow-mode`: `text-overflow-mode` sets where the hint character should appear, and `text-overflow-ellipsis` controls what should appear.

`text-overflow-ellipsis` has three unique values, each of which can take strings of text to help define what is displayed: `ellipsis-end`, `ellipsis-after` and a URL value. The `ellipsis-end` value allows you to set a specific string or character as the "hint" character within the line of text that has overflowed. `ellipsis-after` does the same, but instead of placing the text or character at the end of a line of text, it is instead placed *after* (that is, outside of) the text flow. The URL value allows you to point to an image file containing whatever you want to use as a hint character. `text-overflow-ellipsis` can also take the `initial` and `inherit` values. The `initial` value is equivalent to the default, which in this case is `ellipsis-end`, and displays a typical ellipsis character ("..."). `inherit` takes on any available parent value for this property.

10.25 text-overflow Property

The text-overflow property is the head of the sub-family of text overflow properties, working as a shortcut property for text-overflow-mode and text-overflow-ellipsis. It takes on all of the values belonging to those two other properties, namely clip, ellipsis, and ellipsis-word, plus the ellipsis-end, ellipsis-after and URL values followed by a string. initial and inherit are also available.

The following code snippet shows how this property might be put to work, in this case adding an ellipsis hint image in place of the final word that would have been clipped.

```
<style>
overflow: clip
text-overflow: ellipsis-word
URL(http://www.fakesite.com/ellipsis-image.gif)
</style>
```

10.26 kerning-mode Property

The kerning-mode property controls kerning effects. Kerning refers to the spaces in between individual letters comprising a word — a word that does not use kerning generally occupies more horizontal space than one that is kerned.

kerning-mode has three unique values in addition to the initial and inherit values common to all CSS3 properties: none, pair and contextual. The none value is the default, and does not set any kerning value. The pair value enables what is known as pair kerning, which removes excess space between adjacent letter pairs. For example, it would remove the space between the overlying part of the letter "Y" when it is adjacent to a small letter like "o." This value is for use with Western languages, as well as Greek and Cyrillic languages. The contextual value is meant for Asian character sets, and, like pair, it removes any space it can between characters, depending, of course, on the individual characters. The initial value takes on the default value for kerning-mode, which in this case is none, and the inherit value takes on whatever parent value may pre-exist for kerning-mode.

10.27 kerning-pair-threshold Property

The `kerning-pair-threshold` property controls the font-size value at which pair kerning is activated. This value exists because when font sizes are very small, kerning may make letters run together and thus make words unreadable.

The `kerning-pair-threshold` property has two unique values, `auto` and a length value, in addition to the usual `initial` and `inherit` values. The `auto` value is the default and tells the browser to choose its own value for when pair kerning should kick in. The length value explicitly tells the browser the font size at which (or above) pair kerning should take effect. The `initial` value forces the default value, and the `inherit` value takes on whatever parent value may already be set.

The following code snippet shows how this might be used — for example, if a script font is being used throughout a sample page at various sizes; the `kerning-pair-threshold` property kicks in only when, in this case, the font size being used is 12 points in size:

```
<style>
body {font-family: Vladimir Script; font-size: 12pt}
div {font-size: 11pt}
kerning-pair-threshold: 12pt
</style>
```

10.28 punctuation-trim Property

The `punctuation-trim` property is designed to be used with Asian character sets and tells the browser whether or not it should trim the leading space around punctuation characters — such as brackets — when they are adjacent to a character.

The `punctuation-trim` property has two unique values, `none` and `start`, as well as the ubiquitous `initial` and `inherit` values. The `none` value tells the browser not to trim the leading edge off of a punctuation mark, so it takes up the same width as a typical character; this is the default value. The `start` value instead tells the browser to remove any leading space in front of a punctuation mark. The `initial` value takes on the default value, and the `inherit` value takes on whatever parent value that may exist.

Figure 10–11 shows the intended difference between the two values for `punctuation-trim`. Notice how the bracket characters and the period all take up the same amount of leading space as a full character.

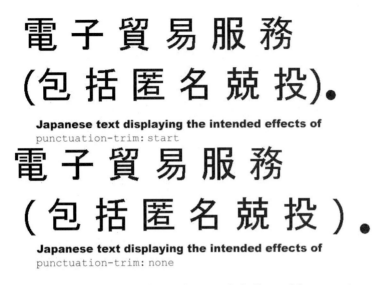

Figure 10–11 Mock-up displaying the intended effects of the two unique values for punctuation-trim.

10.29 text-line-through Set of Properties

The `text-line-through` set of properties is a collection of four proposed properties designed to control the type of line that can be displayed through text — usually called "struck-through." This effect is usually reserved for denoting deleted text that needs to remain visible. In addition to the shortcut `text-line-through` property, this family contains `text-line-color`, `text-line-through-mode` and `text-line-through-style`.

This family of properties works in exactly the same way as its "sister" families `text-overline` and `text-underline` — the functionality is equivalent save for where the "line" decoration is placed in relation to the text.

text-line-through-color Property

The `text-line-through-color` property allows you to set the color of a struck-through line. It can either take the browser's default value (if it is explicitly not set) or a specific color value, using the full gamut of color naming conventions available under CSS (named color values, RGB, hexadecimal color values, compressed hex and so on — for more details on setting color values, see Chapter 13, "Color").

In addition to explicit color values, `text-line-through-color` can also take on the values `initial` and `inherit`. `initial` takes on the default value, which may differ from browser to browser, but in most cases will be black. The `inherit` value takes on whatever parent value may already have been applied to this property.

text-line-through-mode Property

The `text-line-through-mode` property determines whether only the words meant to be struckthrough are in fact struckthrough, or if the white space between words is also struckthrough. There are two unique values: `continuous` and `words`; `continuous` is the default value.

The `continuous` value is how struckthrough lines are currently rendered in all browsers. If you strike through more than one word, the space between those words will also be display as being struckthrough. The `words` value enables the Web author to set things so that only the words are actually struckthrough.

In addition to the unique values for this property, `text-line-through-mode` can also take on the values `initial` and `inherit`. `initial` uses the default value, and `inherit` takes on whatever parent value may apply to this property.

text-line-through-style Property

The `text-through-style` property can take any one of nine unique values: `none`, `solid`, `double`, `dotted`, `thick`, `dashed`, `dot-dash`, `dot-dot-dash` and `wave`. These values are modeled on equivalent values available for the `border` family of properties (for those unfamiliar with them, the last three values — `dot-dash`, `dot-dot-dash` and `wave` — are proposed additions to the `border` family under CSS3). These values are all self-descriptive, displaying exactly the type of struck-through line you'd expect from their names.

In addition to these unique values, `text-line-through-style` can also take on the values `initial` and `inherit`. `initial` is equal to the default value, which in this case is `none`, and the `inherit` value takes on whatever parent value may apply to this property.

text-line-through Property

The `text-line-through` property is the shortcut property for this sub-family of properties, allowing you to quickly set several strike-through values at once. As such it can take on all of the values belonging to the other properties: a color value (taken from `text-line-through`), `continuous` and `words` (derived from `text-line-through-mode`), and `none`, `solid`, `double`, `dotted`, `thick`, `dashed`, `dot-dash`, `dot-dot-dash` and wave (taken from `text-line-through-style`), as well as the usual generic `initial` and `inherit` values.

Listing 10.11 depicts several combinations of the values for `text-line-through`, showing the differences in strike-through formatting available. The results of this code are mocked-up in Figure 10–12.

Listing 10.11	*text-line-through Code Example*

```
<html>
<head>
<title>text-line-through Example</title>
<style>
body {font: normal 25px Arial, Helvetica, sans-serif}
</style>
</head>
<body>
<span style="text-line-through: black, continuous, none">This text
is set to the default value for <code>text-line-through</code>, so
no overline is in fact displayed.</span>
<p>
<span style="text-line-through: red, word, none">This text uses
<code>text-line-through</code> to change the color of the text,
and set the overline to word-only mode.</span>
</p>
<p>
<span style="text-line-through: black, continuous, wave">This text
shows how you can use <code>text-line-through</code> to change the
style of overline to a wave.</span>
</p>
<p>
<span style="text-line-through: black, continuous,
dot-dot-dash">This text shows how you can use
<code>text-line-through</code> to change the style of overline to
a dot-dot-dash.</span>
</p>
<p>
<span style="text-line-through: yellow, continuous, dou-ble">This
text shows how you can use <code>text-line-through</code> to
change the style of overline to a yellow double-line.</span>
</p>
```

Listing 10.11	*text-line-through Code Example (continued)*

```
<p>
<span style="text-line-through: green, word, thick">This text
mixes a bunch of values together for
<code>text-line-through</code>; it's green in color, and only the
words are overlined using a thick style.</span>
</p>
</body>
</html>
```

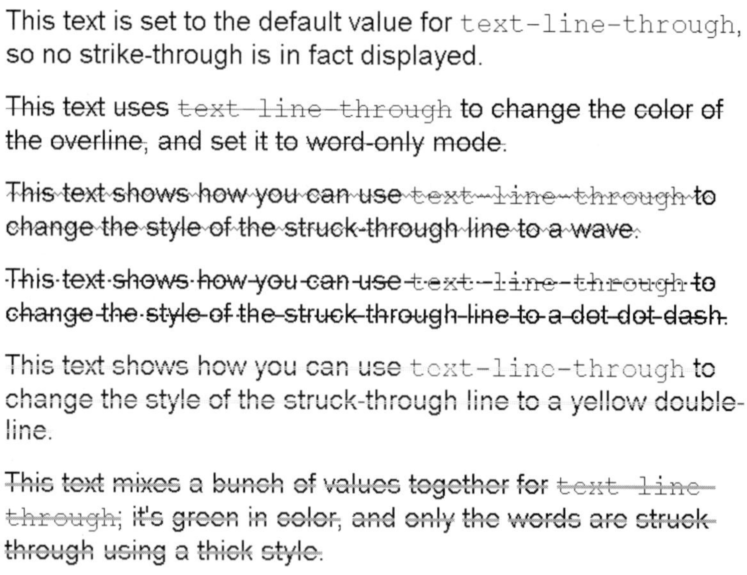

This text is set to the default value for `text-line-through`, so no strike-through is in fact displayed.

~~This text uses~~ ~~text-line-through~~ ~~to change the color of the overline, and set it to word-only mode.~~

~~This text shows how you can use~~ ~~text-line-through~~ ~~to change the style of the struck-through line to a wave.~~

~~This text shows how you can use~~ ~~text-line-through~~ ~~to change the style of the struck-through-line-to-a-dot-dot-dash.~~

This text shows how you can use `text-line-through` to change the style of the struck-through line to a yellow double-line.

~~This text mixes a bunch of values together for~~ ~~text-line-through; it's green in color, and only the words are struck-through using a thick style.~~

Figure 10–12 Various values for text-line-through displayed in a mock-up.

10.30 text-overline Set of Properties

The `text-overline` set of properties is a set of four properties providing control over the type of line that can be displayed above text. Overlines are usually used as a type of emphasis. In addition to the shortcut `text-overline` property, there are also `text-overline`, `text-overline-mode` and `text-overline-style`.

This family of properties works in exactly the same way as its "sister" properties `text-line-through` and `text-underline` — the functionality is equivalent save for where the "line" decoration is placed in relation to the text.

text-overline-color Property

The `text-overline-color` property allows you to set the color of an overline. It can either take the default auto value (which in most cases is black, *not* "link blue") or a specific color value, using the full gamut of color naming conventions available under CSS (named color values, RGB, RGBA, hexadecimal color values and so on — for more details on setting color values, see Chapter 13, "Color").

In addition to explicit color values, `text-overline-color` can also take on the values `initial` and `inherit`. `initial` takes on the default value — which may differ from browser to browser, but in most cases will be black. The `inherit` value takes on whatever parent value may apply to this property.

text-overline-mode Property

The `text-overline-mode` property determines whether only the words meant to be overlined are in fact overlined, or if the whitespace between words is also overlined. There are two unique values, `continuous` and `words`; `continuous` is the default value.

The `continuous` value is how overlining is currently done in all browsers. If you overline more than one word, the space between those words will also display an overline. The `words` value enables the Web author to set things so that only the words are actually overlined instead.

In addition to the unique values for this property, `text-overline-mode` can also use the values `initial` and `inherit`. `initial` takes on the default value, which in this case is `continuous`, and the `inherit` value takes on whatever parent value may apply to this property.

text-overline-style Property

The `text-overline-style` property can take any one of nine unique values: `none`, `solid`, `double`, `dotted`, `thick`, `dashed`, `dot-dash`, `dot-dot-dash` and `wave`. These values are modeled on equivalent values available for the `border` family of properties (for those unfamiliar with them, the last three values — `dot-dash`, `dot-dot-dash` and `wave` — are proposed additions to the `border` family under CSS3). These values are all self-descriptive, displaying exactly the type of overline you'd expect from their names.

In addition to these unique values, `text-overline-style` can also take on the values `initial` and `inherit`. `initial` is equal to the default value, which in this case is none, and the `inherit` value takes on whatever parent value may apply to this property.

text-overline Property

The `text-overline` property is the shortcut property for this sub-family of properties, allowing you to quickly set several overline values at once. As such it can take on all of the values belonging to the other properties: a color value (taken from `text-overline`), `continuous`, `words` (derived from `text-overline-mode`), `none`, `solid`, `double`, `dotted`, `thick`, `dashed`, `dot-dash`, `dot-dot-dash` and `wave` (taken from `text-over-style`), as well as the usual `initial` and `inherit` generic CSS3 values.

Listing 10.12 depicts several combinations of the values for `text-overline`, showing the differences in overline formatting available. The results of this code are mocked-up in Figure 10–13.

Listing 10.12	*text-overline Example Code*

```
<html>
<head>
<title>text-overline Example</title>
<style>
body {font: normal 25px Arial, Helvetica, sans-serif}
</style>
</head>
<body>
<span style="text-overline: black, continuous, none">This text is
set to the default value for <code>text-overline</code>, so no
overline is in fact displayed.</span>
<p>
<span style="text-overline: red, word, none">This text uses
<code>text-overline</code> to change the color of the text, and
set the overline to word-only mode.</span>
</p>
<p>
<span style="text-overline: black, continuous, wave">This text
shows how you can use <code>text-overline</code> to change the
style of overline to a wave.</span>
</p>
<p>
<span style="text-overline: black, continuous, dot-dot-dash">This
text shows how you can use <code>text-overline</code> to change
the style of overline to a dot-dot-dash.</span>
</p>
```

Listing 10.12	*text-overline Example Code (continued)*

```
<p>
<span style="text-overline: yellow, continuous, double">This text
shows how you can use <code>text-overline</code> to change the
style of overline to a yellow double-line.</span>
</p>
<p>
<span style="text-overline: green, word, thick">This text mixes a
bunch of values together for <code>text-overline</code>; it's
green in color, and only the words are overlined using a thick
style.</span>
</p>
</body>
</html>
```

This text is set to the default value for text-overline, so no overline is in fact displayed.

This text uses text-overline to change the color of the overline, and set it to word-only mode.

This text shows how you can use text-overline to change the style of overline to a wave.

This text shows how you can use text-overline to change the style of overline to a dot-dot-dash.

This text shows how you can use text-overline to change the style of overline to a yellow double-line.

This text mixes a bunch of values together for text-overline; it's green in color, and only the words are overlined using a thick style.

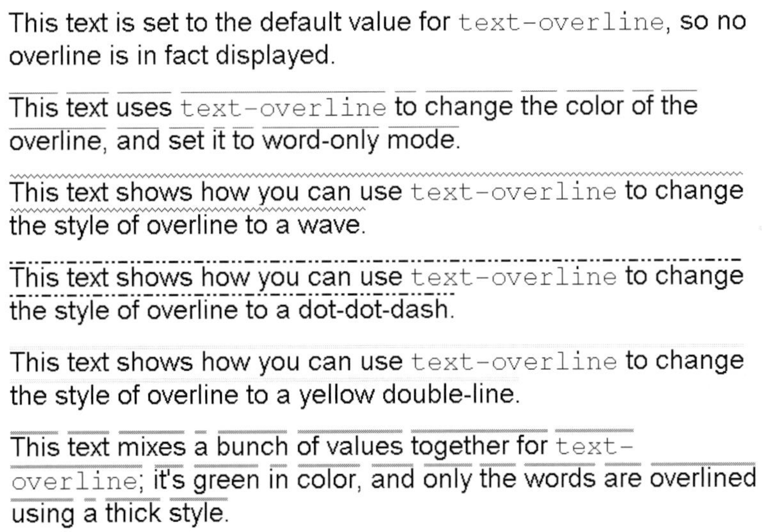

Figure 10–13 Various values for text-overline displayed in a mock-up.

10.31 text-underline Set of Properties

The `text-underline` set of properties is a set of five new properties providing greater control over the type of underline displayed under text. Underlines usually provide emphasis. In effect, these properties are intended to replace the deprecated <u> tag, and greatly expand it capabilities. In addition to the shortcut `text-underline` property, there are also `text-underline-color`, `text-underline-mode`, `text-underline-style` and `text-underline-position`.

This family of properties works in exactly the same way as its "sister" properties `text-overline` and `text-line-through` — its functionality is equivalent save for where the "line" decoration is placed.

text-underline-color Property

The `text-underline-color` property allows you to specifically set the color of an underline. It can either take the default `auto` value (which in most cases will render an underline in black, *not* "link blue") or a specific color value, using the full gamut of color naming conventions available under CSS (named color values, hexadecimal color values, compressed hex, RGBA and so on — for more details on setting color values, see Chapter 13, "Color").

In addition to explicit color values, `text-underline-color` can also take on the values `initial` and `inherit`. `initial` takes on the default value — which may differ from browser to browser, but in most cases is black. The `inherit` value takes on whatever parent value may apply to this property.

text-underline-mode Property

The `text-underline-mode` property determines whether only the words meant to be underlined are in fact underlined, or if the whitespace between words is also underlined. There are two unique values, `continuous` and `words`; `continuous` is the default value.

The `continuous` value is how underlining is currently done in all browsers. If you underline more than one word, the space between those two words will also display an underline. The `words` value enables the Web author to set things so that only the words are actually underlined instead.

In addition to the unique values for this property, `text-underline-mode` can also take on the values `initial` and `inherit`. `initial` takes on the default value, which in this case is `continuous`, and the `inherit` value takes on whatever parent value may apply to this property.

text-underline-style Property

The text-underline-style property can take any one of nine unique values: none, solid, double, dotted, thick, dashed, dot-dash, dot-dot-dash and wave. These values are modeled on equivalent values available for the border family of properties (for those unfamiliar with them, the last three values — dot-dash, dot-dot-dash and wave — are proposed additions to the border family under CSS3). These values are all self-descriptive, displaying exactly the type of underline you'd expect from their names.

In addition to these unique values, text-underline-style can also take on the values initial and inherit. initial is equal to the default value, which in this case is none, and the inherit value takes on whatever parent value may apply to this property.

text-underline-position Property

In Western languages, underlines typically run underneath the text they emphasize — there is a reason why they are called *under*lines, after all. But there are some circumstances where you might want to have the underline closer or further away from the text it is meant to emphasize. This is part of the intent of the text-underline-position property. It can take on one of four unique values: auto-pos, before-edge, after-baseline and after-edge. This property is unique to the sub-family of text-underline properties — neither text-overline nor text-line-through has an equivalent property.

When used with text in a horizontal layout — typical of Western languages — the auto-pos value will place the underline underneath the run of text; when applied specifically to a vertical run of Japanese text (set using lang), auto-pos will instead place the underline prior to the edge of the text. The before-edge value explicitly tells the browser to place the underline prior to the edge of the text, so the effect is as if the letters are sitting directly on the underline, rather than floating above it. This value is the same as when auto-pos is set to Japanese text, but in this case before-edge can be used against any language. The after-baseline value positions the underline immediately under the baseline — this is "closer" to the letters than the default, and can be expected to cut across any letters that descend across the baseline of the text. The after-edge value produces what is known as an "accounting" underline, which places the underline well underneath the baseline, ensuring that it does not cut across any descending letters. The intent in accounting circles with this type of underlining is to ensure that the underline does not cut across things like commas separating values, ensuring that the value can still be easily read.

In addition to its unique values, text-underline-position can also take on the values initial and inherit. initial takes on the default value, in this case auto-pos , and the `inherit` value takes on whatever parent value may apply to this property.

text-underline Property

This property is the shortcut property for the `text-underline` sub-family of properties, allowing you to quickly set several underline values at once. As such it can take on all of the values belonging to the other properties: a color value (derived from `text-underline-color`), continuous, `words` (derived from `text-underline-mode`), none, solid, double, dotted, thick, dashed, dot-dash, dot-dot-dash and `wave` (taken from `text-underline-style`), and auto-pos , before-edge, after-baseline and `after-edge` (from `text-underline-position`), as well as the usual `initial` and `inherit` CSS3 values.

Listing 10.13 depicts several combinations of the values for `text-underline`, showing the differences in underline formatting available. The results of this code are mocked-up in Figure 10–14.

Listing 10.13	*text-underline Example Code*

```
<html>
<head>
<title>text-underline Example</title>
<style>
body {font: normal 25px Arial, Helvetica, sans-serif}
</style>
</head>
<body>
<span style="text-underline: black, continuous, none,
auto-pos">This text is set to the default value for
<code>text-underline</code>, so no underline is in fact
displayed.</span>
<p>
<span style="text-underline: red, word, none, auto-pos">This text
uses <code>text-underline</code> to change the color of the
underline, and set it to word-only mode.</span>
</p>
<p>
<span style="text-underline: black, continuous, wave,
auto-pos">This text shows how you can use
<code>text-underline</code> to change the style of underline to a
wave.</span>
</p>
```

| Listing 10.13 | *text-underline Example Code (continued)* |

```
<p>
<span style="text-underline: green, continuous, none,
after-edge">This text shows how you can use
<code>text-underline</code> to change the position of the
underline, which is far away from the letter (as well as its
color).</span>
</p>
<p>
<span style="text-underline: yellow, continuous, none,
before-edge">This text shows how you can use
<code>text-underline</code> to change the position of the
underline so that the letters "sit" on it; the color has also been
changed.</span>
</p>
<p>
<span style="text-underline: purple, word, dot-dot-dash,
after-baseline">This text mixes a bunch of values together for
<code>text-underline</code>; it's purple in color, only the words
are underlined using a dot-dot-dash style, and appears just under
the baseline.</span>
</p>
</body>
</html>
```

This text is set to the default value for text-underline, so no underline is in fact displayed.

This text uses text-underline to change the color of the underline, and set it to word-only mode.

This text shows how you can use text-underline to change the style of underline to a wave.

This text shows how you can use text-underline to change the position of the underline, which is far away from the letters (as well as its color).

This text shows how you can use text-underline to change the position of the underline so that the letters "sit" on it; the color has also been changed.

This text mixes a bunch of values together for text-underline; it's purple in color, only the words are underlined using a dot-dot-dash style, and appears just under the baseline.

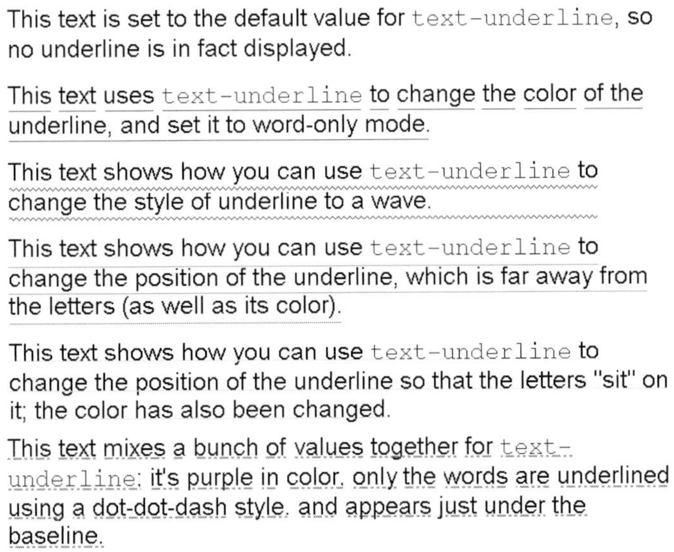

Figure 10–14 Various values for text-underline displayed in a mock-up.

10.32 text-blink Property

The text-blink property is intended solely to set text to blink — or not. In this way it works exactly the same as the relatively non-descriptive text-decoration property when set to the blink value.

The text-blink property has two values: none (the default) and blink. Once text is set to blink using this property, there is still no way to govern the rapidity or duration of the blinking text. The following code snippet provides an idea of how it could be put to use:

```
<em style="text-blink: blink">This text blinks. Annoying, isn't
it?</em>
```

This property also takes on the ubiquitous CSS3 values initial (which in this case is none) and inherit, which takes on any available parent value that may be present.

TEXT PROPERTY EXTENSIONS

Topics in This Chapter

- Internet Explorer Text-Formatting CSS Extensions
- `layout-flow` Property
- `writing-mode` Property
- layout-grid Sub-Family of Properties
- `text-autospace`
- `text-justify`
- `text-kashida-space`
- `text-underline-position`
- `word-break`
- `text-align-last`

11.1 Internet Explorer Text-Formatting CSS Extensions

In additional to the large number of font and text formatting CSS properties, Microsoft has been adding a number of its own such properties since version 5 of Internet Explorer. Many of these properties are designed to aid with the layout of text meant to be read vertically, as many Asian languages are often displayed. Still others are there to deal with the finer points of justification, how exactly words should "break," spacing out multilingual text and more. Microsoft has submitted many of these properties for consideration to the World Wide Web Consortium for inclusion in the official CSS3 specification.

This chapter is devoted wholly to looking at these extra text-layout CSS properties available in Internet Explorer. It also looks at any variations that may exist in the equivalent CSS3 modules for these properties.

11.2 layout-flow Property

The `layout-flow` property is designed to set the flow of text on the page. By "flow," we mean how successive words are laid out on a page, either horizontally, as with most Western languages, or vertically, as in many Asian languages. This property was first introduced in Internet Explorer 5.0 and continues to work in subsequent versions of this browser. This property has been deprecated in favor of the equally browser-specific `writing-mode` property, but it serves as a good introduction to the subject of laying out Asian character sets.

It has two values: `horizontal` (which is the default) and `vertical-ideographic`. The horizontal value is familiar to anyone reading this book: text flows from left to right, and from the top down. The `vertical-ideographic` setting is designed for dealing with Asian character layout, and sets the flow of the text from top to bottom, with subsequent text appearing to the left of the first line of characters.

Writing Chinese or other Asian character sets for use within a Web browser is usually done using a special program or interface designed for the purpose, and the resulting Web code is rendered as a Unicode character entity, which displays the appropriate symbol. So, for example, "歡" produces the Chinese character "歡", and &#36814 is rendered as "迎". Note also that you have to specify the correct font and have to have the Chinese language (or whatever language you are working with) plug-in for Internet Explorer. Typically you will be automatically prompted to download the correct language plug-in when code that calls for a different character set than you have on your system appears on a given Web page.

Listing 11.1 shows a mix of English and Chinese text rendered in first horizontal and vertical layout modes; the results are illustrated in Figure 11–1.

Listing 11.1	*layout-flow Example #1*

```
<html>
<head>
<title>layout-flow Example</title>
</head>
<style>
span.chinese {font-family: ËÎÌå,MingLiU; font-weight: bold;
font-size: 40pt}
span.english {font-family: arial; font-weight: bold;
font-size: 40pt}
</style>

<body>

<div style="layout-flow: horizontal">
<span class="chinese">
&#27489;&#36814;&#28459;&#28216;</span>
<span class="english">PanelX &#150;</span>
<span class="chinese">
&#24179;&#38754;&#39023;&#31034;&#23631;&#26989;&#30028;&#30340;
</span>
```

| Listing 11.1 | *layout-flow Example #1 (continued)* |

```
<span class="english">Portal </span>
<span class="chinese">&#21450;</span>
<span class="english">Exchange</span>
</div>

<hr />

<div style="layout-flow: vertical-ideographic">
<span class="chinese">
&#27489;&#36814;&#28459;&#28216;</span>
<span class="english">PanelX &#150;</span>
<span class="chinese">
&#24179;&#38754;&#39023;&#31034;&#23631;&#26989;&#30028;&#30340;
</span>
<span class="english">Portal </span>
<span class="chinese">&#21450;</span>
<span class="english">Exchange</span>
</div>
</body>
</html>
```

Figure 11–1   Sample Chinese and English text displayed in horizontal and vertical formats using layout-flow.

Notice the flow of characters in Figure 11–1: the flow of characters for the second `layout-flow: vertical-ideographic` example runs from the top-left of its section and then down, and renders the text and characters that follow it in successive lines to the left of the first line of text. When using `layout-flow` on a page that has paragraphs of alternate Western text and Asian characters, ensure you use a block-level element in order to ensure they do not run into each other on the page.

As you can see from Figure 11–1, the way Asian character sets are typically rendered in Internet Explorer is independent of the orientation of the flow of text, so each character appears the right way up regardless of the setting used for `layout-flow`. Not so for the English text used in this example, which as you can see, is rotated 90 degrees. This can be fixed, by setting the English text specifically to the horizontal setting, as you can see in Listing 11.2, whose results are seen in Figure 11–2.

Listing 11.2	*layout-flow Example #2*

```
<html>
<head>
<title>layout-flow Example 2</title>
</head>
<style>
span.chinese {font-family: ËÎÌå,MingLiU; font-weight: bold; font-
size: 35pt}
span.english {font-family: arial; font-weight: bold; font-size:
35pt}
span.english-horizontal {font-family: arial; font-weight: bold;
font-size: 35pt; layout-flow: horizontal}
</style>
<body>

<div style="layout-flow: vertical-ideographic">
<span class="chinese" lang="zh-tw">
&#27489;&#36814;&#28459;&#28216;</span>
<span class="english">PanelX &#150;</span>
<span class="chinese">
&#24179;&#38754;&#39023;&#31034;&#23631;&#26989;&#30028;&#30340;<
/span>
<span class="english">Portal </span>
<span class="chinese">&#21450;</span>
<span class="english">Exchange</span>
</div>

<hr />
```

Listing 11.2	*layout-flow Example #2 (continued)*

```
<div style="layout-flow: vertical-ideographic">
<span class="chinese" lang="zh-tw">
&#27489;&#36814;&#28459;&#28216;</span>
<span class="english-horizontal">PanelX &#150;</span>
<span class="chinese">
&#24179;&#38754;&#39023;&#31034;&#23631;&#26989;&#30028;&#30340;<
/span>
<span class="english-horizontal">Portal </span>
<span class="chinese">&#21450;</span>
<span class="english-horizontal">Exchange</span>
</div>

</body>
</html>
```

Figure 11–2 Combined Chinese and English text displayed first in vertical format, and then in a combined vertical and horizontal formats.

As you can see from Figure 11–2, the English text is rendered in horizontal format, but is still contained within the vertical format of the Chinese characters on the page. This does not simply rotate the English characters 90 degrees counterclockwise as you might expect, but renders the whole English word horizontal. Depending on your needs, you may find that the text layout is too wide when rendered in this manner, but it is worth knowing that it is available.

The `layout-flow` property sets the height of each vertical column automatically, dependent on the amount of content to be displayed. This can be overridden using the `height` property set to a specific value. All text that exceeds the selected value overflows into the following left column of characters.

Even though this is an addition first introduced in Internet Explorer 5.5, by version 6.0 of the browser this property has been deprecated by Microsoft in favor of the `writing-mode` property.

11.3 writing-mode Property

The `writing-mode` property was first introduced in a beta version of Internet Explorer 5.5, and has since become the favored way for handling the flow of non-Western character sets on a Web page. This is due to the fact that an expanded version of the `writing-mode` property has been incorporated into the CSS3 specification, and clearly sets the way in which text layout for different language sets is going to be accomplished in future standards-compatible browsers.

Like the `layout-flow` property, at the moment `writing-mode` has two working values which equate roughly with the text layout styles for Western and Asian languages. The default value is `lr-tb`, which stands for left-to-right, top-to-bottom, and equates with Western styles of text layout. The other value is `tb-rl`, which stands for top-to-bottom, right-to-left, which is the setting to be used for Asian languages. At first, this wouldn't seem to be radically different from the `layout-flow` property, and in fact, it isn't — the two properties are functionally equivalent. Like `layout-flow`, `writing-mode` does not rotate English or other Western letters back to their proper orientation automatically, a point which is illustrated in Figure 11–3, which compares equivalent code for `layout-flow` against `writing-mode`, as depicted in Listing 11.3.

Listing 11.3	*layout-flow versus writing-mode*

```
<html>
<head>
<title>writing-mode Example</title>
</head>
<style>
span.chinese {font-family: ËÎÌå,MingLiU; font-weight: bold; font-
size: 34pt}
span.english-horizontal-lf {font-family: arial; font-weight: bold;
font-size: 34pt; layout-flow: horizontal}
```

Listing 11.3 *layout-flow versus writing-mode (continued)*

```
span.english-horizontal-wm {font-family: arial; font-weight: bold;
font-size: 34pt; writing-mode: lr-tb}
</style>
<body>

<strong>Using <code>layout-flow</code></strong>
<div style="layout-flow: vertical-ideographic">
<span class="chinese">
&#27489;&#36814;&#28459;&#28216;</span>
<span class="english-horizontal-lf">PanelX &#150;</span>
<span class="chinese">
&#24179;&#38754;&#39023;&#31034;&#23631;&#26989;&#30028;&#30340;<
/span>
<span class="english-horizontal-lf">Portal </span>
<span class="chinese">&#21450;</span>
<span class="english-horizontal-lf">Exchange</span>
</div>

<hr />
<strong>Using <code>writing-mode</code></strong>
<div style="writing-mode: tb-rl">
<span class="chinese">
&#27489;&#36814;&#28459;&#28216;</span>
<span class="english-horizontal-wm">PanelX &#150;</span>
<span class="chinese">
&#24179;&#38754;&#39023;&#31034;&#23631;&#26989;&#30028;&#30340;<
/span>
<span class="english-horizontal-wm">Portal </span>
<span class="chinese">&#21450;</span>
<span class="english-horizontal-wm">Exchange</span>
</div>

</body>
</html>
```

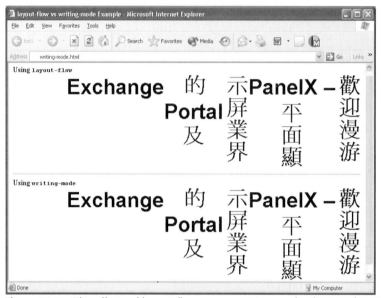

Figure 11–3   The effects of layout-flow versus writing-mode; they are functionally equivalent.

CSS3 and writing-mode

Under the CSS3 specification, in addition to the existing `lr-tb` and `tb-rl` values, there are four additional values: `rl-tb`, `tb-lr`, `bt-lr` and `bt-rl`. The `rl-tb` value flows the text from right-to-left, then top-to-bottom, a layout typical for both Hebrew and Arabic text. The `tb-lr` value displays the text from top-to-bottom, from left-to-right, which is as an alternate way of flowing Chinese and Japanese text. The `bt-lr` value flows text from bottom-to-top and then from left-to-right, a layout typical of the Mongolian language. Finally, the `bt-rl` value flows text from bottom-to-top, from right-to-left. There is no known writing system that actually uses a bottom-to-top, from right-to-left layout, but it is included solely for consistency's sake. None of these other values as yet work in Internet Explorer, but they are expected to when it fully adopts the CSS3 values for this property. An illustration of how the CSS3 values for `writing-mode` would be displayed can be seen in Figure 11–4, using English text.

writing-mode: lr-tb

The quick brown fox jumped
over the lazy dog.

writing-mode: rl-tb

depmuj xof nworb kciuq ehT
.god yzal eht revo

writing-mode: tb-rl

```
t f T        T f t            . r n          n r .
h o h        h o h            g e w          w e g
e x e        e x e            o v o          o v o
                              d o r          r o d
l j q        q j l              b            b
a u u        u u a          y d                d y
z m i        i m z          z e k          k e z
y p c        c p y          a p c          c p a
  e k        k e            l m i          i m l
d d            d d            u u            u u
o   b        b   o          e j q          q j e
g o r        r o g          h                    h
. v o        o v .          t x e          e x t
  e w        w e              o h          h o
  r n        n r              f T          T f
```

         writing-mode: tb-lr   **writing-mode: bt-rl**

Figure 11–4   The intended effects of the CSS3 writing-mode values on some sample text.

Figure 11–4 does takes some liberties, most notably by displaying English text in various non-standard formats instead of using the horizontal, left-to-right layout we've seen, but this example is just to show how these text flows would work while still retaining some legibility for English readers. Keep in mind that as of Internet Explorer 6.0 (or any other browser of the same vintage) none of these other CSS3 values work.

11.4 layout-grid Sub-Family of Properties

Beginning with Internet Explorer 5.0, Microsoft included a sub-family of properties relating to how Asian character sets should be spaced on a page. Though the analogy isn't exact, rough equivalents can be found for Western language sets with formatting properties like `line-height` and `letter-spacing` or `word-spacing`, which set how far apart lines of text should be from each other, and how those individual characters and words should be separated from each other. Asian character sets often use an explicit grid layout in which to set their characters, and the `layout-grid` sub-family of properties is designed to accommodate Web designers aiming to lay out text in Asian languages.

The layout-grid sub-family of properties consists of four separate main properties — `layout-grid-mode`, `layout-grid-type`, `layout-grid-line` and `layout-grid-char` — as well as the `layout-grid` shortcut property, which allows the user to set various aspects of the main properties all at once. None of these properties is typically used in isolation, as they are designed to be used together to achieve a particular layout effect.

layout-grid-mode Property

The `layout-grid-mode` property is used to set the type of grid to be employed, if any. It has four values: `both`, `none`, `line` and `char`. The `both` value, which is the default, enables both line and character grid types, and is designed primarily for text that may contain both block and inline elements — such as paragraph and blockquote elements for example. The `none` value ensures that no grid is present. The `line` value sets an element to only use a line grid, which is the setting recommended for use with inline elements, like blockquotes. The obverse of this value is the `char` value which sets a character grid for an element, and this is recommended for block-level elements.

For the most part, it is likely that you'll want to defer to the default `both` value, unless you want to set special formatting for any particular inline elements that you want to have stand out.

layout-grid-type Property

The `layout-grid-type` property controls the type of layout grid for rendering an element's content. There are three different values for it: `loose`, `strict` and `fixed`. `loose` is the default value, and is the setting designed to be employed for Japanese and Korean character sets. The `strict` value is designed for use for Chinese character sets, as well as Japanese Genko characters. The `fixed` value is the grid layout to be used when you want to display characters in a monospaced fashion, where each character takes up the same amount of space as every other character.

Listing 11.4 uses the `loose` and the `strict` values for `layout-grid-type` on the same piece of Chinese text, making it easier to see the difference it makes. You can see the results of this in Figure 11–5.

Listing 11.4 *layout-grid-type Sample Code*

```
<html>
<head>
<title>layout-grid-type Example</title>
</head>

<style>
div {font-family: PMingLiU; layout-grid-mode: both; layout-flow:
vertical-ideographic; font-weight: bold; font-size: 15pt}
</style>
<body>
<code>layout-grid-type: loose</code>
<div style="layout-grid-type: loose">
&#20320;&#21487;&#23559;&#20320;&#35201;&#20834;&#25237;&#30340;&
#36008;&#29289;&#21152;&#35387;&#25104;&#29305;&#23531;&#38917;&#
30446;&#65292;&#25110;&#29305;&#21029;&#35201;&#27714;&#38917;&#3
0446;&#12290;&#25152;&#26377;&#29305;&#23531;&#38917;&#30446;&#25
110;&#29305;&#21029;&#35201;&#27714;&#38917;&#30446;&#22343;&#263
71;&#24471;&#21040;&#29305;&#21029;&#34389;&#29702;
&#12290;&#20363;&#22914;&#65306;&#23427;&#20497;&#26371;&#34987;&
#25918;&#32622;&#22312;&#20834;&#25237;&#32178;&#38913;&#30340;&#
39318;&#38913;&#12289;&#21450;&#22312;&#20854;&#20182;&#32178;&#3
8913;&#19978;&#29992;&#21152;
&#31895;&#23383;&#39636;&#39023;&#31034;&#12290;&#21152;&#35387;&
#36027;&#29992;&#28858;&#27599;&#38917;&#32654;&#20803;&#20116;&#
21313;&#20803;&#12290;
</div>
<code>layout-grid-type: strict</code>
<div style="layout-grid-type: strict">
&#20320;&#21487;&#23559;&#20320;&#35201;&#20834;&#25237;&#30340;&
#36008;&#29289;&#21152;&#35387;&#25104;&#29305;&#23531;&#38917;&#
30446;&#65292;&#25110;&#29305;&#21029;&#35201;&#27714;&#38917;&#3
0446;&#12290;&#25152;&#26377;&#29305;&#23531;&#38917;&#30446;&#25
110;&#29305;&#21029;&#35201;&#27714;&#38917;&#30446;&#22343;&#263
71;&#24471;&#21040;&#29305;&#21029;&#34389;&#29702;
&#12290;&#20363;&#22914;&#65306;&#23427;&#20497;&#26371;&#34987;&
#25918;&#32622;&#22312;&#20834;&#25237;&#32178;&#38913;&#30340;&#
39318;&#38913;&#12289;&#21450;&#22312;&#20854;&#20182;&#32178;&#3
8913;&#19978;&#29992;&#21152;
&#31895;&#23383;&#39636;&#39023;&#31034;&#12290;&#21152;&#35387;&
#36027;&#29992;&#28858;&#27599;&#38917;&#32654;&#20803;&#20116;&#
21313;&#20803;&#12290;
</div>
</body>
</html>
```

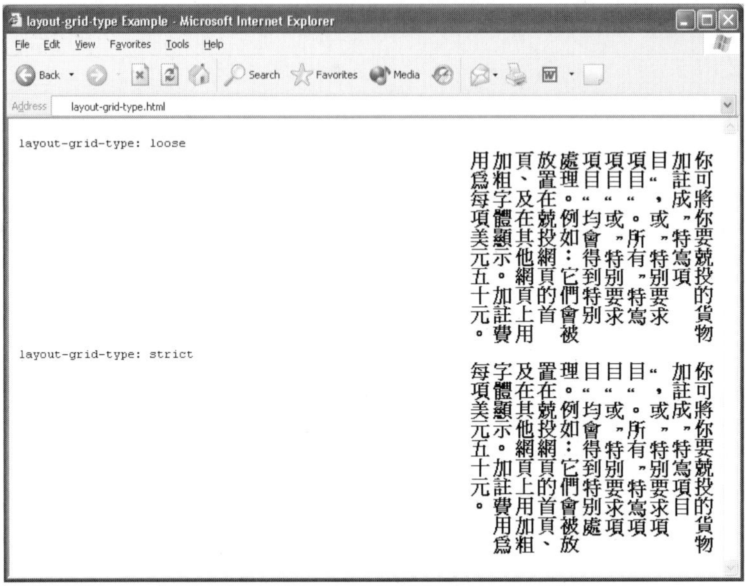

layout-grid-type: loose

layout-grid-type: strict

Figure 11–5   Internet Explorer showing the differences between a loose and a strict setting on the same Chinese text.

Though the difference between the two texts is subtle, it can be discerned in Figure 11–5. The initial block of Chinese text is set to `loose`, and the second to `strict`. With the `strict` setting, on average there are more characters contained within each vertical line. This is because only the ideographs, kanas and wide characters are snapped to the layout grid under the `strict` setting, and it also disables normal text justification — hence you tend to get more characters displayed in each vertical line.

With the `loose` setting, a constant width value is used on each character — so wide characters are narrowed, and narrow characters are widened slightly. The end result tends to be fewer characters per vertical line. The `fixed` value rigidly constrains all of the characters to fit into the same space, with any justification turned off.

layout-grid-line and layout-grid-char Properties

The `layout-grid-line` and `layout-grid-char` properties share a common purpose: they are there to help the Web author set the dimensions of the grid that the characters will be displayed upon. Too low a value, and the characters will begin to merge together, too high and you end up wasting space. The `layout-grid-line` is used to set the distance between vertical lines of characters, while `layout-grid-char` sets the spacing value for the character values contained within the line. The rough equivalent for each property in Western terms would be `line-height` and `letter-spacing`, respectively, except that we are talking about characters displayed vertically rather than horizontally.

Both properties can take the same types of values, consisting of any one of four properties: `none` (the default), `auto` (an optimal value determined by the browser), a measurement value or a percentage value.

The best way to explain these properties is to look at their effects. Listing 11.5 shows two samples of Chinese text — the first without any layout-grid-line value set and the second set to a relatively wide value. The results can be seen in Figure 11–6.

| Listing 11.5 | *layout-grid-line Sample Code* |

```
<html>
<head>
<title>layout-grid-line Example</title>
</head>
<style>
div {font-family: PMingLiU; layout-grid-mode: both; layout-flow:
vertical-ideographic; font-weight: bold; font-size: 15pt}
</style>
<body>
Chinese text with no <code>layout-grid-line</code> value set
(<code>font-size</code> set to 15pt)
<div>
&#20320;&#21487;&#23559;&#20320;&#35201;&#20834;&#25237;&#30340;&
#36008;&#29289;&#21152;&#35387;&#25104;&#29305;&#23531;&#38917;&#
30446;&#65292;&#25110;&#29305;&#21029;&#35201;&#27714;&#38917;&#3
0446;&#12290;&#25152;&#26377;&#29305;&#23531;&#38917;&#30446;&#25
110;&#29305;&#21029;&#35201;&#27714;&#38917;&#30446;&#22343;&#263
71;&#24471;&#21040;&#29305;&#21029;&#34389;&#29702;
&#12290;&#20363;&#22914;&#65306;&#23427;&#20497;&#26371;&#34987;&
#25918;&#32622;&#22312;&#20834;&#25237;&#32178;&#38913;&#30340;&#
39318;&#38913;&#12289;&#21450;&#22312;&#20854;&#20182;&#32178;&#3
8913;&#19978;&#29992;&#21152;
&#31895;&#23383;&#39636;&#39023;&#31034;&#12290;&#21152;&#35387;&
#36027;&#29992;&#28858;&#27599;&#38917;&#32654;&#20803;&#20116;&#
21313;&#20803;&#12290;
</div>
Same Chinese set to <code>layout-grid-line: 25pt</code>
<div style="layout-grid-line: 25pt">
&#20320;&#21487;&#23559;&#20320;&#35201;&#20834;&#25237;&#30340;&
#36008;&#29289;&#21152;&#35387;&#25104;&#29305;&#23531;&#38917;&#
30446;&#65292;&#25110;&#29305;&#21029;&#35201;&#27714;&#38917;&#3
0446;&#12290;&#25152;&#26377;&#29305;&#23531;&#38917;&#30446;&#25
110;&#29305;&#21029;&#35201;&#27714;&#38917;&#30446;&#22343;&#263
71;&#24471;&#21040;&#29305;&#21029;&#34389;&#29702;
```

Listing 11.5	*layout-grid-line Sample Code (continued)*

```
&#12290;&#20363;&#22914;&#65306;&#23427;&#20497;&#26371;&
#25918;&#32622;&#22312;&#20834;&#25237;&#32178;&#38913;&#30340;&#
39318;&#38913;&#12289;&#21450;&#22312;&#20854;&#20182;&#32178;&#3
8913;&#19978;&#29992;&#21152;
&#31895;&#23383;&#39636;&#39023;&#31034;&#12290;&#21152;&#35387;&
#36027;&#29992;&#28858;&#27599;&#38917;&#32654;&#20803;&#20116;&#
21313;&#20803;&#12290;
</div>
</body>
</html>
```

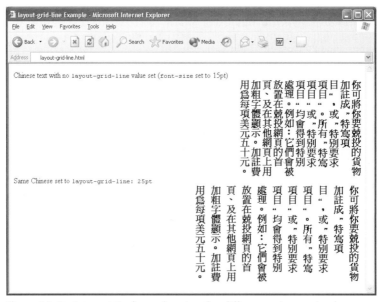

Figure 11–6   Internet Explorer showing the differences in spacing between vertical lines of text when a value is set to layout-grid-line.

As you can plainly see from Figure 11–6, `layout-grid-line` spaces the lines of characters out on the page. Using this property you can more easily control how much content is used to fill up a page, by essentially adding padding between the lines of characters.

Be careful when using the percentage value with `layout-grid-line`, as it is applied relative to the height of the line. A setting of `layout-grid-line: 0%` equals the regular default value, whereas a value of `layout-grid-line: 100%` will space each and every line of characters by their height. Don't use large percentage values unless you want to give your readers some practice using the horizontal scrollbar in order to view all of the text on your page. Also, it should be noted that `layout-grid-line` does not accept negative values — if you try, it will set the text to the default `layout-grid-line` value.

As mentioned earlier, `layout-grid-char` works in roughly the same way as the `letter-spacing` property for Western languages, though in this case it sets a spacing value between *vertical* characters. It gives the Web author greater control over the spacing of characters across the page. As with the previous sample code, Listing 11.6 shows two samples of Chinese text — the first does not have a `layout-grid-char` value set and the second is set to a relatively high value. The results can be seen in Figure 11–7.

Listing 11.6 *layout-grid-char Sample Code*

```
<html>
<head>
<title>layout-grid-char Example</title>
</head>
<style>
div {font-family: PMingLiU; layout-grid-mode: both; layout-flow:
vertical-ideographic; font-weight: bold; font-size: 15pt}
</style>
<body>
Chinese text with no <code>layout-grid-char</code> value set
(<code>font-size</code> set to 15pt)
<div>
&#20320;&#21487;&#23559;&#20320;&#35201;&#20834;&#25237;&#30340;&
#36008;&#29289;&#21152;&#35387;&#25104;&#29305;&#23531;&#38917;&#
30446;&#65292;&#25110;&#29305;&#21029;&#35201;&#27714;&#38917;&#3
0446;&#12290;&#25152;&#26377;&#29305;&#23531;&#38917;&#30446;&#25
110;&#29305;&#21029;&#35201;&#27714;&#38917;&#30446;&#22343;&#263
71;&#24471;&#21040;&#29305;&#21029;&#34389;&#29702;
&#12290;&#20363;&#22914;&#65306;&#23427;&#20497;&#26371;&#34987;&
#25918;&#32622;&#22312;&#20834;&#25237;&#32178;&#38913;&#30340;&#
39318;&#38913;&#12289;&#21450;&#22312;&#20854;&#20182;&#32178;&#3
8913;&#19978;&#29992;&#21152;
&#31895;&#23383;&#39636;&#39023;&#31034;&#12290;&#21152;&#35387;&
#36027;&#29992;&#28858;&#27599;&#38917;&#32654;&#20803;&#20116;&#
21313;&#20803;&#12290;
</div>
```

Listing 11.6	*layout-grid-char Sample Code (continued)*

```
Same Chinese text set to <code>layout-grid-char: 15pt</code>
<div style="layout-grid-char: 15pt">
&#20320;&#21487;&#23559;&#20320;&#35201;&#20834;&#25237;&#30340;&
#36008;&#29289;&#21152;&#35387;&#25104;&#29305;&#23531;&#38917;&#
30446;&#65292;&#25110;&#29305;&#21029;&#35201;&#27714;&#38917;&#3
0446;&#12290;&#25152;&#26377;&#29305;&#23531;&#38917;&#30446;&#25
110;&#29305;&#21029;&#35201;&#27714;&#38917;&#30446;&#22343;&#263
71;&#24471;&#21040;&#29305;&#21029;&#34389;&#29702;
&#12290;&#20363;&#22914;&#65306;&#23427;&#20497;&#26371;&#34987;&
#25918;&#32622;&#22312;&#20834;&#25237;&#32178;&#38913;&#30340;&#
39318;&#38913;&#12289;&#21450;&#22312;&#20854;&#20182;&#32178;&#3
8913;&#19978;&#29992;&#21152;
&#31895;&#23383;&#39636;&#39023;&#31034;&#12290;&#21152;&#35387;&
#36027;&#29992;&#28858;&#27599;&#38917;&#32654;&#20803;&#20116;&#
21313;&#20803;&#12290;
</div>
</body>
</html>
```

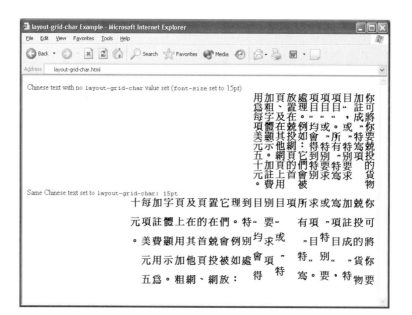

Figure 11–7   Internet Explorer showing the differences in spacing between vertical characters when a value is set to layout-grid-char.

Figure 11–7 shows the effects of `layout-grid-char` on our sample of Chinese text — the section where it has been applied expands the spacing between vertical characters, displaying five characters per line instead of ten characters per line in the default sample. The way this setting works is that it sets the spacing value between each character. So in the second example, the `layout-grid-char` value is set to equal that of the font-size of the Chinese characters, so it ends up placing half as many characters along each vertical line, and twice as many lines are needed to display all of the characters. Even though there is significant spacing between the characters in the second example, the spacing of the lines remains the same — there may be more lines of characters, but `layout-grid-char` does not affect the spacing between the lines of characters.

As with `layout-grid-line`, `layout-grid-char` does not take negative values, and it must be applied to a block-level elements.

According to Microsoft's documentation, in order for these properties to work, `layout-grid-mode` must be set to either `line` or `both` — though in our tests it did not matter if `layout-grid-mode` was present, as the presence of `layout-grid-line` or `layout-grid-char` seemed to be enough to do the trick.

layout-grid Property

The `layout-grid` property is a shortcut property to all of the rest of the layout-grid family of properties, and like all other such shortcut properties, it allows Web authors to quickly set multiple parameters at once. The values must be placed in this order: first the `layout-grid-mode` value, then `layout-grid-type` followed by `layout-grid-line` and `layout-grid-char`. The default setting for `layout-grid` is the default value for each of these individual properties in succession: `both loose none none`.

Using this shortcut property you can easily and quickly make formatting changes to sections or all of the Asian text on your Web pages. The default setting for displaying such text on a Web page tends to be very compact, which can make the characters hard to read, especially if the characters are rather small. Using `layout-grid` you can make wholesales changes all at once.

Listing 11.7 shows some Japanese text, the first without any special `layout-grid` settings, the second using `layout-grid: both loose 10pt 5pt`. The results can be see in Figure 11–8.

Listing 11.7 *layout-grid Sample Code*

```
<html>
<head>
<title>layout-grid Example</title>
</head>
<style>
div {font-family: "MS Mincho"; layout-flow: vertical-ideographic;
font-size: 15pt}
</style>
<body>
Unformatted Japanese text
<div>
&#12399;&#12501;&#12521;&#12483;&#12488;&#12497;&#12493;&#12523;&
#12487;&#12451;&#12473;&#12503;
&#12524;&#12452;&#26989;&#30028;&#12398;&#29420;&#31435;&#12375;&
#12383;&#12509;&#12540;&#12479;
&#12523;&#12469;&#12452;&#12488;&#12391;&#12289;&#38651;&#23376;&
#21462;&#24341;&#12469;&#12540;
&#12499;&#12473;&#12434;&#34892;&#12387;&#12390;&#12362;&#12426;&
#12414;&#12377;&#12290;&#39321;
&#28207;&#12289;&#12488;&#12525;&#12531;&#12488;&#65288;&#12459;&
#12490;&#12480;&#65289;&#12289;
&#12525;&#12531;&#12489;&#12531;&#65288;&#12452;&#12462;&#12522;&
#12473;&#65289;&#12395;&#12354;
&#12427;&#31169;&#12393;&#12418;&#12398;&#12458;&#12501;&#12451;&
#12473;&#12424;&#12426;&#12289;
&#12450;&#12472;&#12450;&#12289;&#12520;&#12540;&#12525;&#12483;&
#12497;&#12289;&#12450;&#12513;
&#12522;&#12459;&#12434;&#12459;&#12496;&#12540;&#12375;&#12390;&
#12362;&#12426;&#12414;&#12377;
&#12290;&#31169;&#12393;&#12418;&#12399;<b>&#12464;&#12525;&#1254
0;&#12496;&#12523;</b>&#12394;
&#27963;&#21205;&#12434;&#34892;&#12387;&#12390;&#12362;&#12426;&
#12289;&#12414;&#12383;&#31478;
&#22770;&#12399;<b>&#21311;&#21517;</
b>&#12392;&#12375;&#12390;&#12362;&#12426;&#12414;&#12377;
&#12290;&#31169;&#12393;&#12418;&#12399;&#30342;&#27096;&#12364;&
#19990;&#30028;&#20013;&#12398;
&#12497;&#12540;&#12488;&#12490;&#12540;&#12392;&#21311;&#21517;&
#12395;&#12390;&#12362;&#21462;
&#24341;&#12391;&#12365;&#12427;&#12424;&#12358;&#25903;&#25588;&
#12373;&#12379;&#12390;&#12356;
&#12383;&#12384;&#12356;&#12390;&#12362;&#12426;&#12414;&#12377;&
#12290;
</div>
Same Japanese text using <code>layout-grid: both loose 10pt 5pt
</code>
```

Listing 11.7 *layout-grid Sample Code (continued)*

```
<div style="layout-grid: both loose 10pt 5pt">
&#12399;&#12501;&#12521;&#12483;&#12488;&#12497;&#12493;&#12523;&#12487;&#12451;&#12473;&#12503;
&#12524;&#12452;&#26989;&#30028;&#12398;&#29420;&#31435;&#12375;&#12383;&#12509;&#12540;&#12479;
&#12523;&#12469;&#12452;&#12488;&#12391;&#12289;&#38651;&#23376;&#21462;&#24341;&#12469;&#12540;
&#12499;&#12473;&#12434;&#34892;&#12387;&#12390;&#12362;&#12426;&#12414;&#12377;&#12290;&#39321;
&#28207;&#12289;&#12488;&#12525;&#12531;&#12488;&#65288;&#12459;&#12490;&#12480;&#65289;&#12289;
&#12525;&#12531;&#12489;&#12531;&#65288;&#12452;&#12462;&#12522;&#12473;&#65289;&#12395;&#12354;
&#12427;&#31169;&#12393;&#12418;&#12398;&#12458;&#12501;&#12451;&#12473;&#12424;&#12426;&#12289;
&#12450;&#12472;&#12450;&#12289;&#12520;&#12540;&#12525;&#12483;&#12497;&#12289;&#12450;&#12513;
&#12522;&#12459;&#12434;&#12459;&#12496;&#12540;&#12375;&#12390;&#12362;&#12426;&#12414;&#12377;
&#12290;&#31169;&#12393;&#12418;&#12399;<b>&#12464;&#12525;&#12540;&#12496;&#12523;</b>&#12394;
&#27963;&#21205;&#12434;&#34892;&#12387;&#12390;&#12362;&#12426;&#12289;&#12414;&#12383;&#31478;
&#22770;&#12399;<b>&#21311;&#21517;</b>
&#12392;&#12375;&#12390;&#12362;&#12426;&#12414;&#12377;
&#12290;&#31169;&#12393;&#12418;&#12399;&#30342;&#27096;&#12364;&#19990;&#30028;&#20013;&#12398;
&#12497;&#12540;&#12488;&#12490;&#12540;&#12392;&#21311;&#21517;&#12395;&#12390;&#12362;&#21462;
&#24341;&#12391;&#12365;&#12427;&#12424;&#12358;&#25903;&#25588;&#12373;&#12379;&#12390;&#12356;
&#12383;&#12384;&#12356;&#12390;&#12362;&#12426;&#12414;&#12377;&#12290;
</div>
</body>
</html>
```

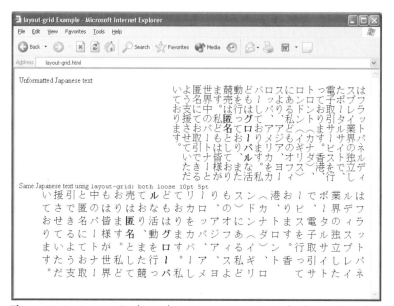

Figure 11–8 Internet Explorer depicting Japanese text: the first with no layout-grid values set, the second using layout-grid: both loose 10pt 5pt.

Here's what's going on in Figure 11–8: the `both` setting (which is the equivalent to `layout-grid-mode: both`) ensures that the formatting is added to both block-level as well as inline elements; `loose` is the correct `layout-grid-type` value for Japanese text; the `10pt` value sets a `10pt` spacing between each successive line (equivalent to `layout-grid-line: 10pt`); and the `5pt` value adds an equivalent spacing between each individual character displayed (same as `layout-grid-char: 5pt`).

The end result as can be seen in Figure 11–8 not only shows the text more spaced out on the page, but it is also arguably easier to make out individual characters, and hence to read the text. Of course there are limits to this — space the text too widely on a page and you'll end up forcing your users to do a lot of horizontal scrolling in order to read all of your text. But used judiciously, `layout-grid` can enhance the overall readability of your text, and display it more elegantly on the Web page.

11.5 text-autospace Property

If you have done much work on creating Web pages destined for an Asian-language audience, you know that there are many occasions when you need to mix in Western-style text with your Asian text. The `text-autospace` property is designed to let you have more control over the spacing between Western characters and your Asian-based character text. In this way, you can help offset, and perhaps emphasize, the Western characters and words that appear in your Asian text.

The `text-autospace` property has five properties: `none`, `ideograph-alpha`, `ideograph-numeric`, `ideograph-parenthesis`, `ideograph-space`. The `none` value is the default, setting no special spacing value between any Asian and Western characters that may appear together on a Web page. The rest of the properties for `text-autospace` describe the conditions under which slightly more space is added when it is next to an Asian ideographic character. So `ideograph-alpha` adds extra space when any regular Western alphabetical characters appear next to Asian ideographs. Similarly, extra space is added between Asian characters and numerals when `ideograph-numeric` is used. `ideograph-parenthesis` is intended to add extra space between Asian characters and information contained in brackets, and when an Asian character is next to a space, `ideograph-space` is intended to make it a slightly larger space.

The effects of these values can be subtle, but the end results are intended to space out the different types of characters from each other in an attempt to make things more readable. Listing 11.8 shows the effects of three of these values set to some nonsensical Chinese text mixed together with English words and numbers.

Listing 11.8   *text-autospace Sample Code*

```
<html>
<head>
<title>text-autospace Example</title>
</head>
<style>
span {font-family: ËÎÏå,MingLiU; font-weight: bold;
font-size: 20pt; layout-flow: vertical-ideographic; height: 400px}
</style>
<body>
<span>text-autospace: none</span>
<span style="text-autospace: none">
&#27489;1&#36814;2&#28459;3&#28216;4
(PanelX) &#150;5
&#24179;6&#38754;7&#39023;8&#31034;9&#23631;10&#26989;11&#30028;1
2&#30340;
Portal 13&#21450; Exchange 14
</span>
<span> </span>
<span>text-autospace: ideograph-alpha</span>
```

| Listing 11.8 | *text-autospace Sample Code (continued)* |

```
<span style="text-autospace: ideograph-alpha">
&#27489;1&#36814;2&#28459;3&#28216;4
(PanelX) &#150;5
&#24179;6&#38754;7&#39023;8&#31034;9&#23631;10&#26989;11&#30028;1
2&#30340;
Portal 13&#21450; Exchange 14
</span>
<span> </span>
<span>text-autospace: ideograph-numeric</span>
<span style="text-autospace: ideograph-numeric">
&#27489;1&#36814;2&#28459;3&#28216;4
(PanelX) &#150;5
&#24179;6&#38754;7&#39023;8&#31034;9&#23631;10&#26989;11&#30028;1
2&#30340;
Portal 13&#21450; Exchange 14
</span>
</body>
</html>
```

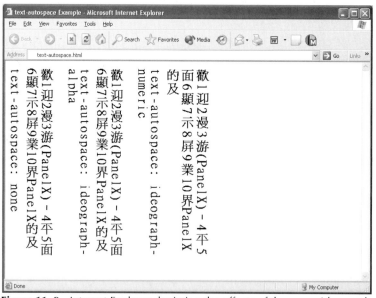

Figure 11–9   Internet Explorer depicting the effects of the none, ideograph-alpha and ideograph-numeric values for text-autospace against a mix of Chinese characters, Western text and numbers.

The effects of these three different values of `text-autospace` can be seen in Figure 11–9. The initial `none` value, seen in the right of Figure 11–9 — which is what you would get as a default — treats the English text, numbers and Chinese text equally, giving them the same amount of spacing. The result is a muddied jumble of all of these characters. The next sample text uses the `ideograph-alpha` value, and though the effect is subtle, there is slight additional spacing added between the English words and their surrounding Chinese characters. The results are more noticeable with the `ideograph-numeric` value, which clearly adds additional space between each individual number and the Chinese characters that surround them. The end effect is to make each block of text more readable.

There is no way to adjust the spacing settings for these `text-autospace` values — you get what you get, which is predetermined by the browser's own settings for handling Asian character sets.

CSS3 and text-autospace

There is an equivalent `text-autospace` property under the CSS3 text module. It has all of the same values as does the Internet Explorer equivalent, and they are designed to work in the same way.

11.6 text-justify Property

Often, when you use a justification value on the text contained within a Web page, you might wish to have greater control over how exactly a line of text is to be justified across the length of a paragraph. For the most part a Web browser will either squeeze the space between letters or expand them slightly, but the adjustments made do not always look good. The `text-justify` property provides much greater control over the type of justification use.

The `text-justify` property has a total of eight separate values: `auto`, `distribute`, `distribute-all-lines`, `inter-cluster`, `inter-ideograph`, `inter-word`, `kashida` and `newspaper`. The `auto` value is the default, allowing the browser to determine how to best justify a line of text. The `distribute` value is intended for use with Asian character sets, and justifies every line of text in a vertical paragraph save for the last line. The `distribute-all-lines` value is also intended for Asian character sets, and works the same way as `distribute`, but it applies the justification to all lines of text in a block of text, including the final line. Both `inter-cluster` and `inter-ideograph` are similarly intended for Asian character sets; the first justifies lines of text containing no inter-word spacing, the second increases or decreases the width between characters or words as necessary. The `inter-word` value increases or decreases the spacing between individual words, though this is applied to the final line of text in the paragraph. The kashida value is specific to Arabic characters, and it justifies the text by exaggerating certain characters at specific points. Finally, the newspaper value increases or decreases the spaces between words, and works the same way as distribute — which similarly does not justify the final line of text — but it is intended for Western text. This property is meant to be used in conjunction with the text-align property set to justify.

Listing 11.9 shows some simple English text on a page using the default auto value as well as the distribute-all-lines values for text-justify.

| Listing 11.9 | *text-justify Sample Code* |

```
<html>
<head>
<title>text-justify Example</title>
<style>
body {font-size: 20pt}
p {text-align:justify; width: 550px; font-weight: bold}
</style>
</head>
<body>
text-justify: auto (the default)
<p style="text-justify: auto">
The quick fox jumped over the lazy dog.
The quick fox jumped over the lazy dog.
The quick fox jumped over the lazy dog.
The quick fox jumped over the lazy dog.
</p>
text-justify: distribute-all-lines
<p style="text-justify: distribute-all-lines">
The quick fox jumped over the lazy dog.
The quick fox jumped over the lazy dog.
The quick fox jumped over the lazy dog.
The quick fox jumped over the lazy dog.
</p>
</body>
</html>
```

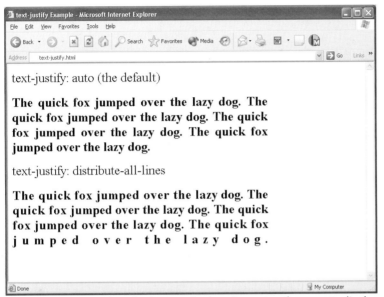

Figure 11–10 Two values for Internet Explorer's text-justify property displayed.

The effects of the `text-justify` values can be seen in Figure 11–10. The first paragraph really just displays the effects of `text-align: justify` which is set to both paragraphs on the page, but the second shows the distinct effect of `distribute-all-lines` value for `text-justify`, which justifies each and every line of text by increasing the space between individual letters and words in the final line of the paragraph.

CSS3 and text-justify

The CSS3 text module introduces a new property called `text-script` which copies many of the value names for `text-justify`. The `text-justify` property shares the values `auto`, `distribute`, `inter-cluster`, `inter-ideograph`, `inter-word`, `kashida` and `newspaper` (as well as the ubiquitous CSS3 values `initial` and `inherit`) but dispenses with `distribute-all-lines`. Given that Microsoft, which makes Internet Explorer, is a member of the World Wide Web Consortium, they are likely to implement these values as the `text-script` property. For more information on this property, see the section devoted to this property in Chapter 10, "Text Properties."

11.7 text-kashida-space Property

Arabic text is typically justified on a line by expanding individual characters at certain, pre-determined points. This type of justification on Arabic text is called kashida. The `text-kashida-space` property gives you fine control over this type of justification, setting the ratio of kashida to white-space expansion.

The `text-kashida-space` has two properties: a percentage value and `inherit`. The `inherit` value takes on whatever parent value may already be set.

The effects of `text-kashida-space` are subtle but definite. The effect is not so much to justify the line of characters across a line, but instead to stretch the very characters themselves in order to fill in a line. It is meant to be used in conjunction with `text-align: justify` and `text-justify: kashida`, and Listing 11.10 shows how they all work together to produce an effect.

Listing 11.10	*text-kashida-space Sample Code*

```
<html dir="rtl" lang="ar">
<head>
<title>text-kashida-space Example</title>
<meta http-equiv="Content-Type" content="text/html;
charset=windows-1256">
<style>
p.koran {font-size: 25pt; width: 550px; font-family: "Traditional
Arabic"; font-weight: bold; text-align: justify; text-justify:
kashida}
</style>
</head>
<body>
:The following are the first few lines of the Koran
<p class="koran" style="text-kashida-space: 0%">
ÈöÓúãö Çááåö ÇáÑøøóÍúãäãö ÇáÑøøóÍöíããöö
ÇáúÍóãÜÏö ááøåö ÑóÈøø ÇáúÚóÇáóãöíäö
ÇáÑøøóÍúãäÜÜÜÜÜÜÜÜÜÜöö ÇáÑøøóÍöíãö
ãóÇáößö íóæúãö ÇáÏøøíäö
ÅöíøóÇßó äóÚúÈõÏõ æÅöíøóÇßó äóÓúÊóÚöíäö
ÇáÏöÇáÅÚÜÜÜÜÜÜÜÜ
```

Listing 11.10 *text-kashida-space Sample Code (continued)*

```
<p class="koran" style="text-kashida-space: 10%">
ÈöÓúãö Çáááåö ÇáÑøóÍúãäö ÇáÑøóÍöíãöö
ÇáúÍóãúÏõ ááøåö ÑóÈøö ÇáúÚóÇáóãöíäó
ÇáÑøóÍúãÜäö ÇáÑøóÍöíãö
ãóÇáößö íóæúãö ÇáÏøöíäö
ÅöíøóÇßó äóÚúÈõÏõ æÅöíøóÇßó äóÓúÊóÚöíäõ
ÇåÏöäóÜÇ ÇáÕøöÑóÇØó ÇáãõÓÊóÞöíãó
ÕöÑóÇØó ÇáøóÐöíäó ÃóäÚóãÊó
Úóáóíåöãú ÛóíÑö ÇáãóÛÖõæÈö Úóáóíåöãú æóáÇó
ÇáÖøóÇáøöíäó
</p>
</body>
</html>
```

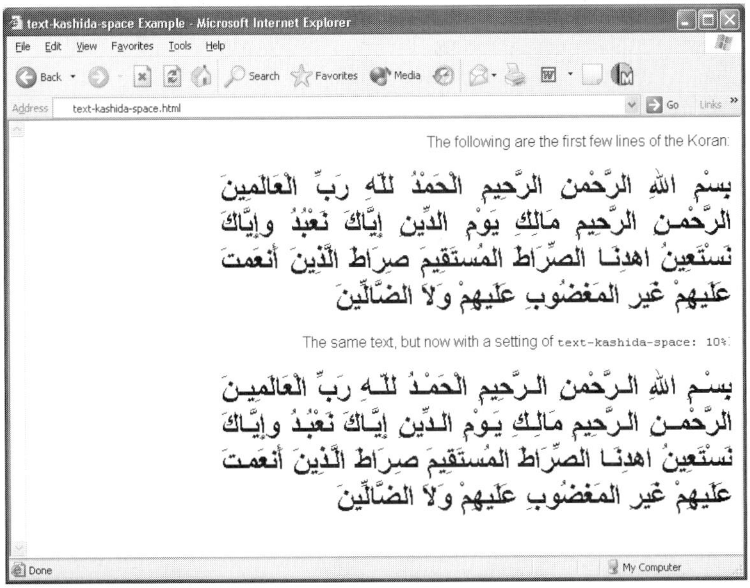

Figure 11–11 Sample Arabic text displayed using different text-kashida-space values.

Figure 11–11 shows the difference between Arabic text that uses the default value, and with a `text-kashida-space` value set to 10%. While the effect can be seen throughout the whole of second paragraph of text, in this case the effect is perhaps most clearly seen on the first line: the individual words are expanded and the space between them decreased.

CSS3 and text-kashida-position

This is another case of Microsoft being very successful in pitching its ideas for CSS properties to the World Wide Web Consortium — the equivalent `text-kashida-position` property in the CSS3 text module works in exactly the same way as it currently functions within Internet Explorer.

11.8 text-underline-position Property

The `text-underline-position` property does exactly what you would think it would do: allow you to set the position of an underline in relation to some text. It is meant to be used in conjunction with `text-decoration: underline`, which sets the line to the text. You might think that there would only be two values, but in fact there are four: `above`, `below`, `auto` and `auto-pos`. The first two are self-explanatory and were first introduced in Internet Explorer 5.0, with `below` being the old default; the `auto` and `auto-pos` values were only introduced with the launch of Internet Explorer 6.0. The `auto` value is the new default value, which sets the line underneath Western text, and has the added flexibility over the `below` value to set it inline if the text setting for the page is explicitly set to Japanese, and `writing-mode` is set to `tb-rl`. The `auto-pos` value is functionally equivalent to `auto`.

Listing 11.11 shows the various values of `text-underline-position` put to the test. The results of this code can be seen in Figure 11–12.

Listing 11.11	*text-underline-position Sample Code*

```
<html>
<head>
<title>text-underline-position Example</title>
<style>
p {text-decoration: underline; font-size: 20pt; font-weight: bold;
font-family: arial}
</style>
</head>
<body>
text-underline-position: above
<p style="text-underline-position: above">
The quick fox jumped over the lazy dog.
</p>
text-underline-position: below
<p style="text-underline-position: below">
The quick fox jumped over the lazy dog.
</p>
```

Listing 11.11	*text-underline-position Sample Code (continued)*

```
text-underline-position: auto
<p style="text-underline-position: auto">
The quick fox jumped over the lazy dog.
</p>
text-underline-position: auto-pos
<p style="text-underline-position: auto-pos">
The quick fox jumped over the lazy dog.
</p>
</body>
</html>
```

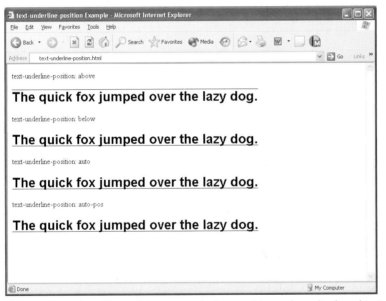

Figure 11–12 The effects of the text-underline-position values displayed in Internet Explorer 6.0.

CSS3 and text-underline-position

The auto and auto-pos values are taken from what is arguably a better-thought-out way of handling underlines that was proposed in the CSS3 text module. The original above and below values for this property made sense when applied to Western character sets, but made little sense when applied to vertically aligned Asian text.

The `auto-pos` position is available in Internet Explorer because it is the default value under the CSS3 text module for this property. In addition to the `auto-pos` value there are three others: `before-edge`, `after-baseline` and `after-edge`. All of these values are set relative to an EM box, which is the virtual, vertically aligned block that surrounds Asian characters on a page. When `before-edge` is used, the underline will appear before the edge of the EM box containing Asian characters. If `after-baseline` is set, the underline will appear after the baseline of the characters, and may end up cutting across any descenders (i.e., the parts of letters that dangle, like the lower parts of the letters y, g, p and q). The `after-edge` property sets the underline to appear after the edge of the EM box, and is designed not to cut across any descenders.

11.9 word-break Property

The `word-break` property is designed to give the Web author control over how line breaks should occur within words, especially in cases where the content is comprised of text from more than one language.

There are three values for this property: `normal`, `break-all` and `keep-all`. The `normal` value is the default, which allows line-breaking behavior within words. The `break-all` value works the same way as `normal`, but is intended for Asian characters, and yet is designed to allow any non-Asian characters to break as they normally might. The third, `keep-all` value, is designed not to allow word breaks for Chinese, Japanese or Korean characters, though it works the same way as `normal` for any non-Asian language.

Listing 11.12 shows a combination of English and Chinese text, and does not use a vertical layout in order to more clearly show the effects of all of the `word-break` properties.

Listing 11.12	*word-break Sample Code*

```
<html>
<head>
<title>word-break Example</title>
</head>
<style>
span.japanese {font-family:"MS Mincho"; font-size: 17pt}
span.english {font-family: arial; font-weight: bold;
font-size: 17pt}
```

Listing 11.12	*word-break Sample Code (continued)*

```
div {layout-grid-type: both; layout-grid-char:1pt;
layout-grid-line:1pt}
</style>
<body>
word-break: normal
<div style="word-break: normal">
<span class="english">PanelX</span>
<span
class="japanese">&#12399;&#12501;&#12521;&#12483;&#12488;&#12497;
&#12493;&#12523;&#12487;&#12451;&#12473;&#12503;&#12524;&#12452;&
#26989;&#30028;&#12398;&#29420;&#31435;&#12375;&#12383;&#12509;&#
12540;&#12479;&#12523;&#12469;&#12452;&#12488;&#12391;&#12289;&#3
8651;&#23376;&#21462;&#24341;&#12469;&#12540;&#12499;&#12473;&#12
434;&#34892;&#12387;&#12390;&#12362;&#12426;&#12414;&#12377;&#122
90;</span>
</div>
<hr />
word-break: break-all
<div style="word-break: break-all">
<span class="english">PanelX</span>
<span
class="japanese">&#12399;&#12501;&#12521;&#12483;&#12488;&#12497;
&#12493;&#12523;&#12487;&#12451;&#12473;&#12503;&#12524;&#12452;&
#26989;&#30028;&#12398;&#29420;&#31435;&#12375;&#12383;&#12509;&#
12540;&#12479;&#12523;&#12469;&#12452;&#12488;&#12391;&#12289;&#3
8651;&#23376;&#21462;&#24341;&#12469;&#12540;&#12499;&#12473;&#12
434;&#34892;&#12387;&#12390;&#12362;&#12426;&#12414;&#12377;&#122
90;</span>
</div>
<hr />
word-break: keep-all
<div style="word-break: keep-all">
<span class="english">PanelX</span>
<span
class="japanese">&#12399;&#12501;&#12521;&#12483;&#12488;&#12497;
&#12493;&#12523;&#12487;&#12451;&#12473;&#12503;&#12524;&#12452;&
#26989;&#30028;&#12398;&#29420;&#31435;&#12375;&#12383;&#12509;&#
12540;&#12479;&#12523;&#12469;&#12452;&#12488;&#12391;&#12289;&#3
8651;&#23376;&#21462;&#24341;&#12469;&#12540;&#12499;&#12473;&#12
434;&#34892;&#12387;&#12390;&#12362;&#12426;&#12414;&#12377;&#122
90;</span>
</div>
```

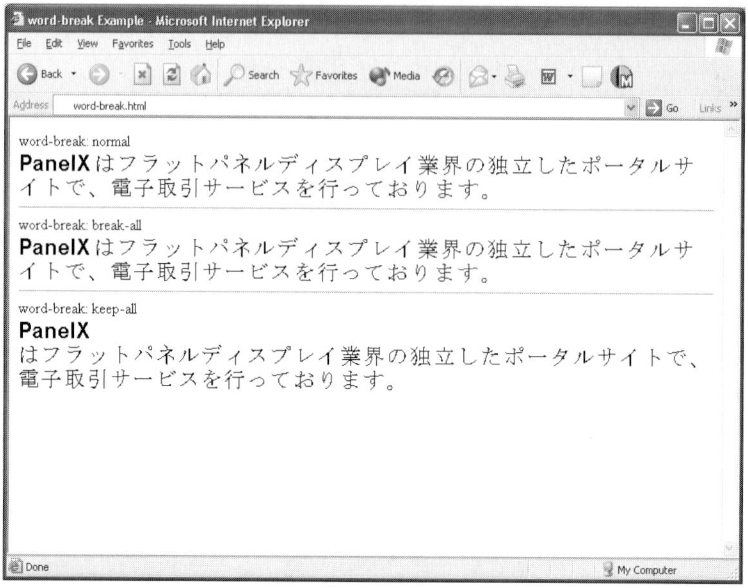

Figure 11–13 The values of word-break used with the same English/Chinese text, viewed in Internet Explorer.

There is no discernable difference between the effects of the normal and break-all values as seen in Figure 11–13. However, it does show the difference the keep-all value makes to the same piece of text: not only is the English text PanelX isolated on its line, but the subsequent Chinese text breaks only at the comma on the second line of text. Be careful using the keep-all value, as a long line of unpunctuated Asian text could cause the user to do a lot of scrolling to be able to read it fully.

CSS3 and word-break

The CSS3 text module word-break property has a few extra values over its current Internet Explorer counterpart. In the CSS3 text module, word-break is in fact a shortcut property for two other properties, word-break-CJK and word-break-inside. The Internet Explorer word-break property is equivalent to the CSS3 property word-break-CJK (the "CJK" references the languages it is designed to work with: Chinese, Japanese and Korean), as it does not incorporate any of the values associated with word-break-inside.

For more information on these CSS3 text properties, see Chapter 10, "Text Properties."

11.10 text-align-last Property

The `text-align-last` property is an Internet Explorer-only property, and is designed to alter the way the very last line of text in a given paragraph is formatted. It is meant to be used in conjunction with the `text-align` property, but it overrules its behavior when it comes to the final line of a paragraph.

The `text-align-last` property has a total of six values: the five belonging to `text-align` — `left`, `right`, `center`, `justify` and `inherit` — and the additional `auto` value. This last value is the default, setting the final line of text to whatever value has been set for `text-align`.

It should be noted that the default layout for the last line of text in a paragraph in Internet Explorer — even when the text is set to `text-align: justify` — is to align the text the left. The example code seen in Listing 11.13 contains three paragraphs which are all set to `text-align: justify`, but the latter two use the additional `text-align-last` property. You can see its effect in Figure 11–14.

Listing 11.13	*text-align-last Example Code*

```
<html>
<head>
<title>text-align-last Example</title>
<style>
body {font-size: 18pt}
</style>
</head>
<body>
<p style="text-align: justify">
This line contains justified text. To ensure you can really see
the effect of this, we need a few sentences so that the effect can
easily be seen. Despite the fact that the <code>text-align-last</
code> property is not being used, the default behavior is that the
last line is <em>not</em> justified.
</p>
<p style="text-align: justify; text-align-last: center">
This line contains justified text. To ensure you can really see
the effect of this, we need a few sentences so that the effect can
easily be seen. This paragraph uses <code>text-align-last</code>
set to <code>center</code>, so the last line is centered.
</p>
```

Listing 11.13	*text-align-last Example Code (continued)*

```
<p style="text-align: justify; text-align-last: right">
This line contains justified text. To ensure you can really see
the effect of this, we need a few sentences so that the effect can
easily be seen. This paragraph uses <code>text-align-last</code>
set to <code>right</code>, so the last line is right-aligned.
</p>
</body>
</html>
```

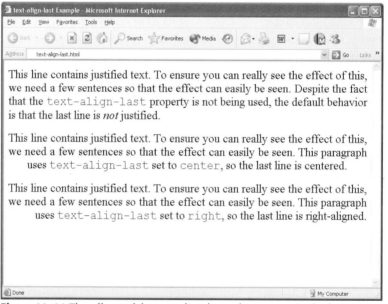

Figure 11–14 The effects of the text-align-last value as seen in the last two paragraphs of this Web page as seen in Internet Explorer 6.0.

Browser Compatibility

At the moment the `text-align-last` property is an Internet Explorer-only property. It was first implemented in version 5.5 of the browser.

CSS3 and text-align-last

The text-align-last property has been adopted within the text module of CSS3, but names of some the values assigned to it are different than those used by Internet Explorer. Internet Explorer uses the values auto, left, right, center, justify and inherit. The CSS3 equivalent values for this property are instead auto, start, end, center, justify, inherit, initial and size. In this case Internet Explorer's left and right values are the same as CSS3's start and end. The initial value is CSS3's way of specifying the default value for a given property (which in this case is also auto), but the size value is something new.

When text-align-last is set to size, the browser is supposed to scale the content on the last line to fit across the whole of the line — which means that the *font size* for the text in the final line may be changed in order to help make the text stretch across it. In order to set constraints on how much (or how little) the browser should scale the size of the font, CSS3 also introduces the min-font-size and max-font-size properties to set the minimum and maximum font size to be applied in this case. (For more information on these two properties, see Chapter 10, "Text Properties.")

BOX PROPERTIES

Topics in This Chapter

- border-"style" Properties
- border-color, border-bottom, -left, -right and -top
- border-width, border-bottom-, -left-, -right- and -top-width
- border
- border-radius
- border-image and border-image-transform
- border-fit and border-break
- box-shadow
- clear, clear-after, float, float-displace
- indent-edge-reset
- height and width
- padding-"side" and margin-"side" Properties
- min-width, max-width, min-height and max-height
- fit and fit-position
- marquee

Chapter

The box family of CSS properties is the largest CSS family, containing almost 50 separate properties. While this sounds impressive, the majority of these properties are only a slight variation upon a common formatting theme. Most of these properties can be collected together into one of three sub-groups of similar properties (they share the same name prefix): the border, margin, and padding groups. The border sub-group controls the type, color and placement of borders around elements on a Web page. The margin sub-group handles where margins should appear between elements on a Web page, and the padding sub-group takes care of spacing between a Web element and a border. There are four additional properties (`clear`, `float`, `height` and `width`) that do not fit neatly into one of these categories, but these "miscellaneous" properties all have a role to play in placing and sizing elements on a Web page.

All of these properties refer to the spacing, placement or size of elements that appear onscreen. The family name "box" is derived from the fact that all of these properties are designed to work with block-level elements and control how they are placed or otherwise arranged on a Web page. The three main categories of properties actually determine the placement of elements on a Web page in concentric rectangles. Margin values set the distance between the edge of the browser window and the border (if any) that appears around text or images on a Web page. Padding, in turn, separates the text from the border. In essence, what you get is a bunch of nested "boxes," one fitting neatly inside the other. Figure 12–1 provides a good example of this.

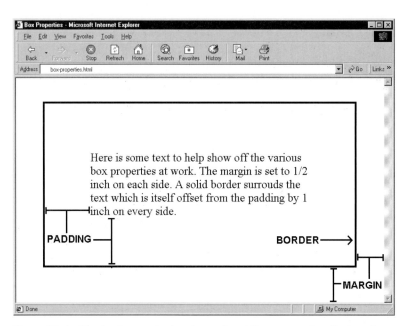

Figure 12–1 The basic margin, border and padding properties displayed.

12.1 border-"style" Properties

The border-"style" sub-family properties are a set of properties that determine the type of border than can be displayed around a given element on a Web page, such as text or an image. This sub-family consists of the following properties:

- `border-style`
- `border-top-style`
- `border-right-style`
- `border-bottom-style`
- `border-left-left`

The `border-style` property is the shortcut property for the group, and all of the values that can be applied to it can be applied to the other properties in this sub-group, which each control one side of a border.

12.2 border-style Property

The border-style property determines the type of border that the browser will display around a given element on a Web page, such as text or an image. Using this property, you can add stylish and eye-catching borders to your Web page. Up until now, the only HTML equivalent was to create a table and turn on the border attribute. There is no way to otherwise change the solid border that would be displayed. With border-style you can play with up to a dozen different values for the type of border that can be displayed, although until recently only a few of these values were supported in Netscape Navigator or Internet Explorer.

There are a number of 2D and 3D border types. The 2D borders are created by the values dashed, dotted, double and solid, while the 3D borders are created by the inset, outset, groove and ridged values. Of the 2D border types, the dashed value displays a border made up of dashes, the dotted value displays a border made from small dots, the double value creates a border made from a double line, and solid displays a solid border style. Of the 3D border types, inset creates a border that appears recessed, while outset creates a border that appears the opposite of inset. groove displays a 3D grooved border line and ridge creates a 3D ridged border line. The value none ensures that no border is displayed. The CSS2 specification added a further variant on none called hidden, which has the same effect, but is supposed to be used in conjunction with table elements to resolve any possible conflicts that might arise. Then there's the inherit value, which takes on any border value previously assigned to a parent element.

You can see all of these properties (save for hidden and inherit) put to use in Listing 12.1, whose effects can be seen in Figure 12–2.

Listing 12.1 *border-style Example*

```
<html>
<head>
<title>border-style Example</title>
</head>
<body style="font-size: medium; font-weight: bold">
<p align="center" style="border-style: dashed; border-color: gray;
border-width: thick">Text surrounded by a dashed border style.</p>
<p align="center" style="border-style: dotted; border-color: gray;
border-width: thick">Text surrounded by a dotted border style.</p>
<p align="center" style="border-style: double; border-color: gray;
border-width: thick">Text surrounded by a double border style.</p>
<p align="center" style="border-style: solid; border-color: gray;
border-width: thick">Text surrounded by a solid border style.</p>
<p align="center" style="border-style: inset; border-color: gray;
border-width: thick">Text surrounded by an inset border style.</p>
```

Listing 12.1	*border-style Example (continued)*

```
<p align="center" style="border-style: outset; border-color: gray;
border-width: thick">Text surrounded by an outset border
style.</p>
<p align="center" style="border-style: groove; border-color: gray;
border-width: thick">Text surrounded by a grooved border
style.</p>
<p align="center" style="border-style: ridge; border-color: gray;
border-width: thick">Text surrounded by a ridged border style.</p>
<p align="center" style="border-style: none; border-color: gray;
border-width: thick">Text surrounded by no border style.</p>
</body>
</html>
```

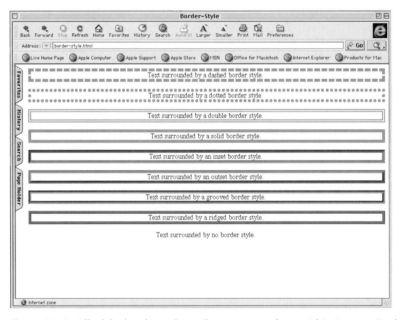

Figure 12–2   All of the border-style attributes as seen from within Internet Explorer 4.5 for the Macintosh.

The current draft of the CSS3 borders module will add three more types of border values: dot-dash, dot-dot-dash and wave. The names for the border types are self-descriptive: dot-dash produces a border using a repeated dot-and-dash sequence, dot-dot-dash does the same thing with two dots followed by a dash, and `wave` produces a sinuous line for a border. The intent of these three additional CSS3 border values can be seen in Figure 12–3.

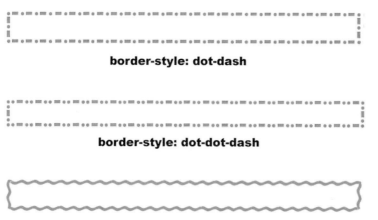

border-style: dot-dash

border-style: dot-dot-dash

border-style: wave

Figure 12–3 Mock-up displaying the three additional border styles proposed under CSS3.

One last thing — try not to use the values "ridged" or "grooved" when you mean to "ridge" or "groove," a common slip-up when setting these values.

Browser Compatibility

This property has is widely adopted, although in Netscape Navigator this has only been the case since version 6.0.

- Internet Explorer 3.0: Unsafe.
- Internet Explorer 4.0: Partial.
- Internet Explorer 4.0 – 4.5 (Mac): Safe.
- Internet Explorer 5.0: Partial.
- Internet Explorer 5.1 – 5.2 (Mac): Safe.
- Internet Explorer 5.5: Safe.
- Internet Explorer 6.0: Safe.
- Netscape Navigator 4.0 – 4.79: Partial.
- Netscape Navigator 4.0 (Mac & UNIX): Partial.
- Netscape Navigator 6.0: Safe.
- Netscape Navigator 7.0: Safe.
- Mozilla 1.0: Safe.
- Opera 3.6 – 4.0: Safe.

- Opera 5.0 – 6.0: Safe.
- Konqueror: Safe.

The `border-style` property has been implemented successfully in Internet Explorer since Windows version 5.5, and in the Macintosh since version 4.0. Prior to these versions, the Partial ratings are applicable only because they did not support the `dotted` border style. It should also be noted that the dotted border, when implemented in the Windows version of this browser, displays a diamond shape, whereas the Macintosh versions display a rounded circle. A minor display difference, but it underscores the fact that each browser tends to display border values slightly differently. None of the CSS3 values are supported.

Like the earlier versions of Internet Explorer, the 4.0 version of Netscape Navigator gets a Partial rating because it did not implement the `dotted` value. Subsequently, version 6.0 implemented it fully. Ditto Mozilla 1.0. It should be pointed out that Netscape Navigator and Internet Explorer both display slightly different-looking borders for the same values, though in most cases it is only due to a difference in shading. The dotted value in Netscape Navigator/Mozilla appears as a small square. None of the CSS3 values are supported.

Opera was an early implementer of the `border-style` property, and has been fully implemented since version 3.6 of that browser. In terms of the "look" of the `border-style` values, Opera's borders follow Netscape Navigator's border model — even the `dotted` value appears as squares. None of the CSS3 values are supported.

Konqueror fully implements all CSS values for this property. Like Opera, the "look" of Konqueror's borders resembles that of Netscape Navigator.

12.3 border-color Property

The `border-color` property sets the color for the border to be displayed. Previous to the introduction of this property, the only way you could add color to borders was to use the `bordercolor` attribute, or the Internet Explorer-only `bordercolorlight` or `bordercolordark` in conjunction with the `<table>` HTML tag. The `border-color` property opens things up so that a Web author can add color to any block-level element.

The `border-color` property, like all other color CSS properties, allows Web authors to set a color value in a variety of ways. For example, it can take a standard color name (such as "red") or a hexadecimal color value (such as "#FF0000", which is also red), both of which are standard ways of setting color values in HTML. In CSS, you can also specify color using a "compressed" hexadecimal color value (such as "#0F0", which is green). You can also use a three-digit RGB ("Red Green Blue") color value where rgb(0,0,255) is blue, and a three-digit RGB percentage color value where rgb(0%,0%,100%) is blue. The CSS3 color module will probably introduce some new ways of setting color (and transparency) values — for more information on ways of specifying color, please see Chapter 13, "Color." Listing 12.2, whose results can be seen in Figure 12–4, demonstrates the different ways of implementing color — save those of the yet to be implemented CSS3 color module — with the `border-color` property in a single Web page.

Listing 12.2	*border-color*

```
<html>
<head>
<title>border-color Example</title>
<style>
p {font : 27px Verdana, Geneva, Arial, Helvetica, sans-serif}
</style>
</head>
</html>
<body style="font-size: large;">
<p style="border-color: red; border-style: solid; border-width:
thick">This paragraph is surrounded by a solid red border.</p>
<p style="border-color: #00ff00; border-style: ridge;
border-width: thick">This paragraph is surrounded by a ridged
green border.</p>
<p style="border-color: #00f; border-style: outset; border-width:
thick">This paragraph is surrounded by an outset blue border.</p>
<p style="border-color: rgb(255,255,0); border-style: inset;
border-width: thick">This paragraph is surrounded by an inset
yellow border.</p>
<p style="border-color: rgb(0%,100%,100%); border-style: double;
border-width: thick">This paragraph is surrounded by a double cyan
border.</p>
</body>
</html>
```

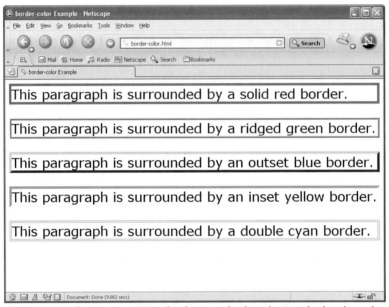

Figure 12–4   The various CSS color formats displayed using the border-color property as seen in Netscape Navigator 7.0.

Browser Compatibility

This property has been widely adopted for a long time, although it should be noted that `border-color` was problematic in Netscape Navigator 4.x

- Internet Explorer 3.0: Unsafe.
- Internet Explorer 4.0: Safe.
- Internet Explorer 4.0 – 4.5 (Mac): Safe.
- Internet Explorer 5.0: Safe.
- Internet Explorer 5.1 – 5.2 (Mac): Safe.
- Internet Explorer 5.5: Safe.
- Internet Explorer 6.0: Safe.
- Netscape Navigator 4.0 – 4.79: Partial.
- Netscape Navigator 4.0 (Mac & UNIX): Partial.
- Netscape Navigator 6.0: Safe.
- Netscape Navigator 7.0: Safe.
- Mozilla 1.0: Safe.
- Opera 3.6 – 4.0: Safe.
- Opera 5.0 – 6.0: Safe.
- Konqueror: Safe.

The `border-color` property has been implemented successfully in Internet Explorer since version 4.0.

Netscape Navigator 4.x is given a Partial rating, although "Buggy" might be more accurate. While it does successfully implement all of the valid ways of implementing color values when setting borders, it only displays a border (and its color) if `border-width` is also set. Under this version of the browser it is also possible to add a border to non-block-level elements, and instead of extending the border across the browser window (as would ordinarily be expected of a block-level element), the border instead only fits the text or other Web page elements it contains. These quirks were all fixed by the 6.0 release. Mozilla 1.0 also fully implemented this property.

Opera was an early implementer of the `border-color` property and has been fully compliant since version 3.6.

Konqueror fully implements the `border-color` property.

12.4 border-width Property

The `border-width` property is used to set the thickness value for the border to be displayed. It can either take an absolute pixel value or any one of three special name values.

This property can take from one to four separate numerical values which set the width of the border selected. If multiple values are to be set using other units of measurement, each value in turn must be set with a specific unit of measurement — one measurement unit value *does not* apply to all automatically. If a single numerical value is present, all borders are set to that value. If two numerical values are present, the top and bottom take the first value, and the side borders take the second. If three values are present, the top, right and left sides, and then the bottom take the numerical values specified. Finally, if four values are present, the top, right, bottom, then left borders take the numerical values specified. When specifying these values, you must separate them by a space, as can be seen in Listing 12.3, whose results are displayed in Figure 12–5.

Listing 12.3	*border-width Example Code Using Pixel Values*

```
<html>
<head>
<title>border-width Example 1</title>
<style>
p {font : 25px Verdana, Geneva, Arial, Helvetica, sans-serif}
</style>
</head>
</html>
```

| Listing 12.3 | *border-width Example Code Using Pixel Values* |

```
<body style="font-size: large;">
<p style="border-width: 15px; border-style: solid">A paragraph
surrounded by a single border 15 pixels in width.</p>
<p style="border-width: 5px 10px; border-style: solid">A paragraph
surrounded by a top borders 5 pixels in width, and side borders 10
pixels in width.</p>
<p style="border-width: 2px 10px 5px; border-style: solid">A
paragraph surrounded by a border that is 2 pixels thick at the top,
10 pixels to the sides and 5 pixels on the bottom.</p>
<p style="border-width: 15px 2px 10px 20px; border-style: solid">A
paragraph surrounded by a border that is 15 pixels on the top, 20
pixels to the left side, 2 pixels to the right side, and 10 pixels
on the bottom.</p>
</body>
</html>
```

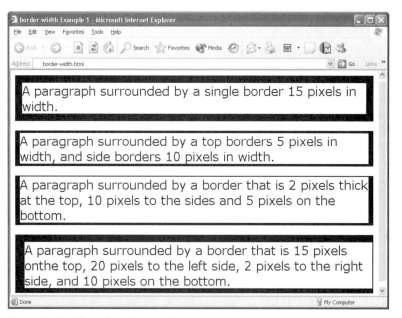

Figure 12–5   The sides of several boxes set to various pixel values using border-width, as seen in Internet Explorer 6.0.

The border-width property can take one of three specific name values: thin, medium and thick. It is also possible to combine one or more of these named values in the same way as with the numerical values. Examples of all of these named values can be seen in Listing 12.4; the results of the code are displayed in Figure 12–6.

Listing 12.4	*Border-Width #2*

```
<html>
<head>
<title>border-width #2</title>
</head>
</html>
<body style="font-size: large;">
<p style="border-width: thin; border-style: solid">A paragraph
surrounded by a thin border.</p>
<p style="border-width: medium; border-style: solid">A paragraph
surrounded by a medium border.</p>
<p style="border-width: thick; border-style: solid">A paragraph
surrounded by a thick border.</p>
<p style="border-width: thin thick; border-style:
solid">A paragraph surrounded by a border that is thin on top
and thick to the sides.</p>
</body>
</html>
```

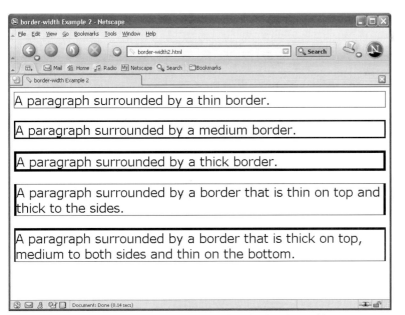

Figure 12–6 The three name values applied to the border-width property as seen in Netscape Navigator 7.0.

Browser Compatibility

The `border-width` property has been adopted at least partially by the major browsers for a long time, although Netscape Navigator only got it right by version 6.0.

- Internet Explorer 3.0: Unsafe.
- Internet Explorer 4.0: Safe.
- Internet Explorer 4.0 – 4.5 (Mac): Safe.
- Internet Explorer 5.0: Safe.
- Internet Explorer 5.1 – 5.2 (Mac): Safe.
- Internet Explorer 5.5: Safe.
- Internet Explorer 6.0: Safe.
- Netscape Navigator 4.0 – 4.79: Partial.
- Netscape Navigator 4.0 (Mac & UNIX): Partial.
- Netscape Navigator 6.0: Safe.
- Netscape Navigator 7.0: Safe.
- Mozilla 1.0: Safe.
- Opera 3.6 – 4.0: Safe.
- Opera 5.0 – 6.0: Safe.
- Konqueror: Safe.

The `border-width` property has been implemented successfully in Internet Explorer since version 4.0.

Netscape Navigator 4.x is given a Partial rating, due to the way this version of the browser implements the border properties, "Buggy" is a better description. It implements all of the `border-width` values accurately, but it is also possible to add a border to non-block-level elements. This and all of the other border problems were fixed by the 6.0 release. Mozilla 1.0 also fully implemented this property.

Opera was an early implementer of the `border-width` property, and has been fully compliant since version 3.6.

Konqueror fully implements the `border-width` property.

12.5 border-bottom Property

The `border-bottom` property sets the value to be assigned to the border at the bottom of the box *only*. It can take on all of the values belonging to the `border-style`, `border-color` and `border-width` properties. It functions in the same way as its sibling properties `border-top`, `border-right` and `border-left`.

The `border-bottom` property is something of a "shortcut" property, as it is capable of taking on all of the other values associated with `border-style`, `border-color` and `border-width` properties. It can take a single numerical or named value that sets the width, color value and border style. What the `border-bottom` property does is to set the display properties that are applied to the bottom border only — no other borders are affected. Listing 12.5, whose results can be seen in Figure 12–7, shows how it can be used.

Listing 12.5 *border-bottom Example Code*

```
<html>
<head>
<title>border-bottom Example</title>
</head>
<style>
p {font: 25px Verdana, Geneva, Arial, Helvetica, sans-serif}
</style>
</html>
<body style="font-size: x-large;">
<p style="border-bottom: thin solid blue">Paragraph with a thin
blue bottom border.</p>
<p style="border-bottom: thick double #ff0000">Paragraph with a
thick, red double bottom border.</p>
<p style="border-bottom: 2cm purple groove">Paragraph with a 2
centimeter thick, purple grooved bottom border.</p>
<p style="border-bottom: 20px #0f0 dotted">Paragraph with a 20
pixel thick, green, dotted bottom border.</p>
<p style="border-bottom: 10px #000 dashed">Paragraph with a 10
pixel thick, black dashed bottom border.</p>
</body>
</html>
```

In the future, `border-bottom` will incorporate the many new values associated with its "kin" `bottom border` properties described in the CSS3 border module. These new values will allow you to do such things as add border-images, transform them so that they properly span a border, create rounded edge effects to your borders and more. At the time of writing no major browser implements any of the CSS3 values for `border-bottom`. All of these new properties are covered later in this chapter.

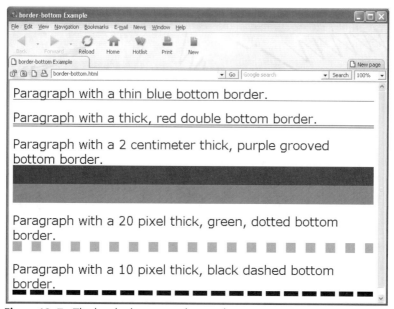

Figure 12–7   The border-bottom code sample as seen in Opera 6.0.

Browser Compatibility

The compatibility rating for `border-bottom` depends at least in part on how the border properties as a whole are implemented within a browser. Each of the browsers with at least a Partial rating implement this property, although the browser may not be able to support other standard border features (such as the `dotted` or `dashed` values for `border-style`, for example).

- Internet Explorer 3.0: Unsafe.
- Internet Explorer 4.0: Partial.
- Internet Explorer 4.0 – 4.5 (Mac): Safe.
- Internet Explorer 5.0: Partial.
- Internet Explorer 5.1 – 5.2 (Mac): Safe.
- Internet Explorer 5.5: Safe.
- Internet Explorer 6.0: Safe.
- Netscape Navigator 4.0 – 4.79: Partial.
- Netscape Navigator 4.0 (Mac & UNIX): Partial.
- Netscape Navigator 6.0: Safe.
- Netscape Navigator 7.0: Safe.
- Mozilla 1.0: Safe.
- Opera 3.6 – 4.0: Safe.

- Opera 5.0 – 6.0: Safe.

- Konqueror: Safe.

The `border-bottom` property has been implemented successfully in Internet Explorer since version 5.0 (Windows). The Partial rating for the earlier 4.0 version has to do with a lack of implementation for `border-style`'s `dotted` and `dashed` values in conjunction with this property.

Similarly Netscape Navigator 4.x is given a Partial rating, since it also did not implement the `dotted` and `dashed` values for `border-style`. It also allowed you to add borders to non-block-level elements, which is not, strictly speaking, correct. All of this was fixed by Netscape Navigator's 6.0 release. Mozilla 1.0 fully implements this property.

Traditionally ahead of the pack, Opera 3.6 had implemented `border-bottom` property fully.

Konqueror fully implements the `border-bottom` property.

12.6 border-left Property

The `border-left` property works in exactly the same manner as `border-bottom`, but in this case sets the value to be assigned to the border to the left of the box *only*. It can take on all of the values belonging to the `border-style`, `border-color` and `border-width` properties. It functions in the same way as its sibling properties `border-top`, `border-right` and `border-bottom`.

The `border-left` property is a "shortcut" property, as it is capable of taking on all of the other values associated with the `border-style`, `border-color` and `border-width` properties. It can take a single numerical or named value that sets the width, color value and border style. What the `border-left` property does is to set the display properties that are applied to the left border only — no other borders are affected. Listing 12.6, which is depicted in Figure 12–8 using Opera 6.0, shows how it can be implemented.

Listing 12.6	*border-left Example Code*

```
<html>
<head>
<title>border-left Example</title>
</head>
```

Listing 12.6   *border-left Example Code (continued)*

```
<style>
p {font: 25px Verdana, Geneva, Arial, Helvetica, sans-serif}
</style>
</html>
<body>
<p style="border-left: medium solid red">A paragraph with a thin
red left border.</p>
<p style="border-left: 1cm ridge #0000ff">A paragraph with a 1
centimeter thick, blue ridged left border.</p>
<p style="border-left: 1in green double">A paragraph with a 1 inch
thick, green double border to the left.</p>
<p style="border-left: 20px dotted #f00">A paragraph with a 20
pixel thick, red dotted border to the left.</p>
<p style="border-left: 10px dashed rgb(0%,0%,100%)">A paragraph
with a 10 pixel thick, blue dashed border to the left.</p>
</body>
</html>
```

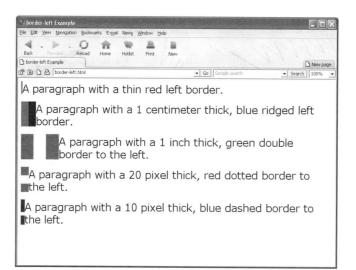

Figure 12–8   The border-left code sample as seen in Opera 6.0.

In the future, `border-left` will have added to it all of the new values described in the CSS3 border module, allowing you to create borders with rounded edges, add border images, tell the browser how to break a border when it crosses a page break and so on. At the moment no major browser implements any of these CSS3 values for `border-left`. All of these new properties are covered later in this chapter.

Browser Compatibility

As with `border-bottom` (and `border-right` and `border-top`) the compatibility rating for `border-left` depends at least in part on how the border properties as a whole are implemented within a browser. Each of the browsers with at least a Partial rating implement this property, although the browser may not be able to support other standard border features (such as the `dotted` or `dashed` values for `border-style`, for example).

- Internet Explorer 3.0: Unsafe.
- Internet Explorer 4.0: Partial.
- Internet Explorer 4.0 – 4.5 (Mac): Safe.
- Internet Explorer 5.0: Partial.
- Internet Explorer 5.1 – 5.2 (Mac): Safe.
- Internet Explorer 5.5: Safe.
- Internet Explorer 6.0: Safe.
- Netscape Navigator 4.0 – 4.79: Partial.
- Netscape Navigator 4.0 (Mac & UNIX): Partial.
- Netscape Navigator 6.0: Safe.
- Netscape Navigator 7.0: Safe.
- Mozilla 1.0: Safe.
- Opera 3.6 – 4.0: Safe.
- Opera 5.0 – 6.0: Safe.
- Konqueror: Safe.

The `border-left` property has been implemented successfully in Internet Explorer since version 5.0 (Windows). The Partial rating for the earlier 4.0 version has to do with a lack of implementation for `border-style`'s `dotted` and `dashed` values in conjunction with this property.

Similarly Netscape Navigator 4.x is given a Partial rating, since it also did not implement the `dotted` and `dashed` values for `border-style`. It also allowed you to add borders to non-block-level elements, which is not, strictly speaking, correct. All of this was fixed by Netscape Navigator's 6.0 release. Mozilla 1.0 fully implements this property.

Traditionally ahead of the pack, Opera 3.6 had implemented `border-left` property fully.

Konqueror fully implements the `border-left` property.

12.7 border-right Property

The `border-right` property works in exactly the same manner as the `border-left`, `border-top` and `border-bottom` properties, but in this case sets the value to be assigned to the border to the right of the box *only*. It can take on all of the values belonging to the `border-style`, `border-color` and `border-width` properties. It functions in the same way as its sibling properties `border-top`, `border-left` and `border-bottom`.

The `border-right` property is a type of "shortcut" property, capable of taking on all of the other values associated with `border-style`, `border-color` and `border-width` properties. It can take a single numerical or named value that sets the width, color value and border style. What the `border-right` property does is to set the display properties that are applied to the right border only — no other borders are affected. Listing 12.7 is sample code that shows how `border-right` can be used. Its results can be seen in Opera 6.0 in Figure 12–9.

| Listing 12.7 | *border-right Example Code* |

```
<html>
<head>
<title>border-right Example</title>
</head>
<style>
p {font: 25px verdana, geneva, arial, helvetica, sans-serif}
</style>
</html>
<body>
<p style="border-right: medium solid red">A paragraph with a thin
red right border.</p>
<p style="border-right: thick ridge #0000ff">A paragraph with a
thick, blue ridged right border.</p>
<p style="border-right: 1in green double">A paragraph with a 1
inch thick, green double border to the right.</p>
<p style="border-right: 20px rgb(0%,100%,0%) dotted">Paragraph
with a 20 pixel thick, green and dotted right border.</p>
<p style="border-right: 5px #000 dashed">Paragraph with a 10 pixel
thick, black and dashed right border.</p>
</body>
</html>
```

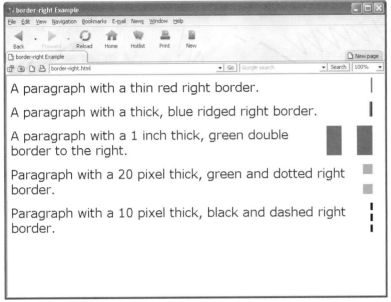

Figure 12–9   The border-right code sample as seen in Opera 6.0.

At some point in the future, `border-right` will incorporate all of the additional values referenced in the CSS3 border module, such as those creating borders with rounded edges, adding border images and so on. At the moment no major browser implements any of these CSS3 values for `border-right`, but they are all covered as individual properties later in this chapter.

Browser Compatibility

As with `border-left`, `border-bottom` (and `border-top`) the compatibility rating for `border-right` depends at least in part on how the border properties as a whole are implemented within a browser. Each of the browsers with at least a Partial rating implement this property, although the browser may not be able to support other standard border features (such as the `dotted` or `dashed` values for `border-style`, for example).

- Internet Explorer 3.0: Unsafe.
- Internet Explorer 4.0: Partial.
- Internet Explorer 4.0 – 4.5 (Mac): Safe.
- Internet Explorer 5.0: Partial.
- Internet Explorer 5.1 – 5.2 (Mac): Safe.
- Internet Explorer 5.5: Safe.

- Internet Explorer 6.0: Safe.

- Netscape Navigator 4.0 – 4.79: Partial.

- Netscape Navigator 4.0 (Mac & UNIX): Partial.

- Netscape Navigator 6.0: Safe.

- Netscape Navigator 7.0: Safe.

- Mozilla 1.0: Safe.

- Opera 3.6 – 4.0: Safe.

- Opera 5.0 – 6.0: Safe.

- Konqueror: Safe.

The `border-right` property has been implemented successfully in Internet Explorer since version 5.0 (Windows). The Partial rating for the earlier 4.0 version has to do with a lack of implementation for `border-style`'s `dotted` and `dashed` values in conjunction with this property.

Similarly Netscape Navigator 4.x is given a Partial rating, since it also did not implement the `dotted` and `dashed` values for `border-style`. It also allowed you to add borders to non-block-level elements, which is not, strictly speaking, correct. All of this was fixed by Netscape Navigator's 6.0 release. Mozilla 1.0 fully implements this property.

Traditionally ahead of the pack, Opera 3.6 had implemented `border-right` property fully.

Konqueror fully implements the `border-right` property.

12.8 border-top Property

The `border-top` property works in exactly the same manner as its sibling properties `border-right`, `border-left` and `border-bottom`, which we have already looked at, and sets the value to be assigned to the border to the top of the box *only*. It can take on all of the values belonging to the `border-style`, `border-color` and `border-width` properties.

The `border-top` is capable of taking on all of the other values associated with `border-style`, `border-color` and `border-width` properties. It can take a single numerical or named value that sets the width, color value and border style. The `border-top` property sets the display properties that are applied to the top border only — no other borders are affected. Listing 12.8 depicts sample code that shows how `border-top` can be implemented. Its results can be seen in Opera 6.0 in Figure 12–10.

Listing 12.8	*border-top Example Code*

```
<html>
<head>
<title>border-top Example</title>
</head>
<style>
p {font: 25px verdana, geneva, arial, helvetica, sans-serif}
</style>
</html>
<body>
<p style="border-top: thin solid blue">A paragraph with a thin and
blue top border.</p>
<p style="border-top: thick double #ff0000">A paragraph with a
thick, red and double top border.</p>
<p style="border-top: groove 2cm #daa520">A paragraph with a 2
centimeter thick, goldenrod and grooved top border.</p>
<p style="border-top: 20px dotted rgb(50%,50%,50%)">A paragraph
with a 10 pixel thick, grey dotted border on the top.</p>
<p style="border-top: 10px #0ff dashed">Paragraph with a 10 pixel
thick, aqua and dashed top border.</p>
</body>
</html>
```

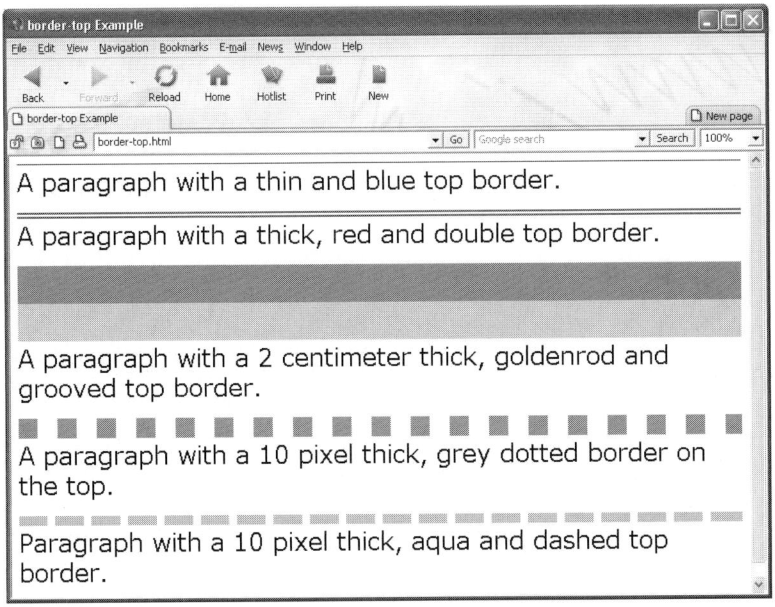

Figure 12–10 The border-top code sample as seen in Opera 6.0.

Finally, it should be noted that ultimately this property will incorporate all of the additional values described in the CSS3 border module, such as those dealing with adding border images, fitting those images properly to the border and many others. At the moment no major browser implements any of these CSS3 values for `border-top`; however, they are all covered as individual properties later in this chapter.

Browser Compatibility

Along with its sibling properties `border-left`, `border-bottom` and `border-right` the compatibility rating for `border-top` depends in part on how the border properties as a whole are implemented within a browser. Each of the browsers with at least a Partial rating implement this property, although the browser may not be able to support other standard border features (such as the `dotted` or `dashed` values for `border-style`, for example).

- Internet Explorer 3.0: Unsafe.
- Internet Explorer 4.0: Partial.
- Internet Explorer 4.0 – 4.5 (Mac): Safe.
- Internet Explorer 5.0: Partial.
- Internet Explorer 5.1 – 5.2 (Mac): Safe.
- Internet Explorer 5.5: Safe.
- Internet Explorer 6.0: Safe.
- Netscape Navigator 4.0 – 4.79: Partial.
- Netscape Navigator 4.0 (Mac & UNIX): Partial.
- Netscape Navigator 6.0: Safe.
- Netscape Navigator 7.0: Safe.
- Mozilla 1.0: Safe.
- Opera 3.6 – 4.0: Safe.
- Opera 5.0 – 6.0: Safe.
- Konqueror: Safe.

The `border-top` property has been implemented successfully in Internet Explorer since version 5.0 (Windows). The Partial rating for the earlier 4.0 version has to do with a lack of implementation for `border-style`'s `dotted` and `dashed` values in conjunction with this property.

Similarly Netscape Navigator 4.x is given a Partial rating, since it also did not implement the `dotted` and `dashed` values for `border-style`. It also allowed you to add borders to non-block-level elements, which is not, strictly speaking, correct. All of this was fixed by Netscape Navigator's 6.0 release. Mozilla 1.0 fully implements this property.

Traditionally ahead of the pack, by Opera 3.6 `border-top` was properly implemented.

Konqueror fully implements the `border-top` property.

12.9 border-bottom-width Property

The `border-bottom-width` property is designed to change the display of the bottom border. It differs from the `border-bottom` property in that it also displays a full border around all of the other sides of the box — only the bottom border is altered. It can take on all of the values belonging to the `border-width` property. It functions in the same way as its sibling properties `border-top-width`, `border-right-width` and `border-left-width`.

`border-bottom-width` can take one of two different sets of values: either a numeric value that sets the size of the border, or a name value. The name value can be `thin`, `medium` or `thick`, where `medium` is the default border width. If a numeric value is given and no measurement unit is specified, the value is set to a pixel width. Remember that when you are using this property, you are only setting the thickness value for the bottom width of the border, so this property is most often used in conjunction with other border family properties that set the display characteristics for the rest of the border. Listing 12.9, whose results can be seen in Internet Explorer 6.0 in Figure 12–11, gives you an idea of its effect.

Listing 12.9 *border-bottom-width Example Code*

```
<html>
<head>
<title>border-bottom-width Example</title>
<style>
body {font-size: large}
</style>
</head>
</html>
<body>
<p style="border-bottom-width: thin; border-style: solid">A
paragraph with a thin bottom border.</p>
<p style="border-bottom-width: medium; border-style: solid">A
paragraph with a medium bottom border (which is the default, so
there is no visible difference).</p>
<p style="border-bottom-width: thick; border-style: solid">A
paragraph with a thick bottom border.</p>
<p style="border-bottom-width: 1cm; border-style: double">A
paragraph with a 1 centimeter thick bottom doubled border.</p>
<p style="border-bottom-width: 20px; border-style: dotted">A
paragraph with a 1 centimeter thick bottom dotted border.</p>
<p style="border-bottom-width: 0.25in; border-style: dashed">A
paragraph with a quarter-inch thick bottom dashed border.</p>
</body>
</html>
```

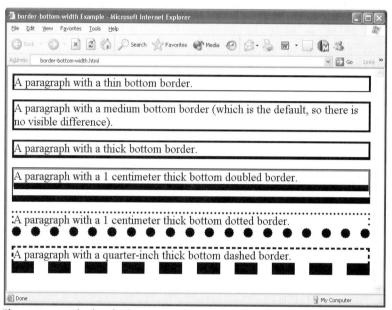

Figure 12–11 The border-bottom-width sample code as seen in Internet Explorer 6.0.

Browser Compatibility

The rating given to a browser for handling the `border-bottom-width` property (along with its sibling properties `border-left-width`, `border-right-width` and `border-top-width`) correctly depends in part on how the browser implements the border properties as a whole.

- Internet Explorer 3.0: Unsafe.
- Internet Explorer 4.0: Partial.
- Internet Explorer 4.0 – 4.5 (Mac): Safe.
- Internet Explorer 5.0: Partial.
- Internet Explorer 5.1 – 5.2 (Mac): Safe.
- Internet Explorer 5.5: Safe.
- Internet Explorer 6.0: Safe.
- Netscape Navigator 4.0 – 4.79: Partial.
- Netscape Navigator 4.0 (Mac & UNIX): Partial.
- Netscape Navigator 6.0: Safe.
- Netscape Navigator 7.0: Safe.
- Mozilla 1.0: Safe.
- Opera 3.6 – 4.0: Safe.
- Opera 5.0 – 6.0: Safe.

- Konqueror: Safe.

The `border-bottom-width` property has been implemented successfully in Internet Explorer since version 5.5 for the Windows version, and 4.0 for the Macintosh version. The Partial ratings handed out for prior versions of Internet Explorer have to do with its not implementing the `dotted` and `dashed` values associated with `border-style`.

While Netscape Navigator 4.x did not implement `border-style`'s `dotted` and `dashed` values either, it also treated `border-bottom-width` as if it were `border-bottom`; in other words, it only displays the bottom border, instead of just enhancing it. In addition, this property is supposed to work if no `border-style` property is set, but Netscape Navigator 4.x required it. It is given a "Partial" rating instead of an "Unsafe" rating because it does at least attempt to provide a bottom border. All of these problems were fixed by version 6.0. Similarly, Mozilla 1.0 fully implements this property.

Opera has supported this property fully since version 3.6.

Konqueror fully implements the `border-bottom-width` property.

12.10 border-left-width Property

The `border-left-width` property is designed to change the display of the left border. It differs from the `border-left` property in that it also displays a full border around all of the other sides of the box — only the left border is altered. It can take on all of the values belonging to the `border-width` property. It functions in the same way as its sibling properties `border-top-width`, `border-right-width` and `border-bottom-width`.

`border-left-width` can take one of two different sets of values: either a numeric value that sets the size of the border, or a name value. The name value can be `thin`, `medium` or `thick`, where `medium` is the default border width. If a numeric value is given and no measurement unit specified, the value is set to a pixel width. Remember that when you are using this property, you are only setting the thickness value for the left width of the border, so this property is most often used in conjunction with other border family properties that set the display characteristics for the rest of the border. Listing 12.10, whose results are seen within Internet Explorer 6.0 in Figure 12–12, gives you an idea of its effect.

Listing 12.10	*border-left-width Example Code*

```
<html>
<head>
<title>border-left-width Example</title>
```

Listing 12.10   *border-left-width Example Code (continued)*

```
<style>
body {font-size: large}
</style>
</head>
<body>
<p style="border-left-width: thin; border-style: solid">A
paragraph with a thin left border.</p>
<p style="border-left-width: medium; border-style: solid">A
paragraph with a medium left border (which is the default, so
there is no visible difference).</p>
<p style="border-left-width: thick; border-style: solid">A
paragraph with a thick left border.</p>
<p style="border-left-width: 1cm; border-style: double">A
paragraph with a 1 centimeter thick left doubled border.</p>
<p style="border-left-width: 15px; border-style: dotted">A
paragraph with a 15 pixel thick left dotted border. Here's some
extra text to ensure it is visible.</p>
<p style="border-left-width: 3mm; border-style: dashed">A
paragraph with a 3 millimeter thick left dashed border. Here's
some extra text to ensure it is visible.</p>
</body>
</html>
```

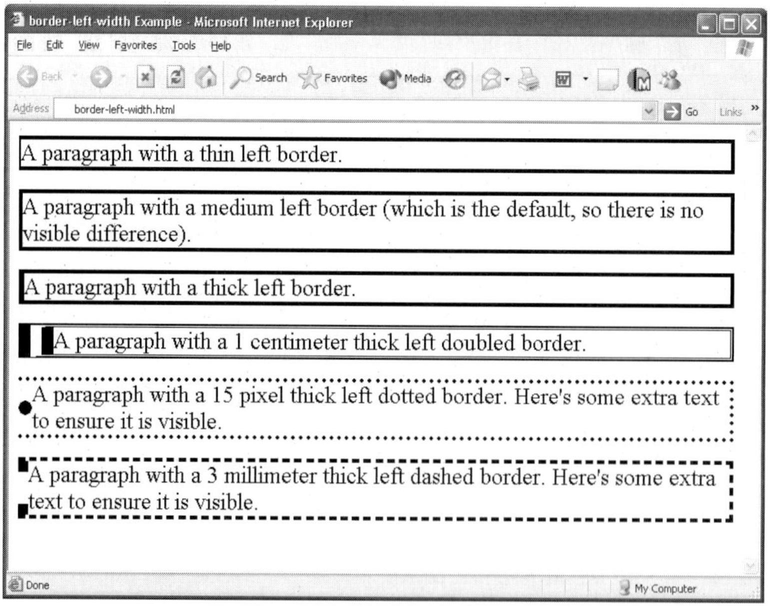

Figure 12–12 The border-left-width sample code as seen in Internet Explorer 6.0.

Browser Compatibility

The rating given to a browser for handling the `border-left-width` property (along with its sibling properties `border-bottom-width`, `border-right-width` and `border-top-width`) correctly depends in part on how that version of the browser implements the border properties as a whole.

- Internet Explorer 3.0: Unsafe.
- Internet Explorer 4.0: Partial.
- Internet Explorer 4.0 – 4.5 (Mac): Safe.
- Internet Explorer 5.0: Partial.
- Internet Explorer 5.1 – 5.2 (Mac): Safe.
- Internet Explorer 5.5: Safe.
- Internet Explorer 6.0: Safe.
- Netscape Navigator 4.0 – 4.79: Partial.
- Netscape Navigator 4.0 (Mac & UNIX): Partial.
- Netscape Navigator 6.0: Safe.
- Netscape Navigator 7.0: Safe.
- Mozilla 1.0: Safe.
- Opera 3.6 – 4.0: Safe.
- Opera 5.0 – 6.0: Safe.
- Konqueror: Safe.

The `border-left-width` property has been implemented successfully in Internet Explorer since version 5.5 for the Windows version, and 4.0 for the Macintosh version. The Partial ratings handed out for prior versions of Internet Explorer have to do with its not implementing the `dotted` and `dashed` values associated with `border-style` since version 4.0 (Windows).

While Netscape Navigator 4.x did not implement `border-style`'s `dotted` and `dashed` values either, it also treated `border-left-width` as if it were `border-left`; in other words, it only displays the left border, instead of just enhancing it. In addition, this property is supposed to work if no `border-style` property is set, but Netscape Navigator 4.x required it. It is given a "Partial" rating instead of an "Unsafe" rating because it does at least attempt to provide a left border. All of these problems were fixed by version 6.0. Similarly, Mozilla 1.0 fully implements this property.

Opera has supported this property fully since version 3.6.

Konqueror fully implements the `border-left-width` property.

12.11 border-right-width Property

The `border-right-width` property is designed to change the display of the right border. It differs from the `border-right` property in that it also displays a full border around all of the other sides of the box — only the right border is altered. It can take on all of the values belonging to the `border-width` property. It functions in the same way as its sibling properties `border-top-width`, `border-bottom-width` and `border-left-width`.

`border-right-width` can take one of two different sets of values: either a numeric value that sets the size of the border, or a name value. The name value can be `thin`, `medium` or `thick`, where `medium` is the default border width. If a numeric value is given and no measurement unit specified, the value is set to a pixel width. Remember that when you are using this property, you are only setting the thickness value for the right width of the border, so this property is most often used in conjunction with other border family properties that set the display characteristics for the rest of the border. Listing 12.11 provides an idea of its effect (its results displayed within Internet Explorer 6.0 in Figure 12–13).

Listing 12.11	*border-right-width Example Code*

```
<html>
<head>
<title>border-right-width Example</title>
<style>
body {font-size: large}
</style>
</head>
</html>
<body>
<p style="border-right-width: thin; border-style: solid">A
paragraph with a thin right border.</p>
<p style="border-right-width: medium; border-style: solid">A
paragraph with a medium right border (which is the default, so
there is no visible difference).</p>
<p style="border-right-width: thick; border-style: solid">A
paragraph with a thick right border.</p>
<p style="border-right-width: 1cm; border-style: double">A
paragraph with a 1 centimeter thick right doubled border.</p>
<p style="border-right-width: 15px; border-style: dotted">A
paragraph with a 15 pixel thick right dotted border. Here's some
extra text to ensure it is visible.</p>
```

| Listing 12.11 | *border-right-width Example Code (continued)* |

```
<p style="border-right-width: 3mm; border-style: dashed">A
paragraph with a 3 millimeter thick right dashed border. Here's
some extra text to ensure it is visible.</p>
</body>
</html>
```

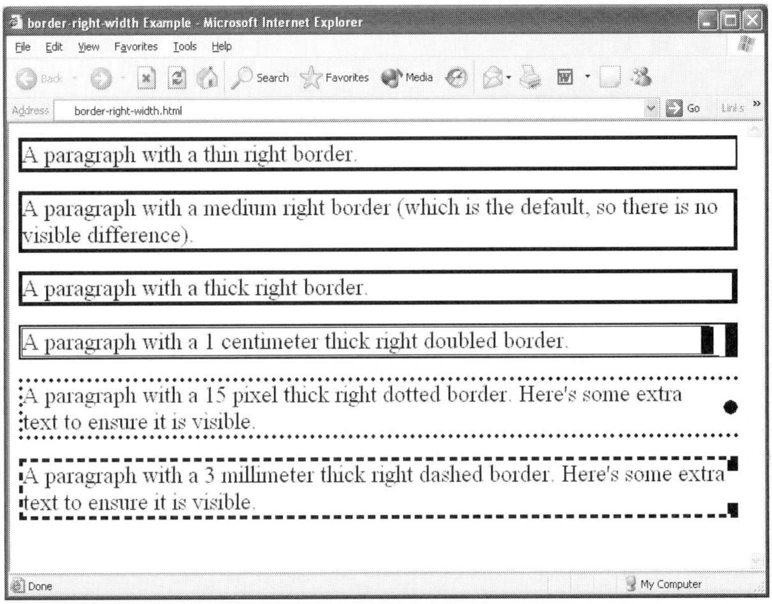

Figure 12–13 The border-right-width sample code as seen in Internet Explorer 6.0.

Browser Compatibility

The rating given to a browser for handling the `border-right-width` property (along with its sibling properties `border-bottom-width`, `border-left-width` and `bor-der-top-width`) correctly depends in part on how that version of the browser implements the border properties as a whole.

- Internet Explorer 3.0: Unsafe.
- Internet Explorer 4.0: Partial.
- Internet Explorer 4.0 – 4.5 (Mac): Safe.
- Internet Explorer 5.0: Partial.
- Internet Explorer 5.1 – 5.2 (Mac): Safe.

- Internet Explorer 5.5: Safe.
- Internet Explorer 6.0: Safe.
- Netscape Navigator 4.0 – 4.79: Partial.
- Netscape Navigator 4.0 (Mac & UNIX): Partial.
- Netscape Navigator 6.0: Safe.
- Netscape Navigator 7.0: Safe.
- Mozilla 1.0: Safe.
- Opera 3.6 – 4.0: Safe.
- Opera 5.0 – 6.0: Safe.
- Konqueror: Safe.

The `border-right-width` property has been implemented successfully in Internet Explorer since version 5.5 for the Windows version, and 4.0 for the Macintosh version. The Partial ratings handed out for prior versions of Internet Explorer have to do with its not implementing the `dotted` and `dashed` values associated with `border-style` since version 4.0 (Windows).

While Netscape Navigator 4.x did not implement `border-style`'s `dotted` and `dashed` values either, it also treated `border-right-width` as if it were `border-right`; in other words, it only displays the right border, instead of just enhancing it. In addition, this property is supposed to work if no `border-style` property is set, but Netscape Navigator 4.x required it. It is given a "Partial" rating instead of an "Unsafe" rating because it does at least attempt to provide a right border. All of these problems were fixed by version 6.0. Similarly, Mozilla 1.0 fully implements this property.

Opera has supported this property fully since version 3.6.

Konqueror fully implements the `border-right-width` property.

12.12 border-top-width Property

The `border-top-width` property is designed to change the display of the top border. It differs from the `border-top` property in that it also displays a full border around all of the other sides of the box — only the top border is altered. It can take on all of the values belonging to the `border-width` property. It functions in the same way as its sibling properties `border-left-width`, `border-right-width` and `border-bottom-width`.

`border-top-width` can take one of two different sets of values: either a numeric value that sets the size of the border, or a name value. The name value can be any one of the following: `thin`, `medium` or `thick`, where `medium` is the default border width. If a numeric value is given and no measurement unit specified, the value is set to a pixel width. Remember that when you are using this property, you are only setting the thickness value for the top width of the border, so this property is most often used in conjunction with other border family properties that set the display characteristics for the rest of the border. Listing 12.12, whose results can be seen in Internet Explorer 6.0 in Figure 12–14, gives you an idea of its effect.

Listing 12.12 *border-top-width Example Code*

```
<html>
<head>
<title>border-top-width Example</title>
<style>
body {font-size: large}
</style>
</head>
</html>
<body>
<p style="border-top-width: thin; border-style: solid">A paragraph
with a thin top border.</p>
<p style="border-top-width: medium; border-style: solid">A
paragraph with a medium top border (which is the default, so there
is no visible difference).</p>
<p style="border-top-width: thick; border-style: solid">A
paragraph with a thick top border.</p>
<p style="border-top-width: 1cm; border-style: double">A paragraph
with a 1 centimeter thick top doubled bor-der.</p>
<p style="border-top-width: 15px; border-style: dotted">A
paragraph with a 15 pixel thick top dotted border. Here's some
extra text to ensure it is visible.</p>
<p style="border-top-width: 3mm; border-style: dashed">A paragraph
with a 3 millimeter thick top dashed border. Here's some extra
text to ensure it is visible.</p>
</body>
</html>
```

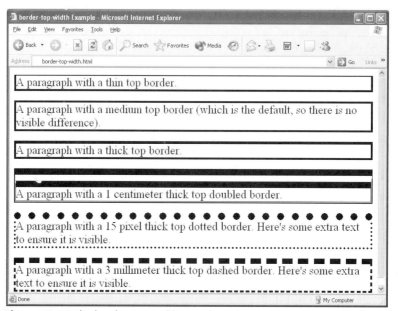

Figure 12–14 The border-top-width sample code as seen in Internet Explorer 6.0.

Browser Compatibility

The rating given to a browser for handling the border-top-width property (along with its sibling properties border-left-width, border-right-width and border-bottom-width) correctly depends in part on how the browser implements the border properties as a whole.

- Internet Explorer 3.0: Unsafe.
- Internet Explorer 4.0: Partial.
- Internet Explorer 4.0 – 4.5 (Mac): Safe.
- Internet Explorer 5.0: Partial.
- Internet Explorer 5.1 – 5.2 (Mac): Safe.
- Internet Explorer 5.5: Safe.
- Internet Explorer 6.0: Safe.
- Netscape Navigator 4.0 – 4.79: Partial.
- Netscape Navigator 4.0 (Mac & UNIX): Partial.
- Netscape Navigator 6.0: Safe.
- Netscape Navigator 7.0: Safe.
- Mozilla 1.0: Safe.
- Opera 3.6 – 4.0: Safe.
- Opera 5.0 – 6.0: Safe.

- Konqueror: Safe.

The `border-top-width` property has been implemented successfully in Internet Explorer since version 5.5 for the Windows version, and 4.0 for the Macintosh version. The Partial ratings handed out for prior versions of Internet Explorer have to do with its not implementing the `dotted` and `dashed` values associated with `border-style` since version 4.0 (Windows).

While Netscape Navigator 4.x did not implement `border-style`'s `dotted` and `dashed` values either, it also treated `border-top-width` as if it were `border-top`; in other words, it only displays the top border, instead of just enhancing it. In addition, this property is supposed to work if no `border-style` property is set, but Netscape Navigator 4.x required it. It is given a "Partial" rating instead of an "Unsafe" rating because it does at least attempt to provide a top border. All of these problems were fixed by version 6.0. Similarly, Mozilla 1.0 fully implements this property.

Opera has supported this property fully since version 3.6.

Konqueror fully implements the `border-top-width` property.

12.13 border Property

The `border` property is a type of "shortcut" property that can allow the Web author to set most, but not all, of the properties normally reserved for the other border sub-family of properties.

Using `border`, you can use all of the border styles you could normally set through the `border-style` property, set the width normally reserved for the `border-width` property, and set the color normally reserved for the `border-color` property. You cannot set the values normally associated with `border-top`, `border-right`, `border-bottom`, `border-left`, `border-top-width`, `border-right-width`, `border-bottom-width` and `border-left-width`. Put simply, you can only set global border values. This means `border` can only take one numerical or name value to substitute for `border-width`, and if you need to set one border value different than another, you will have to use `border` with one of the other properties that control that type of thing. In addition, when using `border`, you must set the border style to be displayed — without a typical `border-style` property value set, nothing is displayed. Listing 12.13, whose effects are illustrated in Figure 12–15, gives you an idea of how it works:

Listing 12.13	*border Example*

```
<html>
<head>
<title>border Example</title>
</head>
</html>
<body style="font-size: large">
<p style="border: thin solid gray">
Paragraph surrounded by a solid gray border.
</p>
<p style="border: 15mm groove #0000ff">
Paragraph surrounded by a 15 millimeter thick, blue grooved border
</p>
<p style="border: thick double">
Paragraph surrounded by a thick, doubled border.
</p>
<p style="border: 1cm ridge; border-bottom-width: 0.5cm">
Paragraph surrounded by a 1 centimeter thick ridged border, and a
1/2 centimeter thick bottom border.
</p>
</body>
</html>
```

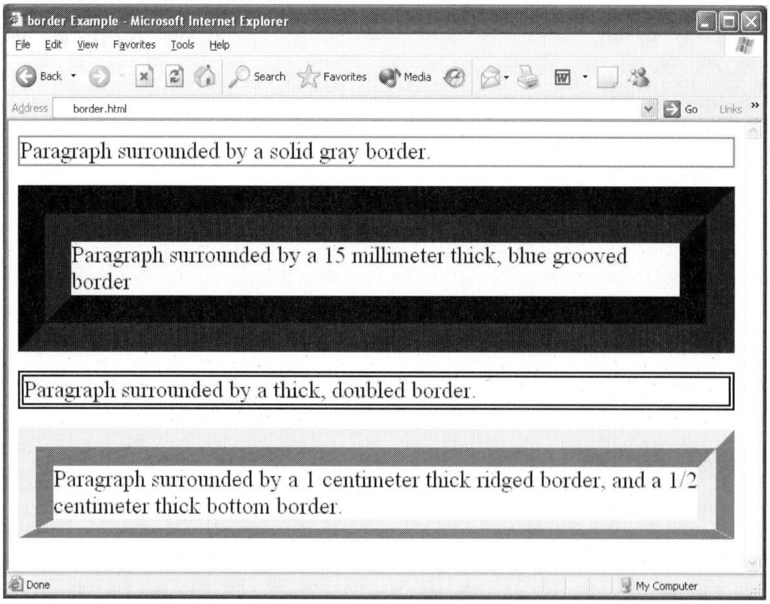

Figure 12–15 The border example code as seen in Internet Explorer 6.0.

At some point in the future, `border` will incorporate all of the additional values referenced in the CSS3 border module, such as those for creating borders with rounded edges, adding border images and so on. All of these properties are individually covered later in the chapter.

Browser Compatibility

Ultimately the compatibility rating given to border depends on how its sub-properties are implemented in the major browsers.

- Internet Explorer 3.0: Unsafe.
- Internet Explorer 4.0: Partial.
- Internet Explorer 4.0 – 4.5 (Mac): Safe.
- Internet Explorer 5.0: Partial.
- Internet Explorer 5.1 – 5.2 (Mac): Safe.
- Internet Explorer 5.5: Safe.
- Internet Explorer 6.0: Safe.
- Netscape Navigator 4.0 – 4.79: Partial.
- Netscape Navigator 4.0 (Mac & UNIX): Partial.
- Netscape Navigator 6.0: Safe.
- Netscape Navigator 7.0: Safe.
- Mozilla 1.0: Safe.
- Opera 3.6 – 4.0: Safe.
- Opera 5.0 – 6.0: Safe.
- Konqueror: Safe.

The `border` property has been implemented successfully in Internet Explorer since version 5.0 (Windows). The Partial rating for the earlier 4.0 version has to do with a lack of implementation for `border-style`'s `dotted` and `dashed` values in conjunction with this property.

Similarly Netscape Navigator 4.x is given a Partial rating, since it also did not implement the `dotted` and `dashed` values for `border-style`. It also allowed you to add borders to non-block-level elements, which is not, strictly speaking, correct. All of this was fixed by Netscape Navigator's 6.0 release. Mozilla 1.0 fully implements this property.

Traditionally ahead of the pack, Opera 3.6 properly implemented `border-top`.

Konqueror fully implements the `border-top` property.

12.14 border-radius Set of Properties

Up to now we have looked at all of the border properties first introduced under CSS1 and CSS2 that control the look of the sides of the border. The proposed CSS3 borders module takes the next natural step and provides a set of properties giving you more control over how "rounded" the corners are displayed by using the `border-radius` set of properties.

There are five `border-radius` properties: four controlling each specific corner and one shortcut property that governs them all. Beginning with the top-left corner and moving clockwise, the individual properties are `border-top-left-radius`, `border-top-right-radius`, `border-bottom-right-radius` and `border-bottom-left-radius`. The shortcut property for them all is `border-radius`. These properties all govern the "roundedness" of a corner by using a pair of values that describe the radius of an ellipse. The first value sets the horizontal radius (the distance "in"), and the second value sets the vertical radius (the distance from the top or bottom). If the values are set to 0, you get the default square border edge. The greater the value of the ellipse you create, the more rounded the border will be. If only one value is used instead of two, it will be applied equally to both the horizontal and vertical values, producing a more circular, rather than elliptical, edge. (The examples that follow use circularly rounded corners — at the time of writing the specification does not say how dual values should be separated, although it will likely either use a comma or space to separate each value from another; single values are used here, since they should prove to be valid code.)

Let's say you want to produce a relatively large rounded border that is used on all four corners. The following code snippet using `border-radius` shows how you could accomplish this:

```
<style>
div.rounded {border-radius: 100px}
</style>
```

This would produce a block whose border is highly rounded, much like the one illustrated at the top of Figure 12–16.

If you are trying to produce a block whose border contains many different rounded corners, the following code snippet shows how to make one:

```
<style>
div.rounded {border-top-left-radius: 50px;
border-top-right-radius: 0px; border-bottom-right-radius: 200px;
border-bottom-left-radius: 15px}
</style>
```

This code would produce a block whose rounded corners would look something like the bottom image in Figure 12–16.

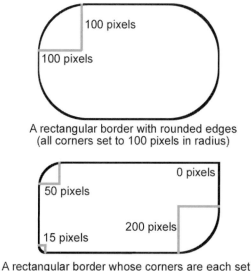

A rectangular border with rounded edges
(all corners set to 100 pixels in radius)

A rectangular border whose corners are each set
to different border-radius values

Figure 12–16 Sample border-radius values mocked up, each illustrating the "depth" value set for the rounding ellipse.

There are a few things to be aware of when using any of these properties. First of all, keep in mind that any content contained within the block will necessarily be "indented" so that it does not overflow the boundary of the rounded edge. So using a rounded border for a block means you can expect to pack less content into a block. Also, if you are using non-Western text and have set `writing-mode: vertical` (a setting typical of many Asian languages), the initial horizontal value is applied to the vertical value instead, and the vertical to the horizontal.

The `border-radius` property is a shortcut property allowing you to set all four corner rounding values at once. The initial code snippet shows how you could use a single value to set all four corners to the same roundedness value. As a shortcut property, `border-radius` should also be able to allow you to set individual corner values sequentially, but this is not spelled out in the specification at the time of writing. It is *likely* that you would be able to accomplish this with comma-separated values, either beginning with the top-left or top-right corner and working clockwise through each corner, but this will only be confirmed when the specification is finally fixed for this set of properties.

12.15 border-image Set of Properties

The CSS3 border module will enable future Web authors to create borders out of images using the extensive set of `border-image` properties. There are in fact three sets of `border-image` properties: one used to specify the image or images to be used, another describing how they should fit together, and a third that allows you to do simple flipping and rotating of a given border image, conserving the total number of border images that need to be used to create a border. This section looks at the first of those sets of properties, which is used to place images to frame the sides and corners of a border.

For setting images for borders, there are two separate sets of border image properties governed by the separate `border-image` and `border-corner-image` shortcut properties. Both of these shortcut properties incorporate the values of four separate sub-properties controlling the four edges and four corners. For `border-image` there are the `border-top-image`, `border-right-image`, `border-bottom-image` and `border-left-image` sub-properties; for `border-corner-image` there are the `border-top-left-image`, `border-top-right-image`, `border-bottom-right-image` and `border-bottom-left-image` sub-properties. Each of these sub-properties can be set to a series of up to three URL values, each pointing to a border image file. If a single image is specified, only it is used for the border. If two are set, then the first is placed to the top or left side, the second to the bottom or right. If three are used, the first image is set to the middle, the second to the top or left and the third to the bottom or right. In practice though, it is more likely that you will be using a single image, if only for simplicity's sake. In addition to these values, you can also set these sub-properties to `none` (the default) and to `inherit`, which will take on any parent value that may be present. All of the border-corner properties have an additional value, called `continue`, which when set to 0 (the default) allows the border side image(s) to run fully into the corner. When a corner value is set, it essentially covers its corner, and hopefully is aligned so that it forms a continuous border with its side image border elements (assuming that they are used at all).

The shortcut properties `border-image` and `border-corner-image` are each designed to take four URL values, each of which sets a single image for each side or corner, respectively. They can also take on the `none` and `inherit` values, while `border-corner-image` can additionally take on `continuous`. While not explicitly spelled out in the CSS3 border specification at the time of writing, the ubiquitous CSS3 value `initial` also likely applies to all of these properties. Since the `initial` value is an explicit way of setting the default value for a property, in this case it would set them to be equivalent to `none` for the `border-image` properties, and `continuous` for the `border-corner-image` properties.

It is easy to come up with some eye-catching borders using these properties along with some well-chosen frame and corner images. For example, to create the top image in Figure 12–17 using the same image twice as the left and right borders you could use the following code snippet:

```
<style>
div.egyptian {border-image-left:
http://www.afakeurl.com/egyptian-column.jpg; border-image-right:
http://www.afakeurl.com/egyptian-column.jpg}
</style>
```

In this case the `border-image-left` and `border-image-right` properties are set to a single image of an Egyptian column, which will bracket the content it contains.

It is also possible to create a stunning border made solely of corner images, such as that depicted in the middle of Figure 12–17. Creating it could be accomplished by using the following code snippet:

```
<style>
div.cornerize {border-corner-image:
http://www.afakeurl.com/ornate1.jpg,
http://www.afakeurl.com/ornate2.jpg,
http://www.afakeurl.com/ornate3.jpg,
http://www.afakeurl.com/ornate4.jpg}
</style>
```

In this piece of code the `border-corner-image` property is set to a series of four separate border images, all of which comprise a complete corner-based "frame."

You can also make a complete mix of side and corner border images as well, much like that seen at the bottom of Figure 12–17. The following code snippet depicts how you can create such an image border collage:

```
<style>
div.collage {border-top-left-image:
http://www.afakeurl.com/ornate1.jpg; border-top-image:
http://www.afakeurl.com/frilly-bow-border.jpg;
border-top-right-image: http://www.afakeurl.com/woodcut-sun.jpg;
border-bottom-right-image: http://www.afakeurl.com/ornate3.jpg;
border-bottom-image: http://www.afakeurl.com/scrolled-wood.jpg;
border-bottom-left-image:
http://www.afakeurl.com/woodcut-sun.jpg}
</style>
```

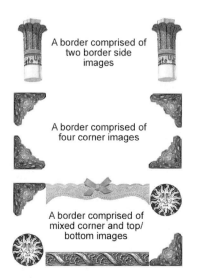

A border comprised of
two border side
images

A border comprised of
four corner images

A border comprised of
mixed corner and top/
bottom images

Figure 12–17 Sample border-image values mocked up.

In addition to the sets of `border-image` and `border-corner-image` properties are related properties that control how border images are "fitted" together, and those used for rotating or "flipping" the image files in order re-use the same image onscreen several times instead of having to load separate image files for each border or corner element.

12.16 border-fit Set of Properties

While the `border-image` set of properties are designed to let you place which image where on a given border or corner, they do not tell the browser how they should interact with each other. That's where the `border-fit` set of properties comes in.

There are in fact three sets of `border-fit` properties: those governing length, those governing width and another set that deal exclusively with corner images (the `border-corner-fit` properties). Including shortcut properties, there are a whopping 20 separate properties in the `border-fit` set of properties. But for the most part they use the same seven values: `clip`, `overflow`, `overwrite`, `repeat`, `scale`, `space` and `stretch`. The `clip` value tells the browser to display the image — without repeating it — and remove (i.e., "clip") any overflow. The `overflow` value does the same thing as `clip`, except that the image is allowed to overflow the border area if necessary. The `overwrite` value displays the image without any scaling, and any overflow isn't clipped. The `repeat` value is used to tile a given image many times over until it fills its space, with any overflow clipped. `scale` is similar to `repeat`, but when the border space is filled prior to an overflow, all of the images are scaled up in size in order to fit. With `space`, the image is repeated as often as possible to fill up a given border area without overflowing, and then space is added between them for a perfect fit. Finally, `stretch` is used so that a single image is expanded or contracted enough to fill the border space. The default value for all of the `border-fit` properties is `repeat`, and for the `border-corner-fit` properties it is `overwrite`, so corner images take precedence over "side" images, which are repeated as necessary to fill the border space. In addition to these values one should not forget the ubiquitous `inherit` value, which would take on any available parent value for the border side or corner. And while it is not explicitly stated in the latest draft of the CSS3 border specification, it would make sense if the CSS3 `initial` value is applicable to these properties. `initial` is a way of explicitly setting a given property to its default value: for the `border-fit` properties it is `repeat`, and it is `overwrite` for the `border-corner-fit` properties.

The set of `border-fit` properties consists of the following: `border-top-fit-length`, `border-right-fit-length`, `border-bottom-fit-length`, `border-left-fit-length`, `border-top-fit-width`, `border-right-fit-width`, `border-bottom-fit-width`, `border-left-fit-width`, `border-fit-length`, `border-fit` and `border-fit-width`. These comprise all of the properties controlling the fit of a border image for the "sides" of the border. If you look closely, you'll see there are three distinct types of properties present here: those that govern length for a side, those that govern its width, and shortcut properties. The shortcut properties `border-fit-length`, `border-fit-width` can take up to four separate values apiece, each of which is applied to each side in turn. The `border-fit` property can take two values: the first is applied to all side lengths, the second to all side widths. If only one value is present for `border-fit`, it is applied to both side lengths and widths.

The set of `border-corner-fit` properties mirrors that for the `border-fit` properties, and it consists of the following individual properties: `border-top-left-fit-length`, `border-top-right-fit-length`, `border-bottom-right-fit-length`, `border-bottom-left-fit-length`, `border-top-left-fit-width`, `border-top-right-fit-width`, `border-bottom-right-fit-width`, `border-bottom-left-fit-width` and `border-corner-fit`. In this case there is only the one shortcut property, `border-corner-fit`, and it can take up to four values. If four values are present, they set the dimensions for the top-left, top-right, bottom-right, and bottom-left corners respectively. If only two values are present for `border-corner-fit`, the first is applied to the vertical dimension, the second to the horizontal. If only one value is stated, it is applied equally to all four corners.

For all of these values, it is permissible for the border image to overflow into the content area, though not into the space beyond the boundaries of the block element it is set to.

Figure 12–18 provides several illustrations of how a single image can be applied as an image border and shaped using the `border-top-fit-length` property, which serves as a good example for all of the other such "side" formatting properties in this section.

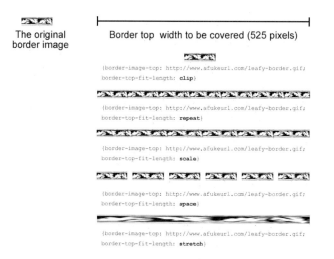

Figure 12–18 Several values for a sample border-top-fit-length border image mocked up.

As you can see from Figure 12–18, several different values are applied to a relatively small border image ("`leafy-border.gif`") across a top border. In the first case, `clip` is used. Since it is not supposed to repeat the image, all you see in this case is a single image centered in the middle of the border area. You would get the same effect if you used the `overwrite` value in this case, because the image is too small to cover the intended border area — so these values work best when larger border images are used, or a small border area is being covered. The second example shows the effect of the `repeat` value, which copies the initial image across the border, and is finally clipped at the end (in this case, the image is clipped in the middle). The third example shows the effects of `scale`, which in this case increases the size of the image just enough so that it can completely fill the border space required. The fourth example shows `space` put to work, which repeats the image at its original size evenly across the border, evenly spaced out. The final version shows `stretch` being used, which creates a distorted looking border — this value is best used for images that more closely resemble the intended size of the border. These same values apply equally well to the `border-corner-fit` properties.

12.17 border-image-transform Set of Properties

The final set of properties relating to adding images to borders is the `border-image-transform` set of properties. Compared to the myriad of properties comprising the `border-image` and `border-fit` sets of properties, the `border-image-transform` set of properties is made up of only two separate properties: `border-image-transform` and `border-corner-image-transform`. The former is for use on "side" border images, while the latter is for use on corner images. The idea with these properties is that you set one corner or side image, and then tell it how it should be reflected or otherwise "transformed" for display on the other three corners or sides, respectively. With `border-image-transform` it applies its transformation on whatever image is set to `border-top-image` (i.e., the image set to the top border), and for `border-corner-image-transform` it is the image assigned to `border-top-left-image` (i.e., the top-left corner). Using these properties you can easily conserve on the total number of images used for your border, letting the browser do all the work of inverting, flipping and rotating border images for you.

The `border-image-transform` property comes with five primary values: `none`, `rotate`, `reflect-xy`, `reflect-right` and `reflect-left`. The `none` value is the default, and leaves the image as is — that is, nothing is done to it and it is not reflected on the other four sides of the border. The `rotate` value simply takes the initial image and rotates it first 90 degrees for the right side, 180 degrees for the bottom side, and 270 degrees for the left side — in all cases the "inner" part of the border image continues to point to the inside of the block. With `reflect-xy`, what happens is that the bottom border image is a reflection of the top, and the right border image is a reflection of that seen on the left. Using `reflect-right`, the top border image is rotated 90 degrees and used for the right side; it is then reflected to the left side, and the top image is similarly reflected to the bottom. `reflect-left` uses the same idea, but instead places the rotated image to the left border first, which is then reflected to the right; the bottom image is still a reflection of that used on the top. All of this may seem hard to visualize, but you can see clear illustrations of the effects of each of these values in the first two rows of Figure 12–19.

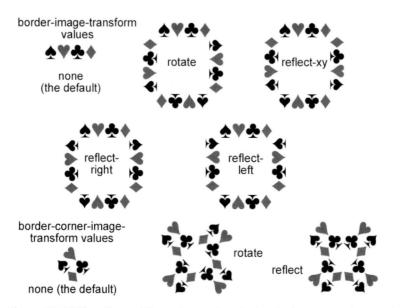

Figure 12–19 The effects of the various values for border-image-transform and border-corner-image-transform illustrated.

The `border-corner-image-transform` property works in a similar fashion, although it only has three values: `none`, `rotate` and `reflect`. The `none` value does nothing; the image is not repeated on any other corner. With `rotate` the corner image is rotated 90 degrees for each succeeding corner, the inner edge of the corner image always pointing inwards. Using `reflect` the original image is reflected from the top-left corner to the bottom-right corner, and the top-right corner is similarly reflected to the bottom-left corner. You can see the effects of all of these values depicted along the bottom row of Figure 12–19.

In addition to all of these values, you can safely assume that `inherit` also applies, so if a parent value is available, it will be applied. Although not explicitly stated, it can also be assumed that the `initial` value also applies to these properties, which sets the property explicitly to its default value. For both `border-image-transform` and `border-corner-image-transform` this value would be `none`.

12.18 border-break Property

`border-break` is another property proposed under the CSS3 border module, and it is designed to tell the browser how to (or not to) break a border when the block displaying the border is spread out over more than one page.

It can take a `border-style` or `border-image` as its value, or the value `none`. `none` is the default, and it does not add any padding or border to a block's border when it is spread across a page break. If a `border-style` or `border-image` is used instead, at the end of the first page and at the beginning of the second it is used to close off the box between the two pages. You can see the effects of both types of values illustrated in Figure 12–20.

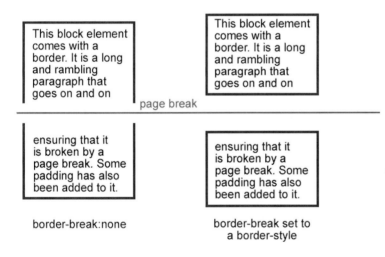

Figure 12–20 Illustrating the effects of the border-break property.

In addition to these values, there is the `inherit` value, taking on whatever parent value may be available. Although not explicitly stated in the CSS3 border module, it can also be assumed that the `initial` value also applies to these properties, which sets `border-break` to its default, which is `none`.

12.19 box-shadow Property

Using the CSS3 border module property `box-shadow` you can add a shadow effect attached to the border of any block element, ensuring that it stands out from the page. Any shadows created in this manner do not otherwise affect the flow of content — for example, if some text immediately follows a block that is set to box-shadow, the shadow is blended into it. If the border is rounded (using one of the border-radius properties), the shadow will also be rounded.

The box-shadow property takes a set of three comma-separated length values followed by a color value. The first length value draws the horizontal offset for the shadow, the second the vertical offset value, and the third sets the blur radius for the shadow. For the latter, a sharp shadow is equal to 0; any other value leads to a larger, more diffuse shadow. The color value that follows these length values sets the color of the shadow. Listing 12.14 shows how this property might be put to use, and its effects are illustrated in Figure 12–21.

Listing 12.14   *box-shadow Example Code*

```
<html>
<head>
<title>box-shadow Example</title>
</head>
<style>
h1 {border: thick solid red; box-shadow: 20px 20px 5px red}
span.square {border: thin solid blue; box-shadow: 1em 1em 5px
blue}
span.round {border: thin solid lime; border-radius: 15px;
box-shadow: 1em 1em 5px lime}
body {font-size: x-large}
</style>
<body>
<h1>This border has a red drop shadow</h1>
This text contains some inline text that features a border that
also <span class="square">sports a drop shadow</span>.
<p>
This text contains some inline text that features a rounded border
with a drop shadow, so necessarily its shadow <span
class="round">should appear rounded</span>.
</p>
</body>
</html>
```

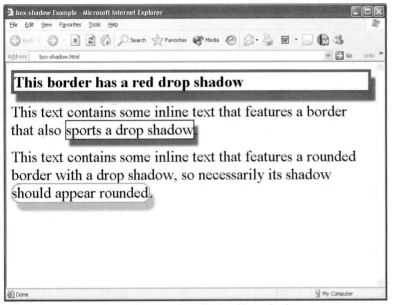

Figure 12–21 A mock-up showing the effects of box-shadow.

It should be noted that a similar mechanism exists for the Internet Explorer browser: the `DropShadow` filter. This is a browser-specific filter, and the effects and even the methods of achieving them are similar. It is covered in depth in Chapter 25, "Filters and Transitions."

12.20 clear Property

The `clear` property belongs to the family of boxes and margins. It is designed to tell the browser where textual elements should appear onscreen. The `clear` property is used to set how the specified element will allow other Web page elements to "float" along its sides, determining where the text that appears after the element should appear in relation to it. In this way, it works in exactly the same manner as the `clear` attribute as used with the `<br>` HTML tag.

When text follows an image, it generally flows immediately after it in the same vertical space occupied by the image. Using the `clear` property, you can control where text should appear in relation to the image. This can be handy when you have multiple images appearing on a Web page, and you want to be sure that your text is associated with the right image, and that the images don't appear in a jumble on the page. For example, the following code will create such a jumble:

```
<img src="trajan.jpg" align="left">
this text should appear beside the previous image.
<img src="trajan.jpg" align="left">
```

What you will get is the first image appearing on the left, some text appearing to its right, and the next image appearing underneath the text and to the right of the first image. Not pretty. To solve this problem, you could can use `<br clear="all">` after the text to force the second image to appear below the first, eliminating the jumble on screen. You can now also use the `clear` CSS property to accomplish the same thing.

The `clear` property uses the following values: `left`, `right`, `both` and `none`. `left` tells the browser to display the text below the image when the image is set to `align="left"`. `right` tells the browser to display the text below the image when the image is set to `align="right"`. `both` should be used when you have two images aligned left and right, and you want text to appear *beneath* both of them. Finally, `none` places the text *between* two images aligned left and right. Listing 12.15, whose effects are displayed in Figure 12–22, demonstrates all of these elements put to use:

Listing 12.15	*clear*

```
<html>
<head>
<title>clear Example</title>
</head>
<body>
<img src="smaller_trajan.jpg" align="left"><b style="clear:
left">This paragraph should appear below an image that is left
aligned.</b>
<br clear="all"><img src="smaller_trajan.jpg" align="right">
<b style="clear: right">This paragraph should appear below an
image that is right aligned.</b>
<p>
<br clear="all"><img src="smaller_trajan.jpg" align="left"><img
src="smaller_trajan.jpg" align="right">
<b style="clear: both">This line of text appears <i>below</i> the
two images.</b>
</p>
<p>
<br clear="all"><img src="smaller_trajan.jpg" align="left"><img
src="smaller_trajan.jpg" align="right">
<b style="clear: none">This line of text appears <i>between</i>
the two images.</b>
</p>
</body>
</html>
```

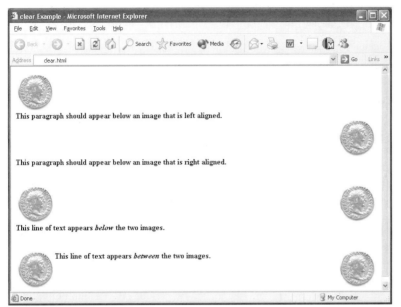

Figure 12–22 Sample code for clear displayed.

CSS3 and clear

The CSS3 box model module proposes a number of new properties to clear: top, bottom, inside, outside, start and end. The top value is meant to be used for vertically flowing text, and in this context it is the equivalent of left when used with that standard, left-right flow of Western text; similarly bottom is equivalent to right for vertically flowing text. inside has the same effect as left for non-paged media, and outside the same effect as right for non-paged media. The start value is dependent on the direction of text in the block it is contained within. It is equivalent to left-top when direction: ltr, and right-bottom when direction: rtl. end works in the same, but opposite way; in other words it is set to right-bottom when direction: ltr, and left-top when direction: rtl.

Browser Compatibility

Other than a few glitches here and there — primarily with early versions of Internet Explorer and Netscape Navigator — the clear property (except for the CSS3 values) has been well supported.

- Internet Explorer 3.0: Unsafe.
- Internet Explorer 4.0: Partial.

- Internet Explorer 4.0 – 4.5 (Mac): Safe.
- Internet Explorer 5.0: Safe.
- Internet Explorer 5.1 – 5.2 (Mac): Safe.
- Internet Explorer 5.5: Safe.
- Internet Explorer 6.0: Safe.
- Netscape Navigator 4.0 – 4.79: Partial.
- Netscape Navigator 4.0 (Mac & UNIX): Partial.
- Netscape Navigator 6.0: Safe.
- Netscape Navigator 7.0: Safe.
- Mozilla 1.0: Safe.
- Opera 3.6 – 4.0: Safe.
- Opera 5.0 – 6.0: Safe.
- Konqueror: Safe.

The `clear` property has been implemented successfully in Internet Explorer since version 5.0 for Windows and version 4.0 for the Macintosh. The Partial rating for the earlier 4.0 version for Windows had to do with problems it encountered when used in conjunction with `float`.

Netscape Navigator 4.x was also problematic when you used `clear` in conjunction with `float`. Subsequent versions of Netscape Navigator, as well as Mozilla, got this combination right.

Ever since Opera version 3.6 `clear` has been implemented properly.

Konqueror fully implements the `clear` property.

12.21 clear-after Property

The `clear-after` property is a proposed CSS3 addition, and is designed to ensure that the bottom border of a box goes below any floating elements that may appear on a page. This property is intended to prevent elements on a Web page from overlapping when `clear` and `float` are used multiple times on a page.

`clear-after` has a total of nine values: `none`, `left`, `right`, `top`, `bottom`, `inside`, `outside`, `start` and `end`. The `none` value is the default, and tells the browser to do nothing. For `left` and `top`, only elements floating to the left and top are accounted for, and for `right` and `bottom` only those elements floating to the right and bottom are considered. If the bottom of an element occurs on a right-hand page, `inside` only works with left-floating elements, and has the opposite effect on a left-hand page. Similarly, `outside` works the same way as `inside`, but with the opposite effect. The `start` value is dependent on the direction of text in the block it is contained within, and is equivalent to left-top when `direction: ltr`, and right-bottom when `direction: rtl`. `end` works in the same, but opposite way; in other words it is set to right-bottom when `direction: ltr`, and left-top when `direction: rtl`. Finally, `both` considers the left/top and right/bottom floats that may be present.

12.22 float Property

The `float` property determines how a specified element wraps around another "parent" element as it floats on a Web page. While it sounds simple, it is arguably one of the hardest things for browsers to get right, and at the moment no browser is fully capable of rendering it properly. The `float` property belongs to the CSS family of boxes and margins, and is most typically used to tell a browser where to place text either immediately before or after an image. To put things in more concrete terms, think of an image on a Web page and some text that follows immediately after it. Browsers typically place the text flush to the bottom of the image. The `float` property is designed to allow the Web author to have that text appear beside that image instead. This is handy, because otherwise the image would take over the Web page, especially if the image is a large one.

`float` can take on one of three properties: `left`, `right` and `none`. `left` displays the element to the left margin of the object specified, `right` displays the element to the right margin, and `none` sets the float value to the browser default (which should be flush with the bottom of the image). Probably the best way to understand how this works is to look at some code and then see the results. Take a look at the following code snippet, for example:

```
<img src="aurelian.jpg">This is the default value
for the browser. <br clear="all">
```

What you will get is an image that appears with some text displayed flush with the bottom of the image. What `float` does is very similar to the function of the `align` attribute for the `<img>` tag. The following two lines of code produce the same results:

```
<p>
<img src="aurelian.jpg" style="float: left">image set to
style="float: left".
<br clear="all">
</p>


<p>
<img src="aurelian.jpg" align="left">image set to
align="left".
</p>
```

If you substitute `align="left"` with `style="float:  left"` or `style="float: right"` with `align="right"` you will get the same results.

As for the value `none`, it should work in the same way as the browser's default value when no float setting is given. All three values for `float` are displayed in the following code, whose results can be seen in Figure 12–23.

Listing 12.16   *float Example #1*

```
<html>
<head>
<title>Float Example #1</title>
</head>
<body style="font-size: x-large">
<img src="aurelian.jpg" style="float: none">Image set to
style="float: none".<br clear="all">
<p>
<img src="aurelian.jpg" style="float: left">image set to
style="float: left".
<br clear="all">
</p>
<p>
<img src="aurelian.jpg" style="float: right">image set to
style="float: right".
</p>
</body>
</html>
```

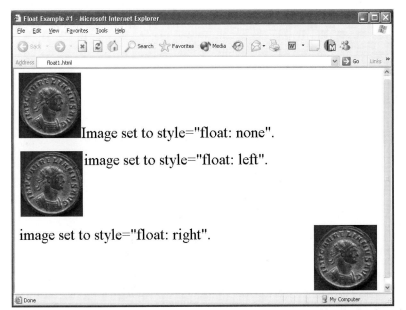

Figure 12–23 Sample code for float when used with an image file, as displayed in Internet Explorer 6.0.

When `float` is used where margins are set, the resulting text or other elements that follow a floated element should also float in relationship to the margins that are set. In Listing 12.17, you can see the difference between non-floated and floated text appearing after an image floats in a margin. In the first example, the text appears flush with the bottom of the text, but in the second, the text appears flush to the top of the margin area, not with the image, which is as it should be. You can see the results of this code displayed correctly in Internet Explorer 6.0 in Figure 12–24.

Listing 12.17	*float Example #2*

```
<html>
<head>
<title>float Example #2</title>
</head>
<body style="font-size: x-large">
<img src="aurelian.jpg" style="margin-top: 0.5in; margin-left:
0.5in">the image appears half an inch down and in
from the top-left of the browser window. The text is not
set to any float value.<br clear="all">
<p>
<img src="aurelian.jpg" style="margin-top: 0.5in; margin-left:
0.5in; float: left">The image appears half an inch
down from the last line of text. In this case the value
float: left has been set, and the text appears just below
the last text from the previous example.<br clear="all">
</body>
</html>
```

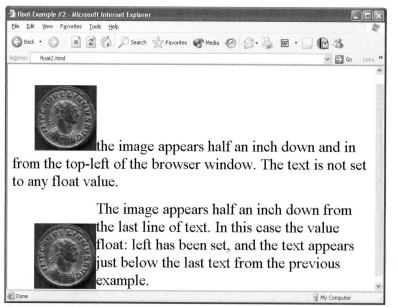

Figure 12–24 The float property used in conjunction with margins set to an image as displayed in Internet Explorer.

Any float-ed images should also be able to operate in series without any problem. In other words, you should be able to set several elements on a line without having them interfere with each other. You can see this in Listing 12.18, which displays in turn three images that should appear on the same line, one after the other, then a sentence whose words should appear on a single line, and then a sentence created using the value float: right — which was written in reverse. You can see the results of this code displayed in Internet Explorer in Figure 12–25:

Listing 12.18 *float Example #3*

```
<html>
<head>
<title>float Example #3</title>
</head>
<body style="font-size: x-large">
<img src="aurelian.jpg" style="float: left">
<img src="aurelian.jpg" style="float: left">
<img src="aurelian.jpg" style="float: left">
<br clear="all">
<p style="float: left">Floated </p>
<p style="float: left"> elements </p>
<p style="float: left">  in a series.</p>
<br clear="all">
<p style="float: right"> code.</p>
<p style="float: right"> in</p>
<p style="float: right"> backwards</p>
<p style="float: right"> written</p>
<p style="float: right"> was</p>
<p style="float: right"> sentence</p>
<p style="float: right">This</p>
</body>
</html>
```

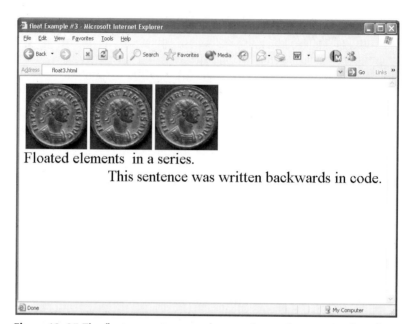

Figure 12–25 The float property set to elements in a series contained on the same horizontal line, as displayed in Internet Explorer 6.0.

Notice that a non-breaking space character (" ") has been added before each word in each sentence. This is because the float property would otherwise put each word flush with each other, turning the sentence into a long one-word nonsense sentence.

CSS3 and float

The current draft CSS3 box model module proposes a number of new properties to float: top, bottom, inside, outside, start and end. These work exactly the same way as these additional values work for the clear property under CSS3. To re-iterate: the top value is meant to be used for vertically flowing text, and in this context it is the equivalent to left when used with the standard left-right flow of Western text; similarly bottom is equivalent to right for vertically flowing text. inside has the same effect as left for non-paged media, and outside the same effect as right for non-paged media. The start value is dependent on the direction of text in the block it is contained within, and is equivalent to left-top when direction: ltr, and right-bottom when direction: rtl. end works in the same, but opposite way; in other words it is set to right-bottom when direction: ltr, and left-top when direction: rtl.

Browser Compatibility

Full support for the `float` property (except for the CSS3 values) is a relatively recent affair — earlier browsers were known to mangle Web pages that used `float` extensively. It should still be used with caution when considering earlier browsers.

- Internet Explorer 3.0: Unsafe.
- Internet Explorer 4.0: Partial.
- Internet Explorer 4.0 – 4.5 (Mac): Partial.
- Internet Explorer 5.0: Safe.
- Internet Explorer 5.1 – 5.2 (Mac): Safe.
- Internet Explorer 5.5: Safe.
- Internet Explorer 6.0: Safe.
- Netscape Navigator 4.0 – 4.79: Unsafe.
- Netscape Navigator 4.0 (Mac & UNIX): Partial.
- Netscape Navigator 6.0: Safe.
- Netscape Navigator 7.0: Safe.
- Mozilla 1.0: Safe.
- Opera 3.6 – 4.0: Safe.
- Opera 5.0 – 6.0: Safe.
- Konqueror: Safe.

The `float` property has been implemented successfully in Internet Explorer since version 5.0 for Windows. It did not work at all under Internet Explorer 3.0, and would produce unpredictable results in version 4.0 of this browser. The general rule with version 4.0 was the more that `float` was used, the less predictable the results.

Similarly, Netscape Navigator 4.x produced highly variable results when `float` was used. This version of Netscape Navigator supported some of the basic values for `float`, but it fell down when trying to handle anything complicated. This was fixed by version 6.0, as it was for Mozilla 1.0.

Ever since Opera version 3.6 `float` has been implemented properly.

Konqueror fully implements the `float` property.

12.23 float-displace Property

This is another CSS3 property introduced under the box model module. It determines how lines of text are wrapped when floats are present.

The `float-displace` property can take one of four values: `line`, `indent`, `block` and `block-within-page`. The `line` value is the default, and it tells the browser to shorten a line of text in order to avoid a floated element. The `indent` value adds a browser-determined spacing between a line of text and a floated element. The `block` value reduces the value of the block containing the text to avoid running into any floated elements; the intended effect is to resize blocks of text to whatever maximum spacing is available between floats. Finally, the `block-within-page` value works the same as `block`, but is designed to be more flexible, adjusting the width of the text block more specifically to its circumstance on multiple pages.

12.24 indent-edge-reset Property

When the CSS3 property `float-displace` is set to `indent`, the `indent-edge-reset` property is there to determine which edge should be the reference indent page, enabling the browser to figure out how much indenting space to reserve.

It can take one of six different values: `none`, `margin-edge`, `border-edge`, `padding-edge`, `content-edge` and `inherit`. `none` is the default, and tells the browser not to introduce a reference edge. `margin-edge`, `border-edge`, `padding-edge` and `content-edge` all tell the browser to use the selected edge as the reference edge. Finally, the `inherit` value takes on whatever parent value may already be present.

12.25 height Property

The `height` property is used to scale an element (typically an image) to the desired vertical length on a Web page. It can take one of three different properties: a unit of measurement value, a percentage value, and the name value `auto`, which sets the element to its default size. It has a sibling property, `width`, which does the exact same thing to horizontal length.

The `auto` setting is used to set an image to its normal size. `height` can also take a specific measurement value, which sizes the height of the image to the desired value. It can also take a percentage value that sizes the height of the image in relation to the overall height of the browser window. When it is applied to an object like an image, it scales the image so that the width of the object is also changed. You can see all of these values for `height` exhibited in Listing 12.19 and displayed within Netscape Navigator 7.0 in Figure 12–26.

Listing 12.19	*height Example*

```html
<html>
<head>
<title>height Example</title>
</head>
<body style="font-size: 14pt">
<img style="height: auto" src="gordian3.jpg">This is the normal
size for this image, which is set to <code>height: auto</code>.
<p>
<img style="height: 25px" src="gordian3.jpg">This image is set to
25 pixels in height.
</p>
<p>
<img style="height: 50%" src="gordian3.jpg">The image is now set
to 50% of the browser window's height.
</p>
</body>
</html>
```

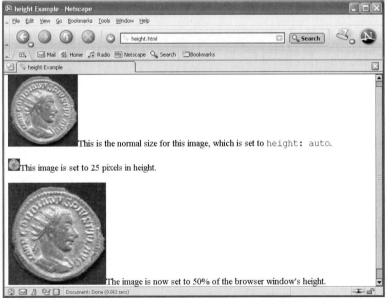

Figure 12–26 Sample height code examples as seen in Netscape Navigator 7.0.

The `height` property is really meant for non-text elements, such as pictures or tables. It is not designed for use with text. When `height` is used in conjunction with text, it does not appreciably affect the display of text on a Web page. There are many other CSS properties more suited to sizing text size (such as `font-size` or `line-height`), so this particular use for the `height` property is not recommended.

CSS3 and height

The only major addition the CSS3 box model module adds to the `height` property is a proposed intrinsic numeric value that can be added in addition to a measured value or a percentage value. The intrinsic value for `height` is the same as `auto`: whatever default value is defined within the browser. In other words, `auto` would equal an intrinsic value of "1". This means that you can also set multiples of this value, so a value of "2" would be twice the automatic value of `height` for that browser.

Browser Compatibility

Although `height` is now widely implemented, it should be noted that earlier browsers had some real problems implementing `height` properly.

- Internet Explorer 3.0: Unsafe.
- Internet Explorer 4.0: Safe.
- Internet Explorer 4.0 – 4.5 (Mac): Safe.
- Internet Explorer 5.0: Safe.
- Internet Explorer 5.1 – 5.2 (Mac): Safe.
- Internet Explorer 5.5: Safe.
- Internet Explorer 6.0: Safe.
- Netscape Navigator 4.0 – 4.79: Unsafe.
- Netscape Navigator 4.0 (Mac & UNIX): Unsafe.
- Netscape Navigator 6.0: Safe.
- Netscape Navigator 7.0: Safe.
- Mozilla 1.0: Safe.
- Opera 3.6 – 4.0: Safe.
- Opera 5.0 – 6.0: Safe.
- Konqueror: Safe.

The `height` property has been implemented successfully in Internet Explorer since version 4.0, though it should be noted that it did not work at all under Internet Explorer 3.0.

Netscape Navigator 4.x is considered Unsafe, since its implementation was highly buggy, and is not recommended. This was fixed by version 6.0, as it was for Mozilla 1.0.

Ever since Opera version 3.6 `height` has been implemented properly.

Konqueror fully implements the `height` property.

12.26 width Property

The `width` property is used to scale an element (typically an image) to the desired vertical length on a Web page. It can take one of three different properties: a unit of measurement value, a percentage value, and the name value `auto`, which sets the element to its default size. It has a sibling property `height`, which does the exact same thing, but to vertical length.

The `auto` setting is used to set an image to its normal size. `width` can also take a specific measurement value, which sizes the height of the image to the desired value. It can also take a percentage value that sizes the width of the image in relation to the overall width of the browser window. You can see all of these values for `width` exhibited in Listing 12.20, whose results can be seen in Figure 12–27.

Listing 12.20	*width Example*

```
<html>
<head>
<title>width Example</title>
</head>
<body style="font-size: 14pt">
<img style="width: auto" src="vitellius.jpg">This is the normal
size for this image, which is set to <code>width: auto</code>.
<p>
<img style="width: 25px" src="vitellius.jpg">This image is set
to 25 pixels in width.
<p>
<img style="width: 25%" src="vitellius.jpg">The image is now set
to 25% of the browser window's width.
</body>
</html>
```

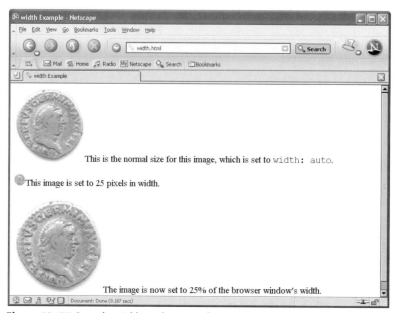

Figure 12–27 Sample width code examples as seen in Netscape Navigator 7.0.

The `width` property is really meant for non-text elements, such as pictures or tables, and in most cases (save for some earlier browsers) it will not display an appreciable effect when applied to text. There are other CSS properties more suited to sizing text horizontally within a Web browser (such as the margin or padding sub-family of properties, which are also examined in this chapter), so this particular use for the `width` property is not recommended.

CSS3 and width

The only major addition the CSS3 box model module adds to the `width` property is a proposed intrinsic numeric value that can be added in addition to a measured value or a percentage value. The intrinsic value for `width` is the same as `auto`: whatever default value is defined within the browser. In other words, `auto` would equal an intrinsic value of "1". This means that you can also set multiples of this value, so a value of "2" would be twice the automatic value of `width` for that browser.

Browser Compatibility

Although `width` is now widely implemented, it should be noted that earlier browsers had some problems implementing `width` properly.

- Internet Explorer 3.0: Unsafe.
- Internet Explorer 4.0: Safe.
- Internet Explorer 4.0 – 4.5 (Mac): Safe.
- Internet Explorer 5.0: Safe.
- Internet Explorer 5.1 – 5.2 (Mac): Safe.
- Internet Explorer 5.5: Safe.
- Internet Explorer 6.0: Safe.
- Netscape Navigator 4.0 – 4.79: Unsafe.
- Netscape Navigator 4.0 (Mac & UNIX): Unsafe.
- Netscape Navigator 6.0: Safe.
- Netscape Navigator 7.0: Safe.
- Mozilla 1.0: Safe.
- Opera 3.6 – 4.0: Safe.
- Opera 5.0 – 6.0: Safe.
- Konqueror: Safe.

The `width` property has been implemented successfully in Internet Explorer since version 4.0, although it should be noted that it did not work at all under Internet Explorer 3.0.

Netscape Navigator 4.x partially implemented `width`. This version of Netscape Navigator did not support the use of `width` with such elements as images, but it did when it came to text. If you set a paragraph to a value of `width: 50%`, under Netscape Navigator 4.x the text will be displayed from the left margin to the center of the browser window, but it failed utterly when it came to formatting images. This was fixed by version 6.0, as well as for Mozilla 1.0.

Ever since Opera version 3.6 `width` has been implemented properly.

Konqueror fully implements the `width` property.

12.27 padding-bottom Property

The `padding-bottom` property is used to add space between one element and another onscreen. It differs from the margin set of properties in that margins are meant to offset text or other objects from the sides of the browser window, whereas padding "indents" an object on the page from another object — such as multiple images or text from the box it is contained within. As values it can take either a specific unit of measure or a percentage value. It works in essentially the same way as its sibling properties `padding-left`, `padding-right` and `padding-top`.

`padding-bottom` can be used to help space out objects on a Web page — a block-level element, such as a paragraph surrounded by a border, for example. In this case, the `padding-bottom` property can be used to add space between the text and the bottom of the border. You can see the use of `padding-bottom` in Listing 12.21, (whose results are seen in Figure 12–28), which separates the top paragraph from the second paragraph, and adds space between the text and the border that surrounds it.

Listing 12.21   *padding-bottom Example*

```
<html>
<head>
<title>padding-bottom Example</title>
</head>
<body style="font-size: large; font-family: sans-serif">
<p style="padding-bottom: 25%">This paragraph is separated from
the next paragraph by a quarter of the browser window's
<em>horizontal</em> width.
</p>
<p style="padding-bottom: 1in; border-style: double; border-width:
thick">There is a 1 inch space between the bottom of the text in
this paragraph and the bottom of the border that surrounds it.
</p>
</body>
</html>
```

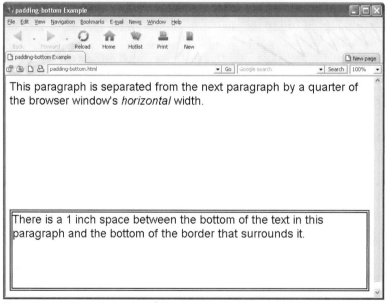

Figure 12–28 The effects of padding-bottom displayed within Opera 6.0.

The `auto` value sets the padding to its default value, which may be browser-dependent.

Browser Compatibility

As with all of the other padding properties, `padding-bottom` has been widely supported and implemented in all but the very earliest CSS-compliant browsers.

- Internet Explorer 3.0: Unsafe.
- Internet Explorer 4.0: Safe.
- Internet Explorer 4.0 – 4.5 (Mac): Safe.
- Internet Explorer 5.0: Safe.
- Internet Explorer 5.1 – 5.2 (Mac): Safe.
- Internet Explorer 5.5: Safe.
- Internet Explorer 6.0: Safe.
- Netscape Navigator 4.0 – 4.79: Safe.
- Netscape Navigator 4.0 (Mac & UNIX): Safe.
- Netscape Navigator 6.0: Safe.
- Netscape Navigator 7.0: Safe.
- Mozilla 1.0: Safe.
- Opera 3.6 – 4.0: Safe.
- Opera 5.0 – 6.0: Safe.
- Konqueror: Safe.

Though it was wholly unsupported in version 3.0, ever since version 4.0 of Internet Explorer `padding-bottom` has been successfully implemented.

`padding-bottom` has been successfully implemented in Netscape Navigator since version 4.x.

Similarly, Opera has implemented `padding-bottom` since version 3.6.

Konqueror fully implements the `padding-bottom` property.

12.28 padding-left Property

The `padding-left` property is used to add space between one element and another onscreen. It can be used to add a specific measurement or percentage value between elements. It shares the same values as its sibling properties `padding-bottom`, `padding-right` and `padding-top`.

`padding-left` is designed to space out objects on a Web page — such as between an image and text or between adjacent blocks of text. In Listing 12.22 `padding-left` is used to add space between the text and the left of the border. You can see the effects of this code in the Opera browser in Figure 12–29.

Listing 12.22	*padding-left Example*

```
<html>
<head>
<title>padding-left Example</title>
</head>
<body style="font-size: large; font-family: sans-serif">
<p style="padding-left: 25%">This paragraph is spaced out from the
left margin by a quarter of the browser window's
<em>horizontal</em> width.
</p>
<p style="padding-left: 1in; border-style: double; border-width:
thick">There is a 1 inch space inserted between the left of the
text in this paragraph and the left side of the border that
surrounds it.
</p>
</body>
</html>
```

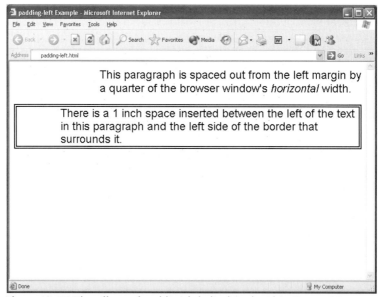

Figure 12–29 The effects of padding-left displayed within Opera 6.0.

The `auto` value sets `padding-left` to its default value, which may be browser-dependent.

Browser Compatibility

As with all of the other padding properties, `padding-left` has been widely supported and implemented in all but the very earliest CSS-compliant browsers.

- Internet Explorer 3.0: Unsafe.
- Internet Explorer 4.0: Safe.
- Internet Explorer 4.0 – 4.5 (Mac): Safe.
- Internet Explorer 5.0: Safe.
- Internet Explorer 5.1 – 5.2 (Mac): Safe.
- Internet Explorer 5.5: Safe.
- Internet Explorer 6.0: Safe.
- Netscape Navigator 4.0 – 4.79: Safe.
- Netscape Navigator 4.0 (Mac & UNIX): Safe.
- Netscape Navigator 6.0: Safe.
- Netscape Navigator 7.0: Safe.
- Mozilla 1.0: Safe.
- Opera 3.6 – 4.0: Safe.
- Opera 5.0 – 6.0: Safe.
- Konqueror: Safe.

Though it was wholly unsupported in version 3.0, ever since version 4.0 of Internet Explorer `padding-left` has been successfully implemented.

`padding-left` has been successfully implemented in Netscape Navigator since version 4.x.

Similarly, Opera has implemented `padding-left` since version 3.6.

Konqueror fully implements the `padding-left` property.

12.29 padding-right Property

Like its sibling properties `padding-left`, `padding-bottom` and `padding-top`, the `padding-right` property is used to add space between one element and another. Like its sibling properties `padding-right` can take either a specific measurement value or percentage value.

You can see the effects of `padding-right` in Listing 12.23, whose effects are displayed within the Opera 6.0 browser in Figure 12–30. In this case, the top paragraph is separated from the right margin, and the text in the second paragraph is offset from the right side border in which it is enclosed.

Listing 12.23	*padding-right Example*

```
<html>
<head>
<title>padding-right Example</title>
</head>
<body style="font-size: large; font-family: sans-serif">
<p style="padding-right: 25%">This paragraph is spaced out from
the right margin by a quarter of the browser window's horizontal
width.
</p>
<p style="padding-right: 1in; border-style: double; border-width:
thick">There is a 1 inch space inserted between
the right of the text in this paragraph and the left side of the
border that surrounds it.
</p>
</body>
</html>
```

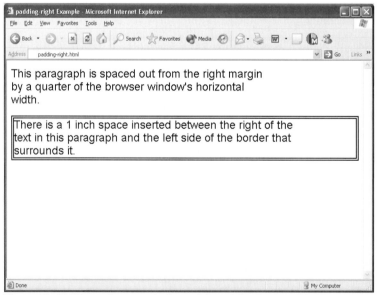

Figure 12–30 The code example for padding-right displayed in Opera 6.0.

The `auto` value sets `padding-right` to its default value, which may be browser-dependent.

Browser Compatibility

As with all of the other padding properties, `padding-right` has been widely supported and implemented in all but the very earliest CSS-compliant browsers.

- Internet Explorer 3.0: Unsafe.
- Internet Explorer 4.0: Safe.
- Internet Explorer 4.0 – 4.5 (Mac): Safe.
- Internet Explorer 5.0: Safe.
- Internet Explorer 5.1 – 5.2 (Mac): Safe.
- Internet Explorer 5.5: Safe.
- Internet Explorer 6.0: Safe.
- Netscape Navigator 4.0 – 4.79: Safe.
- Netscape Navigator 4.0 (Mac & UNIX): Safe.
- Netscape Navigator 6.0: Safe.
- Netscape Navigator 7.0: Safe.
- Mozilla 1.0: Safe.
- Opera 3.6 – 4.0: Safe.
- Opera 5.0 – 6.0: Safe.
- Konqueror: Safe.

Though it was wholly unsupported in version 3.0, ever since version 4.0 of Internet Explorer `padding-right` has been successfully implemented.

`padding-right` has been successfully implemented in Netscape Navigator since version 4.x.

Similarly, Opera has implemented `padding-right` since version 3.6.

Konqueror fully implements the `padding-right` property.

12.30 padding-top Property

Like its sibling properties `padding-left`, `padding-right` and `padding-bottom`, the `padding-top` property is used to add space between one element and another. Like its sibling properties `padding-top` can take either a specific measurement value or percentage value.

You can see the effects of `padding-top` in the Listing 12.24, whose results are displayed within the Opera 6.0 browser in Figure 12–31. In this case, the top paragraph is separated from the top of the browser window, and the second paragraph uses the property to add space between the text and the top of the border that surrounds it.

| Listing 12.24 | *padding-top Example* |

```
<html>
<head>
<title>padding-top Example</title>
</head>
<body style="font-size: large; font-family: sans-serif">
<p style="padding-top: 25%">
This paragraph is spaced out from the top of the browser by a
quarter of the browser window's <em>horizontal</em> width.
</p>
<p style="padding-top: 1in; border-style: double; border-width:
thick">
There is a 1 inch space inserted between the top of the text in
this paragraph and the top border that surrounds it.
</p>
</body>
</html>
```

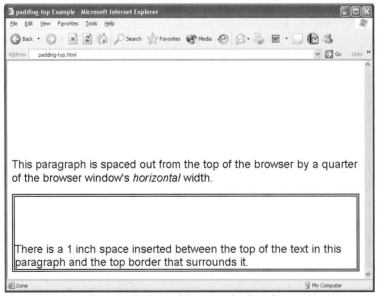

Figure 12–31 Code example for padding-top displayed in Opera 6.0.

The `auto` value sets `padding-top` to its default value, which may be browser-dependent.

Browser Compatibility

As with all of the other padding properties, `padding-top` has been widely supported and implemented in all but the very earliest CSS-compliant browsers.

- Internet Explorer 3.0: Unsafe.
- Internet Explorer 4.0: Safe.
- Internet Explorer 4.0 – 4.5 (Mac): Safe.
- Internet Explorer 5.0: Safe.
- Internet Explorer 5.1 – 5.2 (Mac): Safe.
- Internet Explorer 5.5: Safe.
- Internet Explorer 6.0: Safe.
- Netscape Navigator 4.0 – 4.79: Safe.
- Netscape Navigator 4.0 (Mac & UNIX): Safe.
- Netscape Navigator 6.0: Safe.
- Netscape Navigator 7.0: Safe.
- Mozilla 1.0: Safe.
- Opera 3.6 – 4.0: Safe.
- Opera 5.0 – 6.0: Safe.
- Konqueror: Safe.

Though it was wholly unsupported in version 3.0, ever since version 4.0 of Internet Explorer `padding-top` has been successfully implemented.

`padding-top` has been successfully implemented in Netscape Navigator since version 4.x.

Similarly, Opera has implemented `padding-top` since version 3.6.

Konqueror fully implements the `padding-top` property.

12.31 padding Property

The `padding` property exists as a type of "shortcut" property that allows Web authors to set the values that belong to `padding-top`, `padding-bottom`, `padding-left` and `padding-right` quickly and easily. As with all of the other properties in its sub-family, `padding` is used to add spacing between elements on a Web page.

This property can take from one to four separate numerical values, which set the width of the padding. The default unit is pixels, so if no measurement unit is specified, the value given is assumed to be a pixel value. If a single numerical value is present, all padding values are set to that value. If two numerical values are present, these padding values are passed on to the top and bottom, and the sides, respectively. If three values are present, the top, right and left, and then bottom take the numerical padding values specified. Finally, if four values are present, the top, right, bottom, then left sides take the numerical padding values specified. When specifying these values, they must be separated by a space, as can be seen in Listing 12.25. You can see the effects of the code in Listing 12.25 in Figure 12–32.

Listing 12.25	*padding Example Using Specific, Measured Values*

```html
<html>
<head>
<title>padding Example</title>
</head>
<body style="font-size: large; font-family: sans-serif">
<p style="padding: 5mm; border-style: solid">
This paragraph is spaced out 5 millimeters on each side.
</p>
<p style="padding: 2mm 5mm; border-style: solid;">
This paragraph is spaced out 2 millimeters from the top and
bottom, and 5 millimeters to the left and right sides.
</p>
<p style="padding: 2mm 15mm 10mm; border-style: solid">
This paragraph is spaced out 2 millimeters from the top, 15
millimeters to the left and right sides and 10 millimeters from
the bottom.
</p>
<p style="padding: 2mm 7mm 7mm 7mm; border-style: solid">
This paragraph is spaced out 2 millimeters from the top, and 7
millimeters from all of the other sides.
</p>
</body>
</html>
```

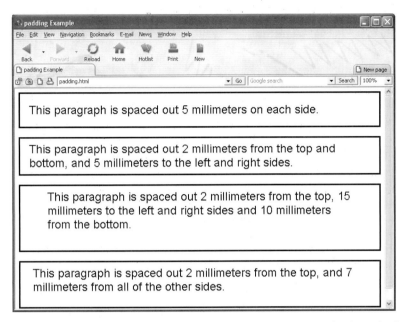

Figure 12–32 Code example for padding using specific measured values displayed in Opera 6.0.

The borders added to each paragraph in the example code simply make it easier to see how and where the padding values are taking effect. If you are playing around with the `padding` property, using `border-style` will help you place your `padding` values correctly.

`padding` can also take a percentage value. Listing 12.26 shows how this can be done.

Listing 12.26   *padding Example Using a Percentage Value*

```
<html>
<head>
<title>padding Example #2</title>
</head>
<body style="font-size: large; font-family: sans-serif">
<p style="padding: 15%; border-style: solid">
This paragraph is spaced by 15% of the browser width on all sides.
</p>
</body>
</html>
```

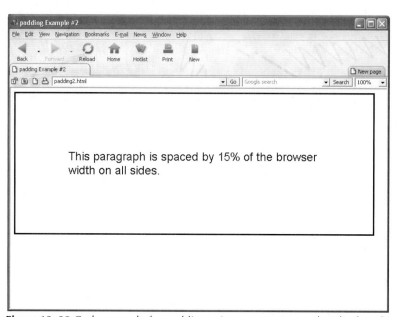

Figure 12–33 Code example for padding using a percentage value displayed in Opera 6.0.

The auto value sets padding to its default.

Browser Compatibility

As with all of the other padding properties, padding has been widely supported and implemented in all but the very earliest CSS-compliant browsers.

- Internet Explorer 3.0: Unsafe.
- Internet Explorer 4.0: Safe.
- Internet Explorer 4.0 – 4.5 (Mac): Safe.
- Internet Explorer 5.0: Safe.
- Internet Explorer 5.1 – 5.2 (Mac): Safe.
- Internet Explorer 5.5: Safe.
- Internet Explorer 6.0: Safe.
- Netscape Navigator 4.0 – 4.79: Safe.
- Netscape Navigator 4.0 (Mac & UNIX): Safe.
- Netscape Navigator 6.0: Safe.
- Netscape Navigator 7.0: Safe.
- Mozilla 1.0: Safe.
- Opera 3.6 – 4.0: Safe.
- Opera 5.0 – 6.0: Safe.

- Konqueror: Safe.

Though it was wholly unsupported in version 3.0, ever since version 4.0 of Internet Explorer `padding` has been successfully implemented.

`padding` has been successfully implemented in Netscape Navigator since version 4.x.

Similarly, Opera has implemented `padding` since version 3.6.

Konqueror fully implements the `padding` property.

12.32 margin-bottom Property

The `margin-bottom` property is used to add space between the browser window and an onscreen element. In terms of functionality, it is equivalent to the padding sub-family of properties, but the padding properties are meant to set the spacing between the border and the content of a box-level element, or to set relative spacing between two or more elements. The margin sub-family of properties instead sets the space between the browser window and a given box property, such as a paragraph, header or image. The difference between the margin set of properties and padding properties is that the margin sets the spacing value *outside* of the box, whereas the padding set of properties sets the spacing value *inside* the boundaries of the box. While they are designed for different purposes, the two sets of properties produce the same sorts of effects. `margin-bottom` can be used to add a specific measurement or percentage value between elements. It shares the same values as its sibling properties `margin-left`, `margin-right` and `margin-top`.

`margin-bottom` can take one of three different types of values: an `auto` value that sets things to the default spacing value between elements, a precise unit of measurement value or a percentage value. You can see the effects of a measurement value and a percentage value applied to the following code, as seen in Figure 12–34.

| Listing 12.27 | *margin-bottom Example* |

```
<html>
<head>
<title>margin-bottom Example</title>
</head>
<body style="font-size: large; font-family: sans-serif">
<p style="margin-bottom: 0.25in">
This paragraph is separated from the next by a quarter inch.
</p>
<p style="margin-bottom: 25%; border-style: solid">
The following image of a coin of the Emperor Commodus is separated
from this sentence by 25% of the browser window's width.
</p>
<img src="commodus.jpg">
</body>
</html>
```

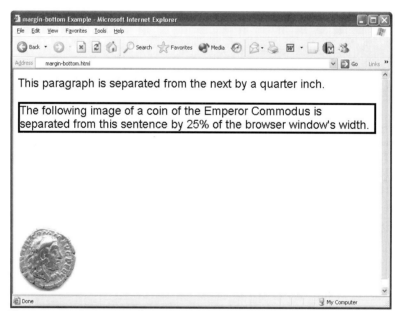

Figure 12–34 Code example using a set measurement value and a percentage value with the margin-bottom property.

Note that in this code example, the image and the second sentence are separated by a distance equivalent to a quarter of the browser window's *width*. This is not what you may expect; it would seem to make more sense that the browser's windows *height* be used. In fact, when a percentage value is used with `margin-bottom`, it takes as the base value the width of the element in which it is set. In this case, it takes as its value the width of the sentence, which stretches across the width of the browser's window. It is important to keep this in mind whenever you try to set a percentage value with `margin-bottom` or `margin-top`.

Browser Compatibility

`margin-bottom` has been widely supported and implemented in all but the very earliest CSS-compliant browsers, although it should be noted that the `auto` value was buggily implemented in Netscape Navigator 4.x.

- Internet Explorer 3.0: Unsafe.
- Internet Explorer 4.0: Safe.
- Internet Explorer 4.0 – 4.5 (Mac): Safe.
- Internet Explorer 5.0: Safe.
- Internet Explorer 5.1 – 5.2 (Mac): Safe.
- Internet Explorer 5.5: Safe.
- Internet Explorer 6.0: Safe.
- Netscape Navigator 4.0 – 4.79: Partial.
- Netscape Navigator 4.0 (Mac & UNIX): Partial.
- Netscape Navigator 6.0: Safe.
- Netscape Navigator 7.0: Safe.
- Mozilla 1.0: Safe.
- Opera 3.6 – 4.0: Safe.
- Opera 5.0 – 6.0: Safe.
- Konqueror: Safe.

Though it was wholly unsupported in version 3.0, ever since version 4.0 of Internet Explorer `margin-bottom` has been successfully implemented.

`margin-bottom` is given a Partial rating for Netscape Navigator 4.x, since it used a different definition of the `auto` value, which ignored any previously set margin. The result is that it placed a Web element immediately underneath the previous element to appear onscreen. This was fixed by version 6.0, as it was for Mozilla 1.0 upon which it and all subsequent versions of Netscape Navigator are based.

Opera has implemented `margin-bottom` since version 3.6.

Konqueror fully implements the `margin-bottom` property.

12.33 margin-left Property

The `margin-left` property is used to add space between the browser window and an onscreen element. In terms of functionality, it is equivalent to the padding sub-family of properties, but the padding properties are meant to set the spacing between the border and the content of a box-level element, or set relative spacing between two or more elements. The margin sub-family of properties instead sets the space between the browser window and a given box property, such as a paragraph, header or image. The difference between the margin set of properties and padding properties is that the margin sets the spacing value *outside* of the box, whereas the padding set of properties sets the spacing value *inside* the boundaries of the box. While they are designed for different purposes, the two sets of properties produce the same sorts of effects. `margin-left` can be used to add a specific measurement or percentage value between elements. It shares the same values as its sibling properties `margin-top`, `margin-right` and `margin-bottom`.

margin-left can take one of three different types of values: an `auto` value that sets things to the default spacing value between elements, a precise unit of measurement value or a percentage value. You can see the effects of a measurement value, a percentage value and a negative value applied to the code seen in Listing 12.28, whose results can be seen in Figure 12–35.

Listing 12.28   *margin-left Example*

```
<html>
<head>
<title>margin-left Example</title>
</head>
<body style="font-size: large; font-family: sans-serif">
<p style="margin-left: 1in">This paragraph is separated from the
left of the browser window by one inch.
</p>
<p style="margin-left: 25%; border-style: solid">
This paragraph is separated from left of the browser window by 25%
of the browser window's width.
</p>
<p>
<img src="addison55.jpg" style="margin-left: -100px">
The preceding image has a margin-left setting of -100 pixels, so
it appears "chopped".
</p>
</body>
</html>
```

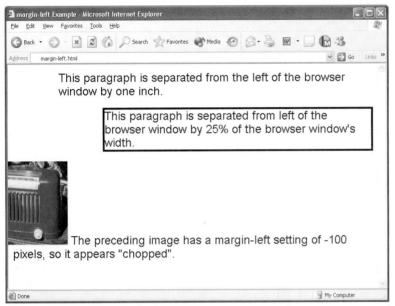

Figure 12–35 Code example using a set measurement value, a percentage value and a negative value with the margin-left property.

Notice how in this code example that negative values are also possible with this property, as with all of the other properties in this family.

Browser Compatibility

The `margin-left` property has been widely supported and implemented in all but the very earliest CSS-compliant browsers, although it should be noted that the `auto` value was buggily implemented in Netscape Navigator 4.x.

- Internet Explorer 3.0: Unsafe.
- Internet Explorer 4.0: Safe.
- Internet Explorer 4.0 – 4.5 (Mac): Safe.
- Internet Explorer 5.0: Safe.
- Internet Explorer 5.1 – 5.2 (Mac): Safe.
- Internet Explorer 5.5: Safe.
- Internet Explorer 6.0: Safe.
- Netscape Navigator 4.0 – 4.79: Partial.
- Netscape Navigator 4.0 (Mac & UNIX): Partial.
- Netscape Navigator 6.0: Safe.
- Netscape Navigator 7.0: Safe.

- Mozilla 1.0: Safe.

- Opera 3.6 – 4.0: Safe.

- Opera 5.0 – 6.0: Safe.

- Konqueror: Safe.

Though it was wholly unsupported in version 3.0, ever since version 4.0 of Internet Explorer `margin-left` has been successfully implemented.

`margin-left` is given a Partial rating for Netscape Navigator 4.x, since it used a different definition of the `auto` value, which ignored any previously set margin. The result is that it placed a Web element immediately underneath the previous element to appear on screen. This was fixed by version 6.0, as it was for Mozilla 1.0 upon which it and all subsequent versions of Netscape Navigator are based.

Opera has implemented `margin-left` since version 3.6.

Konqueror fully implements the `margin-left` property.

12.34 margin-right Property

The `margin-right` property is used to add space between the browser window and an onscreen element. In terms of functionality, it is equivalent to the padding sub-family of properties, but the padding properties are meant to set the spacing between the border and the content of a box-level element, or set relative spacing between two or more elements. The margin sub-family of properties instead sets the space between the browser window and a given box property, such as a paragraph, header or image. The difference between the margin set of properties and padding properties is that the margin sets the spacing value *outside* of the box, whereas the padding set of properties sets the spacing value *inside* the boundaries of the box. While they are designed for different purposes, the two sets of properties produce the same sorts of effects. `margin-right` can be used to add a specific measurement or percentage value between elements. It shares the same values as its sibling properties `margin-left`, `margin-bottom` and `margin-top`.

`margin-right` can take one of three different types of values: an `auto` value that sets things to the default spacing value between elements, a precise unit of measurement value or a percentage value. You can see the effects of a measurement value, a percentage value and a negative value applied to the code seen in Listing 12.29, whose results can be seen in Figure 12–36.

Listing 12.29 *margin-right Example*

```
<html>
<head>
<title>margin-right Example</title>
</head>
<body style="font-size: 23px; font-family: sans-serif">
<p style="margin-right: 1in">
This paragraph is separated from the right of the browser window
by one inch. Here is some more text to make the effect more
apparent.
</p>
<p style="margin-right: 25%; border-style: solid">
This paragraph is separated from the right of the browser window
by 25% of the browser window's width. Here is some more text to
make the effect more apparent.
</p>
<p>
<img src="addison55.jpg" style="margin-right: -100px">The
preceding image has a margin-right setting of -100 pixels, so the
first part of the text that follows it is "chopped" as it begins
100 pixels "into" and behind the image.
</p>
</body>
</html>
```

Notice that the text is all indented from the right margin of the browser window by the amounts specified in the code. The only effect that may surprise some people is that of a negative value applied to the image, and its effects on the text that follows it, with the first couple of words covered or partially obscured by the image. This effect occurs because the negative value applied to `margin-right` is applied within the boundary of the image itself. Therefore the text begins 100 pixels "within" the right margin of the image itself.

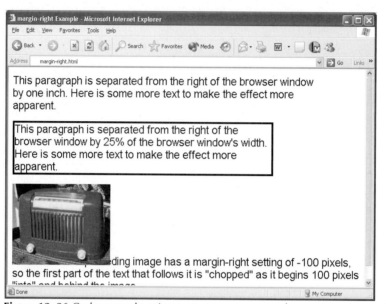

Figure 12–36 Code example using a set measurement value, a percentage value and a negative value with the margin-right property.

Browser Compatibility

The `margin-right` property has been widely supported and implemented in all but the very earliest CSS-compliant browsers, though it should be noted that the `auto` value was buggily implemented in Netscape Navigator 4.x.

- Internet Explorer 3.0: Unsafe.
- Internet Explorer 4.0: Safe.
- Internet Explorer 4.0 – 4.5 (Mac): Safe.
- Internet Explorer 5.0: Safe.
- Internet Explorer 5.1 – 5.2 (Mac): Safe.
- Internet Explorer 5.5: Safe.
- Internet Explorer 6.0: Safe.
- Netscape Navigator 4.0 – 4.79: Partial.
- Netscape Navigator 4.0 (Mac & UNIX): Partial.
- Netscape Navigator 6.0: Safe.
- Netscape Navigator 7.0: Safe.
- Mozilla 1.0: Safe.
- Opera 3.6 – 4.0: Safe.

- Opera 5.0 – 6.0: Safe.
- Konqueror: Safe.

Though it was wholly unsupported in version 3.0, ever since version 4.0 of Internet Explorer `margin-right` has been successfully implemented.

`margin-right` is given a Partial rating for Netscape Navigator 4.x, since it used a different definition of the `auto` value, which ignored any previously set margin. The result is that it placed a Web element immediately underneath the previous element to appear on screen. This was fixed by version 6.0, as it was for Mozilla 1.0 upon which it and all subsequent versions of Netscape Navigator are based.

Opera has implemented `margin-right` since version 3.6.

Konqueror fully implements the `margin-right` property.

12.35 margin-top Property

The `margin-top` property is used to add space between the browser window and an onscreen element. In terms of functionality, it is equivalent to the padding sub-family of properties, but the padding properties are meant to set the spacing between the border and the content of a box-level element, or set relative spacing between two or more elements. The margin sub-family of properties instead sets the space between the browser window and a given box property, such as a paragraph, header or image. The difference between the margin set of properties and padding properties is that the margin sets the spacing value *outside* of the box, whereas the padding set of properties sets the spacing value *inside* the boundaries of the box. While they are designed for different purposes, the two sets of properties produce the same sorts of effects. `margin-top` can be used to add a specific measurement or percentage value between elements. It shares the same values as its sibling properties `margin-left`, `margin-right` and `margin-bottom`.

`margin-top` can take one of three different types of values: an `auto` value that sets things to the default spacing value between elements, a precise unit of measurement value or a percentage value. You can see the effects of a measurement value, a percentage value and a negative value applied to the code seen in Listing 12.30, whose results can be seen in Figure 12–37.

Listing 12.30	*margin-top Example*

```
<html>
<head>
<title>margin-top Example</title>
</head>
<body style="font-size: large; font-family: sans-serif">
<p style="margin-top: 1in">
This paragraph is separated from the top of the browser window by
one inch.
</p>
<p style="margin-top: 25%; border-style: solid">
This paragraph is separated from the previous one by 25% of the
browser window's width.
</p>
</body>
</html>
```

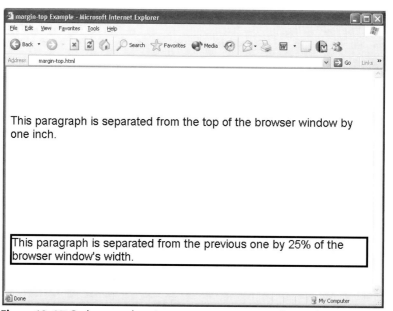

Figure 12–37 Code example using a set measurement value and a percentage value with the margin-top property.

Note that in the code example, the image and the second sentence are separated by a distance equivalent to a quarter of the browser window's *width*. This is not what you may expect; it would seem to make more sense to take a percentage value relative to the browser's window *height*. In fact, when a percentage value is used with margin-top, it takes as the base value the width of the element in which it is set. In this case, it takes as its value the width of the sentence, which stretches across the width of the browser's window. It is important to keep this in mind whenever you try to set a percentage value with margin-top or any of its sibling properties.

Browser Compatibility

The margin-top property has been widely supported and implemented in all but the very earliest CSS-compliant browsers, although it should be noted that the auto value was buggily implemented in Netscape Navigator 4.x.

- Internet Explorer 3.0: Unsafe.
- Internet Explorer 4.0: Safe.
- Internet Explorer 4.0 – 4.5 (Mac): Safe.
- Internet Explorer 5.0: Safe.
- Internet Explorer 5.1 – 5.2 (Mac): Safe.
- Internet Explorer 5.5: Safe.
- Internet Explorer 6.0: Safe.
- Netscape Navigator 4.0 – 4.79: Partial.
- Netscape Navigator 4.0 (Mac & UNIX): Partial.
- Netscape Navigator 6.0: Safe.
- Netscape Navigator 7.0: Safe.
- Mozilla 1.0: Safe.
- Opera 3.6 – 4.0: Safe.
- Opera 5.0 – 6.0: Safe.
- Konqueror: Safe.

Though it was wholly unsupported in version 3.0, ever since version 4.0 of Internet Explorer margin-top has been successfully implemented.

margin-top is given a Partial rating for Netscape Navigator 4.x, since it used a different definition of the auto value, which ignored any previously set margin. The result is that it placed a Web element immediately underneath the previous element to appear on screen. This was fixed by version 6.0, as it was for Mozilla 1.0 upon which it and all subsequent versions of Netscape Navigator are based.

Opera has implemented margin-top since version 3.6.

Konqueror fully implements the margin-top property.

12.36 margin Property

This is a "shortcut" property that allows the Web author to quickly set margins that can combine the values of the rest of the margin sub-family of properties: `margin-top`, `margin-bottom`, `margin-left` and `margin-right`. In fact, this property makes things easier if you intend to set margin values for more than one side of a Web element.

This property can take from one to four separate numerical values, which work in exactly the same manner as the `padding` and `border` properties. In this case, it sets the width of the selected margin. The default unit is pixels, so if no measurement unit is specified, the value given is assumed to be a pixel value. If a single numerical value is present, all borders are set to that value. If two numerical values are present, the top and bottom and then the side borders take on those values, respectively. If three values are present, the top, right and left and then the bottom take the numerical values specified. Finally, if four values are present, the top, right, bottom, then left border take the numerical values specified. When specifying these values, they must be accompanied by the measurement value to be used and they must all be separated by a space, as can be seen in Listing 12.31 (whose results can be seen in Figure 12–38).

Listing 12.31	*margin Example*

```
<html>
<head>
<title>margin Example</title>
</head>
</html>
<body style="font-size: large">
<p style="margin: 1cm; border-style: solid; border-width: 1px">
Paragraph surrounded by a 1 centimeter margin on all sides.
</p>
<p style="margin: 1cm 2cm; border-style: solid; border-width:
1px">
Paragraph with a 2 centimeter margin to the left and right, and a
1 centimeter margin to the top and bottom.
</p>
<p style="margin: 1cm 2cm 3cm; border-style: solid; border-width:
1px">
Paragraph with a 2 centimeter margin to the left and right, a 1
centimeter margin to the top and a 3 centimeter margin to the
bottom.
</p>
```

Listing 12.31	*margin Example (continued)*

```
<p style="margin: auto; border-style: solid; border-width: 1px">
Margin is set to auto for this paragraph.
</p>
</body>
</html>
```

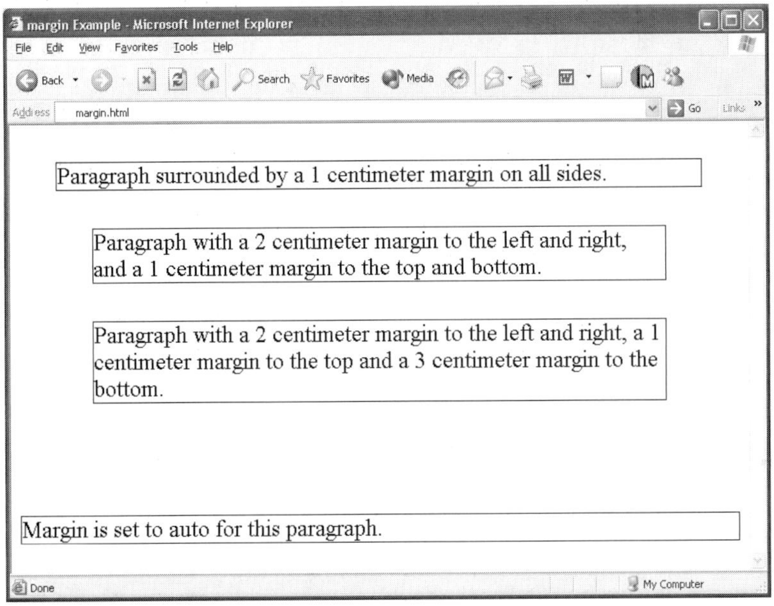

Figure 12–38 Code example for margin as seen in Internet Explorer 7.0.

As you can see in Figure 12–38, in the first example a 1-centimeter margin is set around the paragraph on all sides. In the second, a 2-centimeter margin is set on the left and right sides while a 1-centimeter margin is set between to its top and bottom sides. The third example is like the second, except that there is a 3-centimeter margin between it and the fourth paragraph. Note how the fourth value is set to the value auto, which takes on whatever the browser default value is for margin.

margin can also take a percentage value, which works in exactly the same way as the other margin sub-family of properties. When a percentage value is used with margin, it takes as the base value the *width* of the element in which it is set, since this value is meant to be applied to box-level elements that stretch across the width of the browser window.

Browser Compatibility

The margin property has been widely supported and implemented in all but the very earliest CSS-compliant browsers, though it should be noted that the auto value was buggily implemented in Netscape Navigator 4.x.

- Internet Explorer 3.0: Unsafe.
- Internet Explorer 4.0: Safe.
- Internet Explorer 4.0 – 4.5 (Mac): Safe.
- Internet Explorer 5.0: Safe.
- Internet Explorer 5.1 – 5.2 (Mac): Safe.
- Internet Explorer 5.5: Safe.
- Internet Explorer 6.0: Safe.
- Netscape Navigator 4.0 – 4.79: Partial.
- Netscape Navigator 4.0 (Mac & UNIX): Partial.
- Netscape Navigator 6.0: Safe.
- Netscape Navigator 7.0: Safe.
- Mozilla 1.0: Safe.
- Opera 3.6 – 4.0: Safe.
- Opera 5.0 – 6.0: Safe.
- Konqueror: Safe.

Though it was wholly unsupported in version 3.0, ever since version 4.0 of Internet Explorer margin has been successfully implemented.

margin is given a Partial rating for Netscape Navigator 4.x, since it used a different definition of the auto value, which ignored any previously set margin. The result is that it placed a Web element immediately underneath the previous element to appear on screen. This was fixed by version 6.0, as it was for Mozilla 1.0 upon which it and all subsequent versions of Netscape Navigator are based.

Opera has implemented margin since version 3.6.

Konqueror fully implements the margin property.

12.37 min-width, max-width, min-height and max-height Properties

The min-width, max-width, min-height and max-height properties are CSS3 properties designed to allow the Web author to specifically set the size of the content area within a given box element. They are there primarily to ensure that the box element is large enough — but not too large — to fit specific content.

The `min-width` and `min-height` properties can take a specific length or percentage value. The `max-width` and `max-height` properties go a bit further, and can take these values in addition to an `auto` or `inherit` value; the former value is set to the browser's default for a given box property, and the latter value tells the browser to take on any available parent value for these properties.

In case of any conflict, `min-width` overrides a smaller value for `max-width` set in error, and both automatically override any previously set `width` value. `min-height` and `max-height` work the same way. The following code snippet shows how you could use these values in context:

```
<div style="min-width: 500px; max-width: 525px; min-height: 50px;
max-height: 60px">

<img src="hadrian.jpg" style="width: 500px; height: 50px">

</div>
```

In this case, these properties work together to ensure that the block created by the div tags is large enough to accommodate the image contained within it.

12.38 fit and fit-position Properties

These CSS3 properties are designed to tell the browser how to scale an image if its width or height values are not explicitly set.

The `fit` property can take one of four values: `fill`, `none`, `meet` and `slice`. `fill` is the default, and tells the browser to scale the object to fit the "box" it is contained within. The `none` value tells the browser to do nothing, and leave the image as is. The `meet` value also tells the browser to scale the object, but unlike `fill`, `meet` tells the browser to keep the aspect ratio of the image intact. Finally, `slice` is an odd opposite of `meet`: the browser must preserve the aspect ratio first, scaling the image to fit the size of the box so that the likely result you will get from this is a "slice" of the original image showing. Figure 12–39 gives you an idea as to how all of these different values for `fit` would work (note that the images would be clipped outside of the box area — they are left intact in this example to better illustrate the differences between the values).

 **Original size of the image**

| fill | none | meet | slice |

Figure 12–39 The intended effects of the values for fit.

Where `fit` is used to size an image to fit a given space, `fit-position` is used for aligning that image within that space. It can take anywhere from one to three different sets of values depending on the circumstance. For example, it can take a pair of percentage values, where "`0% 0%`" places an image in the top-left of a box, and "`100% 100%`" places it to the bottom-right. It can also take a pair of measured values, so a value of "`2mm 2mm`" places the image 2 millimeters to the right and then down from the top-left edge of the box. `fit-position` can also take a number of particular combinations of named values in twos or threes: "`top left, left top`" is the same as "`0% 0%`"; "`top, top center, center top`" has the effect of centering the image at the top of the box; "`right top, top right`" sets the image to the top right corner of the box. "`left, left center, center left`" is the same as "`0% 50%`", "`center, center center`" places the image squarely in the center of the box, "`right, right center, center right`" is the same as "`100% 50%`", "`bottom left, left bottom`" is the same as "`0% 100%`", "`bottom, bottom center, center bottom`" is the same as "`50% 100%`", and "`bottom right, right bottom`" is equivalent to "`100% 100%`". There is also an `auto` value, which places the image in the default corner of the box, dependent on whatever writing-mode value is set; for Western text it would place the image in the top-left corner, whereas for Hebrew ("`rl-tb`") it would be the top-right corner, and for Japanese or Chinese ("`tb-rl`") it would also be the top-right corner.

12.39 marquee Properties

The proposed CSS3 marquee sub-family of properties is used to produce a scrolling display of text or other block-level elements on a page. In an odd way it resurrects and expands the functionality of the old Internet Explorer-specific <marquee> tag, which could be used to create a scrolling display of text. Whereas the <marquee> tag was limited only to horizontally scrolling text, these new marquee properties allow images to scroll in addition to text, and they can scroll vertically as well as horizontally.

The set of marquee properties consists of four individual properties and one shortcut property: marquee-style, marquee-direction, marquee-speed, marquee-repetition and marquee.

The marquee-style property determines how the marquee is displayed. It has four possible values: none, slide, scroll and alternate. The none value tells the browser not to scroll the selected element. The slide value starts the content outside of the content box, and then it comes into view and then disappears out the other side. The scroll value does exactly the same thing as slide, but instead of disappearing out the other side, it stops when it reaches the end of the content box. Finally, the alternate value (which is the default) tells the browser to initially display the marquee content and then "bounce" it between the two edges of the content box.

The marquee-direction property tells the browser in which direction the selected marquee element should go. It has nine individual values: left, right, up, down, forwards, backwards, ahead, reverse and auto. The left, right, up and down values tell the selected element to go in the indicated direction. With the exception of auto, the other values are dependent on any value for writing-mode that may be present, and is designed to work with the "natural" flow of content for that language. If writing-mode is set to rl-tb (typical of Hebrew text for example) the forwards value runs in the same direction. Similarly, backwards under these same conditions would make the text run from left to right instead. Again, assuming writing-mode: rl-tb, the ahead value tells the browser to scroll the content in the direction of block's progression, which in this case is equivalent to "down" (since the "tb" part of "rl-tb" means "top-to-bottom"). Similarly, reverse does the opposite, so in the case of a page where writing-mode: rl-tb, the content scrolls "up" instead. The auto value has the same effect as backwards for Western content, or reverse for non-Western content.

The marquee-speed property sets the velocity of the scrolling content. Its values are slow, normal, fast, a specific length value and a length over time value. The normal value is the default, slow is slower than normal, and fast is faster than normal. When a given length value is used (i.e., "2in") it tells the browser that this is the distance the marquee content should travel per second. Another, more specific length over time value is also possible, so a value of "2in/3sec" tells the browser to scroll the content over 2 inches in 3 seconds. Using negative values with either of these last two values reverses the normal flow of the marquee.

`marquee-repetition` is used to set the number of times the marquee content is to move. It takes either a specific integer value, or the default `infinite` value. So for `marquee-repetition: 4`, the content scrolls four times and then stops.

Finally, the `marquee` property acts as a shortcut property for all of its sibling properties. It takes on the values for these properties in the following order: `marquee-style`, `marquee-direction`, `marquee-speed` and `marquee-repetition`.

For an example as to how this works, take a look at Listing 12.32, which displays equivalent HTML and CSS code for displaying marquees (note that the HTML code will only work in Internet Explorer).

Listing 12.32   *marquee Example*

```
<html>
<head>
<title>marquee Example</title>
</head>
</html>
<body style="font-face: sans-serif; font-size: 50px">
<strong>HTML Marquee:</strong>
<marquee behavior="slide" direction="left" loop="4"
scrolldelay="170">Some marquee sliding text.</marquee>
<marquee behavior="scroll" direction="right" loop="-1"
scrolldelay="85">Some marquee scrolling text.</marquee>
<p>
<strong>CSS Marquee Equivalent:</strong>
<div style="marquee-style: slide; marquee-direction: left;
marquee-repetition:4; marquee-speed: fast">Some marquee sliding
text.</div>
<div style="marquee-style: scroll; marquee-direction: right;
marquee-repetition: infinite; marquee-speed: normal">Some marquee
scrolling text.</div>
</p>
</body>
</html>
```

Color

Topics in This Chapter

- color
- Gamma Correction under CSS3
- opacity
- rendering-intent
- color-profile
- @color-profile
- X-11 Color Keywords

Chapter 13

Under CSS1 and CSS2, color values were rolled together into what was called the Color and Background family of properties. This is because there was only a single color property — color — and it didn't make any sense to put it into its own family, even though its effects were not limited solely to setting colored backgrounds. The new proposed CSS3 color module now puts color into its own separate family, adding a number of related properties to it as well as extending the ways in which you can specify color values. Even without this, the color property provided a much broader range of choices for Web authors than when using HTML. It is really *the* way to set color to any element on a Web page.

Under the CSS3 color module, the new color family consists of four separate properties plus one new at-rule, all relating to color or the visibility of an item on a Web page. The new color family of properties consists of the following: `color`, `opacity`, `color-profile`, `rendering-intent`, and `@color-profile`. CSS3 also formally incorporates the long-standing X-11 color naming scheme. As with any other CSS3 property mentioned in this book, they should be considered a heads up as to the possibilities of new things you can expect to see in future Web browsers, though the final result may not be exactly as described here.

13.1 color Property

The `color` CSS property simply sets the color to be displayed for an associated element. The `color` property works the same way as the `color` attribute does with the `<body>` tag or a number of other XHTML tags.

This property can take any color value type that can be associated with CSS. For example, it can take a standard color name (such as "`blue`") or a hexadecimal color value (such as "`#0000ff`", which is also blue), both of which should be familiar ways of setting color for people used to setting it in HTML. CSS allows you to set color values using four additional color formats: a compressed hexadecimal color value (such as "`#00f`", which again equals blue), a numerical triplet RGB (Red Green Blue) color value where "`rgb(0,0,255)`" is blue, and a three-digit RGB percentage color value where "`rgb(0%,0%,100%)`" is blue. Table 13.1 neatly lays out the different ways you can specify color values numerically in CSS.

Table 13.1 *Different Ways of Expressing Color Numerically Using CSS*

"Full" Hexadecimal	*"Compressed" Hex*	*RGB (numerical triplet)*	*RGB (percentage)*
ff0000	f00	rgb(255,0,0)	rgb(100%,0%,0%)
00ff00	0f0	rgb(0,255,0)	rgb(0%,100%,0%)
0000ff	00f	rgb(0,0,255)	rgb(0%,0%,100%)
333333	333	rgb(51,51,51)	rgb(20%,20%,20%)
666666	666	rgb(102,102,102)	rgb(40%,40%,40%)
999999	999	rgb(153,153,153)	rgb(60%,60%,60%)
cccccc	ccc	rgb(204,204,204)	rgb(80%,80%,80%)
ffffff	fff	rgb(255,255,255)	rgb(100%,100%,100%)

You can see several of these methods used in Listing 13.1 (and displayed in Figure 13–1), which shows how separate HTML and CSS code can produce equivalent results.

Listing 13.1 *HTML vs. CSS in Setting color Values*

```
<html>
<head>
<title>Color: HTML and CSS Renderings</title>
<style>
body {font-size: xx-large}
.red {color: ff0000} /* red */
.yellow {color: yellow}
.blue {color: 00f} /* blue */
</style>
</head>
<body>

<font color="red"><b>Red, bold text</b></font><br>
<font color="yellow"><b>Yellow, bold text</b></font><br>
<font color="blue"><b>Blue, bold text</b></font>

<p>
<strong class="red">Red, bold text</strong><br>
<strong class="yellow">Yellow, bold text</strong><br>
<strong class="blue">Blue, bold text</strong>
</p>

</body>
</html>
```

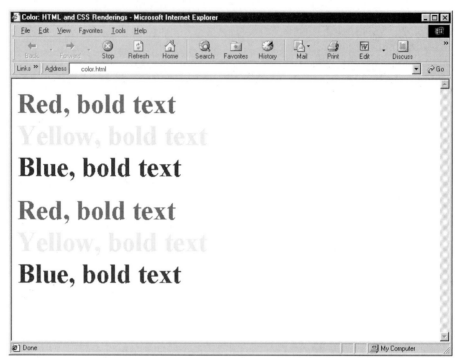

Figure 13–1   The example color code displayed in Internet Explorer 5.5.

While Listing 13.1 uses the old HTML 4.01 `<font>` tag, under the XHTML specification, this tag is deprecated in favor of using a combination of the `color` and `font` CSS properties. While in this case the color values have been added to text, CSS allows you to directly add color to things like borders, backgrounds, user interface elements and more — if it's an object on a Web page, chances are you can add CSS color values to it somehow. In this way the CSS `color` property goes much further than what can be accomplished using standard HTML.

CSS3 goes one step further by adding an additional way of not only specifying color values, but also opacity — in other words, how transparent a color value is. This is accomplished using an RGBA color value, where the A stands for Alpha, a common industry term for dealing with opacity values. This additional alpha value takes a range from `0.0` (fully transparent) to `1.0` (opaque). To specify an RGBA color value, you specify it explicitly using `rgba` and tack on the alpha value to the end of the RGB statement, as Listing 13.2 shows.

Listing 13.2	*CSS3 RGBA Code Example*

```
<html>
<head>
<title>RGBA Example</title>
<style>
h1 {font-size: x-large}
.opaque {color: rgba(0,0,255,1.0)}
.three-quarters-opaque {color: rgba(0,0,255,0.75)}
.half-opaque {color: rgba(0,0,255,0.5)}
.one-quarter-opaque {color: rgba(0,0,255,0.25)}
.transparent {color: rgba(0,0,255,0.0)}
</style>
</head>
<body>
<h1 class="opaque">This header is fully opaque</h1>
<h1 class="three-quarters-opaque">This header is set to 0.75
opaque</h1>
<h1 class="half-opaque">This header is set to 0.5 opacity</h1>
<h1 class="one-quarter-opaque">This header is set to 0.25
opacity</h1>
<h1 class="transparent">This header is fully transparent</h1>
</body>
</html>
```

In this case, what you would see would be blue header text that is increasingly transparent, with the final header effectively being invisible — although any subsequent content would fall below it because it is still there. Invisible text continues to displace any other content that would follow it in the natural flow of objects on the Web page. You can see a mock-up of the code from Listing 13.2 displayed in Figure 13–2.

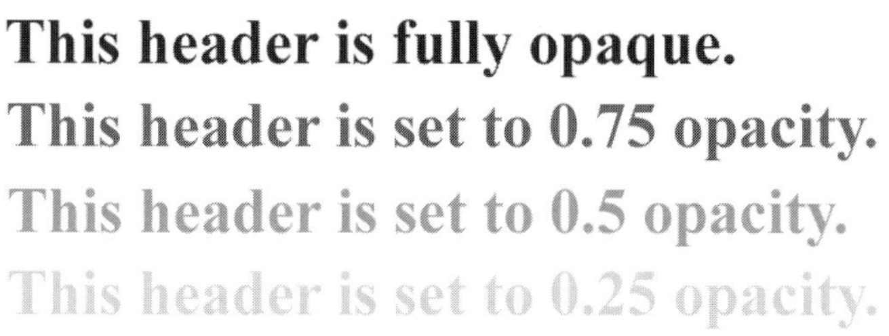

This header is fully opaque.
This header is set to 0.75 opacity.
This header is set to 0.5 opacity.
This header is set to 0.25 opacity.

Figure 13–2 Example of RGBA values set to decreasing opacity values.

Note that you can only do this with either the numerical RGB triplet or percentage methods of specifying colors — the CSS3 color module does not allow you to do this directly using hexadecimal values or color names.

CSS3 introduces a wholly new way of specifying Web color values called HSL, which is short for Hue, Saturation and Lightness. It is arguably the most intuitive way of specifying color values, as it describes color values in terms of their placement on a rainbow color circle, how deep a color is, and how light or dark it is. The first value of HSL is described by a color circle with color values arranged on its circumference. 0 (and 360) degrees is red, green is 120 degrees and blue is 240 degrees. Both saturation and lightness are represented by percentage values. 100% saturation is the full value for a given color, whereas 0% represents the grayest value for that color. 100% lightness is white, 50% is normal and 0% lightness is black. The following code snippet shows how full red, green and blue values would be represented using HSL:

```
{color: hsl(0deg, 100%, 50%)}   /* red */
{color: hsl(120deg, 100%, 50%)} /* green */
{color: hsl(240deg, 100%, 50%)} /* blue */
```

Once you know where a color value lies on the color wheel, it is a relatively easy thing to tweak the value; making a color more green or blue, for example, de-saturating it, or making it darker or brighter as needed.

Since there is a way of specifying transparency values with RGB values with RGBA, it only makes sense to do the same with HSL, and so the CSS3 color module also introduces HSLA, which works exactly the same way as RGBA. Under this scheme, the following rules would be equivalent, producing a paragraph in half-transparent blue:

```
p {color: rgba(0, 0, 255, 0.5)}
p {color: hsla(240deg, 100%, 50%, 0.5)}
```

Finally, the CSS3 color module adds the `transparent` value to all properties that accept color. So, by adding this value, you can make a Web object fully transparent, although still there. This was a value that previously could be applied to background color, but this new arrangement simplifies things considerably, making it easier to directly — and dynamically — change color values for Web objects.

Browser Compatibility

The following browser compatibility statements apply only to CSS1 and CSS2 attributes for the `color` property — the CSS3 attributes are too new to be considered here.

- Internet Explorer 3.0: Safe.
- Internet Explorer 4.0: Safe.

- Internet Explorer 4.0 – 4.5 (Mac): Safe.
- Internet Explorer 5.0: Safe.
- Internet Explorer 5.1 – 5.2 (Mac): Safe.
- Internet Explorer 5.5: Safe.
- Internet Explorer 6.0: Safe.
- Netscape Navigator 4.0 – 4.79: Safe.
- Netscape Navigator 4.0 (Mac & UNIX): Safe.
- Netscape Navigator 6.0: Safe.
- Netscape Navigator 7.0: Safe.
- Mozilla 1.0: Safe.
- Opera 3.6 – 4.0: Safe.
- Opera 5.0 – 6.0: Safe.
- Konqueror: Safe.

This is one of those properties where every browser manufacturer realized its advantages early on. It is completely safe to use in all browsers.

Core Tip

A note of warning to non-American readers of this book: make sure you use the American spelling of the word "color" — the British spelling (colour) does not work in CSS code.

13.2 Gamma Correction under CSS3

In a nutshell, gamma describes the brightness of a computer display. On average, PC (Personal Computer) displays tend to be darker, and hence have a lower gamma value, than Macintosh, Silicon Graphics or NeXT computer displays.

There are no proposed properties that would allow the Web author direct control over the gamma value of their Web page; it would appear as though it is up to the browser developers to implement this function. Under this scheme, the default gamma value would apparently match that of typical PC systems running under MS-Windows. Many other systems operate at gamma levels that are brighter than those typically used by a PC. Under this system, a typical PC system would have a gamma correction value of 0, a Macintosh would be 1.45, an SGI system would be brighter still at 1.7 and a NeXT system brightest at 2.22.

If this is how things work out, it will eliminate the differences in color displays across different computer systems, although this may take some getting used to by users of brighter computer systems.

As this is a CSS3 development, there is no direct support for this in current browsers.

13.3 opacity Property

By default, all objects on a Web page are fully opaque. The opacity property would give Web authors the ability to change that, setting a value that tells the browser how opaque an object would be, allowing for interesting visual blending effects.

opacity takes a decimal value ranging between 0.0 (fully transparent) and 1.0 (fully opaque) — any value greater or lower than this is clipped to stay within this range. The opacity value is applied across the entire element — any outline, border or background that may be associated with a selected element is rendered using the same opacity value.

Listing 13.3 shows how the opacity property could be used, with its results seen in Figure 13–3.

Listing 13.3	*opacity Example Code*

```
<html>
<head>
<title>opacity Example</title>
<style>
h1 {font-size: x-large}
.opaque {opacity: 1.0}
.point-eight-opaque {opacity: 0.8}
.point-six-opaque {opacity: 0.6}
.point-four-opaque {opacity: 0.4}
.point-two-opaque (opacity: 0.2)
.transparent {opacity: 0.0}
</style>
</head>
<body>
<h1 class="opaque">This header is fully opaque</h1>
<h1 class="point-eight-opaque">This header is set to 0.8
opacity</h1>
<h1 class="point-six-opaque">This header is set to 0.6
opacity</h1>
<h1 class="point-four-opaque">This header is set to 0.4
opacity</h1>
<h1 class="point-two-opaque">This header is set to 0.2
opacity</h1>
```

| Listing 13.3 | *opacity Example Code (continued)* |

```
<h1 class="transparent">This header is fully transparent</h1>
Some extra text to display the effects of the transparent header.
</body>
</html>
```

This header is fully opaque.
This header is set to 0.8 opacity.
This header is set to 0.6 opacity.
This header is set to 0.4 opacity.
This header is set to 0.2 opacity.

Some extra text to display the effects of the transparent header.

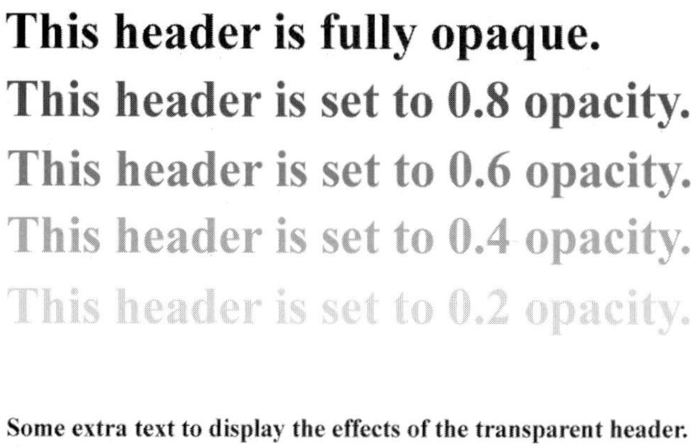

Figure 13–3   A sample of how the opacity property could be displayed.

Remember that this property is still — at the time of writing — not finalized in the CSS3 color module. So while things may be different in the final version of the specification, this still provides an idea of what to expect in future browsers.

13.4 rendering-intent Property

Reproducing color values across different media is not easy, as anybody who has tried to do professional color matching between print and onscreen colors will tell you. The International Color Consortium (ICC) set up a color-profile format that tries to deal with these issues, and in particular, what to do with out-of-gamut colors, which are colors that fall outside the range of a particular color profile for a given device. For example, it is very hard to exactly reproduce the bright, onscreen color generated by the hexadecimal value 255,0,0 (color name: red) into print, and it is equally difficult to get an exact match for a printed magenta onscreen. Rendering intent rules have been created to cope with color equivalency between different devices. The rendering-intent property comes with six properties, each with its own unique set of rules for handling color: auto, perceptual, relative-colorimetric, saturation and absolute-colorimetric as well as inherit.

The auto value is the default, and corresponds to the default behavior for the individual browser. The perceptual value renders the full range of color to match the color output of the device, either compressing or expanding the actual color values. It is called perceptual because the intent is to try and shift the color values so that they all match each other even if the match is not exact — a red may become a pink, but it is still red after a fashion. Under this value, the gray balance is preserved. The rela-tive-colorimetric value takes the white value of the original and maps it to the white value of the destination device, shifting all of the other color values along with it in the process. The saturation value is meant to retain the vividness of color val-ues — it preserves the original saturation rather than hue levels, so while a color may shift towards green or red, its "neon-iness" is retained. The absolute-colorimetric value reproduces colors exactly, and converts out-of-gamut colors to the nearest possible hue. The inherit value takes on whatever parent colorimetric value may be present.

The following code snippet provides an example of how this future CSS3 property might be used:

```
@color-profile {rendering-intent: absolute-colorimetric}
```

Since this is a CSS3 property and not officially set, it is not as yet supported by any browser. For more information on @color-profile, read the section on this at-rule later in this chapter.

13.5 color-profile Property

There are some cases where you might want to use a specific color profile that goes beyond what the rendering-intent property can deliver. That's where the color-profile property comes in. It allows the Web author to set a color profile based on information, or force the display device to use an sRGB format.

This property takes one of four values: auto, sRGB, a URL value and inherit. The auto value is the default, which is assumed to be an sRGB format — which is the standard color format for most major computing platforms. The specific sRGB value is there in case the device is not sRGB-based, allowing the Web author to force the device to try and use this format. The URL value allows you to point to an external ICC color profile configuration file. The inherit value takes on any parent value that may have already been set.

The following code snippet shows how this property might be used to force a display device to render an image file according to an external color profile configuration file:

```
<style>
img {color-profile:
"http://www.corecss.com/profiles/dummyfile.icm"}
</style>
```

13.6 @color-profile

`@color-profile` is a new at-rule that essentially allows you to set `rendering-intent` or `color-profiling` for a Web page all at once. Whereas you might expect to use `rendering-intent` or `color-profile` for particular objects on a page (individual images, for example), the `@color-profile` at-rule will allow you to set color profiling to the whole of the color-based contents on the page.

`@color-profile` essentially combines all of the values available to `rendering-intent` and `color-profile`: `auto`, `perceptual`, `relative-colorimetric`, `saturation` and `absolute-colorimetric`, `sRGB`, a URL value and `inherit`. All of these values work in exactly the same way as they do with these two properties.

The following code snippet provides an idea as to how the `@color-profile` at-rule could be put to use:

```
@color-profile {rendering-intent: relative-colorimetric}
```

13.7 X11 Color Keywords

If adopted in its current state, the CSS3 color module will also enshrine the X11 set of color names within CSS. This is a listing of 142 color keywords that have long been incorporated within both major browsers (since version 3.0 for Internet Explorer and Netscape Navigator). The X11 color set was first devised for the X Windows System (underlying most UNIX operating systems), and was later widely adopted within other operating systems. While there are 142 keywords, there are in fact only 140 different colors, since there are two cases where the same color value is represented by two keywords; so "Magenta" and "Fuchsia" are two different names for the same color (#FF00FF), as is "Aqua" and "Cyan" (#00FFFF).

Table 13.2 depicts all of the color names contained under the X11 color set in alphabetical order, listing their corresponding hexadecimal RGB, decimal and HSL values.

Table 13.2   *The X11 Color Set*

Color Name	Hex RGB	Decimal	HSL
AliceBlue	#F0F8FF	240,248,255	208deg,6%,100%
AntiqueWhite	#FAEBD7	250,235,215	34deg,14%,98%
Aqua	#00FFFF	0,255,255	180deg,100%,100%
Aquamarine	#7FFFD4	127,255,212	160deg,50%,100%
Azure	#F0FFFF	240,255,255	180deg,6%,100%
Beige	#F5F5DC	245,245,220	60deg,10%,96%
Bisque	#FFE4C4	255,228,196	33deg,23%,100%
Black	#000000	0,0,0	0deg,0%,0%
BlanchedAlmond	#FFEBCD	255,235,205	36deg,20%,100%
Blue	#0000FF	0,0,255	240deg,100%,100%
BlueViolet	#8A2BE2	138,43,226	271deg,81%,89%
Brown	#A52A2A	165,42,42	0deg,75%,65%
BurlyWood	#DEB887	222,184,135	0deg,39%,87%
CadetBlue	#5F9EA0	95,158,160	182deg,41%,63%
Chartreuse	#7FFF00	127,255,0	90deg,100%,100%
Chocolate	#D2691E	210,105,30	25deg,86%,82%
Coral	#FF7F50	255,127,80	16deg,69%,100%
CornflowerBlue	#6495ED	100,149,237	219deg,58%,93%
Cornsilk	#FFF8DC	255,248,220	48deg,14%,100%
Crimson	#DC143C	220,20,60	348deg,91%,86%
Cyan	#00FFFF	0,255,255	180deg,100%,100%
DarkBlue	#00008B	0,0,139	240deg,100%,55%
DarkCyan	#008B8B	0,139,139	180deg,100%,55%

Table 13.2   *The X11 Color Set (continued)*

DarkGoldenrod	#B8860B	184,134,11	43deg,94%,72%
DarkGray	#A9A9A9	169,169,169	0deg,0%,66%
DarkGreen	#006400	0,100,0	120deg,100%,39%
DarkKhaki	#BDB76B	189,183,107	56deg,43%,74%
DarkMagenta	#8B008B	139,0,139	300deg,100%,55%
DarkOliveGreen	#556B2F	85,107,47	82deg,56%,42%
DarkOrange	#FF8C00	255,140,0	33deg,100%,100%
DarkOrchid	#9932CC	153,50,204	280deg,75%,80%
DarkRed	#8B0000	139,0,0	0deg,100%,55%
DarkSalmon	#E9967A	233,150,122	15deg,48%,91%
DarkSeaGreen	#8FBC8F	143,188,143	120deg,24%,74%
DarkSlateBlue	#483D8B	72,61,139	248deg,56%,55%
DarkSlateGray	#2F4F4F	47,79,79	180deg,41%,31%
DarkTurquoise	#00CED1	0,206,209	181deg,100%,82%
DarkViolet	#9400D3	148,0,211	282deg,100%,83%
DeepPink	#FF1493	255,20,147	328deg,92%,100%
DeepSkyBlue	#00BFFF	0,191,255	195deg,100%,100%
DimGray	#696969	105,105,105	0deg,0%,41%
DodgerBlue	#1E90FF	30,144,255	210deg,88%,100%
FireBrick	#B22222	178,34,34	0deg,81%,70%
FloralWhite	#FFFAF0	255,250,240	40deg,6%,100%
ForestGreen	#228B22	34,139,34	120deg,76%,55%
Fuchsia	#FF00FF	255,0,255	300deg,100%,100%
Gainsboro	#DCDCDC	220,220,220	0deg,0%,86%
GhostWhite	#F8F8FF	248,248,255	240deg,3%,100%
Gold	#FFD700	255,215,0	51deg,100%,100%
Goldenrod	#DAA520	218,165,32	43deg,85%,85%

Table 13.2   *The X11 Color Set (continued)*

Gray	#808080	128,128,128	0deg,0%,50%
Green	#008000	0,128,0	120deg,100%,50%
GreenYellow	#ADFF2F	173,255,47	84deg,82%,100%
Honeydew	#F0FFF0	240,255,240	120deg,6%,100%
HotPink	#FF69B4	255,105,180	330deg,59%,100%
IndianRed	#CD5C5C	205,92,92	0deg,55%,80%
Indigo	#4B0082	75,0,130	275deg,100%,51%
Ivory	#FFFFF0	255,255,240	60deg,6%,100%
Khaki	#F0E68C	240,230,140	54deg,42%,94%
Lavender	#E6E6FA	230,230,250	240deg,8%,98%
LavenderBlush	#FFF0F5	255,240,245	340deg,6%,100%
LawnGreen	#7CFC00	124,252,0	90deg,100%,99%
LemonChiffon	#FFFACD	255,250,205	54deg,20%,100%
LightBlue	#ADD8E6	173,216,230	195deg,25%,90%
LightCoral	#F08080	240,128,128	0deg,47%,94%
LightCyan	#E0FFFF	224,255,255	180deg,12%,100%
LightGoldenrodYellow	#FAFAD2	250,250,210	60deg,16%,98%
LightGreen	#90EE90	144,238,144	120deg,39%,93%
LightGrey	#D3D3D3	211,211,211	0deg,0%,83%
LightPink	#FFB6C1	255,182,193	351deg,29%,100%
LightSalmon	#FFA07A	255,160,122	17deg,52%,100%
LightSeaGreen	#20B2AA	32,178,170	177deg,82%,70%
LightSkyBlue	#87CEFA	135,206,250	203deg,46%,98%
LightSlateGray	#778899	119,136,153	210deg,22%,60%
LightSteelBlue	#B0C4DE	176,196,222	214deg,21%,87%
LightYellow	#FFFFE0	255,255,224	60deg,12%,100%
Lime	#00FF00	0,255,0	120deg,100%,100%

Table 13.2   *The X11 Color Set (continued)*

LimeGreen	#32CD32	50,205,50	120deg,76%,80%
Linen	#FAF0E6	250,240,230	30deg,8%,98%
Magenta	#FF00FF	255,0,255	300deg,100%,100%
Maroon	#800000	128,0,0	0deg,100%,50%
MediumAquamarine	#66CDAA	102,205,170	160deg,50%,80%
MediumBlue	#0000CD	0,0,205	240deg,100%,80%
MediumOrchid	#BA55D3	186,85,211	288deg,60%,83%
MediumPurple	#9370DB	147,112,219	260deg,49%,86%
MediumSeaGreen	#3CB371	60,179,113	147deg,66%,70%
MediumSlateBlue	#7B68EE	123,104,238	249deg,56%,93%
MediumSpringGreen	#00FA9A	0,250,154	157deg,100%,98%
MediumTurquoise	#48D1CC	72,209,204	178deg,66%,82%
MediumVioletRed	#C71585	199,21,133	322deg,89%,278%
MidnightBlue	#191970	25,25,112	240deg,78%,44%
MintCream	#F5FFFA	245,255,250	150deg,4%,100%
MistyRose	#FFE4E1	255,228,225	6deg,12%,100%
Moccasin	#FFE4B5	255,228,181	38deg,29%,100%
NavajoWhite	#FFDEAD	255,222,173	36deg,32%,100%
Navy	#000080	0,0,128	240deg,100%,50%
OldLace	#FDF5E6	253,245,230	39deg,9%,99%
Olive	#808000	128,128,0	60deg,100%,50%
OliveDrab	#6B8E23	107,142,35	80deg,75%,56%
Orange	#FFA500	255,165,0	39deg,100%,100%
OrangeRed	#FF4500	255,69,0	16deg,100%,100%
Orchid	#DA70D6	218,112,214	302deg,49%,85%
PaleGoldenrod	#EEE8AA	238,232,170	55deg,29%,93%
PaleGreen	#98FB98	152,251,152	120deg,39%,98%

Table 13.2   *The X11 Color Set (continued)*

PaleTurquoise	#AFEEEE	175,238,238	180deg,26%,93%
PaleVioletRed	#DB7093	219,112,147	340deg,49%,86%
PapayaWhip	#FFEFD5	255,239,213	37deg,16%,100%
PeachPuff	#FFDAB9	255,218,185	28deg,27%,100%
Peru	#CD853F	205,133,63	30deg,69%,80%
Pink	#FFC0CB	255,192,203	350deg,25%,100%
Plum	#DDA0DD	221,160,221	300deg,28%,87%
PowderBlue	#B0E0E6	176,224,230	187deg,23%,90%
Purple	#800080	128,0,128	300deg,100%,50%
Red	#FF0000	255,0,0	0deg,100%,100%
RosyBrown	#BC8F8F	188,143,143	0deg,24%,74%
RoyalBlue	#4169E1	65,105,225	225deg,71%,88%
SaddleBrown	#8B4513	139,69,19	25deg,86%,55%
Salmon	#FA8072	250,128,114	6deg,54%,98%
SandyBrown	#F4A460	244,164,96	28deg,61%,96%
SeaGreen	#2E8B57	46,139,87	146deg,67%,55%
Seashell	#FFF5EE	255,245,238	25deg,7%,100%
Sienna	#A0522D	160,82,45	19deg,72%,63%
Silver	#C0C0C0	192,192,192	0deg,0%,75%
SkyBlue	#87CEEB	135,206,235	197deg,43%,92%
SlateBlue	#6A5ACD	106,90,205	248deg,56%,80%
SlateGray	#708090	112,128,144	210deg,22%,56%
Snow	#FFFAFA	255,250,250	0deg,2%,100%
SpringGreen	#00FF7F	0,255,127	150deg,100%,100%
SteelBlue	#4682B4	70,130,180	207deg,61%,71%
Tan	#D2B48C	210,180,140	34deg,33%,82%
Teal	#008080	0,128,128	180deg,100%,50%

Table 13.2	The X11 Color Set (continued)		
Thistle	#D8BFD8	216,191,216	300deg,12%,85%
Tomato	#FF6347	255,99,71	9deg,72%,100%
Turquoise	#40E0D0	64,224,208	174deg,71%,88%
Violet	#EE82EE	238,130,238	300deg,45%,93%
Wheat	#F5DEB3	245,222,179	39deg,27%,96%
White	#FFFFFF	255,255,255	0deg,0%,100%
WhiteSmoke	#F5F5F5	245,245,245	0deg,0%,96%
Yellow	#FFFF00	255,255,0	60deg,100%,100%
YellowGreen	#9ACD32	154,205,50	80deg,76%,80%

BACKGROUND PROPERTIES

Topics in This Chapter

- `background-color`
- `background-image`
- `background-repeat`
- `background-attachment`
- `background-position`
- `background`
- `background-position-x`
- `background-position-y`
- `background-clip`
- `background-origin`
- `background-size`
- `background-quantity`
- `background-spacing`

Chapter 14

The background family of properties enables Web authors to tile background images with precision. Prior to the advent of the CSS3 specification, various color-related properties used to be part of the same family as the background properties, but as both have been expanded and grown more specialized, they have now been separated into families of properties.

14.1 background-color Property

The `background-color` property sets the background color of an HTML element, and for the most part functions in exactly the same way as the `bgcolor` attribute associated with the body element under the HTML 4.0 specification.

What makes this property so versatile is that it can be added to virtually any Web element. It can take on any type of CSS color value, ranging from standard name values (such as "green" and "aqua") to standard hexadecimals ("#ff0000", which equals red) to rgb color values — in short, any type of color value that the `color` property can take (see Chapter 13, "Color"). It can also take on a transparent value, which is designed to let the immediate "parent" color show through. It can also take on an `inherit` value, which adopts whatever parent value may be available. The code depicted in Listing 14.1 shows some examples of how it can be added to many different Web page elements, and is shown in Figure 14–1.

Listing 14.1 *background-color Example Code*

```
<html>
<head>
<title>background-color</title>
<style>
.demo {background-color: rgb(255,255,255)}
body {font-size: large}
</style>
</head>
<body style="background-color: rgb(0,0,0)">
<h1 style="background-color: aqua">A Light Blue Header</h1>
<em style="background-color: #ffff00">Italicized text on a yellow
background.</em>
<em style="background-color: green">Text with a green background.
<strong style="background-color: transparent">This should be in
green too.</strong>
More text with a green background.</em>
<table border="2" cellpadding="5" style="background-color: lime">
<tr>
<td>A small lime-colored table</td>
</tr>
</table>
<ul style="background-color: yellow">
 <li>List item #1 with a yellow background</li>
 <li style="background-color: #f0f">List item #2 showing cascading
effect (purple background)</li>
 <li>List item #3 with a yellow background</li>
</ul>
<span class="demo">Span using a white background</span>
</body>
</html>
```

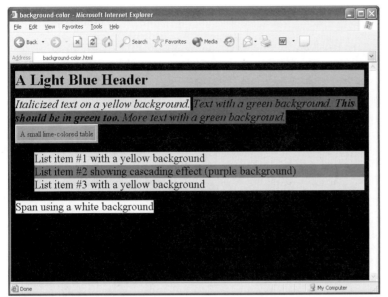

Figure 14–1   background-color example code as depicted in Internet Explorer 6.0.

Browser Compatibility

This property has been widely adopted, and works properly in all but the earliest browsers.

- Internet Explorer 3.0: Unsafe
- Internet Explorer 4.0: Safe
- Internet Explorer 4.0 – 4.5 (Mac): Safe
- Internet Explorer 5.0: Safe
- Internet Explorer 5.1 – 5.2 (Mac): Safe
- Internet Explorer 5.5: Safe
- Internet Explorer 6.0: Safe
- Netscape Navigator 4.0 – 4.79: Partial. All values supported with the exception of `transparent`.
- Netscape Navigator 4.0 (Mac & UNIX): Partial. Ditto above.
- Netscape Navigator 6.0-7.0: Safe. Note that it also sets a background color for spaces leading up to individual list elements. This is within the range of interpretation for the specification. See Figure 14–2 for an example of this behavior.
- Netscape Navigator 7.0: Safe. Ditto above.

- Mozilla 1.0: Safe, though displays same behavior as Netscape Navigator 6.0 when it comes to individual list elements.
- Opera 3.6 – 4.0: Safe.
- Opera 5.0 – 6.0: Safe.
- Konqueror: Safe.

Internet Explorer beginning with version 4.0 fully supports `background-color`.

Netscape Navigator began implementing this feature beginning with version 4.x, but its results have been problematic. The 4.x version of this browser is rated Partial since it does not implement the `transparent` value which is supposed to let the underlying color "show through." In Figure 14–1 (which uses Internet Explorer 6.0), the code that uses `transparent` is displayed as black (the color set to the body element) instead of the green value (set to the `em` element, its immediate parent element) that should be displayed instead. Netscape Navigator 6.0 and 7.0 as well as Mozilla 1.0 remedy this problem, though it should be noted that the color value is added to `ul` and `ol` elements when present, a behavior which does not occur in any other browser, though this is within the range of interpretation for the specification. See Figure 14–2 for an example of this behavior.

Opera began implementing the `background-color` property beginning with version 3.6.

Konqueror also implements this property.

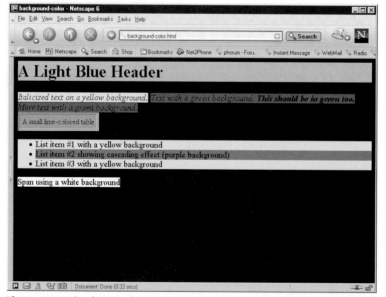

Figure 14–2   background-color example code as depicted in Netscape Navigator 6.0; note the difference in the way the background color is applied to the ul element.

14.2 background-image Property

`background-image` enables a Web author to set a graphic image as the background image for an element on a Web page. It works in much the same manner as does the background attribute to the body element, but its CSS counterpart allows background to be set for pretty much any element on a Web page.

It can take a URL value (or an `inherit` value if it points to an image file), which points to the background image. The browser then takes the image and begins tiling it "under" the element it is associated with. The following code snippet shows how it can be added to a sample Web element (in this case the `body` element):

```
<body style="background-image: url(picture.gif)">
```

If you want to specify an image contained on a different Web server (or just want to point to it in absolute terms), you have to add the full URL, as depicted in the following code snippet:

```
<body style="background-image:
url(http://www.corecss.com/images/picture.gif)">
```

The `background-image` property can be associated with any Web page element that can be displayed on screen. For example, the following Web page (illustrated in Figure 14–3) gives you an idea of how it can be used:

Listing 14.2 *background-image Example Code*

```
<html>
<head>
<title>background-image</title>
<style>
.commodus {background-image: url(commodus.jpg); font-size: large;
color: black}
.claudius {background-image: url(claudius.jpg); font-size: large;
color: silver}
</style>
</head>
<body class="claudius">
The body of this page is tiled using a coin depicting Roman Emperor
Claudius. He was a grandson of the first Roman Emperor Augustus,
and he reigned from 41-54 A.D. The fictional work <cite>I,
Claudius</cite> is based on his life.
```

Listing 14.2	*background-image Example Code (continued)*

```
<table border width="50%" cellpadding="5" class="commodus">
<tr>
<td>This table contains a tiled background image of a coin of
Roman Emperor Commodus. The movie <cite>Gladiator</cite> casts him
as part of the story.</td>
</tr>
</table>

<ol class="commodus">
<li>This list of elements also has a tiled</li>
<li>background of Roman Emperor Aurian</li>
<li>While this page will never win an award</li>
<li>for beauty, it does get the point across that you can add
<code>background-image</code></li>
<li>to just about anything.</li>
</ol>

</body>
</html>
```

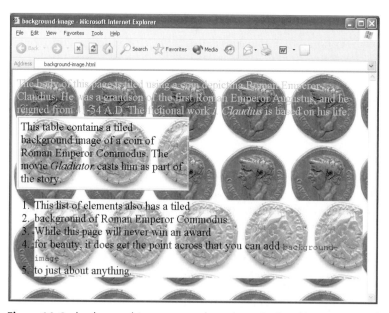

Figure 14–3 background-image example code as depicted in Internet Explorer 6.0.

This property can be thought of as the "foundation" property of the background family of CSS properties, as all of the other properties in this family (with the sole exception of `background-color`) are used to modify its behavior. All of these other properties are treated separately in this chapter.

Browser Compatibility

This property is fully supported in the more recent versions of both Internet Explorer and Netscape Navigator, so it is considered safe to use.

- Internet Explorer 3.0: Unsafe.
- Internet Explorer 4.0: Safe.
- Internet Explorer 4.0 – 4.5 (Mac): Safe.
- Internet Explorer 5.0: Safe.
- Internet Explorer 5.1 – 5.2 (Mac): Safe.
- Internet Explorer 5.5: Safe
- Internet Explorer 6.0: Safe
- Netscape Navigator 4.0 – 4.79: Safe, but quirky.
- Netscape Navigator 4.0 (Mac & UNIX): Safe, but quirky. Ditto above.
- Netscape Navigator 6.0: Safe.
- Netscape Navigator 7.0: Safe.
- Mozilla 1.0: Safe.
- Opera 3.6: Safe.
- Opera 5.0: Safe.
- Opera 6.0: Safe.
- Konqueror: Safe.

Internet Explorer has implemented this property since version 4.0, and is safe to use within this browser.

Netscape Navigator started implementing this feature beginning with version 4.x, but it does have one quirk: if you you are using a universal style sheet, you must use an http reference for the file, as a relative URL will "break" when the CSS page is accessed from a Web page at a lower level (in other words, Netscape Navigator looks at the relative URL in relation to the current page, instead of to the universal style sheet). This can cause problems if you are trying to demonstrate pages run locally without the use of a Web server. It is otherwise completely safe to use (and this problem was fixed in subsequent versions of this browser)

Opera was an early adopter of this property, and it has been implemented since version 3.6.

Konqueror also properly implements this property.

14.3 background-repeat Property

The `background-repeat` property is always used in conjunction with the `back-ground-image` property, and it determines how an image will be tiled on a Web page. The default value is `repeat`, which works the same way that `<body back-ground="image.gif">` or `<body style="background-image: url(image.gif)">` does by simply repeating the background image both across and down the Web page. The `background-repeat` property comes with four other values:

- `repeat-x` tiles the image horizontally,

- `repeat-y` tiles the image vertically,

- `no-repeat` tells the browser not to tile the image at all, and

- `inherit` takes on any parent value that may be present.

As an example, Listing 14.3 tiles the image file in a strip that runs down right side of the Web page, and also across the top of a table.

Listing 14.3	*background-repeat*

```
<html>
<head>
<title>background-repeat example</title>
<style>
body {background-image: url(aurelian.jpg); background-repeat:
repeat-y}
table {background-image: url(aurelian.jpg); background-repeat:
repeat-x}
em {font-size: x-large; color: lime}
table {position: absolute; top: 0; left: 0}
</style>
</head>
<body>

<table>
<tr>
<td>
<em>This page contained tiled images of a coin of the ancient
Roman emperor Aurelian, who reigned from 270 - 275 AD. He managed
to drive the barbarians out of Italy, and restored many provinces
back into the empire. He was murdered by his own guards, the fate
of many Roman emperors.</em>
```

Listing 14.3	*background-repeat (continued)*

```
<p>
<em>Note how the image of the coin is tiled down the left side of
the Web page, while it is tiled across the top of this table. Neat,
eh?</em>
</p>
</em>
</td>
</tr>
</table>

</body>
</html>
```

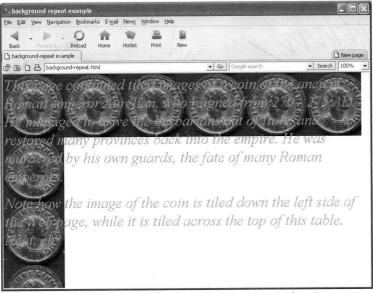

Figure 14–4   The effects of background-repeat as seen within Opera 6.0.

Browser Compatibility

This property is supported fully in the most recent versions of Internet Explorer and Netscape Navigator, though it is worth noting that Netscape Navigator 4.x is given only a "Partial" rating.

- Internet Explorer 3.0: Unsafe.
- Internet Explorer 4.0: Safe.
- Internet Explorer 4.0 – 4.5 (Mac): Safe.
- Internet Explorer 5.0: Safe.
- Internet Explorer 5.1 – 5.2 (Mac): Safe.
- Internet Explorer 5.5: Safe.
- Internet Explorer 6.0: Safe.
- Netscape Navigator 4.0 – 4.79: Partial.
- Netscape Navigator 4.0 (Mac & UNIX): Partial.
- Netscape Navigator 6.0: Safe.
- Netscape Navigator 7.0: Safe.
- Mozilla 1.0: Safe.
- Opera 3.6: Safe.
- Opera 5.0: Safe.
- Opera 6.0: Safe.
- Konqueror: Safe.

Internet Explorer has implemented this property properly since version 4.0.

Netscape 4.x gets a Partial rating. It is safe when only a single background image is used, but if multiple images are displayed, this version of the browser has problems when the page is scrolled. Figure 14–5 displays the effects you can expect to see when multiple background images are used. In some instances it can crash the browser. This also one of those rare occasions when the Macintosh and UNIX versions of this browser diverge from the behavior seen in the Windows version — while it does not have the same problem as the Windows version, it *can* display a background image, its behavior can be quirky, especially when `background-repeat` is combined with `background-position` and the latter is set to a percentage value. These problems were fixed by the time Netscape Navigator 6.0 (and Mozilla 1.0) came on the scene.

Opera adopted this property fully beginning with version 3.6.

Konqueror properly implements this property.

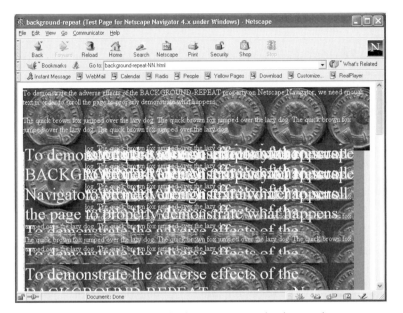

Figure 14–5 The effects of multiple images set to background-repeat as seen within Netscape Navigator 4.79 for Windows.

14.4 background-attachment Property

The background-attachment property is designed to set how the background image should move when the browser window is scrolled. When you scroll a page in a browser, the typical behavior for the background is that it, the text and any other elements on the Web page scroll in unison. With the background-attachment property, you have another choice.

The background-attachment property is always associated with background-image and it can take one of two possible values: scroll and fixed. The scroll value is the default, and is what you typically see when you scroll any Web page with a background image — the background scrolls with you. The fixed value is supposed to keep the background in place while the browser moves the text and other elements of the Web page instead. It can also take on an inherit value, which adopts whatever parent value may be available. You can see the effect of this in Figure 14–6, derived from the code in Listing 14.4: the text in Internet Explorer scrolls, but the background does not. The effect makes it seem as though the text is "floating" above the background image.

Listing 14.4	*background-attachment: fixed Example*

```
<html>
<head>
<title>A PRINCESS OF MARS by Edgar Rice Burroughs
(background-attachment Example)</title>
<style>
body {background-image: url(mars-surface.jpg);
background-attachment: fixed}
p {color: white; font-weight: bold}
</style>
</head>
<body>
<h1>A PRINCESS OF MARS by Edgar Rice Burroughs</h1>
<h2>CHAPTER III</h2>
<h3>MY ADVENT ON MARS</h3>
<p>
I opened my eyes upon a strange and weird landscape.  I knew that
I was on Mars; not once did I question either my sanity or my
wakefulness.  I was not asleep, no need for pinching here; my inner
consciousness told me as plainly that I was upon Mars as your
conscious mind tells you that you are upon Earth.  You do not
question the fact; neither did I.
</p>
<p>
I found myself lying prone upon a bed of yellowish, mosslike
vegetation which stretched around me in all directions for
interminable miles.  I seemed to be lying in a deep, circular
basin, along the outer verge of which I could distinguish the
irregularities of low hills.
</p>
<p>
It was midday, the sun was shining full upon me and the heat of it
was rather intense upon my naked body, yet no greater than would
have been true under similar conditions on an Arizona desert.
Here and there were slight outcroppings of quartz-bearing rock
which glistened in the sunlight; and a little to my left, perhaps
a hundred yards, appeared a low, walled enclosure about four feet
in height.  No water, and no other vegetation than the moss was in
evidence, and as I was somewhat thirsty I determined to do a little
exploring.
</p>
```

| Listing 14.4 | *background-attachment: fixed Example (continued)* |

```
<p>
Springing to my feet I received my first Martian surprise, for the
effort, which on Earth would have brought me standing upright,
carried me into the Martian air to the height of about three yards.
I alighted softly upon the ground, however, without appreciable
shock or jar.  Now commenced a series of evolutions which even then
seemed ludicrous in the extreme. I found that I must learn to walk
all over again, as the muscular exertion which carried me easily
and safely upon Earth played strange antics with me upon Mars.
</p>
<p>
Instead of progressing in a sane and dignified manner, my attempts
to walk resulted in a variety of hops which took me clear of the
ground a couple of feet at each step and landed me sprawling upon
my face or back at the end of each second or third hop.  My
muscles, perfectly attuned and accustomed to the force of gravity
on Earth, played the mischief with me in attempting for the first
time to cope with the lesser gravitation and lower air pressure on
Mars.
</p>
etc...
</body>
</html>
```

Although it has been around for awhile, the `bgproperties="fixed"` attribute for the `body` element is little used, so many users are initially surprised when they see the effect in action. When put into effect (using either HTML or CSS) this "trick" can actually be a little unsettling to the viewer, so it is best used sparingly. In addition, as when choosing any background image, make sure that you are choosing one that will not interfere with the readability of your text.

While it is possible to add this property to other elements on a Web page, it really only makes sense to add the `background-attachment` property to any property where scrolling is involved, such as the `body` and `textarea` elements.

Figure 14–6 background-attachment: fixed example code as displayed within Internet Explorer 6.0 as the page is scrolled.

Browser Compatibility

Beginning as early as Internet Explorer 2.0, there was a browser-specific HTML equivalent for this CSS property: `<body bgproperties="fixed">`. As it was an attribute of the body element introduced into Internet Explorer, it was not supported in versions of Netscape Navigator (or any other browser for that matter). Not surprisingly then, up until the most recent versions of Netscape Navigator, this CSS equivalent property only supported the default `fixed` value.

- Internet Explorer 3.0: Unsafe
- Internet Explorer 4.0: Safe
- Internet Explorer 4.0 – 4.5 (Mac): Safe
- Internet Explorer 5.0: Safe
- Internet Explorer 5.1 – 5.2 (Mac): Safe.
- Internet Explorer 5.5: Safe
- Internet Explorer 6.0: Safe
- Netscape Navigator 4.0 – 4.79: Partial. Only supports the default `fixed` value; `scroll` is not supported, and it behaves as if the value were fixed.
- Netscape Navigator 4.0 (Mac & UNIX): Partial. Same as above.
- Netscape Navigator 6.0: Safe.

- Netscape Navigator 7.0: Safe.
- Mozilla 1.0: Safe.
- Opera 3.6: Safe
- Opera 5.0: Safe
- Opera 6.0: Safe
- Konqueror: Safe.

The `background-attachment` property has been implemented in Internet Explorer since version 4.0.

Netscape Navigator is rated as Partial because it only supports the default `fixed` value; `scroll` is not supported, and it behaves as if the value were set to `fixed`. While it is rated only as Partial here, strictly speaking its behavior does not have to implement this feature according to the specification — so while it is not necessarily in error, it does not perform as some Web authors might expect, hence the Partial rating. This situation was taken care of with the release of Netscape Navigator 6.0 (and Mozilla 1.0), which now displays the effects of the `scroll` value.

Opera has correctly interpreted this property since version 3.6.

Konqueror also correctly interprets this property.

14.5 background-position Property

The `background-position` property provides a feature that is otherwise impossible in regular HTML: the exact positioning of a background image on a Web page. It is always used in conjunction with the `background-image` property, and can take either a precise X,Y pixel value, a percentage value or a special keyword value.

You can set an X,Y value that tells the background image where it should be initially displayed. X is the value in pixels the image will appear from the left of the browser window, and Y is the number of pixels the image will appear from the top of the browser window. It can also take on an `inherit` value, which adopts whatever parent value may be available. The code example Listing 14.5, depicted in Figure 14–7, shows this in action.

Listing 14.5	*background-position Example Set to Specific X and Y Values*

```
<html>
<head>
<title>background-position Example</title>
<style>
body {background-image: url(annie.jpg); background-position: 160px
160px; background-repeat: no-repeat; font-size: x-large}
</style>
</head>
<body>
This background image is positioned 160 pixels from the top of the
browser window and 160 pixels from the left of the browser window.
It does not tile because <code>background-repeat</code> is set to
<code>no-repeat</code>.
</body>
</html>
```

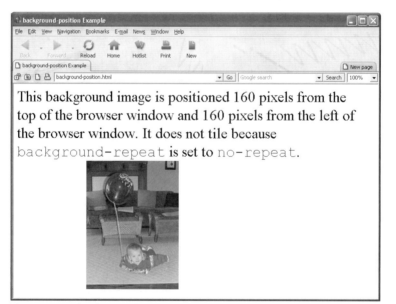

Figure 14–7 background-position example set to a specific X,Y pixel value, with background-repeat set to no-repeat, as seen within Opera 6.0.

What this code does is position the image called `annie.jpg` and begin tiling it 160 pixels from the right and 160 pixels from the top. Notice that the additional property `background-repeat: no-repeat` has been set; this has been done to show off the effect more clearly. When it is removed, the image is simply tiled over the whole of the Web page, with the first image offset by the value determined by background-position, as can be seen in Figure 14–8. (Note that the color of the text has been changed as well in order to make it visible.)

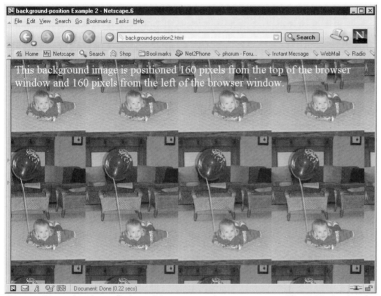

Figure 14–8 background-position example set to a specific X,Y pixel value, with no background-repeat value set, as seen within Netscape Navigator 6.0.

The background-position property can also take a percentage value, where the X and Y values are set relative to the width of the browser's window. If it is set to a value of 50% for both values (as it is in Listing 14.6) the image will be centered in the middle of the browser window.

Listing 14.6	*background-position Example with X and Y Values Set to Percentages*

```
<html>
<head>
<title>background-position Example 3</title>
<style>
body {background-image: url(annie.jpg); background-position: 50%
50%; font-size: x-large; color: white}
</style>
</head>
<body>
This background image is positioned using a value of 50% of the
browser window's height by 50% of the browser's height, which
means it should be centered in the middle of the screen.
<code>background-repeat: no-repeat</code> been added to make the
effect stand out more.
</body>
</html>
```

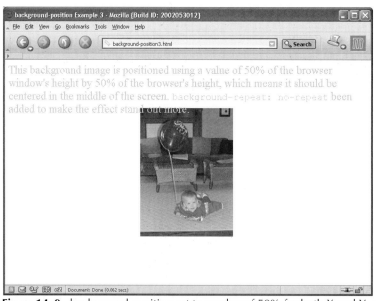

Figure 14–9   background-position set to a value of 50% for both X and Y, centering the background image in the browser's window, as seen within Mozilla 1.0.

A number of keyword values can also be used to position a background image with the `background-position` property. The keywords `left`, `center` and `right` can be used for the X value, and `top`, `center` and `bottom` can be used for the Y value.

These keyword values offer a simple shortcut for Web authors who want to ensure that a background image always begins in any of the corners of a browser window or aligned within its center. This has an edge over percentage or pixel values, as you can never be sure how wide your users will size their browser's window. Listing 14.7, depicted in Figure 14–10, shows the X and Y values set to right and bottom, respectively (again, using `background-repeat: no-repeat` to clearly show the effect).

Listing 14.7	*background-position Example with X and Y Values Set to Percentages*

```
<html>
<head>
<title>background-position Example 4</title>
<style>
body {background-image: url(annie.jpg); background-position: right
bottom; background-repeat: no-repeat; font-size: x-large}
</style>
</head>
<body>
This background image is positioned with the X and Y values set to
<code>right</code> and <code>bottom</code> respectively.
<code>background-repeat: no-repeat</code> has been added to make
the effect stand out more.
</body>
</html>
```

This property is arguably most effective (or at least most distinct) when combined with the `background-repeat` property set to `no-repeat`, as can be seen in the many code examples in this section. If you want the background image to stand out on your Web page, you can use the `background-position` and `background-repeat` properties effectively for this purpose.

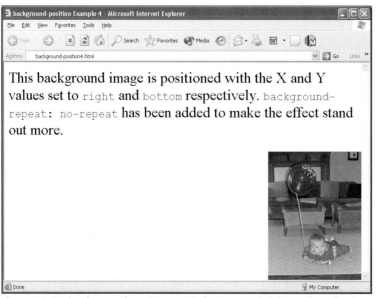

Figure 14–10 background-position set to bottom and right, with no background-repeat set to no-repeat, as seen with Internet Explorer 6.0.

Browser Compatibility

This is another property that was first implemented fully within Internet Explorer (and Opera) well before it was adopted within Netscape Navigator. Versions of Netscape Navigator including and prior to 4.79 should be considered unsafe for using this property.

- Internet Explorer 3.0: Unsafe.
- Internet Explorer 4.0: Safe.
- Internet Explorer 4.0 – 4.5 (Mac): Safe.
- Internet Explorer 5.0: Safe
- Internet Explorer 5.1 – 5.2 (Mac): Safe.
- Internet Explorer 5.5: Safe
- Internet Explorer 6.0: Safe
- Netscape Navigator 4.0 – 4.79: Unsafe. Image is tiled as if `background-position` were not present.
- Netscape Navigator 4.0 (Mac & UNIX): Unsafe. Ditto above.
- Netscape Navigator 6.0: Safe.
- Netscape Navigator 7.0: Safe.
- Mozilla 1.0: Safe.

- Opera 3.6: Safe
- Opera 5.0: Safe
- Opera 6.0: Safe
- Konqueror: Safe.

Internet Explorer began implementing this property beginning with version 4.0.

This property is not safe to use in Netscape Navigator 4.x, as the image is tiled as if `background-position` were not present. This problem was corrected by the launch of Netscape Navigator 6.0 (and Mozilla 1.0).

Opera was an early adopter of this property, first incorporating it within version 3.6.

Konqueror implements this property fully.

14.6 background Property

The `background` property is a "shortcut" property, allowing Web authors quick access to all of the values contained in the rest of the background family of properties, namely `background-color, background-image, background-repeat, background-attachment` and `background-position`. It works in much the same manner as the `font` property in providing quick access to all of the values contained in the font family. It should also be noted that when the background-related properties that appear in the CSS3 specification begin to be adopted within popular browsers, they will also be applicable to this shortcut property.

All of the values associated with `background` property have already been discussed in detail with each of the other background family properties. `background` is a handy shortcut for setting all of the values you need quickly. The following two code samples are equivalent to each other, and are depicted in Figure 14–11:

Listing 14.8 *background Put to Use as a "Shortcut" Property*

```
<html>
<head>
<title>background Example</title>
<style>
body {background: silver url(rufus_s-202.jpg) repeat-y fixed top
right; font-size: large;  margin-right: 55%}
</style>
</head>
```

Listing 14.8   *background Put to Use as a "Shortcut" Property*

This page presents a coin of Senator Rufus, who issued coins
during the Republican period of the ancient Roman state (prior to
the advent of the first Roman emperor Augustus).
```
<p>
```
The head of Sol the sun god is depicted on one side, and the other
side shows him in a chariot being pulled across the sky by four
horses.
```
</p>
</body>
</html>
```

Listing 14.9   *Various Background Properties the Equivalent of the Previous Background Code Example*

```
<html>
<head>
<title>background Example 2 (Long form)</title>
<style>
body {background: silver; background-image: url(rufus_s-202.jpg);
background-repeat: repeat-y; background-attachment: fixed;
background-position: top right; font-size: large;  margin-right:
55%}
</style>
</head>
<body>
```
This page presents a coin of Senator Rufus, who issued coins
during the Republican period of the ancient Roman state (prior to
the advent of the first Roman emperor Augustus).
```
<p>
```
The head of Sol the sun god is depicted on one side, and the other
side shows him in a chariot being pulled across the sky by four
horses.
```
</p>
</body>
</html>
```

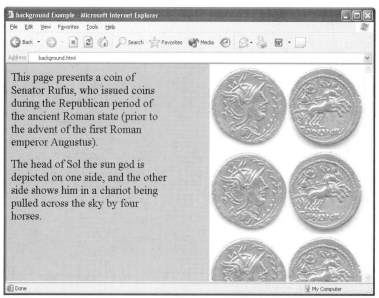

This page presents a coin of Senator Rufus, who issued coins during the Republican period of the ancient Roman state (prior to the advent of the first Roman emperor Augustus).

The head of Sol the sun god is depicted on one side, and the other side shows him in a chariot being pulled across the sky by four horses.

Figure 14–11 The background property "in action," as seen with Internet Explorer 6.0.

As you can easily see, the first code sample using only the `background` property is much more concise.

Unlike the somewhat finicky `font` shortcut property, it is possible to rearrange the ordering of the various values for background without interfering with the presentation of the elements displayed on screen.

Browser Compatibility

Given the fact that this property is a shortcut property for all of the other properties in the `background` family, it necessarily inherits all of the functionality (or lack thereof) supported by a particular browser.

- Internet Explorer 3.0: Unsafe.
- Internet Explorer 4.0: Partial.
- Internet Explorer 4.0 – 4.5 (Mac): Safe.
- Internet Explorer 5.0: Safe
- Internet Explorer 5.1 – 5.2 (Mac): Safe.
- Internet Explorer 5.5: Safe
- Internet Explorer 6.0: Safe
- Netscape Navigator 4.0 – 4.79: Partial. Only supports the values associated with `background-image` fully.

- Netscape Navigator 4.0 (Mac & UNIX): Partial. Same as above.

- Netscape Navigator 6.0: Safe.

- Netscape Navigator 7.0: Safe.

- Mozilla 1.0: Safe.

- Opera 3.6: Safe.

- Opera 5.0: Safe.

- Opera 6.0: Safe.

- Konqueror: Safe.

Internet Explorer has fully implemented the `background` property since version 4.0.

Netscape Navigator 4.x only rates a Partial as it only supports the values associated with `background-image` fully. Netscape Navigator 6.0 (and Mozilla 1.0) on up support all of the attributes for the `background` property.

This property has been fully implemented since version 3.6 of Opera.

It is also fully supported within Konqueror.

14.7 background-position-x and background-position-y Properties

In order to provide Web authors with greater control over exactly where background images can begin tiling themselves as a background, Microsoft introduced two new, browser-specific background properties with the release of version 5.5 of Internet Explorer: `background-position-x` and `background-position-y`. Both properties are used in conjunction with the `background-image` property, and are used to set the position where the background image begins to start tiling. Note that this does not mean that you can set exactly where the background-image is to start tiling within an element on a Web page; instead they position the background image relative to *itself* — so a setting of `0,0` does not refer to the top-leftmost portion of the background element, but the top-leftmost position of the image itself.

Both `background-position-x` and `background-position-y` can take percentage and specific length measures. A value of 50% means that the background image should start tiling at exactly half of its vertical (or horizontal) dimension. When a length measure — such as pixels — is used, Internet Explorer begins tiling the background image at the point specified. Listing 14.10 shows how these values can be applied using the background-position-x property:

Listing 14.10	*Various Background Properties the Equivalent of the Previous Background Code Example*

```html
<html>
<title>background-position-x Example 1</title>
<style>
div.fixed-length {background-image: url(antony_rsc-12.jpg);
background-position-x: 0 px; height: 140px; width: 400px; font:
large Arial, Helvetica, sans-serif; color: navy}
div.percentage {background-image: url(antony_rsc-12.jpg);
background-position-x: 50%; height: 140px; width: 400px; font:
large Arial, Helvetica, sans-serif; color: navy}
div.negative-value {background-image: url(antony_rsc-12.jpg);
background-position-x: -100px; height: 140px; width: 400px; font:
large Arial, Helvetica, sans-serif; color: navy}
code {font: large Arial, Helvetica, sans-serif; color: navy;
background-color: white}
</style>
</head>
<body>
<p>
<div class="fixed-length">This image is positioned using
<code>background-position-x: 0 pixels</code> (so it appears as it
would normally be tiled).</div>
</p>
<p>
<div class="percentage">This image is positioned using
<code>background-position-x: 50%</code>.</div>
</p>
<p>
<div class="negative-value">This image is positioned using
<code>background-position-x: -100 pixels</code>.</div>
</p>
</body>
</html>
```

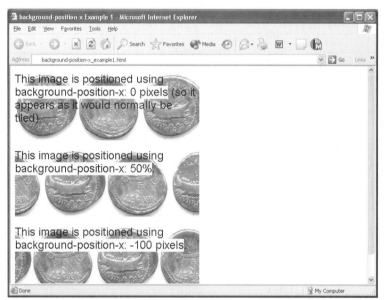

Figure 14–12 The background-position-x property using fixed-length, percentage and negative values, as seen with Internet Explorer 6.0.

As this example shows, it is also possible to set a negative value to `background-position-x` (and `background-position-y`). In this case the negative value tells the browser to start tiling the image beginning 100 pixels "in" to the left side of the image.

Both `background-position-x` and `background-position-y` also have specific named values as well: `background-position-x` can take on `left`, `center` and `right`; `background-position-y` can take `top`, `center` and `bottom`. These values behave slightly different than the percentage and length values — these values do not refer to a coordinate within the image, but how the background image is initially positioned within a Web element containing the background image. So a value of `right` tells the browser to put the "first" background image on the right-hand side, and begin tiling leftward and down from there. A value of "`bottom`" tells the browser to put the initial background image at the bottom of the element to tile up from there. Figure 14–13 shows how the three values for `background-position-x` can be used.

Listing 14.11	*background-position-x Example Using the left, center and right Values*

```
<html>
<head>
<title>background-position-x Example 2 (left, center and right
values)</title>
<style>
div.left {background-image: url(antony_rsc-12.jpg);
background-position-x: left; height: 140 px; width: 400 px; font:
large Arial, Helvetica, sans-serif; color: navy}
div.center {background-image: url(antony_rsc-12.jpg);
background-position-x: center; height: 140 px; width: 400 px;
font: large Arial, Helvetica, sans-serif; color: navy}
div.right {background-image: url(antony_rsc-12.jpg);
background-position-x: right; height: 140 px; width: 400 px; font:
large Arial, Helvetica, sans-serif; color: navy}
code {font: large Arial, Helvetica, sans-serif; color: navy;
background-color: white}
</style>
</head>
<body>
<p>
<div class="left">This image is positioned using
<code>background-position-x: left</code> (the default
setting).</div>
</p>
<p>
<div class="center">This image is positioned using
<code>background-position-x: center</code>.</div>
</p>
<p>
<div class="right">This image is positioned using
<code>background-position-x: right</code>.</div>
</p>
</body>
</html>
```

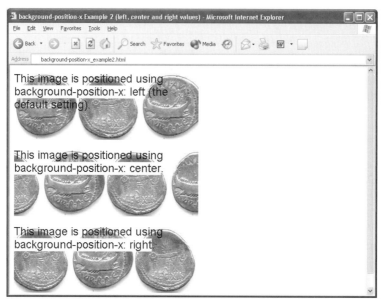

Figure 14–13 The background-position-x property using left, center and right values, as seen with Internet Explorer 6.0.

Core Tip

There's one other little trick you have to know about if you intend to use these properties — ensure that you are using the proper `<!doctype>` *statement. When using* `background-position-x` *or* `background-position-y` *make sure you do not use the standard XHTML* `<!doctype>` *declaration — these properties will only work when the document is set as a transitional or frameset HTML 4.0 document (i.e.,* `<!doctype html public "-//W3C//DTD HTML 4.0 Transitional//EN">` *or* `<!doctype html public "-//W3C//DTD HTML 4.0 Frameset//EN">`*). If* `<!doctype>` *is set to strict HTML 4.0 or XHTML 1.0, the effect of these properties will be "turned off" when viewed under Internet Explorer 6.0, as it has the ability to process the contents of a Web page in accordance with the* `<!doctype>` *setting.*

14.8 CSS3 Properties

The CSS3 specification introduces several new properties that give even greater control to Web authors seeking to control backgrounds contained within elements on a Web page. The CSS3 specification adds an additional five properties to the background family. They are:

- `background-clip`
- `background-origin`
- `background-size`
- `background-quantity`
- `background-spacing`

All of these new properties are there to support existing CSS properties (notably, `background-image`), providing further "fine tuning" over the placement and display of images.

14.9 background-clip Property

This property is designed to control whether a background extends into the border area — meaning the natural "padding" value that most browsers by default will indent the content of a Web page — or not.

This property comes with two values: `border` and `padding`. By default the value is `border`, which means that the browser tiles the image beginning at the top-left position of the Web page (coordinates `0,0` of the element in absolute terms). If the value is set to `padding`, the background is clipped (not repositioned) so that the border area around the page is transparent. The following code snippet shows how it might be used:

```
<style>
table.example1 {background-image: url("caligula.jpg")
background-clip: padding}
table.example2 {background-image: url("caligula.jpg")
background-clip: border}
</style>
```

The primary purpose for this property would seem to be to enable Web authors to retain a transparent border setting even when a background image has been applied. While this would make the element "stand-out," it would be particularly useful when applied to block elements that display a visible border, as the lines demarking the object would be clear, making individual elements contained with the border (such as cells in a table) more distinct. The following mock-up illustration (Figure 14–14) makes this feature of the property clear.

background-clip: padding

background-clip: border

Figure 14–14 Mock-up illustrating the possible effects of the background-clip property.

In the mock-up example illustrated in Figure 14–14, you can clearly see the difference between the border and padding values: with `border` the background image extends into the border area, and with `padding` it is clipped at the border edge.

14.10 background-origin

This property will be used to set the initial status for how the `background-position` property will be calculated. Like `background-clip`, it takes the `border` and `padding` values, plus one additional value: `content`. The default value is `padding`, telling `background-position` that any background image will begin within the padding zone (i.e., the top-left, or coordinates 0,0 of a given element). When `border` is used, the browser is supposed to start tiling an image within the border zone. Finally, the `content` value tells the browser to position the background image so that it starts at the top-left of the content contained within an element, which is typically indented slightly from the outside edges of the "box" it is contained within.

The following code snippet shows how it might be used:

```
<style>

table.example1 {background-image: url("caligula.jpg")
background-clip: padding; background-origin: padding}

table.example2 {background-image: url("caligula.jpg")
background-clip: padding; background-origin: content}

table.example3 {background-image: url("caligula.jpg")
background-clip: padding; background-origin: border}

</style>
```

Figure 14–15 is a mock-up that shows how this sample code might be rendered in a compliant browser.

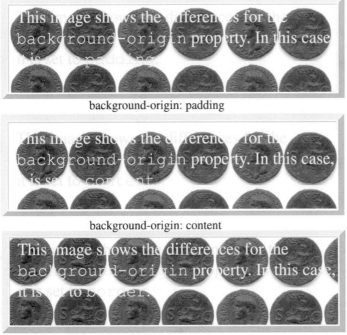

background-origin: padding

background-origin: content

background-origin: border

Figure 14–15 Mock-up illustrating the intended effects of the background-origin property.

The mock-up shows the intended effects clearly: with `padding` the image begins tiling within the area of the border; with `content` the background only begins to tile at the beginning of the text content of the table, and with `border` the background image begins to tile within the border of the table.

14.11 background-size

The background-size property is intended to give the Web author more control over the exact sizing of a background image. This is a much welcomed property as it enables the Web author to precisely size the image under the intended space in which it is to serve as a background.

It can take three types of value. auto, a specific set of numerical values or a percentage value. The auto value is the default, and sets the image to display at its normal size. The property can also take either a single or a pair of specific length values; if a single value is specified it is applied to both the width and height, and if two values are supplied they specify the width and height, respectively. So a value of 50px sets the image to a square 50 pixels on a side, whereas a value of 50px 100px sets the background image to a size of 50 pixels in width by 100 pixels in height. The background-size property can also take a percentage value, which is applied relative to the box containing the image. A setting of 100% stretches the image to fit the height and width of the box it is contained within. A setting of 50% ensures that two background images fill the space, a setting of 25% gives you four background images and so on. The following code snippet shows how this property could be used (its effects illustrated in Figure 14–16):

```
<style>
table.example1 {background-image: url("caligula.jpg")
background-size: auto}
table.example2 {background-image: url("caligula.jpg")
background-size: 100px}
table.example3 {background-image: url("caligula.jpg")
background-size: 50%}
</style>
```

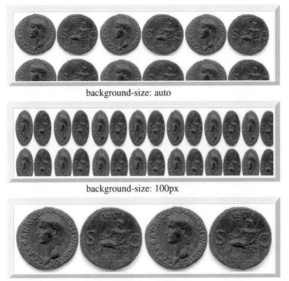

background-size: auto

background-size: 100px

background-size: 50%

Figure 14–16 Mock-up illustrating several effects of the background-size property.

As you can see from Figure 14–16, the `auto` value depicts the original size of the image, a value of `100px` sets the image to a size of 100 pixels square, and then begins to tile it, and finally, a value of `50%` puts two sets of the coin image stretched across the background of the table.

14.12 background-quantity

The `background-quantity` property is designed to be used in conjunction with the `background-image` property to set how many times the background image repeats. It can take one of three values: `infinite`, a specific numeric value and `inherit`. The `infinite` value is the default value, which tiles the background image over the entire area selected. The numeric value tells the browser how many times the image should tile, which can lead to some interesting looking effects. Interestingly enough, there is an `inherit` value, which is particularly useful in this case, as it is easy to think of a case where you'd want to ensure that the background image tiles the same number of time across different Web elements. The following code snippet shows how this property could be used (its effects illustrated in Figure 14–17):

```
<style>
table.example1 {background-image: URL(caligula.jpg);
background-quantity: infinite}
table.example2 {background-image: URL(caligula.jpg);
background-quantity: 3}
table.example3 {background-image: URL(caligula.jpg);
background-quantity: 5}
</style>
```

background-quantity: infinite

background-quantity: 3

background-quantity: 5

Figure 14–17 Mock-up illustrating several values attached to the background-quantity property.

14.13 background-spacing

This new property is designed to work in conjunction with the `background-image` property to set the spacing between individual background images as they are tiled across the background of an element. By default, there is no spacing value between background images, so this property finally gives the Web author some control over this. It can take either one or two numeric values as well as `inherit`. If a single numerical value is specified, it sets the distance between adjacent background images both vertically and horizontally. If two numeric values are used, the first applies to the horizontal dimension, the second to the vertical. The following code snippet shows how this property could be used (its effects illustrated in Figure 14–18):

```
<style>
table.example1 {background-image: url(caligula.jpg)}
table.example2 {background-image: url(caligula.jpg);
background-spacing: 20px}
table.example3 {background-image: url(caligula.jpg); background-
spacing: 20px 30px}
</style>
```

no background-spacing value set

background-spacing: 20px

background-spacing: 20px 30px

Figure 14–18 Mock-up illustrating several spacing values set to the background-spacing property.

CLASSIFICATION PROPERTIES AND GENERATED/AUTOMATIC CONTENT

Topics in This Chapter

- white-space
- list-style-type
- list-style-image
- list-style-position
- list-style
- content property plus the before and after Pseudo-Elements
- quotes
- counter-increment
- counter-reset
- marker-offset

Chapter 15

The classification family of properties is a powerful group of elements that can fundamentally change the way a particular CSS property functions. These properties are designed to classify elements into categories, and not just to set a specific onscreen display.

Unfortunately, several of these properties are still rather poorly supported within the major browsers, and at the time of writing, *none* of them can be considered completely safe to use.

15.1 white-space Property

The white-space property is designed to add extra spaces (i.e., "white space") between words. It does not function in the same way as word-spacing or letter-spacing do by setting a fixed value that is used to separate the individual letters or words. Instead, it more closely resembles the <pre> HTML tag. The white-space property can take one of three different values: normal, nowrap and, tellingly, pre.

One of the tenets of Web formatting is that you are not normally allowed to have more than one horizontal space separating words in a line. In the days prior to the advent of the word processor, most typists added a couple of spaces between the end of one sentence and the beginning of another. The common form these days is to only have a single space between sentences. Accordingly, whenever somebody adds more than one space between the words in a sentence, the Web browser automatically subtracts them so that only a single space remains. Before the `white-space` property, Web authors either had the choice of adding multiple non-breaking spaces ("` `") between words, or using the `<pre>` ("preformatted text") HTML tag. The `normal` value for `white-space` simply tells the browser to format a line of text as it normally would by removing excess spaces that appear between words. `pre` works exactly like the `<pre>` HTML tag, retaining the original spacing and carriage returns between letters and words on a page. The `nowrap` ignores any carriage returns, and sets the text as a single, unbroken line, independent of the width of the browser; using this property, you would have to insert a line break ("`<br />`") to insert a carriage return. You can see all three properties put to use in Listing 15.1, whose results are depicted in Figure 15–1.

Listing 15.1	*white-space Example Code*

```
<html>
<head>
<title>white-space Example</title>
</head>
<body style="font-size: x-large">
<p style="white-space: normal">
While there   are extra white   spaces contained in this sentence
at code    level,   it   will be  displayed    normally.
</p>
<p style="white-space: pre">
The extra white spaces and carriage
returns in this sentence
are displayed. It works in exactly the
same manner as does the &lt;pre&gt; HTML tag.
</p>
<p style="white-space: nowrap">
This line of text <strong>should</strong> be displayed all as a
single
line of unbroken text, and will likely run off the
end of the page, forcing you to scroll in order to
see its end.
</p>
</body>
</html>
```

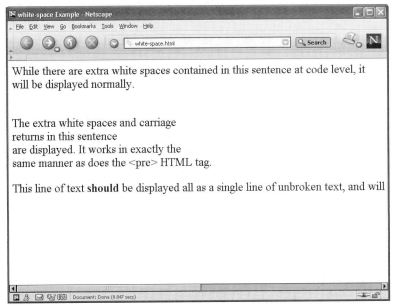

Figure 15–1   white-space example code displayed in Netscape Navigator 7.0.

Browser Compatibility

Unfortunately, `white-space` has relatively poor support in the major browsers; there is support for it within the latest versions of Netscape Navigator, but it is not considered safe for general usage.

- Internet Explorer 3.0: Unsafe.
- Internet Explorer 4.0: Unsafe.
- Internet Explorer 4.0 – 4.5 (Mac): Unsafe.
- Internet Explorer 5.0: Partial.
- Internet Explorer 5.1 – 5.2 (Mac): Partial. Only `normal` and `nowrap` values supported.
- Internet Explorer 5.5: Partial. Ditto above.
- Internet Explorer 6.0: Partial. Ditto above.
- Netscape Navigator 4.0 – 4.79: Partial. Only `pre` and `normal` values supported.
- Netscape Navigator 4.0 (Mac & UNIX): Partial. Ditto above.
- Netscape Navigator 6.0: Safe.
- Netscape Navigator 7.0: Safe.
- Mozilla 1.0: Safe.
- Opera 3.6 – 4.0: Unsafe

- Opera 5.0 – 6.0: Safe.
- Konqueror: Partial. Only `pre` and `normal` values supported.

Internet Explorer has only recently begun to implement this property, although even the most recent version gets only a Partial rating, as it only implements the default `normal` and the `nowrap` values.

Support for this property in Netscape Navigator has fared better. It rates a Partial rating for version 4.x, as it supported the `pre` value, in addition to the default `normal` value. By version 6.0 (and Mozilla 1.0) it had fully supported all three values for this property.

Opera began supporting this property beginning with version 5.0.

Konqueror gets only a Partial rating, since it, like Netscape Navigator 4.x, only supports the `pre` and `normal` values.

15.2 list-style-type Property

The `list-style-type` property is one of a sub-family of list properties, also including `list-style-image`, `list-style-position` and `list-style`, designed to alter the way the list marker at the beginning of a list element appears. Normally, when you create an unordered list ("`<ul>`"), a simple black circle precedes every list element ("`<li>`"). If you create an ordered list ("`<ol>`"), each list element is preceded by a number. Under the initial CSS1 specification for this property the `list-style-type` property provides support for displaying various types of graphical "dots" used as bullets, as well as upper- or lowercase roman numerals. CSS2 went further by providing support for initial lettering under such languages as Hebrew and Armenian, plus their equivalents under several types of Chinese and Japanese character systems. CSS3 proposes to take this to the next logical step, supporting initial lettering schemes for more than 30 additional languages and character sets.

There are three different values for setting the type of "dot" list marker that can appear: `disc`, `circle` and `square`. `disc` produces the default filled-in black "dot" most commonly associated with individual list elements appearing in an unordered list. `circle` displays an unfilled, white-centered circle on screen, and `square` displays a black-filled square. Here's a list showing what you should expect to see for each type:

- list item preceded by a disc
- list item preceded by a circle
- list item preceded by a square.

There are five different values that can be set for the type of alphanumeric list markers that most commonly appear before ordered list elements: `decimal`, lower-alpha, upper-alpha, lower-roman and upper-roman. decimal displays a regular number, which is the default value for all ordered list elements. lower-alpha and upper-alpha display lower- and uppercase letters in alphabetical order for each list element. Similarly, lower-roman and upper-roman display lower- and uppercase roman numerals in numerical order for each list element, as demonstrated in the following list:

- Decimal: 1, 2, 3...
- Lower-Alpha: a, b, c...
- Upper-Alpha: A, B, C...
- Lower-Roman: i, ii, iii...
- Upper-Roman: I, II, III...

In addition to these values, there is none, which displays no list marker before a list element, but still indents each list item as usual. You can see all of these values used in the example code in Listing 15.2, which is displayed in Figure 15–2.

Listing 15.2	Example Code for list-style-type Using CSS1 Values

```
<html>
<head>
<title>list-style-type Example (CSS1 values)</title>
</head>
<body>
<table style="font-size: 28px">
<tr>
<td valign="top">
<ul style="list-style-type: disc">
<li>list items
<li>preceded by
<li>discs (the default value)
</ul>
<ul style="list-style-type: circle">
<li>list items
<li>preceded by
<li>hollow circles
</ul>
<ul style="list-style-type: square">
<li>list items
<li>preceded by
<li>solid squares
</ul>
</td>
```

| Listing 15.2 | *Example Code for list-style-type Using CSS1 Values (continued)* |

```html
<td valign="top">
<ol style="list-style-type: lower-roman">
<li>list items
<li>preceded by
<li>lowercase roman numerals
</ol>
<ol style="list-style-type: upper-roman">
<li>list items
<li>preceded by
<li>uppercase roman numerals
</ol>
<ol style="list-style-type: lower-alpha">
<li>list items
<li>preceded by
<li>lowercase letters
</ol>
</td>
<td valign="top">
<ol style="list-style-type: upper-alpha">
<li>list items
<li>preceded by
<li>uppercase letters
</ol>
<ul style="list-style-type: decimal">
<li>list items
<li>preceded by
<li>numbers
</ul>
<ul style="list-style-type: none">
<li>list items
<li>preceded by
<li>...nothing!
<li>(but still indented like a regular list)
</ul>
</td>
</tr>
</table>
```

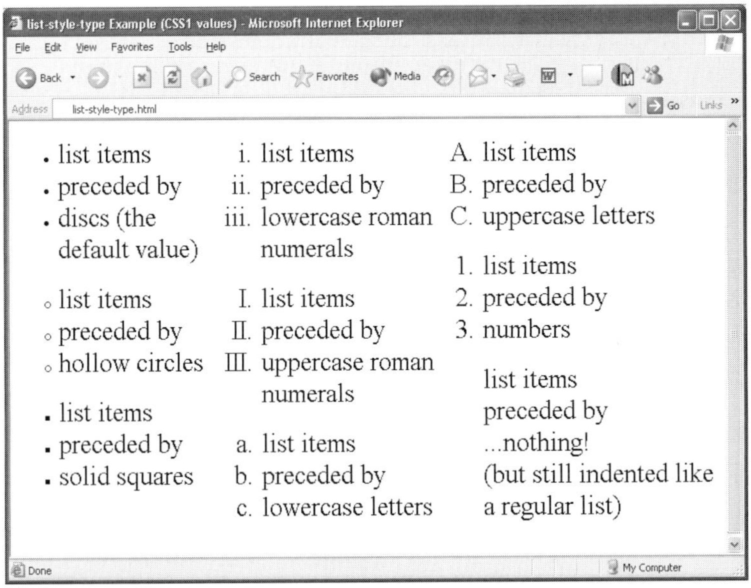

Figure 15–2 All of the CSS1 list-style-type property values displayed within Internet Explorer.

You can actually achieve these same effects within HTML by using the `type` attribute with either the unordered or ordered list tags. For example, the two sets of code seen in Listing 15.3 — alternately using CSS and HTML — are equivalent. You can see the results of this code displayed within the Opera 6.0 browser in Figure 15–3.

Listing 15.3	*Equivalent List Element Formatting Using CSS and HTML*

```
<html>
<head>
<title>CSS and Equivalent HTML Code for List Elements</title>
</head>
<body>
<h1>Lists Elements Formatted Using CSS</h1>
<ul style="list-style-type: square">
<li>List items
<li>preceded by
<li>solid squares
</ul>
<ol style="list-style-type: upper-roman">
<li>List items
```

Listing 15.3	*Equivalent List Element Formatting Using CSS and HTML (continued)*

```html
<li>preceded by
<li>upper case roman numerals
</ol>

<h1>Lists Elements Formatted Using HTML</h1>
<ul type="square">
<li>List items
<li>preceded by
<li>solid squares
</ul>
<ol type="I">
<li>List items
<li>preceded by
<li>upper case roman numerals
</ol>

</body>
</html>
```

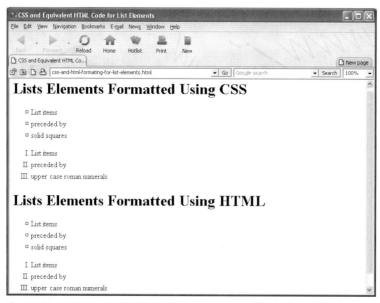

Figure 15–3 Equivalent CSS and HTML code for list elements displayed in Opera 6.0.

For all of the unordered list markers, you would use the same names in CSS as you would in HTML (e.g., disc, circle and square). For the ordered list markers in HTML, however, you use the first "number" to appear in the form you want it to take; so, as in the preceding code example, to begin a list consisting of uppercase roman numerals, you use the first roman numeral ("I"). Similarly, for lowercase roman you'd specify "i", for uppercase alpha you'd use "A", and for lowercase alpha you'd use "a".

list-style-type takes a wider variety of values under CSS2 than CSS1. Other than inherit, list-style-type also takes the following new values: armenian, cjk-ideographic, decimal-leading-zero, georgian, hiragana, hiragana-iroha, hebrew, katakana, katakana-iroha and lower-greek. The decimal-leading-zero value adds a numerical value that always displays at least two digits, with "0" leading the number if it is lower than the value "10". lower-greek adds Greek letters in low-ercase prior to each list item, functioning in much the same way that the CSS1 values lower-alpha and lower-roman do. The rest of the new values all add alphabetical listings in the native letter type of the specified language. Listing 15.4 arranges all of these CSS2 values on a single Web page, whose results can be see in Figure 15–4 in Netscape Navigator 7.0.

Listing 15.4	*Example Code for list-style-type Using CSS2 Values*

```
<html>
<head>
<title>list-style-type Example (CSS2 values)</title>
</head>
<body>
<table style="font-size: 20px">
<tr>
<td valign="top">
<ul style="list-style-type: armenian">
<li>List items
<li>preceded by an
<li>alphabetical listing
<li>of Armenian characters
</ul>
<ul style="list-style-type: cjk-ideographic">
<li>List items
<li>preceded by an
<li>alphabetical listing
<li>of CJK-Ideographic characters
</ul>
<ol style="list-style-type: decimal-leading-zero">
<li>List items
<li>preceded by
```

Listing 15.4	*Example Code for list-style-type Using CSS2 Values (continued)*

```
<li>decimal-leading-zero
<li>values
</ol>
<ul style="list-style-type: georgian">
<li>List items
<li>preceded by an
<li>alphabetical listing
<li>of Georgian characters
</ul>
</td>
<td>
<ul style="list-style-type: hiragana">
<li>List items
<li>preceded by an
<li>alphabetical listing
<li>of Hiragana characters
</ul>
<ul style="list-style-type: hiragana-iroha">
<li>List items
<li>preceded by an
<li>alphabetical listing
<li>of Hiragana-Iroha characters
</ul>
<ul style="list-style-type: hebrew">
<li>List items
<li>preceded by an
<li>alphabetical listing
<li>of Hebrew characters
</ul>
<ul style="list-style-type: inherit">
<li>List items
<li>preceded by an
<li>regular bullets, which are inherited
</ul>
</td>
<td>
<ul style="list-style-type: katakana">
<li>List items
<li>preceded by an
<li>alphabetical listing
<li>of Katakana characters
</ul>
<ul style="list-style-type: katakana-iroha">
<li>List items
<li>preceded by an
<li>alphabetical listing
```

| Listing 15.4 | *Example Code for list-style-type Using CSS2 Values (continued)* |

```
<li>of Katakana-Iroha characters
</ul>
<ul style="list-style-type: lower-greek">
<li>List items
<li>preceded by
<li>lowercase
<li>Greek characters
</ul>
</td>
</tr>
</table>
```

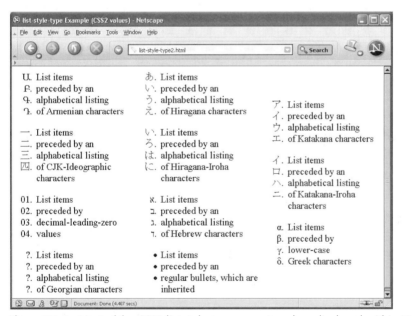

Figure 15–4 Most of the CSS2 list-style-type property values displayed within Netscape Navigator 7.0.

Note the question marks that appear prior to where the Georgian characters should appear — this is a case of the browser not recognizing a specific numbering system, and falling back on something it can support, all according to the specification. The default value is a disc glyph, but if more than one value for `list-style-type` is specified, then the browser will chose something it can render.

The CSS3 list module — which is not confirmed at the time of writing — adds a further 30 plus languages — primarily East Asian and African in origin — to `list-style-type`: `arabic-indic`, `bengali`, `cjk-earthly-branch`, `cjk-heavenly-stem`, `devanagari`, `ethiopic-abegede`, `ethiopic-halehame`, `ethiopic-numeric`, `gujarait`, `gurmukhi`, `hangul`, `hangul-consonant`, `hangule-consonant` (which is an alternate spelling), `japanese-formal`, `japanese-informal`, `kannada`, `khmer`, `lao`, `malayalam`, `myanmar`, `oriya`, `persian`, `simp-chinese-formal`, `simp-chinese-informal`, `tamil`, `telugu`, `thai`, `trad-chinese-formal`, `trad-chinese-informal` and `urdu`. None of these is as yet supported in the major browsers.

Browser Compatibility

The CSS1 values for `list-style-type` are now universally adopted in the major browsers, but the CSS2 values are only spottily supported. The following list only looks at CSS1 support for this property, although the relative acceptance of CSS2 values is detailed.

- Internet Explorer 3.0: Unsafe.
- Internet Explorer 4.0: Safe.
- Internet Explorer 4.0 – 4.5 (Mac): Safe.
- Internet Explorer 5.0: Safe.
- Internet Explorer 5.1 – 5.2 (Mac): Safe.
- Internet Explorer 5.5: Safe.
- Internet Explorer 6.0: Safe.
- Netscape Navigator 4.0 – 4.79: Safe.
- Netscape Navigator 4.0 (Mac & UNIX): Safe.
- Netscape Navigator 6.0: Safe.
- Netscape Navigator 7.0: Safe.
- Mozilla 1.0: Safe.
- Opera 3.6 – 4.0: Safe.
- Opera 5.0 – 6.0: Safe.
- Konqueror: Safe.

Internet Explorer has supported all of the CSS1 values for `list-style-type` since version 4.0. The latest version — version 6.0 — does not support *any* of the CSS2 values.

Netscape Navigator also contained early support for the CSS1 values for this property, incorporating them into version 4.x of its browser. It also fares best when it comes to supporting the CSS2 values. Beginning with version 6.0, it supported the following CSS2 values: `cjk-ideographic`, `decimal-leading-zero`, `hiragana`, `hiragana-iroha`, `hebrew`, `katakana`, `katakana-iroha` and `lower-greek`. It did not support the `armenian` or `georgian` values. As you can see from Figure 15–4, Netscape Navigator 7.0 (and Mozilla 1.0) now support all but the `georgian` value.

Opera has supported all of the CSS1 values for `list-style-type` beginning with version 3.6. Oddly enough, Opera 6.0 supports the one CSS2 value Netscape Navigator 7.0 doesn't: `georgian`. None of the other CSS2 values are supported in version 6.0.

Konqueror fully supports all of the CSS1 values, and as yet supports none of the CSS2 values.

15.3 list-style-image Property

Along with the `list-style-type`, `list-style-position` and `list-style`, `list-style-image` is designed to alter the way the list marker at the beginning of a list element appears. The idea behind `list-style-image` is that sometimes you may want something other than a standard, plain old list marker to appear in front of each element in a list. If you want to put a colorful 3D button, a picture of the Mona Lisa or any other image in front of a list item, `list-style-type` is the property for you.

`list-style-type` has two possible values: `none` and a URL that links to the desired image. `none` is the default value, and, not surprisingly, it doesn't add a picture before a list element (it appears as a regular list item). By adding a URL value that links to an image, that image can become the "list marker" at the beginning of the list. The URL must be specified in the CSS manner (see the URL section in Chapter 6, "CSS Units" for more detailed information on specifying URLs in CSS).

Listing 15.5 is some sample code that adds a different image immediately before each list item. It's results can be seen in Figure 15–5.

Listing 15.5	*list-style-image Example Code*

```
<html>
<head>
<title>list-style-image Example</title>
</head>
<body style="font-size: x-large; padding-left: 100px">
<ul>
<li style="list-style-image: url(hadrian.jpg)">Emperor Hadrian,
117-158 AD
<li style="list-style-image: url(gordian3.jpg)">Emperor Gordian
III, 238-244 AD
<li style="list-style-image: url(aurelian.jpg)">Emperor Aurelian,
270-275 AD
</ul>
</body>
</html>
```

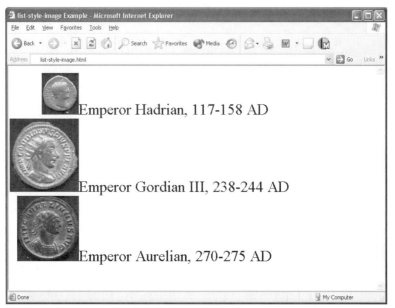

Figure 15–5   Sample list-style-image code displayed within Internet Explorer 6.0.

This code example is extreme, for as you can see in Figure 15–5 the images are too large to be practical, but it gets the idea across. Notice the `padding-left: 100px` value that has been added to the `<body>` element in Listing 15.5 — it was necessary in this case because by default only a small value for the indentation of the image is allowed for, normally about 10 pixels or so — and this behavior is consistent across the major browsers. So try not to go to extremes with the size of your images when using this property, as it is really only meant for small, icon-size images.

Also note that this extreme example demonstrates that the images are displayed at their regular size. This is important to know if you intend to mix images using the `list-style-image` property, as such CSS sizing properties as `height` and `width` do *not* work in conjunction with the URL value.

Browser Compatibility

This property is well supported in the latest versions of the major browsers, although Konqueror and early versions of Netscape Navigator have problems with it.

- Internet Explorer 3.0: Unsafe.
- Internet Explorer 4.0: Safe.
- Internet Explorer 4.0 – 4.5 (Mac): Safe.
- Internet Explorer 5.0: Safe.

- Internet Explorer 5.1 – 5.2 (Mac): Safe.
- Internet Explorer 5.5: Safe.
- Internet Explorer 6.0: Safe.
- Netscape Navigator 4.0 – 4.79: Unsafe.
- Netscape Navigator 4.0 (Mac & UNIX): Unsafe.
- Netscape Navigator 6.0: Safe.
- Netscape Navigator 7.0: Safe.
- Mozilla 1.0: Safe.
- Opera 3.6 – 4.0: Safe
- Opera 5.0 – 6.0: Safe.
- Konqueror: Partial.

Internet Explorer has implemented `list-style-image` properly since version 4.0.

Netscape Navigator 4.x did not support this property. It defaults to displaying circle bullets when confronted with the code seen in Listing 15.5. This property became fully supported by version 6.0.

Opera was an early adopter of this property and supported it fully beginning with version 3.6.

Konqueror gets only a Partial rating, since it automatically assumes small values for the bullet images, which in the extreme example seen in Listing 15.5 cause a real jumble of overlapping images and consequently unreadable text. When the images are small, it behaves as it should, but Web authors should be aware of the situation when the images are larger than the browser expects.

15.4 list-style-position Property

The `list-style-position` property, like all of the other sub-family of list style properties, is designed to alter the way the list marker at the beginning of a list element appears. This property does not cover where a list or the list element markers appear onscreen as its name might lead you to believe. Instead, it positions the multiple lines of text after the list marker.

The `list-style-position` property has two values: `inside` and `outside`. The effects of both of these values can only be seen when there are multiple lines of text appearing after a list element. `outside` is the default value, and it essentially sets a margin value flush with the beginning of the first word that appears in the first line after the list marker. All subsequent lines of text that appear after it are flush against that value. `inside` removes this margin, and subsequent lines of text appear *under* the list marker. In addition, the `inside` value moves the margin of the list item in slightly. The effects are slightly different when used with the unordered list ("`<ul>`") tag than with the ordered list ("`<ol>`") tag. When the `inside` value is applied to the unordered list tag, the next line of text appears directly underneath the list element marker. When applied to the ordered list tag, it appears under the period following the number — it does not appear flush underneath the number.

You can see both values used with the unordered and ordered list tags in Listing 15.6, whose results are displayed in Netscape Navigator 7.0 in Figure 15–6.

Listing 15.6   *list-style-position Example Code*

```
<html>
<head>
<title>list-style-position Example</title>
</head>
<body style="font-size: 25px">
<ul style="list-style-position: outside">
<li>The lines of text appearing after this bullet will appear as
they normally do, with all subsequent lines indented the same
amount as the first line.
</ul>
<ul style="list-style-position: inside">
<li>Notice how the text in the second line of this bullet item
begins underneath the bullet rather than directly under the first
word, and how the bullet is indented.
</ul>
<ol style="list-style-position: outside">
<li>The text for this bullet item will be displayed normally, the
second line of text beginning in a position directly underneath
the first word.
</ol>
<ol style="list-style-position: inside">
<li>Notice how the text in the second line of this bullet item
begins underneath the period that appears after the number rather
than directly under the first word, and how the bulleted number is
indented.
</ol>
</body>
</html>
```

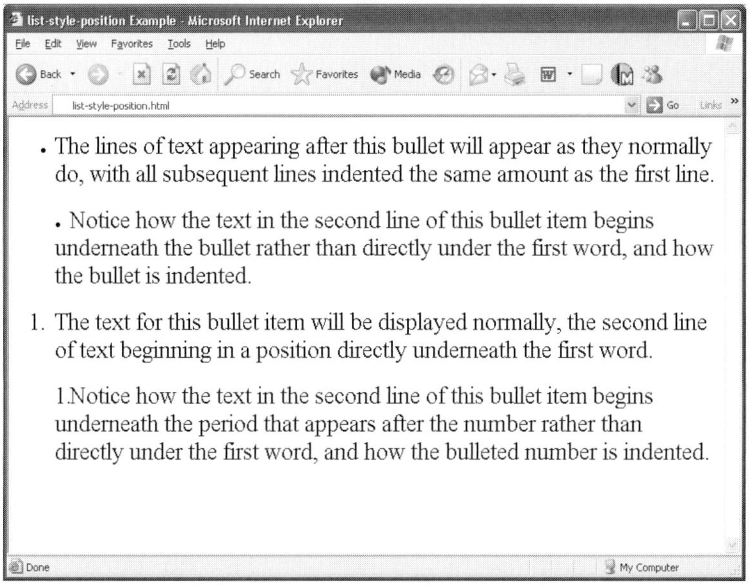

Figure 15–6 Sample list-style-position code displayed within Netscape Navigator 7.0.

This particular CSS property is really a typographic nicety — it is an effect sometimes used in desktop publishing, primarily to save margin space. On the whole, though, the consensus is that the alternate `inside` display value is not as "clean" as the default `outside` value. Just because a property exists doesn't mean you have to use it — but it is a nice option if you are tight on space.

Browser Compatibility

This property is well supported in the latest versions of the major browsers, but early versions of Netscape Navigator had problems with it.

- Internet Explorer 3.0: Unsafe.
- Internet Explorer 4.0: Safe.
- Internet Explorer 4.0 – 4.5 (Mac): Safe.
- Internet Explorer 5.0: Safe.
- Internet Explorer 5.1 – 5.2 (Mac): Safe.
- Internet Explorer 5.5: Safe.
- Internet Explorer 6.0: Safe.
- Netscape Navigator 4.0 – 4.79: Unsafe.
- Netscape Navigator 4.0 (Mac & UNIX): Unsafe.
- Netscape Navigator 6.0: Safe.

- Netscape Navigator 7.0: Safe.
- Mozilla 1.0: Safe.
- Opera 3.6 – 4.0: Safe
- Opera 5.0 – 6.0: Safe.
- Konqueror: Safe.

Internet Explorer has implemented `list-style-position` properly since version 4.0.

Netscape Navigator 4.x did not support this property. This version of the browser simply ignored the `inside` value for `list-style-position` and positioned all such instances as if they were the default `outside` value. This property became fully support by version 6.0 of Netscape Navigator.

Opera was an early adopter of this property, and supported it fully beginning with version 3.6.

Konqueror fully supports this property.

15.5 list-style Property

The `list-style` property is a "shortcut" property that incorporates all of the features contained within its sibling properties `list-style-type`, `list-style-position` and `list-style-image`. It is a convenient way to either set list display values that belong to its sibling properties, or to mix and match some of them.

`list-style` can take the six CSS1 values that belong to the `list-style-type` property: `decimal`, `lower-alpha`, `upper-alpha`, `lower-roman`, `upper-roman` and `none`. `decimal` displays a regular number, which is the default value for all ordered list elements. `lower-alpha` and `upper-alpha` display lower- and uppercase letters in alphabetical order for each list element. Similarly, `lower-roman` and `upper-roman` display lower- and uppercase roman numerals in numerical order for each list element. The value `none` (shared with `list-style-image`) is the default value, and it doesn't do anything (in other words, the list appears the same as a regular, non-CSS altered list). Under CSS2 and a proposed CSS3 module, `list-style` now also accepts the myriad of other values now associated with `list-style-type`.

`list-style` can take on the URL value that belongs to `list-style-image`. By adding a URL value that links to an image, that image can become the "list marker" at the beginning of the list. The URL must be specified in the CSS manner (see the URL section in Chapter 6, "CSS Units" for more detailed information on specifying URLs in CSS).

`list-style` can also take the two values that belong to `list-style-position`: `inside` and `outside`. `outside` is the default value, and it essentially sets a margin value flush with the beginning of the first word that appears in the first line after the list marker. All subsequent lines of text that appear after it are flush against that value. `inside` removes this margin, and subsequent lines of text appear under the list marker.

You can see a mix of all of these values displayed in Listing 15.7 (whose results are displayed in Figure 15–7).

Listing 15.7 *list-style Example Code*

```html
<html>
<head>
<title>list-style Example</title>
</head>
<body style="font-size: x-large">
<ul style="list-style: circle outside">
<li>List items
<li>preceded by
<li>hollow circles
</ul>
<ol style="list-style: lower-roman inside">
<li>List items
<li>preceded by
<li>lower-case roman numerals. To see the effect of the
<code>inside</code> value, we'll need to add some more text.
</ol>
<ul style="list-style: url(pulsing_bullet.gif) lower-roman
inside">
<li>List items
<li>preceded by
<li>a pulsing animated bullet image. To see the effect of
the <code>inside</code> value, we'll need to add some more text.
Notice how the value <code>lower roman</code> is ignored and not
displayed.
</ul>
</body>
</html>
```

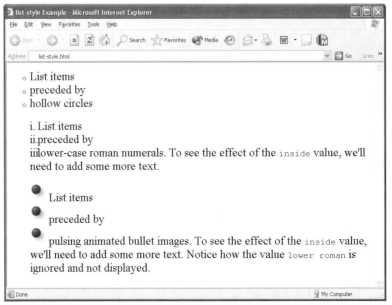

Figure 15–7 Sample `list-style` code displayed within Internet Explorer.

You will have noticed from Figure 15–7 that not all of the values can exist with each other. It is impossible to mix the values belonging to the `list-style-type` property when an image has already been set for the list marker using the URL value associated with the `list-style-image` property. Specifically, notice how, in the third group of list items, the value "`url(pulsing_bullet.gif)`" overrules the "`lower-roman`" value. Neither of these sets of values conflict with the values associated with the `list-style: inside` or `outside`. You can see from the first two groups of lists where the `inside` and `outside` values are mixed with `circle` and `lower-roman`.

Browser Compatibility

Since `list-style` is a shortcut property, its level of support in the major browsers depends on how its related properties are supported.

- Internet Explorer 3.0: Unsafe.
- Internet Explorer 4.0: Safe.
- Internet Explorer 4.0 – 4.5 (Mac): Safe.
- Internet Explorer 5.0: Safe.
- Internet Explorer 5.1 – 5.2 (Mac): Safe.
- Internet Explorer 5.5: Safe.

- Internet Explorer 6.0: Safe.
- Netscape Navigator 4.0 – 4.79: Unsafe.
- Netscape Navigator 4.0 (Mac & UNIX): Unsafe.
- Netscape Navigator 6.0: Safe.
- Netscape Navigator 7.0: Safe.
- Mozilla 1.0: Safe.
- Opera 3.6 – 4.0: Safe
- Opera 5.0 – 6.0: Safe.
- Konqueror: Partial.

Internet Explorer has implemented `list-style` since version 4.0. Note version 6.0 does not support any of the CSS2 values associated with `list-style-type`.

Netscape Navigator 4.x has problems with the `list-style-image` and `list-style-type` values. These properties became fully supported by version 6.0 of Netscape Navigator. Versions 6.0 and 7.0 implement a significant amount of the CSS2 values for `list-style-type`, and they are similarly supported under `list-style` (for more detailed information, see the Browser Compatibility section for `list-style-type`).

Opera was an early adopter of this property, and supported it fully beginning with version 3.6. Opera 6.0 supports a single CSS2 value for `list-style-type: georgian`. None of the other CSS2 values for `list-style-type` are supported in version 6.0.

Konqueror has problems with the `list-style-image` values, especially when the images are larger than the browser expects. See the Browser Compatibility section for `list-style-image` for more information.

15.6 The content Property plus the before and after Pseudo-Elements

There is little point in talking about the `content` property without also talking about the `before` and `after` pseudo-elements, since their functions are so inextricably intertwined. The `content` property is used to set the type of content (i.e., an HTML tag) with which the `before` and `after` pseudo-elements are associated. The `content` property is *always* used in conjunction with the `before` and `after` pseudo-classes. This collection of CSS2 functions enables Web authors to set such things as audio cues to be spoken immediately before or after certain elements, or to add formatting to specific onscreen elements.

These functions are also used extensively by all of the other properties contained within the generated content, automatic numbering and lists family.

The before pseudo-element inserts a string and/or otherwise modifies the display at the beginning of the selected Web element, and the after pseudo-element inserts a string and/or otherwise modifies the display at the end of the selected Web element. The before and after pseudo-classes are meant to be used in a global context. content, before and after are designed for use in the header of a Web page, or in a separate Web page containing CSS information meant to be applied to more than one Web page.

The content property is capable of taking a wide range of values in addition to its common usage with the before and after pseudo-classes. It can take a string value (i.e., text) that is set by the Web author to be used as an identifier. It can also take a URL value to point to Web content, such as an image or sound file. It can also take on the values counter-increment and counter-reset, which set a counter value for the associated element (much like an ordered list).

content can return a text string value by using the value attr along with the name of the string. It is also capable of being used with a number of quotation-mark-related properties — open-quote, close-quote, no-open-quote and no-close-quote — which insert the correct type of quotation mark, depending on context. Since counter values and the quotation-mark values are closely tied to other properties in this family, they will be examined in detail later in this section. content can also take on the ubiquitous CSS2 value inherit, so that it will take on whatever parent value has already been set for content.

Listing 15.8, whose results are displayed in the Netscape Navigator 7.0 in Figure 15–8, depicts a basic example of the before and after pseudo-classes at work, along with examples of content taking a URL and a string value.

Listing 15.8	content Example Code

```
<html>
<head>
<title>Content Example</title>
<style>
img:before {content: url("This_Is_An_Image.wav")}
body:after {content: "That's All Folks!"; display: block;
margin-top: 1cm; text-align: right; color: navy; font-size:
xx-large;}
</style>
</head>
<body style="font-size: x-large">
The image on this Web page is preceded by an audio
introduction, announcing it to be an image, primarily for
the benefit of those using audio browsers.
```

| Listing 15.8 | content Example Code (continued) |

```
<P>
<img src="fokker.jpg">
</body>
</html>
```

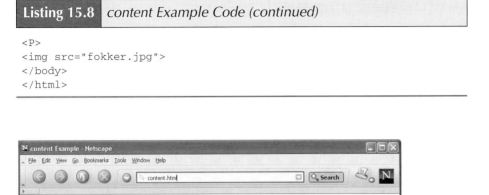

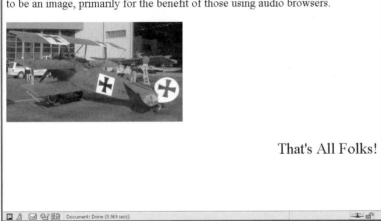

Figure 15–8   Content example code displayed in Netscape Navigator 7.0.

 While the initial example can't be properly "displayed" within a book, the sound file ("this_is_an_image.wav") would be played immediately prior to the image when the text on the Web browser is read aloud. In this way, an audio cue can be presented before a specific element to notify those who may be "viewing" the page using only an audio browser about the type of content appearing on the screen. The after pseudo-element is associated with the <body> element, so at the conclusion of the Web page, the phrase "That's all folks!" appears. In this latter case, you can see that the content tag is very flexible, and that it is possible to set a number of different display attributes for the text string.

Browser Compatibility

Since the `content` property plus the `before` and `after` pseudo-elements were first introduced under CSS2, the earliest browsers do not support them.

- Internet Explorer 3.0: Unsafe.
- Internet Explorer 4.0: Unsafe.
- Internet Explorer 4.0 – 4.5 (Mac): Unsafe.
- Internet Explorer 5.0: Unsafe.
- Internet Explorer 5.1 – 5.2 (Mac): Unsafe.
- Internet Explorer 5.5: Unsafe.
- Internet Explorer 6.0: Unsafe.
- Netscape Navigator 4.0 – 4.79: Unsafe.
- Netscape Navigator 4.0 (Mac & UNIX): Unsafe.
- Netscape Navigator 6.0: Safe.
- Netscape Navigator 7.0: Safe.
- Mozilla 1.0: Safe.
- Opera 3.6 – 4.0: Unsafe
- Opera 5.0 – 6.0: Safe.
- Konqueror: Unsafe.

Internet Explorer does not as yet support the `content` property or the `before` and `after` pseudo-elements.

Netscape Navigator 4.x didn't support this property or its associated pseudo-elements. They were supported beginning with Netscape Navigator 6.0 (and Mozilla 1.0).

Opera began supporting this property and its associated pseudo-elements beginning with version 5.0.

Konqueror does not support the `content` property or its associated pseudo-elements.

15.7 quotes Property

The `quotes` property is always used in conjunction with the `content` property and its associated pseudo-classes `before` and `after`. Using this property, it is possible to set different types of quotation marks to appear — primarily to set the appropriate quotation symbol for a given language.

The sole purpose of the `quotes` property is to set the type of quotation marks to be displayed in relation to generated content. `quotes` can take three different values: a text string, the named value `none` (which tells the browser not to display any quotation marks) and `inherit`, which takes on any parent value for `quotes`.

The most interesting value here is the string value, which is set to the type of quotation marks you wish to display. Two sets of strings must be specified: the open and close quotation marks for two different levels, with the second set denoting the quotation marks to be displayed when a quote is nested within a quote. The following code snippet shows how you can do this for a typical set of English quotation marks:

```
q:lang(en) {quotes: '"' '"' "'" "'"}
```

A property such as this is crucial when you are generating quotation marks using automatically generated content, as you need to be able to tell the browser what to display when one quote is contained within another. It also provides Web authors with the possibility of setting alternate quotation marks, such as those used in other languages. For example, the following code snippet shows how you could set this up for French quotation marks:

```
q:lang(fr) {quotes: '«' '»' "<" ">"}
```

You can see how this can be applied to generated content in the code sample Listing 15.9, whose results can be seen in Opera 6.0 in Figure 15–9.

Listing 15.9 *quotes Example*

```
<html lang="en">
<head>
<title>quotes Example</title>
<style>
blockquote:before {content: open-quote; color: yellow; font-size:
30pt)}
blockquote:after {content: close-quote; color: red; fontsize:
30pt)}
q:lang(en) {quotes: '"' '"' "'" "'"}
q:before {content: open-quote; color: navy; font-size: 30pt)}
q:after {content: close-quote; color: fuchsia; font-size: 30pt)}
</style>
</head>
<body style="font-size: 30pt">
<p>
<blockquote>
The text in this blockquote will be preceded by an extra-large
yellow open-quote mark, and will finish with an extra-large red
close-quote mark.
</blockquote>
```

Listing 15.9	*quotes Example (continued)*

```
<p>
In the lecture the professor said <q>Shakespeare was the one who
said the immortal words <q>to thine own self be true</q></q>
</body>
</html>
```

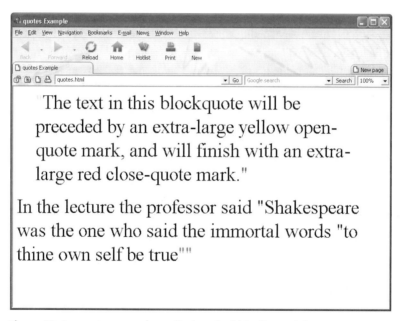

Figure 15–9   quotes example as displayed within Opera 6.0.

As you can see in Figure 15–9, the code is displayed properly within Opera. While the browser is capable of making the distinction between the types of quotation marks to be displayed around the `<blockquote>` and `<q>` tags, it does not do a proper job of setting the type of nested quotation marks to be displayed within the `<q>` section. At the time of writing, none of the major browsers gets this quite right, but the generated content feature does at least work.

The code in Listing 15.9 shows how the `open-quote` and `close-quote` value can be used with the `content` tag. Two other quotation-mark values are available for `content`: `no-open-quote` and `no-close-quote`. These two values are to be used when you want quoted text to be nested within a quote, but do not want to have the quote marks displayed.

Browser Compatibility

Since the `quotes` property was first introduced under CSS2, the earliest browsers do not support this property.

- Internet Explorer 3.0: Unsafe.
- Internet Explorer 4.0: Unsafe.
- Internet Explorer 4.0 – 4.5 (Mac): Unsafe.
- Internet Explorer 5.0: Unsafe.
- Internet Explorer 5.1 – 5.2 (Mac): Unsafe.
- Internet Explorer 5.5: Unsafe.
- Internet Explorer 6.0: Unsafe.
- Netscape Navigator 4.0 – 4.79: Unsafe.
- Netscape Navigator 4.0 (Mac & UNIX): Unsafe.
- Netscape Navigator 6.0: Partial.
- Netscape Navigator 7.0: Partial.
- Mozilla 1.0: Safe.
- Opera 3.6 – 4.0: Unsafe
- Opera 5.0 – 6.0: Partial.
- Konqueror: Unsafe.

Internet Explorer does not as yet support the `quotes` property.

Netscape Navigator 4.x did not support the `quotes` property. It was supported beginning with Netscape Navigator 6.0 (and Mozilla 1.0), although it only gets a Partial rating as it is unable to deal properly with nested quotes.

Opera began supporting the `quotes` property beginning with version 5.0, but gets a Partial rating as it also doesn't know how to deal with nested quotes properly.

Konqueror does not support the `quotes` property.

15.8 counter-increment and counter-reset Properties

The `counter-increment` and `counter-reset` properties are both used to increase the range of automatic numbering options available within browsers. Using these properties, you can now automatically set such things as chapter headings with sub-sections. The `counter-increment` property is used to establish which Web tag begins a sequence and when a value of "1" should be added to subsequent instances of that tag within the page. The `counter-reset` property determines which element should reset the counting for properties on the Web page (i.e., turn the increment value back to "0").

Both the `counter-increment` and `counter-reset` properties take the same values: a text string that sets the identifier for the element to be incremented, as well as the value by which it should be incremented, plus the named values `none` (which tells the browser not to increment) and `inherit` (which takes on any parent value for these properties). The string set for the `counter-increment` and `counter-reset` properties works similarly for both properties. The text string works as an "identifier" to be associated with the property. These values are then defined. The following code snippet should make things clear:

```
h1:before {content: "floor " counter(floor) " ";
counter-increment: floor; counter-reset: room;}
```

Again, the `content` property plays a crucial role in how this works. It takes a text value and a special algorithm defined by two text values. In this case, whenever an `<h1>` appears on the page, the word "`Floor `" (note the extra space) should appear, followed by the number as set by the formula "`counter(floor)`". An extra space (" ") separates this in turn from whatever text is contained in this header. This is how the `attr(x)` value for `counter` works. You can actually use the named value `attr` with a string value representing the arbitrary value "X". The value for counter is set by `counter-increment`, and it should be reset whenever it meets the value set by the word "`room`", as defined by `counter-reset`.

In Listing 15.10, the result should be an incremented list of the floors of a building along with the sections contained on each floor; the code example is depicted within Opera 6.0 in Figure 15–10.

Listing 15.10	*counter-increment and counter-reset Example Code*

```
<html>
<head>
<title>counter-increment and counter-reset Example</title>
<style>
h1:before {content: "floor " counter(floor) " "; counter-incre-
ment: floor; counter-reset: room; font-size: large}
h2:before {content: counter(floor) "-" counter(room) " ";
counter-increment: room; font-size: large; font-weight: bold}
</style>
</head>
<body>
<h1>Basement</h1>
<h2>Storage space</h2>
<h1>Main Floor</h1>
<h2>Reception</h2>
<h2>Restaurant</h2>
<h2>Frank's Fish &amp; Steak House</h2>
```

Listing 15.10	*counter-increment and counter-reset Example Code (continued)*

```
<h1>Second Floor</h1>
<h2>Croecko Incorporated</h2>
</body>
</html>
```

Figure 15–10 counter-increment and counter-reset example code as displayed within Opera 6.0.

As you can see, as we go up a floor, each of the floor numbers is incremented, but the areas on each floor are reset after every floor.

Browser Compatibility

The `counter-increment` and `counter-reset` properties are not supported within the major browsers. At the time of writing, they are only supported within the latest version of Opera.

- Internet Explorer 3.0: Unsafe.
- Internet Explorer 4.0: Unsafe.

- Internet Explorer 4.0 – 4.5 (Mac): Unsafe.
- Internet Explorer 5.0: Unsafe.
- Internet Explorer 5.1 – 5.2 (Mac): Unsafe.
- Internet Explorer 5.5: Unsafe.
- Internet Explorer 6.0: Unsafe.
- Netscape Navigator 4.0 – 4.79: Unsafe.
- Netscape Navigator 4.0 (Mac & UNIX): Unsafe.
- Netscape Navigator 6.0: Partial.
- Netscape Navigator 7.0: Partial.
- Mozilla 1.0: Safe.
- Opera 3.6 – 4.0: Unsafe
- Opera 5.0 – 6.0: Partial.
- Konqueror: Unsafe.

Internet Explorer does not as yet support the `counter-increment` and `counter-reset` properties.

No version of Netscape Navigator as yet supports the `counter-increment` and `counter-reset` properties either.

Opera began supporting the `counter-increment` and `counter-reset` properties beginning with version 5.0, and at the moment is the only browser that supports them.

Konqueror does not support the `counter-increment` and `counter-reset` properties.

15.9 marker-offset Property

The `marker-offset` property is designed to create some extra "space" at the beginning of a list item. Some generated content may go outside of the normal bounds of the markers for most list items, so the `marker-offset` property gives Web authors the leeway of adding extra room to accommodate the expanded marker. However, this property has never been supported by any browser, and has since been deprecated in CSS3. As such, it is a bit of a "white elephant."

`marker-offset` takes three different values: a numerical length value, the named value `auto` (which uses the browser's default value for spacing markers from the content of the list item), and `inherit` (which assigns the parent value for `marker-offset`). The sample code from the property listing provides a good example of `marker-offset` at work. It is set to a value of `5em`, which means that it is offset by a space equal to 5 em in the font that is being used. This should provide ample room in which generated content can appear due to the associated `content` property.

Listing 15.11	*marker-offset Example Code*

```
<html>
<head>
<title>marker-offset Example</title>
<style>
p {margin-left: 10em} /* Make space for counters */
li:before {display: marker; marker-offset: 5em; content:
counter(mycounter, upper-alpha) "."; counter-increment:
mycounter;}
</style>
</head>
<body>
<p>
<ol>
<li> Here is the first item.
<li> Here is the second item.
<li> Here is the third item.
</ol>
<p>
</body>
</html>
```

As noted, the `margin-offset` property has been made obsolete in the proposed CSS3 lists module, and has been deprecated in favor of the new `margin-end` property.

Browser Compatibility

This particular property has never received strong support within the major browsers, and now that it has been rendered obsolete in the proposed CSS3 lists module, it is unlikely to gain further support.

- Internet Explorer 3.0: Unsafe.
- Internet Explorer 4.0: Unsafe.
- Internet Explorer 4.0 – 4.5 (Mac): Unsafe.
- Internet Explorer 5.0: Unsafe.
- Internet Explorer 5.1 – 5.2 (Mac): Unsafe.
- Internet Explorer 5.5: Unsafe.
- Internet Explorer 6.0: Unsafe.
- Netscape Navigator 4.0 – 4.79: Unsafe.

- Netscape Navigator 4.0 (Mac & UNIX): Unsafe.
- Netscape Navigator 6.0: Unsafe.
- Netscape Navigator 7.0: Unsafe.
- Mozilla 1.0: Unsafe.
- Opera 3.6 – 4.0: Unsafe
- Opera 5.0 – 6.0: Safe.
- Konqueror: Unsafe.

Internet Explorer does not support `marker-offset`.
Netscape Navigator does not support `marker-offset`.
Neither Opera nor Konqueror supports `marker-offset` either.

VISUAL FORMATTING AND DETAILED VISUAL FORMATTING

Topics in This Chapter

- `display`
- Positioning Properties: `position, top, left, right` and `bottom`
- `z-index`
- `direction` and `unicode-bidi`
- `min-width, max-width, min-height` and `max-height`

Chapter  16

CSS2 introduced a new family of properties known as the visual formatting set of properties. This set of largely new or greatly expanded properties provides Web authors with much greater control over the display of elements on screen. The properties in this family include those that enable Web authors to exercise precise positioning of onscreen elements (also known as CSS positioning), to control the "level" in which a stack of 3D objects can appear on screen, and also to manage the direction in which text for other languages is displayed onscreen.

16.1 display Property

Under CSS1, the `display` property falls under the set of classification properties. Under CSS2, it now falls under the set of visual formatting properties, but it retains its original purpose of being able to fundamentally alter or set the nature of a Web tag with which it is associated. Under CSS2, its role is expanded, and it has a number of new values.

Under CSS1, the `display` property had the following four values: `block`, `inline`, `list-item` and `none`. CSS2 added another fifteen: `compact`, `run-in`, `marker`, `table`, `table-caption`, `table-cell`, `table-column`, `table-column-group`, `table-footer-group`, `table-header-group`, `table-row`, `table-row-group`, `inline-table`, `inline-block` and `inherit`. The current draft of the CSS3 version of this property adds five more: `ruby`, `ruby-base`, `ruby-text`, `ruby-base-group` and `ruby-text-group`.

The compact and run-in values are designed to set either a block or an inline box, depending on the context of the selected Web element. A block-level element set to compact will, in effect, "compress" the size of the box under certain circumstances in an effort to conserve space. This is particularly handy with such things as lists, where you may not want the description of a list item to take up an extra line of space if it can "fit" in the same line as that of any content that might precede it. Similarly, run-in will enable a block element to behave like an inline element, so that space can be saved. If the element so chosen doesn't take the full width of the browser display, it is rendered as an inline element. Listing 16.1 shows how these two values are meant to work.

| Listing 16.1 | *display Example #1* |

```
<html>
<head>
<title>display Example #1</title>
<style>
dt {display: compact}
dd {margin-left: 2.5cm}
body {font-size: 26px; font-weight: bold}
h1 {display: run-in}
</style>
</head>
<body>
<h1>Some Parts of a Car:</h1>
<p>(a short list of parts and descriptions that go into making
a car.)</p>
<dl>
<dt>Tires:
<dd><p>made of rubber and are in contact with the ground.</p>
<dt>Windshield:
<dd><p>made of glass and keeps bugs and debris from hitting
the driver.</p>
<dt>Seats:
<dd><p>driver and passenger(s) sit in these.</p>
</dl>
</body>
</html>
```

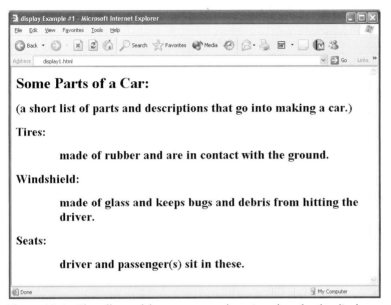

Figure 16–1 The effects of the compact and run-in values for the display property as seen within Opera 6.0.

As you can see from Listing 16.1, the header at the top of the page is set to run-in, so the text in the following paragraph is not displayed on the next line down as it usually would be, but is instead displayed immediately after the header, saving space on the page. The compact value has been added to the `<dt>` ("Definition Term") tag, and the `<dd>` ("Definition Description") tag has the value margin-left: 2.5cm attached to it. This means that if the definition term text is shorter than 2.5 centimeters in size, the definition description should follow immediately after the definition term, instead of on the next line down from it. You can see how the description follows the definition on the same line with the relatively short words "Tires:" and "Seats:" and how they are compacted; "Windshield:" is too long, however, and cannot be compacted.

The desired effect of the marker value is in specifying how a generated marker should appear on screen, and setting the characteristics that distinguish it from the other content with which it is associated. The marker value is meant to be used only with the before and after pseudo-classes, and is designed to declare the selected content to be a marker in automatically generated content. marker content is formatted only on a single line, and is only created if the content property associated with the before or after pseudo-classes actually generates content. Marker boxes can have padding and even borders, but cannot take margin values. Listing 16.2 provides an idea as to how it should work.

Listing 16.2 *display Example #2*

```
<html>
<head>
<title>display Example #2</title>
<style>
li:before {display: marker; content: "[" counter(counter) "]";
counter-increment: counter; width: 2cm; text-align:
left}
body {font-size: xx-large;}
</style>
</head>
<body>
<ol>
<li style="list-style-type: none">Here is an item</li>
<li style="list-style-type: none">Here is another item</li>
<li style="list-style-type: none">Here is a third item</li>
<li style="list-style-type: none">Here is the final, fourth
item.</li>
</ol>
</body>
</html>
```

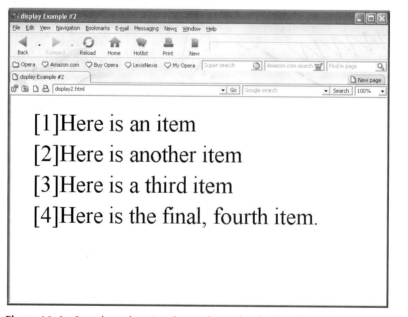

Figure 16–2 Sample code using the marker value for the display property, as seen within Opera 6.0.

Notice in the code listing how `list-style-type: none` has been added to each list item. This is done to suppress the normal numbers that would occur in an ordered list — if not present, you would get two sets of numbers displayed in order, with only the second number contained within square brackets.

As you can see from this example, the parameters determine how the generated `marker` content should appear onscreen. Each of the list items is preceded by a number contained within square brackets, and each of these "markers" is left-aligned (most list markers are indented slightly); the text that follows them is spaced 2 centimeters from the marker.

Under CSS2, `display` also carries a number of HTML table-tag related values: `table`, `table-caption`, `table-cell`, `table-column`, `table-column-group`, `table-footer-group`, `table-header-group`, `table-row`, `table-row-group` and `inline-table`. In each case, these values set the associated Web element to appear as an equivalent to the HTML table-tag value. Some of these values may be unfamiliar to you, as they correspond to rarely used but valid table tag values (such as `<col>`, `<colgroup>`, `<tfoot>` and `<thead>`, for example) under the official HTML 4.0 specification. There are one-to-one relationships between each of the HTML 4.0 table-tags and their `display` property equivalents, as can be seen in Table 16.1.

Table 16.1 *HTML 4.0 Table Tags and Their CSS2 display Property Equivalents*

HTML	*display Equivalent*
`<caption>`	`{display: table-caption}`
`<col>`	`{display: table-column}`
`<colgroup>`	`{display: table-column-group}`
`<table>`	`{display: table}`
`<tbody>`	`{display: table-row-group}`
`<td>`	`{display: table-cell}`
`<tfoot>`	`{display: table-footer-group}`
`<th>`	`{display: table-cell}`
`<thead>`	`{display: table-header-group}`
`<tr>`	`{display: table-row}`

These values are not meant to supercede the existing HTML tags, but rather to be used by other document languages (such as the eXtended Markup Language, better known as "XML") that do not have predefined table elements. This CSS2 scheme essentially allows XML applications (or similar languages) to incorporate tables by using what is effectively a "port" of CSS to whatever document language is being used. They can be used to create "table-less" tables, as can be seen in Listing 16.3, whose results are depicted within Figure 16–3.

Listing 16.3	*display Example #3*

```
<html>
<head>
<title>display Example #3</title>
<style>
body {font-size: 50px}
.column {display: table-column; border: thin solid red}
</style>
</head>
<body>
<div style="display: table; border: dotted thick black">
<div style="display: table-caption; color: navy">A Table-less
Table</div>
<div style="display: table-row">
<span style="display: table-cell; width: 125px; text-align: cen-
ter">A</span>
<span style="display: table-cell; width: 125px; text-align: cen-
ter" class="column">B</span>
<span style="display: table-cell; width: 125px; text-align: cen-
ter">C</span>
</div>
<div style="display: table-row">
<span style="display: table-cell; width: 125px; text-align: cen-
ter">1</span>
<span style="display: table-cell; width: 125px; text-align: cen-
ter" class="column">2</span>
<span style="display: table-cell; width: 125px; text-align: cen-
ter">3</span>
</div>
</div>
</body>
</html>
```

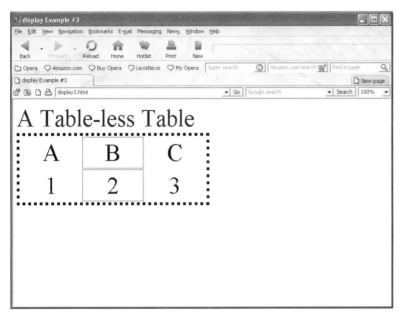

Figure 16–3 Example code showing the effects of the table group of values, as seen within Opera 6.0.

There is only one problem with the way this code is interpreted as seen in Figure 16–3: the "B" and "2" are part of a column group to which a thin red border has been added, but that border should only appear on the circumference of the group, so they should not appear as separate cells, as they do here.

In addition to these table values is the `inline-block` value, which makes a selected element behave as if it were a block element contained within a line. Unlike all of the other values for `display`, there is no direct HTML equivalent tag for expressing this type of situation. Finally, there is the `inherit` named value for `display`, which simply takes on whatever parent value has already been set for display.

The currently proposed CSS3 version of this property includes five additional properties, most of them belonging to the relatively recent ruby text formatting model. Just like the table values for `display`, the ruby values correspond to the equivalent display properties for ruby formatting, as you can see from Table 16.2.

Table 16.2 *HTML Ruby Tags and Their CSS2 display Property Equivalents*

HTML	*display Equivalent*
`<ruby>`	`{display: ruby}`
`<rb>`	`{display: ruby-base}`
`<rt>`	`{display: ruby-text}`
`<rbc>`	`{display: ruby-base-group}`
`<rtc>`	`{display: ruby-text-group}`

The `<rbc>` and `<rtc>` tags (which stand for "ruby base container" and "ruby text container," respectively) are recent additions to the ruby specification and have not been adopted within any major browser as yet. For more information on Ruby formatting, see Chapter 22, "Ruby."

Browser Compatibility

Browser compatibility for the `display` property is poor. At the moment, there isn't a single browser that gets all of it right. This property should be used with caution.

- Internet Explorer 3.0: Unsafe.
- Internet Explorer 4.0: Partial.
- Internet Explorer 4.0 – 4.5 (Mac): Partial.
- Internet Explorer 5.0: Partial.
- Internet Explorer 5.1 – 5.2 (Mac): Partial.
- Internet Explorer 5.5: Partial.
- Internet Explorer 6.0: Partial.
- Netscape Navigator 4.0 – 4.79: Partial.
- Netscape Navigator 4.0 (Mac & UNIX): Partial.
- Netscape Navigator 6.0: Partial.
- Netscape Navigator 7.0: Partial.
- Mozilla 1.0: Partial.
- Opera 3.6 – 4.0: Partial.
- Opera 5.0 – 6.0: Partial.
- Konqueror: Partial.

The initial 3.0 version of Internet Explorer did not support `display` at all. While Internet Explorer implemented the `none` value beginning with version 4.x, it was only beginning with version 5.x that real support for this value started coming through, with support for the `inline` and `block` values as well as the `table-header-group` and `table-footer-group` values. Version 6.x started supporting the `list-item` value. It also attempts to interpret some of the other table values for property, but does so oddly: for example, it displays the code from Listing 16.3 with a border appearing outside all of the content, ignoring the `table-caption` value and placing the border around it as well.

Netscape only fares marginally better than Internet Explorer when it comes to supporting the `display` property. Netscape Navigator 4.x supports the `none`, `block`, and `list-item` values. Beginning with Mozilla 1.x and Netscape Navigator 6.x, the `inherit`, `inline`, `table-header-group`, `table-footer-group`, `table`, `table-caption`, `table-cell`, `table-row` and `table-row-group` values were supported. It does not yet support the `marker`, `compact` or `run-in` values, and support for `table-column` and `table-column-group` is incomplete — for example, it displays the same problem handling the table-column value as does Opera 6.0 in the example seen in Figure 16–3.

Not surprisingly, given its track record of adopting CSS, Opera provides the best coverage for this property. Version 3.6 supported the `none`, `inline` and `block` values. Version 4.0 supported the `list-item`, `marker`, `compact`, `run-in` and all of the table values save for the `table-column` and `table-column-group` values, which don't fully jibe with the expected behavior for these values; elements in a columnar format are not properly formatted (see Figure 16–3).

Konqueror does not support the `run-in` and `inline-block` values for this property. Otherwise, its support is good.

16.2 Positioning Properties: position, top, left, right and bottom

One of the long standing concerns in Web-page design is the positioning of elements on a Web page. How many times have you wanted to add some image or text to a *specific* point on a Web page and found that this seemingly simple task tried your patience? Over time, people have attempted such tricks as transparent images, indented unordered list tags and maddeningly intricate sets of tables in order to get something exactly where they wanted it to be.

The set of positioning properties — consisting of `position`, `top`, `left`, `right` and `bottom` — were among the earliest of the post-CSS1 properties to be suggested, and in terms of browser compatibility, among the first group of CSS2 properties to be adopted within the major browsers. Collectively, these properties are part of a new sub-set of properties known as CSS positioning properties, often called "CSS-P" for short. Using them, you can state exactly where you want a Web element to appear on-screen.

The position property has five values: absolute, relative, static, fixed and inherit. position is meant to be associated with at least one (and usually more) of its other associated positioning properties left, right, bottom and top, which take a unit of measurement value, a percentage value, the named value auto (which uses the default value normally used) or the ubiquitous inherit (which uses the parent value, if any, already set for any of these properties). Given the specific nature of the positioning element with reference to a computer screen, the default measurement value used is pixels.

The absolute value for position is the easiest to understand and is typically the most used. When you use the absolute value, your element is positioned "absolutely" with reference to the top-left corner of the browser window. In other words, the top-left of your browser window represents the coordinates 0, 0, and you position your element with reference to that value. If you wanted to position an image to appear 25 pixels over and 100 down, you could write the following code:

```
<img src="my-image.jpg" style="position: absolute;
left: 250; top: 100">
```

This means that the top-left corner of the image "my-image.gif" is positioned 250 pixels to the right and 100 pixels down from the top of the browser window. Absolutely positioned elements are removed from the normal flow of elements onscreen, however, so any "normal" onscreen elements will flow underneath the absolutely positioned element. A good example of this can be seen in Listing 16.4, whose results can be seen within Internet Explorer 6.0 in Figure 16–4.

Listing 16.4	*position Example #1*

```
<html>
<head>
<title>position Example #1</title>
</head>
<body style="font-size: xx-large">
<img src="fokker.jpg" style="position: absolute; left: 250; top:
100">
The quick brown fox jumped over the lazy dogs.
The quick brown fox jumped over the lazy dogs.
The quick brown fox jumped over the lazy dogs.
The quick brown fox jumped over the lazy dogs.
The quick brown fox jumped over the lazy dogs.
The quick brown fox jumped over the lazy dogs.
The quick brown fox jumped over the lazy dogs.
</body>
</html>
```

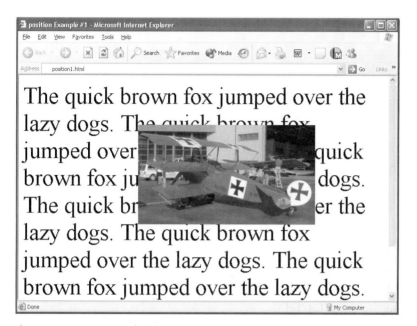

Figure 16–4 An example of position: absolute as seen within Internet Explorer 6.0.

As you can see, in Figure 16–4 the flow of the text on the page continues as if the image of the old warplane were not there.

With the `relative` value, you can specify where you want an onscreen element to go *in relation to* other onscreen elements. Whereas an element positioned with `absolute` is set apart from other elements on a page, `relative` is set with respect to these other elements. Elements that are positioned using `relative` have their own box, and can influence subsequent elements. The following code shows `relative` being used to offset a picture of a Sopwith Camel airplane from that of the Fokker (which, in this case, does not use any special positioning values):

Listing 16.5   *position Example #2*

```
<html>
<head>
<title>position Example #2</title>
</head>
<body style="font-size: x-large; font-family: sans-serif">
<img src="fokker.jpg">
<img src="sopwith.jpg" style="position: relative; top: 45;
left: 100">
```

Listing 16.5	*position Example #2 (continued)*

```
<p>
The image of the Sopwith Camel is positioned in relation to that of
the Fokker, and it does not otherwise interfere with the flow of
this text onscreen. (Note that the Sopwith image overlaps the text
slightly).
</body>
</html>
```

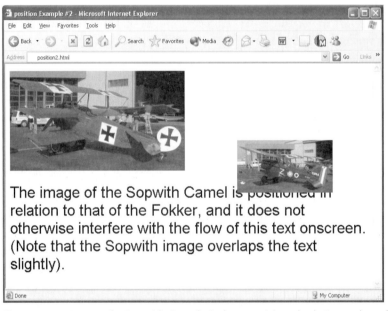

Figure 16–5   Image of a Sopwith Camel airplane positioned relative to that of the Fokker airplane, as seen within Internet Explorer 6.0.

As you can see from this example, the image of the Sopwith Camel airplane is positioned 100 pixels to the left of and 45 pixels down from the image of Fokker airplane. Relative positioning is always relative to the previous element that has been set. If there were two images of the Fokker airplane set one after the other, the Sopwith Camel would be positioned relative to the second one. This does not just apply to images; this applies equally to text or other elements that may appear previous to the relatively positioned object. Note that the 45 pixels down value is with respect to the image of the Fokker as a whole, rather than from the top of the Fokker image; otherwise the Sopwith Camel image would have overlapped that of the Fokker. Also note that the Sopwith image does not interfere with the normal flow of text on the page, and in facts overlaps some of it.

The static value is the default value for the position property, and it essentially sets things to return to the normal flow on a page. Occasions for wanting to use this particular value would be rare. As an example, the following two lines of code would be displayed in an identical manner:

```
<em style="position: static">Back to the normal flow!</em>
<em>Back to the normal flow!</em>
```

The fixed value behaves in much the same way as the absolute value, but while the item will scroll with the page with the absolute value, it will not with the fixed value. In Figure 16–6 — whose code in Listing 16.6 is similar to that used to demonstrate the absolute value in Listing 16.4 — you can see how the text "behind" the fixed image scrolls, but the image itself does not.

Listing 16.6	*Position Example #3*

```
<html>
<head>
<title>position Example #3</title>
</head>
<body style="font-size: xx-large">
<img src="fokker.jpg" style="position: fixed; left: 250; top:
100">
The quick brown fox jumped over the lazy dogs.
The quick brown fox jumped over the lazy dogs.
The quick brown fox jumped over the lazy dogs.
The quick brown fox jumped over the lazy dogs.
The quick brown fox jumped over the lazy dogs.
The quick brown fox jumped over the lazy dogs.
The quick brown fox jumped over the lazy dogs.
The quick brown fox jumped over the lazy dogs.
The quick brown fox jumped over the lazy dogs.
The quick brown fox jumped over the lazy dogs.
The quick brown fox jumped over the lazy dogs.
The quick brown fox jumped over the lazy dogs.
The quick brown fox jumped over the lazy dogs.
The quick brown fox jumped over the lazy dogs.
The quick brown fox jumped over the lazy dogs.
</body>
</html>
```

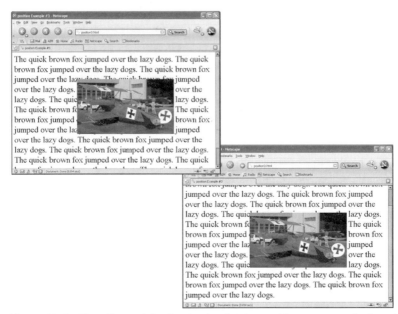

Figure 16–6 The effects of the fixed value for the position property displayed within Netscape Navigator 7.0 as it is scrolled.

One note of caution when using the `fixed` value — it is really designed for use on dynamic displays, and not for other media, such as print. With the introduction of media types under CSS2 (see Chapter 8, "Media Types and Media Queries"), Web authors must be concerned with such things, so it is advisable to set things so that the `fixed` value is only utilized in the "right" media. The following code snippet gives you an idea of how you can differentiate between different media while using the `fixed` value effectively:

```
<style>
@media screen {h1#initial {position: fixed}}
@media print {h1#initial {position: static}}
</style>
```

Finally, the `inherit` value simply takes on whatever parent value may have already been set for `position`.

These examples might imply that you always have to position items to the left and down from any previous element on the Web page. You can certainly use the `right` and `bottom` properties. You can also use negative values for these, as well as for `left` and `top`. Using negative values means that you can position elements off the screen if you like. When you combine this feature with some JavaScript, it becomes possible to add dynamic CSS-based displays and to make text or images appear or disappear at will.

Browser Compatibility

The `position` property is only fully implemented in the more recent versions of Opera and Netscape Navigator. Its sibling properties `top`, `left`, `right` and `bottom` have been relatively better supported in the major browsers, with `top` and `left` receiving the most consistent report.

position

- Internet Explorer 3.0: Unsafe.
- Internet Explorer 4.0: Partial.
- Internet Explorer 4.0 – 4.5 (Mac): Partial.
- Internet Explorer 5.0: Partial.
- Internet Explorer 5.1 – 5.2 (Mac): Partial.
- Internet Explorer 5.5: Partial.
- Internet Explorer 6.0: Partial.
- Netscape Navigator 4.0 – 4.79: Partial.
- Netscape Navigator 4.0 (Mac & UNIX): Partial.
- Netscape Navigator 6.0: Safe.
- Netscape Navigator 7.0: Safe.
- Mozilla 1.0: Safe.
- Opera 3.6: Unsafe
- Opera 4.0: Partial
- Opera 5.0 – 6.0: Safe.
- Konqueror: Safe.

The initial 3.0 version of Internet Explorer did not support `position`. Beginning with version 4.x Internet Explorer supported the `absolute`, `relative` and `static` values. This have changed little since then, and version 6.x of the browser still lacks support for the `fixed` and `inherit` values.

Netscape Navigator 4.x only supported the `absolute`, `relative` and `static` values for `position`. Version 6.0 (and Mozilla 1.x) supported all of the remaining values fully.

The initial version of Opera did not support the `position` property, but it was fully implemented by version 5.x.

Konqueror fully supports the `position` property.

top and left

- Internet Explorer 3.0: Unsafe.
- Internet Explorer 4.0: Partial.
- Internet Explorer 4.0 – 4.5 (Mac): Partial.
- Internet Explorer 5.0: Partial.
- Internet Explorer 5.1 – 5.2 (Mac): Partial.
- Internet Explorer 5.5: Partial.
- Internet Explorer 6.0: Partial.
- Netscape Navigator 4.0 – 4.79: Partial.
- Netscape Navigator 4.0 (Mac & UNIX): Partial.
- Netscape Navigator 6.0: Safe.
- Netscape Navigator 7.0: Safe.
- Mozilla 1.0: Safe.
- Opera 3.6 – 4.0.: Unsafe
- Opera 5.0 – 6.0: Safe.
- Konqueror: Safe.

The initial 3.0 version of Internet Explorer did not support `top` or `left`. Real support for these properties began with version 4.x, when it fully supported the length and percentage values for the property, as well as the default `auto` value. Version 6.x still does not support the `inherit` value.

Netscape Navigator 4.x only supported the length and percentage values for `top` and `left`. With the advent of Mozilla 1.x/Netscape 6.x the remaining `auto` and `inherit` values had been adopted.

Opera 3.6 did not support `top` or `left`, but version 4.x supported the length, percentage and `auto` values. Version 5.x got things completely right when it adopted the `inherit` value.

Konqueror fully supports `top` and `left`.

bottom and right

- Internet Explorer 3.0: Unsafe.
- Internet Explorer 4.0: Unsafe.
- Internet Explorer 4.0 – 4.5 (Mac): Unsafe.
- Internet Explorer 5.0: Unsafe.
- Internet Explorer 5.1 – 5.2 (Mac): Partial.
- Internet Explorer 5.5: Partial.
- Internet Explorer 6.0: Partial.
- Netscape Navigator 4.0 – 4.79: Unsafe.
- Netscape Navigator 4.0 (Mac & UNIX): Unsafe.
- Netscape Navigator 6.0: Safe.
- Netscape Navigator 7.0: Safe.

- Mozilla 1.0: Safe.

- Opera 3.6 – 4.0: Partial.

- Opera 5.0 – 6.0: Safe.

- Konqueror: Safe.

The `bottom` and `right` properties were not supported in Internet Explorer in Windows until version 5.5 (and version 5.x in the Macintosh version). Much improved, though still not perfect, support for these properties began with version 6.x, when Internet Explorer fully supported the length and percentage values for the property, as well as the default `auto` value. Version 6.x still does not support the `inherit` value.

Netscape Navigator only began supporting the values for `bottom` and `right` beginning with Mozilla 1.x/Netscape 6.x.

Opera 3.6 did not support `bottom` or `right`, but version 4.x supported the length, percentage and `auto` values. Version 5.x got things completely right when it adopted the `inherit` value.

Konqueror fully supports `bottom` and `right`.

16.3 z-index Property

On a Web page, Web elements exist in only two dimensions: the X- (horizontal) and Y- (vertical) axes. On a regular Web page, elements are either above or below, or to the right or left of, another element. With the advent of the `position` property, a third dimension is added, so that things can appear either "in front of" or "behind" other elements. This third axis is known as the Z-axis, and elements can be controlled in this fashion by using the `z-index` property.

`z-index` can take one of three values: an integer value that corresponds to the "stacking" level of the specified element's box; `auto`, which makes the stack value the same as its parent's; and `inherit`, which in this case ought to work the same way as `auto`. `z-index` is always used in conjunction with the `position` property.

The integer value is the value that is most often used. It sets the "stacking" level, which determines where elements fall within the stack. Lower numbers are at the "bottom" of the stack; those with higher numbers appear "above" those below them. Any element that is not assigned a stack level falls below the lowest stacked item, and either does not appear (if the object on top is large enough) or flows underneath it. A good example of how this works can be seen in Listing 16.7, as seen within Internet Explorer 6.0 in Figure 16–7.

Listing 16.7 *z-index Example*

```
<html>
<head>
<title>z-index Example</title>
<style>
body {font-family: sans-serif; font-size: 16px; font-weight: bold}
</style>
</head>

<body>
<div style="position: absolute; left: 75px; top: 155px; z-index:
4; background-color: white">
This text should sit on top of all of the images.
</div>
<div style="position: absolute; left: 30px; top: 100px; z-index:
1">
<img src="fokker.jpg" width="369" height="201" border="0"
alt="z-index: 1">
</div>
<div style="position: absolute; top: 200px; right: 250px; z-index:
2">
<img src="fokker.jpg" width="369" height="201" border="0"
alt="z-index: 2">
</div>
<div style="position: absolute; left: 200px; top: 110px; position:
absolute; z-index: 3">
<img src="fokker.jpg" width="369" height="201" border="0"
alt="z-index: 3">
</div>
</body>
</html>
```

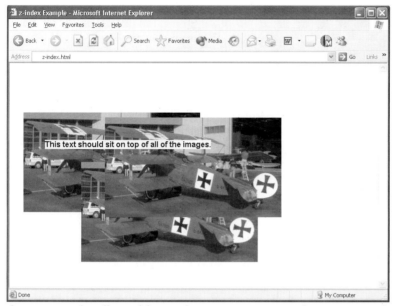

Figure 16–7   The effects of the z-index property as seen within Internet Explorer 6.0.

The pictures of the airplane you can see in Figure 16–7 from left-to-right have a stacking order of "1", "2" and "3" respectively, so the final picture sits on top of the other two. The text is set to "z-index: 4", and so sits on top of all of the images.

Browser Compatibility

Support for this property varies. At the moment it can only be called Safe in the latest versions of the major browsers except Internet Explorer.

- Internet Explorer 3.0: Unsafe.
- Internet Explorer 4.0: Partial.
- Internet Explorer 4.0 – 4.5 (Mac): Partial.
- Internet Explorer 5.0: Partial.
- Internet Explorer 5.1 – 5.2 (Mac): Partial.
- Internet Explorer 5.5: Partial.
- Internet Explorer 6.0: Partial.
- Netscape Navigator 4.0 – 4.79: Unsafe.
- Netscape Navigator 4.0 (Mac & UNIX): Unsafe.
- Netscape Navigator 6.0: Safe.
- Netscape Navigator 7.0: Safe.
- Mozilla 1.0: Safe.

- Opera 3.6 – Unsafe.
- Opera 4.0 – Partial.
- Opera 5.0 – 6.0: Safe.
- Konqueror: Safe.

Beginning with version 4.x, Internet Explorer adopted the numeric and `auto` values for `z-index`. As of version 6.x it has still not implemented the `inherit` value.

Netscape Navigator 4.x supported the numeric and `auto` values for `z-index`, and with the advent of Mozilla 1.x/Netscape 6.x fully supported the property, including the `inherit` value.

Opera 3.6 did not support `z-index`, but version 4.x supported the numeric and `auto` values for it. By version 5.x the `inherit` value had been adopted.

Konqueror fully supports the `z-index` property.

16.4 direction and unicode-bidi Properties

There are many languages that read from right-to-left, such as Arabic and Hebrew, instead of the left-to-right typical of European languages. When characters from both types of writing systems are present in a single document, it is known as bidirectional text: some text is to be read in one direction, and some in the other. The `direction` and `unicode-bidi` properties are designed to help Web authors render this type of display onscreen.

The direction property has three values: `ltr` ("left-to-right"), `rtl` ("right-to-left") and `inherit`. In essence, this property is used to flip around the way the text should be displayed. This does not mean that if you took the English proper name "Keith Schengili-Roberts" and used the `rtl` value on it, it would come out as "streboR-ilignehcS htieK". Instead, it tells the browser which way the text is supposed to flow on the page, and whether it should begin from the left side of the browser window or from the right — the ordering of the individual letters or other characters is not affected. The `direction` property was designed for use with the `unicode-bidi` property, helping to set the direction for the text display of other languages.

Every browser has an implicit understanding of how text from various languages should appear on screen. This is handled by the Unicode specification. The `unicode-bidi` property enables Web authors to explicitly set the direction in which text and associated content should appear in Web pages that use languages meant to be read in different directions. Whereas `direction` can be used within a Web document, `unicode-bidi` essentially has the same purpose, but applies instead to the whole of a Web document (or Web documents).

The `unicode-bidi` property has four named properties: `normal`, `embed`, `bidi-override` and `inherit`. The `normal` value does not alter the default bidirectional setting for the display of text. The `embed` value is meant for use with inline Web elements, in which it sets up an additional level of embedding with respect to the bidirectional algorithm. If the `bidi-override` value is used, this value overrides the value already in place, keeping with the values set by the `direction` property. It is meant for use in inline and block-level elements. Finally, the `inherit` value takes the same value for `unicode-bidi` as that set for the property of the parent element. Of these values, `embed` is the one most likely to see use, as it is the most versatile. Listing 16.8 provides an example of how the `unicode-bidi` and `direction` properties can be used:

Listing 16.8   *unicode-bidi and direction Example*

```
<html>
<head>
<title>unicode-bidi and direction Example</title>
<style>
.arabic {direction: rtl; unicode-bidi: embed}
.english {direction: ltr; unicode-bidi: embed}
.hebrew {direction: rtl; unicode-bidi: embed}
body {font-size: xx-large; font-family: sans-serif}
</style>
</head>
<body>
<div class="english">english 1</div>
<div class="arabic">arabic 1</div>
<div class="hebrew">hebrew 1</div>
<div class="english">english 1 english 2, english 3.</div>
<div class="arabic">arabic 1, arabic 2, arabic 3.</div>
<div class="hebrew">hebrew 1, hebrew 2, hebrew 3.</div>
</body>
</html>
```

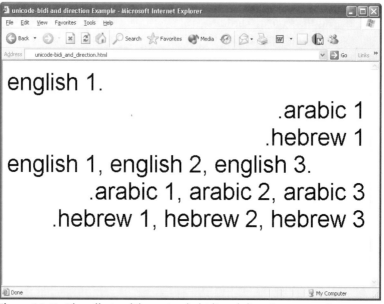

Figure 16–8   The effects of the unicode-bidi and direction properties as seen within Internet Explorer 6.0.

As you can see from Figure 16–8, the order of the characters comprising individual words has not changed, but both the "Arabic" and "Hebrew" text begin from the right side of the browser window and end — note the placement of the periods — to the left.

Browser Compatibility

- Internet Explorer 3.0: Unsafe.
- Internet Explorer 4.0: Unsafe.
- Internet Explorer 4.0 – 4.5 (Mac): Unsafe.
- Internet Explorer 5.0: Safe.
- Internet Explorer 5.1 – 5.2 (Mac): Safe.
- Internet Explorer 5.5: Safe.
- Internet Explorer 6.0: Safe.
- Netscape Navigator 4.0 – 4.79: Unsafe.
- Netscape Navigator 4.0 (Mac & UNIX): Unsafe.
- Netscape Navigator 6.0: Safe.
- Netscape Navigator 7.0: Safe.
- Mozilla 1.0: Safe.
- Opera 3.6 – 4.0: Unsafe.

- Opera 5.0 – 6.0: Unsafe.
- Konqueror: Safe.

As these are CSS2 properties, support for `direction` and `unicode-bidi` did not begin until version 5.x for Internet Explorer, which implements them fully.

Netscape Navigator began implementing these properties fully starting with version 6.x (and Mozilla 1.0).

Oddly enough, the Opera browser at the time of writing still does not support these two properties.

Konqueror fully supports both `direction` and `unicode-bidi`.

16.5 min-width, max-width, min-height and max-height Properties

The `min-height` and `max-height` properties work in much the same way as the `min-width` and `max-width` properties, by setting the height (vertical) value or the width (horizontal) value for a block element. It is important to note that while you can set the height or width of the box within which an element is contained, the elements contained within the box are not stretched or condensed to fit.

The `min-width` and `max-width` properties are designed to enable Web authors to set the smallest and largest possible width values for box elements. You now have control over the minimum and maximum width for any given box element, and can better set how a particular Web element should appear on screen.

Both `min-width` and `max-width` take the same values: either a numeric unit of measurement value, a percentage value relative to the width of the containing block, `none` (which does not set a specific width value for the box), and `inherit` (which takes its value from that of the parent).

The `min-width` property is handy when you want to ensure that a Web element runs to at least a given minimum on the Web page; if, for example, you set the contents of a header to a size of 2 centimeters, no matter how much text is contained in the header, it will be at least 2 centimeters in width. Of course, it can be bigger than 2 centimeters. It is important to note that while you can set the minimum width of the box within which an element is contained, the elements contained within the box are not made to "fit" this space.

`max-width` is more likely to see common usage than `min-width`, as it constrains the box element to a certain maximum width on the Web page. Listing 16.9, whose effects are illustrated in Figure 16–9, shows two examples of `max-width` at work:

Listing 16.9   *min-width and max-width Example*

```
<html>
<head>
<title>min-width and max-width Example</title>
<style>
body {font-size: 16px; font-family: sans-serif; font-weight: bold}
</style>
</head>
<body>
<h1 style="min-width: 2cm">This header must be no smaller than 2cm
in width; that's easy enough...</h1>
<h1 style="max-width: 5cm">This header must be no wider than
5cm</h1>
<h1 style="max-width: 75%">This header has a maximum width of 75%
the browser window's width</h1>
</body>
</html>
```

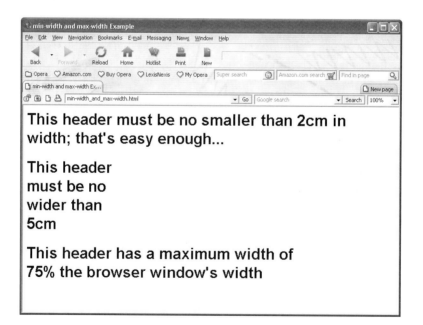

Figure 16–9   The effects of min-width and max-width properties as seen within Opera 6.0.

Both `min-height` and `max-height` take the same values: a numeric unit of measurement value, a percentage value relative to the width of the containing block, plus the two named values `none` (the default, which only applies to `max-height` — the default value for `min-height` is "0") and `inherit` (which takes its value from that of the parent).

The `min-height` property is handy when you want to ensure that a Web element runs to at least a given height on the Web page. If, for example, you set the contents of a header to a size of 5 centimeters in height, the box containing the header will be at least that size on the Web page. You might think that `max-height` would constrain the box element to a certain maximum height on the Web page, but in effect it simply ensures that the containing box is no bigger than that — if content overflows it, it does not clip it. Listing 16.10 and Figure 16–10 show these two properties at work.

Listing 16.10	*min-height and max-height Example*

```
<html>
<head>
<title>min-height and max-height Example</title>
</head>
<body>
<h1 style="min-height: 5cm">This header must be at least 5cm in
height</h1>
<h1 style="max-height: 1cm">This header must be no bigger than
1cm</h1>
</body>
</html>
```

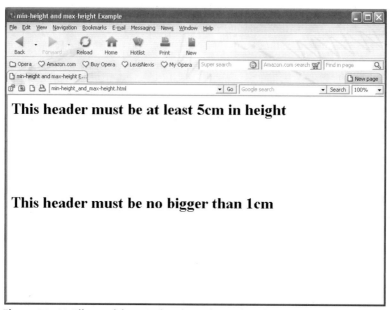

Figure 16–10 Effects of the min-height and max-height properties displayed within the Opera 6.0 browser.

Notice how in the Figure 16–10 the top header is contained within a "box" that is 5 centimeters in height. The text in the box is not "stretched to fit"; it is instead rendered normally, but the next Web element appears 5 centimeters underneath the box containing the top header. Note how the second header is set to only 1 centimeter in height, and as the header is no larger than this, the browser displays it properly. This does not mean that overflowing content would necessarily be clipped, however, as this property does not restrict content in that way.

Browser Compatibility

min-width and max-width

Being CSS2 properties automatically excludes the earliest browsers from implementing min-width and max-width. Support is restricted to Netscape/Mozilla among the major browsers.

- Internet Explorer 3.0: Unsafe.
- Internet Explorer 4.0: Unsafe.
- Internet Explorer 4.0 – 4.5 (Mac): Unsafe.
- Internet Explorer 5.0: Unsafe.

- Internet Explorer 5.1 – 5.2 (Mac): Unsafe.
- Internet Explorer 5.5: Unsafe.
- Internet Explorer 6.0: Unsafe.
- Netscape Navigator 4.0 – 4.79: Unsafe.
- Netscape Navigator 4.0 (Mac & UNIX): Unsafe.
- Netscape Navigator 6.0: Safe.
- Netscape Navigator 7.0: Safe.
- Mozilla 1.0: Safe.
- Opera 3.6 – 4.0: Unsafe.
- Opera 5.0 – 6.0: Unsafe.
- Konqueror: Unsafe.

min-height

Being a CSS2 property automatically excludes the earliest browsers from implementing `min-height`, and only Netscape/Mozilla support it fully. The versions of Internet Explorer rated as Partial support the length and percentage values, but not the `inherit` value.

- Internet Explorer 3.0: Unsafe.
- Internet Explorer 4.0: Unsafe.
- Internet Explorer 4.0 – 4.5 (Mac): Unsafe.
- Internet Explorer 5.0: Unsafe.
- Internet Explorer 5.1 – 5.2 (Mac): Unsafe.
- Internet Explorer 5.5: Partial.
- Internet Explorer 6.0: Partial.
- Netscape Navigator 4.0 – 4.79: Unsafe.
- Netscape Navigator 4.0 (Mac & UNIX): Unsafe.
- Netscape Navigator 6.0: Safe.
- Netscape Navigator 7.0: Safe.
- Mozilla 1.0: Safe.
- Opera 3.6: Unsafe.
- Opera 4.0 – 6.0: Unsafe.
- Konqueror: Unsafe.

max-height

Being a CSS2 property automatically excludes the earliest browsers from implementing `max-height`. Support is restricted to Netscape/Mozilla among the major browsers.

- Internet Explorer 3.0: Unsafe.
- Internet Explorer 4.0: Unsafe.
- Internet Explorer 4.0 – 4.5 (Mac): Unsafe.

- Internet Explorer 5.0: Unsafe.
- Internet Explorer 5.1 – 5.2 (Mac): Unsafe.
- Internet Explorer 5.5: Unsafe.
- Internet Explorer 6.0: Unsafe.
- Netscape Navigator 4.0 – 4.79: Unsafe.
- Netscape Navigator 4.0 (Mac & UNIX): Unsafe.
- Netscape Navigator 6.0: Safe.
- Netscape Navigator 7.0: Safe.
- Mozilla 1.0: Safe.
- Opera 3.6: Unsafe.
- Opera 4.0 – 6.0: Unsafe.
- Konqueror: Unsafe.

VISUAL EFFECTS

Topics in This Chapter

- overflow
- overflow-x and overflow-y
- clip
- visibility
- zoom
- ime-mode

Chapter 17

The set of visual effects properties is designed to enable Web authors to control how text or other Web elements are displayed when they exceed the dimensions of the box within which they are contained. With the introduction of absolute positioning and fixed height and width, it becomes necessary to tell the browser what to do on those occasions when content ends up exceeding its box. The `overflow`, `clip` and `visibility` properties are three recent CSS2 properties introduced in order to aid Web authors in determining how material should be displayed under such circumstances. In addition to these values are three other properties — `overflow-x`, `overflow-y` and `zoom` — introduced by Microsoft in versions of Internet Explorer that further expand the possibilities of positioning elements onscreen. Another Internet Explorer-specific property, `ime-mode`, provides visual assistance to users seeking to enter Asian characters within forms.

17.1 overflow Property

The `overflow` property tells the browser what to do whenever the content contained within the bounding box of a block-level element extends beyond the dimensions of the box. Using this property, you can tell the browser to simply not display the content that "overflows" the boundary of the box, display a scrollbar so that the user can see the full content of the box if they desire, and more.

The overflow property can take any one of five different named values: visible, hidden, scroll, auto and inherit. With the visible value, the content contained within the box is not clipped, but is instead displayed, thereby forcing the box to fit the size of the content it contains.

With the hidden value, the content is simply clipped and there is no way for the viewer to see the remaining content. scroll and auto both display scrollbars for the user to see any content that would otherwise have been clipped; the difference between the two is that with scroll the scrollbars always appear, and with auto the scrollbars only appear if the situation requires. The inherit value simply takes on whatever parent value already exists for overflow.

The value most likely to see used is auto, which automatically adds a scrollbar to the content so that people can view the content within the restraining box. It has the advantage over scroll of adding a scrollbar only if it is needed. Listing 17.1 shows three examples of the overflow property at work.

Listing 17.1   *overflow Example*

```
<html>
<head>
<title>overflow Example #1</title>
<style>
body {font-size: 15px; font-family: sans-serif; font-weight: bold}
</style>
</head>
<body>
<b>The author then said:</b>
<p>
<blockquote style="width: 1.5in; height: 1in; overflow: auto">
If this quote runs too long, a scrollbar will appear so that the
viewer can continue to read the somewhat lengthy and definitely
meandering quotation.
</blockquote>
<p style="width: 3.5in; height: 1.25in; overflow: auto">
<img src="tiberius.jpg">
</p>
<p style="width: 3.5in; height: 1.25in; overflow: hidden">
<img src="tiberius.jpg">
</p>
</body>
</html>
```

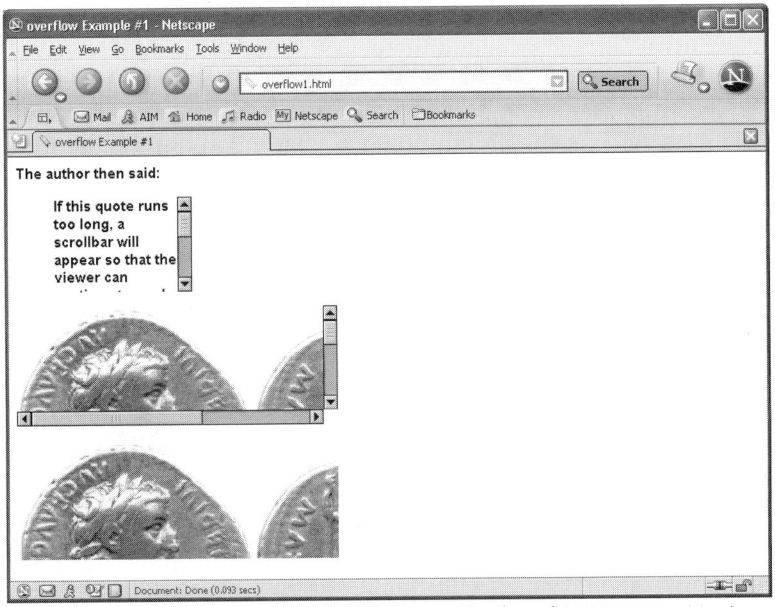

Figure 17–1   Effects of the overflow property displayed in Netscape Navigator 7.0.

Note in Figure 17–1 how a single scrollbar appears with the text example, but two scrollbars appear in the first example associated with the picture. This is because the text itself is not constrained to a certain width, and it is only the overflow text at the bottom that needs to be scrolled. Since the image has a set width and height and is not clipped, scrollbars appear at the side and the bottom so the viewer can observe the full image. The second image uses overflow: hidden, so there is no way to scroll to see the rest of the image.

Browser Compatibility

Browser compatibility for the overflow property is mixed, with only the recent versions of Internet Explorer and Netscape Navigator getting things right.

- Internet Explorer 3.0: Unsafe.
- Internet Explorer 4.0: Unsafe.
- Internet Explorer 4.0 – 4.5 (Mac): Unsafe.
- Internet Explorer 5.0: Safe.
- Internet Explorer 5.1 – 5.2 (Mac): Safe.
- Internet Explorer 5.5: Safe.
- Internet Explorer 6.0: Safe.
- Netscape Navigator 4.0 – 4.79: Unsafe.

- Netscape Navigator 4.0 (Mac & UNIX): Unsafe.

- Netscape Navigator 6.0: Safe.

- Netscape Navigator 7.0: Safe.

- Mozilla 1.0: Safe.

- Opera 3.6 – 4.0: Unsafe.

- Opera 5.0 – 6.0: Partial.

- Konqueror: Partial.

This property became fully supported within Internet Explorer beginning with version 5.0.

Netscape Navigator only began to support `overflow` beginning with version 6 (and Mozilla 1.0).

Recent versions of Opera only support the `hidden`, `visible` and `inherit` values for `overflow`, and do not support the critical `scroll` or `auto` values.

Konqueror can only claim partial support for `overflow`, as it does not support the `scroll` and `auto` values either.

17.2 overflow-x and overflow-y Properties

Specific to Internet Explorer 5.x and up, the `overflow-x` and `overflow-y` properties work in the same way as `overflow`, but for a specific direction. `overflow-x` is meant for content that might overflow horizontally, and `overflow-y` is for content that might overflow vertically.

Each can use any one of four common values: `visible`, `scroll`, `hidden` and `auto`. These are the same values shared by the `overflow` property, and they work in exactly the same way: the default `visible` value does not attempt to clip the content, `scroll` adds scrollbars, `hidden` clips the image and `auto` adds scrollbars only if they are needed.

Listing 17.2 shows how they can be applied to a couple of images, using the `scroll` value to display scrollbars along the vertical and horizontal axes in turn, respectively.

Listing 17.2 *overview-x and overview-y Example*

```
<html>
<head>
<title>overflow-x and overflow-y Example</title>
<style>
body {font-size: 15px; font-family: sans-serif; font-weight: bold}
</style>
</head>
<body>
<p style="width: 3.5in; height: 1.25in; overflow-y: scroll">
<img src="tiberius.jpg">
</p>
<p style="width: 3.5in; height: 1.25in; overflow-x: scroll">
<img src="tiberius.jpg">
</p>
</body>
</html>
```

Figure 17–2 Effects of the overflow-x and overflow-y properties displayed within Internet Explorer 6.0.

The `overflow-x` and `overflow-y` properties are specific to Internet Explorer 5.x and up, and are not recognized within any other browser.

17.3 clip Property

By default, the bounding box of any given block-level element displays everything contained within it. Using the clip property, it is possible to define what portion of the content contained within the box is actually visible to the viewer.

There are three named values that apply to clip: rect, which defines a rectangle outlined by units of measurement; auto, which sets the clipping value to the default visible value; and inherit, which adopts its value from the parent. Of these three, it is really the rect value that defines the clip property.

rect takes a string of up to four separate measurement values that set the top, right, bottom and left clipping values, respectively. When a unit of measure value is set, it sets the clipping value "in" from the bounding box, so a value of 5px clips content from the inside of the box by 5 pixels. You can see the clipping effect in Listing 17.3 and Figure 17–3, which shows the original picture and a "clipped" version of that same picture within Internet Explorer 6.0.

Listing 17.3   *clip Example #1*

```
<html>
<head>
<title>clip Example #1</title>
<style>
body {font-family: sans-serif; font-size: 16px; font-weight: bold}
</style>
</head>
<body>
<div style="position: absolute; left: 100px; top: 100px; z-index:
1">
<img src="tiberius.jpg" width="504" height="251" border="0"
alt="Unclipped Image">
</div>
<div style="position: absolute; z-index: 2; clip: rect(35px 180px
220px 45px)">
<img src="tiberius.jpg" width="504" height="251" border="0"
alt="Clipped Image">
</div>
<div style="position: absolute; z-index: 3">
Clipped and unclipped image of a coin highlighting the head of
ancient Roman Emperor Tiberius.
</div>
</body>
</html>
```

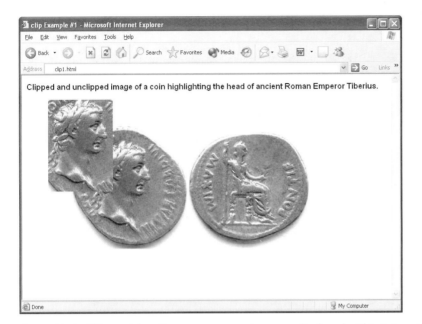

Figure 17–3 Effects of the clip property on an image as displayed within Internet Explorer 6.0.

As you can see from Figure 17–3, a copy of the original image is clipped so as to emphasize part of that image. The code in Listing 17.3 utilizes absolute positioning properties as well as the z-index property to provide a layered effect to the images. While this example shows how you can use clip in a static Web page, arguably the same effect could be achieved by cropping the image using an image editing program. In conjunction with absolute positioning it does allow you to effectively "re-use" a single image for dramatic effect. But Listing 17.4 takes the clipping effect one step further by making the effect dynamic.

Listing 17.4 *clip Example #2*

```
<html>
<head>
<title>clip Example #2</title>
</head>
<body>
<img id="emperor" src="tiberius.jpg" style="position: absolute;
top: 1.5cm; left: 1.5cm">
```

Listing 17.4   *clip Example #2(continued)*

```
<button
onclick="emperor.style.clip='rect(50px,200px,200px,50px)'">Clip
Image</button>
</body>
</html>
```

Figure 17–4   "Before" and "After" shots of dynamic clipping as seen within Internet Explorer 6.0.

As you can see in the "Before" and "After" shots in Figure 17–4, you can dynamically apply clipping to an image. Either the static or dynamic examples of clipping can be used on a Web site to eye-popping effect.

Browser Compatibility

Browser compatibility for the `clip` property is mixed, with Opera lagging behind the pack in terms of implementing `clip`'s values.

- Internet Explorer 3.0: Unsafe.
- Internet Explorer 4.0: Unsafe.

- Internet Explorer 4.0 – 4.5 (Mac): Unsafe.
- Internet Explorer 5.0: Unsafe.
- Internet Explorer 5.1 – 5.2 (Mac): Safe.
- Internet Explorer 5.5: Safe.
- Internet Explorer 6.0: Safe.
- Netscape Navigator 4.0 – 4.79: Unsafe.
- Netscape Navigator 4.0 (Mac & UNIX): Unsafe.
- Netscape Navigator 6.0: Safe.
- Netscape Navigator 7.0: Safe.
- Mozilla 1.0: Safe.
- Opera 3.6 – 4.0: Unsafe.
- Opera 5.0 – 6.0: Unsafe.
- Konqueror: Safe.

Internet Explorer only began supporting the values for `clip` beginning with version 5.5.

Netscape Navigator started implementing `clip` beginning with version 6.0 (as well as in Mozilla 1.0).

Opera has a poor record supporting this property, and its use within this browser cannot be recommended.

Konqueror fully supports `clip`.

17.4 visibility Property

The `visibility` property is available for Web authors who want select which Web elements should and should not be rendered visible onscreen. It can be applied to all onscreen elements.

There are four named values for `visibility`: `visible`, the default value that displays the element onscreen; `hidden`, which prevents the element from being displayed; `collapse`, which is to be used with tables and prevents a column or row from being displayed; and `inherit`, which simply takes on the parent value set for `visibility`. The `visible` and `hidden` values are self-explanatory, and their effects can be seen in Listing 17.5.

You should note that when using the `visibility` property, the box surrounding the element (be it inline or block-level element) does not disappear; it simply "hides" the content from being displayed. The result is a blank space where the content would normally appear, as you can see in Figure 17–5.

Listing 17.5   *visibility Example #1*

```
<html>
<head>
<title>visibility Example #1</title>
<style>
body {font-family: sans-serif; font-weight: bold; font-size: 30px}
</style>
</head>
<body>
<h1 style="visibility: visible">This Header is Visible</h1>
<p>
<h1 style="visibility: hidden">This Header in Invisible</h1>
<p>
<h1 style="visibility: visible">This Header is Also Visible</h1>
<p style="font-size: large">This part of the sentence is visible,
<b style="visibility: hidden">this  is not visible</b>, and this
is also visible.
</p>
</body>
</html>
```

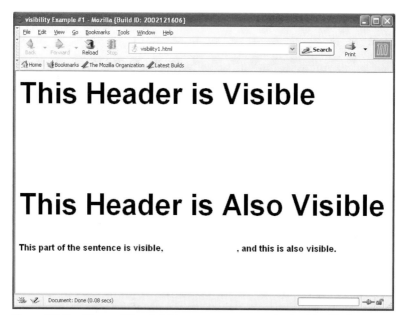

Figure 17–5   Effects of the visibility property as seen in the Mozilla browser.

The `collapse` value is meant to be used with table rows and columns, and is designed to have much the same effect as `hidden`. Instead of leaving the space where an effectively invisible row or column would be displayed, however, it "collapses" the adjoining rows or columns so that it is as if the selected row or column did not exist. You can see an example of this in Listing 17.6, whose results are displayed in Figure 17–6.

Listing 17.6	*visibility Example #2*

```
<html>
<head>
<title>visibility Example #2</title>
</head>
<style>
tr {font-size: 25px; font-weight: bold; font-family: sans-serif}
</style>
<body>
<table>
<tr>
<td valign="top">
<!-- left-hand table -->
<table cellpadding="15" style="border: thick black solid">
<tr>
<td>This will be visible</td>
<td>So will this</td>
</tr>
<tr style="visibility: collapse">
<td>This should not be visible</td>
<td>Neither will this</td>
</tr>
<tr>
<td>This will be visible</td>
<td>So will this</td>
</tr>
</table>
</td>
<td valign="top">
<!-- right-hand table -->
<table cellpadding="15" style="border: thick black solid">
<tr>
<td>This will be visible</td>
<td>So will this</td>
</tr>
<tr style="visibility: hidden">
<td>This should not be visible</td>
<td>Neither will this</td>
</tr>
```

Listing 17.6	*visibility Example #2 (continued)*

```
<tr>
<td>This will be visible</td>
<td>So will this</td>
</tr>
</table>
</td>
</tr>
</table>
</body>
</html>
```

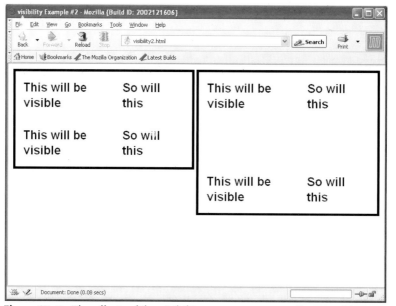

Figure 17–6   The effects of the visibility property on two adjacent tables, one with collapse set to the middle row, and the second with hidden set to the middle row.

You can see the effects of the values `collapse` and `hidden` as applied within two nested tables seen in Figure 17–6. In the first table, it is as if the row never existed (it has been "collapsed"), whereas in the second table, it is clear that there is an invisible row present in the table.

The visibility property really comes into its own when it is applied dynamically. For example, it is sometimes used to help create code-efficient rollover menus on Web sites, or to create simple interactive effects on a Web page. You can see an example of how visibility can be used in this way in Listing 17.7, which combines

JavaScript with CSS in order to make a coin image disappear when the user mouses over some text.

Listing 17.7	*visibility Example #3*

```html
<html>
<head>
<title>visibility Example #3</title>
<style>
.vis1 {visibility: visible}
.vis2 {visibility: hidden}
body {font-family: sans-serif; font-size: 30px;
</style>
</head>
<body>
<img src="tiberius.jpg" alt="Emperor Tiberius" name="coin"
id="coin" width="504" height="251" border="0">
<p onmouseover="coin.className='vis2'" onmouseout="coin.class-
Name='vis1'">
Make the coin disappear! Just mouse over this text.</p>
<p>
</body>
</html>
```

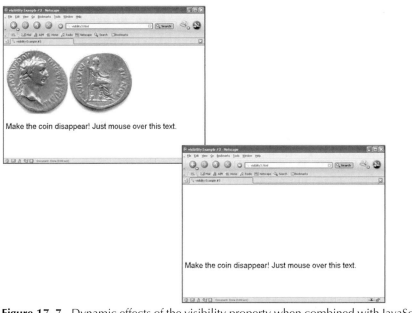

Figure 17–7 Dynamic effects of the visibility property when combined with JavaScript, as displayed in "Before" and "After" images in Netscape Navigator 7.0.

Browser Compatibility

Unlike many of the other properties covered in this section, `visibility` is well supported within the major browsers.

- Internet Explorer 3.0: Unsafe.
- Internet Explorer 4.0: Safe.
- Internet Explorer 4.0 – 4.5 (Mac): Safe.
- Internet Explorer 5.0: Safe.
- Internet Explorer 5.1 – 5.2 (Mac): Safe.
- Internet Explorer 5.5: Safe.
- Internet Explorer 6.0: Safe.
- Netscape Navigator 4.0 – 4.79: Safe.
- Netscape Navigator 4.0 (Mac & UNIX): Safe.
- Netscape Navigator 6.0: Safe.
- Netscape Navigator 7.0: Safe.
- Mozilla 1.0: Safe.
- Opera 3.6 – 4.0: Safe.
- Opera 5.0 – 6.0: Safe.
- Konqueror: Safe.

Only the initial 3.0 version of Internet Explorer does not support `visibility`. It is fully supported in all subsequent versions of this browser.

Netscape Navigator began implementing this property starting with version 4.0.

Opera began supporting `visibility` starting with version 3.6.

Konqueror fully supports this property.

17.5 zoom Property

The `zoom` property is an Internet Explorer-only property, instituted beginning with version 5.5, which sets the magnification level for an element. This property is designed primarily for dynamic use in order to change the size of an element being displayed. Using `zoom`, you can make objects more or less visible depending on the circumstance.

`zoom` can take one of three possible values: the named value `normal`, a numeric value and an integer value. The `normal` value is the default, and objects are displayed at their intrinsic, normal size. Using either a numeric or percentage value with `zoom` you can change the magnification level of an object; a numeric value of `1` is considered equivalent to `normal`, as is a percentage value of `100%`.

Listing 17.8 shows a dynamic Web page where you can increase or decrease the size of a coin image based on a numeric value contained within a drop-down menu.

Listing 17.8	*zoom Example*

```html
<html>
<head>
<title>zoom Example</title>
<script>
function changeZoomage() {
  newZoomage= parseInt(Slider.value)
      Zoomage.style.zoom=newZoomageage+'%';
  }
function changeZoomage2(Select) {
  newZoomage= Select.options[Select.selectedIndex].innerText
      Zoomage.style.zoom=newZoomage;
  }
</script>
</head>
<body onload="Zoomage.style.zoom='100%'" >
<!-- The container for the zoomable area -->
<div style="position: absolute; top:0; left:0; width: 600px;
height: 200px; background-color: navy; vertical-align: middle;
padding: 20px; font-family: sans-serif; font-weight: bold; color:
white; z-index: 3" align="center">
<!-- The zoomable area itself -->
<div id="Zoomage" style="zoom:100%" align="center">
<img src="tiberius.jpg">
<p>
Coin of the Ancient Roman Emperor Tiberius
</p>
</div></div>

<div id="Control" style="position: absolute; top: 334; left: 0;
width: 600px; height: 100px; background-color: gray; color: white;
font-family: sans-serif; font-size: 12; padding: 10px; z-index: 3;
text-align: center; border: 1px solid dotted">
<div style="padding-left:65px">
Change the zoom magnification of the coin image above by changing
the percentage value for the image on the drop-down menu below.
</div>
```

Listing 17.8	*zoom Example (continued)*

```
<div align=center>
<select id="percent" onchange="changeZoomage2(percent); ">
<option selected>Use Percentage Value</option>
<option>10%</option>
<option>25%</option>
<option>50%</option>
<option>75%</option>
<option>100%</option>
<option>150%</option>
<option>200%</option>
</select>
</div>
</body>
</html>
```

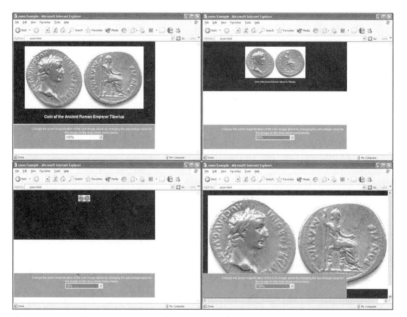

Figure 17–8 The zoom example code displayed in Internet Explorer 6.0 at various resolutions.

In Figure 17–8 you can see how an initial image set to its regular size (zoom: 100%) can be dynamically changed using a drop-down menu which selects different zoom values for the <div>-based container holding the image of the coin.

17.6 ime-mode Property

This is another Internet Explorer-specific property, first incorporated in version 5.x of the browser. The "ime" part of `ime-mode` is short for "Input Method Editor," which is a type of editor used for entering CJK (Chinese, Japanese or Korean) characters. In essence it allows the user to enter these characters in such things as form elements using an ordinary keyboard. Typically a user first selects a base character, which does a look-up of related characters, and then the user chooses the specific character they want displayed. IMEs are automatically included in the localized Chinese, Japanese and Korean versions of MS-Windows.

The `ime-mode` property has four properties: `auto`, `active`, `inactive` and `disabled`. The `auto` value is the default, which means that the Input Method Editor is not specifically invoked, although if the client is using one, its use is not suppressed. With the `active` value all characters are input through an IME, although the client can still deactivate it, and with the `inactive` value characters are not automatically entered via an IME (although the client can still activate one if they chose to do so). The `disabled` value means that the IME is unusable and cannot be optionally turned on by the user.

Listing 17.9 shows all of these options incorporated into a single form on a Web page. These values would only be displayed in a situation where an IME was present and active.

Listing 17.9	*ime-mode Example*

```
<html>
<head>
<title>ime-mode Example</title>
<style>
body {font-size: 25px; font-family: sans-serif}
</style>
</head>
<body>
<form>
<h1>Form containing four different settings for
<code>ime-mode</code></h1>
<p>
<code>ime-mode: auto</code> <input type="text" name="text1"
size="15" maxlength="20" style="ime-mode: auto">
</p>
```

Listing 17.9 *ime-mode Example (continued)*

```
<p>
<code>ime-mode: active</code> <input type="text" name="text2"
size="15" maxlength="20" style="ime-mode: active">
</p>
<p>
<code>ime-mode: inactive</code> <input type="text" name="text3"
size="15" maxlength="20" style="ime-mode: inactive">
</p>
<p>
<code>ime-mode: disabled</code> <input type="text" name="text4"
size="15" maxlength="20" style="ime-mode: disabled">
</p>
</form>
</body>
</html>
```

You can see the results in Figure 17–9, which shows a Chinese IME being used to enter characters — where possible — in Internet Explorer 6.0 displaying the sample code from Listing 17.9.

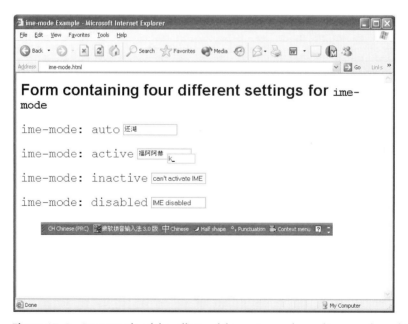

Figure 17–9   An example of the effects of the various values of ime-mode and its effects on an Input Method Editor.

Core Tip

Input Method Editors for various CJK input can be downloaded from the Microsoft Web site directly at: http://www.microsoft.com/windows/ie/downloads/recommended/ime/default.asp.

PAGED MEDIA

Topics in This Chapter

- size
- marks
- Page Break Properties
- page
- orphans
- widows

Chapter

CSS2 introduced the idea of rendering Web pages as "paged media" — in other words, rendering a Web page specifically for print instead of the computer screen. The properties in the paged media family are designed to extend greater control over how Web pages are to be printed.

The paged media properties are intended to solve the long-standing problem of rendering Web pages in a non-continuous medium, such as print. You now have greater control over such things as page breaks, the size of the printed page, setting the margin (i.e., left or right indent) of a page and more.

The CSS2 specification did this by essentially extending the box model to the width of the printed page, making it a page "box" as defined by the various paged media properties. It is then up to the browser to take this information and produce printed output as designed by the Web author.

18.1 size Property

The size property is designed to set the orientation and size of the printed page box. With this property, Web authors can precisely control the dimensions for the printed output of their Web pages, and can even set whether or not the pages should be printed in portrait (the default) or landscape mode.

The size property can take any of the following values: a twin set of numeric values that set the width and height of the page, respectively, and auto, which sets the page box to the size and orientation of the target paper size. There are also two orientation values: `portrait`, the default, which prints the content so it flows down the long side of the page, and `landscape`, which flows the content along the short side of the page. Figure 18–1 makes the distinction between `portrait` and `landscape` orientation clear.

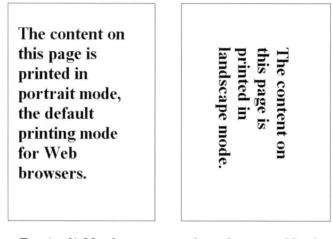

Portrait Mode   **Landscape Mode**

Figure 18–1   Portrait and landscape printing modes displayed.

The `size` property is used exclusively with the `@page` media type. It is used to set a value for the size and orientation of the page within the header of the page, which is the obvious place to set this sort of information for a Web page designed to be printed.

The following example code sets the size of the Web page to a typical 8.5 x 11 inch "letter" format, tells the browser to print the output in landscape mode and sets a 0.5 inch margin on each side of the page:

| Listing 18.1 | *size Example* |

```
<head>
<title>size Example</title>
<style>
@page {size: 8.5in 11in landscape; margin: 0.5in}
</style>
</head>
<body>
The content on this page will be printed in landscape mode, have an
indented margin of 0.5 inches on all four sides, and be set for
printing on regular 8.5 x 11 inch paper.
</body>
</html>
```

Browser Compatibility

- Internet Explorer 3.0: Unsafe.
- Internet Explorer 4.0: Unsafe.
- Internet Explorer 4.0 – 4.5 (Mac): Unsafe.
- Internet Explorer 5.0: Unsafe.
- Internet Explorer 5.5: Unsafe.
- Internet Explorer 6.0: Unsafe.
- Netscape Navigator 4.0 – 4.79: Unsafe.
- Netscape Navigator 4.0 (Mac & UNIX): Unsafe.
- Netscape Navigator 6.0: Unsafe.
- Netscape Navigator 7.0: Unsafe.
- Mozilla 1.0: Unsafe.
- Opera 3.6 – 4.0: Unsafe.
- Opera 5.0 – 6.0: Safe.
- Konqueror: Unsafe.

The size property was first introduced under the CSS2 specification, and hence came out after the release of the earliest browsers capable of displaying some CSS properties.

The only browser that implements the size property is Opera, beginning from version 5.0 and up.

Internet Explorer 6.0, Netscape Navigator 7.0 and Mozilla 1.1 do not support this feature.

18.2 marks Property

The marks property is designed to set the type of sign (or "mark") to appear defining the boundaries of the printed page. In a print shop, these marks define where the pages would be trimmed before binding, or where the pages should be aligned. In this case, it really just defines the printable area of the Web page.

The marks property is used in conjunction with the @page media type. The marks property can take one of four different named values: crop, which adds a crop mark to a page; cross, which adds a cross mark used to align sheets; none (the default), where no mark is visible; and the ubiquitous inherit, which takes on whatever parent value may have already been set for the property. You can see how this property can be used in Listing 18.2.

Listing 18.2	*marks Example*

```
<head>
<title>marks Example</title>
<style>
@page {size: 8.5in 11in portrait; margin: 0.5in; marks: cross}
</style>
</head>
<body>
The content on this page will be printed in landscape mode, have an
indented margin of 0.5 inches on all sides, and be set for printing
on regular 8.5 x 11 inch paper.
</body>
</html>
```

The crop and cross values are handy for determining the boundary of printing margins for the page, giving Web authors a better idea as to where the margins on the printed page appear. The difference between the two types of marks can be seen in the following illustration:

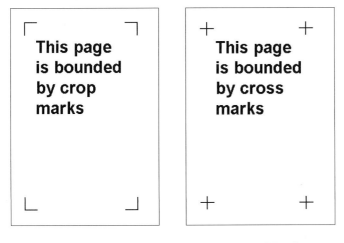

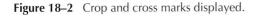

Figure 18–2   Crop and cross marks displayed.

Browser Compatibility

- Internet Explorer 3.0: Unsafe.
- Internet Explorer 4.0: Unsafe.
- Internet Explorer 4.0 – 4.5 (Mac): Unsafe.
- Internet Explorer 5.0: Unsafe.
- Internet Explorer 5.5: Unsafe.
- Internet Explorer 6.0: Unsafe.
- Netscape Navigator 4.0 – 4.79: Unsafe.
- Netscape Navigator 4.0 (Mac & UNIX): Unsafe.
- Netscape Navigator 6.0: Unsafe.
- Netscape Navigator 7.0: Unsafe.
- Mozilla 1.0: Unsafe.
- Opera 3.6 – 4.0: Unsafe.
- Opera 5.0 – 6.0: Unsafe.
- Konqueror: Unsafe.

The marks property is not yet supported in any major browser.

18.3 Page-Break Properties

The paged media family comes with three properties specifically designed to set where page breaks should (or should not) occur within Web pages when they are printed: `page-break-before`, `page-break-after` and `page-break-inside`. The first two accomplish the task of inserting a page break. `page-break-inside` operates using a sub-set of values assigned to both `page-break-before` and `page-break-after` and is used to prevent a page break within a particular part of the Web page. All three are used in conjunction with block-level properties, so page breaks are not set from within a line of text.

Both `page-break-before` and `page-break-after` share the following values: `auto`, `avoid`, `left`, `right`, `always` and `inherit`. The `auto` value is the default setting, and neither forces nor prohibits a page break from occurring at a specific point. `avoid` tells the browser to specifically avoid forcing a page break before a given block-level element. The `left` value forces a page break to occur so that subsequent text appears on a left-facing page, and the `right` value forces a page break to occur so that the subsequent text appears on a right-facing page. When using the `left` and `right` values, be aware that in order for the browser to produce a subsequent page that is either to be printed as a left- or right-facing page, a blank page may need to be inserted. For example, if the previous page is left-facing and `left` is used, then a blank right page would have to be present before the next left-facing page could appear.

The `always` value sets the page break after a given block-level element when used in `page-break-after`, and before it in `page-break-before`. The `inherit` value takes on whatever page-break value has already been set by the parent. While `page-break-before` and `page-break-after` share all of these values, `page-break-inside` only takes on `auto`, `avoid` and `inherit`.

The `page-break-before` property is used when you want to set a page break immediately before a given block-level element, as the example code in Listing 18.3 shows.

Listing 18.3 *page-break-before Example*

```
<html>
<head>
<title>page-break-before Example</title>
<style>
h1 {page-break-before: always;}
</style>
</head>
<body>
Here is some text.
<h1>This header will appear on a new printed page</h1>
</body>
</html>
```

In this particular case, the browser has been instructed to put in a page break immediately before any top-level header that appears on the Web page. This scenario makes a lot of sense if you want each top-level header to be displayed on a new page. You could also set things so that you could have every paragraph on a Web page printed on a different page, as the `page-break-after` code example seen in Listing 18.4 depicts.

Listing 18.4 *page-break-after Example*

```
<html>
<head>
<title>page-break-after Example</title>
<style>
p {page-break-after: always}
</style>
</head>
<body>
<p>
Each subsequent paragraph will be forced onto a new printed page.
</p>
<p>
This is on a second printed page.
</p>
<p>
This will be printed on a third page.
</p>
</body>
</html>
```

Use the `page-break-inside` property when you deliberately want to make sure that a page break does *not* occur within a given block-level element. Using this property ensures that whatever Web element you select remains on the same printed page, as with the code example in Listing 18.5.

Listing 18.5 *page-break-inside Example*

```
<html>
<head>
<title>page-break-inside Example</title>
<style>
blockquote {page-break-inside: avoid}
</style>
</head>
<body>
<blockquote>no matter how long this quote may be, the
page-break-inside property will ensure that a page break does
not occur inside of it, breaking it across more than one
page.
</blockquote>
</body>
</html>
```

The obvious disadvantage of using this value for `page-break-inside` is that if you have a longish paragraph or two, you could end up forcing the use of more paper when printing out your Web page than is absolutely necessary. Keep that in mind when using this value.

Together, all three properties present Web authors with the opportunity to explicitly set where printed page breaks should or should not occur.

Browser Compatibility

page-break-before and page-break-after

- Internet Explorer 3.0: Unsafe.
- Internet Explorer 4.0: Unsafe.
- Internet Explorer 4.0 – 4.5 (Mac): Unsafe.
- Internet Explorer 5.0: Unsafe.
- Internet Explorer 5.5: Safe.
- Internet Explorer 6.0: Safe.
- Netscape Navigator 4.0 – 4.79: Unsafe.
- Netscape Navigator 4.0 (Mac & UNIX): Unsafe.
- Netscape Navigator 6.0: Unsafe.

- Netscape Navigator 7.0: Unsafe.
- Mozilla 1.0: Unsafe.
- Opera 3.6 – 4.0: Unsafe.
- Opera 5.0 – 6.0: Safe.
- Konqueror: Unsafe.

The `page-break-before` and `page-break-after` properties are supported in Internet Explorer beginning with version 5.5.

These properties are similarly supported within Opera, beginning with version 5.0.

The `page-break-before` and `page-break-after` properties are not supported within recent versions of Netscape, Mozilla or Konqueror.

page-break-inside

- Internet Explorer 3.0: Unsafe.
- Internet Explorer 4.0: Unsafe.
- Internet Explorer 4.0 – 4.5 (Mac): Unsafe.
- Internet Explorer 5.0: Unsafe.
- Internet Explorer 5.5: Unsafe.
- Internet Explorer 6.0: Unsafe.
- Netscape Navigator 4.0 – 4.79: Unsafe.
- Netscape Navigator 4.0 (Mac & UNIX): Unsafe.
- Netscape Navigator 6.0: Unsafe.
- Netscape Navigator 7.0: Unsafe.
- Mozilla 1.0: Unsafe.
- Opera 3.6 – 4.0: Unsafe.
- Opera 5.0 – 6.0: Safe.
- Konqueror: Unsafe.

Despite the fact that the `page-break-before` and `page-break-after` properties are supported within Internet Explorer 5.5 and up, the `page-break-inside` property is not.

The only browser that as yet supports this feature is Opera 5.0 (and up).

18.4 page Property

The `page` property is used to set a specific printed property to elements contained within a printed Web page. In other words, it allows Web authors to specify how certain elements within a page should appear. If, for example, you wanted all tables to be printed in landscape mode, you simply attach a name to the `page` property and then associate that name with the specific tables you want printed in landscape mode.

There are two possible values for `page`: a name value set by the Web author (which could be anything), and `auto` (the default), which follows the automatic formatting for the given element.

Listing 18.6 shows how the `page` property could be put to use. In this case, the content on the page is printed as usual, but when the printer meets the table contained on the page, the `page` property associated with it tells the printer to print the table on a separate page and in landscape mode rather than portrait mode.

Listing 18.6 *page Example*

```
<html>
<head>
<title>page Example</title>
<style>
@page regular {size 8.5in 11in; margin: 1.5in;}
@page landscape {size: landscape;}
div {page: regular;}
table {page: landscape;}
</style>
</head>
<body>
<div>
The idea behind the <code>page</code> property is to create a page
break <i>and</i> enable the Web author to format the content of
the subsequent page in a different manner than that which went
before it.
</div>
<table>
<tr>
<td>The content in this table will be set in a new page, and will
appear in a landscape format.</td>
</tr>
</table>
</body>
</html>
```

Browser Compatibility

- Internet Explorer 3.0: Unsafe.
- Internet Explorer 4.0: Unsafe.
- Internet Explorer 4.0 – 4.5 (Mac): Unsafe.
- Internet Explorer 5.0: Unsafe.

- Internet Explorer 5.5: Unsafe.

- Internet Explorer 6.0: Unsafe.

- Netscape Navigator 4.0 – 4.79: Unsafe.

- Netscape Navigator 4.0 (Mac & UNIX): Unsafe.

- Netscape Navigator 6.0: Unsafe.

- Netscape Navigator 7.0: Unsafe.

- Mozilla 1.0: Unsafe.

- Opera 3.6 – 4.0: Unsafe.

- Opera 5.0 – 6.0: Safe.

- Konqueror: Unsafe.

The `page` property is only supported within Opera 5.0 on up.

This property is not currently supported in any of the major browsers, including the most recent versions of Internet Explorer, Netscape Navigator and Konqueror.

18.5 windows and orphans Properties

"Widows" and "orphans" are old printing terms used to specify the minimum amount of lines of text that should appear at the top and bottom of a printed page, respectively. The CSS2 properties accomplish the same thing, ensuring that a minimum amount of text appears at the top and bottom of each page.

Both the `widows` and `orphans` properties share the same values: an integer value that assigns the number of lines that must appear in a paragraph before it is forced to move to another page (one way or the other), and the named value `inherit`, which takes on whatever parent value may have already been set. The default numeric value for both `widows` and `orphans` is 2, ensuring that at least two lines of text in a paragraph are either at the top or bottom of a page before a page break will occur. These properties are designed only to be used with block-level elements, such as `<p>` or `<div>`.

Listing 18.7 shows how the `p` elements on a Web page are set to widow and orphan values of 3, ensuring that at least that many lines appear in a paragraph before forcing the print mechanism to carry a paragraph over onto a subsequent printed page.

Listing 18.7 *widows and orphans Example*

```
<html>
<head>
<title>widows and orphans Example</title>
<style>
@page regular {size 8.5in 11in; margin: 1.5in;}
p {orphans: 3; widows: 3}
body {font-size: x-large}
</style>
</head>
<body>
The paragraphs on this page has been set to a value of
<code>orphans: 3</code> and <code>widows: 3</code>, which  means
that at least three lines of text in a paragraph are necessary at
the top or bottom of a page before a page-break will occur while
printing.
<p>
What follows is "filler" text to help make this effect apparent
while printing.
<p>
Sed ut perspiciatis unde omnis iste natus error sit voluptatem
accusantium doloremque laudantium, totam rem aperiam, eaque ipsa
quae ab illo inventore veritatis et quasi architecto beatae vitae
dicta sunt explicabo. Nemo enim ipsam voluptatem quia voluptas sit
aspernatur aut odit aut fugit, sed quia consequuntur magni dolores
eos qui ratione voluptatem sequi nesciunt. Neque porro quisquam
est, qui dolorem ipsum quia dolor sit amet, consectetur, adipisci
velit, sed quia non numquam eius modi tempora incidunt ut labore
et dolore magnam aliquam quaerat voluptatem. Ut enim ad minima
veniam, quis nostrum exercitationem ullam corporis suscipit labo-
riosam, nisi ut aliquid ex ea commodi consequatur? Quis autem vel
eum iure reprehenderit qui in ea voluptate velit esse quam nihil
molestiae consequatur, vel illum qui dolorem eum fugiat quo volup-
tas nulla pariatur?
<p>
Lorem ipsum dolor sit amet, consectetaur adipisicing elit, sed do
eiusmod tempor incididunt ut labore et dolore magna aliqua. Ut
enim ad minim veniam, quis nostrud exercitation ullamco laboris
nisi ut aliquip ex ea commodo consequat. Duis aute irure dolor in
reprehenderit in voluptate velit esse cillum dolore eu fugiat
nulla pariatur. Excepteur sint occaecat cupidatat non proident,
sunt in culpa qui officia deserunt mollit anim id est laborum.
</body>
</html>
```

Be careful when assigning numeric values for either widows or orphans, as too large a value will only add to the amount of white space added to each page.

Browser Compatibility

- Internet Explorer 3.0: Unsafe.
- Internet Explorer 4.0: Unsafe.
- Internet Explorer 4.0 – 4.5 (Mac): Unsafe.
- Internet Explorer 5.0: Unsafe.
- Internet Explorer 5.5: Unsafe.
- Internet Explorer 6.0: Unsafe.
- Netscape Navigator 4.0 – 4.79: Unsafe.
- Netscape Navigator 4.0 (Mac & UNIX): Unsafe.
- Netscape Navigator 6.0: Unsafe.
- Netscape Navigator 7.0: Unsafe.
- Mozilla 1.0: Unsafe.
- Opera 3.6 – 4.0: Unsafe.
- Opera 5.0 – 6.0: Safe.
- Konqueror: Unsafe.

The widows and orphans properties are only supported within Opera 5.0 on up.

This property is not currently supported in any of the other major browsers, including Internet Explorer 6.0, Netscape Navigator 7.0 and Konqueror.

TABLES

Topics in This Chapter

- `caption-side`
- `table-layout`
- `border-collapse`, `border-spacing` and `empty-cells`
- `speak-header`
- Table-like Layout Using CSS

Chapter 19

Another of the new sets of properties that CSS2 introduces is the set of table properties. This set of wholly new properties is designed to provide Web authors with greater control over the appearance of tables and table elements — even how the table contents are spoken aloud.

This chapter also looks at several ways in which you can create table-like layout effects using CSS code instead of HTML-based table code.

19.1 caption-side Property

The `caption-side` property enables Web authors to place the caption box in relation to the rest of the table. It works in much the same fashion as the little-used `<caption>` HTML tag, but allows for greater flexibility in the placement of table captions.

`caption-side` can take any one of up to five different named values: `top`, `bottom`, `left`, `right` and `inherit`. The `<caption>` tag can actually take a similar set of values (`valign=top` or `bottom`, `align=top`, `bottom`, `left`, `right`, or `center`), but the `left` and `right` values for `caption-side` produce different results. The `caption-side` property is designed to work with the `<caption>` element, acting as a substitute for the usual way of setting captions with tables.

When you add a caption to a table, it appears outside the boundaries of the table's contents, but is bound to appear in a space alongside the table itself (in other words, if you set a visible `border` value to the table, the caption will be located outside of the table's border).

When you use the `align=left` or `align=right` value with the `<caption>` tag, it aligns the text in the caption; it does not alter where the caption appears in relation to the table. That is where the `left` and `right` values for `caption-side` come into effect; they place the caption to the left or right, respectively, of the table itself. You can see examples of all four native values for `caption-side` displayed in the following code, with its intended effects seen in Figure 19–1.

Listing 19.1 *caption-side Example*

```
<html>
<head>
<title>caption-side Example</title>
<style>
td,caption {font: bold 25px Verdana, Geneva, Arial, Helvetica,
sans-serif}
table {border : medium solid black}
</style>
</head>
<body>
<table>
<caption style="caption-side: top">Table Caption to the
Top</caption>
<tr>
<td>This text is contained within the table</td>
</tr>
</table>
 
<table>
<caption style="caption-side: bottom">Table Caption to the
Bottom</caption>
<tr>
<td>This text is contained within the table</td>
</tr>
</table>
 
<table>
<caption style="caption-side: left">Caption to the Left</caption>
<tr>
<td>This text is contained within the table</td>
</tr>
</table>
 
```

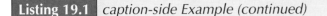

Listing 19.1 *caption-side Example (continued)*

```
<table>
<caption style="caption-side: right">Table Caption to the
Right</caption>
<tr>
<td>This text is contained within the table</td>
</tr>
</table>

</body>
</html>
```

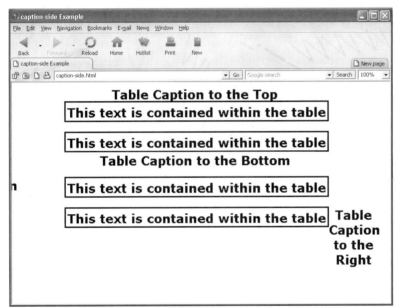

Figure 19–1 The caption-side code example as displayed within Opera 6.0. Note the problem with the left value.

Browser Compatibility

As this property was first introduced in the CSS2 specification, this automatically rules out support for `caption-side` in the earlier versions of the major browsers.

- Internet Explorer 3.0: Unsafe.
- Internet Explorer 4.0: Unsafe.
- Internet Explorer 4.0 – 4.5 (Mac): Unsafe.

- Internet Explorer 5.0: Unsafe.
- Internet Explorer 5.1 – 5.2: Unsafe.
- Internet Explorer 5.5: Unsafe.
- Internet Explorer 6.0: Unsafe.
- Netscape Navigator 4.0 – 4.79: Unsafe.
- Netscape Navigator 4.0 (Mac & UNIX): Unsafe.
- Netscape Navigator 6.0: Partial.
- Netscape Navigator 7.0: Partial.
- Mozilla 1.0: Partial.
- Opera 3.6 – 4.0: Unsafe.
- Opera 5.0 – 6.0: Partial.
- Konqueror: Unsafe.

Internet Explorer flat out does not support `caption-side`. The text contained within any table caption is displayed at the top of the table, which is the default.

Beginning with version 6.0 of Netscape Navigator, there is partial support for `caption-side`. It understands the `top` and `bottom` values for this property, but not the `left` and `right` values.

The only browser that gets `caption-side` mostly right is Opera, beginning with version 6.0. Not only does it display the `top` and `bottom` values, but it also displays the `right` value properly. As seen in Figure 19–1, the caption for the `left` value does appear, but it shifted well to the left, almost completely out of the browser's window. Hence it can only be given a Partial rating.

19.2 table-layout Property

The introduction of the `table-layout` property is designed to enable Web authors to explicitly lay out their tables according to whether or not the width should be dependent on the size of the content of the individual cells comprising the table. By expressing this property, Web authors gain more explicit control over how the table (and its contents) should appear onscreen.

The `table-layout` property has three named values: `auto`, `fixed` and `inherit`. With the `auto` property, the browser must first determine the size of the contents of each cell and the resulting column in which they reside. Once that is calculated, the browser then proceeds to lay out the resulting table. This is the default value. This method is not terribly efficient, since the browser has to do a lot of calculation beforehand in order to present anything. The `fixed` value enables Web authors to set a maximum size for the table to be displayed, which necessarily sets an upper limit on what can be contained within the individual cells and columns of cells within the resulting table. The `inherit` value simply takes whatever parent value may have already been set for `table-layout`.

The code in Listing 19.2 gives an idea of how `table-layout` can be used. In this example there are two tables displayed, both containing an image. In the first case, where the value `auto` is used, the table is sized to fit the size of the image and text. In the second case, the value `fixed` has been applied to the table, in conjunction with specific `width`.

Listing 19.2 *table-layout Example*

```
<html>
<head>
<title>table-layout Example</title>
</head>
<body>
<table>
<tr>
<td>

<table style="table-layout: auto; border: 1px solid black" >
<tr>
<td><img src="fokker.gif"><br />
A picture of a Fokker airplane taken prior to an airshow.
</td>
</tr>
</table>
</td>
<td>

<table style="table-layout: fixed; width: 1.5in; border: 1px solid
black">
<tr>
<td><img src="fokker.gif" style=" overflow: auto"><br />
A picture of a Fokker airplane taken prior to an airshow.</td>
</tr>
</table>

</td>
</tr>
</table>
</body>
</html>
```

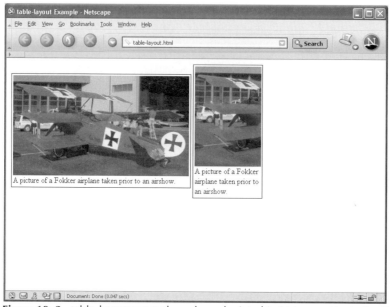

Figure 19–2   table-layout example code as depicted in Netscape Navigator 7.0.

As you can see from Figure 19–2, the image contained in the second table is "chopped," because the picture is larger than the specified width for the cell within the table. Notice also that because there was no restriction set on the cell's height, the text that appears alongside the image stretches the height of the table.

You might think you would be able to use the `overflow` property in order to add scrollbars that would allow you to scroll over to view content not currently visible within a cell, but that property is not available to tables or their cells' content. So be aware of the limitations of using a value like `layout-table: fixed`.

Browser Compatibility

As this is a CSS2 property, early browsers are automatically out of the picture when it comes to compatibility. But even some of the more recent browsers have problems with this property.

- Internet Explorer 3.0: Unsafe.
- Internet Explorer 4.0: Unsafe.
- Internet Explorer 4.0 – 4.5 (Mac): Unsafe.
- Internet Explorer 5.0: Safe.
- Internet Explorer 4.0 – 4.5 (Mac): Safe.
- Internet Explorer 5.5: Safe.

- Internet Explorer 6.0: Safe.
- Netscape Navigator 4.0 – 4.79: Unsafe.
- Netscape Navigator 4.0 (Mac & UNIX): Unsafe.
- Netscape Navigator 6.0: Safe.
- Netscape Navigator 7.0: Safe.
- Mozilla 1.0: Safe.
- Opera 3.6 – 4.0: Unsafe.
- Opera 5.0 – 6.0: Partial.
- Konqueror: Unsafe.

Internet Explorer was a relatively early adopter of this property, implementing it beginning with version 5.5 (although it should be noted that it was not adopted within that Macintosh 5.x version).

Netscape Navigator began to implement this property beginning with version 6.0, as did Mozilla 1.0.

Somewhat oddly for Opera, it was and continues to be behind the curve on implementing this property, ignoring the `layout-table: fixed` value if its content is larger than that set for the size of an individual cell.

Although Konqueror tends to do well in adopting many CSS2 properties, `layout-table` is not one of them.

19.3 border-collapse, border-spacing and empty-cells

There are three properties that handle how borders should be displayed around tables, and they are `border-collapse`, `border-spacing` and `empty-cells`. The first two work in conjunction with each other to tell the browser which border-formatting model to use: either the collapsed or separate model, each of which has its own unique display characteristics. The collapsed border model ensures that all border formatting settings are continuous within the body of the table, and the separate model allows for distinct borders around individual cells. The `empty-cells` property tells the browser how to deal with the special instance of adding borders around cells that do not contain any content.

border-collapse Property

`border-collapse` can take any one of three named values: `collapse`, which sets the table to the standard collapsing borders model; `separate`, which sets the table to the separated borders model (and allows the table to be formatted using the border-spacing property); and the inherit value, which takes on the same value as that set for the parent for border-collapse.

When border-collapse is set to collapse, border values for cells should "attach" to each other and flow without a break throughout the table. This also allows you to do some interesting mixing of border styles within a given table. When set to separate, each cell in a given table will be formatted individually to whatever border values are provided. Listing 19.3 shows two tables that use four distinct border styles, the top one set to border-collapse: collapse and the bottom one to border-collapse: separate. You can easily see the difference in these two different values reflected in Figure 19–3.

Listing 19.3 *border-collapse Example*

```
<html>
<head>
<title>border-collapse Example</title>
<style>
table.collapsed {border-collapse: collapse; border: 5px solid
navy}
table.separate {border-collapse: separate; border: 5px solid navy}
th {border: 10px solid navy; font: bold 25px Arial, Helvetica,
sans-serif}
td {border: 5px solid black; font: bold 20px Arial, Helvetica,
sans-serif}
td.special {border: 7px double lime; font: bold 20px Arial,
Helvetica, sans-serif}
body {font: bold 20px Arial, Helvetica, sans-serif}
</style>
</head>
<body>
Table set to <code>border-collapse: collapse</code>
<table class="collapsed">
<tr>
<th>Item</th>
<th>Description</th>
<th>Price</td>
</tr>
<tr>
<td>Widget</td>
<td>White, with black stripes</td>
<td>$2.50</td>
</tr>
```

| Listing 19.3 | *border-collapse Example (continued)* |

```
<tr>
<td class="special">Thingamabob</td>
<td class="special">Perfect for your thing bobbing needs</td>
<td class="special">$0.25</td>
</tr>
<tr>
<td>Doofinkle</td>
<td>You know what do with this</td>
<td>$1.35</td>
</tr>
</table>

<p>
Table set to <code>border-collapse: separate</code>
<table class="separate">
<tr>
<th>Item</th>
<th>Description</th>
<th>Price</td>
</tr>
<tr>
<td>Widget</td>
<td>White, with black stripes</td>
<td>$2.50</td>
</tr>
<tr>
<td class="special">Thingamabob</td>
<td class="special">Perfect for your thing bobbing needs</td>
<td class="special">$0.25</td>
</tr>
<tr>
<td>Doofinkle</td>
<td>You know what do with this</td>
<td>$1.35</td>
</tr>
</table>
</p>
</div>
</body>
</html>
```

You can see the results of the code from Listing 19.3 in Figure 19–3. The chief thing to note here is not so much the different styles of borders being used, but the effects of the two border-collapse values: how collapse ensures that all of the border formatting "runs together" and that `separate` applies the border formatting to each individual cell.

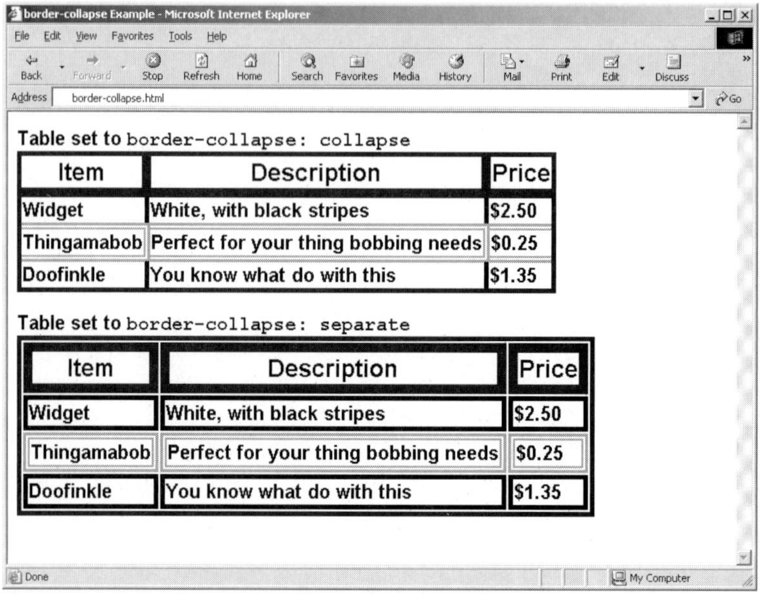

Figure 19–3   Displaying the effects of border-collapse within Internet Explorer 6.0.

Browser Compatibility

As `border-collapse` is a CSS2 property, many of the early browsers are automatically eliminated from the picture. Still, even modern browsers that do implement this feature tend to be buggy.

- Internet Explorer 3.0: Unsafe.
- Internet Explorer 4.0: Unsafe.
- Internet Explorer 4.0 – 4.5 (Mac): Unsafe.
- Internet Explorer 5.0: Partial.
- Internet Explorer 5.5: Partial.
- Internet Explorer 6.0: Partial.
- Netscape Navigator 4.0 – 4.79: Unsafe.
- Netscape Navigator 4.0 (Mac & UNIX): Unsafe.
- Netscape Navigator 6.0: Partial.
- Netscape Navigator 7.0: Partial.
- Mozilla 1.0: Partial.
- Opera 3.6 – 4.0: Unsafe.
- Opera 5.0 – 6.0: Safe.

- Konqueror: Unsafe.

Internet Explorer adopted the use of this property relatively early, starting with version 5.0. It does, however, have a problem whenever a table is set to `border-collapse: collapse` and there is a `cellpadding` attribute set to the table element. The specification says that such values should be overruled by the browser, but instead the `cellspacing` value ends up separating borders that ought to run together.

Beginning with version 6.0, Netscape Navigator treats all instances of `border-collapse` as if they are set to `separate`. The `collapsed` value is not supported.

At the moment, the only browser that displays this property properly is Opera beginning with version 3.6. It also works as it is supposed to when a `cellpadding` value is set.

Konqueror does not support `border-collapse`.

border-spacing Property

The `border-spacing` property typically takes a basic standard unit of measurement value, and must be used in conjunction with `border-collapse: separate`. If a single measurement value is specified, the value is set to all borders, and if two are specified, the first value is taken for horizontal spacing, while the second is used as the vertical spacing value. It can also take the named value `inherit`, which takes on whatever value has been set to the parent for `border-spacing`.

Listing 19.3 depicts a table where the table has simply been set to `border-collapse: separate`, and where a value of `border-spacing: 10px` has additionally been set. The results can be seen in Figure 19–4

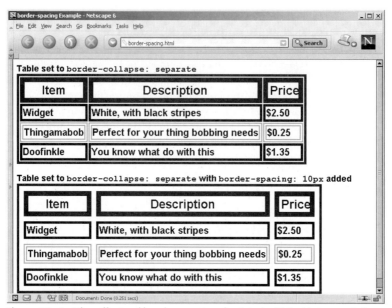

Figure 19–4   The effects of border-spacing depicted within Netscape 6.0.

Browser Compatibility

This is a property first proposed in the CSS2 specification, so many early browsers are ruled out.

- Internet Explorer 3.0: Unsafe.
- Internet Explorer 4.0: Unsafe.
- Internet Explorer 4.0 – 4.5 (Mac): Unsafe.
- Internet Explorer 5.0: Unsafe.
- Internet Explorer 5.1 – 5.2 (Mac): Unsafe.
- Internet Explorer 5.5: Unsafe.
- Internet Explorer 6.0: Unsafe.
- Netscape Navigator 4.0 – 4.79: Unsafe.
- Netscape Navigator 4.0 (Mac & UNIX): Unsafe.
- Netscape Navigator 6.0: Safe.
- Netscape Navigator 7.0: Safe.
- Mozilla 1.0: Safe.
- Opera 3.6 – 4.0: Unsafe.
- Opera 5.0 – 6.0: Safe.
- Konqueror: Safe.

Internet Explorer does not implement this property, even in more recent versions. Oddly enough, when a `border-spacing` value is added, the resulting table is displayed as if `border-collapse: collapse` were set instead.

This property is fully supported within Netscape Navigator beginning with version 6.0 (along with Mozilla 1.0).

This property is fully supported within Opera beginning with version 5.0.

This property is supported within Konqueror.

empty-cells Property

There are often cases when one or more table cells may contain no content whatsoever, but are still needed so that the table display remains intact (i.e., that the number of cells in a row or column equals the number assigned to the table as the whole). In a regular table, cells that contain no content appear "empty" and the border for the table (assuming one exists) seems to fill in and overlay the empty cell. Some Web authors have gotten around this by inserting a non-breaking space ("` `") into the otherwise empty cell, so that it displays an actual cell containing no visible content. The `empty-cells` property is designed to let Web authors automatically specify how empty cells should appear in a given table.

The `empty-cells` property can take any one of three named values: `show`, which displays a full border around the empty cell; `hide`, which does not draw a border around the cell; and `inherit`, which takes whatever parent value has been set for `empty-cells`.

The `show` value is equivalent to adding the non-breaking space character within a table cell, and `hide` is like having a completely empty cell, as displayed in the previous illustration. Using `empty-cells`, Web authors no longer have to "fill in" each empty cell with a non-breaking space in order for the border around the cell to appear. Listing 19.4 shows some code using this property, whose effects can be seen in Figure 19–5.

Listing 19.4	*empty-cells Example*

```
<html>
<head>
<title>empty-cells Example</title>
<style>
td {font-size: xx-large;}
body {font-size: x-large; font-family: verdana}
</style>
</head>
```

Listing 19.4   *empty-cells Example (continued)*

```
<body>
<p>
<div align="center">
The following table has no content in what would be "cell 3"
<code>(empty-cells: hide)</code>:
<table style="empty-cells: hide; width: 50%" border>
<tr>
<td>cell 1</td>
<td>cell 2</td>
</tr>
<tr>
<td></td>
<td>cell 4</td>
</tr>
</table>

The following table has no content in what would be "cell 3"
<code>(empty-cells: show)</code>:
<table style="empty-cells: show; width: 50%" border>
<tr>
<td>cell 1</td>
<td>cell 2</td>
</tr>
<tr>
<td></td>
<td>cell 4</td>
</tr>
</table>
</div>

</div>
</body>
</html>
```

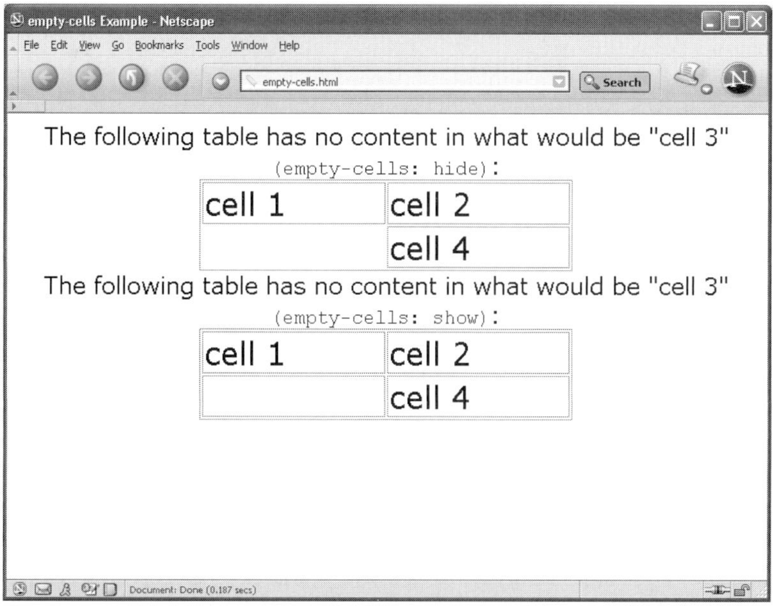

Figure 19–5 The "empty-cell" effect illustrated in Netscape Navigator 7.0.

Browser Compatibility

This CSS2 property is not supported by early browsers.

- Internet Explorer 3.0: Unsafe.
- Internet Explorer 4.0: Unsafe.
- Internet Explorer 4.0 – 4.5 (Mac): Unsafe.
- Internet Explorer 5.0: Unsafe.
- Internet Explorer 4.0 – 4.5 (Mac): Safe.
- Internet Explorer 5.5: Unsafe.
- Internet Explorer 6.0: Unsafe.
- Netscape Navigator 4.0 – 4.79: Unsafe.
- Netscape Navigator 4.0 (Mac & UNIX): Unsafe.
- Netscape Navigator 6.0: Safe.
- Netscape Navigator 7.0: Safe.
- Mozilla 1.0: Safe.
- Opera 3.6: Unsafe.
- Opera 4.0: Safe.
- Opera 5.0 – 6.0: Safe.
- Konqueror: Safe.

The `empty-cells` property is not supported within any version of Internet Explorer.

It is fully supported within Mozilla 1.0 as well as Netscape Navigator 6.0 and up.

It is fully supported in Opera beginning with version 4.0.

Konqueror supports `empty-cells`.

19.4 speak-header Property

The `speak-header` property is actually an aural property specific to the table family. Its job is to speak aloud the headers in a table in the manner prescribed by the Web author. The author can either specify that table headers be read out only once at the beginning of a list of associated cell values, or repeated along with each cell value with which it is associated.

The `speak-header` property can take one of three named values: `once`, in which case the header value is only said aloud one time at the beginning of a list of cell values; `always`, which reads the header value before each associated cell value; and `inherit`, which takes the same value as that set for the property of the parent value set for `speak-header`.

The code standards for this property are not very clear. The W3C (at the time of writing) provides only a single, rather poor example on their Web site using HTML attributes for the `th` element that don't exist. From what I can see, nobody else has been able to figure this one out, and in the absence of any browser that actively makes use of ACCS (Aural Cascading Style Sheet) code, it is hard to put theories to practice. Sensibly, the likely way would be either to set the property to all headers belonging to a table, or to create a class so that only selected headers would be read aloud (which is what the W3C example may be alluding to).

Browser Compatibility

This property depends on Aural Cascading Style Sheets (ACSS) in order to work, and as yet, none of the ACSS properties are supported in the major browsers.

- Internet Explorer 3.0: Unsafe.
- Internet Explorer 4.0: Unsafe.
- Internet Explorer 4.0 – 4.5 (Mac): Unsafe.
- Internet Explorer 5.0: Unsafe.
- Internet Explorer 5.1 – 5.2 (Mac): Unsafe.
- Internet Explorer 5.5: Unsafe.
- Internet Explorer 6.0: Unsafe.
- Netscape Navigator 4.0 – 4.79: Unsafe.

- Netscape Navigator 4.0 (Mac & UNIX): Unsafe.
- Netscape Navigator 6.0: Unsafe.
- Netscape Navigator 7.0: Unsafe.
- Mozilla 1.0: Unsafe.
- Opera 3.6 – 4.0: Unsafe.
- Opera 5.0 – 6.0: Unsafe.
- Konqueror: Unsafe.

For more information on ACCS, see Chapter 21, "Aural Cascading Style Sheets."

19.5 Table-like Layout Using CSS

When most Web authors create tables in their Web pages, they do it in order to better lay out content on their pages, rather than laying out tables of figures or other tabular data. This is where the CSS3 columns module is to come in, but as yet no browser supports those properties, nor is one likely to in the immediate future.

Yet it is possible to do standard columnar layout for a Web page using some relatively safe CSS properties. All of the code in this section displays well in the most recent releases of the major browsers and is relatively safe to use. If your target browsers are capable of doing such things as absolute positioning, basic floats, and using width and margin, you can get away with using these "tables."

One of the chief advantages of using CSS for layout is the compact nature of the code, and the fact that it is very easy to reference. What's more, since loading table structures is a very processor-intensive effort for any browser, you can expect — on average — quicker loading times for your pages.

Two-Column Layout

One of the most common layouts for a Web page is a two-column approach: a narrow column to the left containing links, and a second, wider "body" column where the majority of a page's content resides. Listing 19.5 shows how a page like this might look using regular HTML.

Listing 19.5	*Two-Column Layout Using HTML*

```
<html>
<head>
<title>Basic Two-Column Box Design - Using Tables</title>
</head>
```

Listing 19.5   *Two-Column Layout Using HTML (continued)*

```html
<body>
<table width="780" border="1">
<tr>
<td width="200">
<strong>Left Column</strong><br />
<a href="link1.html">Link 1</a><br />
<a href="link2.html">Link 2</a><br />
<a href="link3.html">Link 3</a>
</td>
<td width="580">
<strong>Body Column</strong><br />
<p>
Here is some basic content designed to fill a 580 pixels wide
"body" box.
</td>
</tr>
</table>
</body>
</html>
```

This same arrangement can also be made using CSS, using the code seen in Listing 19.6.

Listing 19.6   *Similar Two-Column Layout Using CSS*

```html
<html>
<head>
<title>Basic Two-Column Box Design</title>
<style>
#leftcolumn {position:absolute; left:10px; width:200px; border:1px
solid black}
#bodycolumn {margin-left: 199px; margin-right:199px; width:580px;
border:1px solid black; voice-family: "\"}\""; voice-family:
inherit;} html>body #bodycolumn {margin-left: 203px; mar-
gin-right:203px}
p,strong,a {margin:0px 10px 10px 10px}
</style>
</head>
```

Listing 19.6	*Similar Two-Column Layout Using CSS (continued)*

```
<body>
<div id="leftcolumn">
<strong>Left Column</strong><br />
<a href="link1.html">Link 1</a><br />
<a href="link2.html">Link 2</a><br />
<a href="link3.html">Link 3</a>
</div>
<div id="bodycolumn">
<strong>Body Column</strong><br />
<p>
Here is some basic content designed to fill a 580 pixels wide
"body" box. You'll notice that that amount of content contained
within a given box also sets the size of the resulting border
around the box.
</p>
</div>
</body>
</html>
```

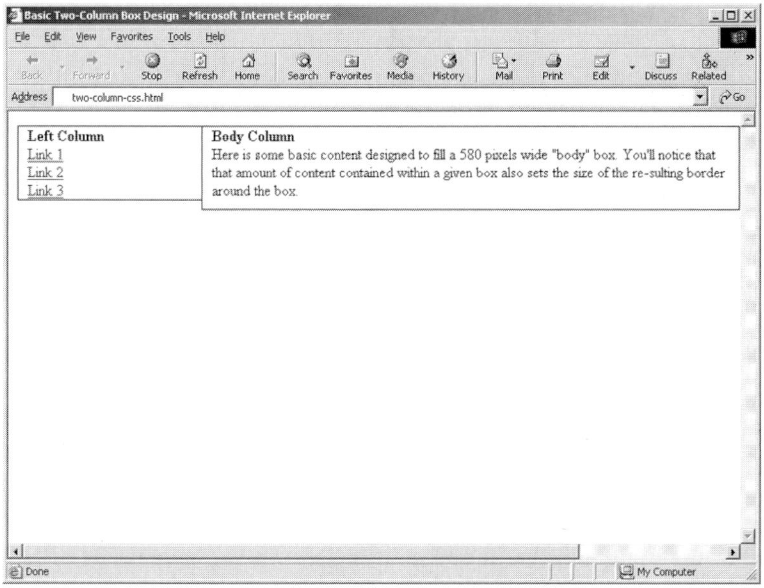

Figure 19–6   Sample two-column layout using CSS.

You can see what the CSS code example looks like in Figure 19–6. (Given the nature of this code, it probably makes more sense to place this in a separate `.css` page that would be referenced using a link element, but for the sake of clarity it is contained within the header of the example code seen in Listing 19.6.)

If you take a look at the code behind this layout, you'll see that the basic concept goes something like this: create a single, absolutely positioned left-hand column set to a given width (200 pixels in this case) and then add a border around it; then create a second column whose margin begins after the absolutely positioned left column, also set to a given width (580 pixels in this case).

But if you take a closer look, you'll see there's some other interesting looking code here — why, for example, are the three pairs of `margin` values here? The extra code is included in order to get around some known bugs in Internet Explorer 5.x. Unfortunately, this browser does not implement the CSS box model correctly, placing such things as padding and borders within its stated width, instead of outside of it. Hence, the first pair of margin values is set to `199px` (so the border values from the left and body columns are overlaid in Internet Explorer 5.0 for the PC).

So why the subsequent `voice-family: "\"}\""; voice-family: inherit;` code? That's because this browser contains a bug when it comes to parsing CSS code that contains `"\"}\""` and will prematurely close the CSS style rule. It is enclosed within a `voice-family` property because it can't do any harm to the layout of the page, and the subsequent `voice-family: inherit` statement ensures that any proper value that may be needed for this property can be inherited from the `body` tag. Browsers that do understand the proper box model move past the original code, and cascading rules ensure that the `margin-left: 203px; margin-right: 203px` values overwrite the original ones there solely for Internet Explorer 5.x for the PC.

This table layout is about as browser-compatible as you can expect for any CSS-based construct. It only works in Internet Explorer 5.0 on up, Netscape Navigator 6.0 and higher, Opera 5.0 and later; of all of these, the one you probably have to beware of the most is Netscape Navigator 4.x, which at the time of writing is still in relatively wide circulation. People using earlier browsers will see two horizontally laid out blocks instead of the intended vertical columns.

Three-Column Layout

This is probably one of the most popular layouts on the Web: a standard three-column arrangement, consisting of a navigation column on the left, a "body" column containing the majority of the page's content and an additional narrow column for placing other items and links. To accomplish this, all that needs to be done is to amend the two-column code from the previous example.

To accomplish this using CSS, take a look at Listing 19.7.

Listing 19.7 *Sample Three-Column CSS Layout*

```
<style>
#leftcolumn {position:absolute; left:10px; width:200px;
bor-der:1px solid black}
#bodycolumn {margin-left: 199px; margin-right:199px; bor-der:1px
solid black; voice-family: "\"}\""; voice-family: inherit;}
html>body #bodycolumn {margin-left: 203px; margin-right:203px}
#rightcolumn {position: absolute; top:15px; right:10px;
width:199px; border:1px solid black;
voice-family: "\"}\""; voice-family: inherit;} html>body #right-
column {width:200px; top:8px}
p,strong,a {margin:0px 10px 10px 10px}
</style>
```

There are two main changes to this code: the width value has been removed from the `#bodycolumn` rule, and a new `#rightcolumn` rule has been added. The `#right-column` rule is also set using `position: absolute` but this time it is set to the right instead of the left. The same browser trick seen in the two-column example is being used here to send one set of values (`top:15px; width:199px;`) to Internet Explorer and another set (`width:200px; top:8px;`) to CSS2-compliant browsers, ensuring broad browser compatibility for the layout.

There are other disadvantages to the CSS columnar approach in addition to browser compatibility — content that is too big for a column (such as setting a `<pre>` value containing text too big to wrap) will overflow the content of the "box."

One of the advantages of this approach is that the code is easily modular: all you have to do is create two different id references for the `#bodycolumn` depending on whether you want a two- or three-column layout, and then simply reference the additional `#rightcolumn` rule if required.

In the future you can expect that the CSS3 module on columns will one day come to prominence over other, alternate ways of laying out CSS columns, but until that day, these examples provide enough help to get any Web author started.

Core Tip

Easily one of the best Web sites that looks at the issue of using CSS to create table-like layout is the "CSS Layout Techniques: for Fun and Profit" page by Eric Costello, which can be found at:
http://www.glish.com/css/.

USER INTERFACE

Topics in This Chapter

- `cursor` Property
- `outline` Property
- `outline-width` Property
- `outline-style` Property
- `outline-color` Property
- `accelerator` Property
- CSS3 Properties
- Mozilla User-Interface-Related Extensions

Chapter 20

The user-interface properties were first introduced under the CSS2 specification. These properties are designed to give Web authors greater control over such things as the display of cursors on screen, and the "focus" outline that appears around such elements as buttons and form fields to indicate that they are selected and ready for input.

There are a total of five properties in the user-interface family of properties:

- `cursor`
- `outline`
- `outline-width`
- `outline-style`
- `outline-color`

Of all of these properties, at the time of writing only the `cursor` property has gained much in the way of support in any of the major browsers.

There is also the `accelerator` CSS extension first incorporated into Internet Explorer 5.0 that neatly falls into the user-interface category.

This chapter also looks at a number of new CSS3 user-interface properties, including the following:

- `resizer`
- `key-equivalent`
- `tab-index`
- `user-input`

- `user-modify`
- `user-select`
- `user-focus`
- `user-focus-key`
- `user-focus-pointer`
- `toggle-group`
- `group-reset`

As these are wholly new properties, none of them are as yet implemented in any major browser, but you can expect them to start appearing in browsers of the near future. Having said that, there are a number of parallel, "placeholder" Mozilla CSS extensions introduced within recent versions of the Mozilla browser as well as Netscape Navigator 6.0+ that are briefly looked at.

20.1 cursor Property

The `cursor` property is used to define the type of cursor to be displayed over a given Web element. The purpose of this property is to draw the attention of the user to the element. It can be applied to any element on a Web page: text, images or any other objects.

There are plenty of values available for the cursor property, enabling Web authors to choose from just about the whole range of cursor types available. There are several cursor values designed to produce very specific cursor types. For example, the `crosshair` value is designed to display a symbol that resembles a "+". The `pointer` value shows a typical "pointing" cursor, which is typically a small, upper-left pointing arrow.

Then there are a number of cursors normally used to indicate that an edge or corner can be moved. These cursor values are `e-resize`, `ne-resize`, `nw-resize`, `n-resize`, `se-resize`, `sw-resize`, `s-resize` and `w-resize`. The letter at the beginning of each of these values designates the cardinal direction of the type of edge or corner cursor to be displayed ("e" for east, "nw" for northwest and so on).

Several cursor values are more dependent on the type of operating system being used. The `move` value should display the type of cursor indicating a Web element can be moved (regardless of whether it can be or not). This type of cursor is commonly displayed as a thick double line, which can be either vertically or horizontally aligned. The `text` value should display the type of cursor that indicates text can be selected. This type of cursor is most typically rendered as an I-bar. The `wait` value should display the type of cursor commonly associated with a computer's "busy-mode" cursor, indicating that the user should be patient while the operation the computer is working on is completed. A good example of this is the standard hourglass cursor. The `help` value should display the type of cursor associated with online help, most typically rendered as either a question mark with pointer or in a separate balloon.

If the `auto` value is used, the browser displays whatever type of cursor would normally be associated with the Web element. Similar to this is the `default` value, which displays the default "pointing" cursor for the browser (most often some form of arrow).

A URL value can also be used with `cursor`, which must point to some sort of cursor resource (presumably a bitmap image of the cursor), which is then loaded by the browser and displayed. The URL value can be cascaded, so that if the first cursor image can't be found, a back-up cursor can be. You can see an example of this in the following code snippet:

```
<h1 style="cursor: url(funkyhand.csr),url(otherhand.cur), text">try
scrolling over this header and see what happens!</h1>
```

It is worth noting that Internet Explorer 6.0 supports this property, but requires that any cursor images be either in a `.cur` or `.ani` (animated cursor) file types.

Finally, there is the `inherit` value, which simply takes on whatever parent value may have already been set for `cursor`.

This may all seem pretty straightforward, but both Microsoft and Netscape added a number of new cursor values in version 6.0 of their respective browsers. Internet Explorer 6.0 supports these additional cursor styles:

- `all-scroll` (produces a up/down/left/right arrow with a dot in the middle, used to indicate the content is scrollable in any direction)
- `col-resize` and `row-resize` (used to indicate that a column or row can be resized, respectively)
- `no-drop` (used to indicate that a dragged object cannot be dropped at the current cursor position)
- `not-allowed` (indicates that the intended action is not allowed)
- `progress` (shows that a background process is running)
- `vertical-text` (indicates that the vertical text is editable)
- `hand` (displays a hand icon; first implemented in version 4).

Netscape Navigator 6.0 also supports a number of custom cursor types, and these are:

- `alias` (shows that a shortcut or alias to some other object is available)
- `cell` (indicates that one or more spreadsheet cells are available)
- `copy` (specifies that the content can be copied)
- `grab` and `grabbing` (the first shows that an object can be "grabbed," and the second shows that it has been "grabbed" and is ready to be moved)

- spinning (used to indicate that a process is going on, but, unlike with "wait", the user interface is still available for use)

Netscape Navigator 6.0 is also supposed to support three other custom cursors — count-down, count-up and count-up-down, indicating that the program is counting down, up, or both in succession, respectively — but they do not appear to work, or have perhaps been discarded in subsequent releases of the browser. It is notable also that the Mozilla browser supports all of the Netscape Navigator-style cursor types — though none of the Internet Explorer types — as well.

Listing 20.1 displays all of the available cursor types that currently work in both browsers.

Listing 20.1	*Valid Cursor Types for Both Major Browsers Used in a Single Web Page*

```
<html>
<head>
<title>cursor Example</title>
<style>
strong {font-family: Arial, Helvetica, sans-serif; font-weight:
bold; font-size: 12px;}
td {font-family: Arial, Helvetica, sans-serif; font-size: 12px}
span {padding: 20px}
</style>
</head>
<p>
<strong>Broadly Adopted Cursor Styles</strong><br/>
<span style="cursor:auto">auto</span>
<span style="cursor:crosshair">crosshair</span>
<span style="cursor:default">default</span>
<span style="cursor:help">help</span>
</p>
<p>
<span style="cursor:move">move</span>
<span style="cursor:text">text</span>
<span style="cursor:wait">wait</span>
<span style="cursor:hand">hand (not supported by NN)</span>
</p>
<p>
<strong>Cursors Types introduced in Internet Explorer
6</strong><br/>
<span style="cursor:all-scroll">all-scroll</span>
<span style="cursor:col-resize">col-resize</span>
<span style="cursor:pointer">pointer</span>
<span style="cursor:progress">progress</span>
</p>
```

Listing 20.1	*Valid Cursor Types for Both Major Browsers Used in a Single Web Page (continued)*

```
<p>
<span style="cursor:no-drop">no-drop</span>
<span style="cursor:not-allowed">not-allowed</span>
<span style="cursor:row-resize">row-resize</span>
<span style="cursor:vertical-text">vertical-text</span>
</p>
<p>
<strong>Directional Cursors (Supported in both IE and
NN)</strong><br/>
<span style="cursor:n-resize">n-resize</span>
<span style="cursor:s-resize">s-resize</span>
<span style="cursor:ne-resize">ne-resize</span>
<span style="cursor:sw-resize">sw-resize</span>
</p>
<p>
<span style="cursor:nw-resize">nw-resize</span>
<span style="cursor:se-resize">se-resize</span>
<span style="cursor:e-resize">e-resize</span>
<span style="cursor:w-resize">w-resize</span>
</p>
<p>
<strong>Extra Cursor Types Supported in Netscape Navigator
6</strong><br/>
<span style="cursor:alias">alias</span>
<span style="cursor:cell">cell</span>
<span style="cursor:copy">copy</span>
<span style="cursor:grab">grab</span>
</p>
<p>
<span style="cursor:grabbing">grabbing</span>
<span style="cursor:pointer">pointer</span>
<span style="cursor:spinning">spinning</span>
</p>
<p>
<strong>Custom Cursors (IE 6 Supports .cur and .ani File
Types)</strong><br/>
<span style="cursor:url(rainbow.cur)">url(rainbow.cur)</span>
<span style="cursor:url(busy.ani)">url(busy.ani)</span>
</p>
</body>
</html>
```

Figure 20–1 illustrates the Listing 20.1 code sample in action, with images of each cursor type attached to each type.

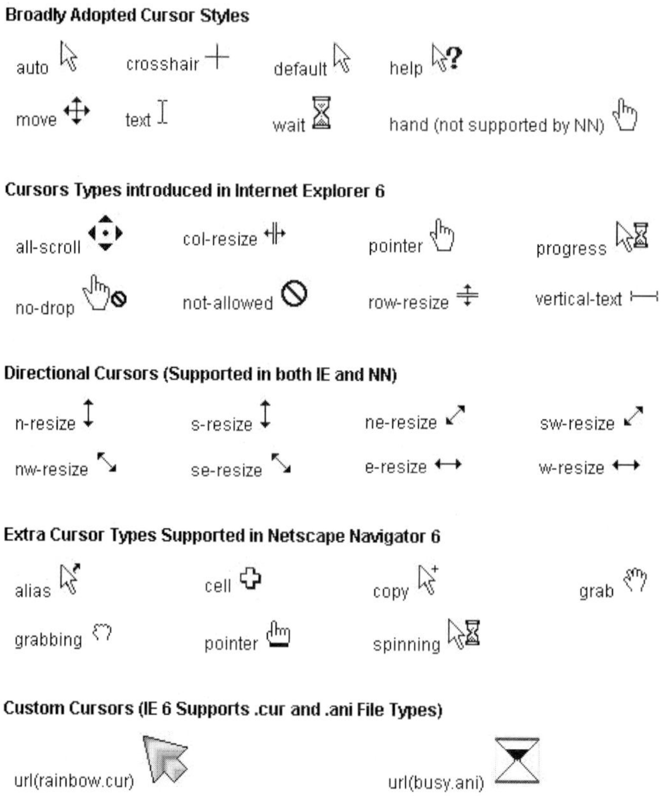

Broadly Adopted Cursor Styles

auto   crosshair   default   help

move   text   wait   hand (not supported by NN)

Cursors Types introduced in Internet Explorer 6

all-scroll   col-resize   pointer   progress

no-drop   not-allowed   row-resize   vertical-text

Directional Cursors (Supported in both IE and NN)

n-resize   s-resize   ne-resize   sw-resize

nw-resize   se-resize   e-resize   w-resize

Extra Cursor Types Supported in Netscape Navigator 6

alias   cell   copy   grab

grabbing   pointer   spinning

Custom Cursors (IE 6 Supports .cur and .ani File Types)

url(rainbow.cur)   url(busy.ani)

Figure 20–1 All usable cursor types displayed under a Windows XP OS.

When using this property, it is important to keep in mind that the type of cursor displayed depends entirely on the operating system of the computer being used by the viewer. The values that have been selected in the CSS2 specification are deliberately generic, though, so you can be assured that your viewers will definitely see something close to your intent.

Browser Compatibility

- Internet Explorer 3.0: Unsafe.
- Internet Explorer 4.0: Unsafe.
- Internet Explorer 4.0 – 4.5 (Mac): Unsafe.
- Internet Explorer 5.0: Unsafe.

- Internet Explorer 5.1 – 5.2 (Mac): Safe.
- Internet Explorer 5.5: Safe.
- Internet Explorer 6.0: Safe.
- Netscape Navigator 4.0 – 4.5: Unsafe.
- Netscape Navigator 4.0 (Mac & UNIX): Unsafe.
- Netscape Navigator 6.0: Safe.
- Netscape Navigator 7.0: Safe.
- Mozilla 1.0: Safe.
- Opera 3.6 – 4.0: Unsafe.
- Opera 5.0 – 6.0: Safe.
- Konqueror: Unsafe.

Internet Explorer only began supporting the `cursor` property beginning with the Macintosh version 5.1, and version 5.5 in Windows.

Netscape Navigator did not support this property in version 4.x, but did starting with version 6.0 (as well as Mozilla 1.0).

Opera started supporting this property beginning with version 5.0.

This property is still unsupported in Konqueror.

cursor and CSS3

It is worth noting that the CSS3 specification tacks on a number of new values for this property. In total, ten further cursor values are added, and they are `copy`, `alias`, `context-menu`, `cell`, `grab`, `grabbing`, `spinning`, `count-up`, `count-down` and `count-up-down`. If some of these seem familiar it is because these are all values supported within recent versions of Netscape Navigator, with the exceptions of `count-up`, `count-down` and `count-up-down` which are recognized by Netscape Navigator but do not seem to currently work. As such, these properties are among the select few CSS3 properties which are already supported, albeit only in recent versions of Netscape Navigator (and Mozilla, from which Netscape Navigator is derived).

20.2 outline Sub-Family of Properties

Under CSS2, it became possible for Web authors to create visual outlines around objects on a Web page, such as buttons, active form fields, imagemaps and other objects, in order to make them stand out to viewers. The sub-family of `outline` properties is designed to add a border to these types of objects. These outlines do not take up any space on the page (in other words, they do not expand the box within which the element is contained), and they can be non-rectangular in shape (which is typical of most imagemaps). This is simply an extension of what is already present in most operating systems, in signaling to the viewer what is known as "focus" (i.e., that a particular element is currently selected). For example, if you are presented with a Web-based form while using a typical MS-Windows computer, you will notice that a cursor will typically appear in the field in which you can currently type, and if you hit the TAB button on your keyboard a few times, you will notice that the cursor jumps to the next field down. If you keep doing this and a button, checkbox or radio button is selected, you will discover that the selected object is usually surrounded by a thin border. This is exactly the type of border that can be explicitly set using the set of `outline` properties.

The sub-family consists of four different properties: `outline-width`, `outline-style`, `outline-color` and the shortcut property `outline`. These properties are meant to be set globally across a Web page, not to a specific element, so these properties should be set within the header of a Web page.

20.3 outline-width Property

The `outline-width` property is used to set a width for the border that appears around an active object. It can take a variety of values, both numeric and named. Its numeric values mirror those that can be set for such properties as `margin` or `border-width`, in that it can take from one to four separate numerical values that set the width of the outline.

The default value is pixels, so if no measurement unit is specified, the value given is assumed to be a pixel value. Having said that, adding a measurement unit after the numeric value at least makes it clear what the numbers are referring to in this case. If multiple values are to be set using other units of measurement, each value, in turn, must be set with a specific unit of measurement — one measurement unit value *does not* automatically apply to all. If a single numerical value is present, all borders are set to that value. If two numerical values are present, the top, bottom and side borders take on those values, respectively. If three values are present, the top, right and left, and then the bottom take the numerical values specified. Finally, if four values are present, the top, right, bottom, then left borders (i.e., clockwise from the top) take the numerical values specified.

When you specify these values, they must all be separated by a space, as can be seen in Listing 20.2.

Listing 20.2 *outline-width Example Using Numerical Values*

```
<html>
<head>
<title>outline-width Example</title>
<style>
input {outline-width: 10px 15px 5px 20px}
</style>
</head>
<body>
The following individual checkboxes should have a solid,
thick-looking "box" appear around them when given focus by the
user:
<p>
<input type="checkbox" name="outline-test" value="One" />One
<input type="checkbox" name="outline-test" value="Two" />Two
<input type="checkbox" name="outline-test" value="Three" />Three
</p>
</body>
</html>
```

`outline-width` can also take a number of named values, such as the following pre-set values: `thin`, `medium` and `thick`. These set relative thickness values for the outline. It is also possible to set a different named value for all four sides of the outline by arranging them like their numeric equivalents, following the same ordering structure, as you can see in Listing 20.3.

Listing 20.3 *outline-width Example Using Name Values*

```
<html>
<head>
<title>outline-width Example 2</title>
<style>
input {outline-width: thin medium thin thick}
</style>
</head>
<body>
The following individual checkboxes should have a solid "box"
(with varying thickness along each of its edges) appear around
them when given focus by the user:
```

Listing 20.3 *outline-width Example Using Name Values (continued)*

```
<p>
<input type="checkbox" name="outline-test" value="One" />One
<input type="checkbox" name="outline-test" value="Two" />Two
<input type="checkbox" name="outline-test" value="Three" />Three
</p>
</body>
</html>
```

`outline-width` can also take the named value `inherit`, which takes the same value as that set for the parent value for `outline-width`, if it has already been set.

Browser Compatibility

- Internet Explorer 3.0: Unsafe.
- Internet Explorer 4.0: Unsafe.
- Internet Explorer 4.0 – 4.5 (Mac): Unsafe.
- Internet Explorer 5.0: Unsafe.
- Internet Explorer 5.1 – 5.2 (Mac): Safe.
- Internet Explorer 5.5: Unsafe.
- Internet Explorer 6.0: Unsafe.
- Netscape Navigator 4.0 – 4.5: Unsafe.
- Netscape Navigator 4.0 (Mac & UNIX): Unsafe.
- Netscape Navigator 6.0: Unsafe.
- Netscape Navigator 7.0: Unsafe.
- Mozilla 1.0: Unsafe.
- Opera 3.6 – 6.0: Unsafe.
- Konqueror: Unsafe.

The only browser which supports this property so far is the Macintosh version of Internet Explorer 5.1 and 5.2.

20.4 outline-style Property

The `outline-style` property sets the type of outline to be displayed around a given object on a Web page. This property accepts the same values as those used for the `border-style` property.

There are a number of 2D and 3D outline types available for `outline-style`. The 2D outlines are created by the values `dashed`, `dotted`, `double` and `solid`, while the 3D outlines are created by the `inset`, `outset`, `groove` and `ridged` values. For the 2D outline types, the `dashed` value displays an outline made up of dashes, the `dotted` value displays an outline made from small dots, the `double` value creates an outline made from a double line, and `solid` displays a solid outline style. For the 3D outline types, `inset` creates an outline that appears recessed, while `outset` creates an outline that appears the opposite of `inset`. `groove` displays a 3D grooved outline, and `ridge` creates a 3D ridged outline. The value `none` ensures that no outline is displayed. The code example seen in Listing 20.4 would display a prominent 3D groove that would appear around whatever button is currently selected on the Web page.

Listing 20.4	*outline-style Used to Implement a Grooved Outline to Input Elements*

```
<html>
<head>
<title>outline-style</title>
<style>
input {outline-style: groove}
</style>
</head>
<body>
The following individual checkboxes should have a solid,
thick-grooved "box" appear around them when given focus by the
user:
<p>
<input type="checkbox" name="outline-test" value="One" />One
<input type="checkbox" name="outline-test" value="Two" />Two
<input type="checkbox" name="outline-test" value="Three" />Three
</p>
</body>
</html>
```

`outline-style` can also take the named value `inherit`, which takes the same value as that set for the parent value for `outline-style`, if it has already been set.

Browser Compatibility

- Internet Explorer 3.0: Unsafe.
- Internet Explorer 4.0: Unsafe.
- Internet Explorer 4.0 – 4.5 (Mac): Unsafe.
- Internet Explorer 5.0: Unsafe.
- Internet Explorer 5.1 – 5.2 (Mac): Safe.
- Internet Explorer 5.5: Unsafe.
- Internet Explorer 6.0: Unsafe.
- Netscape Navigator 4.0 – 4.5: Unsafe.
- Netscape Navigator 4.0 (Mac & UNIX): Unsafe.
- Netscape Navigator 6.0: Unsafe.
- Netscape Navigator 7.0: Unsafe.
- Mozilla 1.0: Unsafe.
- Opera 3.6 – 6.0: Unsafe.
- Konqueror: Unsafe.

The only browser which supports this property so far is the Macintosh version of Internet Explorer 5.1 and 5.2.

20.5 outline-color Property

The `outline-color` property sets the color for the outline to be displayed around a given object on a Web page that can currently accept input from the user. This property accepts the same values as those used for the `border-color` property.

The `outline-color` property, like all other color CSS properties, allows Web authors to set a color value in a variety of ways. For example, it can take a standard color name (such as "`yellow`") or a hexadecimal color value (such as "#ffff00", which also produces yellow), both of which are standard ways of setting color values in HTML. In CSS, you can also specify color using a "compressed" hexadecimal color value (such as "#00f", which is blue). You can also use a three-digit RGB ("Red Green Blue") color value (where `rgb[0,255,0]` is green), and a three-digit RGB percentage color value (where `rgb[100%,100%,100%]` is white). (For more information on these latter ways of specifying color, please see the "Color Formats" section in the CSS Units chapter).

Listing 20.5 shows how you could set a thick green border color for the selected buttons on a Web page.

Listing 20.5	*outline-color Used to Set a Thick Green Border Color for Input*

```
<html>
<head>
<title>outline-color</title>
<style>
input {outline-color: green; outline-width: thick}
</style>
</head>
<body>
The following individual checkboxes should have a solid, thick
green "box" appear around them when given focus by the user:
<p>
<input type="checkbox" name="outline-test" value="One" />One
<input type="checkbox" name="outline-test" value="Two" />Two
<input type="checkbox" name="outline-test" value="Three" />Three
</p>
</body>
</html>
```

outline-color can also take the named value invert, which uses the color opposite the one currently used by the background. So, if the background is white, a black
outline will be displayed. This is a fairly common programmer's trick, designed to
ensure that the outline will always be visible no matter what the circumstance.

outline-color can also take the named value inherit, which takes the same
value as that set for the parent value for outline-color, if it has already been set.

Browser Compatibility

- Internet Explorer 3.0: Unsafe.
- Internet Explorer 4.0: Unsafe.
- Internet Explorer 4.0 – 4.5 (Mac): Unsafe.
- Internet Explorer 5.0: Unsafe.
- Internet Explorer 5.1 – 5.2 (Mac): Safe.
- Internet Explorer 5.5: Unsafe.
- Internet Explorer 6.0: Unsafe.
- Netscape Navigator 4.0 – 4.5: Unsafe.
- Netscape Navigator 4.0 (Mac & UNIX): Unsafe.
- Netscape Navigator 6.0: Unsafe.
- Netscape Navigator 7.0: Unsafe.
- Mozilla 1.0: Unsafe.
- Opera 3.6 – 6.0: Unsafe.
- Konqueror: Unsafe.

The only browser which supports this property so far is the Macintosh version of Internet Explorer 5.1 and 5.2.

20.6 outline Property

The outline property is a "shortcut" property that allows Web authors to set all of the properties normally reserved for the other outline sub-family of properties. In this fashion, it is modeled on another shortcut property, border.

Using outline, you can use all of the border styles you could normally set through the outline-style property, set the width normally reserved for the outline-width property, and determine the color normally reserved for the outline-color property (see these properties for a full explanation of the relevant values). Using outline, it is possible to set all of the outline values for the selected elements on a Web page quickly and easily, as Listing 20.6 shows, combining values found in the outline-style, outline-width and outline-color.

Listing 20.6 *outline as a "Shortcut" Property*

```
<html>
<head>
<title>outline</title>
<style>
input {outline: thick red groove}
</style>
</head>
<body>
The following individual checkboxes should have a solid, thick red
and grooved "box" appear around them when given focus by the user:
<p>
<input type="checkbox" name="outline-test" value="One" />One
<input type="checkbox" name="outline-test" value="Two" />Two
<input type="checkbox" name="outline-test" value="Three" />Three
</p>
</body>
</html>
```

Browser Compatibility

- Internet Explorer 3.0: Unsafe.
- Internet Explorer 4.0: Unsafe.
- Internet Explorer 4.0 – 4.5 (Mac): Unsafe.

- Internet Explorer 5.0: Unsafe.
- Internet Explorer 5.1 – 5.2 (Mac): Safe.
- Internet Explorer 5.5: Unsafe.
- Internet Explorer 6.0: Unsafe.
- Netscape Navigator 4.0 – 4.5: Unsafe.
- Netscape Navigator 4.0 (Mac & UNIX): Unsafe.
- Netscape Navigator 6.0: Unsafe.
- Netscape Navigator 7.0: Unsafe.
- Mozilla 1.0: Unsafe.
- Opera 3.6 – 6.0: Unsafe.
- Konqueror: Unsafe.

The only browser which supports this property so far is the Macintosh version of Internet Explorer 5.1 and 5.2.

20.7 accelerator Property

The `accelerator` property is a browser-specific extension available within Internet Explorer, and it enables Web authors to turn off the underlines under "accelerated" items. An accelerator is the keyboard shortcut that activates a particular feature, for example, in Word, ALT + F activates the File menu. The word "File" in this case has an underlined letter "F," showing the user that this is the key that, combined with holding the ALT key, will activate the feature. The `accelerator` property allows the Web author to turn this feature "on" or "off."

Accordingly, the `accelerator` property has two values: `true` and `false`. For reasons that should be obvious, it makes the most sense to combine this with the underline HTML element (though keep in mind that this is a deprecated element). It must also be used in conjunction with the label element in order to tell the browser that the underlined element is selectable. Listing 20.7 shows how this property could be effectively used.

Listing 20.7	Web Page Incorporating the accelerator Property

```
<html>
<head>
<title>accelerator Property Example</title>
<style>
u {accelerator: true}
body {font-size: large; font-family: Arial, Helvetica, sans-serif}
</style>
```

Listing 20.7	Web Page Incorporating the accelerator Property (continued)

```
</head>
<body>
When you hit the ALT key, underlines will appear underneath the
"F" under "First Name" and the "L" under "Last Name".
<p>
<ul>
<li>Hitting ALT+F simultaneously will move focus automatically to
the First Name input text field.</li>
<li>Hitting ALT+L simultaneously will move focus automatically to
the Last Name input text field.</li>
</ul>
</p>
<form action="goes-nowhere.php" method="post" name="erewhon">
<label id="fname"><u>F</u>irst Name: </label><input type="text"
accesskey="f" name="fname" size="10" max-length="15" />
<label id="lname"><u>L</u>ast Name: </label><input type="text"
accesskey="l" name="lname" size="15" max-length="25" />
</form>
</body>
</html>
```

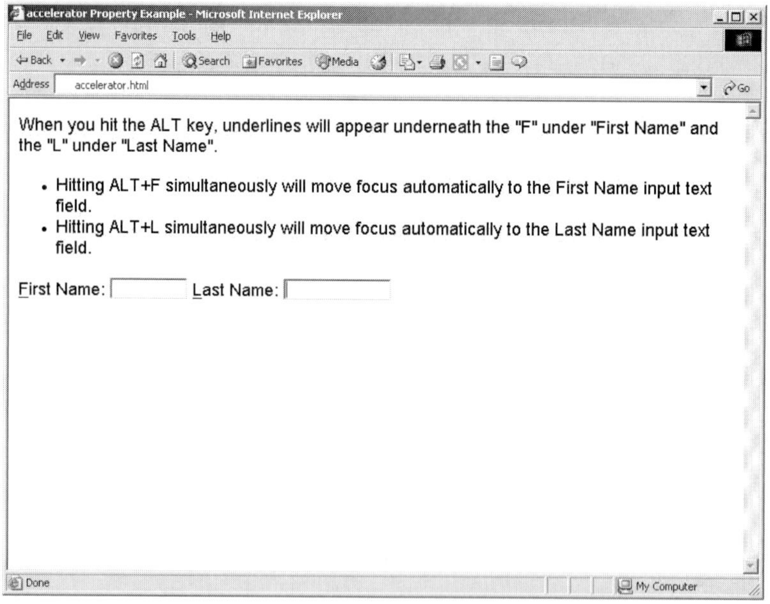

Figure 20–2   The accelerator code example as seen within Internet Explorer 6.0, as the user hits ALT + L (note the cursor appearing in the Last Name text field).

You can see how this is displayed in Figure 20–2, which shows the code example displayed within Internet Explorer 6.0 when a user has hit the ALT + L key. As you can see, the cursor appears in the "Last Name" text field.

Browser Compatibility

The `accelerator` property is supported solely within versions of Internet Explorer 5.5 on up. It is not supported within any other browser. Having said that, it appears to be a relatively harmless enhancement, as it is unlikely to interfere with functionality when the page is viewed in other browsers (while the sample code did not work on the other browsers listed here, neither did it appear to cause any problems). However, unless you tell the user about this feature, it is unlikely that a user will find it (they would have to accidentally hit the ALT key to discover it otherwise).

20.8 CSS3 Properties

When it came to the user-interface properties, the CSS3 specification aimed at trying to pick up where things had been left in the CSS2 specification and extend them further, with the aim of giving Web authors much more control over the user-interface "experience." In particular they give the Web author finer control over the behavior of non-scrollable elements, how form-related elements can be selected via a keyboard, which properties can and cannot be selected (or copied, or read) and more.

20.9 resizer Property

With the advent of being able to set specific widths and heights to elements on a Web page, there are situations where a user might find that a given non-scrollable element in fact obstructs the view of other elements on a Web page. The `resizer` property exists to allow — or disallow — viewers from resizing a specific element. Strictly speaking, this property is designed to be set to a root `<html>` element on a Web page, though it can be set on any element that may contain scrollbars.

The `resizer` property has size attributes: `auto`, `both`, `horizontal`, `vertical`, `none` and `inherit`. The `auto` value is whatever the default behavior for that particular element is. The `both` value allows for bidirectional (i.e., both horizontal and vertical) resizing of the element. The `horizontal` value only allows for horizontal resizing of the element, and the `vertical` value allows for only vertical resizing. The `none` value does not permit the viewer under any circumstances to resize the element, and finally the `inherit` value takes on whatever inheritable values may be present.

The following code snippet shows how this property might be utilized against the root `html` element, as well as a `div` element:

```
<style>
html {width: 400px; height: 400px; overflow: clip; resizer: none}
div {width: 200px; height: 50px; overflow: scroll; resizer:
vertical}
</style>
```

In this case what you would get would be a Web page that would be "box" 400 pixels in width and height that is not resizable by the user. Any `div` elements contained within this page would be 200 pixels wide, 50 pixels in height and could be vertically resized to display its full content.

20.10 key-equivalent Property

The `key-equivalent` property is designed to be a CSS equivalent to the `accesskey` attribute found on certain HTML 4.0 tags. This attribute, which is available to the `<input>` and `<anchor>` tags, allows the Web author to assign a specific keyboard key value so that when that key is pressed by the user, that particular link or input on a form is selected, and can then be used. The `key-equivalent` property goes further than that, giving the Web author the ability to specify which key or key combination triggers a particular event on a Web page.

This property can take one of four sets of values: `none`, a `<key-press-combination>`, a `<system-key-equivalent>` and `inherit`. The `none` value ensures that no key equivalent is set for a given element, and the `inherit` value sets a key equivalent value to whatever inheritable value may be present.

The interesting values here are the `<key-press-combination>` and `<system-key-equivalent>`. The `<key-press-combination>` takes a bunch of space-separated values representing valid keystrokes that can initiate focus (or some other event) set to an element. In this way it works very much the way in which font families are listed using the `fontfamily` property. If you want to indicate a key combination instead of a single key, the individual keys are joined together by dashes ("-"). The following code snippet shows how various keys can signal an "exit" from a particular function:

```
input.end {key-equivalent: esc ctrl-x brk cmd-.}
```

In this case the Escape key, Control + X, the Break key and Command when pressed will all tell the browser to activate `input.end`. Note that while in the example everything is rendered in lowercase text, this property is not case-sensitive. This means that "x" and "X" are equivalent — "x" does not equal "shift-x".

The `<system-key-equivalent>` is available so that Web authors can easily utilize system keys that certain operating systems use. An equivalent `<system-key-equiva-lent>` example for the previous code sample could look like this:

```
input.end {key-equivalent: system-cancel}
```

In this case it is up to the browser manufacturer to determine which key on a given operating system (if any) is equivalent to the `system-cancel` value assigned.

20.11 tab-index Property

The `tab-index` property is designed to be a direct replacement for the HTML 4 attribute `tabindex`. It works in the same fashion as the old HTML 4 attribute, speci-fying the position of the tabbing order for elements on a page (i.e., which element is selected first, second, third and so on at each press of the TAB key).

This property can take one of three values: `none`, a numeric value and `inherit`. The `none` value ensures that an element is not selectable via tabbing, and the `inherit` value sets whatever inheritable value may be present for an element. The numeric value runs down from the highest value of "1," so any element assigned with this value will automatically be selected first when the TAB key is hit. Subsequent numerical values (i.e., 2, 3, 4, etc.) will be selected next in sequence. Any remaining selectable elements not assigned a value are then selected next. The following code snippet shows how this property could work:

```
Address: <input type="text" name="address" style="tab-index: 3"
size="20" maxlength="35" /><br/>
First Name: <input type="text" name="fname" style="tab-index: 1"
size="10" maxlength="15" /><br/>
Last Name: <input type="text" name="lname" style="tab-index: 2"
size="20" maxlength="25" /><br/>
City:  <input type="text" name="city" size="10" maxlength="15"
/><br/>
<input type="reset" style="tab-index: none" value="Reset" />
<input type="submit" value="Submit" />
```

In this case, when the user hits the TAB key, it will first go to the First Name text field, rather than to the Address field (which is what would happen if `tab-index` were not present). Subsequent tabbing would then focus on the Last Name field (with `tab-index` value of "2") and then Address (with `tab-index` value of "3"), then City, then Submit, neither of which have a `tab-index` value explicitly set, so they are selected because they are next in sequence. The Reset button with a `tab-index` value of "`none`" would not be selectable via tabbing.

20.12 user-input Property

The user-input property is designed to allow a Web author to specify whether a given user-interface element can accept input from the user. The principle reason for having such a property is to selectively enable or disable inputs interactively. For example, say you have a form where you are seeking the user's address. If the user lives in a city, you might want to disable a rural route setting. If the user lives in a house, you might want to disable a post office box field or an apartment box field selectively — and the user-input property will enable you to do these things when used in a program.

The user-input property can take one of four values: none, enabled, disabled and inherit. The none value ensures that an element is not available for user input, and the inherit value sets whatever inheritable value may be present. The enabled value allows for user input on an element, and disabled does the opposite. The following code snippet shows how this could be put to use:

```
<style>
input.enable {user-input: enabled}
input.disable {user-input: disabled}
</style>
```

The idea would be to add programming code that could selectively enable and disable individual input elements on the page using these lines of CSS3 code. One other thing worth noting about this property is that it is not allowed to be combined with the :enabled or :disabled pseudo-classes, since this could allow for having an enabled or disabled pseudo-class — an event that would be likely to crash any self-respecting browser.

20.13 user-modify Property

The user-modify property is designed to allow Web authors to set which fields in a form can and cannot be modified by the user. At first this may seem like an odd concept, but it allows for fields which can be "pre-filled" programmatically that can be seen by the user but not changed. This differs from a setting like user-input disabled in that the user can select a form element and copy its contents if necessary.

This property takes one of four values: read-only, read-write, write-only and the ubiquitous inherit. The read-only value allows the user to see but not change anything, read-write (which would be the default) gives the user full control over adding or changing input. The write-only value is an incongruous setting, which only allows the user to select and edit the contents, but not see what they are or copy them out. This would probably behave in much the same way as current password fields do (each character typed in is displayed as an asterisk or an equivalent character) though one has to wonder how a person could effectively "edit" such a field, except by removing its contents and re-writing them.

The following code snippet shows how this property could be put to use:

```
<style>
input.read-only {user-modify: read-only}
input.regular {user-modify: read-write}
</style>
```

As with user-input, again the idea would be to add programming code to selectively "enable" (i.e., user-modify: read-write) and "disable" (i.e., user-modify: read-only) individual input elements on the page with this CSS3 code.

20.14 user-select Property

The user-select property is designed to allow Web authors to determine which elements on an Web page are "selectable." For example, using this property it would theoretically be possible to enable the text on buttons to be selected and copied (by default, most browsers do not allow this). The purpose of this property is to allow the Web author to explicitly set these types of conditions to elements on a Web page.

This property can take one of seven values: none, text, toggle, element, elements, all and inherit. The none value ensures that an element is not selectable, text specifies that only the text contained by an element is selectable and toggle allows the content selectability to be switched "on" or "off." The element value only allows one element at a time to be selected, whereas elements allows for multiple element selection (i.e., by holding down the Control key while selecting individual elements). The all value allows the element to be wholly selectable by a user. The inherit value takes on any existing parent value that may have been previously set.

Perhaps the most important value of these is none, as it is a key value that enables various user elements to function properly. When you click a button, you do not want to inadvertently select any text it may contain (though a setting of user-select: text would make this possible), as that element would continue to be selected unless you explicitly click (or tab) to the next element.

The following code snippet shows how this might be used:

```
<style>
input.no-select {user-select: none}
input.text {user-select: text}
</style>
```

20.15 user-focus, user-focus-key and user-focus-pointer Properties

The `user-focus` set of properties all give the Web author greater control over what can happen to an element when it is has been given focus by the user. The `user-focus-key` property is there to determine what happens to an element when a user specifically clicks on it using their mouse, and `user-focus-pointer` determines what happens to a given element when a user "tabs" over to it. The `user-focus` property acts as a shortcut property, incorporating all of the functions of `user-focus-key` and `user-focus-pointer`.

They all share the following eight properties: `auto`, `normal`, `select-all`, `select-before`, `select-after`, `select-same`, `select-menu` and `inherit`. The `auto` value is whatever the default value is for a given element, and `inherit` takes on whatever parent value may be present. The `normal` value means that when an element acquires focus, it does nothing else. When `select-all` is used, the whole of an element's contents are selected (this could be text within a text field for example). When an element is selected that uses `select-before`, the cursor appears at the beginning of the contents of that element, and when an element uses `select-after`, the cursor appears at the end of the contents of that element (again, think in terms of a text field to get an idea as to why these values would be used). When `select-same` is used, whatever element last had focus is given focus again. The following code snippet shows how these might be put to use:

```
<style>
input.focus-text {user-focus: select-before}
input.focus-number {user-focus: select-after}
</style>
```

Presumably you would be able to set the tabbing behavior for an element to be different than when it is simply pointed at, though there are no occasions I can think of where this would be truly useful. This is the likely reason for the `user-focus` shortcut property, which would set the same value to an element no matter whether it was tabbed to or pointed to.

20.16 toggle-group and group-reset Properties

Both the `toggle-group` and `group-reset` properties are related in function, where `toggle-group` defines a set of toggle controls (such as radio buttons) and the `group-reset` property serves as a "reset" function for a specified group or groups of toggle controls.

Both properties take pretty much the same values: a name identifying the group (or groups, with `group-reset`) of toggles, `none` and `inherit`. The `none` value means that a toggle group is not explicitly identified as such and `inherit` takes on whatever parent value may be present. The identifying value is what makes these two properties "tick"; with `toggle-group` it is used to give a name to a bunch of toggles, and with `group-reset` it serves to identify which toggle group or groups of toggles are to be reset. The following code snippet (derived from the W3C original) shows how these two properties might work to style three sets of radio button toggles:

```
<style>
.radiogroup1 {group-reset: group-a}
.radiobutton {toggle-group: group-a; display: inline-block;
white-space: nowrap; cursor: auto; user-input: enabled;
user-modify: read-only; user-select: toggle; user-focus: normal}
.radiobutton:before {content: radio}
</style>
```

Both of these properties respond to cascading rules in the same manner as the `counter-reset` and `counter-increment` properties.

20.17 Mozilla User-Interface-Related Extensions

While none of the CSS3 properties covered in this section are supported in any of the major browsers, it is interesting to note that since Netscape Navigator 6.0, *some* of these properties have received limited support, albeit in a browser-specific manner.

Unlike the CSS extensions Microsoft has added to versions of Internet Explorer, the Netscape-specific extensions are meant as "placeholders" — extensions the developers have thrown in, presumably in an attempt to build-in features in anticipation of a finalized CSS3 specification. All of these extensions come with the prefix "moz" (named after the "Mozilla" browser the 6.x and greater versions of Netscape Navigator are built upon), followed by the name of a draft CSS3 property — or something close to it.

In the user-interface category, these Mozilla extensions are:

- `-moz-resizer` (resizer)
- `-moz-key-equivalent` (key-equivalent)
- `-moz-user-input` (user-input)

- `-moz-user-modify (user-modify)`
- `-moz-user-select (user-select)`
- `-moz-user-focus (user-focus)`
- `-moz-outline-radius`
- `-moz-outline-radius-topleft`
- `-moz-outline-radius-top-right`
- `-moz-outline-radius-bottom-left`
- `-moz-outline-radius-bottom-right`

All but the last five properties have direct equivalents in the CSS3 specification.

None of these properties are documented in Netscape, so they don't "officially" exist. There is also no guarantee a property introduced in one version of Netscape Navigator or Mozilla will be present in subsequent releases. So for these reasons it is not recommended that you use these properties extensively, but they are certainly useful to "play" with, if only to get a feel for how future CSS3 properties might be implemented. Try using the sample code from the CSS3 section, try putting "`-moz`" before them and see what happens — and keep in mind that there's *no* guarantee that things will work the way you expect, if they work at all.

The following looks at some of the key differences between the Mozilla user-interface property that have close CSS3 equivalents:

- `-moz-resizer` — no *apparent* differences in values from CSS3 equivalent
- `-moz-key-equivalent` — no *apparent* differences in values from CSS3 equivalent
- `-moz-user-input` — exactly the same as in CSS3 specification
- `-moz-user-modify` — exactly the same as in CSS3 specification
- `-moz-user-select` — incorporates all of the CSS3 values and includes two new values, `tri-state` and `-moz-all`, the former of which is presumably for a toggle with three states (instead of the usual two) and the latter appears to be equivalent to "`all`"
- `-moz-user-focus` — may not incorporate full set of CSS3 values, and includes one new value, `ignore`, which presumably would work the same way as `none`, or perhaps override the existing behavior

Perhaps the most interesting of the Mozilla user-interface extensions is the `-moz-outline-radius` set of properties. They appear to let Web authors set rounded — as opposed to square — outlines around elements, by means of controlling the "roundedness" values for the corners. There are four properties that control the roundedness value for each of the corners for an outlined element, and running in clockwise order they are `-moz-outline-radius-top-left`, `-moz-outline-radius-top-right`, `-moz-outline-radius-bottom-left` and `-moz-outline-radius-bottom-right`. The `-moz-outline-radius` property is a shortcut property which can easily control the roundedness values for all four corners at once. They can all take a simple numeric size value, a percentage value (percentage of what exactly is not known) and an `inherit` value. It behaves like most properties it is akin to: one numeric value will control the roundedness of all four corners, two values will control the top-left and bottom-right, and the top-right and bottom-left values, respectively, and four separate values will control each corner in a clockwise fashion from top-right.

It is worth noting that there is a parallel `-moz-border-radius` set of properties, which appears to work in exactly the same way. I say "appears" because at the moment this is theoretical — at the time of writing I could not get these properties to display any functional differences, but this may change in later builds of Mozilla and Netscape. (Remember what I said earlier about these being "placeholder" properties.)

20.18 CSS3 Additions to Existing User-Interface Properties

The CSS3 specification also adds a bunch of new values to existing properties, such as `color`, `font`, `box-sizing`, `display`, `inline-block`, `content` and `list-style-type`. The CSS3 additions to these properties are covered in their respective sections in this book.

AURAL CASCADING STYLE SHEETS

Topics in This Chapter

- speak Property
- volume Property
- pause, pause-before and pause-after Properties
- cue, cue-before and cue-after Properties
- play-during Property
- azimuth Property
- elevation Property
- speech-rate Property
- voice-family Property
- pitch and pitch-range Properties
- stress Property
- richness Property
- speak-punctuation and speak-numeral Properties

Chapter

One of the most significant innovations instituted in the CSS2 specification is the introduction of aural style sheets. With aural style sheets, you can now set the way a Web page should sound. More specifically, aural style sheet properties are designed to tell the Web browser how it should read aloud the text on a Web page. Using the various aural style sheet properties available under CSS2, Web masters can set the type of voice to be played, where the sound should be placed within the stereo sound field, set pauses and cues, add sound effects, move the sound around in the sound-scape and even determine whether the voice should be female or male. Using the aural style sheet properties (also known as "ACSS"), you can easily make the Web browser your stage and your text the players upon it.

There are nineteen aural style sheet properties in the CSS2 specification, all of which are discussed in the following sections. The intent of these properties is to turn your ordinary browser into a "talking browser," allowing the "viewer" to hear the textual content of a Web page. This frees the user from having to necessarily be in front of a computer screen when surfing the Web, for example. Talking browsers offer future Web users the possibility of surfing from just about anywhere. A "Web-Walkman" may appear in the not-too-distant future. "Talking browsers" are also designed to aid the visually impaired, opening up the Web to a wider range of potential surfers.

Whenever you are using sound of any sort, you should remember that not all computers are equipped with sound cards, so it is important for Web authors not to rely upon spoken cues to get the point of a Web page across to the viewer. Having said that, it is likely that these aural style sheet properties will not adversely affect the function of the Web page for those Web browsers not equipped for sound — so in other words, play with these properties and try them out!

At the time of writing, none of these properties are implemented in any *major* browser. However, there is at least one browser that does: Emacspeak, a freely available browser available only for the Linux operating system (downloadable from http://emacspeak.sourceforge.net/). As support for the CSS2 increases, expect other browsers to incorporate aural cascading style sheet properties. It's also worth noting that there are voice synthesizers capable of reading the content of a Web page, and that they may not necessarily interpret your aural style sheet code.

21.1 speak Property

The speak property is used to set those parts of the Web page whose text is to be spoken aloud by the browser. If you want the content of your pages to be spoken aloud, you need to use this property. (This is only true of any browser that is ACSS compatible — there are many voice synthesizers which may read the content of a Web page and completely ignore the ACCS code underlying it.)

This particular property can be used to tell the browser not only what parts to speak, but also how it should speak them.

The speak property has four separate named values: none, normal, spell-out and inherit. The value none does what you would expect — it tells the browser not to speak aloud the selected part of the Web site. You would use the none property for those sections of a Web page — for whatever reason — you would not want to have read aloud. An ideal way of using this value would be in conjunction with the <div> tag, making it easy to set up distinct areas of the Web page text that are "silent." The normal value is the default browser-speak setting, which should be a normal speaking voice. The spell-out value is to be used in those situations where you want to spell out the individual letters that comprise a word. This is particularly useful for such acronyms as "U.S.," which might otherwise be rendered aloud by the browser as "us." It could also be used to deliberately spell out the letters in a word for any another reason, as the following Web code example displays.

The fourth property, inherit, takes on whatever the parent value is set to for the speak property. For example, if the example code in Listing 21.1 did not explicitly close off the spell-out value, inherit could be used in a subsequent paragraph to return the following text that is read aloud back to the parent speak:normal setting embedded in the <body> element.

Listing 21.1	*speak Example*

```
<html>
<head>
<title>Speak Example</title>
</head>
<body>
<p style="speak: normal">
<img src="mom.gif" />
Don't tell our daughter that she's about to have a <em
style="speak:spell-out">bath</em>.
<img src="dad.gif" />
</p>
</body>
</html>
```

21.2 volume Property

The volume property behaves much like the "volume" knob on your radio or television — it regulates the "loudness" level of the sound being played back. The aural style sheet volume property is designed to control the sound level of the speech being played over the computer's speakers. It is a very versatile property, giving Web authors complete control over sound level.

The volume property can take a wide range of values, covering the complete spectrum from near-quiet to deafening loudness. It can take a numeric value that ranges from "0" to "100," where "0" is equivalent to near-silence, and "100" is the loudest possible sound the Web browser can produce. The volume property can also take a percentage value, where a value of "0%" is the same as near-silence (or "0"), and "100%" is full volume (or "100" in numerical terms).

You may ask yourself why the value "0" is equivalent to "near-quiet" instead of complete silence. This is because the CSS2 specification does not set the value of "0" to equal no sound at all — it merely means the lowest possible audible setting available that still produces sound. Instead, there is a named value, called silent, which takes care of that.

Table 21.1 lists the six named properties for volume that correspond to preset volume levels: silent, x-soft, soft, medium, loud and x-loud. These values work in very much the same way the xx-small to xx-large values work with the font-size property, providing a range of set values applied to the sound level produced by the browser when reading the page aloud. The silent value is equivalent to no sound at all — for reasons already discussed, the value of silent is in fact "lower" than the value "0". x-soft is the equivalent to a very low volume level, and it is this sound level that is equivalent to the numerical value "0." soft is a low volume level equivalent to the numerical value "25." medium is a medium volume level which is the same as the numerical value "50." Note that the medium level means that it is exactly half as loud a sound as the Web browser is able to produce. The loud value is equivalent to the numerical value "75," and, finally, x-loud is the loudest sound volume level possible, equivalent to the numerical value "100." The following table lays out the numerical equivalent for the name sound values:

Table 21.1   *volume Example*

Name Value	*Equivalent Numeric Value*
silent	0 (or simply equivalent to no sound at all)
x-soft	0
soft	25
medium	50
loud	75
x-loud	100

volume can also take the named value inherit, which in this case means that the text takes on whatever the parent sound level is set to. Volume, when applied to speech, is a highly variable thing. The actual sound level in speech always varies (unless the voice is speaking in a monotone).

In any speech, there will be peaks and valleys, which can be used for emphasis by the speaker. The specification takes this into account, and allows for some latitude in the interpretation of these values by the browser. Keep in mind also that there could also be differences in the actual sound level produced by different browsers on different computers. A value of "50" may not necessarily be equivalent to the same value on a different computer — especially since most computers that have sound cards often have different sound levels set by their users. If and when this particular CSS2 property is widely implemented by the major browsers, keep in mind that what may seem like a medium sound level to you may be loud on a different system. This is still a very useful property for setting the emphasis of the speaking voice. Listing 21.2 provides an example of this.

Listing 21.2 *volume Example*

```
<html>
<head>
<title>volume Example</title>
</head>
<body>
<p style="volume:medium">
I'm the big gruff bear.
</p>
<img src="bear.gif" />
<strong style="volume:loud">Roar!</strong>
</body>
</html>
```

21.3 Pause Sub-Set of Properties

The sub-set of pause-related properties is designed to stop speech briefly immediately before or after a specific Web element, lending emphasis to the sentence being spoken by the Web browser. There are three properties in this sub-set: pause-before, pause-after and pause. The pause-before property is designed to stop speech briefly *before* a specific Web element, and the pause-after property does the same, but instead stops speech immediately *after* a given Web element. The pause property is a shortcut property that enables Web authors to simply set a pause before and/or after a given Web element.

This particular set of aural sub-properties is meant to let Web authors better imitate the natural rhythm of human speech, and to lend further emphasis to the text being read by the browser.

All three properties can take any of three different values: a numerical value representing the time of the pause, a percentage value set relative to the rate at which the text is being read, and the ubiquitous CSS2 named value inherit.

The most straightforward setting for this is the numeric time value you can set with these properties. Simply set a numerical value, and then set whether or not this value should be expressed in milliseconds (ms) or seconds (s). In order to set a half-second pause value, you would use a value of 500 milliseconds (1,000 milliseconds go into 1 second), or you can simply state it as a decimal fraction of a second. Listings 21.3 and 21.4 show how you can use a numeric value with the pause-before and pause-after properties:

| Listing 21.3 | *Pause Properties Example 1* |

```
<html>
<head>
<title>pause-before Example</title>
</head>
<body style="speak:normal">
Need a dramatic pause?
<p style="pause-before:50ms">You just got one</p>
</body>
</html>
```

| Listing 21.4 | *Pause Properties Example 2* |

```
<html>
<head>
<title>pause Example</title>
</head>
<body style="speak:normal">
<p>
The title of this play is:
</p>
<h1 style="pause:1s 2s">The Tempest</h1>
<p>
by William Shakespeare
</p>
</body>
</html>
```

In this example, a one-second pause is inserted immediately before and after the text in the header (*The Tempest*) is read aloud. With the `pause-before` example, a half-second pause is associated with the paragraph tag ("`<p>`"), so the pause occurs immediately before the presence of the tag. With the `pause-after` example, a half-second pause appears at the close of the paragraph tag it is associated with ("`</p>`"). Things are slightly different with the `pause` property. It can take two separate numeric values. If two values are specified, the first pause value is applied before the Web element, and the second value is applied after; so in Listing 21.4, there is a 1-second pause before *The Tempest* is spoken aloud, and a 2-second pause is inserted after it. If only one value is specified (as in Listing 21.5), the `pause` value is applied both before *and* after the Web element.

The pause properties can also take a percentage value, which relates to the speed at which the text is being read aloud by the browser. This value is set in relation to the `speech-rate` property (covered later in this chapter), or the default value for it used by the browser if it is not explicitly set. When a `pause` value is expressed in percentage terms, the length of the pause is in fact determined by the length of time it takes for a single word to be spoken. So if `speech-rate` is set at an extremely pedestrian 60 words per minute — which means that one word is spoken every second — then a pause value set to 100% means that you will end up with a one-second pause. The following code shows how you can get different lengths of pauses depending on the value of the `speech-rate` property.

Listing 21.5	*Pause Properties Example 3*

```
<html>
<head>
<title>pause-before and speech-rate Example</title>
</head>
<body style="speak:normal; speech-rate:120">
In this section of the Web page the speech is rendered at 120 words
per minute.
<p style="pause-before:100%">The pause before this text lasts for
half a second.</p>
<p style="pause-before:200%">The pause before this text lasts for
one second.</p>
<p style="pause-before:50%">The pause before this text lasts for a
quarter of a second.</p>
<div style="speech-rate:60">
In this section of the Web page the speech is rendered at a very
slow 60 words per minute.
<p style="pause-before:100%">The pause before this text lasts for
one second.</p>
<p style="pause-before:200%">The pause before this text lasts for
two seconds.</p>
<p style="pause-before:50%">The pause before this text lasts for
half a second</p>
</div>
</body>
</html>
```

Notice how in this last example, despite having the same percentage values, the lengths of the pauses are quite different, depending wholly on the value to which `speech-rate` has been set.

Finally, the pause properties can also take the named value `inherit`, which derives its value from the parent value set for any of the pause properties. If the `pause-before` value for `<body>` is set to one second, then the declaration `p {pause-before: inherit}` would add a one-second pause to the beginning of each paragraph.

21.4 Cue Sub-Set of Properties

Just as there is a sub-set of pause-related properties, so too is there a sub-set of cue-related properties. In this case, however, instead of attaching a pause value to a Web element, the cue essentially adds the equivalent of a "sound effect." If you wanted to add the sound of a creaking door, a doorbell, a ghostly wail or anything else you can think of, you can do so using the set of cue properties. There are three properties in this sub-set of properties: `cue-before`, `cue-after` and `cue`. The `cue-before` property is designed to add a sound effect *before* a specific Web element, and the `cue-after` property adds a sound effect *after* a given Web element. The shortcut property `cue` works in much the same way as the `pause` property, in that it can take two URL values. If two values are specified, the first sound file is played before the Web element, and the second sound file reference is played after it. If only one sound file is specified, the same sound is played before *and* after the Web element. Note: when a cue property is used, the sound appears either before or after the text being read by the browser, not along with it.

The cue properties can take any one of two different values: a URL that points to a sound file the browser is capable of playing back, and the named property `inherit`.

The CSS2 specification does not standardize the types of sound files that any particular browser must be capable of playing back; therefore the implementation of valid sound file formats will likely depend on the browser being used.

Listing 21.6 shows all three properties in action.

Listing 21.6	*Cue Properties Example*

```
<html>
<head>
<title>Cue Properties Example</title>
</head>
<body>
<h1 style="cue-before:bong.wav">Hamlet: Act I, Scene I</h1>
You can get there by <a href="link.html"
style="cue-after:click.wav">Clicking  here</a>.
```

| Listing 21.6 | *Cue Properties Example (continued)* |

```
<p>
A single sound appears before and after this <a href="link.html"
style="cue:bada-bing.wav">link</a>.
</p>
<p>
Two different sounds appear before and after this
<a href="link.html" style="cue:bada-bing.wav
bada-boom.wav">link</a>.
</p>
</body>
</html>
```

In the `cue-before` example, the sound "`bong.wav`" is played immediately before the text contained in the header. With the `cue-after` example, the sound is played at the end of the link. There are also two examples of the `cue` property in action. With the first, only a single sound file ("`bada-bing.wav`") is specified, so it is played both before and after the link. In the second, two sound files are specified, so the first sound file ("`bada-bing.wav`") is played before the link, and the second ("`bada-boom.wav`") is played after it.

The cue properties can also take on the named `inherit` value, so that if a parent value is set for a particular sound, any Web element can call it by using the `inherit` value.

21.5 play-during Property

The `play-during` property is used to set a sound file to play "behind" specified text on a Web page. In this way, you can add a sound effect or music that is played continuously behind your text as it is being read by the browser. It differs from the cue sub-set of properties in that it does not interrupt the flow of the text as it is read, but instead is designed to be "background" sound.

Like the `cue` sub-set of properties, the `play-during` property takes a URL to specify the name of the sound file to be played. The same browser restrictions regarding the types of sound files that can be played under the cue properties apply to the `play-during` property.

In addition to the URL used to specify the sound file, `play-during` can also take the following named values: `mix`, `repeat`, `auto`, `none` and `inherit`. The `mix` value is used to "mix" or add in any sound from a previously set `play-during` sound. Thus, you can have multiple background sounds playing at once. The `repeat` value is designed to play a sound file multiple times under a given selection of text. You would use this value when you have a relatively short sound file you want to use to "fill up" a given section of text, you want to add continuous background music or you simply wish to ensure that a "parent" background sound is played throughout the reading of the text on the page.

The `auto` value is designed to let any parent background sound continue to play under a given Web element. The `none` value effectively "turns off" any sound that is playing, creating silence. The `inherit` value explicitly sets the sound to whatever parent sound has previously been set. Listing 21.7, which stages a scene from *Hamlet*, shows several of these values put into action.

Listing 21.7	*play-during Example*

```
<html>
<head>
<title>play-during Example</title>
<style>
body {speak: normal; play-during:windy-outdoors.wav}
p.ghost {play-during:ghostly.wav mix repeat}
</style>
</head>
<body>
Hamlet: Whither wilt thou lead me? Speak! I'll go no further.
<p class="ghost">
Ghost: Mark me.
</p>
<p>
Hamlet: I will.
</p>
<p class="ghost">
Ghost: My hour is almost come, when I to sulph'rous and tormenting
flames must render up myself.
</p>
</body>
</html>
```

In this brief scene, two sound files are played: `windy-outdoors.wav` and `ghostly.wav`. The `windy-outdoors.wav` — combined with the `repeat` value — is set to the `<body>` element, so that sound will be played throughout the reading of the Web page. The `ghostly.wav` file is set up so that it is associated only with those lines spoken by the ghost, designed to lend a special mood to his lines. The `mix` value is used whenever the `ghostly.wav` file is played, so it is played over the `windy-out-doors.wav`, instead of simply displacing it.

21.6 azimuth Property

The azimuth property is used to describe the location of a sound in a flat circle surrounding the Web page "viewer" (or, more properly, "listener"). It, along with the elevation property, is designed to allow the Web author to "place" where speech and sound will appear in a three-dimensional sound space. In simpler terms, the azimuth property sets where the sound is placed "around" the listener, and the elevation property sets where the sound is in terms of its "height" above or below the listener.

The azimuth property can take both a numeric value and several preset named values. The numeric value is set in degrees (deg) with a range in angle values from 0 to 360. In this scheme, a value of 0deg places a sound directly in front of the listener, 180deg places it behind the listener, 90deg is to the right, and 270deg is to the left. These numeric values can also be expressed in negatives, so that 90deg is equivalent to -270deg, 180deg is the same as -180deg, 270deg is the same as -90deg, and -0deg is the same as -360deg.

There are also a number of convenient named values that are preset equivalents of various numeric values. These named values are: left-side, far-left, left, center-left, center, center-right, right, far-right, right-side and behind. There are also three name values that can be used in conjunction with these other values: behind, leftwards and rightwards. Finally, there is the inherit value, which takes on the value of any parent value set for azimuth on the Web page.

As seen from in Figure 21–1, starting from the leftmost value and going clockwise, the values run in the following order: left-side (270deg), far-left (300deg), left (320deg), center-left (340deg), center (0deg), center-right (20deg), right (40deg), far-right (60deg), and right-side (90deg). If the value behind is combined with any of these values — with the exception of left-side and right-side values — it inverts or "mirrors" the value, placing it at the same angle *behind* the listener. Continuing the circle going clockwise, the values are far-right behind (120deg), right-behind (140deg), center-right behind (160deg), behind (180deg), center-left behind (200deg), left behind (220deg) and far-left behind (240deg). Figure 21–1 shows how the sound can be placed all around the listener using these named values.

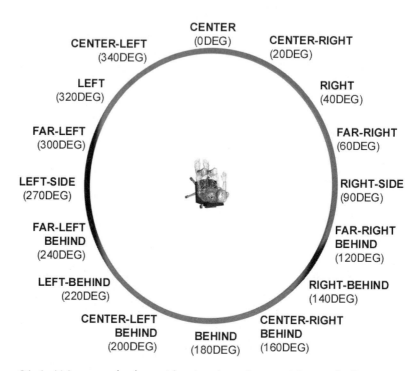

Figure 21–1 Using named values with azimuth to place sound around a listener.

There are two other named values used to shift sound from the last location: leftwards and rightwards. leftwards moves the sound 20 degrees to the left (counterclockwise) from its last position, and rightwards moves the sound 20 degrees to the right (clockwise) from its last position. In Listing 21.8 you can see how the various players are placed around the listener. Hamlet and Laertes are positioned to the left-side, while the King and Queen are positioned to the right side, and the rest of the royal court are placed behind the listener. All of the positions are static, indicating where particular players are. Movement is suggested by the use of the rightwards value as Hamlet goes over to stab the King. Using all of these values with the azimuth property, it is possible to create a moving, dynamic soundscape, very much like listening to a recorded play.

Listing 21.8	*azimuth Example*

```html
<html>
<head>
<title>azimuth Example</title>
<style>
body {speak:normal}
p.behind {azimuth:behind}
p.left {azimuth:left}
p.right {azimuth:right}
p.rightwards {azimuth:rightwards}
p.far-right {azimuth:far-right}
p.center {azimuth:center}
</style>
</head>
<body>
<p class="left">Hamlet: How does the Queen?<p>
<p class="right">King: She sounds to see them bleed. </p>
<p class="far-right">Queen: No, no! the drink, the drink! O my
dear Hamlet! The drink, the drink! I am poison'd.</p>
<p class="center">[Dies]</p>
<p class="left">Hamlet: O villany! Ho! let the door be lock'd.
Treachery! Seek it out.</p>
<p class="far-left">Laertes: It is here, Hamlet. Hamlet, thou art
slain; No medicine in the world can do thee good. In thee there is
not half an hour of life. The treacherous instrument is in thy
hand, Unbated and envenom'd. The foul practice Hath turn'd itself
on me. Lo, here I lie, Never to rise again. Thy mother's poison'd.
I can no more. The King, the King's to blame. </p>
<p class="center">[Dies]</p>
<p class="left">Hamlet: The point envenom'd too?</p>
<p class="rightwards">Then, venom, to thy work.</p>
<p class="center">[Hurts the King]</p>
<p class="behind">All: Treason! treason!</p>
</body>
</html>
```

The creation of these effects is entirely up to the technology available to the listener's computer. While most multimedia systems are capable of stereo output, not all systems are necessarily up to a full 360-degree placement of sound. In these situations, the sound system may try to approximate the placement of sound, perhaps by making sounds placed "behind" sounds more distant than those in front. Results are likely to vary, not only between computing systems, but also between individual computers, as well.

21.7 elevation Property

Where the `azimuth` property is used to set the placement of sound around the listener, the `elevation` property is used to set the relative "height" of the sound above or below the plane of the stereo soundscape.

Again, much like the `azimuth` property, the `elevation` property can take either a numeric value or a special named value that is the equivalent of a preset numeric value.

Users can set the height of the sound in a virtual semi-circle that goes from directly below the plane of the listener to directly above. In this scheme, the range in angle runs from `-90deg` (directly below the listener) to `90deg` (directly above the listener).

There are six named values for `elevation`: `below`, `level`, `above`, `higher`, `lower` and `inherit`. The preset values are `below` (equivalent to -90deg), `level` (equivalent to 0deg), and `above` (equivalent to 90deg). You can see all of these represented in Figure 21–2.

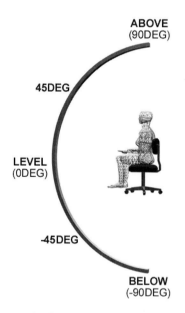

Figure 21–2 Using named values with `elevation` to place sound above and below a listener.

The named value `higher` adds 10 degrees to the current elevation, essentially "raising" the sound up; `lower` subtracts 10 degrees to the current elevation, in effect "lowering" it. The `inherit` value takes on whatever parent value may have been set for `elevation`.

Both `azimuth` and `elevation` are great for placing different sound sources in a soundscape, allowing Web authors to transform the text on their Web pages to become the actors on a sound stage. Listing 21.9 provides a practical demonstration of how you might use `elevation`.

Listing 21.9 | *elevation Example*

```
<html>
<head>
<title>elevation Example</title>
<style>
body {speak: normal}
p.below-ground {elevation:-20deg}
p.above-ground {elevation:20deg}
p.lower {elevation:lower}
p.center {elevation:center}
p.higher {elevation:higher}
</style>
</head>
<body>
<p class="below-ground">
Gravedigger: A pestilence on him for a mad rogue! 'A pour'd a
flagon of Rhenish on my head once. This same skull, sir, was
Yorick's skull, the King's jester.
</p>
<p class="above-ground">
Hamlet: This?
</p>
<p class="below-ground">
Gravedigger: E'en that.
</p>
<p class="lower">
Hamlet: Let me see.
</p>
<p class="center">
[Takes the skull.]
</p>
<p class="higher">
Alas, poor Yorick! I knew him, Horatio. A fellow of infinite jest,
of most excellent fancy.
</p>
</body>
</html>
```

In this example derived from *Hamlet*, the gravedigger is quite naturally placed below the plane of the listener, whereas Hamlet, who is standing on the ground, is placed just above it. Using the `lower` and `higher` value, it would seem to the listener that Hamlet stoops to pick up Yorick's skull, and then stands up again.

21.8 speech-rate Property

The `speech-rate` property is designed to allow the Web author to set the rate at which the speech is played back by the Web browser. It essentially sets the "speed" at which the text on the Web page is read.

The `speech-rate` property can take either a numeric value or one of a series of named values that are the equivalent of preset numeric values. All of these values are designed to set the speaking rate in terms of words read aloud over the course of a minute. Not only can this property be used to simply set the rate at which the text on the page is read, but it can also lend dramatic emphasis to text, if used properly.

A relaxed, typical English speaking voice runs to just under 200 words per minute. A relatively fast speaker talks at a rate of about 300 words per minute. Thanks to computer technology, you can have the computer read text extremely fast, with the limit really being set by the software driving the text-reading program.

There are eight different named values for `speech-rate`: `x-slow`, `slow`, `medium`, `fast`, `x-fast`, `faster`, `slower` and `inherit`. `x-slow` is equivalent to 80 words-per-minute, `slow` to 120 words-per-minute, `medium` to 180–200 words-per-minute, `fast` to 300 words-per-minute and finally `x-fast` to 500 words-per-minute. The `faster` value increases the current speech rate by 40 words-per-minute, and `slower` decreases the speech rate by 40 words-per-minute. The ubiquitous `inherit` property takes the same value as that set for the parent value for `speech-rate`.

It is safe to say that there will be an implicit `speech-rate` value set for any speech-enabled browser. For the most part, Web authors who intend to use this property are likely to either go with the implicit value used by the browser (likely equivalent to a `medium` value in the range of 180–200 words-per-minute) or to set an explicit value in the `<BODY>` tag of the Web page. `speech-rate` can also be used to lend dramatic emphasis to sections of text on a Web page, though, as shown in Listing 21.10.

Listing 21.10   *speech-rate Example*

```
<html>
<head>
<title>speech-rate Example</title>
<style>
body {speak:normal; speech-rate:medium}
p.slow {speech-rate:slow}
p.slower {speech-rate:slower}
p.fast {speech-rate:fast}
p.faster {speech-rate:faster}
</style>
</head>
<body>
[Ghost beckons Hamlet.]
<p class="slower">
Horatio: It beckons you to go away with it, as if it some
impartment did desire to you alone.
</p>
<p class="faster">
Marcellus: Look with what courteous action It waves you to
a more removed ground. But do not go with it!
</p>
<p class="fast">
Horatio: No, by no means!
</p>
<p class="slow">
Hamlet: It will not speak. Then will I follow it.
</p>
</body>
</html>
```

In this brief scene, a whole range of speech-rate values are used. The initial value is set to medium, but Horatio's initial lines are rendered using slower to add weight to his apprehension. Marcellus' exclamation is rendered using faster, and Horatio's imploring of Hamlet uses the fast setting. The contemplative Hamlet's concluding words are rendered using slow.

21.9 voice-family Property

Using the `voice-family` property, you can actually set the "sex" of a speaking voice. Not only can you set a generic sex value to the voice, but you can also add specific voices if they are supported by your browser.

The `voice-family` property can take any of four specific named values: `male`, `female`, `child` and `inherit`. It can also take a specific predefined voice name whose vocal characteristics have previously been set. It is the vocal equivalent of the `font-family` property, allowing Web authors to set several values for a voice; the first value that matches what is available on the browser is the one that is used.

Although it is not explicitly stated in the CSS2 specification, it is assumed that the `male` voice has a relatively deep sound to it; a `female` voice would be rendered in a higher pitch, and a `child`'s voice would be higher still. Since there are no specific values provided, chances are that the results will vary from browser to browser.

The `voice-family` property can also take any predefined voice name that may exist. There is no explanation in the specification as to how this might work in practice, but presumably various standard voice types would be made available to the browser. As a fallback, you can always use the standard sex names as well, in case the specific voices are not universally available. With that in mind, it should be possible to write the following code in Listing 21.11.

In this code example, there are two distinct voices being used: `laertes`, a male voice, and `ophelia`, a female voice. In each case, the specific voice name, such as "`laertes`", is followed up by the name value "`male`". In this way, in case the preset vocal characteristics for the character of `laertes` are not present on a user's system, it will load up the default `male` voice instead.

Listing 21.11	*voice-family Example*

```
<html>
<head>
<title>voice-family Example</title>
<style>
body {speak: normal}
p.laertes {voice-family:laertes, male}
p.ophelia {voice-family:ophelia, female}
</style>
</head>
```

Listing 21.11	*voice-family Example (continued)*

```
<body>
<p class="laertes">
Laertes: Farewell, Ophelia, and remember well what I have said to
you.
</p>
<p class="ophelia">
Ophelia: 'Tis in my memory lock'd, and you yourself shall keep the
key of it.
</p>
<p class="laertes">
Laertes: Farewell.
</p>
</body>
</html>
```

21.10 pitch Property

The `pitch` property is designed to set the pitch level for a given speaking voice. Using this property, you can artificially set up different types of voices to be played back through your browser. The `pitch` property helps Web authors better characterize voices reading text from the Web page.

Another member of the voice characteristics grouping of sub-properties, the `pitch` property enables you to set the current pitch of the voice reading the text aloud. Depending on how widely this property and the `voice-family` properties are eventually implemented in the major browsers, they both seem to be alternate ways of achieving much the same thing: lending character to a given speaking voice.

The average pitch of a given voice will vary depending on the `voice-family` value to which it belongs. For example, a typical male voice is a relatively low 120 Hz, whereas a typical female voice is usually higher, in the range of 210 Hz.

It is possible to either set a numeric value for the speaking voice in Hertz (Hz), or in one of five named values, `x-low`, `low`, `medium`, `high`, `x-high` and `inherit`. The CSS2 specification does not set specific Hertz values for these named values, as they can have different values depending on the `voice-family` value they belong to (a value of "`high`" for a male voice would necessarily be lower than the same value applied to a female voice). All the specification says is that the values must progress from low Hertz values (from "`x-low`") to high Hertz values (to "`x-high`"). The `inherit` value simply takes on whatever `pitch` value has been assigned to the parent property.

Although not specifically referenced in the specification, it is implied that the values for `pitch` are most likely to be used in conjunction with the `voice-family` property, making it possible to vary the standard `voice-family` properties of `male`, `female` and `child`. In this way, it should be relatively easy for a "viewer" to distinguish between different reading voices on a given Web page, as can be seen in Listing 21.12.

Listing 21.12	*pitch Example*

```
<html>
<head>
<title>pitch Example</title>
<style>
body {speak: normal}
p.hamlet {voice-family:male; pitch:medium}
p.horatio {voice-family:male; pitch:low}
p.marcellus {voice-family:male; pitch:x-low}
</style>
</head>
<body>
<p class="hamlet">
Hamlet: What hour now?
</p>
<p class="horatio">
Horatio: I think it lacks of twelve.
</p>
<p class="marcellus">
Marcellus: No, it is struck.
</p>
</body>
</html>
```

In this case, we have three different male characters. Normally, it would be hard to distinguish among them, but by using different values for the `pitch` property, it is possible to do so. The voice assigned to Hamlet has a `pitch` value of `medium`, Horatio has a `pitch` value of `low`, and Marcellus' `pitch` is set to `x-low`.

21.11 pitch-range Property

Another member of the voice characteristics of aural sub-properties, the
`pitch-range` property is meant to be used in conjunction with the `pitch` property,
and is designed to enable the Web author to set the variable range for a given speaking
voice. While the `pitch` property is used to set the average pitch of a given spoken
voice, the `pitch-range` property is essentially used to add the amount of inflection
that is added to a speaking voice. A relatively small value leads to a dry voice, whereas
a high value sets a highly animated voice.

The `pitch-range` property can either take a specific numerical value that falls
anywhere in a range between 0 and 100, and the value `inherit`. A numerical value of
50 is the default value, and is the normal pitch range for a given English-speaking
voice. A value of 0 produces a speaking voice that is a monotone, staying at the value
fixed by `pitch`. A value of 100 produces a highly animated speaking voice. If you
think of things in terms of emotionally charged speaking voices, a 0 value for
`pitch-range` produces a dry, emotionless voice, whereas a value of 100 produces a
highly emotionally charged voice. The named value `inherit` simply takes on whatever parent value may have been set for `pitch-range`. Listing 21.13 tries to add some
emotion to the voices speaking the lines from Shakespeare's *Hamlet*.

Listing 21.13	*pitch-range Example*

```
<html>
<head>
<title>pitch-range Example</title>
<style>
body {speak: normal}
p.ghost {voice-family:male; pitch:low}
p.hamlet {voice-family:male; pitch:medium}
</style>
</head>
<body>
<p class="ghost" style="pitch-range:25">
Ghost: Revenge his foul and most unnatural murder.
</p>
<p class="hamlet" style="pitch-range:80">
Hamlet: Murder?
</p>
```

Listing 21.13   *pitch-range Example (continued)*

```
<p class="ghost" style="pitch-range:35">
Ghost: Murder most foul, as in the best it is; but this most foul,
strange, and unnatural.
</p>
</body>
</html>
```

In this short scene, the Ghost speaks in a cold voice, drained of emotion, whereas Hamlet reacts to the news of his father's murder with a great deal of emotion.

21.12 stress Property

The stress property is used to help "color" a voice, in order to add more inflection or emphasis. This property is a companion to the pitch-range property, aiding it in an effort to add more or less emotional inflection to a given voice.

The stress property can either take a numeric value ranging from 0 to 100, or can take the named property inherit common to all CSS2 properties. English is a language that relies upon stress values within words. The more a word is stressed, the more each syllable in the word is emphasized, and the more inflected it becomes. In the CSS2 scheme, a value of 50 is equal to normally inflected English speech, 0 is equal to very dry, uninflected speech, and 100 is a wildly inflected voice. The inherit property simply takes on whatever parent value may have already been set for the stress property.

Listing 21.14 shows how this property can be put to use in the following excerpt from *Hamlet*.

Listing 21.14   *stress Example*

```
<html>
<head>
<title>stress Example</title>
<style>
body {speak: normal}
p.king {voice-family:male; pitch:low}
p.ophelia {voice-family:male; pitch:high}
</style>
</head>
```

Listing 21.14	*stress Example (continued)*

```
<body>
<p class="king" style="pitch-range:25; stress:40">
King: How do you, pretty lady?
</p>
<p class="ophelia" style="pitch-range:45; stress:95">
Ophelia: Well, God 'ild you! They say the owl was a baker's daugh-
ter. Lord, we know what we are, but know not what we may be. God be
at your table!
</p>
</body>
</html>
```

In this snippet, we see how the King's words are relatively uninflected, with a `stress` value of 40, reflecting how solemn and reserved he is in front of the clearly mad Ophelia. Ophelia, being insane, has highly inflected speech with a `stress` value of 95.

21.13 richness Property

The `richness` property is used to set the "brightness" (also known as "richness") of the speaking voice. This term really refers to the power behind the voice, and its ability to fill a room. A very rich voice fills a room, whereas a smooth voice does not.

The `richness` property can either take a numeric value within a range of 0 to 100, or the named value `inherit`. The higher the numeric value, the more the voice will "carry" and resonate within the room. A lower value produces a softer, more mellifluous voice. The default value for `richness` is 50, equal to that of regular speech. Any Web element set to the `inherit` value will take on whatever value for `richness` has already been set in the parent.

Like many of the other properties in the voice characteristics sub-group, `richness` lends itself well to adding further depth to the characterization of the reading voice. This can be seen in Listing 21.15.

In this scene from *Hamlet*, a dying Hamlet forces the King to drink the poison meant for him. In this emotionally charged scene, both Hamlet and the King have high `richness` values assigned to their voices. Contrast this to the narrator who mentions the King's death, which is rendered in a relatively dry, unobtrusive tone with a low `richness` value.

Listing 21.15	*richness Example*

```
<html>
<head>
<title>richness Example</title>
<style>
body {speak: normal}
p.king {voice-family:male; pitch:low}
p.hamlet {voice-family:male; pitch:high}
p.narration {voice-family:male; pitch:x-low; pitch:high;
pitch-range:20; stress:50; richness:40}
</style>
</head>
<body>
<p class="king" style="pitch-range:25; stress:40; richness:80">
King: O, yet defend me, friends! I am but hurt.
</p>
<p class="hamlet" style="pitch-range:40; stress:80; richness:70">
Hamlet: Here, thou incestuous, murd'rous, damned Dane, Drink off
this potion! Is thy union here? Follow my mother.
</p>
<p class="narration">
[King dies.]
</p>
</body>
</html>
```

21.14 Speech Sub-Group of Properties

There is one final sub-grouping of like properties in the aural style sheets portion of the CSS2 specification. The oddly non-descriptive speech sub-group of properties contains two properties that tell the browser how it should handle reading things like numbers and dates aloud. These two properties are the `speak-punctuation` and `speak-numeral` properties.

The `speak-punctuation` and `speak-numeral` properties are similar in that they allow Web authors to specify exactly how certain parts of a Web page's text should be played back. `speak-punctuation` determines whether the punctuation marks that exist in the text should be named as the text is read aloud ("Hello there semi-colon"), or whether the text should flow normally according to the punctuation rules ("Hello there;"). Similarly, `speak-numeral` determines whether a string of numbers should be read as "one two three" or as "one hundred and twenty-three." Both of the properties can be said to operate in a similar way to the `spell-out` value for the `speech` property.

`speak-punctuation` can take one of three possible named values: `code`, in which punctuation marks (such as periods, commas, brackets and so on) are spoken literally; `none`, in which the punctuation marks are not spoken, but are instead interpreted as natural pauses in speech, and the value `inherit`, which takes on the value for `speak-punctuation` that has been previously set for the parent.

`speak-numeral` works in much the same way. It can also take one of three named properties: `digits`, which pronounces numbers as individual digits; `continous`, which pronounces a string of numbers as one full number, and the value `inherit`, which simply takes on whatever value for `speak-numeral` has been set for the parent.

Listing 21.16 shows both of these properties put into action.

Listing 21.16	*speak-punctuation and speak-numeral Example*

```
<html>
<head>
<title>speak-punctuation and speak-numeral Example</title>
<style>
body {speak: normal}
p.queen {voice-family:female; pitch:high; pitch-range:medium}
p.francisco {voice-family:male; pitch:medium; pitch-range:medium}
p.bernardo {voice-family:male; pitch:medium; pitch-range:high}
</style>
</head>
<body>
In the following sentence, all of the punctuation (periods, excla-
mation marks and  commas) are read aloud.
<p class="queen" style="speak-punctuation: code">
Queen: No, no! the drink, the drink! O my dear Hamlet! The drink,
the drink! I am poison'd.
</p>
<p class="francisco">
Francisco: You come most carefully upon your hour.
</p>
<p class="bernardo" style="speak-numeral: continuous">
Bernardo: 'Tis now struck 12. Get thee to bed, Francisco.
</p>
</body>
</html>
```

These properties may clearly be used for different purposes. There are occasions when you might want the punctuation to be read aloud, to set apart the text from the punctuation. In the course of normal speech, you would probably want to set the `speak-numeral` property to `continous` (as in the previous code example), but there are cases where it would be better to have the individual numerals spoken separately, such as in a table, so that the listener, who may be copying down the figures, has a better chance of recording the right number.

RUBY

Topics in This Chapter

- What Is Ruby?
- The `<ruby>` Tag Set
- `ruby-align`
- `ruby-overhang`
- `ruby-position`

Chapter 22

22.1 What Is Ruby?

Ruby refers to a technique for laying out text used in many Asian character sets, like Japanese (Hiragana, Katakana, Kana and Kanji), Korean (Hangul and Hanja) and Chinese (the Bopomofo characters used in Madarin as an example), where additional characters are used in conjunction with "base" characters as an aid in pronunciation or as an explanatory annotation.

There are three implicit structures for ruby: the initial "base" text (called "ruby base"), the commentary text (called "ruby text") and the bounding box that contains both (the "ruby" itself). Figure 22–1 uses English words to provide an example of what ruby is all about.

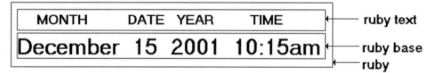

Figure 22–1   The parts of ruby layout.

In this case the specific date and time info ("December 15 2001 10:15am") comprise the ruby base; the text above it ("MONTH", "DATE", "YEAR" and "TIME") are the ruby text. You can also see from this example how ruby text is used to help explain the text contained in the ruby base. The ruby is the bounding box that surrounds both the ruby text and the ruby base, and controls such things as setting the padding around each.

In Asian languages ruby is more typically used to better explain the meaning of obscure or archaic individual characters. With character sets often containing several hundred characters apiece, it is not uncommon that certain rarely used characters may require an explanation or a pronunciation guide. For example, the phonetic Japanese Hiragana alphabet may be set in a ruby text to help "sound out" characters contained in the ruby base area.

Beginning with Internet Explorer 5.0, Microsoft added a new set of ruby CSS properties along with a couple of HTML tags. Ruby is *also* a set of proposals in the forthcoming CSS3 specification, as well as the XHTML 1.1 specification. So while Microsoft is jumping the gun a bit here, it does enable Web developers — especially those creating Web sites using Asian character sets — greater control over how characters should be displayed without having to resort to complicated and fussy HTML table code in order to display text.

22.2 The <ruby> Tag Set

As mentioned earlier, ruby works as both an HTML tag and as a set of CSS attributes. Ruby annotation tags were introduced as an XHTML 1.1 recommendation in May 2001, and it consists of the following tags:

- `<ruby>` — an inline element which encloses all other ruby text elements.
- `<rbc>` — ruby base container, used only in complex ruby markup
- `<rtc>` — ruby text container, used only in complex ruby markup
- `<rb>` — ruby base text
- `<rt>` — ruby text
- `<rp>` — ruby parenthesis

There are two types of ruby markup: simple and complex. Both use the `<ruby>` tag to contain all of the other elements. Simple ruby markup utilizes the `<rb>`, `<rt>` and `<rp>` tags, while complex ruby markup is done using the `<rbc>` and `<rtc>` tags in conjunction with the `<rb>` and `<rt>` tags.

When the text to be contained within the ruby is fairly basic, simple ruby markup should be used. The `<rb>` tag denotes the ruby base text, and the `<rt>` tag encloses the ruby text. An example of this could look like the code seen in Listing 22.1.

Listing 22.1	*A Simple Ruby Example*

```
<ruby>
 <rb>CSS</rb>
 <rt>Cascading Style Sheets</rt>
<ruby>
```

Browsers that do not understand the ruby tags will simply ignore them, and consequently run all of the text together on a single line. The `<rp>` (ruby parenthesis) tag is designed as a fallback mechanism for those browsers that do not know how to render ruby text appropriately, allowing the Webmaster to place parentheses around the ruby text. Browsers that do understand ruby tags will not display the parentheses (or anything else) contained within the `<rp>` tags. Listing 22.2 shows how this can be used.

Listing 22.2	*A More Complex Ruby Example*

```
<ruby>
 <rb>CSS</rb>
 <rt><rp>(</rp>Cascading Style Sheets<rp>)</rp></rt>
<ruby>
```

Browsers that do not render ruby tags will display "CSS (Cascading Style Sheets)," and those that do will render both lines of text in a ruby box, omitting the parentheses.

Complex ruby markup is to be used when you want to associate more than one ruby text with a given base text, or for associating sections of ruby text with parts of base text. Complex ruby markup uses the `<rbc>` and `<rtc>` tags which can enclose multiple instances of the `<rb>` and `<rt>` tags, respectively. The `<rt>` tag can also use the `rbspan` attribute, which works in the same way as the `colspan` attribute works with the `<th>` and `<td>` table tags. Listing 22.3 shows some sample code that uses more complex ruby markup.

Listing 22.3 *An Even More Complex Ruby Example*

```
<ruby>
 <rbc>
  <rb>Dec</rb>
  <rb>15</rb>
  <rb>2001</rb>
  <rb>10:15am</rb>
 </rbc>
 <rtc>
  <rt>Month</rt>
  <rt>Date</rt>
  <rt>Year</rt>
  <rt>Time</rt>
 </rtc>
 <rtc>
  <rt rbspan="4">Current Date/Time</rt>
 </rtc>
</ruby>
```

As mentioned earlier, this is all part of the latest XHTML 1.1 recommendation. A "recommendation" is not the same as an accepted specification however. In other words, this is how ruby text layout is likely to appear in the final XHTML 1.1 specification.

Since this is only a recommendation, the browser manufacturers are not obligated to implement these ruby tags in their browsers. At the time of writing, none of the major browsers had implemented this set of ruby tags, though a subset of these tags — specifically, the <ruby> and <rt> tags were included in Internet Explorer 5.0.

The three CSS properties that can be used along with them are ruby-align, ruby-overhang and ruby-position. The way it works is that the Web author sets the <ruby> tag, and then uses the style attribute to set one of the three CSS properties to it. This is definitely an odd way of doing things — you'd think that the CSS properties could simply be set up as attributes of the <ruby> tag instead, but they *must* be set as styles.

The ruby base text is defined by <ruby>, and the <rt> tag encloses the ruby text. The simplest example code without any CSS values is sufficient to display the intended effect of ruby text, as can be seen in Listing 22.4.

Listing 22.4	*Ruby Web Page Example Code*

```html
<html>
<head>
<title>Ruby Example 1</title>
<style>
body {font-size: xx-large}
</style>
</head>

<body>

<ruby>
Ruby base
<rt>Ruby text</rt>
</ruby>

</body>
</html>
```

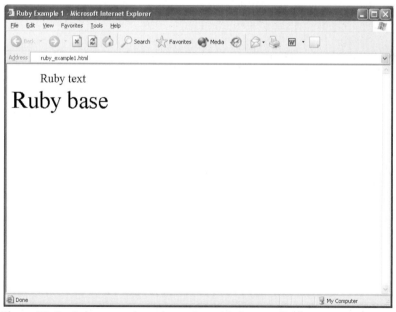

Figure 22–2   Ruby example code as viewed in Internet Explorer.

When viewed in Internet Explorer 5.0 and up, the words "Ruby text" are displayed using a small font centered directly above the words "Ruby base." In many instances this may be enough, but the CSS properties provide greater control over positioning of the ruby text.

The `<ruby>` and `<rt>` tags can each take on all of the standard attributes common to all XHTML tags, `class`, `id`, plus all of the standard JavaScript handles, but for the most part it's the `style` attribute that it is used in order to set the CSS properties for these elements.

22.3 ruby-align Property

The `ruby-align` property is used to set the horizontal positioning of ruby text relative to the ruby base, and it comes with seven separate values: `auto`, `left`, `center`, `right`, `distribute-letter`, `distribute-space` and `line-edge`.

With the `auto` value the browser determines the best arrangement, and the `left`, `center` and `right` alignment values are self-explanatory. The `distribute-letter` value is used when the width of the ruby text is less than that of the ruby base, and each letter (or character) is spaced out evenly across the width of the ruby text box — essentially it "justifies" the characters evenly across the width of the ruby text box. Similarly, `distribute-space` is also used when the ruby text is smaller than that of the ruby base, but instead of justifying it, it adds some spacing to either side equal to half the kerning value of the ruby text. Its effects are similar to `center`, though extra spacing is added between the characters as well as at the "margins." `line-edge` appears to align the ruby text to the line edge of the ruby text bounding box, allowing more "room" for the ruby text to appear within, but this does not seem to be case in practice at the moment. The code in Listing 22.5 when displayed in Internet Explorer 5.0 shows the effect of each property.

Listing 22.5	*ruby-align Example Code*

```
<html>
<head>
<title>ruby-align Example</title>
<style>
ruby {font-size: x-large}
rt {font-size: large}
td {font-size: small}
</style>
</head>
```

Listing 22.5 *ruby-align Example Code (continued)*

```
<body>

<table>
 <tr>
  <td>

auto:<br>
<ruby style="ruby-align: auto">
Ruby base
<rt>Ruby text</rt>
</ruby>

<p>
left:<br>
<ruby style="ruby-align: left">
Ruby base
<rt>Ruby text</rt>
</ruby>
</p>

<p>
center:<br>
<ruby style="ruby-align: center">
Ruby base
<rt>Ruby text</rt>
</ruby>
</p>

<p>
right:<br>
<ruby style="ruby-align: right">
Ruby base
<rt>Ruby text</rt>
</ruby>
</p>

  </td>
  <td valign="top">

<p>
distribute-letter:<br>
<ruby style="ruby-align: distribute-letter">
Ruby base
<rt>Ruby text</rt>
</ruby>
</p>
```

Listing 22.5   *ruby-align Example Code (continued)*

```
<p>
distribute-space:<br>
<ruby style="ruby-align: distribute-space">
Ruby base
<rt>Ruby text</rt>
</ruby>
</p>

<p>
line-edge<br>
<ruby style="ruby-align: line-edge">
Ruby base
<rt>Ruby text with more text than it can conveniently display</rt>
</ruby>
</p>
  </td>
 </tr>
</table>

</body>
</html>
```

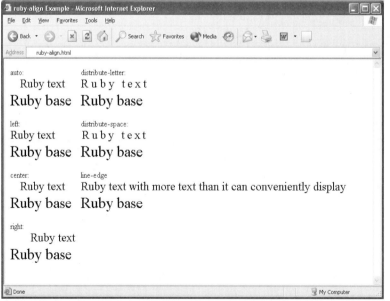

Figure 22–3   ruby-align example code as viewed in Internet Explorer.

Browser Compatibility

At the moment, this element only works in Internet Explorer beginning with version 5.0.

It is worth noting however that this property is contained in the CSS3 specification, so it will likely be incorporated into future browsers. The CSS3 specification contains three additional values for this property: `start`, `end` and `inherit`. The `start` and `end` values are functionally equivalent to the `left` and `right` values, respectively, and are available primarily for those instances when there could be confusion over the alignment of the ruby alignment when the ruby is to be displayed horizontally. The `inherit` value fetches any parent value for the ruby that may be available.

22.4 ruby-overhang Property

`ruby-overhang` is used to set how the browser is to display material adjacent to the ruby content if the ruby text content is wider than the ruby itself.

It takes three values: `auto`, `none` and `whitespace`. The browser tries to determine the best way of positioning things when `auto` is used, `none` tells the browser not to make allowances for it (hence the ruby text may run into adjacent non-ruby elements), and `whitespace` tells the browser to fill in the ruby base text with additional spacing to ensure that the ruby as a whole can accommodate all of the text — in other words, expanding the whole of the ruby in order to make all of its contents "fit," It is likely that the `auto` and `whitespace` values would display very similar results, whereas with none you can expect any text outside of the ruby to flow just outside the ruby base (and possibly flow "through" an oversized ruby text).

This would appear to be how Microsoft intended these settings to work, though in practice this value appears to be a placeholder — as its various values do not appear to influence the display of the ruby text against adjacent text or other items on the page. The code in Listing 22.6 *ought* to produce the effects seen in Figure 22–4 (which is a mock-up).

Listing 22.6 *ruby-overhang Example Code*

```
<html>
<head>
<title>ruby-overhang Example</title>
</head>

<body>

<b>auto</b>
<ruby style="ruby-overhang: auto">
Ruby base
<rt>Ruby text which should be longer than the base</rt>
</ruby>
the quick brown fox jumped over the lazy dog

<p>
<b>none</b>
<ruby style="ruby-overhang: none">
Ruby base
<rt>Ruby text which should be longer than the base</rt>
</ruby>
the quick brown fox jumped over the lazy dog

<p>
<b>whitespace</b>
<ruby style="ruby-overhang: whitespace">
Ruby base
<rt>Ruby text which should be longer than the base</rt>
</ruby>
the quick brown fox jumped over the lazy dog

</body>
</html>
```

auto

the quick brown fox jumped over the lazy dog

<small>Ruby text which should be longer than the base</small>

       Ruby base   the quick brown fox jumped over the lazy dog

none

the quick brown fox jumped over the lazy dog

<small>Ruby text which should be longer than the base</small>

       Ruby base the quick brown fox jumped over the lazy dog

whitespace

the quick brown fox jumped over the lazy dog

<small>Ruby text which should be longer than the base</small>

       Ruby base   the quick brown fox jumped over the lazy dog

Figure 22–4   ruby-align example code mocked up.

Browser Compatibility

At the moment, no browser — oddly enough, not even Internet Explorer 5.0 or 6.0 — supports this property. It is included in the CSS3 specification, so you can expect it to appear in browsers in the near future.

The CSS3 specification contains three additional values: start, end and inherit. The start value tells the browser that the ruby text can overhang the non-ruby text that may precede it, if the ruby text is significantly longer than the ruby base. Similarly, the end value tells the browser that the ruby text can overhang non-ruby text that may flow after it. These two values are illustrated in the mock-up illustration in Figure 22–5.

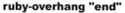

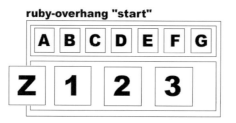

Figure 22–5 Illustrating the intended effects of the ruby-overhang "start" and "end" values.

These values would give Web authors more precise control over how and where non-ruby text can or cannot overflow the ruby base than the values introduced in Internet Explorer 5.0.

The `inherit` value fetches any parent value for the ruby that may be available.

22.5 ruby-position Property

The third ruby CSS property is `ruby-position`, which specifies the position of the ruby text in relation to the ruby base: either above it or on the same level as the base.

Under Internet Explorer 5.x, it takes two values: `above` and `inline`. The default for this value is `above` (which is the normal behavior for ruby) and `inline` essentially places the ruby text immediately after the ruby base (effectively removing the effects of the ruby box).

The code in Listing 22.7, when displayed, shows the difference between the two values.

Listing 22.7 *ruby-position Example Code*

```
<html>
<head>
<title>ruby-position Example</title>
<style>
body {font-size: xx-large}
</style>
</head>

<body>

<p>
<b>above</b><br/>
<ruby style="ruby-position: above">
Ruby base
<rt>Ruby text</rt>
</ruby>
</p>

<p>
<b>inline</b><br/>
<ruby style="ruby-position: inline">
Ruby base
<rt>Ruby text</rt>
</ruby>
</p>

</body>
</html>
```

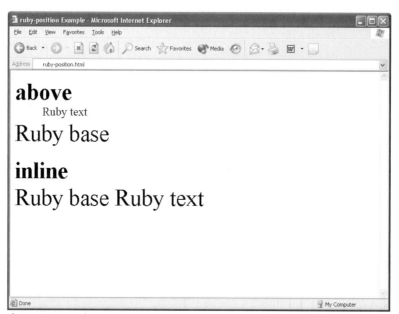

Figure 22–6 ruby-position example code as viewed in Internet Explorer.

Browser Compatibility

At the moment, this element only works in Internet Explorer 5.0 and up. It is included in the CSS3 specification, so you can expect it to appear in other browsers in the near future.

The CSS3 specification outlines other possible useful values for `ruby-position`, including a value `after` that would place ruby text underneath the ruby base text. (It's worth noting that the CSS3 values make much more sense than Microsoft's implementation; `before` and `after` are more readily understood than `above` or `below` when you consider that some Asian characters sets are displayed vertically rather than horizontally.)

Other values contained in the CSS3 draft include `right`, which places the ruby text to the right of the ruby. The effect of this is the same as inline, save for the fact that this value is not relative to the flow of the text. It also includes the standard `inherit` value, which explicitly fetches whatever parent value may be present.

MULTI-COLUMN LAYOUT

Topics in This Chapter

- Introduction
- `column-count`
- `column-width`
- `column-gap`
- `column-width-policy`
- `column-space-distribution`
- Column Rule Properties
- `column-span`

Chapter 23

23.1 Introduction

The CSSS3 specification has laid out a new way for formatting Web pages with the introduction of the set of multi-column layout properties. Using multi-column layouts it is possible to arrange text and other elements on a page as if they were lines of newspaper columns. One of the advantages of using a column layout as opposed to a more traditional table layout (which can otherwise accomplish pretty much the same thing) is that the flow of text and other elements on the page progresses smoothly across the columns — where the text overflows one column, the rest automatically goes into the adjoining column. A comparable table layout would require the Web author to figure out where the text flow should end at the end of a column and begin at the next one.

The CSS properties in this family are designed to allow the Web author complete control over the following characteristics for the column layout:

1. Be able to set the number of columns
2. Set the width of those columns (assuming that there's room)
3. Allow for a spacing gap between the columns

Interestingly enough, there is an old browser-specific HTML tag that accomplished much the same goals as the new CSS properties. The `multicol` element was a Netscape-specific tag that came with three attributes: `cols`, `gutter` and `width`. The `cols` attribute set the number of columns, `gutter` took a pixel value which set the space between the columns and width could take either a pixel or percentage value which set the maximum width for the columnar layout. The following code snippet, whose results are displayed in Figure 23–1, show how this element worked.

```
<multicol cols="3" width="85%" gutter="15">
Interdum volgus videt, est ubi peccat. Si veteres ita miratur
laudatque poetas, ut nihil anteferat, nihil illis comparet,
errat. Si quaedam nimis antique, si peraque dure dicere credit
eos, ignave multa fatetur, et sapit et mecum facit et Iova
iudicat aequo. Non equidem insector delendave carmina Livi esse
reor, memini quae plagosum mihi parvo Orbilium dictare; sed
emendata videri pulchraque et exactis minimum distantia miror.
Inter quae verbum emicuit si forte decorum, et si versus paulo
concinnior unus et alter, iniuste totum ducit venditque poema.
<p>
Indignor quicquam reprehendi, non quia crasse compositum
illepedeve putetur...
</p>
</multicol>
```

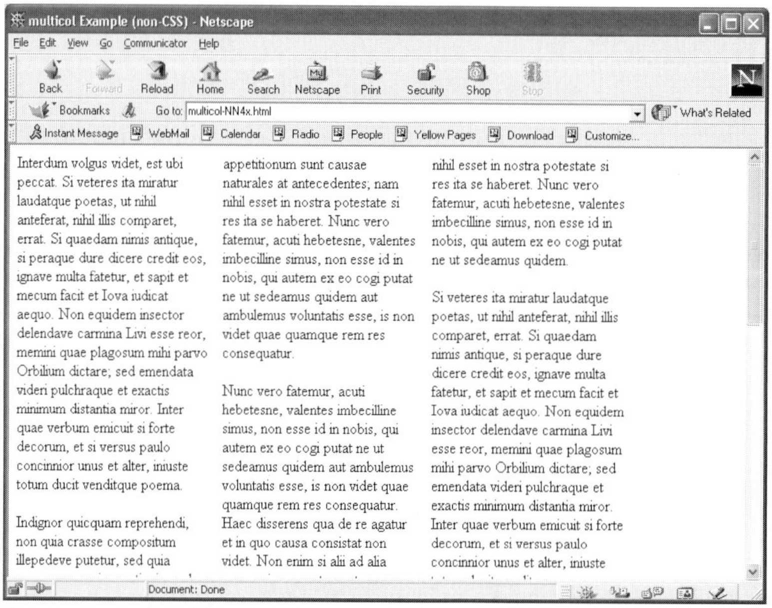

Figure 23–1   The old multicol element as displayed in Netscape Navigator 4.79.

This element was never supported in Internet Explorer, and never became part of any official W3C HTML specification, and so it saw limited use. In order to comply with accepted Web standards, Netscape dropped support for this element from Netscape Navigator 6.0 and subsequent browsers, but if you have a 3.x or 4.x version of Netscape floating around, you can get a taste for how the `multi-column` CSS properties are supposed to work.

Core Tip

Looking for an old version of Netscape Navigator? You can download older versions of this browser from Netscape's archives at:

`http://wp.netscape.com/download/archive.html.`

The set of CSS column properties allow for much greater control over columnar layout than the old `multicol` element could ever hope to do. In addition to new specific properties governing the number of columns, as well as the width and gap between them, there are more refined properties controlling such things as the rule lines between columns and whether or not an element can span columns.

Figure 23–2 shows all of the parts of columnar layout that are possible: the total columnar width and the difference between it and the full browser width, the column gaps separating individual columns and the column rules that can be set between then. Some header text shows how elements can be set to span multiple columns, and how optional borders and padding can also be set.

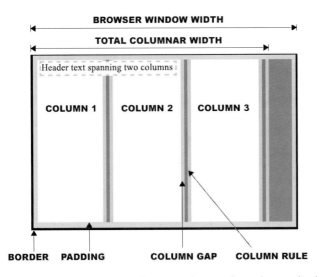

Figure 23–2   All of the major elements of CSS column layout displayed.

23.2 column-count Property

The first thing you have to do to be able to arrange a column layout is to set the number of columns to display. This is handled using the `column-count` property. This property takes one of three values: a numeric value, `auto` and `inherit`. The numeric value allows you to set a specific number of columns to be displayed. The `auto` value leaves the browser to determine how many columns are to be displayed, and is used in conjunction with the values present for the `column-width` and `column-gap` properties. The `inherit` value takes on whatever parent value for `column-count` may already be present. Not surprisingly, the default value for `column-count` is 1, which equates the width of the browser window to a column.

The following code fragment shows how you could set three columns to a `div` element:

```
div.columns {column-count: 3}
```

23.3 column-width Property

This property allows you to set a specific width for the columns that are displayed. It can take a standard length value, a percentage value, `auto` and `inherit`. The default behavior for this property is that if a single value is supplied, it is applied equally across all displayed columns. So if you set a specific length or percentage value, it is applied equally across all of the displayed columns. The `auto` value apportions the same amount of available space to the number of columns that have been set by the `column-count` property. If you want to set a width value for successive columns, you can also do that by setting successive values to this property in order. The following code snippet shows how you could use this property to set three columns, the first of which is set to 150 pixels in width, the second being 35% of the browser window, and third filling the rest of the available space.

```
div.columns {column-count: 3; column-width: 150px 35% auto}
```

It is easy to go wrong with this sort of property by setting larger widths than are possible to be displayed — like setting more than two 50% width values. In cases like these it is possible that content could be "lost" in the process. In these cases it is recommended that `overflow: visible` be used in order to ensure that any content that might overflow the columnar layout might be displayed by default.

23.4 column-gap Property

In order to set some spacing between columns, use the `column-gap` property. This takes the same values as `column-width` (i.e., a standard length value, a percentage value, `auto` and `inherit`) as well as one more: `normal`. This last property is the default, and the specification recommends that it be set to a value of 1 em in width, though individual browsers may differ in how they render this. When the `auto` value is used, it tells the browser to make the gaps between the columns equal to each other.

If column rules are used, they are placed in the middle of the column gaps. It is worth noting that the width value set to any column rules does not affect the width of any column gaps that are set. The following code snippet adds a 15-pixel-wide column gap to a `div` element:

```
div.columns {column-count: 3; column-width: 150px 35% auto;
column-gap: 15px}
```

The only other thing worth noting is that `column-gap` values are not allowed to be negative, as this would allow for a situation where the content from one column could overlap that of an adjacent column.

23.5 column-width-policy Property

In most cases it is desirable to have the whole of the columnar display fit the full width of the available browser window width. In order to do this without having to explicitly set the exact width every time, you can use the `column-width-policy` property.

This property has three values which control the size of the overall columnar display: `flexible`, `strict` and `inherit`. The `flexible` value is the default, which tells the browser to increase the widths of the columns to fit the available space. When `strict` is used — which may be handy in situations where you want to ensure the placement of elements within the flow of the columns — only the explicit column width values that have already been set are used. The `inherit` value would take on any parent value that may already be present.

The following code snippet gives a sense of how this could be used. For example, say you have separate pages where in some cases you want the columnar layout to be strictly the size that you set it to, and in other cases you want that layout to be more flexible. The following code snippet would allow you to set either option to a particular page when called from an external style sheet:

```
div.strict-columns {column-count: 3; column-width: 30%;
column-gap: 10px; column-width-policy: strict}
div.flexible-columns {column-count: 3; column-width: 30%;
column-gap: 10px; column-width-policy: flexible}
```

So in this code example, it is unlikely that three columns set to 30% of the width of the browser window are likely to fill out that space fully, even with the column gap. If you don't care so much about the exact placement of things within the flow of the columns, you would call the `div.flexible-columns` setting, which will increase the size of the columns to make them fit the browser window's width. Using the `div.strict-columns` setting, you ensure that your intended layout remains in place, leaving the unused space to the right side of the columnar space for something else, for example, an absolutely positioned graphic.

23.6 column-space-distribution Property

If you end up using the `strict` value for `column-width-policy`, it is likely that in most cases the total columnar space will be smaller than the available browser window width. In that case, you can use the additional `column-space-distribution` property to tell the browser what to do with that remaining, leftover space.

The `column-space-distribution` property can take any of six values: `start`, `end`, `inner`, `outer`, `between` and `inherit`. The `start` value places the space prior to the initial column, and the `end` value places the leftover space to the right of the final column. The `inner` and `outer` values are to be used only in a printable setting (i.e., with odd and even page settings), and set the spacing to the side closest and furthest from the binding area, respectively. The `between` value distributes any leftover space equally between the column sides, and the `inherit` value takes on whatever parent value may already be in place. Figure 23–3 shows how these values will be displayed against a sample `strict` three column layout that has some leftover space.

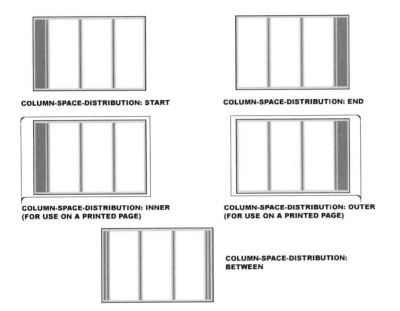

Figure 23–3 column-space-distribution values as they would be displayed in a compatible browser.

The following code snippet shows how you could set the between value for column-space-distribution on a sample strict column layout:

```
div.strict-columns {column-count: 3; column-width: 30%;
column-gap: 10px; column-width-policy: strict;
column-space-distribution: between}
```

23.7 Column Rule Properties

There is a sub-set of column rule properties which tell the browser how rules — which are lines that run in column gaps — should appear in a columnar layout. There are four properties in this sub-set which allow you to set color values, the style of the rule, how wide the rule line should appear and one shortcut property that can do all of these things.

column-rule-color Property

Not surprisingly, the `column-rule-color` property is used to set the color for the rule line. It takes either a standard color value or the `inherit` property, which would take on any parent value which would be available.

The `column-rule-color` property is able to take on any type of color value, including being able to set RGB, Alpha and HSL (Hue Saturation Lightness) ways of setting color allowed by the CSS3 color module. The following code snippet shows the various ways you can set color values for a rule, all of them equivalent to setting a red rule.

```
div.red_name-columns {column-count: 3; column-width: 30%;
column-gap: 10px; column-rule-color: red}

div.red_fullhex-columns {column-count: 3; column-width: 30%;
column-gap: 10px; column-rule-color: #ff0000}

div.red_compressedhex-columns {column-count: 3;
column-width: 30%; column-gap: 10px; column-rule-color: #f00}

div.red_rgb_number-columns {column-count: 3; column-width: 30%;
column-gap: 10px; column-rule-color: rgb(255,0,0)}

div.red_rgb_percentage-columns {column-count: 3; column-width:
30%; column-gap: 10px; column-rule-color: rgb(100%,0,0)}

div.red_rgb_alpha-columns {column-count: 3; column-width: 30%;
column-gap: 10px; column-rule-color: rgba(255,0,0,0.75)} /* red
with an opacity value of 0.75*/

div.red_hsl-columns {column-count: 3; column-width: 30%;
column-gap: 10px; column-rule-color: hsl(0, 100%, 50%)} /* hue,
saturation and lightness value for 'red' */
```

If only the `column-rule-color` is specified, all of the other column-rule properties are assumed and set to their default values.

For more information on color values, see Chapter 13, "Color Properties."

column-rule-style Property

The `column-rule-style` property allows you to set the look of the rule line. It can take on any of the properties belonging to the border sub-set of elements, as well as `inherit`. The set of border properties includes the 2D values `dashed`, `dotted`, `double` and `solid`, as well as the 3D borders values `inset`, `outset`, `groove` and `ridged` values. There's also the `none` value, and the CSS2 variant on `none` called `hidden`, which has the same effect, but is supposed to be used in conjunction with table elements to resolve any possible border conflicts that might arise. CSS3 introduces three further three 2D values: `dot-dash`, `dot-dot-dash` and `wave`. The `dot-dash` value produces a border made of alternating dots and dashes, `dot-dot-dash` produces a similar border containing two dots for every dash, and the `wave` value produces an undulating, sinuous wave pattern for a border. The `inherit` value takes on any parent value that may be present for column-rule style.

The following code snippet shows how you can set a wavy styled rule to a columnar display:

```
div.wavy-columns {column-count: 3; column-width: 30%;
column-gap: 20px; column-rule-style: wave}
```

If only the `column-rule-style` property is set, all of the other column-rule properties are assumed and set to their default values. The specification says nothing about whether separate rule styles are possible between different columns, but the assumption would be that by default if only one value is specified, it is applied to all rule lines, and if multiple values are set, they are displayed in sequence. If `column-rule-style` property is set to `none`, it forces the browser to set `column-rule-width` to 0.

For more information on border styles, see Chapter 12, "Box Properties."

column-rule-width Property

You can set the width of the rule using the `column-rule-width` property. It takes all of the values available to the `border-width` property as well as `inherit`. The `border-width` property can either take a set pixel value or one of three named values: `thin`, `medium` and `thick`. The default display value for `column-rule-width` is `medium`. The `inherit` value takes on any parental value that may be available.

The following code snippet shows how you can set a thick dot-dashed rule line to your columnar layout:

```
div.dotdash-columns {column-count: 3; column-width: 30%;
column-gap: 20px; column-rule-style: dot-dash;
column-rule-width: thick}
```

If only the `column-rule-width` property is set, all of the other column-rule properties are assumed and set to their default values. The specification says nothing about whether separate rule styles are possible between different columns, but the assumption would be that by default if only one value is specified, it is applied to all rule lines, and if multiple values are set — as is permitted with `border-width` — they are displayed in sequence.

For more information on border width values, see Chapter 12, "Box Properties."

column-rule Property

The `column-rule` property is the shortcut property, allowing you to set all of the column-rule values common to the other properties in this sub-set of properties, as well as `inherit`. The order for setting the properties is `column-rule-width`, `column-rule-style` and then `column-rule-color`. So, if you wanted to set a thin `dot-dot-dashed` green rule line, you could use the code in the following snippet to do that:

```
div.thin_green_dotdotdash-columns {column-count: 3; column-width:
30%; column-gap: 20px; column-rule: thin, dot-dot-dash, green}
```

23.8 column-span Property

There will be instances where you will want to be able to have elements — such as pictures or header text — span across several columns, and this is the reason for having the `column-span` property. The `column-span` property has four possible values: an integer value, `none`, `all` and `inherit`.

If an integer value is set, it tells the browser how many columns the element it is attached to is intended to span. If this integer value is greater than the total number of columns displayed, then the element will span all of the displayed columns — it will not overflow. If the `all` value is set, the element will automatically span all of the columns. The `none` value is the default, and restricts the element to be contained within a single column. Finally, the `inherit` value takes on whatever parent value may have already been set for `column-span`. The following code snippet provides a sense of how this property works:

```
<div style="column-count: 3; column-rule: solid black 20px;
column-gap: 30px">
<h1 style="column-span: all; font-size: x-large">Some Header Text
That Spans All Columns</h1>
<p>...</p>
<img src="Vanessa_in_a_tree.jpg" style="column-span: 2" />
<p>...</p>
</div>
```

What is important to note is that when an element spans a column, the content that follows it flows into the adjacent column above it, and then starts again in the first column, and when that is full, begins again below the spanned element in the second column. Taking the previous code snippet as an example, the flow of content would follow the numbered sequence as seen in Figure 23–4.

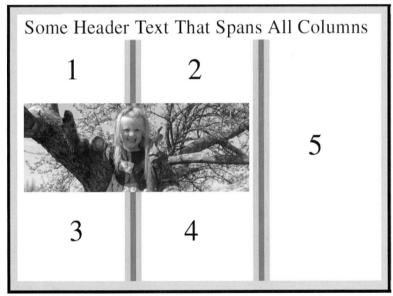

Figure 23–4 Depicting the flow of text in a multi-column display when content spans more than one column.

SCROLLBARS

Topics in This Chapter

- The Parts of a Scrollbar
- Scrollbar Properties

Chapter 24

Have you ever wanted to change the color scheme of the scrollbars that appear alongside your Web pages? Me neither, but apparently some people have, and Microsoft built in some extra CSS properties to handle this. The effect can add a bit of harmless pizzazz to your Web pages.

Scrollbars appear whenever there is more information available that can be displayed. Using a scrollbar — either to scroll a Web page or text in Web elements like text areas with overflowing text — enables the user to move (or "scroll") the text.

24.1 The Parts of a Scrollbar

At the top and bottom of every scrollbar (and I am assuming a vertical scrollbar here) are arrow buttons. In between these two buttons is an area called the scrollbar tray. In the scrollbar tray (assuming that there is scrollable content on the page) there is the scrollbar slider, which is a button that can be directly manipulated by the user. The content the scrollbar affects (i.e., scrolls) is called the viewport. The button elements contain shading elements (which produce the 3D effect) and the slide tray appears to be inset in relation to the buttons, and so is shaded using a dithering process.

These elements can be broken down further: the topmost part of the arrow button and the slider is known as the face. The arrow buttons and slider are set upon a base, and a virtual light source highlights the top and right raised faces of the button, where the left and bottom faces are in a shadow. The other side of the base (also to the left and bottom) is rendered in a dark shadow. Figure 24–1 shows all of these scrollbar elements.

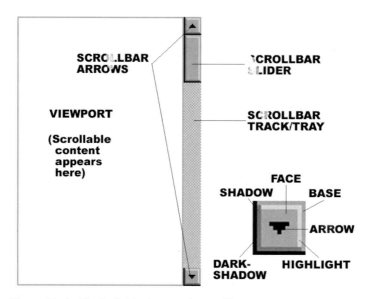

Figure 24–1   The individual parts of a scrollbar.

All of these elements can take on color values under the set of CSS scrollbar extensions first made available in Internet Explorer 5.5.

24.2 Scrollbar Properties

There are eight CSS scrollbar properties: `scrollbar-arrow-color`, `scrollbar-base-color`, `scrollbar-face-color`, `scrollbar-shadow-color`, `scrollbar-darkshadow-color`, `scrollbar-3dlight-color`, `scrollbar-highlight-color` and `scrollbar-track-color`. These properties all control various color aspects of the scrollbar.

`scrollbar-arrow-color` sets the color of an active scrollbar arrow. `scrollbar-base-color` sets the "base" color for the scrollbar elements, setting the color values for the scrollbar button arrows, the arrow on the scrollbar button, the scrollbar slider and scrollbar tray (which is dithered). `scrollbar-face-color` sets the color of the "upper" portions of the scrollbar, namely the arrow button face, the slider face and the slide tray (which is dithered). The difference between the dithering value of the slider tray for `scrollbar-base-color` as opposed to `scrollbar-face-color` is that `scrollbar-face-color` presents a much lighter dithered color. `scroll-bar-shadow-color` sets a color value for the bottom and right edges of the scroll tray and arrows (again, assuming a vertical scrollbar). `scrollbar-darkshadow-color` does the same as `scrollbar-shadow-color`, but the shadow effect is more pronounced. `scrollbar-3dlight-color` sets the color value for the top-left edges of the scroll box and arrow buttons and `scrollbar-highlight-color` sets the top-left edges of the scroll box, the "top" portions of the arrow buttons and the scrollbar tray to the desired color. The `scrollbar-track-color` property controls the color of the track in which the slider slides.

Listing 24.1 sets various parts of the scrollbar to the color maroon in order to illustrate each scrollbar property in turn (whose effects are depicted in the illustration that follows it).

Listing 24.1   *Scrollbar Example 1*

```
<html>
<head>
<title>Scrollbar Example 1</title>
<style>
td {font-family: arial, helvetica, sans-serif; font-size: 12px;
    font-weight: bold}
textarea.3dlight {scrollbar-3dlight-color: maroon}
textarea.arrow {scrollbar-arrow-color: maroon}
textarea.base {scrollbar-base-color: maroon}
textarea.darkshadow {scrollbar-darkshadow-color: maroon}
textarea.face {scrollbar-face-color: maroon}
textarea.highlight {scrollbar-highlight-color: maroon}
textarea.shadow {scrollbar-shadow-color: maroon}
textarea.track {scrollbar-track-color: maroon}
</style>
</head>
<body>

<table>
 <tr>
  <td align="center">
  <form>
  <textarea rows="4" cols="15" wrap="virtual">The quick brown fox
jumps over the lazy dog. The quick brown fox jumps over the lazy
dog.
  </textarea>
  </form>
  Normal scrollbars</td>
```

Listing 24.1   *Scrollbar Example 1 (continued)*

```
  <td align="center">
  <form>
  <textarea class="3dlight" rows="4" cols="15" wrap="virtual">The
quick brown fox jumps over the lazy dog. The quick brown fox jumps
over the lazy dog.
  </textarea>
  </form>
  scrollbar-3dlight-color
  </td>
  <td align="center">
  <form>
  <textarea class="arrow" rows="4" cols="15" wrap="virtual">The
quick brown fox jumps over the lazy dog. The quick brown fox jumps
over the lazy dog.
  </textarea>
  </form>
  scrollbar-arrow-color
  </td>
 </tr>
 <tr>
  <td align="center">
  <form>
  <textarea class="base" rows="4" cols="15" wrap="virtual">The
quick brown fox jumps over the lazy dog. The quick brown fox jumps
over the lazy dog.
  </textarea>
  </form>
  scrollbar-base-color
  </td>
  <td align="center">
  <form>
  <textarea class="darkshadow" rows="4" cols="15" wrap="virtual">
The quick brown fox jumps over the lazy dog. The quick brown fox
jumps over the lazy dog.
  </textarea>
  </form>
  scrollbar-darkshadow-color
  </td>
```

Listing 24.1 *Scrollbar Example 1 (continued)*

```
<td align="center">
<form>
<textarea class="face" rows="4" cols="15" wrap="virtual">The
quick brown fox jumps over the lazy dog. The quick brown fox jumps
over the lazy dog.
</textarea>
</form>
scrollbar-face-color: red
</td>
</tr>
</tr>
<tr>
<td align="center">
<form>
<textarea class="highlight" rows="4" cols="15" wrap="virtual">
The quick brown fox jumps over the lazy dog. The quick brown fox
jumps over the lazy dog.
</textarea>
</form>
scrollbar-highlight-color
</td>
<td align="center">
<form>
<textarea class="shadow" rows="4" cols="15" wrap="virtual">The
quick brown fox jumps over the lazy dog. The quick brown fox jumps
over the lazy dog.
</textarea>
</form>
scrollbar-shadow-color
</td>
<td align="center">
<form>
<textarea class="track" rows="4" cols="15" wrap="virtual">The
quick brown fox jumps over the lazy dog. The quick brown fox jumps
over the lazy dog.
</textarea>
</form>
scrollbar-track-color
</td>
</tr>
</table>

</body>
</html>
```

Note that in Figure 24–2, the "normal" scrollbar is how a typical scrollbar is displayed under the Windows XP operating system — so that when you use any of the scrollbar CSS properties in your code, you effectively turn the scrollbar into a pre-Windows XP (i.e., Windows 95/98/2000) scrollbar display. This could throw off a viewer expecting a "normal" scrollbar, but it is at least guaranteed to stand out. It is ultimately up to the Web author to decide whether or not coloring scrollbars is an effective enhancement or not.

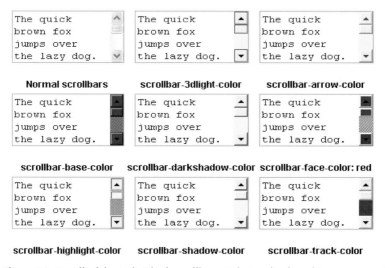

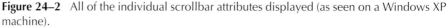

Figure 24–2 All of the individual scrollbar attributes displayed (as seen on a Windows XP machine).

Since this is CSS, you can set the colors using any of the standard CSS color values, including hexadecimal, named values (i.e., "red") or RGB values.

This set of elements can be applied not only to the Web page as a whole, but also to elements within a page, such as a `textarea` element within a form. In fact they can be set to any element that may use scrollbars (this includes the `<applet>`, `<body>`, `<embed>`, `<object>`, `<select>`, `<table>` and `<textarea>` tags, plus any other element which has an overflow CSS property set to `auto` or `scroll`).

Listing 24.2 which changes the colors of certain scrollbar elements within a `textarea` element (whose effects can be seen in Figure 24–3).

Listing 24.2 *Scrollbar Example 2*

```
<html>
<head>
<title>Scrollbar Example 1</title>
<style>
textarea {
scrollbar-face-color: red;
scrollbar-3dlight-color: silver;
scrollbar-track-color: white;
scrollbar-arrow-color: yellow;
}
</style>
<script>
function changeColor(){
if (document.all)
document.body.style.cssText="scrollbar-shadow-color: aqua; scroll-
bar-face-color: black; scrollbar-track-color: black"
}
</script>
</head>
<body>

<form>
<textarea rows="4" name="scroll_example" cols="15" wrap="virtual">
The button faces are red, the button arrows are yellow, the slide
tray is white and the 3d parts of the buttons are silver.
</textarea>

<input type="button" value="Click to alter scrollbar colors"
name="sample_button" onClick="changeColor()">
</form>

</body>
</html>
```

All of these properties can also be applied via JavaScript calls. So, for example, you could change the various colors of elements on your scrollbar as the user's mouse passes over an onscreen element, or click on a button. Try clicking on the button displayed by this code example to see the effect. When you click on the button, you'll notice that the "shadow" portions of the 3D buttons in the text-area scrollbar will be rendered in an aqua color. But the face of the buttons in the text-area are *not* changed to black, because it cannot override the existing, specific value already set to the textarea. This is correct cascading behavior in action: more specific references override less specific references. However, you may have noticed the scrollbar faces for the Web browser *have* been changed to black, since there were no previous scrollbar values to overrule.

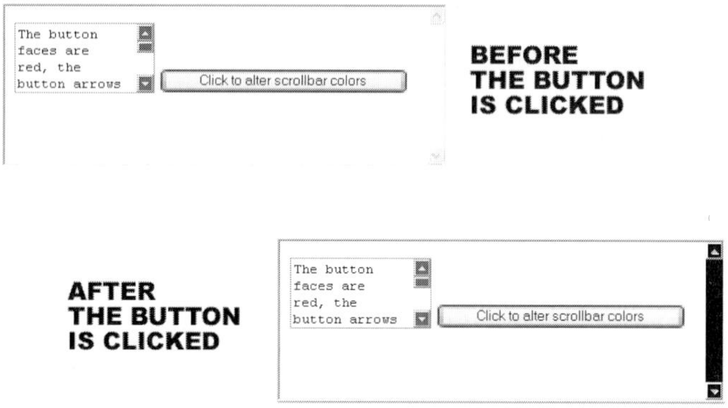

Figure 24–3 The effect on the scrollbars before and after the button is clicked.

Perhaps one of the best uses for this family of CSS extensions is to use them with an eye to helping "color-coordinate" all of the elements on your Web site. Say you have a Web site where many of the elements are set to specific colors. You can then use various scrollbar properties to try to match and further enhance the look of the site. For example, take a look at the following code snippet:

```
body {
scrollbar-face-color: #FF6700;
scrollbar-shadow-color: #003333;
scrollbar-highlight-color: #006633;
scrollbar-3dlight-color: #009933;
scrollbar-darkshadow-color: #333333;
scrollbar-track-color: #003399;
scrollbar-arrow-color: #45618F;
}
```

scrollbar-face-color is set to an orange value, scrollbar-shadow-color is set somewhere between a dark green and a dark blue, scrollbar-highlight-color to a medium green, and scrollbar-darkshadow-color is set to a more vibrant green. Finally, the scrollbar-track-color is set to a deep blue value, and scrollbar-arrow-color to a light blue. These broadly match the colors used on the Web site this example comes from (captmondo.com, the author's "Blogger" site), as you can see in Figure 24–4. While there is no green on the page, the various green values were chosen as they provided the best contrast to the matching elements, and made them stand out more. Other designs could instead try to "merge" color values directly with the rest of the page, so that the line between the scrollbar and Web page is less distinct. If you decide to try and use these properties, the best thing you can do is to play with the colors until you are satisfied with the results.

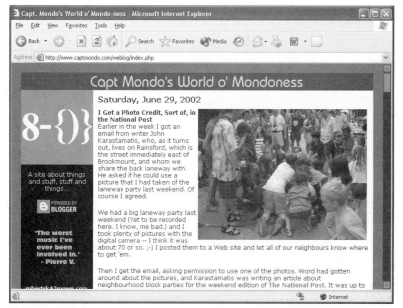

Figure 24–4   An example of "color-coordinating" your scrollbar to match the dominant colors on a Web page.

Core Tip

When applying these values, remember that the spelling of all of these properties uses the American form of "color" (without the "u").

This is a fairly harmless addition to your Web pages. At best you can use it to match the color scheme on the rest of your site, and at worst you'll make your scrollbar invisible.

24.3 Browser Compatibility

All of the scrollbar properties are supported solely within versions of Internet Explorer 5.5 on up. They are not supported within any other browser.

Since the effect isn't displayed in Netscape Navigator, and since it's hard to think of an instance where knowing the color of a scrollbar is crucial to the functioning of a Web page, think of it as a harmless yet snazzy enhancement for the Internet Explorer users who visit your site.

FILTERS AND TRANSITIONS

Topics in This Chapter

- Visual Filters in Internet Explorer
- Static Filters
- Transition Filter Overview

Chapter

25.1 Visual Filters in Internet Explorer

Beginning with Internet Explorer 4, Microsoft began adding a number of programmable visual filter and transition effects to their browser. In fact these new extensions were to be the first CSS-based extension that Microsoft added to their browser. Depending on the filter, their effects can either be modified programmatically via JavaScript, or can be added using CSS elements on a given Web object.

In practice, filters and transitions have seen relatively little use on the Web, as their display properties are exclusive to Internet Explorer, and their effects can be dramatic enough that a page must be viewed using Internet Explorer in order for its content to be readable — in other words, they don't make for browser-compatible code. Having said that, if you are confident that your audience is composed largely of Internet Explorer users — say, on a corporate intranet — or are willing to customize your code on a browser-by-browser basis, you can use these filters and transitions to good effect.

Visual filters and transitions differ from regular CSS properties in that they require the full program code prior to the name of the filter, so the code specified for the `Alpha` filter actually looks something like this code snippet:

```
filter: progid:DXImageTransform.Microsoft.Alpha
```

A given filter's values are further modified by enclosing its values in parentheses, separated by commas, as you can see from the following code snippet:

```
(Opacity=100,FinishOpacity=0, Style=1, StartX=0, FinishX=0,
StartY=0, FinishY=100)
```

At this point you may well be thinking that this is really beginning to stretch the boundaries of CSS, and frankly, you'd be right. In some cases the properties rely upon JavaScript to make them work, so they don't fit the mold of your typical static CSS property used to make some text look nice on a Web page.

Internet Explorer 4.x introduced over a dozen visual filters. All of these original filters were superceded or expanded upon by the release of Internet Explorer 5.5, when Microsoft took the opportunity to rationalize and greatly expand the filtering and transition capabilities within the browser, deprecating several of these earlier filter types in the process.

There are two classes of filters: static filters and transitional filters. The static filters are not always so static, as you will see from some of the examples in this chapter, but their often dynamic effects are rendered on a single selected object. The transition filters are all designed to produce interesting "wipes," slowly revealing new content over the old. This chapter provides an overview of what's available.

Core Tip

For documentation on all of Microsoft's static filters and transition filters, go to the MSDN Library at `http://msdn.microsoft.com/library/`, *and navigate to Web Development and then Web Multimedia section to find it.*

25.2 Static Filters

This section concentrates on the static filters, which are comprised of the following: Alpha, Basicimage, Blur, Chroma, Compositor, DropShadow, Emboss, Engrave, Glow, ICMFilter, Light, Maskfilter, Matrix, MotionBlur, Shadow and Wave. These are all known as "static" filters, because they immediately change the look of an object — in other words, there's no transitional state (this is what sets them apart from the transitional filters also available in Internet Explorer 5.5 and up).

The following is a selection from the numerous static filters you can find in Internet Explorer 5.5 and up.

AlphaFilter Filter

By default all objects on a Web page, such as images and text, are opaque — meaning you can't see through them. With the `AlphaFilter` property you can change the opacity value of an object on a Web page, often to dramatic effect.

The `AlphaFilter` has a number of parameters that allow you to set x/y grid values at which you want the opacity values to change. The `StartX` and `FinishX` values tell Internet Explorer the horizontal beginning and end points for the Alpha filter's effects, and the `StartY` and `FinishY` values do the same thing along the vertical dimension. The `Opacity` value takes a percentage value ranging from `0-100`, and sets the beginning opacity value. The `FinishOpacity` takes a similar percentage value, and sets the end transparency value. Different "styles" of opacity gradients can be set using the `Style` value: `0` is Uniform (or "none"), `1` produces a linear gradation in opacity (i.e., horizontal or vertical), `2` a radial gradation and `3` a rectangular gradation. You can see the first two styles used in the Listing 25.1, whose results can be seen in Figure 25–1.

Listing 25.1 *AlphaFilter Example Code*

```
<html>
<head>
<title>AlphaFilter Example</title>
<style>
div {font: bold 12pt arial}
div.box {width: 250px; height: 250px; padding: 20px;
        font: bold 28pt arial;}
body {font: bold 12pt arial}
</style>
</head>

<body>
<div style="float: left"><code>"Style=1"</code> produces a linear
gradient</div>
<div style="float: right"><code>"Style=2"</code> produces a radial
transparency effect</div>

<div class="box" style="background: red; float: left;
filter: progid:DXImageTransform.Microsoft.Alpha (Opacity=100,
FinishOpacity=0, Style=1, StartX=0, FinishX=0, StartY=0,
FinishY=100)">
Some Sample Text</div>
```

Listing 25.1	*AlphaFilter Example Code (continued)*

```
<div class="box" style="background: blue; float: right;
filter: progid:DXImageTransform.Microsoft.Alpha (Opacity=100,
FinishOpacity=0, Style=2, StartX=0, FinishX=0, StartY=0,
FinishY=100)">
Some Sample Text</div>

<div style="float: left; clear: left"><code>Opacity=100,
FinishOpacity=0, Style=1, StartX=0, FinishX=0, StartY=0,
FinishY=100)</code></div>
<div style="float: right; clear: right"><code>Opacity=100,
FinishOpacity=0, Style=2, StartX=0, FinishX=0, StartY=0,
FinishY=100)</code></div>
</body>
</html>
```

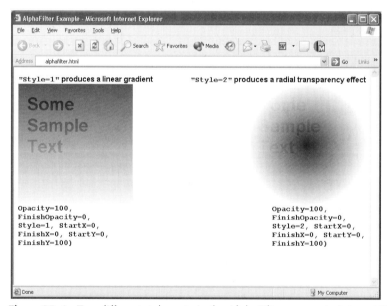

Figure 25–1   Two different styles set via the AlphaFilter as seen in Internet Explorer 6.0.

The code from Listing 25.1 creates a box with a red background that "fades" to white near the bottom of the box, as well as a blue box that uses a radial gradient that is fully opaque in the center and becomes transparent at the edges. Playing around with the `StartX`, `FinishX`, `StartY` and `FinishY` values will change the location at which the opacity values begin and end.

Blur and MotionBlur Filters

There are two types of static blur filters available: one which makes a Web object appear fuzzy, and another which makes a Web object appear as if it has moved rapidly. The first effect is created by the `Blur` filter, the second by the `MotionBlur` filter.

The `Blur` filter takes four values: `makeShadow`, `pixelRadius`, `shadowOpacity` and the near ubiquitous `enabled`. The `enabled` value appears in most of Microsoft's filters, and is there simply to "activate" the filter, and if it is not present, it is activated by default. The most important property of the bunch is arguably `pixelRadius`, which sets the radius of the blur; a higher value makes an object appear more blurry. The `makeshadow` and `shadowOpacity` values are used to set a shadow effect; the first can be set to either `true` or `false`, the second takes a numeric value ranging from `0.0` to `1.0` and sets the "darkness" of the shadow. The last two values are best used in conjunction with images, but the first can produce some impressive blur effects all on its own, as Listing 25.2, whose results are depicted in Figure 25–2, shows.

Listing 25.2	*Blur Filter Example Code*

```
<html>
<head>
<title>Blur Filter Example</title>
<style>
div {font: bold 12pt arial}
div.box {width: 175px; height: 175px; padding: 20px;
         font: bold 28pt arial;}
body {font: bold 12pt arial}
</style>
</head>

<body>
<div style="float: left"><code>PixelRadius='2'</code> is only
slightly blurry</div>
<div style="float: right"><code>PixelRadius='5'</code> is more
blurry</div>
<div class="box" style="background: red; float: left;
clear: left;  filter:
progid:DXImageTransform.Microsoft.Blur(PixelRadius='2')">
Some Sample Text</div>
<div class="box" style="background: blue; float: right; clear:
right;
filter: progid:DXImageTransform.Microsoft.Blur(PixelRadius='5')">
Some Sample Text</div>
```

| Listing 25.2 | *Blur Filter Example Code (continued)* |

```
<div style="float: left; clear: left">
<code>PixelRadius='15'</code> is unreadable</div>
<div style="float: right; clear: right">
<code>PixelRadius='50'</code> begins to warp 
reality</div>
<div class="box" style="background: yellow; float: left;
clear: left;  filter:
progid:DXImageTransform.Microsoft.Blur(PixelRadius='15')">
Some Sample Text</div>
<div class="box" style="background: green; float: right;
clear: right; filter:
progid:DXImageTransform.Microsoft.Blur(PixelRadius='100')">
Some Sample Text</div>
</body>
</html>
```

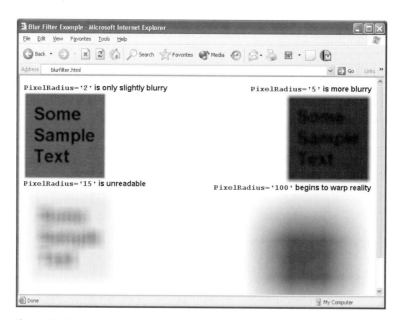

Figure 25–2 Increasing values for PixelRadius produce increasing effects of the Blur filter in Internet Explorer 6.0.

As you can see from Figure 25–2, the higher the numeric value set to `PixelRadius`, the blurrier the image.

The MotionBlur filter produces a similar effect, except that instead of simply making an object appear "fuzzy," it makes it look as if it is moving rapidly. It takes three values: Strength sets the amount in pixels for the motion blur value, and Direction sets the angle in degrees for the motion blur, essentially setting the "course" of the blur. Add can either be set to true, which sets whether the blur effect should overlay the object, or false, which effectively sets the motion blur across the whole of the object. Listing 25.3 puts the MotionBlur filter into action, and its results can be seen in Figure 25–3.

Listing 25.3 *MotionBlur Example Code*

```
<html>
<head>
<title>MotionBlur Filter Example</title>
<style>
div {font: bold 12pt arial}
div.box {width: 175px; height: 175px; padding: 20px;
         font: bold 28pt arial;}
body {font: bold 12pt arial}
</style>
</head>
<body>
<div style="float: left"><code>Add='true'</code></div>
<div style="float: right"><code>Add='false'</code></div>
<div class="box" style="background: red; float: left;
clear: left;  filter:
progid:DXImageTransform.Microsoft.MotionBlur(Strength=20,
Direction=315, Add='true')">
Some Sample Text</div>
<div class="box" style="background: blue; float: right;
clear: right; filter:
progid:DXImageTransform.Microsoft.MotionBlur(Strength=20,
Direction=315, Add='false')">
Some Sample Text</div>

<div style="float: left; clear: left"><code>Strength=50,
Direction=90</code></div>
<div style="float: right; clear: right"><code>Strength=100,
Direction=120</code></div>
<div class="box" style="background: yellow; float: left;
clear: left;  filter:
progid:DXImageTransform.Microsoft.MotionBlur(Strength=50,
Direction=90, Add='true')">
Some Sample Text</div>
```

| Listing 25.3 | *MotionBlur Example Code (continued)* |

```
<div class="box" style="background: green; float: right;
clear: right; filter:
progid:DXImageTransform.Microsoft.MotionBlur(Strength=100,
Direction=120, Add='true')">
Some Sample Text</div>
</body>
</html>
```

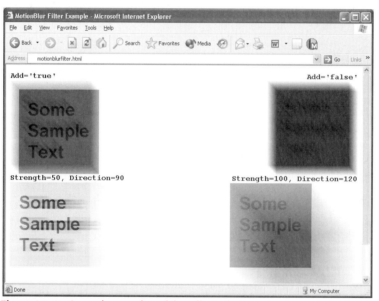

Figure 25–3   Several examples of the effects that can be generated using Internet Explorer's MotionBlur filter.

The effects of the Add value can be seen in the top two squares: the Add="true" value effectively sets a strong opacity value for the final state of the blur, making the text readable; conversely the Add="false" value renders the text contained within its square relatively hard to read, and it appears more blurry. The two lower squares clearly show the effects of Strength and Direction: the larger the Strength value, the more the selected object appears to be in movement, and the Direction value sets the plane along which the motion blur is set.

DropShadow and Shadow Filters

Two types of shadow filters are available: DropShadow and Shadow. The first produces a shadow that seems to fall onto an invisible plane set behind the Web object, whereas the latter produces a shadow that gradually tails from the corners of the selected Web object.

The DropShadow filter takes four values: OffX and OffY take pixel values by which the shadow is offset from the object (the values can either be positive or negative), Color takes any valid color value and Positive either turns the effect on ("true"), or off ("false"). Listing 25.4 show the DropShadow filter put to work.

Listing 25.4	*DropShadow Example Code*

```
<html>
<head>
<title>DropShadow Filter Example</title>
<style>
div {font: bold 12pt arial}
div.box {width: 175px; height: 175px; padding: 20px; font: bold
28pt arial;}
body {font: bold 12pt arial}
</style>
</head>
<body>
<div style="float: left"><code>OffX=10, OffY=10</code></div>
<div style="float: right"><code>OffX=-10, OffY=-10</code></div>
<div class="box" style="background: red; float: left;
clear: left;  filter: progid:DXImageTransform.Microsoft.DropShadow
(OffX=10, OffY=10, Color='black', Positive='true')">
Some Sample Text</div>
<div class="box" style="background: blue; float: right;
clear: right; filter: progid:DXImageTransform.Microsoft.DropShadow
(OffX=-10, OffY=-10, Color='black', Positive='true')">
Some Sample Text</div>

<div style="float: left; clear: left"><code>OffX=50,
OffY=-50</code></div>
<div style="float: right; clear: right">
<code>Positive='false'</code></div>
<div class="box" style="background: yellow; float: left;
clear: left; filter: progid:DXImageTransform.Microsoft.DropShadow
(OffX=50, OffY=-50, Color='black', Positive='true')">
Some Sample Text</div>
```

Listing 25.4	*DropShadow Example Code (continued)*

```
<div class="box" style="background: green; float: right;
clear: right; filter: progid:DXImageTransform.Microsoft.DropShadow
(OffX=10, OffY=10, Color='navy', Positive='false')">
Some Sample Text</div>
</body>
</html>
```

The results of the code in Listing 25.4 can be seen in Figure 25–4. The shadow for the top-right square is offset 10 pixels to the left and below the square, and for the top-left square the object — rather than the shadow — is offset by 10 pixels down and to the right, thanks to the negative values set for OffX and OffY. The lower-left square shows a more extreme version of the effect, and the lower-right square depicts the effect turned "off" when Positive='false'.

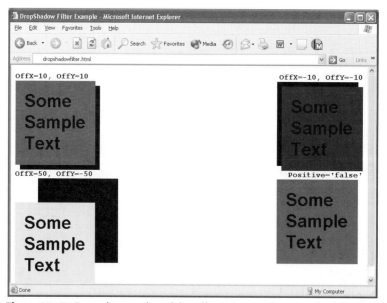

Figure 25–4 Several examples of the effects that can be generated using Internet Explorer's DropShadow filter.

To some eyes, the DropShadow filter effect may appear a bit clunky — it produces a square shadow underneath the selected object, but in the more extreme cases it looks just like a square not necessarily connected to the one "on top" of it. That's where the Shadow filter comes in: it produces a gradient shadow effect, linking the object to its shadow. It takes three values: the color property sets the color of the shadow, `direction` sets the angle value for the shadow, and `strength` sets the distance in pixels that the shadow effect is spread over. Listing 25.5 shows the `Shadow` filter put to use on our usual four colorful squares.

Listing 25.5	*Shadow Example Code*

```
<html>
<head>
<title>Shadow Filter Example</title>
<style>
div {font: bold 12pt arial}
div.box {width: 175px; height: 175px; padding: 20px;
font: bold 28pt arial;}
body {font: bold 12pt arial}
</style>
</head>
<body>
<div style="float: left">
<code>color='blue', Direction=40, Strength=10</code>
</div>
<div style="float: right">
<code>color='black', Direction=120, Strength=10</code>
</div>
<div class="box" style="background: red; float: left;
clear: left;  filter: progid:DXImageTransform.Microsoft.Shadow
(color='blue', Direction=40, Strength=10)">
Some Sample Text</div>
<div class="box" style="background: blue; float: right;
clear: right; filter: progid:DXImageTransform.Microsoft.Shadow
(color='black', Direction=120, Strength=10)">
Some Sample Text</div>

<div style="float: left; clear: left">
<code>color='black', Direction=220, Strength=20</code>
</div>
<div style="float: right; clear: right">
<code>color='green', Direction=320, Strength=25</code>
</div>
<div class="box" style="background: yellow; float: left;
clear: left; filter: progid:DXImageTransform.Microsoft.Shadow
(color='black', Direction=220, Strength=20)">
Some Sample Text</div>
```

Listing 25.5	*Shadow Example Code (continued)*

```
<div class="box" style="background: green; float: right;
clear: right; filter: progid:DXImageTransform.Microsoft.Shadow
(color='green', Direction=320, Strength=25)">
Some Sample Text</div>
</body>
</html>
```

The effects of the `Shadow` filter are plain to see in Figure 25–5. The lower-right square shows an interesting effect when the shadow color matches that of the target object — it begins to look like a cube. Though no example of it is shown here, the shadowing effect is best when applied at a diagonal angle to the object; values of `0`, `90`, `180` or `270` added to `Direction` produce the gradient shadow effect only to the top, right, bottom and left sides, respectively, and the effect looks odd.

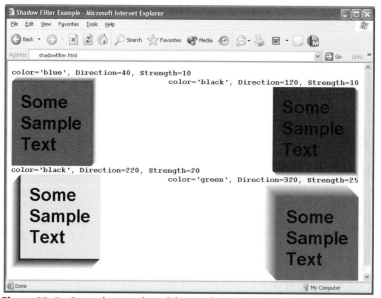

Figure 25–5 Several examples of the gradient shadow effects that can be made using Internet Explorer's Shadow filter.

Emboss and Engrave Filters

There are two filters available in Internet Explorer that can be used to render a simple 3D effect upon a selected Web object: Emboss and Engrave. Both first render the selected Web object into grayscale, and then either make it appear as if it has been punched out of the page (Emboss), or had been chiseled into the page (Engrave).

Both Emboss and Engrave operate in much the same manner — all you have to do is set the filter and you get an effect. They can also both take a bias value which ranges from −1.0 (low brightness) to 1.0 (high brightness). While these filters can be used effectively on text, they produce much more dramatic results when pictures are selected. Listing 25.6 sets the Emboss and Engrave filters on our usual four squares, though due to the grayscale effect, the results are not colorful.

Listing 25.6	*Emboss and Engrave Example Code*

```
<html>
<head>
<title>Emboss and Engrave Filters Example</title>
<style>
div {font: bold 12pt arial}
div.box {width: 175px; height: 175px; padding: 20px;
font: bold 28pt arial;}
body {font: bold 12pt arial}
</style>
</head>
<body>
<div style="float: left"><code>Emboss()</code></div>
<div style="float: right"><code>Emboss(Bias='0.5')</code></div>
<div class="box" style="background: red; float: left;
clear: left;  filter: progid:DXImageTransform.Microsoft.Emboss()">
Some Sample Text</div>
<div class="box" style="background: blue; float: right;
clear: right;
filter: progid:DXImageTransform.Microsoft.Emboss(Bias='0.5')">
Some Sample Text</div>

<div style="float: left; clear: left"><code>Engrave()</code></div>
<div style="float: right; clear: right">
<code>Engrave(Bias='0.5')</code></div>
<div class="box" style="background: yellow; float: left;
clear: left;
filter: progid:DXImageTransform.Microsoft.Engrave()">
Some Sample Text</div>
```

Listing 25.6	*Emboss and Engrave Example Code (continued)*

```
<div class="box" style="background: green; float: right;
clear: right;
filter: progid:DXImageTransform.Microsoft.Engrave(Bias='0.5')">
Some Sample Text</div>
</body>
</html>
```

As you can see in Figure 25–6, the effects produced by the Emboss and Engrave filters are quite distinct. More subtle is the effect of the Bias value in each case (as can be seen in both left-hand squares, which in addition to brightening the object, also makes the effect less distinct).

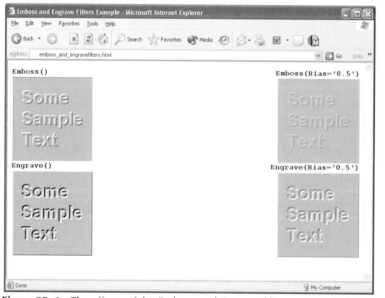

Figure 25–6 The effects of the Emboss and Engrave filters as seen in Internet Explorer 6.0

One part of the code that some people might find puzzling, or merely an oversight, is the fact that color values are still set to these squares. This is deliberate, as the Emboss and Engrave filters require a background field upon which their effects can be stamped. The actual color value doesn't matter as much as the fact that there has to be one for these effects to be visible.

Wave filter

One filter that produces an interesting and unique effect is the `Wave` filter. It takes the selected Web object and adds a sine wave to it, making the object appear to "wobble." The `Wave` filter takes five values: `Add` sets whether or not the wave overlays the original image and takes either a `true` or `false` value; `LightStrength` sets the difference in the intensity of the peaks and troughs of the object; `Phase` sets the phase offset value for the sine wave (default: `0`; ranges from `0 - 360` degrees); `Strength` sets dimensions for the wave effect as a number of pixels; and `Freq` sets the frequency of the sine wave (i.e., how many "ripples" are made).

In Listing 25.7 the effects of the `Add` and the `Freq` values are the only changes made to each of our sample squares in order to isolate these particular effects, whose results can be seen in Figure 25–7.

Listing 25.7	*Wave Filter Example Code*

```
<html>
<head>
<title>Wave Filter Example</title>
<style>
div {font: bold 12pt arial}
div.box {width: 175px; height: 175px; padding: 20px;
font: bold 28pt arial;}
body {font: bold 12pt arial}
</style>
</head>
<body>
<div style="float: left"><code>Add='false' and Freq='1'</code>
</div>
<div class="box" style="background: red; float: left;
clear: left;
filter:
progid:DXImageTransform.Microsoft.Wave(Add='false',LightStrength=
'40',Phase='80',Strength='50',Freq='1')">
Some Sample Text</div>
<div style="float: right"><code>Add='false' and Freq='3'</code>
</div>
<div class="box" style="background: blue; float: right;
clear: right;
filter:
progid:DXImageTransform.Microsoft.Wave(Add='false',LightStrength=
'40',Phase='80',Strength='50',Freq='3')">
Some Sample Text</div>
```

Listing 25.7 *Wave Filter Example Code (continued)*

```
<div style="float: left; clear: left"><code>Add='true' and
Freq='1'</code></div>
<div style="float: right; clear: right"><code>Add='true' and
Freq='3'</code></div>
<div class="box" style="background: yellow; float: left;
clear: left;
filter:
progid:DXImageTransform.Microsoft.Wave(Add='true',LightStrength='
40',Phase='80',Strength='50',Freq='1')">
Some Sample Text</div>
<div class="box" style="background: green; float: right;
clear: right;
filter:
progid:DXImageTransform.Microsoft.Wave(Add='true',LightStrength='
40',Phase='80',Strength='50',Freq='3')">
Some Sample Text</div>
</body>
</html>
```

It is easy to make out the effect of the Freq value on the four colored squares in Figure 25–7; those on the left contain one set of ripples, while those on the right are more wavy, containing three sets of ripples. The Add value is significant to the legibility of the text contained in the boxes. In the two top examples, where Add='false', the text is warped along with the rest of the box they are contained within. In the two bottom boxes the original box and text is intact, and the wave is applied "underneath." A greater numeric value set to LightStrength will emphasize the object over the wave effect applied to it. A greater Strength value would increase the "depth" of the waves created. Changing the Phase value changes where the beginning of the sine wave is applied to the object.

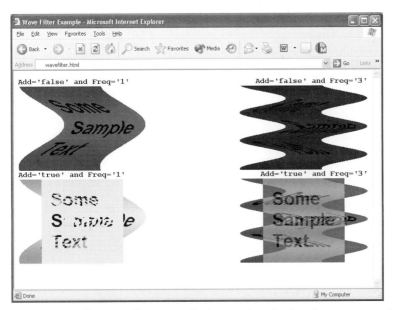

Figure 25–7   The Wave filter as applied to a series of colored squares containing text as seen in Internet Explorer 6.0.

BasicImage Filter

The `BasicImage` filter contains a grab-bag of values which control the rotation, opacity and color processing done to a selected object. Though not exactly a shortcut property — its values don't correspond exactly to the other properties that control such things as opacity, for example — it does allow you to easily set multiple effects on an object all at once.

The `BasicImage` filter takes a set of six values, most of which take either a 0 or 1 value which equates to "off" and "on." `Grayscale` can set the object to a monochrome value. `Xray` can produce interesting effects, especially on images, setting them to grayscale but emphasizing edges. `mirror` produces a mirror image of the object, and `invert` switches it around internally. The two sets of values that differ from this on/off mechanism are `rotation`, which can take an integer value from 0 – 4 (0 being no rotation, 1 being 90 degrees, 2 is 180 degrees, 3 is 270 degrees and 4 being 360 degrees), and `opacity`, which can take a range of values between 0.0 (transparent) – 1.0 (opaque).

Listing 25.8 isolates the effects of the `rotation` and `opacity` values for `BasicImage`. To make the opacity effect more clear, all of the squares have been set to the same color (red).

Listing 25.8	*BasicImage Filter Example Code Isolating the Effects of Rotation and Opacity*

```
<html>
<head>
<title>BasicImage Filter Example #1</title>
<style>
div {font: bold 12pt arial}
div.box {width: 175px; height: 175px; padding: 20px;
font: bold 28pt arial;}
body {font: bold 12pt arial}
</style>
</head>
<body>
<div style="float: left"><code>opacity=0.25 and rotation=0</code>
</div>
<div class="box" style="background: red; float: left;
clear: left;
filter: progid:DXImageTransform.Microsoft.BasicImage(grayscale=0,
xray=0, mirror=0, invert=0, opacity=0.25, rotation=0)">
Some Sample Text</div>
<div style="float: right"><code>opacity=0.5 and rotation=1</code>
</div>
<div class="box" style="background: red; float: right;
clear: right;
filter: progid:DXImageTransform.Microsoft.BasicImage(grayscale=0,
xray=0, mirror=0, invert=0, opacity=0.5, rotation=1)">
Some Sample Text</div>

<div style="float: left; clear: left">
<code>opacity=0.75 and rotation=2</code></div>
<div style="float: right; clear: right">
<code>opacity=1.0 and rotation=3</code></div>
<div class="box" style="background: red; float: left; clear: left;
filter: progid:DXImageTransform.Microsoft.BasicImage(grayscale=0,
xray=0, mirror=0, invert=0, opacity=0.75, rotation=2)">
Some Sample Text</div>
<div class="box" style="background: red; float: right;
clear: right;
filter: progid:DXImageTransform.Microsoft.BasicImage(grayscale=0,
xray=0, mirror=0, invert=0, opacity=1.0, rotation=3)">
Some Sample Text</div>
</body>
</html>
```

Figure 25–8 shows how progressive values added to both the `rotation` and `opacity` values increase the level of rotation and decrease the transparency value for the square.

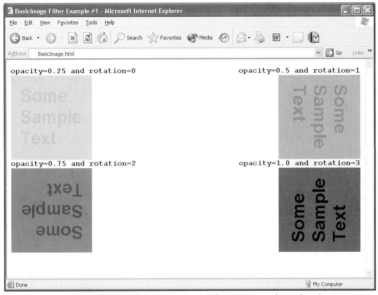

Figure 25–8 The effects of the opacity and rotation values for the BasicImage filter isolated in four example squares.

The effects of the other values are demonstrated in Listing 25.8, where each of the other values are sequentially turned "on," and the `opacity` and `rotation` values are set to their defaults. The effects of this code can be seen in Figure 25–9. The `grayscale` setting converts the red square and black text to levels of gray, eliminating any color contained in the object. The `xray` value also turns the object to grayscale, but turns the black text to white. This is because the text overlaying the square is considered "thicker," and like a bone in an actual X-ray image, the denser parts appear lighter. The square on the bottom right shows the effect of the `mirror` value turned "on," which essentially takes the object and produces a mirror image of it. Finally, the effect of the `invert` value is that it displays the opposite color values for a given object, so the red background becomes blue, and the black text becomes white.

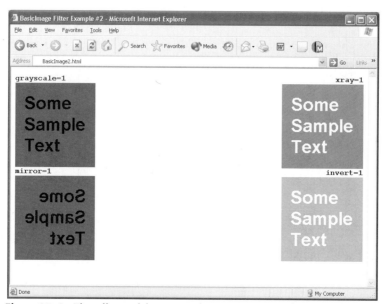

Figure 25–9   The effects of the grayscale, xray, mirror and invert values for the BasicImage filter isolated in four example squares.

Glow Filter

The Glow filter is another simple static filter which enables you to add a funky, radiant halo-like effect to such things as text on a page. It takes three values: color, strength and enabled. The color value can take any color name or numeric color value, strength sets the spread of the Glow in pixels, and enabled tells the browser whether or not to apply the filter (this is the default).

Listing 25.9 depicts ever-increasing values for the Glow filter added to successive blocks of text.

Listing 25.9   *Glow Filter Example Code*

```
<html>
<head>
<title>Glow Filter Example</title>
<style>
div {font: bold 12pt arial}
div.box {width: 175px; height: 175px; padding: 20px; font: bold
23pt arial;}
</style>
</head>
```

| Listing 25.9 | *Glow Filter Example Code (continued)* |

```
<body>
<div style="float:
left"><code>color='red',strength='1'</code></div>
<div style="float:
right"><code>color='blue',strength='5'</code></div>
<div class="box" style="float: left;  clear: left;
filter:progid:DXImageTransform.Microsoft.Glow(color='red',strengt
h='1')">
Sample red glowing text
</div>
<div class="box" style="float: right;  clear: right;
filter:progid:DXImageTransform.Microsoft.Glow(color='blue',streng
th='5')">
Sample blue glowing text
</div>

<div style="float: left; clear:
left"><code>color='yellow',strength='10'</code></div>
<div style="float: right; clear:
right"><code>color='green',strength='25'</code></div>
<div class="box" style="float: left; clear: left;
filter:progid:DXImageTransform.Microsoft.Glow(color='yellow',stre
ngth='10')">
Sample yellow glowing text
</div>
<div class="box" style="float: right; clear: right;
filter:progid:DXImageTransform.Microsoft.Glow(color='green',stren
gth='25')">
Sample green glowing text
</div>
</body>
</html>
```

The effects of the code from Listing 25.9 can be readily seen in Figure 25–10. As you can see, when you change the strength value you find that the strength of the glow also determines a "glow indent" value — if you set the strength of the glow to 100 pixels, the text will be indented from the top and left margins by that same value. Also, like many other of these filters Glow requires some sort of basic layout property — such as width or height, or its position set to absolute — be applied to the target object for the filter to work.

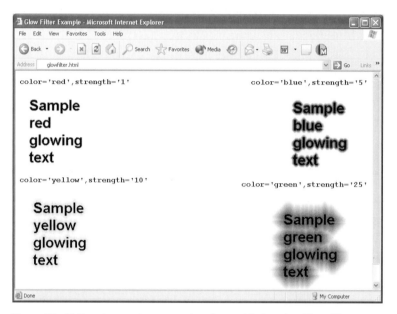

Figure 25–10 Ever-increasing strength values added to the Glow filter, as seen in Internet Explorer 6.0.

Chroma Filter

Internet Explorer's `Chroma` filter is designed to make a specified color transparent. The `Chroma` filter takes two values: `color` (followed either by a color name or numerical color value) and `enabled`, which is the default value. This filter could conceivably be used to remove such things as links for which you have specified a particular color value, or colored text that you want to disappear under certain circumstances.

Listing 25.10 shows how, when you combine the `Chroma` filter with some JavaScript, you can "knock out" an existing color in use on a Web page.

Listing 25.10	*Chroma Filter Example Code*

```
<html>
<head>
<title>Chroma Filter Example</title>
<style>
span {font: bold 24pt arial}
</style>
</head>
```

Listing 25.10	*Chroma Filter Example Code (continued)*

```
<body>
<button
onclick="oFilterDIV.filters.item('DXImageTransform.Microsoft.Chro
ma').color = 'black'">Clear Black Text, Restore Other
Colors</button><br/>
<button
onclick="oFilterDIV.filters.item('DXImageTransform.Microsoft.Chro
ma').color = 'red'">Clear Red Text, Restore Other
Colors</button><br/>
<button
onclick="oFilterDIV.filters.item('DXImageTransform.Microsoft.Chro
ma').color = 'green'">Clear Green Text, Restore Other
Colors</button><br/>
<p>
<div id="oFilterDIV" style="width:340px; height:100px;
filter:progid:DXImageTransform.Microsoft.Chroma(color='white')">
<span style="color: black">This text is black.</span><br/>
<span style="color: red">This text is red.</span><br/>
<span style="color: green">This text is green.</span>
</div>
</p>
</body>
</html>
```

What happens when you run this code in Internet Explorer (as evidenced in Figure 25–11) is that you get three buttons followed by three lines of colored text. When you click a button, it removes the color it represents, and restores another line of colored text if it has been previously cleared. When a button is pressed, the `Chroma` filter is applied to the color value contained within the button [i.e., `('DXImageTransform.Microsoft.Chroma').color = 'black'`] that is then expressed in the line of text containing the same color. If you hit another button, the `Chroma` value is then applied to the new color, and the previously cleared line of text reappears because it is no longer being affected by the filter.

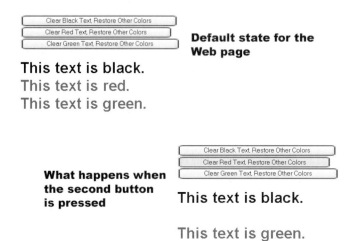

Figure 25–11 The ability of the Chroma filter to "knock out" a specified color value dynamically, as seen in Internet Explorer 6.0.

Despite the JavaScript, the `Chroma` filter is still considered a static filter — the scripting in the example is there primarily to make the effect more evident.

Light Filter

The `Light` filter is used to create the effect of a light source shining on an object. This filter has only one attribute: `enabled`, which is the default. However, this filter is meant to be used in conjunction with a number of different JavaScript methods, which include `addAmbient`, `addCone`, `addPoint`, `changeColor`, `changeStrength`, `clear` and `movelight`. For the record, `addAmbient` throws an ambient, diffuse light on an object, `addCone` casts a conical light source, `addPoint` beams a light source to a particular point which then radiates out, `changeStrength` changes the light source's intensity, and `changeColor`, `clear` and `movelight` all do what you'd think based on their descriptions.

Here's some sample code that shows you how to add the `addAmbient`, `addPoint` and `addCone` filters to a sample image:

Listing 25.11 *Light Filter Example Code*

```
<html>
<head>
<title>Light Filter Example</title>
<style>
div {font: bold 12pt arial}
</style>
<script>
function LightFilter1(){
    greeny.filters.light.addAmbient(0,255,0,100)
    }
function LightFilter2(){
    pointyblue.filters.light.addPoint(100,120,100,0,0,255,100)
    }
function LightFilter3(){
    coneyred.filters.light.addCone(220,120,220,100,150,255,
                          50,50,100,20)
    }
</script>
</head>
<body>
<div style="float: left; clear: left">The original picture</div>
<div style="float: right; clear: right">The same image, but much
greener</div>
<div style="float: left; clear: left"><img src="smaller_annie.jpg"
alt="The original image" width="140" height="187" border="0">
</div>
<div style="float: right; clear: right"><img
src="smaller_annie.jpg" alt="The same image, but much greener"
name="greeny" id="greeny" width="140" height="187" border="0"
style="filter:light" onLoad="LightFilter1()"></div>

<div style="float: left; clear: left"><img src="smaller_annie.jpg"
alt="The same image, but with a blue point source of light added to
it" name="pointyblue" id="pointyblue" width="140" height="187"
border="0" style="filter:light" onLoad="LightFilter2()"></div>
<div style="float: left; clear: left">The same image, but with a
blue point source of light added to it</div>
<div style="float: right; clear: right"><img
src="smaller_annie.jpg" alt="The same image, but with a red cone
of light added to it" name="coneyred" id="coneyred" width="140"
height="187" border="0" style="filter:light"
onLoad="LightFilter3()"></div>
<div style="float: right; clear: right">This time with a red cone
of light added to it</div>
</body>
</html>
```

You get a glimpse of what the `Light` filter does when you see the code in Listing 25.11 run in Internet Explorer, as you can see in Figure 25–12. The top-left image is the original image, the top-right image is the same but with a somewhat diffuse green glow, the bottom-left image uses a blue spotlight that diffuses out, and the bottom-right image contains the same image but with a sharply defined parabola of red light cast upon it.

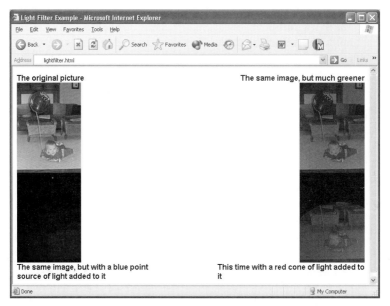

Figure 25–12 Some of the Light filter's effects as seen within Internet Explorer 6.0.

The code behind it needs a bit of explanation. The section contained between the two `<script>` tags contains the JavaScript functions that are activated when the images are loaded via the `onload` statements associated with each individual image. The `LightFilter1()` function uses the `addAmbient` method with a series of values that describe the color of the light in red, green and blue values (ranging from `0` – `255`), followed by a value that describes the strength of the light expressed in a range from `0-100`. So the value "`(0,255,0,100)`" produces a green ambient light filter at full strength. The `LightFilter2()` function uses the `addPoint` method whose first three values equate to the positioning of the point light source from the top, left and then the z-axis (read "distance" from the surface of the picture) of the light source, followed by values for red, green, blue and strength. So the "`(100,34,100,0,0,255,100)`" value adds a point source illumination centered at 100 pixels down and 34 pixels to the right whose source is located 100 pixels "above" the image that is blue and strong. The final `LightFilter3()` function adds a conical light source whose values equate to the left coordinate by the top coordinate by the z-axis for the light *source*, followed by the left and top coordinates for the target of the light's focus, followed by the usual red, green, blue and strength values, plus an additional value describing the spread of the vertical position of the light source and the surface of the displayed object. Whew! In addition, make sure you add the `style="filter:light"` to each image as well as the specific `id` value associated with the function [i.e., `id="pointyblue"` with `LightFilter2()`'s `pointyblue.filters.light.addPoint`].

You can create a lot of these effects by creating equivalent images in graphics programs like PhotoShop or Paint Shop Pro — the advantage of doing things this way is twofold: the code is smaller than an equivalent image file, and you can manipulate it directly — try changing the `onLoad()` statements to `onClick()` in the previous example and then click on the blank picture spaces to get a simple dynamic HTML effect using these filters.

Compositor Filter

The `Compositor` filter is designed to display new content based on a "mix" of the color combinations from two or more objects on a page. It has no value other than itself — it just "does its thing" when it is activated. The effect of the `Compositor` filter is essentially to blend color values between two overlapping objects, making a new display from the two of them.

Listing 25.12 contains three objects: one is an overlaying block of black text on a white background, the second is a hidden block of yellow text on a green background of roughly the same size, though using a different font. The third object is a container which activates the filter when the button on the page is pressed.

| Listing 25.12 | *Compositor Filter Example Code* |

```
<html>
<head>
<title>Compositor Example</title>
<style>
div {position:absolute; left:50; top:50}
</style>
</head>
<body onload="loader()">
<button onClick="filterThing()">Click to See The Compositor Filter
at Work</button><br/>
```

Listing 25.12   *Compositor Filter Example Code (continued)*

```
<div id="container"
style="filter:progid:DXImageTransform.Microsoft.Compositor();
position: absolute; height:500; width:500">
<div style="background: white; color: black; font-family: arial;
font-size: 50pt">Some sample text</div>
</div>
<script>
function loader()
    {
    container.filters.item(0).Apply();
    container.innerHTML = hidden.innerHTML;
    container.filters.item(0).Play();
    }
    function filterThing()
    {
    container.filters.
        item('DXImageTransform.Microsoft.Compositor').Function = 2;
    }
</script>
<div id="hidden" style="display: none">
<div style="background: green; color: yellow; font-family: times;
font-size: 49pt">Some sample text</div>
</div>
</body>
</html>
```

As you can see in Figure 25–13, the effect when activated allows the previously hidden layer to not just appear, but to also blend together with the layer on top of it. As you can see, some of the yellow text and green background come through the top layer, and because the underlying background isn't as large as the top layer, the last couple of letters of the word "sample" remain black.

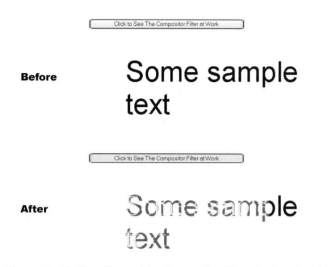

Figure 25–13 The effects of the Compositor filter displayed within Internet Explorer 6.0.

ICMFilter Filter

There are occasions when you want to ensure that an image on a Web page is as good as it can possibly appear onscreen. Though its effects can be subtle the `ICMFilter` is designed to provide more precise color control over objects displayed on a Web page.

The `ICMFilter` filter can take two values: `colorSpace`, which allows the Web author to retrieve a file containing a preset color value; and `intent`, which allows you to pick from four preset values: `Proof`, `Picture`, `Graphic` and `Match`.

The `colorSpace` value is designed to point at a file with an `.icm` extension (the "ICM" stands for "Image Color Management or Image Color Matching" depending on whom you talk to). These files contain a color profile designed for a specific application like a color printer for example. This profile is then taken and adapted for use on a different device, like a computer display. Essentially, this is a means to help you get a better idea onscreen of the true color values of what you can expect to print. The ICM standard was set by the International Color Consortium and is adhered to by such firms as Microsoft, Adobe, Kodak, Fuji, Apple and many more, so you can be confident that any `.icm` file you may get for one computer device is likely to display well in one made by another manufacturer.

The intent value allows you to set more general color value preferences. When it is set to the `Picture` sub-value, the display maintains the relationship between colors for such things as photos and pictures. The `Graphic` setting is meant to be used on such things as charts, and it retains the image's color saturation levels rather than its hue or lightness, ensuring better contrast. The `Proof` sub-value selects the closest supported color values if your display (or whatever) cannot depict that exact color value. The Match sub-value works the same as graphic, but the white point — which is the chroma value for a display, setting the hue though not the level of brightness — value is preserved.

Listing 25.13 sets the Picture and Proof sub-values for intent against a given image file. The results of this code can be seen in Figure 25–14.

Listing 25.13	*ICMFilter Filter Example Code*

```
<html>
<head>
<title>ICMFilter Filter Example</title>
<style>
div {font: bold 12pt arial}
</style>
</head>
<body>
<div style="float: right; clear: right"><code>ICMFilter
(intent='Picture')</code></div>
<div
style="filter:progid:DXImageTransform.Microsoft.ICMFilter(intent=
'Picture')">
<img src="nerva.jpg" width="446" height="220" alt="Coin of Roman
Emperor Nerva" border="0"></div>
<div style="float: right; clear: right"><code>ICMFilter
(intent='Proof')</code></div>
<div
style="filter:progid:DXImageTransform.Microsoft.ICMFilter(intent=
'Proof')">
<img style="float: left; clear: left" src="nerva.jpg" width="446"
height="220" alt="Coin of Roman Emperor Nerva" border="0"></div>
</body>
</html>
```

Figure 25–14 The effects of two settings for the ICMFilter filter displayed within Internet Explorer 6.0.

The effects of these two `ICMFilter` settings are subtle — and may not be easily discernable in the grayscale Figure 25–14 illustration — but they are there. The image of the ancient Roman coin that uses the `Picture` setting is slightly darker in tone overall than the `Proof` setting, reflecting the fact that the true color of the image is in fact slightly lighter than is good for optimal contrast on a computer screen.

Core Tip

For more information on color profiles, go to the International Color Consortium's Web site at: `http://www.color.org/`.

MaskFilter Filter

The `MaskFilter` can be used to render certain colors transparent, and then overlay them with a color value. In effect, it creates what's known as a "mask" for the selected object, allowing you to invert the existing color value and then apply a new one on top of it.

This was one of the original filters added to Internet Explorer 4.0. While it is still present in more recent versions of the browser, you can do much the same with the more advanced `BasicImage` filter. The `MaskFilter` has two values: `enabled`, which is the default, and `color`, which can take any allowable CSS color value. Any object that this filter is applied to must have some sort of layout directly attached to it, such as `width`, `height` or `position: absolute`. Listing 25.14 shows the effects of this filter against a simple text box. The effects of this code can be seen in Figure 25–15.

Listing 25.14	*MaskFilter Filter Example Code*

```
<html>
<head>
<title>MaskFilter Filter Example</title>
<style>
div {font: bold 14pt arial}
p {border: thick dashed; width: 300px; font: bold 30pt arial}
p.magenta {filter:
progid:DXImageTransform.Microsoft.MaskFilter(color=magenta)}
p.lime {filter:
progid:DXImageTransform.Microsoft.MaskFilter(color=lime)}
p.hexvalue {filter:
progid:DXImageTransform.Microsoft.MaskFilter(color=#ffff33)}
</style>
<body>
<div style="float: left; clear: left">Default</div>
<p style="float: left; clear: left">The quick fox jumped over the
lazy dog.</p>
<div style="float: right; clear: right">
<code>MaskFilter(color=magenta)</code></div>
<p class="magenta" style="float: right; clear: right">The quick
fox jumped over the lazy dog.</p>

<div style="float: left; clear: left">
<code>MaskFilter(color=lime)</code></div>
<p class="lime" style="float: left; clear: left">The quick fox
jumped over the lazy dog.</p>
<div style="float: right; clear: right">
<code>MaskFilter(color=#ffff33)</code></div>
<p class="hexvalue" style="float: right; clear: right">The quick
fox jumped over the lazy dog.</p>
</body>
</html>
```

The initial text box contained in Figure 25–15 shows some black text surrounded by a thick, black dashed border. The filter has been applied to the other three boxes on the page, in effect changing the color of the black text and border to white, and applying the chosen color to the sections of the original text box that were white. As you can see, this filter can create a rather dramatic effect, especially since the inverted border value creates a "spiky box" effect, something otherwise not as easy to set using standards-compliant CSS properties.

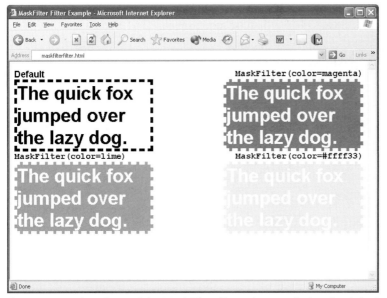

Figure 25–15 The effects of the MaskFilter filter when applied to the default text box.

It should also be noted that the `MaskFilter` filter does not affect the color values of any images that it may be set to alter.

Matrix Filter

The `Matrix` filter allows you to resize, rotate, or reverse the characteristics of the selected object. This filter creates a transform of the selected object, creating a 2 x 2 matrix which is in turn augmented by a linear vector. Complicated stuff. A good understanding of linear algebra will go a long way in helping you work with this particular filter.

The `Matrix` filter contains a wealth of values: `Dx`, `Dy`, `enabled`, `FilterType`, `M11`, `M12`, `M21`, `M22` and `SizingMethod`. The `Dx` and `Dy` values set the x- and y-values for the linear transformation. The `enabled` value is the default value for this property, and `FilterType` sets the method used to define the new content, and it can take either a `bilinear` or `nearest neighbor`, each of which are ways of determining new color values for the target. The `M11` and `M12` values set the first row/first column and first row/second column for the linear transform. Similarly the `M21` and `M22` values set the second row/first column and second row/second column for the linear transform.

The `SizingMethod` value determines whether or not the content is confined to a container or not; `clip to original` keeps the size and `auto expand` increases the size of the container to fit its content.

Listing 25.15 shows a rather complex set of equations (adapted from Microsoft's documentation on this filter) that depicts a light green box of text that spins and expands slightly with each click, as can be seen in Figure 25–16.

Listing 25.15   *Matrix Filter Example Code*

```
<html>
<head>
<title>Matrix Filter Example</title>
<script>
<!-- SetTheRotation function -->
var deg2radians = Math.PI * 260 / 360;
function SetTheRotation(Obj, deg)
{
    rad = deg * deg2radians ;
    costheta = Math.cos(rad);
    sintheta = Math.sin(rad);
    Obj.filters.item(0).M11 = costheta;
    Obj.filters.item(0).M12 = -sintheta;
    Obj.filters.item(0).M21 = sintheta;
    Obj.filters.item(0).M22 = costheta;
}
<!-- ResizeTheBox function -->
function ResizeTheBox(Obj, Multiplier)
{
    Obj.filters.item(0).M11 *= Multiplier;
    Obj.filters.item(0).M12 *= Multiplier;
    Obj.filters.item(0).M21 *= Multiplier;
    Obj.filters.item(0).M22 *= Multiplier;
}
var Count = 800;
<!-- SpinIt function -->
function SpinIt(Obj)
{
<!-- The function chosen for Multiple defines size changes in the
animation. -->
    var Multiple = Count/720;
    Count += 8;
```

| Listing 25.15 | *Matrix Filter Example Code (continued)* |

```
<!-- Set the number of 360-degree rotations -->
    if (Count>=360*4)
{
    Obj.onclick = null;
}
    SetTheRotation(Obj, Count);
    ResizeTheBox(Obj, Multiple);
}
</script>
</head>
<body>
<!-- When loaded, the onfilterchange event is fired as the filter
makes its initial settings.  This starts the animation.-->
<div style="position: absolute;
filter:progid:DXImageTransform.Microsoft.Matrix(sizingMethod='aut
o expand')"
onclick="SpinIt(this)">
<div style="background-color: lightgreen; padding: 5">
Click on me<br/>
and see<br/>
me spin!<br/>
</div>
</div>
Some regular text<br />
positioned "underneath"<br />
the box.
</body>
</html>
```

In the code listing seen in Listing 25.15 you see functions that set the light green text box object to "spin." The initial settings control the amount of the rotation, how the box is successively resized during each part of the rotation, and how many total rotations the text box will experience. As you can see, this filter does not affect any text or other object that may be "underneath" it.

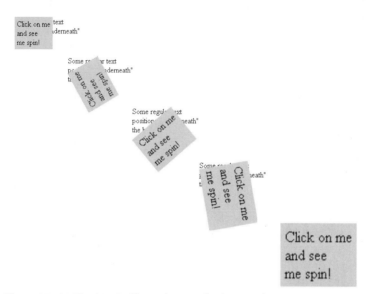

Figure 25–16 The Matrix filter when applied to an object, as seen in successive clicks of the screen within Internet Explorer 6.0.

This is a very interesting filter, though a knowledge of linear algebra should be considered a must before tackling it.

25.3 Transition Filter Overview

In addition to the standard static filters that have already been covered in this chapter, Microsoft has also introduced a number of "transition" filters. These enable Web authors to create some funky, eye-catching effects when moving from one object on a Web page to another. Many people will be familiar with these types of transitions from television or movies where various editing "wipes" are used to go from one sequence to another. Their effects are pure "eye candy" — they serve no other useful purpose than to catch a viewer's attention, which they are pretty much guaranteed to do.

For those Web developers working on Web sites tailored to versions of Internet Explorer 5.5 and above, there are 17 different transitions, and they are Barn, Blinds, Checkerboard, Fade, GradientWipe, Inset, Iris, Pixelate, RadialWipe, RandomBars, RandomDissolve, Slide, Spiral, Stretch, Strips, Wheels and Zigzag. Using a combination of CSS extensions and JavaScript, it is relatively easy to implement these transitions on a Web page.

Each of these transition filters requires at least two objects on a Web page: one visible and one invisible, both preferably occupying the same space on a Web page. This can be done using absolute positioning and the CSS `visibility` element. Then all you have to do is to plug in the transition filter code along with something to "activate" it in order to see the effect. The code listing in Listing 25.16 provides a relatively simple "template" upon which you can change the transition filter settings — all you have to do to swap in different transition filter code snippets to make the transitions.

Listing 25.16	A Simple "Template" for Viewing Transition Filter Code

```
<html>
<head>
<script>
var transitionState=0;
function transition() {
    transitionSpace.filters[0].Apply();
    if (transitionState=='0') {
        transitionState=1;
        otho.style.visibility="visible";
        galba.style.visibility="hidden";}
    else {
        transitionState=0;
        otho.style.visibility="hidden";
        galba.style.visibility="visible";}
        transitionSpace.filters[0].Play();}
</script>
</head>

<body>
<button onclick="transition()">Activate Transition</button>
<div id="transitionSpace" style="position:absolute; top: 0px;
left: 0px; width: 260px; height:300px;
filter:progid:DXImageTransform.Microsoft.Barn(orientation=vertica
l, motion=in, duration=2)">

<div id="galba" style="position:absolute; top:50px; left:10px;
width:250px; height:200px; background:ffffcc; border-style:dotted;
border-color:black; border-width:medium" align="center">
<img src="galba.jpg" width="150" height="150" alt="Galba"
border="0"><br>Emperor Galba AD 68-69</div>
```

Listing 25.16	*A Simple "Template" for Viewing Transition Filter Code (continued)*

```
<div id="otho" style="position:absolute; top:50px; left:10px;
width:250px; height:200px; background: ccffff; border-style:solid;
border-color:red; border-width:medium; visibility:hidden"
align="center"><img src="otho.jpg" width="150" height="150"
alt="Otho" border="0"><br>Emperor Otho AD 69</div>
</body>
</html>
```

Listing 25.16 contains two separate Web objects, with only the first one (identified as `id="galba"`) visible, and the second one (identified as `id="otho"`) invisible, though occupying the same space thanks to absolute positioning (i.e., `position: absolute; top:50px; left:10px;`). They depict coins of two ancient Roman emperors, Galba and Otho, the latter succeeding — or transitioning — to the throne upon the death of the former. One of the better ways of overlaying the transition effect is to create another `<div>` block which overlays the position of the previous code, and to which we will directly apply the transition effect. We still need some JavaScript code in order to make the transition from the first object to the second one function. The JavaScript code requires the `Apply` and/or `Play` methods in order to do this, which can be seen in the header of the Web page. When the `transition()` function is activated, it applies the effects of the transition filter to the overlaying Web object (called `transitionSpace`), which makes the previously invisible Web object `"otho"` visible, while making the original one (`"galba"`) invisible in the process. The script is designed so that if triggered again, it reverses this process. To trigger the transition, there's a simple button with a JavaScript trigger that activates the `transition()` function.

The code outlined here serves as a good base, and all you need to do in most instances is to simply change the active filter code (which is in bold) in the `transitionSpace` Web object to apply different filters. Listing 25.16 uses the `Barn` transition filter. To try the other transition filters, simply replace the code with the pertinent code snippets for each transition filter to get the effect you want.

Blinds and Barn Transition Filters

If you tried out the code in Listing 25.16, you'll already have a sense of how the `Barn` transition works. The `Barn` transition creates an effect like a door opening or closing. It has four attributes: `duration`, `enabled`, `motion` and `orientation`. The `duration` attribute sets the time value for the transition, specified in seconds and milliseconds (`0.0000`), and the `enabled` attribute is a standard attribute common to most filters and transitions. By default `enabled` is always set to "on," even when it is not specified.

The `motion` attribute has two values: `out` (the transition moves from the center on out) and `in` (the transition moves in from the borders). The `orientation` attribute has two self-descriptive values: `horizontal` and `vertical`.

The following code snippet contains the active transition filter code, which is spelled out fully in Listing 25.16. Its effects can be seen in successive frames in Figure 25–17.

```
filter:progid:DXImageTransform.Microsoft.Barn(orientation=vertical,
motion=in, duration=2)">
```

Figure 25–17 The successive effects of the Barn filter transition, as seen in Internet Explorer 6.0.

The `Blinds` transition filter works in a similar manner, and shares half of the same attributes as the `Barn` transition filter. It also has four attributes: `bands`, `direction`, `duration` and `enabled`. The `bands` attribute sets the number of "blinds" that appear, and it takes a numeric value. The `direction` attribute takes one of four self-describing values: `up`, `down`, `right` or `left`. The `duration` and `enabled` attributes work in exactly the same way as the equivalent attributes with the `Barn` transition filter.

The following code snippet shows the `Blinds` filter set to four vertical bands which move to the right when run. Simply swap this code for the section in bold in Listing 25.16 to see the effect depicted in Figure 25–18.

```
filter:progid:DXImageTransform.Microsoft.Blinds(direction=left,
duration=2)
```

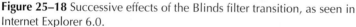

Figure 25–18 Successive effects of the Blinds filter transition, as seen in Internet Explorer 6.0.

Checkerboard and Fade Transition Filters

The Checkerboard filter creates a transition which looks like a regular pattern of checkerboard squares "uncovered" to reveal the object underneath. It takes three attributes: direction, squaresX and squaresY. The direction attribute works the same way as it does with the Blinds transition. The squaresX and squaresY attributes each take numeric values which must be greater than two, each of which sets the "size" of the checkerboard squares. If you have matching values (i.e., squaresX=4, squaresY=4), you will get squares. If the two values are different, you'll end up with rectangles instead. To see this in action, replace the bold filter statement in Listing 25.16 with the following line of code:

```
filter:progid:DXImageTransform.Microsoft.Checkerboard(squaresX=4,
squaresY=4,direction=right)
```

This produces the effect seen in Figure 25–19, where you can see a checkerboard-like pattern reveal the new content.

Figure 25–19 The effects of the Checkerboard filter transition as seen in Internet Explorer 6.0.

The `Fade` filter creates a transition that reveals new content by "fading out" the original content. It takes three attributes: `duration`, `enabled` and `overlap`. The only new attribute here is `overlap`, which can take on a value from `0.0` to `1.0` and sets the transition's duration in which both the original and the new content are displayed. Here's how it works: if you set duration to 10 seconds and overlap to 0.4, for the first three seconds the original content begins to fade out, then over the next four seconds displays a merging effect when both the original content and new content appear at once — this is the overlap segment. The final three seconds see the new content fully "fade in." Here's how such code would look:

```
filter:progid:DXImageTransform.Microsoft.Fade(duration=10,
overlap=0.4)
```

START

STEP 2

STEP 3

FINISH

Figure 25–20 The effects of the fade filter transition as seen in Internet Explorer 6.0.

In Figure 25–20 you can see how in Step 2 the initial image begins to "fade away"; and Step 3 shows the brief merged effect that happens as the second image begins to transition into the frame.

GradientWipe, RadialWipe and Strips Transition Filters

The GradientWipe transition creates a gradual dissolve using a gradient band that progresses across the original image, and reveals the new one. It takes any of the following attributes: duration, enabled, gradientSize, motion as well as the JavaScript property wipeStyle. The duration attribute sets the time value for the transition, specified in seconds and milliseconds (0.0000). The enabled attribute is a standard attribute common to most filters and transitions, and by default is "on," even when not specified. The gradientSize attribute sets the value for the gradient wipe, ranging from 0.0 to 1.0. If set to 0.5, the gradient wipe covers 50% of the object during the wipe. The wipeStyle property works in conjunction with motion; wipeStyle and sets whether the gradient moved horizontally (0) or vertically (1), and motion can be set to either forward or reverse.

To see a demonstration of this at work, replace the filter statement in Listing 25.16 with the following piece of code:

```
filter:progid:DXImageTransform.Microsoft.Wipe(GradientSize=0.5,
wipeStyle=0, motion=forward)
```

The effects of this transition filter can be seen in Figure 25–21.

Figure 25–21 The effects of the GradientWipe filter transition as seen in Internet Explorer 6.0.

Another type of wipe transition can be created by using the `RadialWipe` filter, which reveals the content of a new object using a windshield-wiper blade effect, or like the sweeping hand of a clock. The `RadialWipe` filter has the following attributes: `duration`, `enabled` and `wipeStyle`. The first two have already been covered, and in this case `wipeStyle` is an attribute instead of a property, presumably because it takes a different set of values: `clock`, `wedge` and `radial`. The `clock` value creates a sweeping wipe like the hands of a clock, `wedge` sweeps around the center from both directions starting from the top, and `radial` sweeps from the top to the left side, anchored in the upper-left corner. To see the clock transition in effect, replace the `filter` statement in Listing 25.16 object with this piece of code:

```
filter:progid:DXImageTransform.Microsoft.RadialWipe(wipeStyle=clock)
```

The effects of this transition filter can be seen in Figure 25–22.

Figure 25–22 The effects of the RadialWipe filter transition as seen in Internet Explorer 6.0.

The `Strips` filter creates a saw-toothed type of wipe. `Strips` can take on any of three attributes: `duration`, `enabled` and `motion`. The `motion` attribute takes on a different set of values from those seen with `GradientWipe`, and these are `leftdown`, `leftup`, `rightdown` and `rightup`. The values refer to the corner in which the wipe effect ends up. To see the `Strips` transition in action, insert the following code snippet in place of the `filter` statement in Listing 25.16:

```
filter:progid:DXImageTransform.Microsoft.Strips(duration=5,
motion-rightdown)
```

This produces a saw-toothed wipe leading from the top-left corner to the bottom-right, as can be seen in Figure 25–23.

Figure 25–23 The effects of the Strips filter transition as seen in Internet Explorer 6.0.

RandomBars and RandomDissolve Transition Filters

There are two types of randomized transitions available: `RandomBars` and `RandomDissolve`. Both are pretty self-descriptive: `RandomBars` reveals the new content by exposing random lines of pixels and `RandomDissolve` reveals new content by exposing random pixels over the object. `RandomBars` can take the `duration`, `enabled` and `orientation` attributes while `RandomDissolve` only takes `duration` and `enabled`. The `RandomBars'` `orientation` attribute can take one of two values: `horizontal` or `vertical`.

To see the transition effect `RandomBars` causes, replace the bold code for the existing `filter` statement in Listing 25.16 with this code snippet:

```
filter:progid:DXImageTransform.Microsoft.RandomBars
(orientation=vertical)
```

Figure 25–24 The RandomBars filter as applied to two images as seen in Internet Explorer 6.0.

The effects of the `RandomDissolve` transition filter can be seen by inserting the following piece of code in Listing 25.16 instead:

```
filter:progid:DXImageTransform.Microsoft.RandomDissolve
(duration=0.75)
```

Figure 25–25 The RandomDissolve filter as applied to two images as seen in Internet Explorer 6.0.

Iris and Spiral Transition Filters

There are a number of transitions that allow you to set specific transition shapes, such as the `Iris` and `Spiral`.

If you are looking for that "007" look in your transitions, the `Iris` filter is for you. The `Iris` filter can take on the following attributes: `duration`, `enabled`, `irisStyle` and `motion`. The only new attribute here is `irisStyle`, which can take any one of six shape values, `diamond`, `circle`, `cross`, `plus`, `square` or `star`. `motion` takes the values `out` or `in`. If you want the James Bond-style of wipe, try the following piece of code in place of the existing `filter` statement in Listing 25.16, and you'll get the effect as seen in Figure 25–26:

```
filter:progid:DXImageTransform.Microsoft.Iris(irisStyle=circle,
motion=out)
```

Figure 25–26 Using the Iris transition filter to get that "007" effect between images in Internet Explorer 6.0.

The `spiral` filter reveals a new object using a spiral motion. The `spiral` filter can take on any of the following four attributes: `duration`, `enabled`, `gridSizeX` and `grid-SizeY`. The two unique attributes here are `gridSizeX` and `gridSizeY`, which determine the size of the grid columns to be used for the spiral, ranging from `0 - 100`. The larger the value set for each of these, the smaller the size of the "block" that leads the spiral effect. The following code, inserted into Listing 25.16 in the bold area, will get you the type of effect seen in Figure 25–27:

```
filter:progid:DXImageTransform.Microsoft.Spiral(GridSizeX=65,
GridSizeY=65,duration=1.0)
```

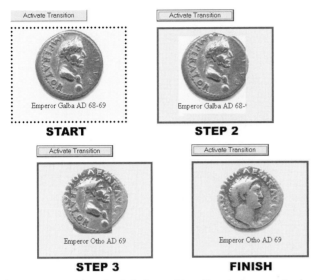

Figure 25–27 Using the Spiral transition filter in Internet Explorer 6.0.

Stretch and Slide Transition Filters

There are other transition filters that create stretching and sliding effects: Stretch and Slide. The Stretch filter has three attributes: duration, enabled and stretch-Style. stretchStyle can take one of three attributes: hide, push or spin. The hide value stretches new content over the old from left to right; push stretches new content "in" while squeezing old content "out" from left to right, much like the effect of a rotating cube; and spin stretches the new content over the old from the center outwards. To see the Stretch transition filter in action, insert the following piece of code into the bold area of Listing 25.16, to get the type of effect seen in Figure 25–28:

```
filter:progid:DXImageTransform.Microsoft.Stretch(stretchStyle=spin)
```

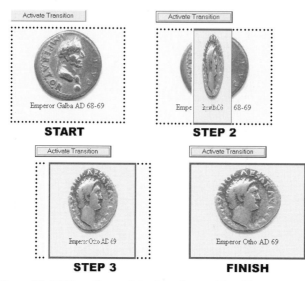

Figure 25–28 The effects of the Stretch transition filter as seen in Internet Explorer 6.0.

The `Slide` filter works by "sliding" new content into place. This filter has four attributes: `bands`, `duration`, `enabled` and `slideStyle`. The two unique attributes here are `bands` and `slideStyle`. `bands` works by setting a numerical value for the number of strips the new content is divided into during the transition, and `slide-Style` takes values similar to those of the `Stretch` filter: `hide`, `push` and `swap`. The `hide` value slides bands of the old content out, exposing the new content, `push` slides bands of new content in, pushing the old out, and `swap` slides in alternating bands of new content while sliding out the old.

To see this in action, try out the following piece of code in place of the bold area of Listing 25.16, to get the type of effect seen in Figure 25–29:

```
filter:progid:DXImageTransform.Microsoft.Slide(slideStyle=swap,
bands=4)
```

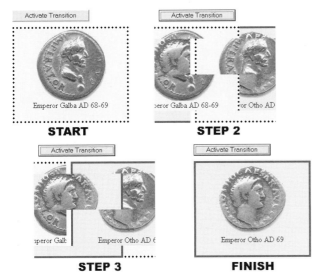

Figure 25–29 The effects of the Slide transition filter as seen in Internet Explorer 6.0.

Inset Transition Filter

The `Inset` transition filter creates a diagonal wipe in the shape of a square across the selected object. It takes two attributes: `enabled` and `duration`. The `enabled` attribute is the default, and is active even when it is not present in the code. The `duration` attribute sets the time value for the transition, specified in seconds and milliseconds (`0.0000`).

To see its effect, insert the following code snippet into the bold area of Listing 25.16, to get the type of effect seen in Figure 25–30:

```
filter:progid:DXImageTransform.Microsoft.Inset()
```

Figure 25–30 The effects of the Inset transition filter as seen in Internet Explorer 6.0.

Pixelate Transition Filter

If you ever wanted to get a computer-retro look with a transition, try using the `Pixelate` transition filter Microsoft provides in Internet Explorer. During the transition it fades the selected objects in and out of a "low-res" mode. The final object then appears to be "sharpened" and is finally fully revealed.

The `Pixelate` transition filter takes three attributes: `duration`, `enabled` and `maxSquare`. The first two attributes should already be familiar: The `enabled` attribute is the default, and the `duration` attribute sets the time value for the transition, specified in seconds and milliseconds (`0.0000`) — it should be noted that you get the best initial results in this case when `enabled` is set to `false`, otherwise the Pixelate effect is applied to the static initial image prior to any action taken by the user. The `maxSquare` attribute sets the size of the squares in pixels — the larger the value, the more "low-res" the transition will look.

To see the effect, insert the following code snippet into the bold area of Listing 25.16, to get the type of effect seen in Figure 25–31:

```
filter:progid:DXImageTransform.Microsoft.Pixelate(MaxSquare=30,
Duration=2,Enabled=false)
```

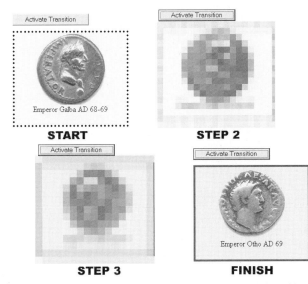

Figure 25–31 The low-res transition effect of the Pixelate filter as seen in Internet Explorer 6.0.

Wheel Transition Filter

The `Wheel` transition filter reveals new content using a rotating motion, like the moving spokes of a wheel. The end effect is like having a bunch of radial pie slices revealing a new object underneath them.

This transition filter takes three values: `enabled`, `duration` and `spokes`. The `duration` attribute sets the time value for the transition, specified in seconds and milliseconds (`0.0000`), and the `enabled` attribute is a standard attribute common to most filters and transitions. The `spokes` attribute is the one specific to this transition filter, and it sets the number of `spokes` of the wheel to be displayed. The higher the number for `spokes`, the more "pie slices" that appear during the transition.

Insert the following code into the bold area of Listing 25.16 to view the effect seen in Figure 25–32:

```
filter:progid:dximagetransform.microsoft.wheel(spokes=3)
```

Figure 25–32 The rotating-wheel wipe you get with the Wheel transition filter as seen in Internet Explorer.

Zigzag Transition Filter

Last but not least is the `zigzag` transition filter, which is used to create a back-and-forth transition that moves down the old object to reveal the new content. The effect is a bit like having a transparent snake slowly eating away line-by-line at the existing content in order to reveal the new. It takes four values: `enabled`, `duration`, `gridSizeX` and `gridSizeY`. The `enabled` attribute is the default, and is active even when it is not present in the code. The `duration` attribute sets the time value for the transition, specified in seconds and milliseconds (`0.0000`). The two new attributes here are `gridSizeX` and `gridSizeY` which each take a pixel value, setting the size of the "head" of that snake that eats away the old content.

Replace code from the bold area of Listing 25.16 with the following code to see the effect seen in Figure 25–33:

```
filter:progid:DXImageTransform.Microsoft.zigzag(GridSizeX=8,
GridSizeY=8)
```

Figure 25–33 The Zigzag transition filter's effects as seen in Internet Explorer.

CSS1 AND CSS2 COMPATIBILITY CHARTS

Appendix A

This appendix provides a useful reference of the browser compatibility of each CSS1 and CSS2 element. The browser compatibility of each element is listed as Safe, Partial (Partially Safe), or Unsafe as shown below:

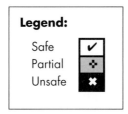

CSS Elements	@media	@font-face	azimuth	background	background-attachment	background-color	background-image	background-position	background-repeat	border	border-bottom	border-bottom-width	border-collapse
Konqueror 2.2	✓	✗	✗	✓	✓	✓	✓	✓	✓	✓	✓	✓	✓
Opera 6.0	✓	✗	✗	✓	✓	✓	✓	✓	✓	✓	✓	✓	✓
Opera 5.0	✓	✗	✗	✓	✓	✓	✓	✓	✓	✓	✓	✓	✓
Opera 4.0	✗	✗	✗	✓	✓	✓	✓	✓	✓	✓	✓	✓	✓
Opera 3.6	✗	✗	✗	✓	✓	✓	✓	✓	✓	✓	✓	✓	✓
Mozilla 1.0	✓	✗	✗	✓	✓	✓	✓	✓	✓	✓	✓	✓	❖
NN 7.0	✓	✗	✗	✓	✓	✓	✓	✓	✓	✓	✓	✓	❖
NN 6.0	✓	✗	✗	✓	✓	✓	✓	✓	✓	✓	✓	✓	❖
NN 4.0 (Mac & UNIX)	✗	✗	✗	❖	❖	❖	✓	✗	❖	❖	❖	❖	✗
NN 4.x	✗	✗	✗	❖	❖	❖	✓	✗	❖	❖	❖	❖	✗
IE 6.0	✓	✗	✗	✓	✓	✓	✓	✓	✓	✓	✓	✓	❖
IE 5.5	✓	✗	✗	✓	✓	✓	✓	✓	✓	✓	✓	✓	❖
IE 5.x (Mac)	✓	✗	✗	✓	✓	✓	✓	✓	✓	✓	✓	✓	✓
IE 5.0	✗	✗	✗	✓	✓	✓	✓	✓	✓	❖	❖	❖	❖
IE 4.x (Mac)	✗	✗	✗	✓	✓	✓	✓	✓	✓	✓	✓	✓	✗
IE 4.x	✗	✗	✗	✓	✓	✓	✓	✓	✓	❖	❖	❖	✗
IE 3.02	✗	✗	✗	✗	✗	✗	✗	✗	✗	✗	✗	✗	✗

CSS Elements	border-color	border-left	border-left-width	border-right	border-right-width	border-spacing	border-style	border-top	border-top-width	border-width	bottom	caption-side	clear
Konqueror 2.2	✓	✓	✓	✓	✓	✓	✓	✓	✓	✓	✓	◈	✓
Opera 6.0	✓	✓	✓	✓	✓	✓	✓	✓	✓	✓	✓	◈	✓
Opera 5.0	✓	✓	✓	✓	✓	✓	✓	✓	✓	✓	✓	◈	✓
Opera 4.0	✓	✓	✓	✓	✓	✗	✓	✓	✓	✓	◈	✗	✓
Opera 3.6	✓	✓	✓	✓	✓	✗	✓	✓	✓	✓	◈	✗	✓
Mozilla 1.0	✓	✓	✓	✓	✓	✓	✓	✓	✓	✓	✓	◈	✓
NN 7.0	✓	✓	✓	✓	✓	✓	✓	✓	✓	✓	✓	◈	✓
NN 6.0	✓	✓	✓	✓	✓	✓	✓	✓	✓	✓	✓	◈	✓
NN 4.0 (Mac & UNIX)	◈	◈	◈	◈	◈	✗	◈	◈	◈	◈	✗	✗	◈
NN 4.x	◈	◈	◈	◈	◈	✗	◈	◈	◈	◈	✗	✗	◈
IE 6.0	✓	✓	✓	✓	✓	✗	✓	✓	✓	✓	◈	✗	✓
IE 5.5	✓	✓	✓	✓	✓	✗	✓	✓	✓	✓	◈	✗	✓
IE 5.x (Mac)	✓	✓	✓	✓	✓	✗	✓	✓	✓	✓	◈	✗	✓
IE 5.0	✓	◈	◈	◈	✓	✗	◈	◈	◈	✓	✗	✗	✓
IE 4.x (Mac)	✓	✓	✓	✓	✓	✗	✓	✓	✓	✓	✗	✗	✓
IE 4.x	✓	◈	◈	◈	◈	✗	◈	◈	◈	✓	✗	✗	◈
IE 3.02	✗	✗	✗	✗	✗	✗	✗	✗	✗	✗	✗	✗	✗

Legend: ✔ = supported, ✖ = not supported, ◆ = partial support

CSS Elements	clip	color	content	counter-increment	counter-reset	cue	cue-after	cue-before	cursor	direction	display	elevation	empty-cells
Konqueror 2.2	✔	✔	✖	✖	✖	✖	✖	✖	✖	✔	◆	✖	✖
Opera 6.0	✖	✔	✔	◆	◆	✖	✖	✖	✖	✖	◆	✖	✔
Opera 5.0	✖	✔	✔	◆	◆	✖	✖	✖	✖	✖	◆	✖	✔
Opera 4.0	✖	✔	✖	✖	✖	✖	✖	✖	✖	✖	◆	✖	✖
Opera 3.6	✖	✔	✖	✖	✖	✖	✖	✖	✖	✖	◆	✖	✖
Mozilla 1.0	✔	✔	✔	✔	✔	✖	✖	✖	✔	✔	◆	✖	✔
NN 7.0	✔	✔	✔	◆	◆	✖	✖	✖	✔	✔	◆	✖	✔
NN 6.0	✔	✔	✔	◆	◆	✖	✖	✖	✔	✔	◆	✖	✔
NN 4.0 (Mac & UNIX)	✖	✔	✖	✖	✖	✖	✖	✖	✖	✖	◆	✖	✖
NN 4.x	✖	✔	✖	✖	✖	✖	✖	✖	✖	✖	◆	✖	✖
IE 6.0	✔	✔	✖	✖	✖	✖	✖	✖	✔	✔	◆	✖	✖
IE 5.5	✔	✔	✖	✖	✖	✖	✖	✖	✔	✔	◆	✖	✖
IE 5.x (Mac)	✔	✔	✖	✖	✖	✖	✖	✖	✔	✔	◆	✖	✖
IE 5.0	✖	✔	✖	✖	✖	✖	✖	✖	✖	✔	◆	✖	✖
IE 4.x (Mac)	✖	✔	✖	✖	✖	✖	✖	✖	✖	✖	◆	✖	✖
IE 4.x	✖	✔	✖	✖	✖	✖	✖	✖	✖	✖	◆	✖	✖
IE 3.02	✖	✔	✖	✖	✖	✖	✖	✖	✖	✖	✖	✖	✖

CSS Elements	float	font	font-family	font-size	font-size-adjust	font-style	font-stretch	font-variant	font-weight	height	left	letter-spacing	line-height
Konqueror 2.2	✓	✓	✓	✓	✗	✓	✗	✓	✓	✓	✓	✓	✓
Opera 6.0	✓	✓	✓	✓	✗	✓	✗	✓	✓	✓	✓	✓	✓
Opera 5.0	✓	✓	✓	✓	✗	✓	✗	✓	✓	✓	✓	✓	✓
Opera 4.0	✓	✓	✓	✓	✗	✓	✗	✓	✓	✓	✗	✓	✓
Opera 3.6	✓	✓	✓	✓	✗	✓	✗	✓	✓	✓	✗	✓	✓
Mozilla 1.0	✓	✓	✓	✓	✗	✓	✗	✓	✓	✓	✓	✓	✓
NN 7.0	✓	✓	✓	✓	✗	✓	✗	✓	✓	✓	✓	✓	✓
NN 6.0	✓	✓	✓	✓	✗	✓	✗	✓	✓	✓	✓	✓	✓
NN 4.0 (Mac & UNIX)	❖	✗	✓	✓	✗	❖	✗	✗	✓	✗	✗	✗	✓
NN 4.x	✗	✗	✓	✓	✗	❖	✗	✗	✓	✗	✗	✗	✓
IE 6.0	✓	✓	✓	✓	✗	✓	✗	✓	✓	✓	❖	✓	✓
IE 5.5	✓	✓	✓	✓	✗	✓	✗	✓	✓	✓	❖	✓	✓
IE 5.x (Mac)	✓	✓	✓	✓	✗	✓	✗	✓	✓	✓	❖	✓	✓
IE 5.0	✓	✓	✓	✓	✗	✓	✗	✓	✓	✓	❖	✓	✓
IE 4.x (Mac)	❖	✓	✓	✓	✗	✓	✗	✓	✓	✓	❖	✓	✓
IE 4.x	❖	✓	✓	✓	✗	✓	✗	✓	✓	✓	❖	✓	✓
IE 3.02	✗	✗	✗	✓	✗	❖	✗	✗	✗	✗	✗	✗	❖

CSS Elements	list-style*	list-style-image	list-style-position	list-style-type*	margin	margin-bottom	margin-left	margin-right	margin-top	marker-offset	marks	min-height	min-width
Konqueror 2.2	◆	◆	✓	✓	✓	✓	✓	✓	✓	✗	✗	✗	✗
Opera 6.0	✓	✓	✓	✓	✓	✓	✓	✓	✓	✓	✗	✗	✗
Opera 5.0	✓	✓	✓	✓	✓	✓	✓	✓	✓	✓	✗	✗	✗
Opera 4.0	✓	✓	✓	✓	✓	✓	✓	✓	✓	✗	✗	✗	✗
Opera 3.6	✓	✓	✓	✓	✓	✓	✓	✓	✓	✗	✗	✗	✗
Mozilla 1.0	✓	✓	✓	✓	✓	✓	✓	✓	✓	✗	✗	✓	✓
NN 7.0	✓	✓	✓	✓	✓	✓	✓	✓	✓	✗	✗	✓	✓
NN 6.0	✓	✓	✓	✓	✓	✓	✓	✓	✓	✗	✗	✓	✓
NN 4.0 (Mac & UNIX)	✗	✗	✗	✓	◆	◆	◆	◆	◆	✗	✗	✗	✗
NN 4.x	✗	✗	✗	✓	◆	◆	◆	◆	◆	✗	✗	✗	✗
IE 6.0	✓	✓	✓	✓	✓	✓	✓	✓	✓	✗	✗	◆	✗
IE 5.5	✓	✓	✓	✓	✓	✓	✓	✓	✓	✗	✗	◆	✗
IE 5.x (Mac)	✓	✓	✓	✓	✓	✓	✓	✓	✓	✗	✗	✗	✗
IE 5.0	✓	✓	✓	✓	✓	✓	✓	✓	✓	✗	✗	✗	✗
IE 4.x (Mac)	✓	✓	✓	✓	✓	✓	✓	✓	✓	✗	✗	✗	✗
IE 4.x	✓	✓	✓	✓	✓	✓	✓	✓	✓	✗	✗	✗	✗
IE 3.02	✗	✗	✗	✗	✗	✗	✗	✗	✗	✗	✗	✗	✗

CSS Elements	max-height	max-width	orphans	outline	outline-color	outline-style	outline-width	overflow	padding	padding-bottom	padding-left	padding-right	padding-top
Konqueror 2.2	✗	✗	✗	✗	✗	✗	✗	◈	✓	✓	✓	✓	✓
Opera 6.0	✗	✗	✓	✗	✗	✗	✗	◈	✓	✓	✓	✓	✓
Opera 5.0	✗	✗	✓	✗	✗	✗	✗	◈	✓	✓	✓	✓	✓
Opera 4.0	✗	✗	✗	✗	✗	✗	✗	◈	✓	✓	✓	✓	✓
Opera 3.6	✗	✗	✗	✗	✗	✗	✗	✗	✓	✓	✓	✓	✓
Mozilla 1.0	✓	✓	✗	✗	✗	✗	✗	✓	✓	✓	✓	✓	✓
NN 7.0	✓	✓	✗	✗	✗	✗	✗	✓	✓	✓	✓	✓	✓
NN 6.0	✓	✓	✗	✗	✗	✗	✗	✓	✓	✓	✓	✓	✓
NN 4.0 (Mac & UNIX)	✗	✗	✗	✗	✗	✗	✗	✗	✓	✓	✓	✓	✓
NN 4.x	✗	✗	✗	✗	✗	✗	✗	✗	✓	✓	✓	✓	✓
IE 6.0	✗	✗	✗	✗	✗	✗	✗	✓	✓	✓	✓	✓	✓
IE 5.5	✗	✗	✗	✗	✗	✗	✗	✓	✓	✓	✓	✓	✓
IE 5.x (Mac)	✗	✗	✗	✓	✓	✓	✓	✓	✓	✓	✓	✓	✓
IE 5.0	✗	✗	✗	✗	✗	✗	✗	✓	✓	✓	✓	✓	✓
IE 4.x (Mac)	✗	✗	✗	✗	✗	✗	✗	✗	✓	✓	✓	✓	✓
IE 4.x	✗	✗	✗	✗	✗	✗	✗	✗	✓	✓	✓	✓	✓
IE 3.02	✗	✗	✗	✗	✗	✗	✗	✗	✗	✗	✗	✗	✗

CSS Elements	page	page-break-after	page-break-before	page-break-inside	pause	pause-after	pause-before	pitch	pitch-range	play-during	position	quotes	richness
Konqueror 2.2	✗	✗	✗	✗	✗	✗	✗	✗	✗	✗	↘	✗	✗
Opera 6.0	✗	↘	↘	↘	✗	✗	✗	✗	✗	✗	↘	✧	✗
Opera 5.0	✗	↘	↘	↘	✗	✗	✗	✗	✗	✗	↘	✧	✗
Opera 4.0	✗	✗	✗	✗	✗	✗	✗	✗	✗	✗	✧	✗	✗
Opera 3.6	✗	✗	✗	✗	✗	✗	✗	✗	✗	✗	✗	✗	✗
Mozilla 1.0	✗	✗	✗	✗	✗	✗	✗	✗	✗	✗	↘	↘	✗
NN 7.0	✗	✗	✗	✗	✗	✗	✗	✗	✗	✗	↘	✧	✗
NN 6.0	✗	✗	✗	✗	✗	✗	✗	✗	✗	✗	↘	✧	✗
NN 4.0 (Mac & UNIX)	✗	✗	✗	✗	✗	✗	✗	✗	✗	✗	✧	✗	✗
NN 4.x	✗	✗	✗	✗	✗	✗	✗	✗	✗	✗	✧	✗	✗
IE 6.0	✗	↘	↘	✗	✗	✗	✗	✗	✗	✗	✧	✗	✗
IE 5.5	✗	↘	↘	✗	✗	✗	✗	✗	✗	✗	✧	✗	✗
IE 5.x (Mac)	✗	↘	↘	✗	✗	✗	✗	✗	✗	✗	✧	✗	✗
IE 5.0	✗	✗	✗	✗	✗	✗	✗	✗	✗	✗	✧	✗	✗
IE 4.x (Mac)	✗	✗	✗	✗	✗	✗	✗	✗	✗	✗	✧	✗	✗
IE 4.x	✗	✗	✗	✗	✗	✗	✗	✗	✗	✗	✧	✗	✗
IE 3.02	✗	✗	✗	✗	✗	✗	✗	✗	✗	✗	✗	✗	✗

CSS Elements	right	size	speech-rate	speech-numeral	speech-punctuation	speak	speak-header	stress	table-layout	text-align	text-decoration	text-indent	text-shadow
Konqueror 2.2	✓	✗	✗	✗	✗	✗	✗	✗	✗	✓	❖	✓	✗
Opera 6.0	✓	✓	✗	✗	✗	✗	✗	✗	❖	✓	✓	✓	✗
Opera 5.0	✓	✓	✗	✗	✗	✗	✗	✗	❖	✓	✓	✓	✗
Opera 4.0	❖	✗	✗	✗	✗	✗	✗	✗	✗	✓	✓	✓	✗
Opera 3.6	❖	✗	✗	✗	✗	✗	✗	✗	✗	✓	✓	✓	✗
Mozilla 1.0	✓	✗	✗	✗	✗	✗	✗	✗	✓	✓	✓	✓	✗
NN 7.0	✓	✗	✗	✗	✗	✗	✗	✗	✓	✓	✓	✓	✗
NN 6.0	✓	✗	✗	✗	✗	✗	✗	✗	✓	✓	✓	✓	✗
NN 4.0 (Mac & UNIX)	✗	✗	✗	✗	✗	✗	✗	✗	✗	✓	❖	✓	✗
NN 4.x	✗	✗	✗	✗	✗	✗	✗	✗	✗	✓	❖	✓	✗
IE 6.0	❖	✗	✗	✗	✗	✗	✗	✗	✓	✓	❖	✓	✗
IE 5.5	❖	✗	✗	✗	✗	✗	✗	✗	✓	✓	❖	✓	✗
IE 5.x (Mac)	❖	✗	✗	✗	✗	✗	✗	✗	✓	✓	❖	✓	✗
IE 5.0	✗	✗	✗	✗	✗	✗	✗	✗	✓	✓	❖	✓	✗
IE 4.x (Mac)	✗	✗	✗	✗	✗	✗	✗	✗	✗	❖	❖	✓	✗
IE 4.x	✗	✗	✗	✗	✗	✗	✗	✗	✗	✓	❖	✓	✗
IE 3.02	✗	✗	✗	✗	✗	✗	✗	✗	✗	❖	❖	✓	✗

Legend: ✓ = supported, ✗ = not supported, ◐ = partial support

CSS Elements	text-transform	top	unicode-bidi	vertical-align	visibility	voice-family	volume	white-space	widows	width	word-spacing	z-index
Konqueror 2.2	✓	✓	✓	✓	✓	✗	✗	◐	✗	✓	✓	✓
Opera 6.0	✓	✓	✗	✓	✓	✗	✗	✓	✓	✓	✓	✓
Opera 5.0	✓	✓	✗	✓	✓	✗	✗	✓	✓	✓	✓	✓
Opera 4.0	✓	✗	✗	◐	✓	✗	✗	✗	✗	✓	◐	◐
Opera 3.6	✓	✗	✗	◐	✓	✗	✗	✗	✗	✓	◐	✗
Mozilla 1.0	✓	✓	✓	✓	✓	✗	✗	✓	✗	✓	✓	✓
NN 7.0	✓	✓	✓	✓	✓	✗	✗	✓	✗	✓	✓	✓
NN 6.0	✓	✓	✓	✓	✓	✗	✗	✓	✗	✓	✓	✓
NN 4.0 (Mac & UNIX)	✓	◐	✗	✗	✓	✗	✗	◐	✗	◐	✗	✗
NN 4.x	✓	◐	✗	✗	✓	✗	✗	◐	✗	◐	✗	✗
IE 6.0	✓	◐	✓	✓	✓	✗	✗	◐	✗	✓	✓	◐
IE 5.5	✓	◐	✓	✓	✓	✗	✗	◐	✗	✓	✗	◐
IE 5.x (Mac)	✓	◐	✓	✓	✓	✗	✗	◐	✗	✓	✓	◐
IE 5.0	✓	◐	✓	✓	✓	✗	✗	◐	✗	✓	✗	◐
IE 4.x (Mac)	✓	◐	✗	◐	✓	✗	✗	✗	✗	✓	✓	◐
IE 4.x	✓	◐	✗	◐	✓	✗	✗	✗	✗	✓	✗	◐
IE 3.02	✗	✗	✗	◐	✗	✗	✗	✗	✗	✗	✗	✗

CSS Elements	Basic Concepts			Selectors						
	Containment in HTML	Grouping	Inheritance	Adjacent Sibling Selectors	Attribute Selectors	Child Selectors	class and id as Selectors	Comments	Contextual Selectors	Universal Selector
Konqueror 2.2	✓	✓	✓	✓	✓	✓	✓	✓	✓	✓
Opera 6.0	✓	✓	✓	✓	✓	✓	✓	✓	✓	✓
Opera 5.0	✓	✓	✓	✓	✓	✓	✓	✓	✓	✓
Opera 4.0	✓	✓	✓	✗	✗	✗	✓	✓	✓	✓
Opera 3.6	✓	✓	✓	✗	✗	✗	✓	✓	✓	✗
Mozilla 1.0	✓	✓	✓	✓	✓	✓	✓	✓	✓	✓
NN 7.0	✓	✓	✓	✓	✓	✓	✓	✓	✓	✓
NN 6.0	✓	✓	✓	✓	✓	✓	✓	✓	✓	✓
NN 4.0 (Mac & UNIX)	◈	✓	✓	✗	✗	✗	◈	✓	✓	✗
NN 4.x	◈	✓	✓	✗	✗	✗	◈	✓	✓	✗
IE 6.0	◈	✓	✓	✗	✗	✗	✓	✓	✓	✓
IE 5.5	◈	✓	✓	✗	✗	✗	✓	✓	✓	✓
IE 5.x (Mac)	◈	✓	✓	✓	✗	✓	◈	✓	✓	✓
IE 5.0	◈	✓	✓	✗	✗	✗	◈	✓	✓	✓
IE 4.x (Mac)	◈	✓	◈	✗	✗	✗	◈	✓	✓	✗
IE 4.x	◈	✓	✓	✗	✗	✗	◈	✓	✓	✗
IE 3.02	◈	✗	✗	✗	✗	✗	✗	✗	✓	✗

CSS Elements

Pseudo-Classes and Pseudo-Elements

Browser	anchor	first-child	firstline	firstletter	focus and hover	before and after	lang	!important	Cascade Order
Konqueror 2.2	✓	✓	✓	✓	✓	✗	✗	✓	✓
Opera 6.0	✓	✗	✓	✓	✓	✓	✗	✓	✓
Opera 5.0	✓	✗	✓	✓	✓	✓	✗	✓	✓
Opera 4.0	✓	✗	✓	✓	✗	✗	✗	✓	✓
Opera 3.6	✓	✗	✓	✓	✗	✗	✗	✓	✓
Mozilla 1.0	◆	✓	✓	✓	✓	✓	✗	✓	✓
NN 7.0	◆	✓	✓	✓	✓	✓	✗	✓	✓
NN 6.0	◆	✓	✓	✓	✓	✓	✗	✓	✓
NN 4.0 (Mac & UNIX)	◆	✗	✗	✗	✗	✗	✗	✗	◆
NN 4.x	◆	✗	✗	✗	✗	✗	✗	✗	◆
IE 6.0	✓	✗	✓	✓	✓	✗	✗	✓	✓
IE 5.5	✓	✗	✓	✓	✓	✗	✗	✓	✓
IE 5.x (Mac)	✓	✗	✓	✓	✓	✗	✗	✓	◆
IE 5.0	✓	✗	✗	✗	✓	✗	✗	✓	◆
IE 4.x (Mac)	✓	✗	✗	✗	✓	✗	✗	✓	✗
IE 4.x	✓	✗	✗	✗	✓	✗	✗	✓	✗
IE 3.02	✗	✗	✗	✗	✗	✗	✗	✗	✗

The Cascade columns: !important, Cascade Order

CSS Elements

Units	Angle Units	Color Units	Frequency Units	Length Units	Percentage Units	Strings	Time Units	URLs
Konqueror 2.2	✗	✓	✗	✓	✓	✗	✗	✓
Opera 6.0	✗	✓	✗	✓	✓	✢	✗	✓
Opera 5.0	✗	✓	✗	✓	✓	✢	✗	✓
Opera 4.0	✗	✓	✗	✢	✓	✢	✗	✓
Opera 3.6	✗	✓	✗	✢	✓	✗	✗	✓
Mozilla 1.0	✗	✓	✗	✢	✓	✗	✗	✓
NN 7.0	✗	✓	✗	✢	✓	✢	✗	✓
NN 6.0	✗	✓	✗	✢	✓	✢	✗	✓
NN 4.0 (Mac & UNIX)	✗	✓	✗	✢	✓	✗	✗	✓
NN 4.x	✗	✓	✗	✢	✓	✗	✗	✓
IE 6.0	✗	✓	✗	✓	✓	✗	✗	✓
IE 5.5	✗	✓	✗	✓	✓	✗	✗	✓
IE 5.x (Mac)	✗	✓	✗	✢	✓	✗	✗	✓
IE 5.0	✗	✓	✗	✢	✓	✗	✗	✓
IE 4.x (Mac)	✗	✢	✗	✢	✓	✗	✗	✓
IE 4.x	✗	✓	✗	✢	✓	✗	✗	✓
IE 3.02	✗	✢	✗	✢	✓	✗	✗	✓

✢ Only applies to CSS1 values for this property

ALPHABETICAL LISTING OF CSS PROPERTIES AND VALUES

Appendix B

This appendix provides a handy alphbetical reference of all CSS1, CSS2 and Internet Explorer-specific properties. Each entry includes its origin and details on its valid values.

accelerator

Description: Enables Web author to turn off the underlines under "accelerated" (i.e., highlighted keyboard shortcut) items.

Media Group: User Interface

CSS Family Type: User Interface

Originated with: Internet Explorer 5.5 *(browser-specific)*

Values:

- `true` — turns the accelerator feature "on"
- `false` — turns the accelerator feature "off"

Sample Code:

```
<style>
u {accelerator: true}
</style>
```

azimuth

Description: Sets the "angle" in which a sound is positioned in a sound space surrounding the viewer.
Media Group: Aural
CSS Family Type: Aural (Sub-family: Spatial Properties)
Originated with: CSS2
Values:

- n deg — The angle in degrees in which a sound is located. The range of the angle is from 0deg to 360deg. In this scheme, a value of 0deg is directly ahead of the viewer, 180deg is behind the viewer, 90deg is to the right, and 270deg is to the left. These values can also be expressed as negative values, so 90deg is equivalent to -270deg and 270deg is the same as -90deg.
- left-side — Equivalent to 270deg. If behind is also set, its value does not change.
- far-left — Equivalent to 300deg. If behind is also set, the value becomes 240deg.
- left — Same as 320deg. If behind is also set, the value becomes 220deg.
- center-left — Equivalent to 340deg. If behind is also set, the value becomes 200deg.
- center — Equivalent to 0deg. If behind is also set, the value becomes 180deg.
- center-right — Equivalent to 20deg. If behind is also set, the value becomes 160deg.
- right — Equivalent to 40deg. If behind is also set, the value becomes 140deg.
- far-right — Equivalent to 60deg. If behind is also set, the value becomes 120deg.
- right-side — Equivalent to 90deg. If behind is also set, its value does not change.
- behind — Equivalent to 180deg. Can also be used to modify other named values, taking a position that was in front and "mirroring" it to the same location behind the viewer.
- leftwards — Moves the sound 20 degrees to the left (counterclockwise) of its current position.
- rightwards — Moves the sound 20 degrees to the right (clockwise) of its current position.
- inherit — Takes the same value as that set for the property of the parent element, if allowed.

Sample Code:

```
<p azimuth: left>
Hamlet: How does the Queen?
</p>
<p azimuth: right>
King: She sounds to see them
bleed.
</p>
<p azimuth: far-right>
Queen: No, no! The drink,
The drink! O my dear Hamlet!
The drink, the drink! I am poison'd.
</p>
```

background

Description: Sets the background color or image. It can take on any value contained in the background family of properties.
Media Group: Visual
CSS Family Type: Backgrounds
Originated with: CSS1
Values:

- *color name* or *numerical color value*
- *url(image)*
- `scroll` — Image moves when the browser window is scrolled.
- `fixed` — Image does not move when the browser window is scrolled.
- `transparent` — renders the specified element transparent
- *x% y%* — Percentage is in reference to the dimensions of the browser window display.
- *x y* — Represents absolute coordinate position of the image.
- (`left`/`center`/`right`) | (`top`/`center`/`bottom`) — Keywords representing screen positions. Left keyword is the x-position and the right keyword is the y-position for the image.
- `repeat` — Image is horizontally and vertically tiled.
- `repeat-x` — Image is horizontally tiled.
- `repeat-y` — Image is vertically tiled.
- `no-repeat` — The image is not repeated.
- `inherit` — *(CSS2)* Takes the same value as that set for the property of the parent element, if allowed.

Sample Code:
```
<strong style="background: green">This text is displayed against
a green background.</strong>
```

background-attachment

Description: If `background-image` property is set, this element specifies how the background image should move when the browser window is scrolled.
Media Group: Visual
CSS Family Type: Backgrounds
Originated with: CSS1
Values:

- `scroll` — Image moves when the browser window is scrolled.
- `fixed` — Image does not move when the browser window is scrolled.
- `inherit` — *(CSS2)* Takes the same value as that set for the property of the parent element, if allowed.

Sample Code:
```
<body style="background-image: url(canvas.gif); background-
attachment: fixed">
```

background-color

Description: Sets the background color of an element.
Media Group: Visual
CSS Family Type: Backgrounds
Originated with: CSS1
Values:

- *color name* or *numerical color value*
- `transparent` — renders the specified element transparent
- `inherit` — *(CSS2)* Takes the same value as that set for the property of the parent element, if allowed.

Sample Code:
```
<em style="background-color: ffff00">Italicized text on a yellow
background.</em>
```

background-image

Description: Sets a graphic image as a background image.
Media Group: Visual
CSS Family Type: Backgrounds
If this element is specified, the CSS elements `background-repeat`, `background-attachment` and `background-position` can also be used with it. A color value can also be added.
Originated with: CSS1
Values:

- `url(image)`
- `inherit` — (CSS2) Takes the same value as that set for the property of the parent element, if allowed.

Sample Code:
```
<body style="background-image: url(canvas.gif)">
```

background-position

Description: If the background-image element is specified, this element specifies where the image first appears, and then describes how it should be tiled.
Media Group: Visual
CSS Family Type: Backgrounds
Originated with: CSS1
Values:

- `x% y%` — Percentage is in reference to the dimensions of the browser window display.
- `x y` — Represents the absolute coordinate position of the image.
- `(left/center/right)` | `(top/center/bottom)` — Keywords representing screen positions. Left keyword is the x-position and the right keyword is the y-position for the image.
- `inherit` — (CSS2) Takes the same value as that set for the property of the parent element, if allowed.

Sample Code:
```
<body style="background-image: url(victorinus.jpg); background-position: 100 50">
```

background-position-x

Description: Provides more precise control over exactly where background images can begin horizontally tiling — within themselves — before tiling the rest of the page as a background.
Media Group: Visual
CSS Family Type: Backgrounds
Originated with: Internet Explorer 5.5 *(browser-specific)*
Values:

- `% value` — Sets a percentage value for the horizontal spacing of the background; value is a percentage value of the width in which the image starts tiling within itself (and not to the browser window)
- `length (units)` — Specifies the length value for the horizontal spacing of the background image telling the browser where to begin tiling the image; value is a measure of the width in which the image starts tiling within itself (and not to the browser window)

Sample Code:
```
<style>
div.fixed-length {background-image: url(antony_rsc-12.jpg); back-
ground-position-x: 0px; height: 140px; width: 400px; font: large
Arial, Helvetica, sans-serif; color: navy}
</style>
```

background-position-y

Description: Provides more precise control over exactly where background images can begin vertically tiling — within themselves — before tiling the rest of the page as a background.
Media Group: Visual
CSS Family Type: Backgrounds
Originated with: Internet Explorer 5.5 *(browser-specific)*
Values:

- `% value` — Sets a percentage value for the vertical spacing of the background; value is a percentage value of the width in which the image starts tiling within itself (and not to the browser window)
- `length (units)` — Specifies the length value for the vertical spacing of the background image telling the browser where to begin tiling the image; value is a measure of the height in which the image starts tiling within itself (and not to the browser window)

Sample Code:
```
<style>
div.percentage {background-image: url(antony_rsc-12.jpg); back-
ground-position-y: 50%; height: 140px; width: 400px; font: large
Arial, Helvetica, sans-serif; color: navy}
</style>
```

background-repeat

Description: If the `background-image` element is set, this additional element speci-
fies how the image is repeated on the Web page.
Media Group: Visual
CSS Family Type: Backgrounds
Originated with: CSS1
Values:

- `repeat` — Image is horizontally and vertically tiled.
- `repeat-x` — Image is horizontally tiled.
- `repeat-y` — Image is vertically tiled.
- `no-repeat` — The image is not repeated.
- `inherit` — (CSS2) Takes the same value as that set for the property of
  the parent element, if allowed.

Sample Code:
```
<body style="background-image: url(gordian3.jpg); background-
repeat: repeat-x">
```

border

Description: This is an abbreviated element that allows the Web author to specify
`border-top`, `border-right`, `border-bottom` and `border-left` elements easily.
Media Group: Visual
CSS Family Type: Boxes (Sub-family: Borders)
Originated with: CSS1
Values:

- `n measurement units` — Sets the thickness of the border.
- `thin | medium | thick` — Sets the relative thickness of the border.
- `color name` or `numerical color value` — Sets the color for the
  border.
- `dashed` — A dashed border line is displayed.

- `dotted` — A dotted border line is displayed.
- `double` — A double line is displayed.
- `inset` — A 3D inset line is displayed.
- `groove` — A 3D grooved line is displayed.
- `none` — No border is displayed, no matter what border-width value is present.
- `outset` — A 3D outset line is displayed.
- `ridge` — A 3D ridged line is displayed.
- `solid` — A solid border line is displayed.
- `hidden` — *(CSS2)* Same effect as `none`. It is designed to suppress border displays when used in tables.
- `inherit` — *(CSS2)* Takes the same value as that set for the property of the parent element, if allowed.

Sample Code:

```
<strong style="border: ridge red">A strong statement.</strong>
```

border-bottom

Description: Sets the display value for the bottom border of the specified HTML tag.
Media Group: Visual
CSS Family Type: Boxes (Sub-family: Borders)
Originated with: CSS1
Values:

- *n measurement units* — Sets the thickness of the border.
- `thin` | `medium` | `thick` — Sets the relative thickness of the border.
- *color name* or *numerical color value* — Sets the color for the border.
- `dashed` — A dashed border line is displayed.
- `dotted` — A dotted border line is displayed.
- `double` — A double line is displayed.
- `inset` — A 3D inset line is displayed.
- `groove` — A 3D grooved line is displayed.
- `none` — No border is displayed, no matter what border-width value is present.
- `outset` — A 3D outset line is displayed.
- `ridge` — A 3D ridged line is displayed.
- `solid` — A solid border line is displayed.
- `hidden` — *(CSS2)* Same effect as `none`. It is designed to suppress border displays when used in tables.

- `inherit` — *(CSS2)* Takes the same value as that set for the property of the parent element, if allowed.

Sample Code:

```
<em style="border-bottom: double blue">Text with a double blue
underline.</em>
```

border-bottom-color

Description: Specifies the color for the bottom border.
Media Group: Visual
CSS Family Type: Boxes (Sub-family: Borders)
Originated with: CSS2
Values:

- *color name* or *numerical color value* — Sets the color for the border.
- `inherit` — Takes the same value as that set for the property of the parent element, if allowed.

Sample Code:

```
<h3 style="border-bottom-color: lime">Third-Level Header with a
Lime Colored Bottom Border</h3>
```

border-bottom-style

Description: Sets the type of bottom border to be displayed.
Media Group: Visual
CSS Family Type: Boxes (Sub-family: Borders)
Originated with: CSS2
Values:

- `dashed` — A dashed border line is displayed.
- `dotted` — A dotted border line is displayed.
- `double` — A double line is displayed.
- `inset` — A 3D inset line is displayed.
- `groove` — A 3D grooved line is displayed.
- `none` — No border is displayed, no matter what border-width value is present.
- `outset` — A 3D outset line is displayed.
- `ridge` — A 3D ridged line is displayed.
- `solid` — A solid border line is displayed.

- `hidden` — Same effect as `none`. It is designed to suppress border displays when used in tables.
- `inherit` — Takes the same value as that set for the property of the parent element, if allowed.

Sample Code:
```
<p style="border-bottom-style: solid">Paragraph with a solid bot-
tom border.</p>
```

border-bottom-width

Description: Sets the thickness of the bottom border.
Media Group: Visual
CSS Family Type: Boxes (Sub-family: Borders)
Originated with: CSS1
Values:

- `n measurement units` — Sets the thickness of the bottom border.
- `thin | medium | thick` — Sets the relative thickness of the border.
- `inherit` — *(CSS2)* Takes the same value as that set for the property of the parent element, if allowed.

Sample Code:
```
<blockquote style="border-bottom-width: thick">"This is an impor-
tant quote,"</blockquote> he said.
```

border-collapse

Description: Selects the table border to be used.
Media Group: Visual
CSS Family Type: Tables
Originated with: CSS2
Values:

- `collapse` — Table is set to the collapsing borders model.
- `separate` — Table is set to the separated borders model.
- `inherit` — Takes the same value as that set for the property of the parent element, if allowed.

Sample Code:

```
<html>
<head>
<title>Border-Collapse</title>
<style>
table {border: outset 15pt; border-collapse:
separate; border-spacing: 15pt;}
td {border: inset 15pt; font-size: xx-large;}
</style>
</head>
<body>
<table>
<tr>
<td>Cell 1</td>
<td>Cell 2</td>
<td>Cell 3</td>
</tr>
</table>
</body>
</html>
```

border-color

Description: Sets the color of the border sides.
Media Group: Visual
CSS Family Type: Boxes (Sub-family: Borders)
Originated with: CSS1
Values:

- *color name* or *numerical color value* — Sets the color for the border.
- `inherit` — (*CSS2*) Takes the same value as that set for the property of the parent element, if allowed.
- `transparent` — (*CSS2*) Renders the border transparent.

Sample Code:

```
<h3 style="border-color: olive">Header with a Colored Border</h3>
```

border-left

Description: Specifies how the left border associated with an HTML tag should be displayed.
Media Group: Visual
CSS Family Type: Boxes (Sub-family: Borders)
Originated with: CSS1
Values:

- `n measurement units` — Sets the thickness of the border.
- `thin | medium | thick` — Sets the relative thickness of the border.
- `color name` or `numerical color value` — Sets the color for the border.
- `dashed` — A dashed border line is displayed.
- `dotted` — A dotted border line is displayed.
- `double` — A double line is displayed.
- `inset` — A 3D inset line is displayed.
- `groove` — A 3D grooved line is displayed.
- `none` — No border is displayed, no matter what border-width value is present.
- `outset` — A 3D outset line is displayed.
- `ridge` — A 3D ridged line is displayed.
- `solid` — A solid border line is displayed.
- `inherit` — *(CSS2)* Takes the same value as that set for the property of the parent element, if allowed.

Sample Code:

```
<h1 style="border-left: 1in teal">Check out the thick teal border
to the left</h1>
```

border-left-color

Description: Specifies the color for the left border.
Media Group: Visual
CSS Family Type: Boxes (Sub-family: Borders)
Originated with: CSS2
Values:

- `color name` or `numerical color value` — Sets the color for the border.
- `inherit` — Takes the same value as that set for the property of the parent element, if allowed.

Sample Code:
```
<h2 style="border-left-color: silver">Second-Level Header with a
Silver Colored Left Border</h2>
```

border-left-style

Description: Sets the type of left border to be displayed.
Media Group: Visual
CSS Family Type: Boxes (Sub-family: Borders)
Originated with: CSS2
Values:

- `dashed` — A dashed border line is displayed.
- `dotted` — A dotted border line is displayed.
- `double` — A double line is displayed.
- `inset` — A 3D inset line is displayed.
- `groove` — A 3D grooved line is displayed.
- `none` — No border is displayed, no matter what border-width value is present.
- `outset` — A 3D outset line is displayed.
- `ridge` — A 3D ridged line is displayed.
- `solid` — A solid border line is displayed.
- `hidden` — Same effect as `none`. It is designed to suppress border displays when used in tables.
- `inherit` — Takes the same value as that set for the property of the parent element, if allowed.

Sample Code:
```
<p style="border-left-style: inset">Paragraph with an inset left
border.</p>
```

border-left-width

Description: Sets the thickness of the left border.
Media Group: Visual
CSS Family Type: Boxes (Sub-family: Borders)
Originated with: CSS1
Values:

- `n measurement units` — Sets the thickness of the left border.

- thin | medium | thick — Sets the relative thickness of the border.
- inherit — *(CSS2)* Takes the same value as that set for the property of the parent element, if allowed.

Sample Code:
```
<h4 style="border-left-width thin">Text with a thin border to the
left.</h4>
```

border-right

Description: Specifies how the right border associated with an HTML tag should be displayed.
Media Group: Visual
CSS Family Type: Boxes (Sub-family: Borders)
Originated with: CSS1
Values:

- *n measurement units* — Sets the thickness of the border.
- thin | medium | thick — Sets the relative thickness of the border.
- *color name* or *numerical color value* — Sets the color for the border.
- dashed — A dashed border line is displayed.
- dotted — A dotted border line is displayed.
- double — A double line is displayed.
- inset — A 3D inset line is displayed.
- groove — A 3D grooved line is displayed.
- none — No border is displayed, no matter what border-width value is present.
- outset — A 3D outset line is displayed.
- ridge — A 3D ridged line is displayed.
- solid — A solid border line is displayed.
- hidden — *(CSS2)* Same effect as none. It is designed to suppress border displays when used in tables.
- inherit — *(CSS2)* Takes the same value as that set for the property of the parent element, if allowed.

Sample Code:
```
<blockquote style="border-right: thin inset yellow">"This quote
stands out with its right border."</blockquote>
```

border-right-color

Description: Specifies the color for the right border.
Media Group: Visual
CSS Family Type: Boxes (Sub-family: Borders)
Originated with: CSS2
Values:

- *color name* or *numerical color value* — Sets the color for the border.
- `inherit` — Takes the same value as that set for the property of the parent element, if allowed.

Sample Code:

```
<h1 style="border-right-color: teal">Top-Level Header with a Teal
Colored Bottom Border</h1>
```

border-right-style

Description: Sets the type of right border to be displayed.
Media Group: Visual
CSS Family Type: Boxes (Sub-family: Borders)
Originated with: CSS2
Values:

- `dashed` — A dashed border line is displayed.
- `dotted` — A dotted border line is displayed.
- `double` — A double line is displayed.
- `inset` — A 3D inset line is displayed.
- `groove` — A 3D grooved line is displayed.
- `none` — No border is displayed, no matter what border-width value is present.
- `outset` — A 3D outset line is displayed.
- `ridge` — A 3D ridged line is displayed.
- `solid` — A solid border line is displayed.
- `hidden` — Same effect as `none`. It is designed to suppress border displays when used in tables.
- `inherit` — Takes the same value as that set for the property of the parent element, if allowed.

Sample Code:

```
<p style="border-right-style: ridge">Paragraph with a ridged
right border.</p>
```

border-right-width

Description: Sets the thickness of the right border.
Media Group: Visual
CSS Family Type: Boxes (Sub-family: Borders)
Originated with: CSS2
Values:

- `n measurement units` — Sets the thickness of the right border.
- `thin | medium | thick` — Sets the relative thickness of the border.
- `inherit` — Takes the same value as that set for the property of the parent element, if allowed.

Sample Code:

```
<tt style="border-right-width 1in">Teletype script with a 1 inch
thick right border.</tt>
```

border-spacing

Description: Sets the distance separating adjacent cell borders. If one value is set, it is used for both height and width. If two values are set, the first is taken for horizontal spacing, while the second is used for vertical spacing.
Media Group: Visual
CSS Family Type: Tables
Originated with: CSS2
Values:

- `n [n] measurement units` — Sets the distance separating cell borders.
- `inherit` — Takes the same value as that set for the property of the parent element, if allowed.

Sample Code:

```
<html>
<head>
<title>Border-Spacing</title>
<style>
table {border: outset 5pt; border-collapse: separate;
```

```
border-spacing: 10pt;}
td {border: inset 5pt;}
</style>
</head>
<body>
<table>
<tr>
<td>Cell 1</td>
<td>Cell 2</td>
<td>Cell 3</td>
</tr>
</table>
</body>
</html>
```

border-style

Description: Sets the type of border to be displayed.
Media Group: Visual
CSS Family Type: Boxes (Sub-family: Borders)
Originated with: CSS1
Values:

- dashed — A dashed border line is displayed.
- dotted — A dotted border line is displayed.
- double — A double line is displayed.
- inset — A 3D inset line is displayed.
- groove — A 3D grooved line is displayed.
- none — No border is displayed, no matter what border-width value is present.
- outset — A 3D outset line is displayed.
- ridge — A 3D ridged line is displayed.
- solid — A solid border line is displayed.
- hidden — (CSS2) Same effect as none. It is designed to suppress border displays when used in tables.
- inherit — (CSS2) Takes the same value as that set for the property of the parent element, if allowed.

Sample Code:
```
<h2 style="border-style: solid">Header with Solid Border.</h2>
```

border-top

Description: Specifies how the top border associated with an HTML tag should be displayed.
Media Group: Visual
CSS Family Type: Boxes (Sub-family: Borders)
Originated with: CSS1
Values:

- `n measurement units` — Sets the thickness of the border.
- `thin | medium | thick` — Sets the relative thickness of the border.
- `color name` or `numerical color value` — Sets the color for the border.
- `dashed` — A dashed border line is displayed.
- `dotted` — A dotted border line is displayed.
- `double` — A double line is displayed.
- `inset` — A 3D inset line is displayed.
- `groove` — A 3D grooved line is displayed.
- `none` — No border is displayed, no matter what border-width value is present.
- `outset` — A 3D outset line is displayed.
- `ridge` — A 3D ridged line is displayed.
- `solid` — A solid border line is displayed.
- `hidden` — *(CSS2)* Same effect as `none`. It is designed to suppress border displays when used in tables.
- `inherit` — *(CSS2)* Takes the same value as that set for the property of the parent element, if allowed.

Sample Code:
```
<tt style="border-top: thin dashed 00ff00">Teletype text with a
top-border</tt>
```

border-top-color

Description: Specifies the color for the top border.
Media Group: Visual
CSS Family Type: Boxes (Sub-family: Borders)
Originated with: CSS2
Values:

- `color name` or `numerical color value` — Sets the color for the border.

- `inherit` — Takes the same value as that set for the property of the parent element, if allowed.

Sample Code:

```
<h1 style="border-top-color: maroon">Top-Level Header with a
Maroon Colored Top Border</h1>
```

border-top-style

Description: Sets the type of top border to be displayed.

Media Group: Visual

CSS Family Type: Boxes (Sub-family: Borders)

Originated with: CSS2

Values:

- `dashed` — A dashed border line is displayed.
- `dotted` — A dotted border line is displayed.
- `double` — A double line is displayed.
- `inset` — A 3D inset line is displayed.
- `groove` — A 3D grooved line is displayed.
- `none` — No border is displayed, no matter what border-width value is present.
- `outset` — A 3D outset line is displayed.
- `ridge` — A 3D ridged line is displayed.
- `solid` — A solid border line is displayed.
- `hidden` — Same effect as `none`. It is designed to suppress border displays when used in tables.
- `inherit` — Takes the same value as that set for the property of the parent element, if allowed.

Sample Code:

```
<p style="border-top-style: dotted">Paragraph with a dotted top
border.</p>
```

border-top-width

Description: Sets the thickness of the top border.
Media Group: Visual
CSS Family Type: Boxes (Sub-family: Borders)
Originated with: CSS1
Values:

- `n measurement units` — Sets the thickness of the top border.
- `thin | medium | thick` — Sets the relative thickness of the border.
- `inherit` — *(CSS2)* Takes the same value as that set for the property of the parent element, if allowed.

Sample Code:
```
<tt style="border-top-width 25px">Teletype script with a 25 pixel
thick top border.</tt>
```

border-width

Description: Sets the thickness of the border for the specified element. One to four border sides can be set.
Media Group: Visual
CSS Family Type: Boxes (Sub-family: Borders)
Originated with: CSS1
Values:

- `n [ n n n] measurement units` — Sets the thickness of the border.
  - If 1 value is present, all borders are set to the numerical value specified
  - If 2 values are present, the top/bottom and side borders take the numerical values specified
  - If 3 values are present, the top, right and left, then bottom take the numerical values specified
  - If 4 values are present, the top, right, bottom, then left borders take the numerical values specified
- `thin | medium | thick` — Sets the relative thickness of the border.
- `inherit` — *(CSS2)* Takes the same value as that set for the property of the parent element, if allowed.

Sample Code:
```
<h2 style="border-width: 5px 5px 15px 5px">Header with Surround-
ing Border</h2>
```

bottom

Description: Specifies the value that the current Web element is positioned above the containing box.
Media Group: Visual
CSS Family Type: Visual Formatting
Originated with: CSS2
Values:

- `n value` — Sets a length unit value.
- `% value` — Sets a length percentage value relative to the width of the containing block.
- `auto` — The default value for the specific element.
- `inherit` — Takes the same value as that set for the property of the parent element, if allowed.

Sample Code:

```
<p style="position: absolute; bottom: 1in">
This header is positioned 1 inch from the containing box, which
in this case is the bottom of the browser window.
</p>
```

caption-side

Description: Specifies where a caption will be in relation to a table.
Media Group: Visual
CSS Family Type: Tables
Originated with: CSS2
Values:

- `top` — Positions the caption above the table.
- `bottom` — Positions the caption below the table.
- `left` — Positions the caption to the left side of the table.
- `right` — Positions the caption to the right side of the table.
- `inherit` — Takes the same value as that set for the property of the parent element, if allowed.

Sample Code:

```
<table style="border: outset 5pt">
<caption style="caption-side: left">A Simple
Table</caption>
<tr>
<td>This text is contained within the table</td>
```

```
</tr>
</table>
```

clear

Description: Sets whether the specified element will allow other elements to "float" along its sides.
Media Group: Visual
CSS Family Type: Boxes
Originated with: CSS1
Values:

- `both` — The specified element will be moved below floating elements on either side.
- `left` — The specified element will be moved below floating elements on the left side only.
- `none` — Any floating elements are allowed on either side of the specified element.
- `right` — The specified element will be moved below floating elements on the right side only.
- `inherit` — *(CSS2)* Takes the same value as that set for the property of the parent element, if allowed.

Sample Code:
```
<strong style="clear: both">This text should appear below the
image.</strong>
```

clip

Description: Defines how much of a Web element is made visible.
Media Group: Visual
CSS Family Type: Visual Effects
Originated with: CSS2
Values:

- `rect[n n n n]` — A rectangle defined by units of length in the following order: top, right, bottom and left. Negative values are permitted. Values are relative to the size of the Web element.
- `auto` — Sets the element to the regular, default visible value for that element. Can be used in conjunction with `rect`.

- `inherit` — Takes the same value as that set for the property of the parent element, if allowed.

Sample Code:
```
<h1>The letters in this header are not "clipped".</h1>
<p>
<h1 style="clip: rect(10px 5px 10px 5px)">The letters in this
header will appear "clipped".</h1>
```

color

Description: Sets the color to be displayed.
Media Group: Visual
CSS Family Type: Backgrounds
Originated with: CSS1
Values:

- *color name* or *numerical color value*
- `inherit` — *(CSS2)* Takes the same value as that set for the property of the parent element, if allowed.

Sample Code:
```
<ul>
<li style="color: ff0000">This is displayed as red text</li>
<li style="color: 00ff00">This is displayed as green text</li>
<li style="color: 0000ff">This is displayed as blue text</li>
</ul>
```

content

Description: Determines the type of content, and, subsequently, how it is to be displayed. This is always used in conjunction with the `before` and `after` pseudo-classes.
Media Group: All
CSS Family Type: Generated Content, Automatic Numbering and Lists
Originated with: CSS2
Values:

- *string* — Refers to regular textual content.
- *url("filename")* — Points to specific Web content (most typically an image or sound file) in a format supported by the browser.

- `counter-increment` | `counter-reset` — These two counter properties can be used in conjunction with content to set a counter value for the associated element.
- `attr(x)` — Returns the string of the value of attribute X for the subject of the selector.
- `open-quote` | `close-quote` — These two values retrieve and insert the string previously set by the quotes property.
- `no-open-quote` | `no-close-quote` — These two values insert nothing, but do increment (or decrement) the nesting level for quotes.
- `inherit` — Takes the same value as that set for the property of the parent element, if allowed.

Sample Code:

```
<html>
<head>
<title>Content Example</title>
<style>
img:before {content: url("This_Is_An_Image.wav")}
body:after {content: "That's All Folks!"; display: block;
margin-top: 1cm; text-align: right; color: navy; font-size:
xx-large;}
</style>
</head>
<body style="font-size: x-large">
The image on this Web page is preceded by an audio
introduction, announcing it to be an image, primarily for
the benefit of those using audio browsers.
<P>
<img src="fokker.jpg" />
</body>
</html>
```

counter-increment

Description: Defines the property to be automatically incremented, and the amount by which it is to be incremented.
Media Group: All
CSS Family Type: Generated Content, Automatic Numbering and Lists
Originated with: CSS2
Values:

- `<identifier> <integer>` — An identifier that selects the element to be incremented, and by how much.
- `none` — The default value.

- `inherit` — Takes the same value as that set for the property of the parent element, if allowed.

Sample Code:

```
<html>
<head>
<title>counter-increment and counter-reset Example</title>
<style>
h1:before {content: "floor " counter(floor) " "; counter-incre-
ment: floor; counter-reset: room; font-size: large}
h2:before {content: counter(floor) "-" counter(room) " ";
counter-increment: room; font-size: large; font-weight: bold}
</style>
</head>
<body>
<h1>Basement</h1>
<h2>Storage space</h2>
<h1>Main Floor</h1>
<h2>Reception</h2>
<h2>Restaurant</h2>
<h2>Frank's Fish &amp; Steak House</h2>
<h1>Second Floor</h1>
<h2>Croecko Incorporated</h2>
</body>
</html>
```

counter-reset

Description: Resets the numerical value set by the `counter-increment` property.
Media Group: All
CSS Family Type: Generated Content, Automatic Numbering and Lists
Originated with: CSS2
Values:

- `<identifier> <integer>` — An identifier that selects the element to be incremented, and by how much.
- `none` — The default value.
- `inherit` — Takes the same value as that set for the property of the parent element, if allowed.

Sample Code:

```
<html>
<head>
<title>counter-increment and counter-reset Example</title>
<style>
```

```
h1:before {content: "floor " counter(floor) " "; counter-incre-
ment: floor; counter-reset: room; font-size: large}
h2:before {content: counter(floor) "-" counter(room) " ";
counter-increment: room; font-size: large; font-weight: bold}
</style>
</head>
<body>
<h1>Basement</h1>
<h2>Storage space</h2>
<h1>Main Floor</h1>
<h2>Reception</h2>
<h2>Restaurant</h2>
<h2>Frank's Fish &amp; Steak House</h2>
<h1>Second Floor</h1>
<h2>Croecko Incorporated</h2>
</body>
</html>
```

cue

Description: Adds sound to a Web element. If a single value is present, the sound is played before and after the element; if two are present, the first sound is played before and the second sound after the element.

Media Group: Aural

CSS Family Type: Aural (Sub-family: Cue Properties)

Originated with: CSS2

Values:

- *url(sound)* — Points to a sound file in a format supported by the browser.
- inherit — Takes the same value as that set for the property of the parent element, if allowed.

Sample Code:

```
A single sound appears before and after this <a href="link.html"
style="cue: badabing.aiff">link</a>.
<p>
Two different sounds appear before and after this
<a href="link.html" style="cue: bada-bing.aiff bada-
boom.aiff">link</a>.
```

cue-after

Description: Adds a sound to be played immediately *after* a Web element. Good for aurally distinguishing significant parts on a Web page.

Media Group: Aural

CSS Family Type: Aural (Sub-family: Cue Properties)

Originated with: CSS2

Values:

- `url(sound)` — Points to a sound file in a format supported by the browser.
- `none` — No sound is played.
- `inherit` — Takes the same value as that set for the property of the parent element, if allowed.

Sample Code:

```
You can get there by <a href="link.html" style="cue-after:
click.wav">Clicking here</a>.
```

cue-before

Description: Adds a sound to be played immediately *before* a Web element. Good for aurally distinguishing significant parts on a Web page.

Media Group: Aural

CSS Family Type: Aural (Sub-family: Cue Properties)

Originated with: CSS2

Values:

- `url(sound)` — Points to a sound file in a format supported by the browser.
- `none` — No sound is played.
- `inherit` — Takes the same value as that set for the property of the parent element, if allowed.

Sample Code:

```
<h1 style="cue-before: bong.au">Hamlet: Act I, Scene I</h1>
```

cursor

Description: Defines the type of cursor to be displayed.
Media Group: Visual, Interactive
CSS Family Type: User Interface
Originated with: CSS2
Values:

- `url` — Points to specific Web content. As the user passes over the link, it will change to the selected cursor type.
- `auto` — Browser displays the type of cursor normally associated with the Web element.
- `crosshair` — A symbol resembling a "+" is displayed.
- `default` — The default cursor type is displayed.
- `pointer` — A pointer cursor (typically a small, upper-left pointing arrow) is displayed.
- `move` — Cursor indicating that a Web element is to be moved.
- `e-resize` | `ne-resize` | `nw-resize` | `n-resize` | `se-resize` | `sw-resize` | `s-resize` | `w-resize` — Cursor associated when an edge or corner that can be moved.
- `text` — Indicates that text can be selected. Typically rendered as an I-bar.
- `wait` — Indicates that the program is busy and that the user should be patient while the operation is completed. Often an hourglass.
- `help` — Online help is available for the object under the cursor. Typically rendered as a question mark with pointer or as a balloon.
- `inherit` — Takes the same value as that set for the property of the parent element, if allowed.

Sample Code:
```
Take aim and fire! <a href="link.html"><img
src="shooting_gallery.gif" style="cursor: crosshair" /></a>
```

direction

Description: Sets the direction for the letters in the text to follow.
Media Group: Visual
CSS Family Type: Visual Formatting
Originated with: CSS2
Values:

- `ltr` — Text is displayed from left to right.

- `rtl` — Text is displayed from right to left.
- `inherit` — Takes the same value as that set for the property of the parent element, if allowed.

Sample Code:
```
<p style="direction: ltr">English1 English2 English3.</p>
<p style="direction: rtl">Arabic1 Arabic2 Arabic3.</p>
```

display

Description: Controls the fundamental nature of the specified HTML tag.
Media Group: All
CSS Family Type: Classification
Originated with: CSS1
Values:

- `block` — Sets the specified element as a block-type element.
- `compact | run-in` — (*CSS2*) Creates either a block or inline box, depending on context.
- `inline` — Sets the specified element as an inline-type element.
- `list-item` — Sets the specified element as a type of list item.
- `marker` — (*CSS2*) This value sets the generated content before or after the box to be a marker. Should be used in conjunction with the `:before` and `:after` pseudo-classes.
- `none` — Switches off the display of the specified element. It does not just create an invisible box; it creates no box at all.
- `table | table-caption | table-cell | table-column | table-column-group | table-footer-group | table-header-group | table-row | table-row-group | inline-table` — (*CSS2*) These values cause the selected element to behave like the table element specified.
- `inherit` — (*CSS2*) Takes the same value as that set for the property of the parent element, if allowed.

Sample Code:
```
<em style="display: list-item">This italicized text is indented
in the same way a list-item would be.</em>
```

elevation

Description: Sets the "angle" in which a sound is played in a sound space that runs from below to above the viewer's position.
Media Group: Aural
CSS Family Type: Aural (Sub-family: Spatial Properties)
Originated with: CSS2
Values:

- `n deg` — The angle in degrees in which a sound is located. The range of the angle is from `-90deg` to `90deg`. In this scheme, a value of `0deg` is directly in front of the viewer, `90deg` is directly above the viewer and `-90deg` is directly below the viewer.
- `below` — Equivalent to `-90deg`.
- `level` — Equivalent to `0deg`.
- `above` — Equivalent to `90deg`.
- `higher` — Adds 10 degrees to the current elevation, in effect, "raising" it.
- `lower` — Subtracts 10 degrees from the current elevation, in effect, "lowering" it.
- `inherit` — Takes the same value as that set for the property of the parent element, if allowed.

Sample Code:

```
<p style="elevation: -20deg">
Gravedigger: A pestilence on him for a mad rogue!
'A pour'd a flagon of Rhenish on my head once.
This same skull, sir, was Yorick's skull, the
King's jester.
</p>
<p style="elevation: 20deg">
Hamlet: This?
</p>
<p style="elevation: -20deg">
Gravedigger: E'en that.
</p>
<p style="elevation: lower">
Hamlet: Let me see.
</p>
<p style="elevation: center">
[Takes the skull.]
</p>
<p style="elevation: higher">
Alas, poor Yorick! I knew him, Horatio. A fellow
of infinite jest, of most excellent fancy.
</p>
```

empty-cells

Description: This property is used to control how table cells containing no content are to be displayed.
Media Group: Visual
CSS Family Type: Tables
Originated with: CSS2
Values:

- show — A border is drawn around the empty cell (the default table value).
- hide — No border is drawn around the empty cell.
- inherit — Takes the same value as that set for the property of the parent element, if allowed.

Sample Code:
```
<table style="empty-cellS: hide; border: inset 15pt">
<tr>
<td>No border should be drawn around the adjacent
cell.</td>
<td></td>
</table>
```

float

Description: Sets how elements can wrap around another "parent" element as it floats on a Web page.
Media Group: Visual
CSS Family Type: Boxes
Originated with: CSS1
Values:

- none — Other elements cannot be displayed to float around the specified element.
- left — Other elements can be displayed to the left margin of the specified element.
- right — Other elements can be displayed to the right margin of the specified element.
- inherit — (CSS2) Takes the same value as that set for the property of the parent element, if allowed.

Sample Code:

```
<img src="aurelian.jpg" style="float: right" />This text floats
to the left of the image.
```

font

Description: This is an abbreviated element that allows the Web author to quickly set fonts in the manner possible under the `font-family`, `font-size`, `font-style`, `font-variant` and `font-weight` CSS elements.
Media Group: Visual
CSS Family Type: Font
Originated with: CSS1
Values:

- `cursive` | `fantasy` | `monospace` | `sans-serif` | `serif` — Sets the type of visual characteristics of font "family" name that can be specified.
- `font_family` — The name of the font to be displayed
- `large` | `medium` | `small` | `x-large` | `x-small` | `xx-large` | `xx-small` — Specifies the size of the text. Values range from `xx-small` (smallest) to `xx-large` (largest).
- `larger` | `smaller` — Changes the size of the current specified element relative to a previously specified value.
- `n value` — Specific unit value for the specified element.
- `% value` — Sets a percentage for the size of a font relative to the base font size.
- `italic` | `normal` — Determines whether or not text is italicized
- `oblique` — Sets an italic-like property if the font used is sans serif.
- `100` | `200` | `300` | `400` | `500` | `600` | `700` | `800` | `900` — Absolute font weight values.
- `bold` | `normal` — Sets whether or not the specified text element uses a bold face.
- `bolder` | `lighter` — Changes the weight of the current specified element relative to a previously specified value.
- `caption` — (CSS2) Sets the system font used for captioned controls, such as buttons.
- `icon` — (CSS2) Sets the system font used to label icons.
- `menu` — (CSS2) Sets the system font used in menus, such as drop down menus.
- `message-box` — (CSS2) Sets the system font used for dialog boxes.
- `small-caption` — (CSS2) Sets the system font used for labeling small controls.

- `status-bar` — (*CSS2*) Sets the system font used for window status bars.
- `inherit` — (*CSS2*) Takes the same value as that set for the property of the parent element, if allowed.

Sample Code:

```
<form style="font: menu italic">
<select name="emperors">
<option>Augustus</option>
<option>Tiberius</option>
<option>Caligula</option>
<option>Claudius</option>
<option>Nero</option>
</select>
</form>
```

font-family

Description: Sets the type of font to be displayed with the specified element.

Media Group: Visual

CSS Family Type: Font

Originated with: CSS1

Values:

- `cursive | fantasy | monospace | sans-serif | serif` — Sets the type of visual characteristics of the font.
- `inherit` — (*CSS2*) Takes the same value as that set for the property of the parent element, if allowed.

Sample Code:

```
<strong style="font-family: serif">This sentence is displayed in
a serif font.</strong>
```

font-size

Description: Sets the display size of text.
Media Group: Visual
CSS Family Type: Font
Originated with: CSS1
Values:

- `large | medium | small | x-large | x-small | xx-large | xx-small` — Sets the size of the text. Values range from `xx-small` (smallest) to `xx-large` (largest).
- `larger | smaller` — Changes the size of the current specified element relative to a previously specified value.
- `n value` — Specific unit value for the specified element.
- `% value` — Sets a percentage for the size of a font relative to the base font size.
- `inherit` — (CSS2) Takes the same value as that set for the property of the parent element, if allowed.

Sample Code:
```
<h1 style="font-size: 68pt">Monster-Sized Heading</h1>
```

font-size-adjust

Description: Sets the aspect value for a selected font element. Useful in keeping the "look" of the size of a substituted font the same or close to that of the intended font.
Media Group: Visual
CSS Family Type: Font
Originated with: CSS2
Values:

- `n` — Sets the aspect value.
- `none` — Browser does not preserve the aspect value between fonts.
- `inherit` — Takes the same value as that set for the property of the parent element, if allowed.

Sample Code:
```
<h1 style="font-size: 12pt; font-family: courier; font-size-
adjust: 1.5">Font-Size-Adjust-ed Header</h1>
```

font-stretch

Description: Sets how condensed or expanded a selected font element should be.
Media Group: Visual
CSS Family Type: Font
Originated with: CSS2
Values:

- `ultra-condensed` | `extra-condensed` | `condensed` | `semi-condensed` | `normal` | `semi-expanded` | `expanded` | `extra-expanded` | `ultra-expanded` — Range of fonts from most condensed to most expanded.
- `wider` — Sets the selected font to a more expanded value.
- `narrower` — Sets the selected font to a more condensed value.
- `inherit` — Takes the same value as that set for the property of the parent element, if allowed.

Sample Code:

```
<h1 style="font-stretch: ultra-condensed">An Ultra-Condensed
Header</h1>
```

font-style

Description: Sets whether or not the displayed font is italicized.
Media Group: Visual
CSS Family Type: Font
Originated with: CSS1
Values:

- `italic` | `normal` — Determines whether or not text is italicized
- `oblique` — To be used to create italicized text (used for fonts that do not understand the term "italic").
- `inherit` — (CSS2) Takes the same value as that set for the property of the parent element, if allowed.

Sample Code:

```
<em style="font: oblique">This text is set to oblique.</em>
```

font-variant

Description: Determines how text is displayed using capital letters.
Media Group: Visual
CSS Family Type: Font
Originated with: CSS1
Values:

- `normal` | `small-caps` — These values are toggles to turn the small-caps effect on and off.
- `inherit` — *(CSS2)* Takes the same value as that set for the property of the parent element, if allowed.

Sample Code:

```
<h1 style="font-variant: small-caps">this text is displayed in
small capital letters</h1>
```

font-weight

Description: Sets the thickness of the displayed font.
Media Group: Visual
CSS Family Type: Font
Originated with: CSS1
Values:

- `100` | `200` | `300` | `400` | `500` | `600` | `700` | `800` | `900` — Absolute font weight values.
- `bold` | `normal` — Sets whether or not the specified text element uses a bold face.
- `bolder` | `lighter` — Changes the weight of the current specified element relative to that of a previously specified value.
- `inherit` — *(CSS2)* Takes the same value as that set for the property of the parent element, if allowed.

Sample Code:

```
<em style="font: bold">This emphasized text is set to bold using
CSS.</em>
```

height

Description: This property scales an element (typically an image) to the specified height.
Media Group: Visual
CSS Family Type: Boxes (Sub-Family: Padding)
Originated with: CSS1
Values:

- `auto` — Specifies that the browser default value should be used.
- `% value` — Sets a percentage value of the element's width.
- `length (units)` — Specifies the length value as a unit of measurement.
- `inherit` — (CSS2) Takes the same value as that set for the property of the parent element, if allowed.

Sample Code:
```
<img src="philco_jnr.jpg" style="height: 2.5in" />
```

layout-flow

Description: Sets the flow of text — either horizontally or vertically — on a page.
Media Group: Visual
CSS Family Type: Text Property Extensions
Originated with: Internet Explorer 5.0 (browser-specific)
Values:

- `horizontal` — Sets the flow of text from left to right, and from the top down, typical of Western text.
- `vertical-ideographic` — Sets the flow of the text from top to bottom, with subsequent text appearing to the left of the first line of characters, which is the typical layout for many Asian languages.

Sample Code:
```
<div style="layout-flow: vertical-ideographic">
<span class="chinese">
&#27489;&#36814;&#28459;&#28216;</span>
<span class="english">PanelX &#150;</span>
<span class="chinese">
&#24179;&#38754;&#39023;&#31034;&#23631;&#26989;&#30028;&#30340;
</span>
<span class="english">Portal </span>
<span class="chinese">&#21450;</span>
```

```
<span class="english">Exchange</span>
</div>
```

layout-grid

Description: Shortcut property for setting Asian characters using a vertical grid framework.

Media Group: Visual

CSS Family Type: Text Property Extensions

Originated with: Internet Explorer 5.0 *(browser-specific)*

Values:

- `% value` — Sets a percentage value for the vertical spacing of characters.

- `length (units)` — Specifies the length value for the vertical spacing of characters.

- `none` — No value is explicitly set for the vertical spacing of characters.

- `auto` — An optimal value for vertical character spacing is determined by the browser.

- `both` — Enables both line and character grid types

- `line` — Sets a line grid for layout purposes.

- `char` — Sets a character grid for layout purposes

- `loose` — A setting designed for use with Japanese and Korean character sets

- `strict` — Designed for use for Chinese character sets and Japanese Genko characters.

- `fixed` — Used in combination with a grid layout when you want to display characters in a monospaced fashion.

Sample Code:

```
<div style="font-family: "MS Mincho"; layout-grid: both loose
10pt 5pt; layout-flow: vertical-ideographic; font-size:
15pt">&#12399;&#12501;&#12521;&#12483;&#12488;&#12497;&#12493;&#
12523;&#12487;&#12451;&#12473;&#12503;&#12524;&#12452;&#26989;&#
30028;&#12398;&#29420;&#31435;&#12375;&#12383;&#12509;&#12540;&#
12479;</div>
```

layout-grid-char

Description: Sets the distance between characters appearing within a line; specific to Asian character layout.
Media Group: Visual
CSS Family Type: Text Property Extensions
Originated with: Internet Explorer 5.0 *(browser-specific)*
Values:

- `% value` — Sets a percentage value for the vertical spacing of characters.
- `length (units)` — Specifies the length value for the vertical spacing of characters.
- `none` — No value is explicitly set for the vertical spacing of characters.
- `auto` — An optimal value for vertical character spacing is determined by the browser.

Sample Code:
```
<div style="font-family: PMingLiU; layout-grid-char: 15pt; lay-
out-grid-mode: both; layout-flow: vertical-ideographic; font-
weight: bold; font-size:
15pt">&#20320;&#21487;&#23559;&#20320;&#35201;&#20834;&#25237;&#
30340;&#36008;&#29289;&#21152;&#35387;&#25104;;</div>
```

layout-grid-line

Description: Sets the distance between vertical lines of characters; specific to Asian character layout.
Media Group: Visual
CSS Family Type: Text Property Extensions
Originated with: Internet Explorer 5.0 *(browser-specific)*
Values:

- `% value` — Sets a percentage value for the vertical spacing of characters.
- `length (units)` — Specifies the length value for the vertical spacing of characters.
- `none` — No value is explicitly set for the vertical spacing of characters.
- `auto` — An optimal value for vertical character spacing is determined by the browser.

Sample Code:

```
<div style="font-family: PMingLiU; layout-grid-line: 25pt; lay-
out-grid-mode: both; layout-flow: vertical-ideographic; font-
weight: bold; font-size:
15pt">&#20320;&#21487;&#23559;&#20320;&#35201;&#20834;&#25237;&#
30340;&#36008;&#29289;&#21152;&#35387;&#25104;</div>
```

layout-grid-mode

Description: Sets the type of grid layout to be used; specific to Asian character layout.
Media Group: Visual
CSS Family Type: Text Property Extensions
Originated with: Internet Explorer 5.0 *(browser-specific)*
Values:

- `both` — Enables both line and character grid types
- `none` — Ensures that no grid is present
- `line` — Sets a line grid for layout purposes.
- `char` — Sets a character grid for layout purposes

Sample Code:

```
<div style="font-family: PMingLiU; layout-grid-mode: both; lay-
out-flow: vertical-ideographic; layout-grid-type:
loose">&#20320;&#21487;&#23559;&#20320;&#35201;&#20834;&#25237;&
#30340;&#36008;&#29289;&#21152;&#35387;&#25104;</div>
```

layout-grid-type

Description: Controls the type of layout grid for rendering an element's content; specific to Asian character layout.
Media Group: Visual
CSS Family Type: Text Property Extensions
Originated with: Internet Explorer 5.0 *(browser-specific)*
Values:

- `loose` — A setting designed for use with Japanese and Korean character sets
- `strict` — Designed for use for Chinese character sets and Japanese Genko characters.
- `fixed` — Used in combination with a grid layout when you want to display characters in a monospaced fashion.

Sample Code:
```
<div style="font-family: PMingLiU; layout-grid-type: loose; lay-
out-grid-mode: both; layout-flow: vertical-ideographic">
&#20320;&#21487;&#23559;&#20320;&#35201;&#20834;&#25237;&#30340;
&#36008;&#29289;&#21152;&#35387;&#25104;;</div>
```

left

Description: Specifies the value that the current Web element is positioned from the left edge of its containing box.
Media Group: Visual
CSS Family Type: Visual Formatting
Originated with: CSS2
Values:

- `n value` — Sets a length unit value.
- `% value` — Sets a length percentage value relative to the width of the containing block.
- `auto` — The default value for the specific element.
- `inherit` — Takes the same value as that set for the property of the parent element, if allowed.

Sample Code:
```
<p style="position: absolute; left: 20px">
This header is positioned 20 pixels from the containing box,
which in this case is the left margin of the browser.
</p>
```

letter-spacing

Description: Specifies the spacing value between letters.
Media Group: Visual
CSS Family Type: Text
Originated with: CSS1
Values:

- `normal` — The browser's default letter-spacing value.
- `length (units)` — Sets the length value between letters as a unit of measurement.
- `inherit` — (CSS2) Takes the same value as that set for the property of the parent element, if allowed.

Sample Code:

```
<strong style="letter-spacing: 1cm">Some wide letter spacing!</
strong>
```

line-break

Description: Sets the type of line-breaking rule to be applied to Chinese, Japanese and Korean (CJK) characters.
Media Group: Visual
CSS Family Type: Text Properties
Originated with: Internet Explorer 5.5 *(browser-specific); also CSS3 proposed*
Values:

- `normal` — Sets the normal line-breaking mode for CJK characters, typically between any small katakana or hiragana characters that may appear on a line
- `strict` — Sets a more strict type of line break whereby small katakana or hiragana characters are not used to start a line of text

Sample Code:

```
<span class="chinese" style="line-break: normal">
&#27489;&#36814;&#28459;&#28216;</span>
```

line-height

Description: Sets the distance between lines of text on a Web page.
Media Group: Visual
CSS Family Type: Font
Originated with: CSS1
Values:

- `normal` — Sets the line height to the default value used by the browser.
- `n` — Sets a multiple value for the current height of the font in use.
- `% value` — Sets a percentage value in relation to the size of the current font in use.
- `length (units)` — Specifies the height value as a unit of measurement.
- `inherit` — *(CSS2)* Takes the same value as that set for the property of the parent element, if allowed.

Sample Code:
```
Baseline<br />
<h1 style="line-height: 2.5in">This appears 2 and a half inches
down from the break element at the top of the page!</h1>
```

list-style

Description: This is an abbreviated element that enables Web authors to quickly set list-item markers in the manner possible under `list-style-position`, `list-style-image` and `list-style-type`.

Media Group: Visual

CSS Family Type: Classification

Originated with: CSS1

Values:

- `circle` | `disc` | `square` — Sets the symbol specified to appear before each list item.
- `decimal` | `lower-alpha` | `lower-roman` | `upper-alpha` | `upper-roman` — Sets the type of alphanumeric symbol to appear before each list item.
- `lower-greek` — *(CSS2)* Sets the type of alphanumeric symbol that appears before each list item.
- `hebrew` | `armenian` | `georgian` | `cjk-ideographic` | `hiragana` | `katakana` | `hiragana-iroha` | `katakana-iroha` — *(CSS2)* Traditional numbering based upon the language type selected.
- `none` — No list marker is to be displayed before a list item.
- `url(image)` — Specifies the URL of the graphic to be used as a list marker.
- `inside` — Displays the text of a list item at a similar indentation level to the list marker.
- `outside` — Displays the text of a list item indented from the list marker.
- `inherit` — *(CSS2)* Takes the same value as that set for the property of the parent element, if allowed.

Sample Code:
```
<ul style="list-style: hebrew">
<li>List items</li>
<li>preceded by</li>
<li>alphabetical Hebrew letters</li>
</ul>
```

list-style-image

Description: Specifies an image to be used as the marker before a list element.
Media Group: Visual
CSS Family Type: Classification
Originated with: CSS1
Values:

- `none` — No list marker is displayed before a list item.
- `url(image)` - Specifies the URL of the graphic to be used as a list marker.
- `inherit` — (CSS2) Takes the same value as that set for the property of the parent element, if allowed.

Sample Code:
```
<ul>
<li style="list-style-image: url(trajan.jpg)">Emperor Trajan, 98-
117 AD</li>
<li style="list-style-image: url(hadrian.jpg)">Emperor Hadrian,
117-158 AD</li>
</ul>
```

list-style-position

Description: Specifies how a list marker is rendered relative to the content of the list item itself.
Media Group: Visual
CSS Family Type: Classification
Originated with: CSS1
Values:

- `inside` — Displays the text of a list item at a similar indentation level to the list marker.
- `outside` — Displays the text of a list item indented from the list marker.
- `inherit` — (CSS2) Takes the same value as that set for the property of the parent element, if allowed.

Sample Code:
```
<ul style="list-style-position: inside">
<li>Notice how the text in the second line of this bullet item
begins underneath the bullet rather than directly under the first
word.</li>
</ul>
```

list-style-type

Description: This element sets the type of list markers that appear before list items.
Media Group: Visual
CSS Family Type: Classification
Originated with: CSS1
Values:

- `circle` | `disc` | `square` — Sets the type of symbol to appear before a list element.
- `decimal` | `lower-alpha` | `lower-roman` | `upper-alpha` | `upper-roman` — Sets the type of alphanumeric symbol that appears before a list marker.
- `decimal-leading-zero` | `lower-greek` | `lower-latin` | `upper-latin` — (CSS2) Sets the type of alphanumeric symbol that appears before a list marker.
- `hebrew` | `armenian` | `georgian` | `cjk-ideographic` | `hiragana` | `katakana` | `hiragana-iroha` | `katakana-iroha` — Traditional numbering based upon the language type selected.
- `none` — No list marker is displayed before a list item.
- `inherit` — (CSS2) Takes the same value as that set for the property of the parent element, if allowed.

Sample Code:
```
<ul style="list-style-type: lower-alpha">
<li>List items</li>
<li>preceded by</li>
<li>lower-case letters</li>
</ul>
```

margin

Description: This is an abbreviated element that enables Web authors to quickly set margin values such as `margin-top`, `margin-right`, `margin-left` or `margin-bottom`.
Media Group: Visual
CSS Family Type: Boxes (Sub-Family: Margin)
Originated with: CSS1
Values:

- `auto` — Specifies that the browser default value should be used.
- `% values` — Sets a percentage value of the element's width.
- `n [ n n n] measurement units` — Sets the thickness of the border.

- If 1 value is present, all borders are set to the numerical value specified
- If 2 values are present, the top/bottom and side borders take the numerical values specified
- If 3 values are present, the top, right and left, then bottom take the numerical values specified
- If 4 values are present, the top, right, bottom, then left borders take the numerical values specified
- `inherit` — *(CSS2)* Takes the same value as that set for the property of the parent element, if allowed.

Sample Code:

```
<h1 style="margin: 2in">This text has a margin set to two
inches.</h1>
```

margin-bottom

Description: Specifies the distance of an element from the bottom edge of the browser window or from the next element that appears below it.
Media Group: Visual
CSS Family Type: Boxes (Sub-Family: Margin)
Originated with: CSS1
Values:

- `auto` — Specifies that the browser default value should be used.
- `% value` — Sets a percentage value of the element's width.
- `length (units)` — Specifies the length value as a unit of measurement.
- `inherit` — *(CSS2)* Takes the same value as that set for the property of the parent element, if allowed.

Sample Code:

```
<tt style="margin-bottom: 1in">This text is indented 1 inch from
the element below it.</tt>
```

margin-left

Description: Specifies the distance of an element from the left edge of the browser window or from the element that appears immediately to the left.
Media Group: Visual
CSS Family Type: Boxes (Sub-Family: Margin)

Originated with: CSS1
Values:

- `auto` — Specifies that the browser default value should be used.
- `% value` — Sets a percentage value of the element's width.
- `length (units)` — Specifies the length value as a unit of measurement.
- `inherit` — (CSS2) Takes the same value as that set for the property of the parent element, if allowed.

Sample Code:
```
<h1 style="margin-left: 2.5in">This header is indented 2 and a
half inches from the left margin.</h1>
```

margin-right

Description: Specifies the distance of an element from the right edge of the browser window or from the next element that appears to its right.
Media Group: Visual
CSS Family Type: Boxes (Sub-Family: Margin)
Originated with: CSS1
Values:

- `auto` — Specifies that the browser default value should be used.
- `% value` — Sets a percentage value of the element's width.
- `length (units)` — Specifies the length value as a unit of measurement.
- `inherit` — (CSS2) Takes the same value as that set for the property of the parent element, if allowed.

Sample Code:
```
<img src="trajan.jpg" style="margin-right: 1in" />This text is
set 1 inch to the right of the adjacent image.
```

margin-top

Description: Specifies the distance of an element from the top edge of the browser window or from the element that appears above it.
Media Group: Visual
CSS Family Type: Boxes (Sub-Family: Margin)
Originated with: CSS1

Values:

- `auto` — Specifies that the browser default value should be used.
- `% value` — Sets a percentage value of the element's width.
- `length (units)` — Specifies the length value as a unit of measurement.
- `inherit` — (CSS2) Takes the same value as that set for the property of the parent element, if allowed.

Sample Code:
```
<h1 style="margin-top: 150px">Header situated 150 pixels from the
top margin.</h1>
```

marker-offset

Description: Sets the distance between the border of a marker box in relation to the principal box with which it is associated.
Media Group: Visual
CSS Family Type: Generated Content, Automatic Numbering and Lists
Originated with: CSS2
Values:

- `n value` — Sets a length unit value.
- `auto` — The default length value.
- `inherit` — Takes the same value as that set for the property of the parent element, if allowed.

Sample Code:
```
<html>
<head>
<title>Marker-Offset</title>
<style>
p {margin-left: 10em} /* Make space for counters */
li:before {display: marker; marker-offset: 5em;
content: counter(mycounter, upper-alpha) ".";
counter-increment: mycounter;}
</style>
</head>
<body>
<p>
<ol>
<li>Here is the first item.</li>
<li>Here is the second item.</li>
<li>Here is the third item.</li>
```

```
</ol>
<p>
</body>
</html>
```

marks

Description: This property sets the type of mark to be displayed, defining the page box. It can be used to add crop marks or cross marks defining the extent of the page.
Media Group: Visual, Paged
CSS Family Type: Paged Media
Originated with: CSS2
Values:

- `crop` — Adds crop marks to a page; used to determine where the page should be cut.
- `cross` — Adds cross marks to a page; used to align sheets.
- `none` — No mark is made visible.
- `inherit` — Takes the same value as that set for the property of the parent element, if allowed.

Sample Code:
```
<html>
<head>
<title>marks Example</title>
<style>
@page {size: 8.5in 11in portrait; margin: 0.5in; marks: cross}
</style>
</head>
<body>
The content on this page will be printed in portrait mode, have
an indented margin of 0.5 inches on all sides, and be set for
printing on regular 8.5 x 11 inch paper.
</body>
</html>
```

max-height

Description: Sets the maximum height for a block element.
Media Group: Visual
CSS Family Type: Visual Formatting (Details)
Originated with: CSS2

Values:

- `n value` — Sets a length unit value.
- `% value` — Sets a length percentage value relative to the height of the containing block.
- `none` — Default value, sets no maximum value for the height of the box.
- `inherit` — Takes the same value as that set for the property of the parent element, if allowed.

Sample Code:

```
<h1 style="max-height: 1cm">This Header Must Be No Bigger than
1cm</h1>
```

max-width

Description: Sets the maximum width for a block element.

Media Group: Visual

CSS Family Type: Visual Formatting (Details)

Originated with: CSS2

Values:

- `n value` — Sets a length unit value.
- `% value` — Sets a length percentage value relative to the width of the containing block.
- `none` — Default value, sets no maximum value for the width of the box.
- `inherit` — Takes the same value as that set for the property of the parent element, if allowed.

Sample Code:

```
<h1 style="max-width: 5cm">This Header Must Be No Wider than
5cm</h1>
```

min-height

Description: Sets the minimum height for a block element.
Media Group: Visual
CSS Family Type: Visual Formatting (Details)
Originated with: CSS2
Values:

- *n value* — Sets a length unit value.
- *% value* — Sets a length percentage value relative to the height of the containing block.
- inherit — Takes the same value as that set for the property of the parent element, if allowed.

Sample Code:

```
<h1 style="min-height: 5cm">This Header Must Be At Least 5cm in
Height</h1>
```

min-width

Description: Sets the minimum width for a block element.
Media Group: Visual
CSS Family Type: Visual Formatting (Details)
Originated with: CSS2
Values:

- *n value* — Sets a length unit value.
- *% value* — Sets a length percentage value relative to the width of the containing block.
- inherit — Takes the same value as that set for the property of the parent element, if allowed.

Sample Code:

```
<h1 style="min-width: 2cm">This Header Must Be No Smaller than
2cm in Width</h1>
```

orphans

Description: Sets the minimum number of lines of a paragraph that must be left at the bottom of a page.
Media Group: Visual, Paged
CSS Family Type: Paged Media
Originated with: CSS2
Values:

- *n* — An integer value that assigns the number of lines that must appear in a paragraph; otherwise, it will be forced to appear on the next page. Default value is 2.
- inherit — Takes the same value as that set for the property of the parent element, if allowed.

Sample Code:
```
<style>
@page {orphans: 3}
</style>
```

outline

Description: A shortcut property that sets a value for the border indicating focus for such things as buttons or form fields.
Media Group: Visual, Interactive
CSS Family Type: User Interface
Originated with: CSS2
Values:

- *n [n n n] measurement units* — Sets the thickness of the border.
  - If 1 value is present, all borders are set to the numerical value specified
  - If 2 values are present, the top/bottom and side borders take the numerical values specified
  - If 3 values are present, the top, right and left, then bottom take the numerical values specified
  - If 4 values are present, the top, right, bottom, then left borders take the numerical values specified
- thin | medium | thick — Sets the relative thickness of the border.
- *color name* or *numerical color value* — Sets the color for the border

- **invert** — Reverses the color currently being used in the background behind the user-interface element.
- **hidden** — Same effect as **none**. It is designed to suppress border displays when used in tables.
- **dashed** — A dashed border line is displayed.
- **dotted** — A dotted border line is displayed.
- **double** — A double line is displayed.
- **inset** — A 3D inset line is displayed.
- **groove** — A 3D grooved line is displayed.
- **none** — No border is displayed, no matter what border-width value is present.
- **outset** — A 3D outset line is displayed.
- **ridge** — A 3D ridged line is displayed.
- **solid** — A solid border line is displayed.
- **inherit** — Takes the same value as that set for the property of the parent element, if allowed.

Sample Code:

```
<style>
buttonstyle {outline: thick red groove}
</style>
```

outline-color

Description: Sets a color value for the border indicating focus for such things as buttons or form fields.
Media Group: Visual, Interactive
CSS Family Type: User Interface
Originated with: CSS2
Values:

- *color name* or *numerical color value* — Sets the color for the border.
- **invert** — Reverses the color currently being used in the background behind the user-interface element.
- **inherit** — Takes the same value as that set for the property of the parent element, if allowed.

Sample Code:

```
<style>
buttonstyle {outline-color: invert}
</style>
```

outline-style

Description: Sets a value for the border style indicating focus for such things as buttons or form fields.
Media Group: Visual, Interactive
CSS Family Type: User Interface
Originated with: CSS2
Values:

- `dashed` — A dashed border line is displayed.
- `dotted` — A dotted border line is displayed.
- `double` — A double line is displayed.
- `inset` — A 3D inset line is displayed.
- `groove` — A 3D grooved line is displayed.
- `none` — No border is displayed, no matter what border-width value is present.
- `outset` — A 3D outset line is displayed.
- `ridge` — A 3D ridged line is displayed.
- `solid` — A solid border line is displayed.
- `inherit` — Takes the same value as that set for the property of the parent element, if allowed.

Sample Code:
```
<style>
buttonstyle {outline-style: double}
</style>
```

outline-width

Description: Sets a value for the border width indicating focus for such things as buttons or form fields.
Media Group: Visual, Interactive
CSS Family Type: User Interface
Originated with: CSS2
Values:

- `n [ n n n] measurement units` — Sets the thickness of the border.
  - If 1 value is present, all borders are set to the numerical value specified
  - If 2 values are present, the top/bottom and side borders take the numerical values specified

- If 3 values are present, the top, right and left, then bottom take the numerical values specified
- If 4 values are present, the top, right, bottom, then left borders take the numerical values specified
- thin | medium | thick — Sets the relative thickness of the outline.
- inherit — Takes the same value as that set for the property of the parent element, if allowed.

Sample Code:
```
<style>
buttonstyle {outline-width: medium}
</style>
```

overflow

Description: Determines how user can access content that would otherwise be hidden from view when it takes up more space than is allotted to it.
Media Group: Visual
CSS Family Type: Visual Effects
Originated with: CSS2
Values:

- visible — The content is not clipped. It is displayed.
- hidden — The content is clipped. No scrollbars are displayed to allow scrolling to view the rest of the content.
- scroll — The content is clipped, but a scrollbar or equivalent mechanism is made available to allow the viewer to scroll through the content.
- auto — A scrolling mechanism is automatically provided should it be needed.
- inherit — Takes the same value as that set for the property of the parent element, if allowed.

Sample Code:
```
<blockquote style="width: 1.5in; height: 1in; overflow: auto">
If this quote runs too long, a scrollbar will appear so that the
viewer can continue to read the somewhat lengthy and definitely
meandering quotation.
</blockquote>
<p style="width: 1.5in; height: 1in; overflow: auto">
<img src="vanessa.jpg" />
</p>
<p style="width: 1.5in; height: 1in; overflow: hidden">
```

```
<img src="vanessa.jpg" />
</p>
```

padding

Description: This is an abbreviated element that enables Web authors to quickly set margin values such as `padding-top`, `padding-right`, `padding-left` or `padding-bottom`.
Media Group: Visual
CSS Family Type: Boxes (Sub-Family: Padding)
Originated with: CSS1
Values:

- `auto` — Specifies that the browser default value should be used.
- `% value` — Sets a percentage value of the element's width.
- `n [ n n n] measurement units` — Sets the thickness of the border.
  - If 1 value is present, all borders are set to the numerical value specified
  - If 2 values are present, the top/bottom and side borders take the numerical values specified
  - If 3 values are present, the top, right and left, then bottom take the numerical values specified
  - If 4 values are present, the top, right, bottom, then left borders take the numerical values specified
- `inherit` — *(CSS2)* Takes the same value as that set for the property of the parent element, if allowed.

Sample Code:
```
<img src="hadrian.jpg" style="padding: 2cm" />
```

padding-bottom

Description: Sets the amount of padding to the bottom of an element.
Media Group: Visual
CSS Family Type: Boxes (Sub-Family: Padding)
Originated with: CSS1
Values:

- `% value` — Sets a percentage value of the element's width.
- `length (units)` — Specifies the length value as a unit of measurement.

- `inherit` — *(CSS2)* Takes the same value as that set for the property of the parent element, if allowed.

Sample Code:

```
<strong style="padding-bottom: 2in">This is padded from the bot-
tom (i.e., from the element below it) by 2 inches.</strong>
<p>
Some extra text to demonstrate the effect.
</p>
```

padding-left

Description: Sets the amount of padding to the left of an element.
Media Group: Visual
CSS Family Type: Boxes (Sub-Family: Padding)
Originated with: CSS1
Values:

- `% value` — Sets a percentage value of the element's width.
- `length (units)` — Specifies the length value as a unit of measurement.
- `inherit` — *(CSS2)* Takes the same value as that set for the property of the parent element, if allowed.

Sample Code:

```
<strong style="padding-left: 15pt">This is padded from the left
by 15 points.</strong>
```

padding-right

Description: Sets the amount of padding to the right of an element.
Media Group: Visual
CSS Family Type: Boxes (Sub-Family: Padding)
Originated with: CSS1
Values:

- `% value` — Sets a percentage value of the element's width.
- `length (units)` — Specifies the length value as a unit of measurement.
- `inherit` — *(CSS2)* Takes the same value as that set for the property of the parent element, if allowed.

Sample Code:

```
<strong style="padding-right: 200px">This text has a padding of
200 pixels from the right. To demonstrate the effect properly,
you need another, long, rambling sentence that just goes on and
on and on and on...</strong>
```

padding-top

Description: Sets the amount of padding to the top of an element.
Media Group: Visual
CSS Family Type: Boxes (Sub-Family: Padding)
Originated with: CSS1
Values:

- `% value` — Sets a percentage value of the element's width.
- `length (units)` — Specifies the length value as a unit of measurement.
- `inherit` — *(CSS2)* Takes the same value as that set for the property of the parent element, if allowed.

Sample Code:

```
<strong style="padding-top: 50mm">This text is padded from the
top by 50 millimeters.</strong>
```

page

Description: Used to set a particular page type to be associated with a particular type of Web element.
Media Group: Visual, Paged
CSS Family Type: Paged Media
Originated with: CSS2
Values:

- `name` — An identifier that is associated with the element.
- `auto` — Follows the automatic formatting for the element. This is the default value.

Sample Code:

```
<html>
<head>
<title>page Example</title>
```

```
<style>
@page regular {size 8.5in 11in; margin: 1.5in;}
@page landscape {size: landscape;}
div {page: regular;}
table {page: landscape;}
</style>
</head>
<body>
<div>
The idea behind the <code>page</code> property is to create a
page break <i>and</i> enable the Web author to format the content
of the subsequent page in a different manner than that which went
before it.
</div>
<table>
<tr>
<td>The content in this table will be set in a new page, and will
appear in a landscape format.</td>
</tr>
</table>
</body>
</html>
```

page-break-after

Description: Tells the browser to insert a page break after the selected block-level element.
Media Group: Visual, Paged
CSS Family Type: Paged Media
Originated with: CSS2
Values:

- `auto` — Neither forces nor prohibits a page break from occurring.
- `always` — Tells the browser to always force a page break to occur after the block-level element.
- `avoid` — Tells the browser to avoid forcing a page break after the block-level element.
- `left` — Forces one or more page breaks to occur after the block-level element so that it appears on a left-hand page.
- `right` — Forces one or more page breaks to occur after the block-level element so that it appears on a right-hand page.
- `inherit` — Takes the same value as that set for the property of the parent element, if allowed.

Sample Code:

```
<html>
<head>
<title>page-break-after Example</title>
<style>
p {page-break-after: always}
</style>
</head>
<body>
<p>
Each subsequent paragraph will be forced onto a new printed page.
</p>
<p>
This is on a second printed page.
</p>
<p>
This will be printed on a third page.
</p>
</body>
</html>
```

page-break-before

Description: Tells the browser to insert a page break before the selected block-level element.
Media Group: Visual, Paged
CSS Family Type: Paged Media
Originated with: CSS2
Values:

- `auto` — Neither forces nor prohibits a page break from occurring.
- `always` — Tells the browser to always force a page break to occur before the block-level element.
- `avoid` — Tells the browser to avoid forcing a page break before the block-level element.
- `left` — Forces one or more page breaks to occur before the block-level element so that it appears on a left-hand page.
- `right` — Forces one or more page breaks to occur before the block-level element so that it appears on a right-hand page.
- `inherit` — Takes the same value as that set for the property of the parent element, if allowed.

Sample Code:
```
<html>
<head>
<title>page-break-before Example</title>
<style>
h1 {page-break-before: always;}
</style>
</head>
<body>
Here is some text.
<h1>This header will appear on a new printed page</h1>
</body>
</html>
```

page-break-inside

Description: Tells the browser whether or not a page break is allowed within the selected block-level element.
Media Group: Visual, Paged
CSS Family Type: Paged Media
Originated with: CSS2
Values:

- `auto` — Neither forces nor prohibits a page break from occurring.
- `avoid` — Tells the browser to avoid forcing a page break within the block-level element.
- `inherit` — Takes the same value as that set for the property of the parent element, if allowed.

Sample Code:
```
<html>
<head>
<title>page-break-inside Example</title>
<style>
blockquote {page-break-inside: avoid}
</style>
</head>
<body>
<blockquote>no matter how long this quote may be, the page-break-
inside property will ensure that a page break does
not occur inside of it, breaking it across more than one
page.
</blockquote>
</body>
</html>
```

pause

Description: A shortcut property that sets a value for a break in speech. The value(s) set is applied to the beginning and end of an element.
Media Group: Aural
CSS Family Type: Paged Media
Originated with: CSS2
Values:

- `n [n]` — Time value for a break in speech expressed in either milliseconds or seconds.
- `% value` — Percentage value expressed in relation to the "speed" of the text being read as set by the `speech-rate` property.
- `inherit` — Takes the same value as that set for the property of the parent element, if allowed.

Sample Code:
```
<p>The title of this play is:</p>
<h1 style="pause: 1s">The Tempest</h1>
<p>by William Shakespeare</p>
```

pause-after

Description: Sets a value for a break in speech occurring immediately after an element.
Media Group: Aural
CSS Family Type: Aural Style Sheets
Originated with: CSS2
Values:

- `n` — Time value for a break in speech expressed in either milliseconds or seconds.
- `% value` — Percentage value expressed in relation to the "speed" of the text being read as set by the speech-rate property.
- `inherit` — Takes the same value as that set for the property of the parent element, if allowed.

Sample Code:
```
<p style="pause-after: 0.5s">
Need a dramatic pause?
</p>
You just got one.
```

pause-before

Description: Sets a value for a break in speech occurring immediately before an element.
Media Group: Aural
CSS Family Type: Aural Style Sheets
Originated with: CSS2
Values:

- n — Time value for a break in speech expressed in either milliseconds or seconds.
- `% value` — Percentage value expressed in relation to the "speed" of the text being read as set by the speech-rate property.
- `inherit` — Takes the same value as that set for the property of the parent element, if allowed.

Sample Code:
```
Need a dramatic pause?
<p style="pause-before: 500ms">
You just got one.
</p>
```

pitch

Description: Sets the average pitch for a given speaking voice. The average pitch for a typical male voice is 120 Hz, while for a female voice it is typically about 210 Hz.
Media Group: Aural
CSS Family Type: Aural (Sub-family: Voice Characteristic Properties)
Originated with: CSS2
Values:

- `n hz` — Sets a numeric value for the speaking voice, in Hertz.
- `x-low` | `low` | `medium` | `high` | `x-high` | — There are no specific pitch settings for these values, as that depends on the voice family being used. The browser should interpret these values from a very low pitch (`x-low`) to a very high pitch (`x-high`).
- `inherit` — Takes the same value as that set for the property of the parent element, if allowed.

Sample Code:
```
<p style="voice-family: male; pitch: medium">
Hamlet: What hour now?
```

```
</p>
<p style="voice-family: male; pitch: low">
Horatio: I think it lacks of twelve.
</p>
<p style="voice-family: male; pitch: x-low">
Marcellus: No, it is struck.
</p>
```

pitch-range

Description: Specifies variation of the pitch for a particular voice.
Media Group: Aural
CSS Family Type: Aural (Sub-family: Voice Characteristic Properties)
Originated with: CSS2
Values:

- n — A numerical value in a range between 0 and 100. A value of 50 is the normal pitch range for a given speaking voice, 0 produces a monotone speaking voice, while 100 produces a highly animated speaking voice.
- inherit — Takes the same value as that set for the property of the parent element, if allowed.

Sample Code:
```
<p style="pitch-range: 25">
Ghost: Revenge his foul and most unnatural murder.
</p>
<p style="pitch-range: 80">
Hamlet: Murder?
</p>
<p style="pitch-range: 35">
Ghost: Murder most foul, as in the best it is; but this most foul,
strange, and unnatural.
</p>
```

play-during

Description: Sets a sound file to be "behind" a particular Web element as it is read.
Media Group: Aural
CSS Family Type: Aural (Sub-family: Mixing Properties)
Originated with: CSS2

Values:

- `url(sound)` — Points to a sound file in a format supported by the browser.
- `mix` — Overlays the specified sound with any other sound values that may be present.
- `repeat` — Keeps repeating the sound for the duration the Web element is present.
- `auto` — Any parent sound present continues to play (instead of simply being restarted) once the selected `play-during` element has finished.
- `none` — No sound; if a parent sound exists, it, too, is turned off.
- `inherit` — Takes the same value as that set for the property of the parent element, if allowed.

Sample Code:

```
<body style="play-during: windy-outdoors.wav repeat">
Hamlet: Whither wilt thou lead me? Speak! I'll go no further.
<p style="play-during: ghostly.wav mix repeat">
Ghost: Mark me.
</p>
Hamlet: I will.
<p style="play-during: ghostly.wav mix repeat">
Ghost: My hour is almost come, when I to sulph'rous and torment-
ing flames must render up myself.
</body>
```

position

Description: Sets the positioning for a box-level element.
Media Group: Visual
CSS Family Type: Visual Formatting
Originated with: CSS2
Values:

- `static` — The box-level element positioning is normal, and is laid out to the normal flow.
- `relative` — The box-level element positioning is calculated with regard to the normal flow, and this element is offset relative to its normal position.
- `absolute` — The box-level element is positioned using the `left`, `right`, `top` and `bottom` properties. Box-level elements positioned this way are separate from the normal flow.

- `fixed` — The box-level element is positioned in the same manner as with `absolute`, but is fixed with regard to some other element.
- `inherit` — Takes the same value as that set for the property of the parent element, if allowed.

Sample Code:

```
<style>
@media screen { {h1#first {position: fixed} }
@media print { {h1#first {position: static} }
</style>
```

quotes

Description: Determines the type of quotation mark to be displayed within embedded quotations.
Media Group: Visual
CSS Family Type: Generated Content, Automatic Numbering and Lists
Originated with: CSS2
Values:

- *string, string* — The open-quote and close-quote values to be used by the content property.
- `none` — No quotation marks are displayed.
- `inherit` — Takes the same value as that set for the property of the parent element, if allowed.

Sample Code:

```
<html lang="en">
<head>
<title>quotes Example</title>
<style>
blockquote:before {content: open-quote; color: yellow; font-size:
30pt)}
blockquote:after {content: close-quote; color: red; fontsize:
30pt)}
q:lang(en) {quotes: """ """ "'" "'"}
q:before {content: open-quote; color: navy; font-size: 30pt)}
q:after {content: close-quote; color: fuchsia; font-size: 30pt)}
</style>
</head>
<body style="font-size: 30pt">
<p>
<blockquote>
```

```
The text in this blockquote will be preceded by an extra-large
yellow open-quote mark, and will finish with an extra-large red
close-quote mark.
</blockquote>
<p>
In the lecture the professor said <q>Shakespeare was the one who
said the immortal words <q>to thine own self be true</q></q>
</body>
</html>
```

richness

Description: Sets the "brightness" (also known as "richness") of the speaking voice being used. The brighter the voice, the better it can be heard from a distance.

Media Group: Aural

CSS Family Type: Aural (Sub-family: Voice Characteristic Properties)

Originated with: CSS2

Values:

- n — Sets the value of brightness in a given voice. Range is between 0 and 100, where a value of 50 is the normal value for a given voice.
- inherit — Takes the same value as that set for the property of the parent element, if allowed.

Sample Code:

```
<p style="voice-family: male; pitch: low; pitch-range:
25; stress: 40"; richness: 80">
King: O, yet defend me, friends! I am but hurt.
</p>
<p style="voice-family: male; pitch: medium;
pitch-range: 40; stress: 80"; richness: 70">
Hamlet: Here, thou incestuous, murd'rous, damned Dane,
Drink off this potion! Is thy union here?
Follow my mother.
</p>
<p style="voice-family: male; pitch: high; pitch-range:
20; stress: 50; richness: 40">
[King dies.]
</p>
```

right

Description: Specifies the value that the current Web element is positioned from the right edge of its containing box.
Media Group: Visual
CSS Family Type: Visual Formatting
Originated with: CSS2
Values:

- `n value` — Sets a length unit value.
- `% value` — Sets a length percentage value relative to the width of the containing block.
- `auto` — The default value for the specific element.
- `inherit` — Takes the same value as that set for the property of the parent element, if allowed.

Sample Code:
```
<p style="position: absolute; right: 2cm">
This header is positioned 2 centimeters from the containing box,
which in this case is the right margin of the browser.
</p>
```

ruby-align

Description: Sets the horizontal positioning of ruby text relative to the ruby base.
Media Group: Visual
CSS Family Type: Ruby
Originated with: Internet Explorer 5.0 *(browser-specific); also CSS3 proposed*
Values:

- `auto` — The browser determines the best arrangement for positioning ruby text.
- `left | center | right` — Aligns the ruby accordingly.
- `distribute-letter` — Spaces each character in the ruby text evenly to match the width of the ruby base.
- `distribute-space` — Adds spacing equal to half the kerning value of the ruby text on either side of the ruby text to make it equal in size to that of the ruby base.
- `line-edge` — Aligns the ruby text to the line edge of the ruby text bounding box, allowing more "room" for the ruby text to appear within.

Sample Code:

```
<html>
<head>
<title>ruby-align Example</title>
<style>
ruby {font-size: x-large}
rt {font-size: large}
td {font-size: small}
</style>
</head>
<body>
left:<br />
<ruby style="ruby-align: left">
Ruby base
<rt>Ruby text</rt>
</ruby>
</body>
</html>
```

ruby-overhang

Description: Tells how the browser is to display material adjacent to ruby content if the ruby text content is wider than the ruby itself.

Media Group: Visual

CSS Family Type: Ruby

Originated with: Internet Explorer 5.0 *(browser-specific)*

Values:

- `auto` — The browser determines the best way of positioning material adjacent to ruby content.
- `none` — Tells the browser to make no special allowances for ruby content.
- `whitespace` — Tells the browser to fill in the ruby base text with additional spacing to ensure that the ruby as a whole can accommodate all of the text it contains.

Sample Code:

```
<ruby style="ruby-overhang: whitespace">
Ruby base
<rt>Ruby text which should be longer than the base</rt>
</ruby>
the quick brown fox jumped over the lazy dog
```

ruby-position

Description: Specifies the position of the ruby text in relation to the ruby base.
Media Group: Visual
CSS Family Type: Ruby
Originated with: Internet Explorer 5.0 *(browser-specific); also CSS3 proposed*
Values:

- `above` — Places the ruby text above the ruby base (which is the normal behavior for ruby).
- `inline` — Places the ruby text immediately after the ruby base.

Sample Code:
```
<ruby style="ruby-position: above">
Ruby base
<rt>Ruby text</rt>
</ruby>
```

scrollbar-3dlight-color

Description: Sets the color value for the top-left edges of the scroll box and arrow buttons.
Media Group: User Interface
CSS Family Type: Scrollbars
Originated with: Internet Explorer 5.5 *(browser-specific)*
Values:

- `color name` or `numerical color value` — Sets the color.

Sample Code:
```
<style>
body {scrollbar-3dlight-color: #009933;}
</style>
```

scrollbar-arrow-color

Description: Sets the color of an active scrollbar arrow.
Media Group: User Interface
CSS Family Type: Scrollbars
Originated with: Internet Explorer 5.5 *(browser-specific)*

Values:

- *color name* or *numerical color value* — Sets the color.

Sample Code:
```
<style>
body {scrollbar-arrow-color: #45618F}
</style>
```

scrollbar-base-color

Description: Sets the "base" color for the scrollbar elements, setting the color values for the scrollbar button arrows, the arrow on the scrollbar button, the scrollbar slider and scrollbar tray (which is dithered).
Media Group: User Interface
CSS Family Type: Scrollbars
Originated with: Internet Explorer 5.5 *(browser-specific)*
Values:

- *color name* or *numerical color value* — Sets the color.

Sample Code:
```
<style>
body {scrollbar-base-color: green}
</style>
```

scrollbar-darkshadow-color

Description: Sets a color value to the bottom and right edges of the scroll tray and arrows; produces a more pronounced effect than `scrollbar-shadow-color`.
Media Group: User Interface
CSS Family Type: Scrollbars
Originated with: Internet Explorer 5.5 *(browser-specific)*
Values:

- *color name* or *numerical color value* — Sets the color.

Sample Code:
```
<style>
body {scrollbar-darkshadow-color: purple;}
</style>
```

scrollbar-face-color

Description: Sets the color of the "upper" portions of the scrollbar, namely the arrow button face, the slider face and the slide tray (which is dithered).
Media Group: User Interface
CSS Family Type: Scrollbars
Originated with: Internet Explorer 5.5 *(browser-specific)*
Values:

- *color name* or *numerical color value* — Sets the color.

Sample Code:
```
<style>
body {scrollbar-face-color: #ff6700;}
</style>
```

scrollbar-highlight-color

Description: Sets the top-left edges of the scroll box, the "top" portions of the arrow buttons and the scrollbar tray to the desired color.
Media Group: User Interface
CSS Family Type: Scrollbars
Originated with: Internet Explorer 5.5 *(browser-specific)*
Values:

- *color name* or *numerical color value* — Sets the color.

Sample Code:
```
<style>
body {scrollbar-highlight-color: #006633;}
</style>
```

scrollbar-shadow-color

Description: Sets a color value to the bottom and right edges of the scroll tray and arrows.
Media Group: User Interface
CSS Family Type: Scrollbars
Originated with: Internet Explorer 5.5 *(browser-specific)*

Values:

- *color name* or *numerical color value* — Sets the color.

Sample Code:
```
<style>
body {scrollbar-shadow-color: lime;}
</style>
```

scrollbar-track-color

Description: Controls the color of the track in which the slider slides.
Media Group: User Interface
CSS Family Type: Scrollbars
Originated with: Internet Explorer 5.5 *(browser-specific)*
Values:

- *color name* or *numerical color value* — Sets the color.

Sample Code:
```
<style>
body {scrollbar-track-color: #003399}
</style>
```

size

Description: Sets the size and orientation of the displayed or printed page.
Media Group: Visual, Paged
CSS Family Type: Paged Media
Originated with: CSS2
Values:

- `n n` — Sets the size for the page box in length units.
- `auto` — The page box is set to the size and orientation of the target sheet.
- `portrait` — Overrides the target's orientation and the shorter sides are horizontal.
- `landscape` — Overrides the target's orientation and the longer sides are horizontal.
- `inherit` — Takes the same value as that set for the property of the parent element, if allowed.

Sample Code:

```
@page {size: 8.5in 11in landscape; margin: 0.5in}
```

speak

Description: Specifies whether text is to be read out loud by the browser.
Media Group: Aural
CSS Family Type: Aural (Sub-family: Speaking Properties)
Originated with: CSS2
Values:

- none — Suppresses the text being read aloud.
- normal — Reads text aloud using the default pronunciation rules.
- spell-out — Spells out text one letter at a time.
- inherit — Takes the same value as that set for the property of the parent element, if allowed.

Sample Code:

```
<p style="speak: normal">
<img src="mom.gif" />
Don't tell the baby that she's about to have a <em style="speak:
spell-out">bath</em>.
<img src="dad.gif" />
</p>
```

speak-header

Description: Determines how a table header is spoken before individual cell values.
Media Group: Aural
CSS Family Type: Tables
Originated with: CSS2
Values:

- once — The header value is only spoken once, at the beginning of a listing of cell values.
- always — The header value is spoken before each associated cell value.
- inherit — Takes the same value as that set for the property of the parent element, if allowed.

Sample Code:

```
<html>
<head>
<style>
th {speak-header: always}
</style>
</head>
<body>
<table>
<tr>
<th>Fruits</th>
<th>Vegetables</th>
</tr>
<tr>
<td>Apple</td>
<td>Carrot</td>
</tr>
</table>
</body>
</html>
```

speak-numeral

Description: Determines how numbers should be read aloud when encountered by the browser.
Media Group: Aural
CSS Family Type: Aural (Sub-family: Speech Properties)
Originated with: CSS2
Values:

- `digits` — Pronounces numbers as individual digits. The number "123" would be spoken as "one two three."
- `continuous` — Pronounces numbers as a full number. The number "123" would be spoken as "one hundred twenty-three."
- `inherit` — Takes the same value as that set for the property of the parent element, if allowed.

Sample Code:

```
<p>
Francisco: You come most carefully upon your hour.
</p>
<p style="speak-numeral: continuous">
Bernardo: 'Tis now struck 12. Get thee to bed, Francisco.
</p>
```

speak-punctuation

Description: Determines how punctuation in text will be read aloud.
Media Group: Aural
CSS Family Type: Aural (Sub-family: Speech Properties)
Originated with: CSS2
Values:

- `code` — Punctuation marks such as periods, commas and brackets are spoken literally.
- `none` — Punctuation marks are not spoken, but are instead interpreted as natural pauses in speech.
- `inherit` — Takes the same value as that set for the property of the parent element, if allowed.

Sample Code:

```
In the following sentence, all of the punctuation (periods,
exclamation marks and commas) are read aloud.
<p style="speak-punctuation: code";>
Queen: No, no! the drink, the drink! O my dear
Hamlet!
The drink, the drink! I am poison'd.
</p>
```

speech-rate

Description: Sets the rate at which words on a Web page are spoken.
Media Group: Aural
CSS Family Type: Aural (Sub-family: Voice Characteristic Properties)
Originated with: CSS2
Values:

- n — Sets the speaking rate in terms of words-per-minute read aloud.
- `x-slow` — Equivalent to 80 words-per-minute.
- `slow` — Equivalent to 120 words-per-minute.
- `medium` — Equivalent to 180–200 words-per-minute.
- `fast` — Equivalent to 300 words-per-minute.
- `x-fast` — Equivalent to 500 words-per-minute.
- `faster` — Increases the current speech rate by 40 words-per-minute.
- `slower` — Decreases the current speech rate by 40 words-per-minute.
- `inherit` — Takes the same value as that set for the property of the parent element, if allowed.

Sample Code:

```
<body style="speech-rate: medium">
[Ghost beckons Hamlet.]
<p style="speech-rate: slower">
Horatio: It beckons you to go away with it, as if it some impart-
ment did desire to you alone.
</p>
<p style="speech-rate: faster">
Marcellus: Look with what courteous action it waves you to a more
removed ground. But do not go with it!
</p>
<p style="speech-rate: fast">
Horatio: No, by no means!
</p>
<p style="speech-rate: slow">
Hamlet: It will not speak. Then will I follow it.
</p>
</body>
```

stress

Description: Sets the amount of stress (i.e., emphasis) of the speaking voice.
Media Group: Aural
CSS Family Type: Aural (Sub-family: Voice Characteristic Properties)
Originated with: CSS2
Values:

- n — Sets the value of stress in a given voice. Range is between 0 and 100, and a value of 50 is the normal stress for a given voice.
- inherit — Takes the same value as that set for the property of the parent element, if allowed.

Sample Code:

```
<p style="voice-family: male; pitch: low; pitch-range: 25;
stress: 40";>
King: How do you, pretty lady?
</p>
<p style="voice-family: female; pitch: high; pitch-range: 45;
stress: 95";>
Ophelia: Well, God 'ild you! They say the owl was a baker's
daughter. Lord, we know what we are, but know not what we may be.
God be at your table!
</p>
```

table-layout

Description: Controls how a table's width is displayed using either a fixed or automatic value.
Media Group: Visual
CSS Family Type: Tables
Originated with: CSS2
Values:

- `auto` — Uses automatic table layout.
- `fixed` — Uses a fixed table layout.
- `inherit` — Takes the same value as that set for the property of the parent element, if allowed.

Sample Code:
```
<table style="table-layout: auto">
<tr>
<td>This text is in the table</td>
</tr>
</table>
```

text-align

Description: Sets the alignment of the text.
Media Group: Visual
CSS Family Type: Text
Originated with: CSS1
Values:

- `center` | `justify` | `left` | `right` — Aligns the text contained by the specified element.
- `inherit` — *(CSS2)* Takes the same value as that set for the property of the parent element, if allowed.

Sample Code:
```
<p style="text-align: center">Centered text</p>
<p style="text-align: justify">Justified text</p>
<p style="text-align: left">Left-aligned text</p>
<p style="text-align: right">Right-aligned text</p>
```

text-align-last

Description: Alters the way in which the last line of a paragraph is formatted.
Media Group: Visual
CSS Family Type: Text Property Extensions
Originated with: Internet Explorer 5.0 *(browser-specific); also CSS3 proposed*
Values:

- `auto` — Text in the final line of the paragraph is set to the same value as for `text-align`.
- `left` — Text in the final line of the paragraph is justified to the left
- `right` — Text in the final line of the paragraph is justified to the right
- `center` — Text in the final line of the paragraph is center justified
- `justify` — Text in the final line of the paragraph is fully justified
- `inherit` — Takes the same value as that set for the property of the parent element, if allowed.

Sample Code:
```
<p style="text-align: justify; text-align-last: center">
This line contains justified text. To ensure you can really see
the effect of this, we need a few sentences so that the effect can
easily be seen. This paragraph uses <code>text-align-last</code>
set to <code>center</code>, so the last line is centered.
</p>
```

text-autospace

Description: Provides control over the spacing between Western characters and Asian-based character text.
Media Group: Visual
CSS Family Type: Text Property Extensions; also CSS3 proposed (all values)
Originated with: Internet Explorer 5.0 *(browser-specific)*
Values:

- `none` — Sets no special spacing value between any Asian and Western characters that may appear together on a Web page.
- `ideograph-alpha` — Adds extra space when any regular Western, "alphabetical" characters appear next to Asian ideographs.
- `ideograph-numeric` — Adds extra space between Asian characters and numerals.
- `ideograph-parenthesis` — Adds extra space between Asian characters and information contained within parentheses.

- `ideograph-space` — Adds extra space when an Asian character is next to a space, making it a slightly larger space.

Sample Code:

```
<span style="font-family: ËÎÎå,MingLiU; text-autospace: ideo-
graph-alpha; font-weight: bold; font-size: 20pt; layout-flow:
vertical-ideographic; height:
400px">&#27489;1&#36814;2&#28459;3&#28216;4(PanelX)
&#150;5&#24179;6&#38754;7&#39023;8&#31034;9&#23631;10&#26989;11&
#30028;12&#30340;Portal 13&#21450; Exchange 14</span>
```

text-decoration

Description: Adds a "decorative" property to the HTML tag specified.
Media Group: Visual
CSS Family Type: Text
Originated with: CSS1
Values:

- `blink` — Text blinks.
- `line-through` — Text contains a line through the middle (strikethrough text).
- `none` — No decoration is added.
- `overline` — Text is displayed with a line running above it.
- `underline` — Text is underlined.
- `inherit` — *(CSS2)* Takes the same value as that set for the property of the parent element, if allowed.

Sample Code:

```
<a href="fred.html" style="text-decoration: none">This link is
not underlined</a>
<h1 style="text-decoration: overline">Header with an Overline</
h1>
<h1 style="text-decoration: underline">Header with an Underline</
h1>
<p style="text-decoration: line-through">Ignore this sentence
<p>
<em style="text-decoration: blink">This text blinks</em>
```

text-indent

Description: Specifies indents from the left margin or from a block element.
Media Group: Visual
CSS Family Type: Text
Originated with: CSS1
Values:

- `length (units)` — Specifies the length value as a unit of measurement.
- `% value` — Specifies the distance as a percentage of the browser window display.
- `inherit` — *(CSS2)* Takes the same value as that set for the property of the parent element, if allowed.

Sample Code:
```
<h1 style="text-indent: 1in">This text is indented from the left
margin by 1 inch.</h1>
```

text-justify

Description: Sets a justification value on text contained within a Web page.
Media Group: Visual
CSS Family Type: Text Property Extensions
Originated with: Internet Explorer 5.0 *(browser-specific)*
Values:

- `auto` — Allows the browser to determine how to best justify a line of text.
- `distribute` — Intended for use with Asian character sets, justifying every line of text in a vertical paragraph save for the final line.
- `distribute-all-lines` — Intended for Asian character sets, justifying every line of text in a vertical paragraph including the final line.
- `inter-cluster` — Intended for Asian character sets, justifying lines of text containing no inter-word spacing.
- `inter-ideograph` — Intended for Asian character sets, this justifies lines of text either by increasing or decreasing the width between characters or words as necessary.
- `inter-word` — This increases or decreases the spacing between individual words for the final line of text in the paragraph.

- `kashida` — Intended for Arabic text, justifying text by exaggerating certain characters at specific points.
- `newspaper` — Increases or decreases the spaces between words, justifying every line of text in a horizontal paragraph save for the final line.

Sample Code:

```
<p style="text-justify: newspaper">
The quick brown fox jumped over the lazy dog. The quick brown fox
jumped over the lazy dog. The quick brown fox jumped over the
lazy dog. The quick brown fox jumped over the lazy dog.
</p>
```

text-kashida-space

Description: Justifies Arabic text by expanding individual characters at certain, pre-determined points.
Media Group: Visual
CSS Family Type: Text Property Extensions
Originated with: Internet Explorer 5.0 *(browser-specific); also CSS3 proposed*
Values:

- `% value` — Sets a percentage value for the amount of kashida justification.
- `inherit` — Takes the same value as that set for the property of the parent element, if allowed.

Sample Code:

```
<p style="text-kashida-space: 10%; font-size: 25pt; width: 550px;
font-family: "Traditional Arabic"; font-weight: bold; text-align:
justify">
ÈöÓúãö Çáááåö ÇáÑøóÍúããö ÇáÑøóÍöíãöö
ÇáúÍóãúÏõ ááøåö ÑóÈøö ÇáúÚóÇáóãöíäó
ÇáÑøóÍúãÜäö ÇáÑøóÍöíãö
ãóÇáößö íóæúãö ÇáÏøöíäö
ÅöíøóÇßó äóÚúÈõÏõ æÅöíøóÇßó äóÓúÊóÚöíäõ
ÇåÏöäóÜÇ ÇáÕøöÑóÇØó ÇáãõÓÊóÞöíãó
ÕöÑóÇØó ÇáøóÐöíäó ÃóäÚóãÊó
Úóáóíåöãú ÛóíÑö ÇáãóÛÖõæÈö Úóáóíåöãú æóáÇó
ÇáÖøóÇáøöíäó
</p>
```

text-overflow

Description: Controls what is displayed at the end of a line when text overflows its boundary.
Media Group: Visual
CSS Family Type: Text Properties
Originated with: Internet Explorer 5.5 *(browser-specific); also CSS3 proposed*
Values:

- `clip` — Content stops at the boundary; no ellipsis is displayed.
- `ellipsis` — Displays ellipses ("…") when text overflows.

Sample Code:
```
<style>
div {overflow: clip; text-overflow: ellipsis}
</style>
```

text-shadow

Description: Adds a shadow effect to text.
Media Group: Visual
CSS Family Type: Text
Originated with: CSS2
Values:

- `none` — No shadow value is set.
- `n n [n]` — Sets a color value plus the unit length of the shadow. At least two length unit values must be present. A comma can separate a chain of overlaying values.
- `color name` or `numerical color value` — Sets the color value for the shadow. Always associated with a length unit value.
- `inherit` — Takes the same value as that set for the property of the parent element, if allowed.

Sample Code:
```
<h1 style="text-shadow: gray 2px 3px, lime -4px 3px 4px">Header
with Drop Shadow Effect</h1>
```

text-transform

Description: Specifies the type of case to be used on the text.
Media Group: Visual
CSS Family Type: Text
Originated with: CSS1
Values:

- `capitalize` — Sets the initial letter of a word in capital letters.
- `lowercase` — Sets all text to lowercase.
- `none` — No transformation is performed.
- `uppercase` — Sets all text to uppercase.
- `inherit` — *(CSS2)* Takes the same value as that set for the property of the parent element, if allowed.

Sample Code:
```
<html>
<head>
<title>text-transform Example</title>
</head>
<body>
<h1 style="text-transform: capitalize">Header in initial caps</
h1>
<h2 style="text-transform: lowercase">HEADER ALL IN LOWERCASE
LETTERS</h2>
<h3 style="text-transform: uppercase">header all in uppercase
letters</h3>
<h4 style="text-transform: none">Nothing special happens with
this header</h4>
</body>
</html>
```

text-underline-position

Description: Allows you to set the position of an underline in relation to text.
Media Group: Visual
CSS Family Type: Text Property Extensions
Originated with: Internet Explorer 5.0 *(browser-specific); also CSS3 proposed*
Values:

- `above` — Positions an underline above the text.
- `below` — Positions an underline below the text.

- `auto` — *(IE6.0)* Sets the line underneath Western text; if set to Japanese, the line is instead positioned inline
- `auto-pos` — *(IE6.0)* Equivalent to `auto` value.

Sample Code:
```
<p style="text-underline-position: below; text-decoration: under-
line">
The quick fox jumped over the lazy dog.
</p>
```

top

Description: Specifies the value that the current Web element is positioned below the containing box.
Media Group: Visual
CSS Family Type: Visual Formatting
Originated with: CSS2
Values:

- `n value` — Sets a length unit value.
- `% value` — Sets a length percentage value relative to the width of the containing block.
- `auto` — The default value for the specific element.
- `inherit` — Takes the same value as that set for the property of the parent element, if allowed.

Sample Code:
```
<p style="position: absolute; top: 1cm">
This header is positioned 1 centimeter from the top of the screen
</p>
```

unicode-bidi

Description: Defines the Unicode text as having bidirectional characteristics, meaning that the text may be rendered from right to left and from left to right in different circumstances.
Media Group: Visual
CSS Family Type: Visual Formatting
Originated with: CSS2

Values:

- `normal` — The selected Web element does not alter the current bidirectional setting.
- `embed` — If the selected Web element is inline, this value sets up an additional level of embedding with respect to the bidirectional algorithm.
- `bidi-override` — If the selected Web element is inline or block level, this value overrides the one in place, keeping with the values set by the `direction` property.
- `inherit` — Takes the same value as that set for the property of the parent element, if allowed.

Sample Code:

```
<style>
arabic {direction: rtl; unicode-bidi: embed}
english {direction: ltr; unicode-bidi: embed}
</style>
```

vertical-align

Description: Sets the vertical positioning of the HTML tag with which it is associated.

Media Group: Visual

CSS Family Type: Text

Originated with: CSS1

Values:

- `baseline` | `bottom` | `middle` | `sub` | `super` | `text-top` | `text-bottom` | `top` — Aligns the text element in relation to the specified value.
- `n value` — Sets a length unit value.
- `% value` — Sets a length percentage value relative to the line height of the containing block.
- `inherit` — (CSS2) Takes the same value as that set for the property of the parent element, if allowed.

Sample Code:

```
<strong style="vertical-align: sub">Subscript-aligned text</
strong> <em style="font-size: 16pt">Large, italicized text.</em>
<strong style="vertical-align: super">Superscript-aligned text</
strong> <em style="font-size: 16pt">Large, italicized text.</em>
```

visibility

Description: Sets whether or not the box associated with an element is rendered.
Media Group: Visual
CSS Family Type: Classification
Originated with: CSS2
Values:

- `visible` — The box generated by the element is displayed.
- `hidden` — The box generated by the element is not displayed.
- `collapse` — When applied to a table element (i.e., a row, row group, column or column group) causes the entire selected row or column to not be displayed.
- `inherit` — Takes the same value as that set for the property of the parent element, if allowed.

Sample Code:
```
<h1 style="visibility: hidden">Header in an Invisible Box</h1>
```

voice-family

Description: Sets a priority list of voice-family names.
Media Group: Aural
CSS Family Type: Aural (Sub-family: Voice Characteristic Properties)
Originated with: CSS2
Values:

- `male | female | child` — A "generic" voice value that sounds male, female and child-like, respectively. Can modify the value of a specific voice.
- `specific-voice name` — A specific, predefined name for a voice value.
- `inherit` — Takes the same value as that set for the property of the parent element, if allowed.

Sample Code:
```
<p style="voice-family: laertes, male">
Laertes: Farewell, Ophelia, and remember well what
I have said to you.
</p>
<p style="voice-family: ophelia, female">
Ophelia: 'Tis in my memory lock'd, and you yourself
shall keep the key of it.
```

```
</p>
<p style="voice-family: laertes, male">
Laertes: Farewell.
</p>
<p style="voice-family: male">
Exit Laertes.
</p>
```

volume

Description: Sets the level for the dynamic range of the sound being played (i.e., its "volume").

Media Group: Aural

CSS Family Type: Aural (Sub-family: Volume Properties)

Originated with: CSS2

Values:

- n — Range is between 0 (near silence) to 100 (full volume)
- `% value` — Range is between 0 (near silence) to 100 (full volume)
- `silent` — Volume is turned off
- `x-soft` — Very low volume level, equivalent to the numerical value "0" (which does not imply silence)
- `soft` — Low volume level, equivalent to the numerical value "25"
- `medium` — Medium volume level, equivalent to the numerical value "50"
- `loud` — Moderately loud volume level, equivalent to the numerical value "75"
- `x-loud` — Very loud volume level, equivalent to the numerical value "100"
- `inherit` — Takes the same value as that set for the property of the parent element, if allowed.

Sample Code:

```
<p style="volume: medium">
I'm the big gruff bear.
<img src="bear.gif" />
<strong style="volume: loud">Roar!</strong>
<p>
```

white-space

Description: This element is used to set white space and the way carriage returns are handled within a Web page.
Media Group: Visual
CSS Family Type: Classification
Originated with: CSS1
Values:

- `normal` — The default browser behavior for the HTML tag this element is associated with.
- `nowrap` — When this value is set, carriage returns and linefeeds are rendered as single space. However, line breaks are not affected.
- `pre` — When this value is set, all spaces, carriage returns, and linefeeds in the document are displayed "as is."
- `inherit` — (CSS2) Takes the same value as that set for the property of the parent element, if allowed.

Sample Code:
```
<p style="white-space: normal">
There    is no extra white space    in
   this sentence.    It is    displayed normally.
</p>
<p style="white-space: pre">
The    extra white    spaces and carriage
 returns in this sentence
    are displayed.
</p>
<p style="white-space: nowrap">
The    extra white   space and carriage
 returns in this sentence
    are <strong>not</strong> displayed.
</p>
```

widows

Description: Sets the minimum number of lines of a paragraph that must be left at the top of a page.
Media Group: Visual, Paged
CSS Family Type: Paged Media
Originated with: CSS2

Values:

- n — An integer value that assigns the number of lines that must appear in a paragraph; otherwise, it will be forced to appear on the previous page. Default value is 2.
- `inherit` — Takes the same value as that set for the property of the parent element, if allowed.

Sample Code:

```
<style>
@page {widows: 3}
</style>
```

width

Description: Scales an element (most typically an image) to the width specified.
Media Group: Visual
CSS Family Type: Boxes
Originated with: CSS1
Values:

- `auto` — Specifies that the browser default value should be used.
- `% value` — Sets a percentage value with respect to the browser window's width.
- `length (units)` — Specifies the length value as a unit of measurement.
- `inherit` — (CSS2) Takes the same value as that set for the property of the parent element, if allowed.

Sample Code:

```
<img src style="width: auto" SRC="gordian3.jpg" />Regular size
(auto setting)
<p>
<img src style="width: 25px" SRC="gordian3.jpg" />Set to 25 pix-
els
<p>
<img src style="width: 25%" SRC="gordian3.jpg" />Set to 25% of
the browser window's width
```

word-break

Description: Provides control over how line breaks should occur within words, particularly in cases where the content is comprised of text from more than one language.
Media Group: Visual
CSS Family Type: Text Property Extensions
Originated with: Internet Explorer 5.0 *(browser-specific); also CSS3 proposed*
Values:

- normal — Allows line-breaking behavior within words
- break-all — Works the same way as normal, but is intended for use with Asian characters
- keep-all — Does not allow word breaks for Chinese, Japanese or Korean words.

Sample Code:
```
<div style=" font-family:"MS Mincho"; word-break: keep-all; font-
size:
17pt">&#12399;&#12501;&#12521;&#12483;&#12488;&#12497;&#12493;&#
12523;&#12487;&#12451;&#12473;&#12503;&#12524;&#12452;&#26989;&#
30028;&#12398;&#29420;&#31435;&#12375;&#12383;&#12509;&#12540;&#
12479;&#12523;&#12469;&#12452;&#12488;&#12391;&#12289;&#38651;&#
23376;&#21462;&#24341;&#12469;&#12540;&#12499;&#12473;&#12434;&#
34892;&#12387;&#12390;&#12362;&#12426;&#12414;&#12377;&#12290;
</div>
```

word-spacing

Description: Sets the spacing between words.
Media Group: Visual
CSS Family Type: Text
Originated with: CSS1
Values:

- normal — The browser default word spacing value is used.
- *length (units)* — Sets the length value between words as a unit of measurement.
- inherit — *(CSS2)* Takes the same value as that set for the property of the parent element, if allowed.

Sample Code:

```
<em style="word-spacing: 1cm">The words in this sentence are all
spaced 1cm apart.</em>
```

writing-mode

Description: Explicitly sets the direction that text should flow on a page.
Media Group: Visual
CSS Family Type: Text Property Extensions
Originated with: Internet Explorer 5.5 *(browser-specific)*; also CSS3 proposed
Values:

- `lr-tb` — Sets text to flow from left-to-right, then top-to-bottom, typical of Western text layout
- `tb-rl` — Sets text to flow from top-to-bottom, then right-to-left, typical of Asian text layout.

Sample Code:

```
<style>
span.english-horizontal-wm {font-family: arial; font-weight:
bold; font-size: 34pt; writing-mode: lr-tb}
</style>
```

z-index

Description: Sets the "stacking level" of the specified box in relation to the current stacking context. It also determines whether the specified box sets up a localized stacking context.
Media Group: Visual
CSS Family Type: Visual Formatting
Originated with: CSS2
Values:

- *n* — An integer value representing the stacking level of the specified element's box. The specified element's box also sets up a local stacking value.
- `auto` — The stack value is the same as its parent's. The specified element's box does not set up a local stacking value.
- `inherit` — Takes the same value as that set for the property of the parent element, if allowed.

Sample Code:

```
<html>
<head>
<title>z-index Example</title>
<style>
.stack {position: absolute; right: 1cm; bottom:
0cm;}
</style>
</head>
<body style="font-size: xx-large; color: yellow">
<p>
<img src="fokker.gif" class="stack" style="z-index: 1"
width="369" height="201" border="0" alt="" />
<div id="text1" class="stack" style="z-index: 3">This text over-
lays image1.</div>
<div id="text2">This text has not been assigned a z-index value,
so it lies beneath everything else.</div>
<div id="text3" class="stack" style="z-index: 2">This text will
underlay text1, but overlay image1.</div>
</body>
</html>
```

CSS3 MOBILE PROFILE

Topics in This Appendix

- Mobile Properties
- At-rules
- Selectors

Appendix C

The CSS Mobile Profile is part of the CSS3 specification, and it describes the CSS properties which should be adopted for use in mobile Web browsers. Since these devices tend to be small, handheld devices, the thought is that it may not be easily possible for hardware manufacturers to incorporate browsers that necessarily incorporate full CSS functionality. For example, there seems little point incorporating the finer points of text alignment, stereo placement of sound or showing print marks on a device probably no bigger than an average cell phone.

Though part of CSS3 (or more properly speaking, a "module" of CSS3) the Mobile Profile only covers values already set in place by the CSS2 specification.

The following table looks at all of the properties, At-rules and selectors that any mobile device should adopt under this profile to qualify for full CSS mobile compliance.

Mobile Properties

The following table looks at both supported and unsupported properties under this profile. In some cases, a given property is only partially supported — in those cases the supported values follow the property in the Supported column and those which are not in the Not Supported column.

Table C.1   *Mobile Properties*

Supported	Not Supported
	azimuth
background: background-color, background-image, background-position, background-repeat, inherit	background: background-attachment
	background-attachment
background-color	
background-image	
background-position	
background-repeat	
border	
	border-collapse
border-color	
	border-spacing
border-bottom	
border-bottom-color	
border-bottom-style	
border-bottom-width	
border-left	
border-left-color	
border-left-style	
border-left-width	
border-right	
border-right-color	
border-right-style	
border-right-width	
border-style	

Table C.1   Mobile Properties (continued)

border-top		
border-top-color		
border-top-style		
border-top-width		
border-width		
	bottom	
	caption-side	
clear		
	clip	
color		
	content	
	counter-increment	
	counter-reset	
	cue	
	cue-after	
	cue-before	
	cursor	
	direction	
display: block, inline, list-item, none	display: compact, inherit, inline-table, marker, run-in, table, table-caption, table-cell, table-column, table-column-group, table-footer-group, table-header-group, table-row, table-row-group	
	elevation	
	empty-cells	
float		
font		
font-family		

Table C.1	*Mobile Properties (continued)*
font-size	
	font-size-adjust
	font-stretch
font-style	
font-variant	
font-weight	
height	
	left
	letter-spacing
	line-height
list-style	
list-style-image	
list-style-position	
list-style-type	
margin	
margin-bottom	
margin-left	
margin-right	
margin-top	
	marker-offset
	marks
	max-height
	max-width
	min-height
	min-width
	orphans
	outline

Table C.1   *Mobile Properties (continued)*

	outline-color
	outline-style
	outline-width
	overflow
padding	
padding-bottom	
padding-left	
padding-right	
padding-top	
	page
	page-break-after
	page-break-before
	page-break-inside
	pause
	pause-after
	pause-before
	pitch
	pitch-range
	play-during
	position
	quotes
	richness
	right
	size
	speak
	speak-header
	numeral

Table C.1   *Mobile Properties (continued)*

	speak-punctuation
	speech-rate
	stress
	table-layout
text-align: center, inherit, justify, left, right	text-align: <string>
text-decoration: inherit, none, underline	text-decoration: line-through, overline
text-indent	
	text-shadow
text-transform	
	top
	unicode-bidi
vertical-align: baseline, sub, super, inherit	vertical-align: <length>, <percentage>, bottom, middle, text-bottom, text-top, top
visibility	
	voice-family
	volume
white-space	
	widows
width	
	word-spacing
	z-index

Mobile At-rules

The following table looks at the At-rules that are and are not supposed to be supported under the CSS3 Mobile Profile.

Table C.2   *At-rule Properties*

Supported	Not Supported
`@import`	
`@charset`	
	`@color-profile`
	`@font-face`
`@media`	
	`@page`

Mobile Selectors

The following table looks at the selectors that are and are not supposed to be supported under the CSS3 Mobile Profile.

Table C.3   *Selectors*

Supported	Not Supported
*	
div.warning	
E	
	E + F
E > F	
E F	
E#myid	
E:active	

Table C.3   *Selectors (continued)*

	E:after
	E:before
	E:first-child
	E:first-letter
	E:first-line
E:focus	
	E:hover
	E:lang(c)
E:link E:visited	
	E[foo]
	E[foo~="warning"]
	E[foo="warning"]
	E[lang|="en"]

Index

A

Accelerator property, 557–59, 707
Accesskey attribute, 18
ACSS. *See* Aural Cascading Style Sheet (ACSS)
Adjacent sibling selectors, 70–71
After pseudo-element, 443–46
All media type, 131
All-space property, 220–21
All-space-treatment property, 220
AlphaFilter property, 639–40
Amaya, 48–49
Anchor pseudo-element
    browser compatibility, 115–16
    overview, 114–15
Angle units
    browser compatibility, 110
    overview, 108–10
Attributes
    accesskey attribute, 18
    class attribute, 21–23, 61–62
    dir attribute, 18
    disabled attribute, 18–19
    id attribute, 21–23, 61–62
    lang attribute, 19
    media attribute, 19
    selectors, 71–77
    tabindex attribute, 19
    type attribute, 19
Aural Cascading Style Sheet (ACSS)
    angle units, 108–10
    frequency units, 110–11
    properties. *See* Aural Cascading Style Sheet properties
    time units, 108
Aural Cascading Style Sheet properties
    azimuth property, 579–81, 708–9
    cue properties, 576–77, 732
    elevation property, 582–84, 736
    overview, 569–70
    pause properties, 573–76
    pitch property, 587–88, 769–70
    pitch-range property, 589–90, 770
    play-during property, 577–78, 770–71
    richness property, 591–92, 773
    speak property, 570–71, 780
    speech properties, 592–94
    speech-rate property, 584–85, 782–83
    stress property, 590–91, 783
    voice-family property, 586–87, 793–94
    volume property, 571–73, 794
Aural media type, 131–32
Azimuth property, 579–81, 708–9

B

Background properties
    background-attachment property, 397–401, 710
    background-clip property, 415–16
    background-color property, 387–90, 710
    background-image property, 391–93, 711
    background-origin property, 416–17
    background-position property, 401–7, 711
    background-position-x property, 410–14, 712
    background-position-y property, 410–14, 712–13
    background property, 407–10, 709–10
    background-quantity property, 419–20
    background-repeat property, 394–96, 713
    background-size property, 418–19
    background-spacing property, 420–21
    CSS3 properties, 415
    overview, 387
Barn Transition filter, 674–75
BasicImage filter, 653–56
Before pseudo-element, 443–46
Berners-Lee, Tim, 3
Blinds filter, 675–76
Blur filter, 641–44
Border-bottom-color property, 715
Border-bottom property, 286–89, 714–15
Border-bottom-style property, 715–16
Border-bottom-width property, 297–99, 716
Border-break property, 319
Border-collapse property, 527–31, 716–17
Border-color property, 280–83, 717
Border-fit properties, 314–16
Border-image properties, 312–14
Border-image-transform properties, 317–18
Border-left-color property, 718–19
Border-left property, 289–91, 718

Border-left-style property, 719
Border-left-width property, 299–301, 719–20
Border property, 307–9, 713–14
Border-radius properties, 310–11
Border-right-color property, 721
Border-right property, 292–94, 720
Border-right-style property, 721–22
Border-right-width property, 302–4, 722
Border-spacing property, 531–33, 722–23
Border-style property, 277–80, 723
Border-top-color property, 724–25
Border-top property, 294–96, 724
Border-top-style property, 725
Border-top-width property, 304–7, 726
Border-width property, 283–86, 726
Bottom property, 727
Box properties
    border-bottom property, 286–89, 714–15
    border-bottom-width property, 297–99, 716
    border-break property, 319
    border-color property, 280–83, 717
    border-fit properties, 314–16
    border-image properties, 312–14
    border-image-transform properties, 317–18
    border-left property, 289–91, 718
    border-left-width property, 299–301, 719–20
    border property, 307–9, 713–14
    border-radius properties, 310–11
    border-right property, 292–94, 720
    border-right-width property, 302–4, 722
    border-style property, 277–80, 723
    border-top property, 294–96, 724
    border-top-width property, 304–7, 726
    border-width property, 283–86, 726
    box-shadow property, 319–21
    clear-after property, 324–25
    clear property, 321–24
    fit-position property, 363–64
    fit property, 363–64
    float-displace property, 331–32
    float property, 325–31, 737–38
    height property, 332–34, 743
    indent-edge-reset property, 332
    margin-bottom property, 349–51
    margin-left property, 352–54, 752–53
    margin property, 360–62, 751–52
    margin-right property, 354–57, 753
    margin-top property, 357–59, 753–54
    marquee properties, 365–66
    max-height property, 362–63
    max-width property, 362–63
    min-height property, 362–63
    min-width property, 362–63
    overview, 275
    padding-bottom property, 337–39, 762–63
    padding-left property, 339–41, 763
    padding property, 345–49, 762

    padding-right property, 341–43, 763–64
    padding-top property, 343–45, 764
    width property, 335–37, 796
Box-shadow property, 319–21
Braille media type, 132
Browser compatibility, 134–35
    accelerator property, 559
    after pseudo-element, 446
    anchor pseudo-element, 115–16
    angle units, 110
    background-attachment property, 400–401
    background-color property, 389–90
    background-image property, 393
    background-position property, 406–7
    background property, 409–10
    background-repeat property, 396
    border-bottom property, 288–89
    border-bottom-width property, 298–99
    border-collapse property, 530–31
    border-color property, 282–83
    border-left property, 291
    border-left-width property, 301
    border property, 309
    border-right property, 293–94
    border-right-width property, 303–4
    border-spacing property, 532–33
    border-style property, 279–80
    border-top property, 296
    border-top-width property, 306–7
    border-width property, 286
    caption-side property, 523–24
    cascading order, 86–87
    class attribute, 61–62
    clear property, 323–24
    clip property, 494–95
    color property, 374–75
    comments, 67
    content property, 446
    contextual selectors, 65–66
    counter-increment property, 451–52
    counter-reset property, 451–52
    CSS1 elements, 694–705
    CSS2 elements, 694–705
    cursor property, 548–49
    direction property, 478–79
    display property, 464–65
    empty-cells property, 535–36
    first-child pseudo-class, 127–28
    first-letter pseudo-element, 121–22
    first-line pseudo-element, 118–19
    float property, 331
    focus pseudo-class, 125
    @font-face pseudo-element, 181
    font-family property, 150
    font property, 170
    font-size-adjust property, 175
    font-stretch property, 172

`font-style` property, 159–60
`font-variant` property, 161–62
`font-weight` property, 167
frequency units, 111
grouping, 55–56
`height` property, 334
`hover` pseudo-class, 125
`id` attribute, 61–62
`!important` property, 89–90
inheritance, 57–58
`lang` pseudo-class, 122
length units, 99–100
`letter-spacing` property, 189–90
`line-height` property, 195
`list-style-image` property, 436–37
`list-style-position` property, 439–40
`list-style` property, 442–43
`list-style-type` property, 434–35
`margin-bottom` property, 351
`margin-left` property, 353–54
`margin` property, 362
`margin-right` property, 356–57
`margin-top` property, 359
`marker-offset` property, 453–54
`marks` property, 511
`max-height` property, 483–84
`max-width` property, 482–83
`min-height` property, 483
`min-width` property, 482–83
`orphans` property, 519
`outline-color` property, 555–56
`outline` property, 556–57
`outline-style` property, 554
`outline-width` property, 552
`overflow` property, 489–90
`padding-bottom` property, 339
`padding-left` property, 341
`padding` property, 348–49
`padding-right` property, 343
`padding-top` property, 345
`page` property, 516–17
percentage units, 103
`position` property, 471–73
`before` pseudo-element, 446
`quotes` property, 449
`ruby-align` property, 605
`ruby-overhang` property, 607–8
`ruby-position` property, 610
scrollbar properties, 634
`size` property, 509
`speak-header` property, 536–37
strings, 107
`table-layout` property, 526–27
`text-align-last` property, 272
`text-align` property, 200–201
`text-decoration` property, 203–4
`text-indent` property, 206

`text-shadow` property, 211
`text-transform` property, 208–9
time units, 108
`unicode-bidi` property, 478–79
URLs, 105
`vertical-align` property, 198
`visibility` property, 500
`white-space` property, 425–26
`widows` property, 519
`width` property, 336–37
`word-spacing` property, 192–93
`z-index` property, 475–76
Browsers
    Amaya, 48–49
    compatibility. *See* browser compatibility
    Emacspeak, 48
    hardware browsers, 50
    Internet Explorer 4.5, 32–33
    Internet Explorer 5.5, 34–35
    Internet Explorer 6.0, 35–36
    Internet Explorer 3.x, 30–31
    Internet Explorer 4.x, 31
    Internet Explorer 5.x, 32–33
    Konqueror, 47–48
    Linux browsers, 47
    Mozilla, 40–46
    Netscape Navigator 4.x, 39–40
    Netscape Navigator 6.x, 40–41
    Netscape Navigator 7.x, 40–41, 46
    Opera 3.5, 37
    Opera 4.x, 38
    Opera 5.x, 38
    Opera 6.x, 38
    support for CSS, 29–30
Browser wars
    CSS properties and, 11
    HTML and, 3–5
    Linux browsers, 11
    Microsoft strategy, 4
    Mozilla browser, 11
    Netscape Navigator and, 11
    Netscape strategy, 3–4
    Opera browser, 11
    origins of, 3–4
    re-emergence of, 10–12

C

`Caption-side` property, 521–24, 727–28
Cascading order
    browser compatibility, 86–87
    overview, 83–86
    sources for, 90–92
Checkerboard filter, 676–77
Child selectors, 68–69
Chroma filter, 658–60
Class attribute, 21–23

browser compatibility, 61–62
overview, 58
as selector, 58–61
Classification properties
content property, 443–46, 729–30
counter-increment property, 449–52, 730–31
counter-reset property, 449–52, 731–32
list-style-image property, 435–37, 750
list-style-position property, 437–40, 750
list-style property, 440–43, 749
list-style-type property, 426–35, 751
marker-offset property, 452–54, 754–55
overview, 423
quotes property, 446–49, 772–73
white-space property, 423–26, 795
Clear-after property, 324–25
Clear property, 321–24, 728
Clip property, 492–95, 728–29
Color
color-profile property, 378–79
@color-profile property, 379
color property, 370–75, 729
opacity property, 376–77
overview, 369
rendering-intent property, 377–78
X11 color set, 379–85
Color-index media query, 138
Color media query, 137–38
Column-count property, 616
Column-gap property, 617
Column rule properties
column-rule-color property, 620
column-rule property, 622
column-rule-style property, 621
column-rule-width property, 621–22
overview, 620
Column-space-distribution property, 618–19
Column-span properties, 622–23
Column-width-policy property, 617–18
Column-width property, 616
Comments
browser compatibility, 67
overview, 66–67
Compositor filter, 663–65
Content property, 443–46, 729–30
Contextual selectors
browser compatibility, 65–66
overview, 62–65
Counter-increment property, 449–52, 730–31
Counter-reset property, 449–52, 731–32
CSS
adding to Web pages, 17–18
browser wars, 11
creation of, 6–7
development of, 7–10
example, 16–17
origin of, 6–7

overview, 6–7, 15–17
tables, used for layout of, 537–41
CSS2
browser compatibility, 694–705
overview, 7–9
selectors. See CSS2 selectors
CSS2 selectors
adjacent sibling selectors, 70–71
attribute selectors, 71–76
child selectors, 68–69
overview, 67
universal selector, 68
CSS3
background properties, 415
clear property, 323
cursor property, 549
float property, 330
font decoration properties. See CSS3 font decoration
      properties
gamma correction, 375–76
height property, 334
mobile At-rules, 807
mobile properties, 801–6
mobile selectors, 807–8
overview, 9–10
properties, 415
selectors. See CSS3 selectors
text-align-last property, 273
text-autospace property, 261
text-justify property, 263
text-kashida-space property, 266
text-underline-position property, 267–68
user-interface properties, 559, 567
width property, 336
word-break property, 270
writing-mode property, 246–47
CSS3 font decoration properties
font-effect property, 182
font-emphasize-position property, 184–85
font-emphasize property, 185
font-emphasize-style property, 184
font-smooth property, 183
overview, 182
CSS3 selectors
attribute selectors, 76–77
non-structural pseudo-class selectors, 79–80
overview, 76
structural pseudo-class selectors, 77–79
Cue-after property, 733
Cue-before property, 733
Cue properties, 576–77, 732
Cursor property, 544–49, 734

D

Device-aspect-ratio media query, 137
Device-height media query, 136–37

Device-width media query, 136–37
Dir attribute, 18
Direction property, 476–79, 734–35
Disabled attribute, 18–19
Display property, 457–65, 735
<div> element, 21–24
DropShadow filter, 645–48

E

Elevation property, 582–84, 736
Emacspeak, 48
Embossed media type, 132
Emboss filter, 649–50
Empty-cells property, 533–36, 737
Engrave filter, 649–50

F

Fade filter, 677–78
Filters
    AlphaFilter property, 639–40
    Barn Transition filter, 674–75
    BasicImage filter, 653–56
    Blinds filter, 675–76
    Blur filter, 641–44
    Checkerboard filter, 676–77
    Chroma filter, 658–60
    Compositor filter, 663–65
    DropShadow filter, 645–48
    Emboss filter, 649–50
    Engrave filter, 649–50
    Fade filter, 677–78
    Glow filter, 656–58
    GradientWipe filter, 678–79
    ICMFilter filter, 665–67
    Inset filter, 687–88
    Iris filter, 683–84
    Light filter, 660–63
    MaskFilter filter, 667–69
    Matrix filter, 669–72
    MotionBlur filter, 641–44
    Pixelate filter, 688–89
    RadialWipe filter, 679–80
    RandomBars filter, 681–82
    RandomDissolve filter, 682–83
    Shadow filter, 645–48
    Slide filter, 686–87
    Spiral filter, 684–85
    static filters, 638–72
    Stretch filter, 685–86
    Strips filter, 680–81
    transition filters, 672–91
    visual filters in Internet Explorer, 637–38
    Wave filter, 651–53
    Wheel filter, 689–90
    Zigzag filter, 690–91

First-child pseudo-class, 125–28
First-letter pseudo-element, 119–22
First-line pseudo-element, 117–19
First pseudo-class, 123
Fit-position property, 363–64
Fit property, 363–64
Float-displace property, 331–32
Float property, 325–31, 331, 737–38
Focus pseudo-class, 123–25
Font-effect property, 182
Font-emphasize-position property, 184–85
Font-emphasize property, 185
Font-emphasize-style property, 184
@font-face pseudo-element, 175–81
Font-family property, 144–50, 739
Font property, 167–70, 738–39
Font-size-adjust property, 173–75, 740, 741
Font-size property
    browser compatibility, 157–58
    overview, 150–52, 740
    percentage value, font-size set to, 155–56
    relative font-size values, 152–54
    units of measure, font-size set to, 154–55
Font-smooth property, 183
Font-stretch property, 170–72, 741
Font-style property, 158–60, 741
Font-variant property, 160–62, 742
Font-weight property, 162–67, 742
Frequency units
    browser compatibility, 111
    overview, 110–11

G

Gamma correction, 375–76
Gates, Bill, 4
Glow filter, 656–58
Glyph-orientation-horizontal property, 211–13
Glyph-orientation-vertical property, 211–13
GradientWipe filter, 678–79
Grid media query, 140
Grouping
    browser compatibility, 55–56
    overview, 53–54
Group-reset property, 564–65

H

Handheld media type, 132
Hardware browsers, 50
Height media query, 136
Height property, 332–34, 743
Hover pseudo-class, 123–25
HTML
    browser wars, 3–5
    <div> element, 21–24
    enhancements before CSS, 4

`<link>` element, 24–27
`<span>` element, 21–24
`<style>` element, 18–20

I

`ICMFilter` filter, 665–67
Id attribute, 21–23
   browser compatibility, 61–62
   overview, 58
   as selector, 58–61
`Ime-mode` property, 503–5
`!important` property, 88–90
Inches, 96
`Indent-edge-reset` property, 332
Inheritance
   browser compatibility, 57–58
   overview, 56–57
`Inset` filter, 687–88
Internet Explorer
   HTML enhancements before CSS, 4
   popularity of, 10
Internet Explorer 4.5, 32–33
Internet Explorer 5.5, 34–35
Internet Explorer 6.0, 35–36
Internet Explorer 3.x, 30–31
Internet Explorer 4.x, 31
Internet Explorer 5.x, 32–33
`Iris` filter, 683–84

K

`Kerning-mode` property, 223
`Kerning-pair-threshold` property, 224
`Key-equivalent` property, 560–61
Konqueror, 47–48

L

Lang attribute, 19
Lang pseudo-class, 122
`Layout-flow` property, 239–44, 743–44
`Layout-grid` properties
   `layout-grid-char` property, 250–55, 745
   `layout-grid-line` property, 250–55, 745–46
   `layout-grid-mode` property, 248, 746
   `layout-grid` property, 255–58, 744
   `layout-grid-type` property, 248–50, 746–47
   overview, 247–48
Left property, 747
Left pseudo-class, 123
Length units
   browser compatibility, 99–100
   inches, 96
   m-length, 96
   overview, 95–98
   picas, 96

   pixels, 96
   points, 96
   x-height, 96
`Letter-spacing` property, 187–90, 747–48
`Light` filter, 660–63
`Line-break` property, 216, 748
`Linefeed-treatment` property, 219
`Line-height` property, 193–95, 748–49
`<link>` element, 24–27
Linux browsers
   browser wars, 11
   overview, 47
Lists, contextual selectors and, 62–65
`List-style-image` property, 435–37, 750
`List-style-position` property, 437–40, 750
`List-style` property, 440–43, 749
`List-style-type` property, 426–35, 751

M

Macintosh
   Internet Explorer 4.5, 32–33
   Internet Explorer 5.x, 32–33
`Margin-bottom` property, 349–51
`Margin-left` property, 352–54, 752–53
`Margin` property, 360–62, 751–52
`Margin-right` property, 354–57, 753
`Margin-top` property, 357–59, 753–54
`Marker-offset` property, 452–54, 754–55
`Marks` property, 510–11, 755
`Marquee` properties, 365–66
`MaskFilter` filter, 667–69
`Matrix` filter, 669–72
`Max-font-size` property, 215
`Max-height` property, 362–63, 479–84, 755–56
`Max-width` property, 362–63, 479–84, 756
Media attribute, 19
Media queries
   `color-index` media query, 138
   `color` media query, 137–38
   `device-aspect-ratio` media query, 137
   `device-height` media query, 136–37
   `device-width` media query, 136–37
   `grid` media query, 140
   `height` media query, 136
   `monochrome` media query, 138–39
   overview, 135–36
   `resolution` media query, 139
   `scan` media query, 139–40
   `width` media query, 136
Media types
   `all` media type, 131
   `aural` media type, 131–32
   `braille` media type, 132
   browser compatibility, 134–35
   `embossed` media type, 132
   `handheld` media type, 132

overview, 131–34
print media type, 132
projection media type, 132
screen media type, 132
tty media type, 132
tv media type, 132
Microsoft strategy in browser wars, 4
Min-font-size property, 215
Min-height property, 362–63, 479–84, 757
Min-width property, 362–63, 479–84, 757
M-length, 96
Mobile At-rules, CSS3, 807
Mobile properties, CSS3, 801–6
Mobile selectors, CSS3, 807–8
Monochrome media query, 138–39
MotionBlur filter, 641–44
Mozilla
    browser wars, 11
    CSS extensions, 42–46
    overview, 40–42
    user-interface properties, extensions for, 565–67
Multi-column layout properties
    column-count property, 616
    column-gap property, 617
    column-rule properties, 620–22
    column-space-distribution property, 618–19
    column-span properties, 622–23
    column-width-policy property, 617–18
    column-width property, 616
    overview, 613–15

N

Netscape Navigator
    browser wars, 3–4, 11
    HTML enhancements before CSS, 4
Netscape Navigator 4.x, 39–40
Netscape Navigator 6.x, 40–41
Netscape Navigator 7.x, 40–41, 46
Non-structural pseudo-class selectors, 79–80

O

Opacity property, 376–77
Opera browser in browser wars, 11
Opera 3.5, 37
Opera 4.x, 38
Opera 5.x, 38
Opera 6.x, 38
Orphans property, 517–19, 758
Outline properties
    outline-color property, 554–56, 759
    outline property, 556–57, 758–59
    outline-style property, 553–54, 760
    outline-width property, 550–52, 760–61
    overview, 549–50
Overflow property, 487–90, 761–62

Overflow-x property, 490–91
Overflow-y property, 490–91

P

Padding-bottom property, 337–39, 762–63
Padding-left property, 339–41, 763
Padding property, 345–49, 762
Padding-right property, 341–43, 763–64
Padding-top property, 343–45, 764
Page-break-after property, 765–66
Page-break-before property, 766–67
Page-break-inside property, 767
Page-break properties, 512–15
Paged media properties
    marks property, 510–11, 755
    orphans property, 517–19, 758
    overview, 507
    page-break properties, 512–15
    page property, 515–17, 764–65
    size property, 507–9, 779–80
    widows property, 517–19, 795–96
Page property, 515–17, 764–65
Pause-after property, 768
Pause-before property, 769
Pause properties, 573–76
Pause property, 768
Percentage units
    browser compatibility, 103
    overview, 101–2
Percentage value, font-size set to, 155–56
Picas, 96
Pitch property, 587–88, 769–70
Pitch-range property, 589–90, 770
Pixelate filter, 688–89
Pixels, 96
Play-during property, 577–78, 770–71
Points, 96
Popularity of Internet Explorer, 10
Position property, 465–73, 771–72
Print media type, 132
Projection media type, 132
Pseudo-classes
    first-child pseudo-class, 125–28
    first pseudo-class, 123
    focus pseudo-class, 123–25
    hover pseudo-class, 123–25
    lang pseudo-class, 122
    left pseudo-class, 123
    right pseudo-class, 123
Pseudo-elements
    after pseudo-element, 443–46
    anchor pseudo-element, 114–16
    combining, 128–29
    first-letter pseudo-element, 119–22
    first-line pseudo-element, 117–19
    @font-face pseudo-element, 175–81

before pseudo-element, 443–46
in selectors, 128–29
Punctuation-trim property, 224–25

Q

Quotes property, 446–49, 772–73

R

RadialWipe filter, 679–80
RandomBars filter, 681–82
RandomDissolve filter, 682–83
Relative font-size values, 152–54
Rendering-intent property, 377–78
Resizer property, 557–60
Resolution media query, 139
Richness property, 591–92, 773
Right property, 774
Right pseudo-class, 123
Ruby
    overview, 597–98
    ruby-align property, 602–5, 774–75
    ruby-overhang property, 605–8, 775
    ruby-position property, 608–10, 776
    <ruby> tag set, 598–602

S

Scan media query, 139–40
Screen media type, 132
Scrollbar-arrow-color property, 776–77
Scrollbar-base-color property, 777
Scrollbar-darkshadow-color property, 777
Scrollbar-3dlight-color property, 776
Scrollbar-face-color property, 778
Scrollbar-highlight-color property, 778
Scrollbar properties
    browser compatibility, 634
    overview, 626–33
Scrollbars
    elements of, 625–26
    overview, 625
    properties, 626–34
Scrollbar-shadow-color property, 778–79
Scrollbar-track-color property, 779
Selectors
    adjacent sibling selectors, 70–71
    attribute selectors, 71–77
    child selectors, 68–69
    class attribute as, 58–61
    contextual selectors, 65–66
    CSS2 selectors. See CSS2 selectors
    CSS3 selectors. See CSS3 selectors
    id attribute as selector, 58–61
    non-structural pseudo-class selectors, 79–80
    pseudo-elements in, 128–29

universal selector, 68
Shadow filter, 645–48
Size property, 507–9, 779–80
Slide filter, 686–87
<span> element, 21–24
Speak-header property, 536–37, 780–81
Speak-numeral property, 781
Speak property, 570–71, 780
Speak-punctuation property, 782
Speech properties, 592–94
Speech-rate property, 584–85, 782–83
Spiral filter, 684–85
Static filters
    AlphaFilter property, 639–40
    BasicImage filter, 653–56
    Blur filter, 641–44
    Chroma filter, 658–60
    Compositor filter, 663–65
    DropShadow filter, 645–48
    Emboss filter, 649–50
    Engrave filter, 649–50
    Glow filter, 656–58
    ICMFilter filter, 665–67
    Light filter, 660–63
    MaskFilter filter, 667–69
    Matrix filter, 669–72
    MotionBlur filter, 641–44
    overview, 638
    Shadow filter, 645–48
    Wave filter, 651–53
Stress property, 590–91, 783
Stretch filter, 685–86
Strings
    browser compatibility, 107
    overview, 106–7
Strips filter, 680–81
Structural pseudo-class selectors, 77–79
<style> element
    accesskey attribute, 18
    and CSS3, 20
    dir attribute, 18
    disabled attribute, 18–19
    lang attribute, 19
    media attribute, 19
    overview, 18
    tabindex attribute, 19
    type attribute, 19
Support for CSS, 29–30

T

Tabindex attribute, 19
Tab-index property, 561
Table properties
    border-collapse property, 527–31, 716–17
    border-spacing property, 531–33, 722–23
    caption-side property, 521–24, 727–28

`empty-cells` property, 533–36, 737
overview, 521
`speak-header` property, 536–37, 780–81
`table-layout` property, 524–27, 784
Tables
   CSS used for layout, 537–41
   properties. *See* table properties
   three-column layout, 540–41
   two-column layout, 537–40
`Text-align-last` property, 271–73, 785
`Text-align` property, 198–201, 784
`Text-autospace` property, 258–61, 785–86
`Text-blink` property, 236
`Text-decoration` property, 201–4, 786
`Text-indent` property, 204–6, 787
`Text-justify` property, 214–15, 261–63, 787–88
`Text-justify-trim` property, 216
`Text-kashida-space` property, 264–66, 788
`Text-line-through` properties
   overview, 225
   `text-line-through-color` property, 225–26
   `text-line-through-mode` property, 226
   `text-line-through` property, 226–28
   `text-line-through-style` property, 226
`Text-overflow-ellipsis` property, 222
`Text-overflow-mode` property, 222
`Text-overflow` property, 223, 789
`Text-overline` properties
   overview, 228–29
   `text-overline-color` property, 229
   `text-overline-mode` property, 229
   `text-overline` property, 230–31
   `text-overline-style` property, 229–30
Text properties
   `all-space` property, 220–21
   `all-space-treatment` property, 220
   `glyph-orientation-horizontal` property, 211–13
   `glyph-orientation-vertical` property, 211–13
   `kerning-mode` property, 223
   `kerning-pair-threshold` property, 224
   `letter-spacing` property, 187–90, 747–48
   `line-break` property, 216, 748
   `linefeed-treatment` property, 219
   `line-height` property, 193–95, 748–49
   `max-font-size` property, 215
   `min-font-size` property, 215
   overview, 187
   `punctuation-trim` property, 224–25
   `text-align` property, 198–201, 784
   `text-blink` property, 236
   `text-decoration` property, 201–4, 786
   `text-indent` property, 204–6, 787
   `text-justify` property, 214–15, 787–88
   `text-justify-trim` property, 216
   `text-line-through` properties, 225–28

`text-overflow-ellipsis` property, 222
`text-overflow-mode` property, 222
`text-overflow` property, 223, 789
`text-overline` properties, 228–31
`text-script` property, 214–15
`text-shadow` property, 209–11, 789
`text-transform` property, 207–9, 790
`text-underline` properties, 232–35
`vertical-align` property, 196–98, 792
`white-space-treatment` property, 219–20
`word-break-cjk` property, 216–17
`word-break-inside` property, 217
`word-break` property, 797
`word-spacing` property, 190–93, 797–98
`wrap-option` property, 218
Text property extensions
   `layout-flow` property, 239–44, 743–44
   `layout-grid` properties, 247–58
   overview, 239
   `text-align-last` property, 271–73, 785
   `text-autospace` property, 258–61, 785–86
   `text-justify` property, 261–63
   `text-kashida-space` property, 264–66, 788
   `text-underline-position` property, 266–68, 790–91
   `word-break` property, 268–70
   `writing-mode` property, 244–47, 798
`Text-script` property, 214–15
`Text-shadow` property, 209–11, 789
`Text-transform` property, 207–9, 790
`Text-underline` properties
   overview, 232
   `text-underline-color` property, 232
   `text-underline-mode` property, 232
   `text-underline-position` property, 233–34, 266–68, 790–91
   `text-underline` property, 234–35
   `text-underline-style` property, 233
Three-column layout for tables, 540–41
Time units
   browser compatibility, 108
   overview, 108
`Toggle-group` property, 564–65
`Top` property, 791
Transition filters
   `Barn Transition` filter, 674–75
   `Blinds` filter, 675–76
   `Checkerboard` filter, 676–77
   `Fade` filter, 677–78
   `GradientWipe` filter, 678–79
   `Inset` filter, 687–88
   `Iris` filter, 683–84
   overview, 672–74
   `Pixelate` filter, 688–89
   `RadialWipe` filter, 679–80
   `RandomBars` filter, 681–82
   `RandomDissolve` filter, 682–83

Slide filter, 686–87
Spiral filter, 684–85
Stretch filter, 685–86
Strips filter, 680–81
Wheel filter, 689–90
Zigzag filter, 690–91
Tty media type, 132
Tv media type, 132
Two-column layout for tables, 537–40
Type attribute, 19

U

Unicode-bidi property, 476–79, 791–92
Units of measure
    angle units, 108–10
    font-size set to, 154–55
    frequency units, 110–11
    length units, 95–100
    percentage units, 101–3
    time units, 108
Universal selector, 68
URLs
    browser compatibility, 105
    overview, 103–4
User-focus-key property, 564
User-focus-pointer property, 564
User-focus property, 564
User-input property, 562
User-interface properties
    accelerator property, 557–59, 707
    CSS3, 559, 567
    cursor property, 544–49, 734
    group-reset property, 564–65
    key-equivalent property, 560–61
    Mozilla extensions, 565–67
    outline properties, 549–57
    overview, 543–44
    resizer property, 557–60
    tab-index property, 561
    toggle-group property, 564–65
    user-focus-key property, 564
    user-focus-pointer property, 564
    user-focus property, 564
    user-input property, 562
    user-modify property, 562–63
    user-select property, 563

V

Vertical-align property, 196–98, 792
Visibility property, 495–500, 793
Visual effects properties
    clip property, 492–95, 728–29
    ime-mode property, 503–5
    overflow property, 487–90, 761–62
    overflow-x property, 490–91

overflow-y property, 490–91
    overview, 487
    visibility property, 495–500, 793
    zoom property, 500–502
Visual formatting properties
    direction property, 476–79, 734–35
    display property, 457–65, 735
    max-height property, 479–84, 755–56
    max-width property, 479–84, 756
    min-height property, 479–84, 757
    min-width property, 479–84, 757
    overview, 457
    position property, 465–73, 771–72
    unicode-bidi property, 476–79, 791–92
    z-index property, 473–76, 798–99
Voice-family property, 586–87, 793–94
Volume property, 571–73, 794

W

Wave filter, 651–53
W3C
    CSS, creation of, 6–7
    overview, 5
Wheel filter, 689–90
White-space property, 423–26, 795
White-space-treatment property, 219–20
Widows property, 517–19, 795–96
Width media query, 136
Width property, 335–37, 796
Word-break-cjk property, 216–17
Word-break-inside property, 217
Word-break property, 217–18, 268–70, 797
Word-spacing property, 190–93, 797–98
World Wide Web Consortium. See W3C
Wrap-option property, 218
Writing-mode property, 244–47, 798

X

X11 color set, 379–85
X-height, 96
XHTML 1.0 standard, 7

Z

Zigzag filter, 690–91
Z-index property, 473–76, 798–99
Zoom property, 500–502

inform IT

www.informit.com

YOUR GUIDE TO IT REFERENCE

Articles

Keep your edge with thousands of free articles, in-depth features, interviews, and IT reference recommendations – all written by experts you know and trust.

Online Books

Answers in an instant from **InformIT Online Book's** 600+ fully searchable on line books. Sign up now and get your first 14 days **free**.

POWERED BY

Safari

Catalog

Review online sample chapters, author biographies and customer rankings and choose exactly the right book from a selection of over 5,000 titles.

Wouldn't it be great

if the world's leading technical publishers joined forces to deliver their best tech books in a common digital reference platform?

They have. Introducing
InformIT Online Books
powered by Safari.

POWERED BY **Safari**

informIT Online Books

informit.com/onlinebooks

■ **Specific answers to specific questions.**
InformIT Online Books' powerful search engine gives you relevance-ranked results in a matter of seconds.

■ **Immediate results.**
With InformIt Online Books, you can select the book you want and view the chapter or section you need immediately.

■ **Cut, paste and annotate.**
Paste code to save time and eliminate typographical errors. Make notes on the material you find useful and choose whether or not to share them with your work group.

■ **Customized for your enterprise.**
Customize a library for you, your department or your entire organization. You only pay for what you need.

Get your first 14 days FREE!

InformIT Online Books is offering its members a 10 book subscription risk-free for 14 days. Visit **http://www.informit.com/onlinebooks** for details.

Prentice Hall Professional Technical Reference

http://www.phptr.com/

Prentice Hall PTR   InformIT   InformIT Online Books   Financial Times Prentice Hall   ft.com   PTG Interactive   Reuters

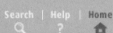

TOMORROW'S SOLUTIONS FOR TODAY'S PROFESSIONALS

Prentice Hall **Professional Technical Reference**

| Browse | Book Series | What's New | User Groups | Alliances | Special Sales | Contact Us |

Search | Help | Home
Q   ?   🏠

Quick Search

PTR Favorites

Find a Bookstore

Book Series

Special Interests

Newsletters

Press Room

International

Best Sellers

Solutions Beyond the Book

 Shopping Bag

Keep Up to Date with
PH PTR Online

We strive to stay on the cutting edge of what's happening in professional computer science and engineering. Here's a bit of what you'll find when you stop by **www.phptr.com**:

What's new at PHPTR? We don't just publish books for the professional community, we're a part of it. Check out our convention schedule, keep up with your favorite authors, and get the latest reviews and press releases on topics of interest to you.

Special interest areas offering our latest books, book series, features of the month, related links, and other useful information to help you get the job done.

User Groups Prentice Hall Professional Technical Reference's User Group Program helps volunteer, not-for-profit user groups provide their members with training and information about cutting-edge technology.

Companion Websites Our Companion Websites provide valuable solutions beyond the book. Here you can download the source code, get updates and corrections, chat with other users and the author about the book, or discover links to other websites on this topic.

Need to find a bookstore? Chances are, there's a bookseller near you that carries a broad selection of PTR titles. Locate a Magnet bookstore near you at www.phptr.com.

Subscribe today! **Join PHPTR's monthly email newsletter!** Want to be kept up-to-date on your area of interest? Choose a targeted category on our website, and we'll keep you informed of the latest PHPTR products, author events, reviews and conferences in your interest area.

Visit our mailroom to subscribe today! **http://www.phptr.com/mail_lists**